Second Edition

CONSTRUCTING CRIME

Perspectives on Making News and Social Problems

Gary W. Potter
Victor E. Kappeler
Eastern Kentucky University

WAVELAND

PRESS, INC.

Long Grove, Illinois

For information about this book, contact:
Waveland Press, Inc.
4180 IL Route 83, Suite 101
Long Grove, IL 60047-9580
(847) 634-0081
info@waveland.com
www.waveland.com

CONTENTS

Part II
Constructing Crime Problems   93

Part III
Effects of Constructing Crime   267

PREFACE

If there is one thing U.S. society has an abundance of, it is images and opinions about crime. Pick up and read a newspaper from any city—Chicago, Boston, Detroit, Los Angeles, Houston, or Tampa. Turn on a TV and flip though the channels; stop on anything—news, talk shows, sitcoms, or soap operas. Stop by a cinema and watch any movie—horror, drama, science fiction, or romance. Ask anyone, anyplace, anytime—a student on campus, a professor in the classroom, a banker at the office, a relative at home, or even a stranger on the street. There is no shortage of talk about crime. It is a central theme running through many forms of communication in modern society.

Crime is a staple on many institutional playing fields. It is a focal concern in our schools; it is the subject of sermons in churches; it anchors political platforms; it permeates discussions of the economy; it frightens families; and it serves as the foundation for our legal institution. Our empirical knowledge and experience with crime pales in comparison to these vicarious experiences. Most of us have never been victims of a violent crime, and the majority of the public has never read a scholarly study of crime. These facts, however, do nothing to mute private and public expressions of opinions. Everyone has an opinion about crime and crime control policy.

In our role as college professors, we often ask students a series of unusual questions on the first day of class. Sometimes we use the language of medicine; other times we adopt the jargon of engineering; and on occasion we drop an example from physics. Simplified, the questions might be posed like this: What do you think about advances in cardiac care? What do you think about the structural quality of this building? or, What do you think about the fact that physicists cannot predict the movement of certain subatomic particles? Responses are remarkably similar (except from the errant physics or health care major)—bright students sit in silence with all expression draining from their faces. As the length of silence grows, gazes begin to be diverted from the inquisitor toward desks or windows. Some students begin to fidget in their seats. Eventually, the uncomfortable silence is broken with yet another series of questions. What do you think about drunk drivers? What are your thoughts on the president's plan to combat terrorism with domestic spying? Should the use of controlled substances be legalized? Expression rushes back to their faces, fidgeting stops, and many lean forward in their seats. The inquisitor has been transformed and is no longer a stranger; a social chord has been struck. The uncomfortable silence is broken in a rush of opinion that has to be diplomatically suppressed to get back to the point of the questions. The purpose, of course, is to demonstrate that while there is a dearth of opinions on many important social and scientific issues, there is no hesitation to express an abundance of opinions about crime and crime control policy.

What explains this sudden break in the silence, the frantic rush to express an opinion, even an uninformed one? To begin to answer this question, we need to look behind the blue haze projected from television and movie screens; to reconsider the reality imprinted in newspapers and magazines, a reality that changes as easily as print ink rubs off onto our fingers; to listen carefully to the crime stories that are told by friends, professors, bankers, relatives, and passing acquaintances. Crime is intricately woven into the very fabric of society.

In this collection, we explore the processes by which the social reality of crime is constructed. Several of the articles included in the anthology are classics, while many of the others merely need a bit of time to demonstrate their contribution to our understanding of crime and the media. Several of the articles were first published during our tenures as a principal reviewer and the editor of *Justice Quarterly*. We were fortunate to be able to work with the authors of several of these articles from their initial submission to the journal through their publication in this anthology.

In putting together the anthology, we attempted to stay true to its primary objective of bringing together a collection of articles devoted to the construction of crime through the making of news and social problems. We have organized the anthology into three distinct sections that reflect this objective. In the first section, we offer an overview of some of the many issues associated with studying crime and the media. The articles in this section provide a foundation for understanding the concepts employed by researchers who study the media and crime as well as an accounting of the many actors, practices, and techniques involved in the construction of crime. In the section that follows, we explore the making of crime problems. In this section various crime issues and types of crime are considered. The section includes media constructions of crime ranging from drug panics to gang rituals to less mature constructions of crime like road warriors. In the final section attention, we turn to the effects of media constructions of crime. In this section the diversity and complexity of media effects are demonstrated—from the impact they have on police and policy to the effects turned inward on the media themselves. We close with a brief epilogue that continues the mirroring process, raising questions about the viability of stripping crime and the media from the broader transformations shaping society.

Gary W. Potter
Victor E. Kappeler
Eastern Kentucky University

INTRODUCTION

There is probably no issue that invokes greater emotion and more consistently influences public opinion than crime. Whether the issue is drug-related crime, violent crime, juvenile crime, child abductions, serial killers, youth gangs, or crime against the elderly, a public consensus exists that crime is rampant, dangerous, and threatening to explode. The dangers of crime are seen as immediate, omnipresent, and almost inescapable. For more than three decades in the United States, the fear of crime has been so real that one can almost reach out and touch it. Politicians, law enforcement executives, the private crime industry, and the media cater to the public mood. Their increasingly draconian responses—in the form of more police, more arrests, longer sentences, more prisons, and more executions—affirm public fears, and that fear grows unabated. Each new crime story, each new crime movie, each new governmental pronouncement on crime increases the public thirst for more crime control, less personal freedom, and greater intervention by the state.

In contrast to seemingly tangible public fear, crime facts are far more difficult to assess. The emotional reaction to crime makes the public policy issue of control intensely sensitive. The issue responds to manipulation and pandering so predictably that advertisers and public relations experts would be envious of the responses elicited. Why are crime facts so difficult to determine but crime fear so easy to manipulate? Through what process do rumors, gossip, urban legends, and apocryphal stories become public "common sense"? Through what mechanisms do isolated and rare incidents weave a tapestry of fear, panic, and hysteria? More importantly, who benefits from the construction of this labyrinth? Those are the questions this book addresses. Whether they can be fully answered is debatable. However, a careful look at crime and crime-related issues can help us see beyond the web of public fear. Public opinion and crime facts demonstrate no congruence. The reality of crime in the United States has been blanketed by a constructed reality. The policies and programs emanating from that constructed reality do far more damage than good to public safety and crime control.

Crime Knowledge

What does the public really know about crime and how do they know it? The most reliable crime data available clearly demonstrate that the vast

1

majority of people living in the United States will never be victims of crime. In fact, over 90 percent of the U.S. population has no direct experience with crime at all (Kappeler & Potter, 2005). Yet the public remains convinced of imminent danger—changing their personal habits and lives to accommodate fears and voting for politicians who promise solutions to the conjured problem. What is the basis for these opinions, fears, and impressions?

In addition to their own experiences, people interpret and internalize the experiences of others. They hear—often second-, third-, or fourth-hand—about crime incidents involving neighbors, relatives, friends, and friends of friends. This process of socialization carries crime "facts" and crime-related experiences from one person to many others like a virus. Crime is a topic of conversation, both public and private. Strong opinions and reactions amplify and extend the content of actual experiences. Lost in the retelling is the relatively isolated aspect of the incidents. Socialization processes, however, have limited utility in explaining the pervasiveness of crime-related concerns. There are other processes at work.

For centuries, the only means of disseminating knowledge from one person to another was oral communication. Reaching larger audiences was a slow, repetitive process limited by time and place. The printing press and public education were important revolutions that allowed written messages from one person to reach many readers. Newer technologies today have created a maelstrom of information. The mass media can disseminate messages literally with the speed of light and sound. Publishers produce thousands of books about crime—some fictional, some true, some simply crude "pot-boilers." Movies make crime a central theme. Producers know that movies like *The Clearing, Kill Bill, Memento, Pulp Fiction, Natural Born Killers,* and *The Usual Suspects* attract large audiences. Television programs also use crime and violence to attract attention. Police programs have been a staple of television programming from *Dragnet* to *CSI.* The creator of the *Law & Order* series, Dick Wolf, comments:

> Crime is a constantly renewable resource. Every day people continue to kill each other in bizarre and unfathomable ways. Even if murder goes down by double digits, there are still thousands of people killed in this country every year and killers who warrant prosecution. (Smith, 2006, p. 16)

Because of the public's fixation on crime, the television industry constructed a new type of programming in 1989—a hybrid between entertainment and crime news called reality TV. By the end of 1993, there were seven national programs fitting this profile. Two survive and continue to attract viewers: *America's Most Wanted* and *Unsolved Mysteries.* The Web site for *America's Most Wanted* advertises its hotline (1-800-CRIME-TV) for tips from viewers and proclaims, "You have helped catch 876 fugitives to date." There is also an AMW case tracker that tells viewers there are 1,185 open cases. You can select the type of crime from a drop-down list, including terrorism, or you can click on an area on the map of the United States and look at crimes by region. Other features of the Web site include: "In the Line of Duty," which claims more than 1,600 law enforcement officers—"an average of one death every 53 hours"—died on the job during the past 10 years and an advertisement for a "fun safety DVD for kids" (AMW, 2006). The portal to the Web site for *Unsolved Mysteries* flashes "missing," "lost love," "homicide," and "fugitive" before showing the title of the program and a button to click to enter the site, where the viewer is told this is one of television's first interactive series (*Unsolved*, 2006).

According to research, the mass media are the basic sources of information on crime, criminals, crime control policies, and the criminal justice system for most people (Barak, 1994; Ericson, Baranek, & Chan, 1989; Graber, 1980; Warr, 1995). Crime themes are a mother lode for the media; crime attracts viewers. More viewers mean greater newspaper and magazine circulations, larger television audiences, and consequently larger advertising fees (Barkan, 1997). The local news and reality crime shows focus on dramatic themes to attract viewers: police "hot pursuits"; violent crimes (particularly strange and heinous crimes with innocent and unsuspecting victims); and crime alleged to be committed by social deviants like drug addicts, pedophiles, prostitutes, and terrorists.

The Portrayal of Crime in the Mass Media

Crime rates have decreased every year since 1991, and victimization surveys indicate that serious crime has been on a perpetual decline since the early 1970s (Kappeler & Potter, 2005). The media, however, provide a distorted view of how much crime there is in society. The media create a wholly inaccurate image of a society in which violent crime is rampant and in which crime is constantly and immutably on the increase. In addition, media coverage of crime seriously distorts public perception of the types of crime being committed and the frequency with which violent crimes occur. The media have a preoccupation with violent crime. Researchers have demonstrated a consistent and strong bias in the news toward murder, sexual crimes, gangs and violence, and drug-related violence (Beirne & Messerschmidt, 1995; Livingston, 1996).

One study looked at local television news programs in 13 major cities and found that crime far outdistanced all other topics in local newscasts, even weather and sports. Commercial advertisements and crime stories dominated the average 30-minute newscast in the study. Crime made up 20 percent of all local TV stories, followed by weather at 11 percent and accidents and disasters at 9 percent (*Public Health Reports*, 1998). The media not only overreport crime, but they also focus on the least common crimes, crimes of violence (Lundman, 2003). Another focus is random violence committed by strangers, despite the fact that violence overwhelmingly occurs among friends and intimates (Feld, 2003).

The less common a crime is, the more coverage it will generate. For example, crimes against small children and wealthy white women are featured in most crime reporting despite the fact that these groups have the lowest victimization rates of any social groups in the United States (Feld, 2003). Sensational and rare crimes that dovetail conveniently into news themes with moralistic messages are particularly popular. Over the years the media have created crime scares by formulating news themes around issues of "white-slavery" in the prostitution industry; sexual psychopaths running rampant in major cities; satanists engaged in mass murder, child sacrifice, and ritualistic child abuse; serial killers roaming the countryside; and many others. As Philip Jenkins (1996) comments:

> If we relied solely on the evidence of the mass media, we might well believe that every few years, a particular form of immoral or criminal behavior becomes so dangerous as almost to threaten the foundations of society. . . . These panics are important in their own right for what they reveal about social concerns and prejudices—often based on xenophobia and anti-immigrant prejudice. (pp. 67–70)

Mass murders by satanic cults, the predations of roaming serial killers, and organized child abuse in day-care centers are so rare as to be total aberrations. The media choose to ignore common, everyday, typical crime. White-collar crimes such as price-fixing, illegal disposal of toxic waste, and unsafe work conditions get little coverage, so the public tends not to view these activities as "real crime."

Crime reports in the media inflame racial tensions and fears through biased and selective coverage. Crime stories on television news programs and in newspapers focus on crimes by African-American and Hispanic offenders, creating a wildly exaggerated view of their involvement in street crime and violent crime (Dorfman & Schiraldi, 2001; Lundman, 2003). The media also distort the race of victims in three important ways. First, newspapers carry a vastly inflated number of stories about white victims when compared to NCVS statistics on victimization. Second, stories featuring white victims are longer and more detailed than stories about African-American victims. Finally, despite the fact that violent crime is overwhelmingly intraracial, newspapers focus on stories involving white victims and African-American offenders (Lundman, 2003).

When a story deals with an African-American or Hispanic offender, the focus is usually on interracial crime as evidenced by accompanying photographs of the offender being taken into police custody or a mug shot of the offender (Chiricos & Eschholz, 2002; Feld, 2003). The impact of this racial profiling by the media is stunning. One study found that 60 percent of the people interviewed recalled an offender being shown in a television news story about crime when no offender images were included. Of those who saw the phantom offender, 70 percent were certain the offender was African American (Gilliam & Iyengar, 2000).

The media are also guilty of bias by age in the depiction of crime and violent crime. Both television and newspaper coverage of crime portrays young people as offenders in violent incidents (Dorfman & Schiraldi, 2001). In fact, the research shows that 68 percent of all television news stories on violent crime highlight youthful offenders, and 55 percent of all stories about young people highlight violence. The reality is that less than 4 percent of all arrests of youths are for violent crime, and less than 16 percent of all crime is committed by young people (FBI, 2005).

The many distortions about crime, types of crime, race, and demographics found in media reporting help explain public ignorance about crime, the criminal justice system, and crime control policy in the United States (Cullen, Fisher, & Applegate, 2000). A study of 500 students taking introductory criminal justice classes found that they estimated the annual number of homicides in the United States at about 250,000 (Vandiver & Giacopassi, 1997, p. 141). In 1997, there were slightly more than 18,208 murders; in 2004 there were 16,137. Similarly a Gallup Poll in 2002 found that 62 percent of the U.S. public thought crime was higher than in 2001, despite a steady ten year drop in crime rates (Maguire & Pastore, 2004).

Media Attention and Citizen Fear of Crime

With such heavy exposure to crime themes in both news and entertainment programming, it would appear to be common sense that more media exposure should be directly related to a greater fear of crime. However, unlike media analysts and news anchors, social scientists are constrained by their craft to be more circumspect in their claims. A correlation between media exposure and concerns about crime is easy to demonstrate, but correlation is a long way from causation. Direct relationships are not easy to prove. For example, it is difficult to demonstrate whether greater media exposure causes fear of crime or whether fear of crime causes greater media exposure because people are staying home watching crime on television. As we pointed out earlier, people are exposed to information other than that provided by the media that may influence their viewpoints (i.e., rumors, gossip, urban legends). In addition, media research is difficult, complex, and subject to many pitfalls. For example, how does one measure the impact of the media? Is viewing time a measure? Do column inches constitute an index? Does the quality and the impact of language and content take precedence? (Miethe & Lee, 1984; Skogan & Maxfield, 1981; Surette, 1998).

Despite the need for caution and the constraints of science, much evidence indicates that the media do influence the level of fear of crime and contribute to the persistence of crime as a major national issue. George Gerbner, a leading media researcher at the Annenberg School of Communications at the University of Pennsylvania, developed cultivation theory—the "mean world" syndrome—to describe the impact of the media. Gerbner argues that research demonstrates that heavy viewers of television violence, whether in entertainment or news mediums, increasingly develop the feeling that they are living in a state of siege. Gerbner's research shows that heavy television viewers: (1) seriously overestimate the probability that they will be victims of violence; (2) believe their own neighborhoods to be unsafe; (3) rank fear of crime as one of their most compelling personal problems; (4) assume crime rates are going up regardless of whether they really are; (5) support punitive anti-crime measures; and (6) are more likely to buy guns and anti-crime safety devices (Gerbner, 1994). Other research demonstrates that "heavy viewers . . . exhibit an exaggerated fear of victimization and a perception that people cannot be trusted." (Carlson, 1995, p. 190).

It is difficult to gauge the impact of the media on fear of crime. One thing, however, is clear from the research: the more you watch television news, the more fearful you are of crime. People who watch more television news and more television crime dramas express dramatically higher rates of fear about crime than those who watch fewer broadcasts (Eschholz, Chiricos, & Gertz, 2003). A study in Philadelphia found that people who watched the television news four times a week were 40 percent more likely to be very worried about crime than those who did not watch the news (Bunch, 1999).

In addition to increasing public fear, media crime coverage has other effects on public perceptions and views of crime. Heavy coverage shapes perceptions and directs much public discourse on the crime issue. For example, the media regularly and falsely direct attention to crimes allegedly committed by young, poor, urban males, who are often members of minority groups (Reiman, 2004). Media coverage directs people's attention to specific crimes and helps to shape those crimes as social problems (i.e., drug use, gangs). Media coverage limits discourse on crime control options to present policies—suggesting that the only options are more laws, more police, longer sentences, and more prisons (Kappeler & Potter, 2005). The impact of media coverage is readily apparent in the creation of crime scares and moral panics.

Moral Panics

The concept of a moral panic was developed by Stanley Cohen (1980). A moral panic occurs when a group or type of activity is perceived as a threat to the stability and well-being of society. The media provide copious details and information (not necessarily accurate); this is followed by attention from law enforcement officials, politicians, and editorial writers who begin to comment on the panic. "Experts" then join the fray and try to explain the panic and offer policy options for dealing with it.

Moral panics direct public attention toward the activity or group and organize public fear for the well-being of society. The attention amplifies the behavior of the groups under scrutiny. Cohen's study looked at media coverage of the "Mods and Rockers" in the 1960s in Britain (Cohen, 1980). The media seriously exaggerated the behaviors of these groups. More importantly, the media played a key role in taking imprecisely defined social groupings (Cohen's "loose stylistic associations") and redefining them into well-organized youth gangs. The "Mods and Rockers" were transformed by media coverage into folk devils, a stereotyped caricature of reality that became the alleged source of great social danger and harm. Media coverage actually heightened the identification of young people with these two groups, an identification that had been marginal at best. The media intensified both the amount of troubling behavior and the numbers of people engaged in that behavior, thereby becoming a self-fulfilling prophecy. Media attention also exacerbated tensions between these two stylized groups and between young people and their communities in general (Cohen, 1980).

Of course, moral panics did not begin with the "Mods and Rockers." In 1922, future Supreme Court Justice Felix Frankfurter and legal scholar Roscoe Pound took the media to task for creating crime scares. Frankfurter and Pound noted that newspapers in Cleveland had dramatically increased their coverage of crime stories during 1919, even though crimes reported to the police had increased only slightly. They charged that the press was needlessly alarming the public and that the effect was a dangerous tendency for the public to pressure police to ignore due process rights and constitutional protections in their pursuit of criminals (Frankfurter & Pound, 1922).

The "sex fiend" panic of the 1930s and 1940s resulted in the passage of sexual psychopath laws in 28 states. One analysis of the development of these laws reveals a key role played by the media (McCaghy & Capron, 1997). Sex fiend panics typically began with the commission of a sex crime, particularly a crime against a child, accompanied by heavy mass media coverage. This panic included estimates, without any basis in fact, that thousands of sex fiends were at large in the community. These "sex crime waves" were not related to any increase in the actual numbers of reported sex crimes; the panic was artificially induced by media coverage of particularly salacious cases (see Sutherland, 1950). The media advocated such solutions as castration, the outlawing of pornography, and life imprisonment for sex offenders. Special sexual psychopath laws were passed that allowed indeterminate confinement for any offender, whether a child molester or an exhibitionist or a fornicator, until the state deemed them to be cured. In some states, the original offense didn't even have to be a sex offense—it could be robbery or arson, as long as a psychiatrist could identify sexual dysfunctions in the accused. The irony, of course, was that a violent rapist or child molester could be arrested and released in a few months, and a masturbator, adulterer, or pickpocket deemed to have an uncorrected sexual dysfunction could sit in prison forever.

In the 1980s the same kind of moral panic surfaced with regard to the use of crack (a smokable form of cocaine hydrochloride). Craig Reinarman and Harry Levine (1989) carefully researched the media's creation of a drug scare surrounding crack. Reinarman and Levine define a "drug scare" as a historical period in which all manner of social difficulties (such as crime, health problems, the failure of the education system) are blamed on a chemical substance. "Drug scares" are not new. Problems of opiate addiction at the turn of the century were blamed on Chinese immigrants; African Americans were portrayed as "cocaine fiends" during the 1920s; violent behavior resulting from marijuana consumption was linked to Mexican farm laborers in the 1920s and 1930s. The construction of the crack scare was similar in that it linked the use of crack-cocaine to inner-city blacks, Hispanics, and youths. In the 1970s, when the use of expensive cocaine hydrochloride was concentrated among affluent whites, both the media and the state focused on heroin, seen as a drug of the inner-city poor. Only when cocaine became available in an inexpensive form, crack, did the scapegoating common to drug scares begin.

The media hype began in 1986, following the spread of crack into poor and working class neighborhoods. *Time* and *Newsweek* ran five cover stories each on crack during 1986. The three major television networks quickly joined the feeding frenzy. NBC did 400 news stories on crack between June and December 1986; in July 1986, all three networks ran 74 drug stories on their nightly newscasts. These stories contained highly inflated estimates of crack use and warnings about the dangers of the drug.

Those news stories were particularly troubling precisely because they were entirely incorrect. Research from the National Institute of Drug Abuse showed that the use of all forms of cocaine by youth and young adults had reached its peak four years earlier and had been declining ever since. Every indicator showed that at the height of the media frenzy crack use was relatively rare (Walker, 1998). Surveys of high school students demonstrated that experimentation with cocaine and cocaine products had been decreasing steadily since 1980. In fact, the government's own statistics showed that 96 percent of young people in the United States had never even tried crack. If there had been an epidemic, it was long over.

Officially produced data strongly refuted other claims about crack use. The media reports claimed that crack and cocaine were highly addictive and that crack, in particular, was so addictive that one experience with the drug could addict a user for life. However, NIDA estimates showed that of the 22 million people who had used cocaine and cocaine-products, very few of them ever became addicted. In fact, very few of them ever escalated to daily use. NIDA's own estimates indicated that fewer than 3 percent of cocaine users would ever become "problem" users (Kappeler & Potter, 2005). The health dangers of cocaine and crack were also widely exaggerated; few users ever required medical treatment because of using the drug.

The impact of the crack scare was tangible and immediate. New laws were passed increasing mandatory sentences for crack use and sales. Ironically, these laws resulted in a situation where someone arrested for crack faced the prospect of a prison sentence three to eight times longer than a sentence for cocaine hydrochloride, the substance needed to produce crack. The drug laws for crack inverted the typical ratio—wholesalers receive less severe sanctions than retailers and users.

Another moral panic centered on juveniles. The Associated Press proclaimed on June 8, 1990, that juvenile crime had increased thirtyfold since 1950. That estimate has been repeated in almost every mass media story on teen crime. These facts are known: (1) the 1950 crime statistics are too incomplete for any comparisons to present crime levels; (2) data comparisons since the 1970s show no increase in juvenile crime in almost three decades. Even more troubling is the misrepresentation of juvenile violence in the media. In 1996, the term "juvenile superpredator" was coined along with a theory about young criminals threatening society.

> America is now home to thickening ranks of juvenile "superpredators"—radically impulsive, brutally remorseless youngsters, including ever more preteenage boys, who murder, assault, rape, rob, burglarize, deal deadly drugs, join gun-toting gangs and create serious communal disorders. (Bennett, DiIulio, & Walters, 1996, p. 27)

The media seized on the theory and repeated inflated estimates of a bloodbath of teenage violence. The numbers were eventually debunked, but the residual fears about threats from teenagers lingered.

Media reports have consistently failed to point out that children are victims more often than perpetrators. For example, 83 percent of murdered children, 50 percent of murdered teenagers, and 85 percent of murdered adults are slain by adults. Every year in the United States about 350,000 children and teenagers are the victims of sexual and physical abuse, with the average age of the perpetrator being about 32. For every sexual and violent crime committed by a teenager, three such crimes are committed by adults against children and teens. The best available estimates tell us that 12 million women in the United States have been raped and that 62 percent of those rapes occurred before age 18. The average age of the rapist was 27. Finally, estimates suggest that between 60 and 90 percent of all prison inmates (and almost all the individuals presently on death row in the United States) were abused as children (Males, 1994). The alleged crime wave by children appears to be more accurately described as a crime wave of children as victims of crime.

Crime Mythology

False beliefs about crime abound in U.S. society and play a disproportionate role in the formulation of government and law enforcement policies. The crime that does exist is not predominantly violent, and violent crime is not as common or debilitating as the media would lead us to believe. The media, the state, and criminal justice officials create and perpetuate crime myths.

Crime myths focus on unpopular, minority, and deviant groups in society. Drug problems have consistently been laid squarely at the feet of immigrant groups, minority groups, and inner-city residents, wholly displacing the reality of drug use. Problems of opiate addiction in the late 1800s and early 1900s were blamed on immigrant Chinese workers, while the actual problem resulted from the overuse of over-the-counter elixirs by white, middle-aged, rural, Protestant women. The reputed cocaine epidemic of the 1980s was blamed on the irresponsible and hedonistic lifestyles of inner-city minorities, while the facts were that cocaine was primarily a drug of choice of affluent, suburban whites. Law enforcement agencies and the media have combined their efforts to tie serial murder, child abduction, ritualistic child abuse, and child sacrifice and murder to the activities of unpopular religious groups and sexual minorities.

Crime myths come in many forms. For example, in the mid-1970s the media reported that children had been murdered as the result of the poisoning of their Halloween candy. However, careful investigation revealed something quite different from a wave of poisoning by strangers. There had been only two incidents: one child died from ingesting heroin he found in his uncle's house; the other child was poisoned by his father, who put cyanide in the boy's candy. As with most crime myths, the truth was ignored while tales of mythical savagery circulated (Best & Horiuchi, 1985). To this day local television stations run cautionary stories before each Halloween.

In the early 1980s the media and the government helped create a panic over the issue of child abduction. It was estimated that somewhere between 1.5 and 2.5 million children were abducted from their homes every year; of that number, 50,000 would never be heard from again, presumably the victims of homicides. Pictures of "missing children" appeared on milk cartons, billboards, in newspapers, and on television. Children and parents were cautioned against contacts with strangers. The police in one town even wanted to etch identification numbers on school children's teeth so their bodies would be easier to identify (Dunn, 1994). The child abduction "epidemic" never existed. About 95 percent of those missing children were runaways (most of whom were home within 48 hours) or children abducted by a parent in a custody dispute. The fact is there are no more than 50 to 150 child abductions by strangers each year in the United States (Kappeler & Potter, 2005).

From 1983 to 1985 official estimates and media hype fueled a serial killer panic. Using FBI estimates of unsolved and motiveless homicides, media sources falsely reported that roughly 20 percent of all homicides, or about 4,000 murders a year, were the handiwork of serial killers. The media fed the myth with shocking and untrue confessions from Henry Lee Lucas, Ted Bundy, and others. Congress funded the Violent Criminal Apprehension Program and a behavioral sciences center for the FBI. When the data was subjected to careful analysis, scholars determined that at most there were 50 or 60 serial killer victims a year and that serial killers could account for no more than 2 percent of all homicides (Jenkins, 1996). Serial murder remains an extremely uncommon event.

The media play a vital role in the construction of crime mythology. Through selective interviewing the media can, and often do, fit isolated and rare incidents into what Fishman calls "news themes" (Fishman, 1978). For example, reporting the details of a crime involving an elderly victim and then interviewing a police official in charge of a special unit targeting crimes against the elderly creates a news theme—and can eventually create both a "crime wave" and a "crime myth." The use of value-laden language also contributes heavily to crime mythology. Youth gang members "prey" upon unsuspecting victims; serial killers "stalk"; child abductors "lurk" in the shadows; organized criminals are "mafiosi." Such language is common in crime news and substantially changes both the content and the context of crime stories. The media also frequently present misleading data. "Crime clocks" portray an exaggerated threat of crime. Uncritical reproduction of officially produced statistics often organizes stories into news themes and deflects alternative interpretations of the data.

Crime myths are not just curiosities or examples of sloppy work by journalists. They have tangible and serious policy implications. Spurred by crime mythology, politicians clamor for ever tougher sanctions against criminals. Crime myths divert attention away from the social and cultural forces that cause crime and toward individual pathologies; they reinforce stereotypes of minorities, poor people, and people who are "different."

Diverting Attention from Serious Social Problems

There is a corollary harm to directing our attention to certain kinds of criminality. Exaggerating the incidence and importance of violent crime, for example, deflects our attention from other serious issues. Consider media portrayals of white-collar crime and crimes against women.

The media pay little substantive attention to corporate crime and other forms of white-collar crime. Since the public is far more likely to be seriously harmed by corporate criminals than by violent criminals, this is a major disservice. In addition, ignoring such offenses encourages corporate crime by removing one of the primary modes of deterring that behavior—publicity. The media's neglect of white-collar crime stems from several sources, including: the risk of libel suits; social relationships between media executives and business executives; a pro-business orientation in the media; and the difficulty of adequately investigating and reporting on white-collar crime. In addition, corporations own the major newspapers, television networks, and television stations. Finally, media revenue comes primarily from advertising purchased by corporations.

The processes through which the media amplify and exaggerate crime and focus our attention on disadvantaged and relatively powerless groups in society are also used to deflect and diffuse concern over other types of crime. A case in point is the media's treatment of crimes against women, particularly rape and wife battering.

The media frequently distort rape coverage by referring to "careless" behavior by the victim or provocative actions or clothing. The fact is that rape is a crime of violence, and the behavior of the perpetrator should be the focus. The media further distort the rape issue by giving primary coverage to stranger rapes, failing to emphasize the far more common case in which rape is committed by acquaintances, relatives, and "friends." Stories about non-stranger rape frequently repeat and reflect police skepticism about such cases. Acquaintance rape stories often emphasize cases of false reporting, a very rare occurrence.

Similarly, the media distort the issue of battering in a variety of ways. First, battering is a relatively uncovered story in a crime-saturated news environment. When battering is reported, it is treated as a bizarre spectacle and news stories make use of euphemistic or evasive language (i.e. marital disputes, domestic disturbance, spouse abuse). Such language obscures the gendered nature of battering and implies the woman may be at fault. Stories on battering often raise the question of why the woman didn't leave her batterer, ignoring the fact that many do try to leave and that many have good reasons not to leave. Battering stories often project a clear implication that women are responsible for their own victimization. In addition, the media frequently overplay the extremely rare occurrences of women abusing their husbands. Rather than focusing on the common crime of spouse battering, media sources often focus on cases where governors have released women from prison who were convicted of murdering abusive husbands. The story often reports that the woman was not living with her husband when she killed him, implying that the danger to the woman had passed. The story usually fails to report that this is precisely the most dangerous time for battered women. News stories frequently imply that pardons and releases encourage battered women to commit acts of violence against their abusers (Barkan, 1997; Devitt, 1992; Devitt & Downey, 1992; Kamen & Rhodes, 1992).

In a particularly egregious example of gender bias, media coverage of school shootings in the 1990s failed to point out that all the offenders were males and a majority of the victims were females (Danner & Carmody, 2001).

Making Sense of Media Representations of Crime

Three fundamental questions for analyzing how the media approach crime issues are: What functions do the media serve?; How do they accomplish those tasks?; and Who benefits from media actions? As one of society's dominant institutions, the media share certain characteristics with other dominant institutions, like the state, corporations, the law enforcement community, and the military. As discussed in the epilogue, the media are increasingly intertwined with other institutions. The three questions help analyze the roles of any influential institution.

The media operate in the same ideological arena as do the educational system, religious institutions, and the family. Ideology is a means of organizing impressions, thoughts, knowledge, and observations to interpret the world around us. The media most frequently voice and, because of their ability to reach such an extensive audience, amplify the views and interests of groups with the greatest political, economic, and social power. Journalists and other media professionals are trained, educated, and socialized to internalize the values and norms of the dominant, mainstream culture. As a result, the media interpret or mediate news, information, and complex issues in a way that is usually consistent with the dominant culture and with the interests of powerful groups. The audience is, of course, free to interpret reports and stories by subjecting them to rigorous analysis, but people generally lack the time, resources, and information to construct alternative definitions and frameworks—in addition to having been socialized in the very same environment that influenced the stories.

The mass media are part of the culture industry that produces tangible products. In general, but not exclusively, the products they produce will reflect the ideas, conceptions, theories, and views of those with power in society. There have been notable examples of investigative reporters whose efforts, for example, have focused attention on abuses in the juvenile justice system in Chicago, forced the San Francisco police department to change how it tracks officers who abuse force, or exonerated inmates on death row (Coen, 2005; Headden, 2006; Worden, 2006). The media more frequently, however, present viewpoints that are consistent with those held by powerful groups. They present those viewpoints as the "obvious" or "natural" perspectives; alternative views, if presented at all, are clearly labeled as deviant, different, or dangerous. The mass media tend to avoid unpopular and unconventional ideas. They repeat widely held views that do not offend audiences, advertisers, or owners.

We discussed media reliance on the portrayal of violence in both news and entertainment programming. These portrayals are not just attention grabbing; they serve other purposes as well. They provide legitimacy to the criminal justice system and the police. They build support for more draconian laws and for more state intervention into people's daily activities. They warn us about people who are different, outsiders, and the dangers of defying social conventions. In other words, they reinforce, they amplify, and they extend the existing state of affairs that makes up the dominant culture and the current distribution of power (Althusser, 1971; Alvarado & Boyd-Barrett, 1992; Hall, 1980; Hall, Critcher, Jefferson, Clarke, & Roberts, 1978; Stevenson, 1995).

Of course, the media are only one half of the equation. The audience is the other half. Are audiences passive individuals who absorb ideological propaganda from newspapers, television, movies, and magazines? Of course not. People rely on other experiences and interactions. Social identities are determined by interactions with all kinds of institutions: the family, the school, the state, language, and the media. However, people generally find their sense of identity and their understanding of the reality around them as a result of social identities molded by those institutions—all of which are "ideological state apparatuses" (Althusser, 1971; Lapley & Westlake, 1988). The media have the capacity to concentrate those definitions and interactions in a way that convinces people that the media are presenting an accurate reflection of everyday lives.

Can audiences resist the power of media representations and definitions? Yes. We have seen that some crime scares and moral panics never get off the ground. Ideological state apparatuses are not always successful in defining people's roles and consciousness. While the mass media relay certain ideological images, the audience—if it has the ability, the resources, and the inclination—can remold, adapt, and integrate those messages into an entirely different system of meaning (Althusser, 1971; Berger, 1991; Hall, 1980; Hall et al., 1978; McQuail, 1994).

Mass media (movies, television, news organizations) form a culture industry in modern capitalist societies. They sell their products. The shape and content of those products will be influenced by the economic interests of the organization producing the products. Businesses operating in the culture industry must cater to the needs of advertisers. News shows are set up in standardized formats that cater to the demands of advertising. News must be fitted into the air time and column inches left over after paid advertising is accounted for. As a result, a standard format with news, weather, and sports segments has evolved around the needs of advertisers. They are unlikely to sponsor programs that attack their interests.

Media businesses must maximize their audiences. They do this in several ways. First, they include heavy doses of sex and violence. Second, they appeal to noncontroversial, mainstream views—trying to achieve a nonoffensive middle-ground on most issues. Finally, they treat the news as light entertainment, something not requiring a great deal of thought or attention on the part of the reader or viewer. In the process, they reduce the danger of alternative interpretations of a story by the audience.

In general we can safely say that: (1) ownership and economic control of the media are important factors in determining the content of media messages and (2) the media are a powerful influence in shaping public consciousness. The media are something of an irresistible force in modern society. The media are instrumental but not the only players in defining the terms through which we think about the world around us (Marcuse, 1991; Strinati, 1995). Stuart Hall points out that there is a "preferred reading" of the media's message that buttresses the dominant political, economic, and social relations in society. However, it is not the only interpretation. Some audiences "negotiate" that message and transform it slightly. Others read that message from a very different perspective and create "oppositional" meanings that are in direct conflict with the views of the powerful.

That is how we should interpret crime news. We must ask questions: Where did that information come from? Who supplied it? Do they have a vested interest in how we react to that information? We must begin to deconstruct the taken-for-granted "common sense" messages of the media. The readings in this volume are road maps through that process of deconstruction. It is up to the audience to follow those maps and to redefine "preferred readings."

References

Althusser, L. (1971). Ideology and ideological state apparatuses. In L. Althusser (Ed.), *Lenin and philosophy and other essays.* London: New Left Books.

Alvarado, M., & Boyd-Barrett, O. (Eds.). (1992). *Media education: An introduction.* London: BFI/Open University.

America's Most Wanted. Accessed February 15, 2006 from http://www.amw.com/

Barak, G. (1994). Media, society, and criminology. In G. Barak (Ed.), *Media, process, and the social construction of crime* (pp. 3–45). New York: Garland Publishing.

Barkan, S. F. (1997). *Criminology: A sociological understanding.* Englewood Cliffs, NJ: Prentice-Hall.

Beirne, P., & Messerschmidt, J. (1995). *Criminology* (2nd ed.). Ft. Worth: Harcourt Brace Jovanovich.

Bennett, W. J., DiIulio, J. J., Jr., & Walters, J. P. (1996). *Body count: Moral poverty and how to win America's war against crime and drugs.* New York: Simon & Schuster.

Berger, A. (1991). *Media analysts' techniques* (Rev. ed.). Newbury Park, CA: Sage.

Best, J., & Horiuchi, G. (1985). The razor and the apple: The social construction of urban legends. *Social Problems, 32,* 488–499.

Bunch, W. (1999). Survey: Crime fear is linked to TV news. *Philadelphia Daily News,* March 16, p. A1.

Carlson, J. (1995). *Prime time enforcement.* New York: Praeger.

Chiricos, T., & Eschholz, S. (2002). The racial and ethnic: Typification of crime and the criminal typification of race and ethnicity in local television news. *Journal of Research in Crime and Delinquency, 39,* 400–420.

Coen, J. (2005, September 5). Report leads to changes in defense for juveniles. *Chicago Tribune,* sec. 4, p. 1.

Cohen, S. (1980). *Folk devils and moral panics: The creation of the mods and rockers.* New York: St. Martin's Press.

Cullen, F., Fisher, B., & Applegate, B. (2000). Public opinion about punishment and corrections. *Crime and Justice: A Review of Research, 27,* 1–79.

Danner, M., & Carmody, D. (2001). Missing gender in cases of infamous school violence: Investigating research and media explanation. *Justice Quarterly, 18,* 87–114.

Devitt, T. (1992). Media circus at Palm Beach rape trial. *Extra!* (Publication of FAIR, Fairness and Accuracy in Reporting). Special issue, 9–10, 24.

Devitt, T., & Downey, J. (1992). Battered women take a beating from the press. *Extra!* (Publication of FAIR, Fairness and Accuracy in Reporting). Special issue, 14–16.

Dorfman, L., & Schiraldi, V. (2001). *Off balance: Youth, race and crime in the news.* Washington, DC: Building Blocks for Youth.

Dunn, K. (1994, April 10). Crime and embellishment. *Los Angeles Times Magazine,* p. 24.

Ericson, R., Baranek, P., & Chan, J. (1989). *Negotiating control: A study of news sources.* Toronto: University of Toronto Press.

Eschholz, S., Chiricos, T., & Gertz, M. (2003). Television and fear of crime: Program types, audience traits, and the mediating effect of perceived neighborhood racial composition. *Social Problems, 50,* 395–415.

Federal Bureau of Investigation. (2005). *Crime in the United States, 2004: Uniform crime reports.* Washington, DC: U.S. Department of Justice.

Feld, B. (2003). The politics of race and juvenile justice: The "due process revolution" and the conservative reaction. *Justice Quarterly, 20,* 765–800.

Fishman, M. (1978). Crime waves as ideology. In this volume, pp. 42–58.

Frankfurter, F., & Pound, R. (1922). *Criminal justice in Cleveland.* Cleveland: The Cleveland Foundation.

Gerbner, G. (1994, July). Television violence: The art of asking the wrong question. *Currents in Modern Thought,* 385–397.

Gilliam, F., & Iyengar, S. (2000). Prime suspects: The influence of local television news on the viewing public. *American Journal of Political Science,* 44, 560–573.

Graber, D. (1980). *Crime news and the public.* New York: Praeger.

Hall, S. (1980). Encoding/decoding. In Centre for Contemporary Cultural Studies (Ed.), *Culture, media, language.* London: Hutchinson.

Hall, S., Critcher, C., Jefferson, T., Clarke, J., & Roberts, B. (1978). *Policing the crisis.* London: Macmillan.

Headden, S. (2006, February 20). A tempest over police shootings. *U.S. News & World Report,* 140, 18.

Jenkins, P. (1988). Myth and murder: The serial killer panic of 1983–5. *Criminal Justice Research Bulletin,* 3, 11, 1–7.

Kamen, P., & Rhodes, S. (1992). Reporting on acquaintance rape. *Extra!* (Publication of FAIR, Fairness and Accuracy in Reporting). Special issue, 11.

Kappeler, V., & Potter, G. (2005). *The mythology of crime and criminal justice* (4th ed.). Long Grove, IL: Waveland Press.

Lapley, R., & Westlake, M. (1988). *Film theory: An introduction.* Manchester, England: Manchester University Press.

Livingston, J. (1996). *Crime & criminology* (2nd ed.). Englewood Cliffs, NJ: Prentice-Hall.

Lundman, R. (2003). The newsworthiness and selection bias in news about murder: Comparative and relative effects of novelty and race and gender typifications in newspaper coverage of homicide. *Sociological Forum,* 18, 257–286.

Maguire, K., & Pastore, A. (Eds.). (2004). *Sourcebook of criminal justice statistics.* [Online]. Available: http://www.albany.edu/sourcebook.

Males, M. (1994). Bashing youth: Media myths about teenagers. *Extra!* (Publication of FAIR, Fairness and Accuracy in Reporting). March/April issue.

Marcuse, H. (1991). *One-dimensional man* (Rev. ed.). Boston: Beacon.

McCaghy, C., & Capron, T. (1997). *Deviant behavior: Crime, conflict and interest groups* (4th ed.). New York: Macmillan.

McQuail, D. (1994). *Mass communication theory* (3rd ed.). London: Sage.

Miethe, T., & Lee, G. (1984). Fear of crime among older people: A reassessment of the predictive power of crime-related factors. *Sociological Quarterly,* 25, 397–415.

Public Health Reports. (1998). Health ranks fifth on local TV news. *Public Health Reports,* 113, 296–297.

Reiman, J. (2004). *The rich get richer and the poor get prison* (7th ed.). Boston: Allyn and Bacon.

Reinarman, C., & Levine, H. (1989). Crack in context: Politics and media in the making of a drug scare. *Contemporary Drug Problems,* 16, 535–577.

Skogan, W., & Maxfield, M. (1981). *Coping with crime: Individual and neighborhood reactions.* Beverly Hills, CA: Sage.

Smith, S. (2006, February 12). Police TV shows are all the rage, and here's why. *Chicago Tribune,* sec. 7, pp. 1, 16.

Stevenson, N. (1995). *Understanding media cultures: Social theory and mass communication.* London: Sage.

Strinati, D. (1995). *An introduction to theories of popular culture.* London: Routledge.

Surette, R. (1998). *Media, crime, and criminal justice: Images and realities* (2nd ed.). Pacific Grove, CA: Brooks/Cole.

Sutherland, E. (1950). The diffusion of sexual psychopath laws. *American Journal of Sociology,* 56, 142–148.

Unsolved Mysteries. Accessed February 15, 2006 from http://www.unsolved.com/

Vandiver, M., & Giacopassi, D. (1997). One million and counting: Students' estimates of the annual number of homicides occurring in the U.S. *Journal of Research in Crime and Delinquency,* 18, 91–131.

Walker, S. (1998). *Sense and nonsense about crime and drugs: A policy guide* (4th ed.). Belmont, CA: Wadsworth.

Warr, M. (1995). Public perceptions of crime and punishment. In J. Sheley (Ed.), *Criminology: A contemporary handbook* (pp. 15–31). Belmont, CA: Wadsworth.

Worden, R. (2006). *Wilkie Collins's "The dead alive": The novel, the case, and wrongful convictions.* Evanston: Northwestern University Press.

PART I

Making News

ENTER MORAL PANICS

Erich Goode & Nachman Ben-Yehuda

The place, Clacton, a small seaside resort community on England's eastern coast, one with an extremely limited range of facilities and amusements for young people. The time, Easter Sunday, 1964. The weather, cold and wet. Hundreds of adolescents and young adults are milling around on the streets and sidewalks, bored and irritated, seeking fun and adventure. A rumor—perhaps true, perhaps false—begins circulating that a bartender refused to serve several young people. A scuffle breaks out on the pavement; factions begin separating out. Youths on motorcycles and scooters roar up and down the street. A starter's pistol is fired into the air. The windows of a dance hall are smashed; some beach huts are destroyed. The damage—perhaps £500 in value, several times that in today's currency. The police, unaccustomed to such rowdiness, overreact by arresting nearly 100 young people, on charges ranging from "abusive behavior" to assaulting a police officer (Cohen, 1972, pp. 29ff).

Media Reaction

While not exactly raw material for a major story on youth violence, the seaside disturbances nonetheless touched off what can only be described as an orgy of sensationalistic news items. On Monday, the day after these events, every national newspaper with the exception of *The Times* ran a lead story on the Clacton disturbances. "Day of Terror by Scooter Groups" screamed the *Daily Telegraph;* claimed the *Daily Express,* "Youngsters Beat Up Town"; the *Daily Mirror* chimed in with, "Wild Ones Invade Seaside." On Tuesday, the press coverage was much the same. Editorials on the subject of youth violence began to appear. The Home Secretary was "urged" to take firm action to deal with the problem. Articles began to appear featuring interviews with Mods and Rockers, the two youth factions, current in Britain at

Goode & Ben-Yehuda (1994), *Moral Panics: The Social Construction of Deviance*, pp. 22–30. Permission granted by Blackwell Publishing.

the time, who were involved in the scuffles and the vandalism. The Mods (the term stood for "modernists") tended to be well-dressed, fashion-conscious teenagers and young adults who frequented discos, listened to the music of the Beatles, the Who, and the Rolling Stones, and, if they were on wheels, rode motor scooters. The Rockers tended to be tougher, more politically reactionary, more classically delinquent; they usually stemmed from a working-class background, and often rode motorbikes.

Theories were articulated in the press attempting to explain what was referred to as the mob violence. Accounts of police and court actions were reported; local residents were interviewed concerning the subject, their views widely publicized. The story was deemed so important that much of the press around the world covered the incidents, with major stories appearing in the United States, Canada, Australia, South Africa, and the European continent. *The New York Times* printed a large photograph of two adolescent girls accompanying its story. The Belgian newspapers captioned one photo "West Side Story on English Coast" (pp. 31ff). Youth fights and vandalism at resorts continued to be a major theme in the British press for some three years. Each time a disturbance broke out, much the same exaggerated, sensationalistic stories were repeated. But by the beginning of 1967, young Britishers no longer identified with the Mods or the Rockers, and the youth-violence angle gave way to other issues.

Enter Stanley Cohen

In 1964, Stanley Cohen was a graduate student at the University of London searching for a research topic for his dissertation. A South African who left his homeland for political reasons, a radical who was attracted to the causes and activities of underdogs and eager to critique the doings of the smug and powerful, Cohen found society's reaction to the exuberant activities of rebellious youth both disturbing and intriguing.

To Cohen, a major issue was the "fundamentally inappropriate" reaction by much of society to certain relatively minor events and conditions. The press, especially, had created a horror story practically out of whole cloth. The seriousness of events were exaggerated and distorted—in terms of the number of young people involved, the nature of the violence committed, the amount of damage inflicted, and their impact on the community, not to mention the importance of the events to the society as a whole. Obviously false stories were repeated as true; unconfirmed rumors were taken as fresh evidence of further atrocities (Cohen, 1972, pp. 31ff). During such times of overheated and exaggerated sense of threat, the society generally, including the press and the police, reacted toward the designated behavior and its enactors in a process Cohen referred to as "community sensitization" (1967, p. 280). Once a class of behavior, and a category of deviants, are identified, extremely small deviations from the norm become noticed, commented on, judged, and reacted to. In the case, the Clacton disturbances, minor offenses, or even gatherings which might become offenses, were instantly the focus of press and police attention. The process of sensitization was summed up in a headline at the time which read: "Seaside Resorts Prepare for the Hooligans' Invasion" (1967, p. 281). Moreover, on more than one occasion, the over-zealousness of the police resulted in an escalation of the conflict, where, for instance, by insisting that the crowd "move along," some of "the more labile members" of a crowd were provoked to resist, blows were exchanged, which led to their arrest (1967, p. 281). To Cohen, the sensitization and escalation processes were central to the public's reaction to the Mods and Rockers.

Cohen launched the term moral panic as a means of characterizing the reactions of the media, the public, and agents of social control to the youthful disturbances. In a moral panic, Cohen wrote:

> A condition, episode, person or group of persons emerges to become defined as a threat to societal values and interests; its nature is presented in a stylized and stereotypical fashion by the mass media; the moral barricades are manned by editors, bishops, politicians and other right-thinking people; socially accredited experts pronounce their diagnoses and solutions; ways of coping are evolved or . . . resorted to; the condition then disappears, submerges or deteriorates and becomes more visible. Sometimes the subject of the panic is quite novel and at other times it is something which has been in existence long enough, but suddenly appears in the limelight. Sometimes the panic passes over and is forgotten, except in folklore and collective memory; at other times it has more serious and long-lasting repercussions and might produce such changes as those in legal and social policy or even in the way society conceives itself. (1972, p. 9)

Actors in the Drama of the Moral Panic

How is this panic expressed? How did Cohen know he had a panic on his hands after the 1964 Clacton disturbances? Cohen looked at the reaction of five segments of society: the press, the public, agents of social control, or law enforcement, lawmakers and politicians, and action groups.

The Press

The way the press handled the seaside events could be characterized by exaggerated attention, exaggerated events, distortion, and stereotyping (1972, pp. 31–8). As we saw, newspapers "over-reported" the events; the scuffles and minor acts of vandalism that took place were accorded a place in the media far out of proportion to their importance. Not only was the focus of attention exaggerated, but the stories describing the events also exaggerated their seriousness. Phrases such as "riot," "orgy of destruction," scenes being "smeared with blood and violence," "battle," and a "screaming mob," were used regularly. If one boat was overturned, reports claimed that "boats" were overturned. One story claimed that, in one resort, the windows of "all" the dance halls by the beach were smashed, which was true—however, the town only had one dance hall, and some of its windows were smashed by youths (1972, pp. 32–3).

The stories also distorted the events and repeated obviously false stories. One youth told a judge that he would pay his fine with a £75 check. This was repeated as long as four years after the event, usually to show that the rebellious youths were affluent hordes whom "fines couldn't touch." In fact, the youth made this statement as a "pathetic gesture of bravado." He not only did not have the money, he didn't even have a bank account, and had never signed a check in his life (1972, p. 33). But because the tale confirmed a certain public image of the events and who perpetrated them, it was repeated and believed as true. Although myth-making characterizes all societies at all times, during times of the moral panic, the process is especially rapid, and a given myth is especially likely to be believed on relatively little evidence (1972, p. 33).

The youth violence and vandalism stories that ran in the British press between 1964 and 1967 tended to follow a stereotypical pattern. For the most part, they put together a composite picture, containing a number of central elements. It was almost as if a new story could be written simply by stitching these elements together. There was very little interest in what actually happened; what counted is how closely a news account conformed to the stereotype. The youths were depicted as being part of gangs, even though all of the youths involved were part of very loose assemblies rather than tightly structured gangs. The seaside villages were said to have been victims of an "invasion from London," even though many—in all likelihood, most—were local youths or came from nearby towns and villages. Few stories omitted the fact that many of the offenders were on motor scooters or motorbikes, even though the overwhelming majority were on foot. Offenders were said to come from affluent families, even though those on whom data could be gathered lived in extremely modest economic circumstances. They were said to have come to the resorts deliberately to make trouble, even though, in reality, nearly all came merely hoping that there would be some trouble to watch. The offenses described in the press were nearly always violent ones, even though only a tenth of the offenders were charged with violent crimes; even most of the offenses that did take place entailed relatively trivial acts such as petty theft, threatening behavior, and obstruction. The financial loss to local businesses was said to have been drastic. If anything, the reverse was true: more people than usual came to the resorts to check out the action. In short, one indication that a moral panic is taking place is the stereotypical fashion in which the subject is treated in the press (1972, pp. 34–8).

The Public

Cohen's conception of moral panics includes the dimension of public concern. There must be some latent potential on the part of the public to react to a given issue to begin with, some raw material out of which a media campaign about a given issue can be built. The public may hold a more sophisticated view of the issue than the press (1972, pp. 65–70), but if the media is infused with hysteria about a particular issue or condition which does *not* generate public concern, then we do not have a moral panic on our hands. The media's exaggerated attention must touch something of a responsive chord in the general public. The disturbances that attracted so much attention broke out in the 1960s, at a time when much of the adult British public, with the Second World War and the postwar era deprivations still fresh on their minds, saw a younger generation growing up in affluence (they "never had it so good," was a common refrain), responding not with gratitude but with disdain, rebellion, and delinquency. The problem was that the younger generation had been coddled, indulged, treated with kid gloves; the solution—a tougher parental hand, stricter social control, harsher penalties for transgressions, stiffer fines and jail sentences. In short, the events at Clacton and other seaside communities were focused on and reacted to by much of the public as a symbol for some of the larger problems plaguing British society. The events themselves were not so important as what they seemed to represent. But in order to see these disturbances as central, it became necessary to exaggerate and distort their reality.

Law Enforcement

In addition to the press and the general public, the actions of the social (or "societal") control culture demonstrated that a moral panic was taking place in Britain in the mid-1960s over the Mods and Rockers (1972, pp. 85ff). In a moral panic, segments of the society are sensitized to trouble from certain quarters (1972, pp. 77ff); the society is said to be faced with a "clear and present danger" the signs of which it is so sharply attuned to. In no sector is this principle more clearly evident than in public attitudes about what the police and the courts—law enforcement—ought to be doing about the perceived threat. Ties between and among local police forces are established and strengthened, and those between the local and national levels of law enforcement are activated, in order to more effectively deal with the problems faced by the putative threat (1972, p. 86). Cohen calls this process *diffusion.*

Efforts are made by officers to broaden the scope of law enforcement and increase its intensity; punitive and overly zealous actions already taken are justified on the basis of the enormity of the threat the society faces (1972, pp. 86–7). Cohen refers to this as *escalation.* New methods of control are proposed both to legislators and to the police: stiffer sentences, expanded police powers, confiscating motor scooters and motorbikes, banning Mod clothing, cutting long hair on youths, drafting troublemakers into the military, and so on (1972, pp. 88–91). Some police practices, previously rarely used, that were called up to deal with unacceptable Mod and Rocker behavior included: riding suspicious youths out of town or to the railroad station; keeping crowds moving along; confiscating studded belts; keeping certain trouble-some locations free of Mods and Rockers; verbally harassing adolescents, par-ticularly in a crowd situation, to "show them up" and "deflate their egos" (1972, p. 95), making immediate (and often wrongful) arrests, and so on (1972, pp. 92–8). The thinking among agents of social control is that "new sit-uations need new remedies"; a national problem called for a drastic solution, and often, this entailed suspending rights and liberties previously enjoyed.

Politicians and Legislators

Members of Parliament (MPs) "took an immediate and considerable interest in disturbances in their own constituencies" (p. 133). Stiffer penalties for youth offenses were called for. Local merchants were assured that "hooli-ganism" would not threaten their economic interests and would not be repeated. Statements by MPs were issued to the press; "Jail These Wild Ones—Call by MPs," ran one such story. A return to corporal punishment for hooliganism was called for by some. Meetings were held between MPs and local police chiefs, and summaries were sent to the Home Secretary. Sug-gestions were made by one MP that Britain revive non-military national ser-vice, such as construction or mining, as a punishment for hooliganism. A suggestion to raise the minimum driving age from 16 to 19 was introduced in the House of Lords. A Malicious Damage Bill was introduced and debated in the House of Commons only a month after the Clacton incident; in further debate on the Bill two months later, the seaside disturbances became the cen-tral imagery dominating the discussion. Though some politicians recognized that the concern was exaggerated, and had a moderating influence on the discussion, the dominant mood among politicians and legislators toward youth crime in the period following the initial incident was angry, self-righ-teous, vindictive, condemnatory, and punitive. Politicians and other groups aligned themselves against a devil and on the side of angels; the fact is, they picked an "easy target," one that "hardly existed." What counted was not the nature of the target but what side they were on and what they were against (1972, p. 138). Such symbolic alignments represent one defining quality of the moral panic.

Action Groups

At some point, moral panics generate appeals, campaigns, and finally, "fully fledged action groups" (p. 119) which arise to cope with the newly-existing threat. These are "moral entrepreneurs" (Becker, 1963, pp. 147ff) who believe that existing remedies are insufficient. Action groups can be seen as "germinal social movements" (Cohen, 1972, p. 120). Often, partic-ipants have something to gain personally from rallying against a problem, but this is not a necessary determinant. The Mods and the Rockers generated two local action groups, one of which proposed that convicted Mods and Rockers be subjected to a penal-style program of discipline and hard labor

(1972, p. 121), and the other of which favored the reintroduction of a variety of harsher penalties, including whippings of young offenders with a birch rod (1972, p. 125). These action groups did not grow into social movements, nor did they survive the demise of the Mods and the Rockers.

There are two additional features that characterize moral panics, two developments that inform the observer that a society is in the grip of a moral panic: the creation of *folk devils* (1972, pp. 40ff) and the development of a *disaster mentality* (pp. 144ff).

Folk Devils

A folk devil is the personification of evil. Folk devils permit instant recognition; they are "unambiguously unfavorable symbols" (Turner and Surace, 1956, pp. 16–20; Cohen, 1972, p. 41), that is, stripped of all favorable characteristics and imparted with exclusively negative ones. In such a symbolization process, "images are made much sharper than reality" (Cohen, 1972, p. 43). While all folk devils are created out of some existing and recognizable elements, a full-scale *demonology* takes place by which the members of a new evil category are placed "in the gallery of contemporary folk devils" (p. 44). Once a category has been identified in the media as consisting of troublemakers, the supposed havoc-wreaking behavior of its members reported to the public, and their supposed stereotypical features litanized, the process of creating a new folk devil is complete; from then on, all mention of representatives of the new category revolves around their central, and exclusively negative, features. All moral panics, by their very nature, identify, denounce, and attempt to root out folk devils. A condition that generates such widespread public concern must have had a personal agent responsible for its inception and maintenance. Such evil does not arise by happenstance or out of thin air; there must be a circle of evil individuals who are engaged in undermining society as we know it. In short, folk devils are *deviants;* they are engaged in wrongdoing; their actions are harmful to society; they are selfish and evil; they must be stopped, their actions neutralized. Only an effort of substantial magnitude will permit us to return to normal.

The Disaster Analogy

And lastly, in moral panics, Cohen argues, preparations are taken very much like those taken before, during, and after a disaster, such as a hurricane, a volcano eruption, or an earthquake. As during disasters, in the moral panic, there are predictions of impending doom, a "warning phase," sensitization to cues of danger, coping mechanisms, frequent overreactions, the institutionalization of threat, rumors speculating about what is happening or will happen, false alarms, and, occasionally, mass delusion (1972, pp. 144–8). The perceived threat to, and subsequent reaction by, conventional society to the projected invasion of hordes of deviants and delinquents has many strong parallels with the steps taken before, during, and after a natural disaster.

The Contribution of the Moral Panics Concept

The concept of the moral panic expands our understanding of social structure, social process, and social change. It ties together concepts from a variety of disparate areas—deviance, crime, collective behavior, social problems, and social movements. Moral panics are likely to "clarify [the] normative contours" and "moral boundaries" of the society in which they occur, demonstrate that there are limits to how much diversity can be tolerated in a society. Focusing on moral panics emphasizes the fact that reactions to unconventional behavior do not arise solely as a consequence of a rational and realistic assessment of the concrete damage that the behavior in question is likely to inflict on the society. Without resorting to conspiratorial thinking, an investigation of the moral panic emphasizes that social reaction to a new and seemingly threatening phenomenon arises as a consequence of that phenomenon's real or supposed threat to certain "positions, statuses, interests, ideologies, and values" (Cohen, 1972, p. 191). The cast of characters Cohen located in the moral panic—the media, the general public, the agents of social control, lawmakers and politicians, and action groups—are distressed by a certain perceived threat for a reason. If all panics entailed a public reaction to a specific, clearly identifiable threat, the magnitude of which can be objectively assessed and readily agreed upon, then such reactions would require no explanation. On the other hand, if, as Cohen argues, the reaction is out of proportion to the threat, we are led to ask why it arises; the panic is problematic—it demands an explanation.

Why a moral panic over *this* supposed threat, but not *that,* potentially even more damaging, one? Why does *this* cast of characters become incensed by the threat the behavior supposedly poses, but not *that* cast of characters? Why a moral panic at this time, but not before or after? How and why do moral panics arise? How and why do they die out? What role do interests play in the moral panic? Are the dynamics of the moral panic different during different historical time periods, or different from one society to another? What does the moral panic tell us about how society is constituted, how it works, how it changes over time? Cohen's concept introduces the observer of society to a wide range of questions and potential explorations.

References

Becker, Howard S. 1963. *Outsiders: Studies in the Sociology of Deviance.* New York: Free Press.

Cohen, Stanley. 1967. "Mods, Rockers, and the Rest: Community Reactions to Juvenile Delinquency." *Howard Journal,* 12(2): 121–30.

_____. 1972. *Folk Devils and Moral Panics: The Creation of the Mods and Rockers.* London: MacGibbon & Kee.

Turner, Ralph H., and Samuel J. Surace. 1956. "Zoot-suiters and Mexicans: Symbols in Crowd Behavior." *American Journal of Sociology,* 62(July): 14–20.

MEDIA CONSTRUCTIONS OF CRIME

Vincent F. Sacco

Crime, like an economic recession, a lack of affordable housing, or inadequate health care, is experienced as both a private trouble and a public issue: Quite obviously, for victims, a criminal offense and the resulting loss or injury present problems of a highly personal nature. For victims and nonvictims alike, however, the "plague of drugs," the "epidemic of random violence," and other manifestations of the crime problem are matters for intense public discussion and political debate.

While the distinction between private troubles and public issues is an important one, these dimensions are not independent.[1] Citizens' personal troubles with crime provide the building blocks out of which public issues are constructed. On the other hand, the warnings of danger implicit in public pronouncements about the seriousness and pervasiveness of crime problems may be a source of private trouble if they exacerbate the fear of crime among those who have routine exposure to such pronouncements.

Central to the interplay between individuals' private troubles with crime and the social issue of crime are the mass media. The news media, in particular, provide an important forum in which private troubles are selectively gathered up, invested with a broader meaning, and made available for public consumption. The dynamic character of these processes and the consequences that they have for public understanding of crime and its solution invite close scrutiny.

From Private Trouble . . .

Numerous studies of media content have documented the fact that crime reports are a durable news commodity.[2] While news about crime figures prominently in all types of media, important differences exist between print and electronic media, between more elite and more popular media, and

From: *Annals of the American Academy of Political & Social Science*, vol. 539, pp. 141–154, copyright 1995. Reprinted by permission of Sage Publications, Inc.

between media markets. Because of this variability, estimates of the proportion of total news that is devoted to crime coverage range from 5 to 25 percent.[3]

News about crime is most frequently news about the occurrence or processing of private trouble in the form of specific criminal events. In her study of crime and justice news in Chicago in the late 1970s, Doris Graber found that while attention to crime varied across media, reports of individual crime dominated for all media.[4] With respect to the three newspapers studied, the coverage of individual crimes surpassed the coverage of Congress and the presidency and equaled or surpassed election coverage.

Analyses of media content demonstrate that the news provides a map of the world of criminal events that differs in many ways from the one provided by official crime statistics. Variations in the volume of news about crime seem to bear little relationship to variations in the actual volume of crime between places or over time.[5] Whereas crime statistics indicate that most crime is non-violent, media reports suggest, in the aggregate, that the opposite is true.[6] While crime news tends to provide only sparse details about victims and offenders, that which is provided is frequently at odds with the official picture. Both offenders and victims, for instance, appear less youthful in media reports than they do in statistical records.[7] In addition, news content does not reflect and frequently even reverses the relationship that, according to much social scientific evidence, exists between minority group membership and criminal offending.[8] With respect to gender, however, both crime statistics and crime news portray offending as predominantly a male activity.[9]

News reports also distort the relationship between crime and legal control. In the news, the police appear to be more effective in apprehending offenders than police data would suggest they are.[10] Moreover, while the activities of the police are prominently featured, the functioning of other actors in the criminal justice system is much less visible.[11] This probably reflects a professional judgment that criminal events are most newsworthy immediately following their occurrence and thus when they are in the early stages of justice system processing, when police activity is prominent.[12]

These images of crime, the criminal, and the victim that appear with patterned regularity in print and broadcast news emerge quite logically from the organizational processes of news production. News stories are most useful to news organizations when they are gathered easily from credible sources; for this reason, policing agencies have become the principal suppliers of these stories.[13] In short, relationships involving news organizations and policing agencies allow the collection of news about common crime to be routinized in a manner that uses the resources of news agencies efficiently.[14] In addition, the public view of the police as apolitical crime experts imbues police-generated crime news with authority and objectivity.

Ease of access to authoritative news is not the only advantage that police-generated crime stories offer, since such stories are consistent with several other professional values that structure the news production process. Much of what we call news consists of reports of specific incidents that have occurred since the publication of the previous day's newspaper or the airing of the previous night's newscast. As discrete incidents that occur at particular times and places, individual crimes conform closely to this requirement of periodicity.

Stories about individual crimes—with their characteristic portrayals of villains and victims—also have dramatic value. The dramatic potential is heightened when the victim or offender is a celebrity, when the incident is of a very serious nature, or when the circumstances of the offense are atypical. In addition, the routine crime story is a rather uncomplicated matter, and it is unnecessary for news workers to assume that readers or viewers require an extensive background in order to appreciate the story. The lack of factual complexity associated with the ordinary individual crime story generally means that it can be easily written and edited by news workers whose professional activities are consistently regulated by rigid deadlines.

The elastic character of the crime news supply offers a further advantage. On any given day, particularly in large metropolitan areas, there is an almost limitless supply of crimes that could be the object of media attention. However, from day to day, or from week to week, the demand of the news agency for crime news may vary due to other events that are seen to demand coverage. Depending on the size of the news hole, crime coverage may be expanded or contracted in compensatory fashion. A study by Sanford Sherizen of crime news in Chicago newspapers found, for instance, that crime reports were often located on the obituary pages so that layout difficulties resulting from the inability to plan these pages could be overcome through the use of crime news filler.[15]

Over the last several years, a number of changes in local and national media environments have altered the nature and extent of crime coverage. The growth of cable stations, for instance, has increased the carrying capacity for news generally and for crime news specifically. More stories can be covered, and those that are judged to be particularly newsworthy can be covered in greater detail. The live television coverage of court proceedings—as in the case of the Menendez brothers, Lorena Bobbit, or O.J. Simpson—has become commonplace. The increasing sophistication of news gathering, surveillance, and home video technologies has meant that it is no longer unusual to capture thefts, robberies, or even homicides on tape. One consequence of the diffusion of these technologies has been to raise to national prominence stories with no real national significance. Crime stories that would have been a purely local affair in an earlier period now attract much wider attention because a videotape of the incident is available for broadcast.

The last two decades have also witnessed a redefinition of what can be considered an appropriate subject for news reporting. Changes in mores relating to public discussion of sex and violence have allowed respectable media outlets to report crimes that would have previously been seen as taboo and to do so at a level of detail that would once have been considered lurid. At the same time, the politicization of crimes such as sexual assault and domestic violence has broadened the range of crime stories that, it can be argued, legitimately require coverage.[16]

Programmatic developments in commercial broadcast media have magnified the impact of these changes. The proliferation of newsmagazines, daytime talk shows, docudramas, and various other forms of infotainment has ushered in a programming cycle that is heavily dependent on crime news and victim accounts. The frequent reliance of many of these programs on dramatic reenactments of real events and their mixing of factual reports with rumor and speculation blurs the basic distinctions that analysts of crime content have traditionally drawn between news and entertainment media.[17]

. . . To Public Issues

Public issues grow up around private troubles when the experiences of individuals are understood as exemplifying a larger social problem, and the news media play a vital role in the construction of such problems.[18] Most notably, professional judgments of newsworthiness and the selective use of news sources allow some groups, rather than others, the opportunity to express a view about what is and what is not a problem and how any such problem should be managed. By implication, the relationships that link the police to news agencies serve law enforcement as well as media interests. The police role as the dominant gatekeeper means that crime news is often police news and that the advancement of a police perspective on crime and its solution is facilitated.[19] It has been argued that this results in the adoption of an uncritical posture with respect to the police view of crime and the measures necessary to control it.[20] More generally, the frame of reference offered by a government bureaucracy or other recognized authority with respect to crime problems may only infrequently be called into question and, as a consequence, competing perspectives may become marginalized.

This tendency may be no less true of in-depth issue coverage than of routine news reporting. Henry Brownstein maintains that during the 1980s, there was relatively little reporting that took issue with the official version of the drug problem constructed by government experts.[21] In a similar way, Philip Jenkins has noted how experts of the Federal Bureau of Investigation were able to present themselves as the authorities on the subject of serial murder and how they made themselves available to journalists who reciprocated with favorable coverage of the agency.[22]

It would be incorrect, however, to suggest that news media are merely the passive conveyors of the claims about problems offered up by government bureaucracies, political candidates, or other self-interested groups, since any such claims must be transformed to meet the requirements of the medium in question. In an analysis of television network news coverage of threats to children, Joel Best argued that "inevitably, network news stories distort the problems they explore,"[23] in large part because news conventions impose severe constraints on how stories are covered. Stories must be told in a few minutes, frequently by reporters who may have little more than a surface familiarity with the complexities of the problem at hand. Moreover, the topic must be viewed as serious enough and as visual enough to be chosen over competing issues. Best found, in the case of child victimization, that the stories used frightening and dramatic examples to typify the problem and that they emphasized the existence of a consensus among knowledgeable experts regarding its scope and seriousness.

In other instances, news media may more actively engage in problem construction. Investigative reporting, or the coverage of an event judged to be especially newsworthy, may contribute to the establishment of a media agenda that finds expression in the reporting of further stories or in more detailed features. A study by David L. Protess and his colleagues revealed how one Chicago newspaper set its own media agenda after an extensive investigative series on rape.[24] The researchers found that while the series did not appear to have a substantial impact on the perceptions of policymakers or the general public, there were significant changes in the extent and depth of rape coverage after the series ended, even though police reports of rape were unchanged. In a related way, during the summer of 1994, the O.J. Simpson case provided an opportunity for sidebar stories relating to the prevalence and causes of domestic violence, the inadequacy of justice system responses, and pending federal and state legislation. Such coverage contextualized the original incident in a way that helped construct the social issue of violence against women at the same time that it legitimated continuing, detailed attention to the original story.

The Content of Crime Problems

Media constructions of crime problems address both the frequency and the substance of private trouble with crime. Rhetoric regarding both of these dimensions serves to impress on readers and viewers the gravity of particular crime problems and the need to confront them in particular ways.

Large numbers of problems provide convincing evidence that problems exist. This is perhaps most evident in the case of crime waves, when it is argued that crime is becoming more frequent. A study by Steven Gorelick, for instance, of an anticrime campaign sponsored by a New York daily newspaper found that crime in the city was frequently described as a "mushrooming cloud," a "floodtide," a "spreading cancer," or in similar terms.[25] Sometimes these claims about the numbers of people affected have greater specificity in that some particular segment of the population is claimed to be experiencing rapidly increasing risks of offending or victimization.[26]

Yet, with respect to many crime waves, it is the belief that crime is increasing, rather than crime itself, that is really on the rise.[27] A study by Mark Fishman of a 1976 New York crime wave against the elderly described how crime waves may be "things of the mind."[28] Fishman found that there was no compelling evidence to indicate that the criminal victimization of the elderly actually increased during the study period. Instead, the crime wave originated in the efforts of journalists to organize individual crime stories around a compelling news theme. The theme of crime against the elderly was elaborated as competing news organizations responded to each other's coverage of the issue. In addition, the police, in their role as gatekeepers of crime news, reacted to the increased media interest by making available more stories that reflected and reinforced the crime-against-the-elderly theme.

A more recent example of a journalistic construction of rapidly rising crime is provided by James D. Orcutt and J. Blake Turner.[29] Their analysis focused on the way in which graphic artists in the national print media transformed survey data, which showed modest yearly changes in drug use, into evidence of a "coke plague." While the numbers were real, their graphical presentation in the weekly periodical under study was misleading. As in the case described by Fishman, the dynamics of competitive journalism created a media feeding frenzy that found news workers "snatching at shocking numbers" and "smothering reports of stable or decreasing use under more ominous headlines."[30]

Claims about statistical frequency are not restricted to reports about how the numbers are increasing, however. With respect to the problem of violence against women, for instance, it is argued that the numbers have always been very high but that the failure to police such incidents, the stigma associated with victimization, and an institutional unwillingness to believe the accounts of victims have resulted in statistical counts that dramatically underestimate the problem. Thus, whether or not the numbers are going up is defined as less salient than the observation that they have always been higher than we have thought.

According to Neil Gilbert, outrageous claims about the prevalence of problems sometimes make their way into news reports in part because of journalists' general inability to evaluate the data supplied to them.[31] Too often, they lack the technical sophistication to critically assess claims about the frequency of crime or victimization in an independent fashion. Instead, they collect and validate information by talking to experts who are expected to offer informed opinions. However, in the case of emergent problems, it is often the problem advocate, interested in advancing a particular point of view, who may be among the first to collect and publicize empirical evidence. As a result, the estimates yielded by advocacy research may be the only ones available at the earliest stages of problem development. Philip Jenkins has argued that the emergence of serial murder as a social issue in the early 1980s was spurred by "epidemic estimates" that placed the number of serial murder victims at between 20 and 25 percent of American homicides.[32] While such numbers continue to circulate through popular and journalistic accounts, more reasoned analysis suggests that the number of serial murder victims is closer to 2 percent of American homicides.

The emergence of crime problems is related not only to claims about the frequency of criminal events but also to claims about their character. Exactly what types of events such incidents are thought to be and who is thought to be typically involved in them matter as much as does the rate at which they are thought to occur.

Any particular social problem can be framed in many ways, and these various frames imply different causal attributions and prospective solutions.[33] Because they are able to legitimate some views and to marginalize others, the news media are an important part of this framing process. Depending on the sources accessed or the type of coverage, rape can be framed as a sex crime or as a crime of violence; the "drug problem" as a product of pushers who hook their victims or as an example of the overreach of criminal law; and violence on the part of youths as a condition necessitating either swift punishment or comprehensive community development.

More generally, when private troubles are constructed as a crime problem of any sort, they are framed in ways that assign primary responsibility for their solution to the criminal justice system. Joel Best has shown how crime problem interpretations of the 1987 freeway shooting incidents in California competed in the relevant news coverage with other interpretations of the incidents.[34] Whereas the crime problem frame implied the need for increased patrols, better investigation, and more effective prosecution, other definitions of the issue—as a gun problem, a traffic problem, or a courtesy problem—suggested other solutions.

In a related way, the social distributional character of victimization is frequently ignored by news coverage that stresses the random character of victimization. While the best social science literature indicates that the risks of crime, like the risks of other misfortunes, are not equally shared, media images often convey a different message. According to Brownstein, for instance, much of the coverage of the drug issue in New York City between 1986 and 1990 emphasized the random character of drug violence even though police statistics indicated that the risks of such violence were extremely low.[35] Themes relating to randomness serve the interests of both news workers and others who seek to frame crime problems. News stories about random crimes have great dramatic value, as the media frenzies that surround serial murders illustrate. Moreover, the advocates to whom news workers have access during the early stages of problem development often stress the random nature of a particular form of victimization since problems must be seen as more urgent when everyone is threatened.

While much routine crime reporting can be understood as maintaining established crime problem frames, new problems are always being discovered as old problem paradigms expand or as novel elements come together with established news themes. The discovery of new problems provides a journalistic opportunity to tell a story that has not been told before, but such stories are told most effectively when they resonate with existing cultural themes. In the 1970s, the problem of crime against the elderly brought together in one package an already familiar concern about crime in the streets and victims' rights with an emerging concern about the aging population.[36] The problem of satanic crime, which received extensive media coverage in the 1980s, combined familiar news themes relating to religious cults, child abuse, and juvenile crime.[37] Media attention to date rape and stalking extends earlier news themes relating to violence against women.

The transition from private troubles to public issues is not always a linear process since media interest in particular crime problems can vary in intensity or decline over time. The 1987 shootings on California freeways never became a well-established problem, despite a strong start.[38] In the case of crimes against the elderly, Fay Lomax Cook and Wesley Skogan observe that while the issue achieved a prominent position on media and other agendas during the early 1970s, by the decade's end, it had declined precipitously.[39] On the other hand, Fishman has argued that as long as police departments are the routine sources of crime news, the media will reinforce a climate of opinion that keeps the attention of the police focused on "crime in the streets." He concludes that while social problems may come and go, "law-and-order news is here to stay."[40]

. . . And Back Again?

There can be little doubt that media consumers have broad and regular exposure to crime news.[41] What are the consequences of this exposure? One potential consequence that has generated considerable interest relates to the deleterious effects that media attention to crime problems may have on audience members' fear of victimization. On the surface, arguments about such effects seem plausible. Public fear of crime is pervasive, and it outstrips measured levels of victimization. By implication, public anxieties would appear to be rooted in vicarious rather than direct experiences, and since messages about crime are so prevalent in the media, it seems reasonable to conclude that much public fear originates in media coverage of crime problems. At issue is whether experience with media treatments of crime as a public issue contributes to fear as a personal trouble. There is a large body of empirical evidence that bears on the relationship between audience exposure to mass media and fear of crime. In the aggregate, however, the findings are equivocal regarding the strength of such a relationship or even whether such a relationship exists.[42]

Some of the inconsistency in this respect is methodological in nature. Considerable variation exists regarding the ways in which crime news, crime news exposure, and fear of crime have been operationalized in the research literature.[43] In addition, since people not only read or watch crime news but also talk about it with friends and neighbors, measured variations in media exposure are not necessarily indicative of exposure to crime news.[44] Nor is it reasonable to assume for research purposes that people are always able to keep clear and report to researchers what is learned in which information channel.[45] Even when such methodological limitations are taken into account, however, the research indicates that the effects of media exposure on fear of crime are less significant than any naive hypothesis would suggest.

Several factors explain this apparent paradox. To begin with, it would be inappropriate to assume that audience members respond passively to the warnings of danger issued by omnipotent news media. Instead, as Paul Williams and Julie Dickinson note, news consumers are actively involved in investing the news with meaning.[46] Audience members bring to the reading and viewing experience their own predispositions, which influence what crime news means for them. These predispositions may include personal experiences with crime or violence,[47] perceptions of the credibility of news media,[48] or the extent of prior concern about personal safety.[49] In the context of cross-sectional research, these predispositions suggest the possibility that the correlation between media usage and fear of crime may be more indicative of selective exposure than of media influence.[50]

While people avidly read and watch crime news, it is unclear that in so doing they extract lessons relating to their own safety. Such lessons, it appears, are more effectively learned in other contexts. The relevant research indicates that the news about crime that travels through interpersonal channels may be more likely to induce fear than is the news that travels through mass channels.[51] To learn about crime by talking to one's neighbors is to learn about victims whose experiences cannot be easily dismissed because they are nameless or faceless or live somewhere else.

By contrast, the typical media crime story is stripped of much of its emotional character and is likely to involve victims about whom the viewer or reader has no personal knowledge. In addition, the average news story may provide readers and viewers with so little information about the victim, the setting in which the crime occurred, or other circumstances of commission that it may be irrelevant to any assessment of personal victimization risks.[52] Most crime news is nonlocal and therefore far removed from judgments that must be made regarding the safety of the immediate environment. Not surprisingly, there is research that suggests that fear is, in fact, related to crime news exposure when local random violent crimes are reported in prominent fashion.[53] Taken together, these findings are consistent with a more general body of research that indicates that people may be less dependent on news media when they seek information about matters close to home.[54]

Overall, it would appear that as crime news relates to matters of personal safety, consumers appear to exercise a healthy dose of skepticism.[55] As Dennis Howitt observes, newspaper readers do not necessarily think that crime rates are going up just because the number of column inches devoted to crime increases.[56] They are more likely to put what is learned from the media in the context of what they learn from other sources, and they may be well aware when media are behaving in a highly sensationalist manner.[57]

Conclusion

If the news business is concerned with the production of crime problems, then the private troubles of criminal offenders and crime victims are the raw materials. These troubles are not simply reported on, however, since they are fundamentally transformed by the news-gathering process. Screened through a law enforcement filter, contextualized by advocacy claims and culturally resonant news themes, and shaped and molded by the conventions and requirements of commercial media, these private troubles become public issues.

While news media coverage of crime may not have a powerful influence on the concern for personal safety, this should not obscure other, perhaps more significant effects. Such effects are not narrowly attitudinal or behavioral but are broadly ideological.

Some critics argue that the police perspective implicit in so much crime news reporting dramatically restricts the parameters of discussion and debate about the problem of crime. As a consequence, the causes of offending are individualized and the relationships that link crime to broader social forces are left largely unexplored.[58] Correspondingly, traditional law-and-order responses are reaffirmed as the most efficient way to manage crime problems. A study of media coverage of attacks against women in Toronto found that explanations of the phenomenon tended to focus attention on the ways in which victims placed themselves in conditions of risk, on offender pathology, and on the need for a more coercive criminal justice response.[59] The authors note that while these terms of reference were not unreasonable, the attention they received left little room for alternative interpretations of the problem, particularly those interpretations that link the victimization of women to structures of gender inequality.

When crime problems are successfully constructed, a consensus emerges regarding what kinds of public issues private troubles represent.[60] Yet the development of such a consensus—regarding what the problems are, who is responsible for them, and how they should be resolved—should not be understood in conspiratorial terms. While both news workers and their sources are interested in offering a convincing and credible construction of reality, for many in the media, the construction of these problems is not a matter of activism but just another day at the office.[61]

As news workers observe and influence each other, and as the line between news and entertainment becomes more confused, public discussion of crime problems reflects and reinforces this consensus, and popular views of these problems begin to assume a taken-for-granted character. Inevitably, but regrettably, the emergence of such a consensus relegates to the margins the search for alternative ways of thinking about crime and its solution.

Notes

[1] C. Wright Mills, *The Sociological Imagination* (New York: Oxford University Press, 1959), pp. 9–11.

[2] See, for example, James Garofalo, "Crime and the Mass Media: A Selective Review of Research," *Journal of Research in Crime and Delinquency*, 18:319–350 (1981); Ray Surette, *Media, Crime and Criminal Justice* (Pacific Grove, CA: Brooks/Cole, 1992); Joseph R. Dominick, "Crime and Law Enforcement in the Mass Media," in *Deviance and Mass Media*, ed. Charles Winick (Beverly Hills, CA: Sage, 1978), pp. 105–128.

[3] Surette, Media, *Crime and Criminal Justice*, p. 62.

4 Doris A. Graber, *Crime News and the Public* (New York: Praeger, 1980).

5 F. James Davis, "Crime News in Colorado Newspapers," *American Journal of Sociology,* 57:325–330 (1952); Wesley G. Skogan and Michael G. Maxfield, *Coping with Crime: Individual and Neighborhood Reactions* (Beverly Hills, CA: Sage, 1981).

6 Garofalo, "Crime and the Mass Media"; Skogan and Maxfield, *Coping with Crime;* Philip Schlesinger, Howard Tumber, and Graham Murdock, "The Media of Politics, Crime and Criminal Justice," *British Journal of Sociology,* 42:397–420 (1991).

7 Margaret T. Gordon and Stephanie Riger, *The Female Fear* (New York: Free Press, 1989), p. 70; Roy Edward Lotz, *Crime and the American Press* (New York: Praeger, 1991).

8 Lotz found, for instance, that in newspapers in New York, Miami, and Philadelphia, white offenders outnumbered black offenders by 7 to 1 in those news reports that allowed for the identification of race. Lotz, *Crime and the American Press,* p. 114.

9 M. A. Bortner, "Media Images and Public Attitudes toward Crime and Justice," in *Justice and the Media,* ed. Ray Surette (Springfield, IL: Charles C Thomas, 1984), pp. 15–30.

10 Harry L. Marsh, "A Comparative Analysis of Crime Coverage in Newspapers in the United States and Other Countries from 1960 to 1989: A Review of the Literature," *Journal of Criminal Justice,* 19:67–80 (1991); Bob Roshier, "The Selection of Crime News by the Press," in *The Manufacture of News: Social Problems, Deviance and the Mass Media,* ed. Stanley Cohen and Jock Young (London: Constable, 1973) pp. 28–39.

11 Steven M. Gorelick, "'Join Our War': The Construction of Ideology in a Newspaper Crime-fighting Campaign," *Crime and Delinquency,* 35:421–436 (1989).

12 Sanford Sherizen, "Social Creation of Crime News: All the News Fitted to Print," in *Deviance and Mass Media,* ed. Charles Winick (Beverly Hills, CA: Sage, 1978), pp. 203–224.

13 Steve Chibnall, *Law-and-Order News: An Analysis of Crime Reporting in the British Press* (London: Tavistock, 1977); Mark Fishman, "Police News: Constructing an Image of Crime," *Urban Life,* 9:371–394 (1981); Richard V. Ericson, "Patrolling the Facts: Secrecy and Publicity in Police Work," *British Journal of Sociology,* 40:205–226 (1989).

14 In comparison to interpersonal crimes like homicide or robbery, corporate crimes are covered with greater difficulty. Generally, corporate crimes are more complex and more difficult to personalize, and well-established source-reporter relationships do not exist for corporate crime as they do for common crimes. Coverage of corporate, white-collar, and organized crime is more common, however, than is sometimes thought. See, for instance, Donna Randall, "The Portrayal of Business Malfeasance in the Elite and General Public Media," *Social Science Quarterly,* 68:28–93 (1987).

15 Sherizen, "Social Creation of Crime News," p. 221.

16 Keith Soothill and Sylvia Walby, *Sex Crime in the News* (London: Routledge, 1991), p. 6.

17 Graeme R. Newman, "Popular Culture and Criminal Justice: A Preliminary Analysis," *Journal of Criminal Justice,* 18:261–274 (1990).

18 Joel Best, ed., *Images of Issues: Typifying Social Problems* (Hawthorne, NY: Aldine de Gruyter, 1989); Joseph R. Gusfield, "Constructing the Ownership of Social Problems: Fun and Profit in the Welfare State," *Social Problems,* 36:431–441 (1989); Joseph W. Schneider, "Social Problems Theory: The Constructionist View," *Annual Review of Sociology,* 11:209–229 (1985).

19 Fishman, "Police News"; Ericson, "Patrolling the Facts."

20 Richard V. Ericson, "Mass Media, Crime, Law and Justice," *British Journal of Sociology,* 31:219–249 (1991); Marjorie S. Zatz, "Chicano Youth Gangs and Crime: The Creation of a Moral Panic," *Contemporary Crises,* 11:129–158 (1987).

21 Henry H. Brownstein, "The Media and the Construction of Random Drug Violence," *Social Justice,* 18:85–103 (1991).

22 Philip Jenkins, *Using Murder: The Social Construction of Serial Homicide* (Hawthorne, NY: Aldine de Gruyter, 1994), pp. 212–213.

23 Joel Best, "Secondary Claims-Making: Claims about Threats to Children on the Network News," *Perspectives on Social Problems,* 1:277 (1989).

24 David L. Protess et al., "Uncovering Rape: The Watchdog Press and the Limits of Agenda Setting," *Public Opinion Quarterly,* 49:19–37 (1985).

[25] Gorelick, "Join Our War," p. 429.

[26] Much has been made in the popular press about, for instance, crime waves that victimize the elderly. See Fay Lomax Cook and Wesley G. Skogan, "Agenda Setting and the Rise and Fall of Policy Issues: The Case of Criminal Victimization of the Elderly," *Environment and Planning C: Government and Policy*, 8:395–415 (1990).

[27] Mary Holland Baker et al., "The Impact of a Crime Wave: Perceptions, Fear, and Confidence in the Police," *Law and Society Review*, 17:317–334 (1983).

[28] Mark Fishman, "Crime Waves as Ideology," *Social Problems*, 25:531 (1978).

[29] James D. Orcutt and J. Blake Turner, "Shocking Numbers and Graphic Accounts: Quantified Images of Drug Problems in the Print Media," *Social Problems*, 40:190–206 (1993).

[30] Ibid., p. 203.

[31] Neil Gilbert, "Miscounting Social Ills," *Society*, 31:24–25 (1994).

[32] Jenkins, *Using Murder*, p. 22.

[33] Gusfield, "Constructing the Ownership of Social Problems"; Schneider, "Social Problems Theory."

[34] Joel Best, "'Road Warriors' on 'Hair-Trigger Highways': Cultural Resources and the Media's Construction of the 1987 Freeway Shootings Problem," *Sociological Inquiry* 61:327–345 (1991).

[35] Brownstein states, for example, that of the 1051 homicides reported in New York City in 1991, less than 2 percent could be categorized as random. Brownstein, "Media and the Construction of Random Drug Violence," p. 95.

[36] Cook and Skogan, "Agenda Setting and the Rise and Fall of Policy Issues."

[37] Ben M. Crouch and Kelly R. Damphousse, "Newspapers and the Antisatanism Movement: A Content Analysis," *Sociological Spectrum*, 12:1–20 (1992), Philip Jenkins and Daniel Maier-Katkin, "Satanism: Myth and Reality in a Contemporary Moral Panic," *Crime, Law and Social Change*, 17:53–75 (1992).

[38] Best, "'Road Warriors' on 'Hair-Trigger Highways.'"

[39] Cook and Skogan, "Agenda Setting and the Rise and Fall of Policy Issues."

[40] Fishman, "Police News," p. 389.

[41] Garofalo, "Crime and the Mass Media"; Skogan and Maxfield, *Coping with Crime*.

[42] For a range of views, see James M. Carlson, *Prime Time Law Enforcement: Crime Show Viewing and Attitudes toward the Criminal Justice System* (New York: Praeger, 1985) Guy Cumberbatch and Alan Beardsworth, "Criminals, Victims and Mass Communications," in *Victims and Society*, ed. Emilio C. Viano (Washington, DC: Visage Press, 1976) pp. 72–90; Anthony N. Doob and Glen E. MacDonald, "Television Viewing and Fear of Victimization: Is the Relationship Causal?" *Journal of Personality and Social Psychology* 37:170–179 (1979); Garofalo, "Crime and the Mass Media"; George Gerbner et al., "The Demonstration of Power: Violence Profile No. 10," *Journal of Communication*, 10:177–196 (1979); Garrett J. O'Keefe. "Public Views on Crime: Television Exposure and Media Credibility," in *Communication Yearbook* 8, ed. Robert N. Bostrom (Beverly Hills, CA: Sage 1984), pp. 514–535; Richard Sparks, Television and the Drama of Crime (Buckingham, England: Open University Press, 1992); Vincent F. Sacco, "The Effects of Mass Media on Perceptions of Crime: A Reanalysis of the Issues," *Pacific Sociological Review*, 25:475–493 (1982).

[43] Glenn G. Sparks and Robert M. Ogles, "The Difference between Fear of Victimization and the Probability of Being Victimized: Implications for Cultivation," *Journal of Broadcasting and Electronic Media*, 34:351–358 (1990).

[44] Anthony N. Doob, "The Role of Mass Media in Creating Exaggerated Levels of Fear of Being the Victim of a Violent Crime," in *Confronting Social Issues: Applications of Social Psychology*, ed. Peter Stringer (Toronto: Academic Press, 1982), pp. 145–159.

[45] Gordon and Riger, *Female Fear*, p. 85.

[46] Paul Williams and Julie Dickinson, "Fear of Crime: Read All about It: The Relationship between Newspaper Reporting and Fear of Crime," *British Journal of Sociology*, 33:34 (1993).

[47] Philip Schlesinger et al., *Women Viewing Violence* (London: BFI, 1992), p.165.

[48] O'Keefe, "Public Views on Crime."

[49] Sacco, "Effects of Mass Media," p. 483.

[50] Williams and Dickinson, "Fear of Crime," p. 51; Dolf Zillmann and Jacob Wakshlag, "Fear of Victimization and the Appeal of Crime Drama," in *Selective Exposure to Communication*, ed. Dolf Zillmann and Jennings Bryant (Hillsdale, NJ: Lawrence Erlbaum, 1987), pp.141–156.

[51] Skogan and Maxfield, Coping with Crime; Susan J. Smith, "Crime in the News," *British Journal of Criminology*, 24:289–295 (1984); Tom R. Tyler, "Assessing the Risk of Crime Victimization: The Integration of Personal Victimization Experience and Socially Transmitted Information," *Journal of Social Issues*, 40:27–38 (1984).

[52] Gordon and Riger, Female Fear, p. 75; Tyler, Assessing the Risk of Crime Victimization," p. 34.

[53] Linda Heath, "Impact of Newspaper Crime Reports on Fear of Crime: Multimethodological Investigation," *Journal of Personality and Social Psychology*, 47:263–276 (1984); Allen E. Liska and William Baccaglini, "Feeling Safe by Comparison: Crime in the Newspapers," *Social Problems*, 37:360–374 (1990). Interestingly, these studies also suggest that coverage of nonlocal violence may decrease fear among news consumers by allowing them to feel safer by comparison.

[54] Philip Palmgreen and Peter Clarke, "Agenda-Setting with Local and National Issues," *Communication Research*, 4:435–452 (1977).

[55] Jack Katz, "What Makes Crime 'News'?" Media, Culture and Society, 9:60 (1987).

[56] Dennis Howitt, *The Mass Media and Social Problems* (Oxford: Pergamon, 1982), pp. 125–126.

[57] Williams and Dickinson, "Fear of Crime," p. 50.

[58] Gorelick, "'Join Our War'"; Drew Humphries, "Serious Crime, News Coverage and Ideology: A Content Analysis of Crime Coverage in a Metropolitan Newspaper," *Crime and Delinquency*, 27:191–205 (1981).

[59] Sophia E. Voumvakis and Richard V. Ericson, *News Accounts of Attacks On Women: A Comparison of Three Toronto Newspapers* (Toronto: University of Toronto, Centre of Criminology, 1984).

[60] Gusfield, "Constructing the Ownership of Social Problems," pp. 434–436.

[61] Stephen Hilgartner and Charles L. Bosk, "The Rise and Fall of Social Problems: A Public Arenas Model," *American Journal of Sociology*, 94:57 (1988).

THREE

CRIME WAVES AS IDEOLOGY

Mark Fishman

When we speak of a crime wave, we are talking about a kind of social awareness of crime, crime brought to public consciousness. It is something to be remarked upon at the corner grocery store, complained about in a community meeting, and denounced at the mayor's press conference. One cannot be mugged by a crime wave, but one can be scared. And one can put more police on the streets and enact new laws on the basis of fear. Crime waves may be "things of the mind," but they have real consequences.

Crime waves are prime candidates for ideology. This study analyzes a specific crime wave that occurred in New York City in late 1976. This case both illustrates and informs my analysis that the crime waves which periodically appear in the press are constructs of the mass media and contribute to an ideological conception of crime in America.[1]

My use of the term ideology follows Dorothy Smith (1972). All knowledge is knowledge from some point of view, resulting from the use of procedures for knowing a part of the world. Ideological accounts arise from "procedures which people use as a means *not to know*" (1972:3, emphasis mine). Routine news gathering and editing involve "procedures not to know." The business of news is embedded in a configuration of institutions. These include a community of news organizations from which journalists derive a sense of "what's news now," and governmental agencies upon which journalists depend for their raw materials. Through their interactions and reliance on official sources, news organizations both invoke and reproduce prevailing conceptions of "serious crime."

Crimes against the Elderly

In late 1976, New York City experienced a major crime wave. The city's three daily newspapers and five local television stations reported a surge of

Social Problems, Vol. 25, No. 5, June 1978, pp. 531–543. Permission granted by University of California Press Journals.

violence against elderly people. The crime wave lasted approximately seven weeks, eventually receiving national television and newspaper coverage.

One consequence of this was the public definition of a new type of crime.[2] "Crimes against the elderly" became a typical crime with typical victims, offenders, and circumstances. Reported muggers, murderers, and rapists of the elderly were usually black or Hispanic youths with long juvenile records. They came from ghetto neighborhoods near enclaves of elderly whites who, for various reasons (usually poverty), had not fled the inner city. Using this scenario, journalists reported incident after brutal incident throughout November and December 1976.

The outcry against these crimes was immediate. The Mayor of New York City, who was preparing to run for re-election, criticized the juvenile justice system and the criminal courts. The New York City Police Department gave its Senior Citizens Robbery Unit (S.C.R.U.) manpower to extend plain-clothes operations. Camera crews from local news stations filmed S.C.R.U. officers dressed as old people and arresting muggers. Local police precincts held community meetings to advise the elderly how to protect themselves. New York State legislators introduced bills to make juvenile records available to a judge at the time of sentencing, to deny sixteen- to nineteen-year-olds juvenile status if they victimized an old person, and to mandate prison sentences for crimes of violence against the aged. These proposals were passed in both the State Senate and Assembly, but were eventually vetoed by the Governor on August 19, 1977—nine months after the crime wave had ended.

A May 1977 Harris poll suggested the crime wave also had a nation-wide effect on people's fear of crime. Moreover, it had an effect on the crime categories which the Harris organization used in its surveys; this poll included a new type of crime, crimes against the elderly, not previously present in Harris polls. Harris found that 60 percent of his respondents felt that assaults against elderly people in their home areas had been going up, and that 50 percent of those age fifty or older said they were more uneasy on the streets than they had been one year ago.[3]

It is doubtful that there really was a crime wave or any unusual surge of violence against elderly people. No one really knows, least of all the journalists who reported the crime wave. The police statistics from the N.Y.P.D. do not show a crime wave.[4] In fact, for one type of crime, homicide, the police showed a 19 percent *drop* over the previous year's rate of elderly people murdered. This is significant because the news media began their reporting with coverage of several gruesome murders. (Twenty-eight percent of the stories reported by the three media organizations I surveyed were stories about homicides. In contrast, the police reported that homicides made up less than 1 percent of crimes against the elderly in 1976.)

For other types of crime with elderly victims police statistics showed an increase over the previous year. Crime victimization, however, rose for all age categories in 1976. In some cases, the increases were greater for elderly victims, in others less. Robbery was up 10 percent in the general population, 19 percent for the elderly. Grand larceny was up 29 percent for the general population, 25 percent for the elderly. In short, police statistics substantiate only that there was a continuing increase in victimization of the elderly (as well as of the general population), not that old people were singled out, as never before. Moreover, the homicide rate contradicts the media presentation of a crime wave.

This article, however, is not a study in the disparity between police statistics and crime news. Prior studies of crime news and crime waves (Davis, 1952; Roshier, 1973), as well as anecdotal reports (Steffens, 1931:285–91), have shown the irony of crime waves: although the public is alarmed and politicians respond to media reports of a dramatic increase in crime, such "waves" have no basis in police statistics. This study goes beyond sociological irony to examine *how and why news organizations construct crime waves*. Crime waves are taken to be waves of coverage of some topic in crime. Crime waves as *media waves* may or may not be related to something happening "on the streets" or in the police crime rates. Studying crime waves means studying processes in the mass media.

Method

I collected two kinds of data. First, two student researchers and I conducted participant observation from November 1976 to April 1977 on a New York City local television station, WAVE (a pseudonym). One student was a full-time WAVE journalist who worked as a news writer, program producer, and assignment editor. We focused on how the assignment editor assembled the daily news program by deciding what major stories would be covered for the day and assigning reporters and camera crews to these stories. In addition, we conducted interviews with journalists from WAVE and the New York *Daily News*.

Second, we kept a record of all news relating to crimes against the elderly reported from September 1976 through February 1977 in two newspapers, the New York *Daily News* and the New York *Post*, and on WAVE, which aired a one-hour newscast in the evening. This enabled us to "locate" the New York crime wave, to determine when it began and ended, and to determine the kind of coverage crimes against the elderly received before, during, and after the crime wave period.

The Crime Wave: A View from the Outside

Over the six-month period of observation the *News*, the *Post*, and WAVE presented eighty-nine stories of crimes against the elderly. Fifty-six stories or 63 percent occurred during the crime wave period. The weekly frequencies of news stories from all three media are shown in the appendix. This graph clearly indicates a wave of media reporting that began in the last week of

October and trailed off by the second week of December. It shows a sharp, swift rise in coverage for the first two weeks, then a slow, uneven decline for the remaining five weeks.

Examining the individual patterns of coverage for each news organization reveals that prior to the crime wave each organization was reporting approximately one story of crime against the elderly every other week. After the wave, coverage in all three media was sporadic, but heavier than coverage during the prewave period, indicating that the media appear to have been sensitized to the topic.

The three individual crime waves in the *News*, the *Post*, and WAVE show that the marked increase in coverage did not coincide in all three media. The *News* had a sudden increase in the third week of October; WAVE and the *Post* did not increase their coverage until the fourth week of October. Further, in this fourth week the two "latecomers" began their increase *simultaneously*. Prior to their increased coverage, the *Post* and WAVE did not parallel each other. It was only after the *News* began reporting a wave that the others developed a synchronous pattern. This trend suggests that the other media simultaneously responded to the *Daily News'* portrayal of a wave of violence against the elderly.

All three media show different crime wave profiles. WAVE steeply increased coverage to a single peak, then had an equally steep decline (seventeen days rising and sixteen days falling). In contrast, the *Daily News* and the *Post* show bimodal curves. In the *News* there was a swift initial rise (ten days), from which coverage subsided slowly, then it turned upward to a second peak (lower than the first), and finally declined.

The unevenness of the *Daily News*'s wave was echoed in the *Post*. The *Post* participated less actively in the crime wave than did the *News* or WAVE. We might even say that the *Post* did not show a crime wave, except that the period of its heaviest coverage coincided with the crime wave period in the other media. Moreover, the *Post*'s pre- and post-wave patterns were similar to [those of] the other media, and during the crime wave it showed a bimodal wave which paralleled that of the *Daily News*. Thus, the *Post*'s wave seems to have been a weak reflection of the *Daily News*'s curve.

How can we explain these bimodal patterns? The likely reason why the *News* and *Post* reduced their coverage after the first peaks involves a major news event coinciding with this drop: the 1976 Presidential Election of November 2. The elections seem to have crowded out crimes against the elderly from the newspapers, but not from local TV news, since stations like WAVE were not trying to compete with network coverage of the presidential race. Thus, during the slow news period after the elections, the *News* and *Post* seemed to have "rediscovered" the crime wave, which was still present in local TV news.

In other words, it seems the *News'* and the *Post*'s second peak was a response to the continuing crime wave in the television media (assuming other TV stations behaved like WAVE). Just as the initial appearance of the crime wave in the *Daily News* seems to have spurred increased coverage by the *Post* and WAVE, so the continuing coverage of the crime wave on television seems to have "re-awakened" interest in the topic by the *Daily News* and the *Post*. Thus, *the behavior of each news organization during the crime wave seems to have been in response to the other media.*

Seeing Themes in Crime: A View from the Inside

How do individual crimes come to be seen as a crime wave? The answer is found in the methods by which news is organized. News workers make crime waves by seeing "themes" in the news. Crime waves are little more than the continued and heavy coverage of numerous occurrences which journalists report as a single topic (for example, "crimes against the elderly").

News themes are various: "everything Jimmy Carter did today," "the taxi cab strike," "Vietnam," "the disintegrating American family," or "labor disputes." A news theme is a unifying concept. It presents a specific news event, or a number of such events, in terms of some broader concept. For example, the mugging of an eighty-two-year-old Bronx woman can be reported as "the latest *instance* of the continuing trend in crimes against the elderly." A news theme allows journalists to cast an incident as an instance of something.

The Glasgow Media Group (1976:355) provides an interesting example of thematized news events from one British television newscast:

> The week had its share of unrest. Trouble in Glasgow with striking dustmen and ambulance controllers, short time in the car industry, no Sunday Mirror or Sunday People today and a fair amount of general trouble in Fleet Street and a continuing rumble over the matter of two builders pickets jailed for conspiracy.

As the authors point out, disparate incidents are reported together under the single theme of "unrest." Calling these things "unrest" imposes order on the events reported. Audience members are meant to see the events as unified, as instances of a single theme.

Themes give news shows and newspapers a presentational order. Items are presented in groups organized around a theme. Some themes are related to others, making it possible for groups of news stories to be placed near each other. For instance, during the crime wave against the elderly, the first ten minutes of a sixty-minute news program at WAVE was organized around interrelated themes:

1. Police apprehend three youngsters who allegedly mugged an elderly Queens couple.

2. Police and senior citizens meet at a Queens precinct to discuss fighting crimes against the elderly.

3. A feature report on the Senior Citizens Robbery Unit.

4. Police seize guns and drugs intended for warring gangs in the Bronx.

5. Two members of a youth gang are arrested for robbing someone at knife point.

6. R.O.T.C. cadet charged in the stabbing death of another cadet.

7. New York State audit finds the city police have been mishandling $9.1 million of federal funds.

8. New York City and the police union are still working on a new contract, at the same time that some laid-off firemen and subway cops will be rehired.

First, there are small groups of stories, each containing a theme that the stories in the group share in common (the first three stories are about "crimes against the elderly" and the next three about "youth crime"). Second, groups of stories are placed next to other groups, since the different themes of each group share common features (the group of crimes against the elderly and the group of youth crimes both can be seen to be about youthful perpetrators and police responses to them).

Journalists do not create themes merely to show an audience the appearance of order. News themes are very useful in the newswork itself. In particular, editors selecting and organizing the day's stories need themes.[5] Every day, news editors face a glut of "raw materials" (wire service reports, press releases, police crime dispatches) out of which they must fashion relatively few news stories. This task involves a selection process which operates somewhat differently in television and newspaper newsrooms. The essentials of the process are the same: individual news items are identified and sorted according to possible themes.

The chances that any event or incident will be reported increase once it has been associated with a current theme in the news. Crime incidents are rarely reported unless news workers see them related to a past or emerging trend in criminality or law enforcement. A brief description of how the assignment editor at WAVE developed the first segment of the news show just cited illustrates this point. The assignment editor determined the top stories for the day when he noticed that several previously unrelated stories were all part of the same current newsworthy theme: crimes against the elderly. And the discovery of this theme was no coincidence: that day's program was in the midst of the crime wave period.

The assignment editor did not begin his day knowing that crime news, and, in particular, the crimes against the elderly, would receive top billing in the evening's news show. When he started work at 8:45 A.M. he already knew of two stories that he would most likely cover.[6] One was a feature report on the Senior Citizens Robbery Unit fighting crimes against the elderly. This feature, which eventually ran as the third story in the evening newscast, had been taped days before; it was part of a continuing series on S.C.R.U. the station had been airing for the past few weeks. The second story was a feature report on a "food fair" that afternoon in Manhattan. The editor planned to send a reporter and camera crew to cover it, but also wanted to line up, as he put it, "some better stories" for the day.

Ten minutes after he arrived in the newsroom the assignment editor began scanning his news sources for lead stories. He sifted through reams of wire service news that had collected overnight under the wire machines; he scanned the police dispatches of the previous night's and that morning's crime incidents (about ten or twelve) received through a teletype called "the police wire." He also looked to other news media for story ideas: he read the *Daily News* and *New York Times* and he listened to an all-news radio station.

In the *Daily News* he found a small story about rehiring firemen and Transit Authority police who had been laid off. He thought this would be a good story because "this indicates things may be turning around in the city." This incident became newsworthy when the assignment editor could see it as part of a current newsworthy theme (New York's fiscal crisis).

Still, the assignment editor despaired that he had "no real news," that this was "a slow news day." However, around ten A.M. two things happened. First: when scanning the police crime dispatches, the assignment editor found that in the 113th precinct in Queens an elderly couple had been mugged, and that one perpetrator was wounded by police. As he was clipping this dispatch, he heard over the all-news radio that the 112th precinct in Queens, very close to where the mugging occurred, was holding a crime prevention meeting with senior citizens. He now knew what his lead stories for the day would be, and he knew what he had to do to line them up:

1. He would send a reporter out to the 113th precinct to find, and get on film whatever he could about the mugging (interviews with police, perhaps with some witnesses or with the victims themselves; and, if he was lucky, film of any suspects that were apprehended).

2. Then the reporter could go over to the nearby 112th precinct to film the police meeting with senior citizens.

3. These two reports would be followed by the pre-taped feature on S.C.R.U.

4. The story on rehiring firemen and Transit police, as well as a few other brief wire service reports relevant to crime which might come in during the rest of the day, would all follow the above three lead stories in some as yet undetermined order. The story on the "food fair" would be placed further back in the show.

Each story, seen independently, might not have merited attention. But seen together, all of them were made newsworthy by the perception of a common theme. The editor's "discovery" of the theme of crime against the elderly made the day's news come together. He knew how to assign a schedule to his reporter and camera crew; and he knew pretty much what the day's work was going to be.

The selection of news on the basis of themes is one component in the ideological production of crime news. It constitutes a "procedure not to know." This procedure requires that an incident be stripped of the actual content of its occurrence so that it may be relocated in a new, symbolic context:

the news theme. Because newsworthiness is based on themes, the attention devoted to an event may exceed its importance, relevance, or timeliness were these qualities determined with reference to some theory of society. In place of any such theoretical understanding of the phenomena they report, news-workers make incidents meaningful only as *instances of themes*—themes which are generated within the news production process. Thus, something becomes a "serious type of crime" on the basis of what is going on inside newsrooms, not outside them.

From Crime Themes to Crime Waves

Crime themes are potential crime waves. A news organization cannot make a crime wave without the collaboration of other media reporting the same crime theme. Crime waves emerge out of an interaction among news organizations.

The Indefinite Overlapping Character of News Judgments

All newsworkers depend on other media organizations for their sense of "what's news today." For example, the WAVE assignment editor began his day by reading the morning papers, the *Daily News* and The *New York Times*, and by listening to an all-news radio station. He later read the New York *Post* and watched when other TV stations aired their news. This editor told me that he did not mind using "anything, any source of news. I'm not proud. I'll steal any source of news."

In reality, stories were not stolen wholesale; rather, the other news media provided an important pool of ideas for story assignments. The noon and evening TV news shows rarely were used for this purpose because, by the time these shows were aired, most of the editor's news was set. The news on other stations mainly confirmed the assignment editor's news judgments, since his planned 10 P.M. news, was, with few exceptions, identical to what his competitors were broadcasting. It seems his competitors were doing just what he was doing: reading the *Times* and the *News*, listening to the all-news radio, and taking stories from the same news sources (wire services, police news dispatches, and press releases).[7]

News judgments continuously overlap in space and time. Editors of after-noon and evening media look for, and are oriented by, the news in the morn-ing media. Editors of the morning media derive their sense of news from afternoon and evening media. Since these media may be in different regions and different cities, news judgments spread throughout an indefinite expanse of territory. The wire services and a few nationally-read newspapers, *The New York Times* and *Washington Post*, increase the diffusion of news judgments through the United States.

Moreover, this overlap provides a continuity of news judgments. A spe-cific incident or theme presented in the morning will be covered in the evening, perhaps with fresh incidents, more details, a new development or a "local angle" on the story. The process may repeat itself the next day, reproducing the theme of the previous evening.

The Crime Wave Dynamic

When journalists notice each other reporting the same crime theme, it becomes entrenched in a community of media organizations. Reporters and editors will know that "this kind of crime is news." To use Sacks's (1972:333) term, journalists have established a "consistency rule": *every crime incident that can be seen as an instance of the theme will be seen and reported as such.* The rule is used to identify the newsworthiness of certain crimes. Reporters and editors will know, for example, that a certain incident is "another one of those crimes against the elderly" and not just an incident that can be categorized in a variety of ways.

Each use of the consistency rule reestablishes the rule. Any use of the principle invites readers or viewers of the news, including other journalists, to use the same principle. In order to recognize a crime incident as an instance of a theme, readers or viewers must use the same consistency rule which was used to produce that news.

Journalists who have not yet seen a particular crime theme learn to see it simply by watching their competition. They are able, using the consistency rule, to report the same crime theme their competition taught them to see. At this point, when a crime theme is beginning to spread through more and more media organizations, the "reality" of the theme is confirmed for the media organizations who first reported it. They now see others using the theme. Moreover, as the theme persists, news organizations already using the theme will not hesitate to report new instances, because they confirm a past news judgment that "this thing really is a type of crime happening now." Thus, each use of the theme confirms and justifies its prior uses.

If it continues long enough, the process constitutes a crime wave dynamic. All crime waves begin as simple themes but by means of this dynamic can swell into waves. Crime themes constantly appear in the media and few reach the proportions of full-scale crime waves. After all, it only takes one editor with a little imagination to introduce a new theme into the news. Why is it that few crime themes go beyond a few days of coverage by one or two news organizations?

Clearly, something more than the crime wave dynamic is necessary for a theme to grow into a wave: *There must be a continuous supply of crime incidents that can be seen as instances of a theme.* Journalists may be primed to report a wave of crime incidents, but they also must know of enough incidents to report the wave. (During the period of my research, New York City journalists had been frustrated in reporting an expected "mafia war." This theme never persisted long enough for lack of enough incidents. Thus, "mafia war" was a hungry crime theme, starved of enough incidents to make it the crime wave it could have become.) The supply of incidents is crucial in determining the growth of crime waves. What are journalists' sources of crime news?

Perpetrators of crime could be a source, but news workers rarely learn of crimes directly from offenders. The primary source is law enforcement agencies.[8] In the newsroom of WAVE, journalists first learned of crime incidents through three sources:[9] the "police wire," the police radio, and other news organizations (wire service reports, the all-news radio station, and the *Daily News*). The first two of these were direct links to the city police. Crime news is really police news. Thus, *the media's supply of crime incidents is a function of the crime reporting practices of law enforcement agencies.* This reliance on law enforcement agencies constitutes another component of the ideological production of crime news. News workers will not know what the police do not routinely detect or transmit to them. What journalists do know of crime is formulated for them by law enforcement agencies.

The Pool of Potential Crime Waves

The police supply news organizations with an assortment of crime incidents every day. For media organizations in towns and small cities this assortment often consists of *all* crimes known to the police in a twenty-four-hour period. But in large urban areas there are far too many crimes known to the police for any reporter to know them all. Therefore, urban journalists depend on the police to provide a "summary" of these incidents.

In New York City, the daily summary is known as the "police wire." All the city's major media have a teletype that receives crime dispatches from the N.Y.P.D.'s Office of Public Information. In one day, this police wire types out anywhere from twelve to twenty-five messages. The crime items appearing over the police wire constitute a "crime wave pool": a collection of crime incidents known to the media and having the potential of being seen as certain crime themes. Crime themes steadily supplied with instances over the police wire can become crime waves.

While journalists may invent crime themes (I suspect the police suggest and encourage many of them), a crime wave needs enough incidents on the police wire to support it. The police have power to both veto and promote the media's construction of crime waves. The collection of crime incidents the police provide to news organizations may systematically preclude certain themes from becoming waves (the veto power). Moreover, the same collection of incidents may contain enough crime items of a certain type to allow only a restricted class of crime themes to become crime waves (the enabling power).

For three ten-day periods from mid-February to the end of March 1977, a copy of all crime dispatches of the police wire was kept. Over this thirty-day period, 468 individual dispatches (averaging 15.6 per day) were received. Of these, I ignored ninety-seven (21%) which the police and journalists did not consider crime items. (They were mostly traffic advisories and non-suspicious fires.)

The remaining 371 crime dispatches reveal that the police wire provides journalists with a heavy and steady diet of "street crimes." Two-thirds (246 items or 66.3%) of the crime items consisted of: a) robberies and burglaries (85 items or 23% of all crime items), b) unspecified shootings and stabbings (156 items or 42%) and c) a sprinkling of other assaults (five items or 1 percent—mostly rapes).

The remaining one-third of the police wire consisted of a variety of incidents: thirteen bombings; nine police suspended or arrested; six demonstrations requiring police action; five hostage situations; four raids for gambling, pornography, and drugs; three people run over by subway trains; one arson, and one hit-and-run. In addition, this third contained incidents which, I assume, the police considered "strange" and consequently of interest to the media (for example, a bus stolen, the theft of a large amount of poisons, a man threatening to set himself on fire, a person crushed by an elevator, and the discovery of a disembodied head).

The first thing worth noting about the police wire is what it does *not* contain: incidents of price-fixing, consumer fraud, sub-standard housing, unhealthy food, environmental pollution, political bribery and corruption, and the like. None appear in this pool of crime incidents from which crime waves arise, yet all of these may occur enough to constitute a crime wave if the media were to have routine access to knowledge of their occurrence.

One reason why these do not appear over the police wire is that agencies other than the city police enforce the laws governing these kinds of crime. Because police manpower is devoted to street crimes, it is street crime reports that the police wire carries. If journalists are to report other kinds of crime, they must draw on other sources (usually the wire services and other media organizations) which provide instances of such crime only sporadically.

Moreover, in the police wire one is unable to find a number of very common crimes which local police *do* know about but consider "uninteresting" and, thus, not worth transmitting to the media.[10] These included what journalists told me were "too common" to be news: everything from bicycle theft, liquor store stick-ups and rapes, to wife beating, child molesting and other "family matters" not resulting in homicide or hospitalization.

It is likely that a large number of the street crimes reported over the police wire were, in fact, family disputes, crimes against women, and racial conflict. But it was difficult to tell this from the information in the crime dispatches. This is particularly true of the large number of shootings and stabbings, which reporters tended to ignore.

Any descriptive features in a crime dispatch provide important clues to newsworkers looking for themes in crime. From reading the police wire, I was struck by the lack of detail. Victims, if they were identified at all, and if they were persons, not businesses, were identified by sex and age. When more was told, they were described as: 1) "elderly" (for homicides and robberies), 2) policemen (for any assaults), or 3) banks (for robberies). Perpetrators (and in the police wire these were always persons, not businesses) were usually identified by sex and a specific age. When more was said, it was almost always in connection with a "youth gang" or the offender's youth.

Victim-offender relationships were rarely mentioned. It was quite difficult to identify cases where the victim and offender knew each other. Thus the police wire gives one the impression most crimes occur between strangers. Finally, the location of a crime was usually provided in terms of a specific address or intersection. But a *type* of location was mentioned only when it could be said the incident occurred in a public or semi-public place, for example, a street, a subway, a schoolyard, or an apartment hallway.

Thus, the kinds of crime items and the descriptions of them in the police wire support only special sorts of crime themes that journalists may report. Crime in public places, crimes between strangers, and crime specific to age are themes that the police wire can and does provide numerous instances of. "Crimes against the elderly" is one theme that has already blossomed into a crime wave with the help of the police wire. But other themes such as "youth gang crime," "subway crime," and "school yard crime" have an excellent chance of becoming new crime waves.

Apparently, the police who transmit crime dispatches to the media select incidents that they think will interest journalists. This criterion of selectivity has two consequences, both keeping the present image of "serious crime" from changing in the news. First, when the police perceive that the media are interested in a certain type of crime (for example, crimes against the elderly), they include instances of it in the police wire whenever they can. Thus, the police bolster emerging crime waves as long as those waves pertain to crimes the police routinely detect (that is, street crime). Second, the police decide what the media are interested in on the basis of what the media have reported before.

The police-supplied incidents that make up the media's crime wave pool all support prevailing notions of "serious crime." The crime wave pool leads the media to reproduce a common image that "real crime" is crime on the streets, crime occurring between strangers, crime which brutalizes the weak and defenseless, and crime perpetrated by vicious youths. Such crimes exist, but this imagery becomes *the only reality of crime* which people will take seriously because it is the only reality impressed upon them in the media. And it is the only reality newsworkers are able to report continuously as themes in crime, and periodically, as full-scale crime waves.

The Role of Authorities

I have described the crime wave pool as if it were only composed of crime incidents. This description is only partially true. During the initial phase of crime waves, media organizations mostly report crime incidents as instances of their theme-becoming-a-wave. But as soon as a crime theme looks like it is catching on and becoming a wave, journalists have another kind of news to report: the responses of politicians, police, and other officials.

The first signs of New York's crime wave against the elderly appeared in the last week of October 1976, when the city's media began reporting incidents of crime against old people. There was widespread coverage of three incidents:

the murder of two aged sisters in their Bronx apartment, the rape-murder of an eighty-five-year-old Manhattan woman, and the release on fifty dollars bail of a youth who beat an elderly person. After this third incident, the first official response appeared: Mayor Beame called a news conference and, with the Police Commissioner at his side, he vowed to make the city safe for old people by beefing up the police's Senior Citizens Robbery Unit and by working for reforms in the criminal justice system. From this point on, "crimes against the elderly" became a favorite topic for political rhetoric and proposed reforms.

Starting from the very first week of the crime wave, the media could report both crimes against the elderly *and* stories of what authorities were saying and doing about it. The entire wave was bolstered throughout its seven-week course by coverage of official statements, possible reforms of the criminal justice system, legislative debate and action, the formation of new police programs, and community conferences on the problem. These kinds of stories made up 35 percent of the crime-wave-related news published during the period.

Officials and authorities were willing to assume from the outset that the crime wave represented something real or, at least, they were unwilling to express any doubts in public. Thus, by making public statements and taking official action on the basis of this assumption, authorities made the wave look even more real. And they guaranteed that the wave would go on for some time. As official responses to "the problem" trailed off in mid-December, so did the number of crime incidents known to the media from the police wire and other police sources. The wave finally died.

It is clear that officials with a stake in "doing something" about crime have power over crime waves. Whether or not they inspire crime waves, they can attempt to redirect the focus of coverage of a crime wave already being reported. Nowhere is this clearer that in the first four weeks of *Daily News* coverage of the wave of crimes against the elderly. News headlines during the first week emphasized "the problem," citing instance after instance. But in the next three weeks the stories (starting with the Mayor's first press conference) shifted focus to "what is being done about the problem."

Politicians and police use their news-making power to channel the coverage of social problems into a definite direction (Molotch and Lester, 1974): news of the problem becomes news of how the system is working to remedy the situation. Authorities may also use their newsmaking powers to stop certain crime themes from becoming crime waves. There is tentative data indicating that another crime theme, "crimes on the subways," was stopped from becoming a full-scale crime wave by the New York City Transit Authority.

In the third week of February 1977, the *Daily News*, the New York *Post*, and WAVE all suddenly increased their coverage of murders and muggings in subways. In the middle of that week the Police Chief of the Transit Authority told a *Daily News* reporter there was not crime wave and, soon thereafter, three senior Transit officials called a news conference to assert that the subways were safer than the city streets. From that point on, coverage of subway crime steadily decreased to its pre-wave level.

If an unwanted crime should arise, officials can use their newsmaking powers to deny the wave's existence or to redirect crime coverage into a "safe" direction. There is some evidence, however, that crimes against the elderly was not an "unwanted crime wave"—at least for some officials in the New York City Police Department.

The *Daily News* reporter who wrote the feature articles which turned out to be the beginning of the crime wave, told me that he received "considerable help" from the Senior Citizens Robbery Unit, whose job it was to catch muggers and murderers of the elderly (and the same unit that the Mayor expanded early in the crime wave). On October seventh, the reporter first wrote a story on two crimes with elderly victims that appeared over the police wire on the same day. This story was published October 8, two weeks before the wave. At that time, a *Daily News* editor thought it would be a good idea for the reporter to do a series of feature stories on "this kind of crime." (Such features had shown up periodically in other media organizations before.)

While he was first researching these feature stories, the reporter was in frequent contact with S.C.R.U. This police unit let him know they felt beleaguered, understaffed, and that they were fighting a battle that deserved more attention. (According to the reporter, "They proselytized a lot.") After he had written his feature stories, police from S.C.R.U. began calling him whenever they knew of a mugging or murder of an elderly person. This enabled the reporter to follow up his series with reports of specific crime incidents. Finally, it was S.C.R.U. which first told the reporter about the youth who was let out on fifty dollars bail after beating an elderly person. All major media in New York quickly picked up this story after the *News* reported it. At that point, the crime wave had begun.

I do not want to assert that from this brief history of one crime wave all waves are inspired by the police or politicians. It is not that simple. The crime wave against the elderly in New York seems to have resulted from a mixture of happenstance and police assistance. The history of this crime wave, however, does show that officials can and do use their positions to nurture fledgling crime themes first identified by journalists. Equally, they may use their position to deny the reality of crime waves.

Summary and Conclusions

Crime waves begin as crime themes that journalists perceive in the process of organizing and selecting news to be presented to a public. Because journalists depend on one another for their sense of "what's news," a crime theme can spread throughout a community of news organizations. As each news organization sees the theme presented by other organizations, they learn to use the theme and present it in their news.

But for this crime wave dynamic to occur, journalists must be able to associate a crime theme with a continuous supply of incidents that can be seen as instances of the theme. Media organizations know of crime almost exclusively through law enforcement agencies. The media's major source of supply for crime incidents in New York City is the N.Y.P.D.'s police wire. Crime dispatches over this wire are largely reports of street crimes: robberies, burglaries, shootings, stabbings, and other assaults. These constitute a pool of potential crime waves, excluding the possibility of certain themes. Non-street crime themes, if they were to receive massive publicity as crime waves, might challenge prevailing notions of "serious crime" in this society.

Moreover, once crime themes receive heavy coverage in the media, authorities can use their power to make news in an attempt to augment, modify, or deny a burgeoning crime wave. Thus, official sources not only control the supply of raw materials upon which crime news is based, but also the growth of crime waves.

While this study has dealt with the generation of crime waves, the news-making processes it reveals have broad implications. News plays a crucial role in formulating public issues and events, and in directing their subsequent course. Just as the interplay between local politics and local media organizations brought about New York City's crime wave, so the interplay between national elites and national media organizations may well have given rise to a number of social issues now widely accepted as fixtures in the recent American political scene.

Consider Watergate. As a few investigative reporters persisted in digging up news about the illegal activities of the Nixon administration, national elites competed among one another to halt, support, or redefine the growing Watergate news theme. Eventually, special prosecutors and Congressional committees were formed; that is, a bureaucratic apparatus was set up which began to feed the media with fresh instances of the Watergate theme. Once Nixon was deposed, this apparatus was dismantled, and so was the Watergate "news wave."

Watergate, the Bert Lance affair, the "death" of political activism of the 1960s, and many other accepted political "realities" may have been produced by the same ideological machinery that underlies crime waves.

Appendix

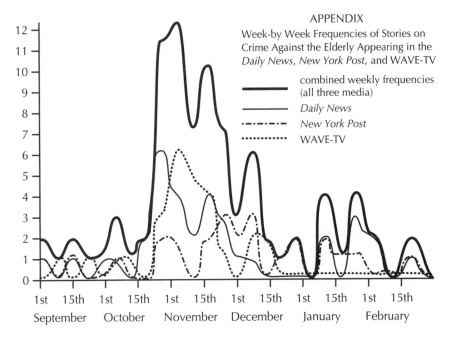

APPENDIX

Week-by Week Frequencies of Stories on
Crime Against the Elderly Appearing in the
Daily News, New York Post, and WAVE-TV

—— combined weekly frequencies
(all three media)

—— *Daily News*

—·—·—· *New York Post*

············ WAVE-TV

Notes

[1] This article focuses on the generation of crime waves, not their effects. Thus, I infer that media crime waves contribute to existing images and fears of crime in society. To substantiate this inference would require a study of crime wave effects with a different method from that used here. There is, however, research indicating that people's fears and images of crime derive, in large part, from the news media. See, for example, Davis (1952:330) and Biderman, et al. (1967:128).

[2] While the New York City crime wave represents the first widely publicized formulation of "crimes against the elderly," the issue was not first defined by the New York media. Fredric DuBow (personal communication) has pointed out that the law enforcement establishment had formulated crimes against the elderly as a new type of crime at least two years prior to the crime wave: Since 1974 it was an important funding theme of L.E.A.A.; in 1975 it was the subject of a major conference; and in February 1976 *Police Chief* devoted a special issue to it.

These earlier law enforcement formulations probably led to the creation of the New York Police Department's Senior Citizens Robbery Unit (S.C.R.U.) well before the city's crime wave. As we shall see, S.C.R.U. played a crucial role in directing media attention to crimes against the elderly in the first stages of the crime wave. Thus, it seems that early "professional formulations" led to the establishment of a specialized agency which, in turn, enabled the media publicly to formulate a category for crimes against the elderly.

[3] Reported in the *New York Post,* May 9, 1977.

[4] Thus far I have been unable to obtain a complete, month-by-month set of 1976 N.Y.P.D. crime rates. Therefore, for all but the homicide rate, the figures described below are tentative, based on partial rates for 1976.

[5] The editor's use of news themes is part of the more general tendency of newsworkers to code and categorize news events in order to "routinize their unexpectedness." See Tuchman, 1973.

[6] The assignment editor started with these two stories because his superior in the newsroom had suggested that they be covered.

[7] While my example of overlapping news judgments is drawn from a local television station, the same phenomenon occurs both on newspapers and national network news (Epstein, 1973:150).

[8] The only exception that comes to mind is the coverage of mafia news by specialized reporters on large New York publications: *The New York Times*, the New York *Daily News*, the *New York Post*, the *Wall Street Journal*, and *Newsday*.

[9] There was an occasional fourth source: phone calls from the police.

[10] There were some exceptions. A handful of common crimes did appear over the police wire (e.g., four rapes in a thirty-day observation period). The journalists I observed could not explain why these were there, and they ignored them.

References

Biderman, Albert, Louise Johnson, Jennie McIntyre, and Adrianne Weir
1967 "Report on a pilot study in the District of Columbia on victimization and attitudes toward law enforcement." Washington, DC: U.S. Government Printing Office.

Davis, F. James
1952 "Crime news in Colorado newspapers." American Journal of Sociology 57:325–30.

Epstein, Edward Jay
1973 News from Nowhere. New York: Random House.

Glasgow Media Group
1976 "Bad news." Theory and Society 3:339–64.

Molotch, Harvey and Marilyn Lester
1974 "News as purposive behavior: the strategic use of routine events, accidents, and scandals." American Sociological Review 39:101–12.

Roshier, Bob
1973 "The selection of crime news in the press." Pp. 28–39 in S. Cohen and J. Young (eds.), The Manufacture of News. Beverly Hills: Sage.

Sacks, Harvey
1972 "On the analyzability of stories by children." Pp. 325–45 in J. Gumperz and D. Hymes (eds.), Directions in Sociolinguistics. New York: Holt, Rinehart and Winston.

Smith, Dorothy
1972 "The very ideological practice of sociology." Unpublished paper, Department of Sociology, University of British Columbia.

Steffens, Lincoln
1931 The Autobiography of Lincoln Steffens. New York: Harcourt Brace.

Tuchman, Gaye
1973 "Making news by doing work: routinizing the unexpected." American Journal of Sociology 79:110–31.

FOUR

FEAR AND LOATHING ON REALITY TELEVISION

AN ANALYSIS OF *AMERICA'S MOST WANTED* AND *UNSOLVED MYSTERIES*

Gray Cavender & Lisa Bond-Maupin

The media serve to stimulate our interest in crime. Newspapers, for example, detail the exploits of criminals, while television news and crime drama focus on crimes. Although most crime drama is fictional representation, programs like *The F.B.I.* modify actual cases.

Recently, a new type of crime program has been presented to the public. *America's Most Wanted* (AMW) and *Unsolved Mysteries* (UM) present vignettes depicting actual crimes in which theories of crime are dramatized. These dramatizations feature actors, actual photographs or film footage, and interviews conducted with participants and the police. Viewers are urged to call the police or program representatives with information related to the crime, and police officers are on standby in the television studio to take these calls.

AMW and UM represent a hybrid programming format in that a news or public service format is superimposed on entertainment to produce a new television genre, reality programming. But the line between fact and fiction is not so distinct in the media (Williams 1989, p. 5). Even the news represents a social construction of reality in which reporters transform occurrences into news events (Molotch and Lester 1974; Tuchman 1978). On television genres tend to blend together (Gitlin 1985, p. 6). However, such blending of fact and fiction represents a defining characteristic of reality programming inasmuch as these programs are intended to draw the audience into their reality through active participation.

Source: *Sociological Inquiry*, Vol. 63, No. 3, August 1993, pp. 305–317. © 1993 by the University of Texas Press. Reprinted with permission.

Crime and Danger in the Media

Scholars analyze media crime depictions ranging from the amount of crime news to the demographics of crime drama. The findings of such studies suggest that newspaper coverage bears little relationship to official crime statistics (Davis 1952; Fishman 1978). Although some analysts are not concerned about the divergence of newspaper coverage from official statistics, because such statistics are, like the news, a social construction (Tuchman 1978; Ericson, Baranek, and Chan 1991, p. 54); still others (Graber 1980) argue that newspapers offer a misleading picture of crime and criminals. Newspapers disproportionately report violent crimes, and reporters tend to focus attention on sensational matters such as the capture of a criminal and high-status offenders (Graber 1980; Garofalo 1981, pp. 323–25; Humphries 1981, pp. 195–96).

Crime news and fiction go hand in hand because a similar pattern emerges in television drama (Katz 1987). Dramatic criminal plots are featured—usually violence against individuals—and the chase is highlighted (Garofalo 1981, p. 327). Television criminals are predominantly male and disproportionately white, over 30 years of age, and members of a profession (Comstock 1978, pp. 289–93; Pandiani 1978). Television crime is detached from the social context in which it is committed, and non-law-enforcement personnel often solve crimes and capture criminals (Humphries 1981; Lichter and Lichter 1983).

Some research addresses the effects of such depictions on the audience, but the scholarly debate continues unresolved as to whether television affects the public's perception of crime (Gerbner and Gross 1976; Hirsch 1980, 1981). Other researchers suggest that the "meaning" of media crime depictions should be addressed prior to evaluating the effects these depictions have on the public (Gitlin 1979).

The ideological and symbolic dimensions of crime are also present. Television crime drama presents mythic morality plays that privilege a social control orientation (Gitlin 1979, p. 257; Schattenberg 1981), while newspaper coverage reinforces the symbolism of the dominant order (Ericson et al. 1991). Still other researchers analyze the newsworthy effect of such stories (Ericson et al. 1991, pp. 140–48), suggesting that these stories are simple, easily dramatized and personalized, and depict the unexpected. Deviance and control stories meet these criteria. Jack Katz (1987, pp. 50–55) offers four additional criteria for newsworthiness of crime stories: (1) they exemplify human viciousness or audacity, (2) collective integrity is threatened, (3) people who violate moral boundaries are featured, and (4) high status criminals are involved.

Jack Katz's newsworthiness of crime stories criteria parallel the elements of urban legends. Urban legends circulate as true stories, referencing frightening strangers who prey upon unsuspecting victims (Best 1990). Urban legends, such as poisoned Halloween candy, symbolize the strains and unpredictability of modern life (Fine 1980, p. 237; Best 1990, p. 142). Newspaper crime stories produce motifs found in urban legends, expressing the frustrations of a world characterized by the fear of violence (Wachs 1988; Oring 1990).

Crime is an ideal idiom for expressing urban fear and a corresponding sense of danger. Sally Merry (1981, pp. 11–13), for example, identifies three aspects of danger that are linked to crime: a cognitive assessment of cues, harm that transcends the risk of crime, and danger, a cultural construct, learned as part of how the world functions. People who occupy ambiguous and interstitial statuses and roles, such as children, are likely victims (Merry 1981, p. 140). Criminals are beyond normal techniques of social control (Douglas 1966; Merry 1981, pp. 125, 163), and the fear of crime justifies increased control over those who are considered "dangerous" (Merry 1981, p. 220).

Television is especially suited for evoking fear. As a visual medium, television conveys situational cues that elicit fear, such as dark, isolated areas or menacing strangers (Merry 1981; Stanko 1990; Warr 1990). Cinematographic techniques make these cues more realistic (Graber 1990; Kellner 1990). In the following section the image of crime, criminals, victims, police, and the world view presented by AMW and UM are analyzed. This analysis also includes images conveyed through cinematographic techniques and formats.

Method

A content analysis was conducted of AMW and UM programs that aired between January 25 and May 31, 1989. These programs were videotaped and a subsample of 16 episodes was randomly selected: nine half-hour-long AMW episodes and seven hour-long UM episodes. The 16 episodes contain 77 vignettes (48 AMW; 29 UM); the vignette serves as the unit of analysis. In the analysis, all percentages are calculated on these numbers of vignettes.

The protocol used for data collection was focused on three aspects of the programming: (1) *demographics*: types of crime and general information on the crime, criminals, and victims; (2) *characterizations*: specific depictions of crime, criminals, and victims, such as brutality, dangerousness, or a victim's vulnerability; (3) *world view*: relative safety of people and places, the terror and randomness of crime, and what the audience should do about crime.

Information about cinematographic techniques (for example, camera angles and soundtrack) was coded across all three categories. Both programs feature updates about fugitives depicted earlier who are sighted or captured. Such updates were coded with the vignettes in which they originally appeared.

Data and Discussion

There are three parts to the analysis. Part one compares AMW with UM with prior research on crime drama. Part two considers the parallels between

AMW and UM's vignettes and urban legends. Part three focuses on the construction and the magnification of the dangers of the modern world depicted in these programs.

Television Crime Drama and Reality Programming

Television depictions differ significantly from official crime statistics. The analysis reveals that AMW and UM's depictions of "real life" crimes and criminals are consistent with crime drama representations.

Television crime is depicted as violent and usually directed against persons. AMW and UM offer a similar view of crime. As shown in table 1, in 92 percent of AMW's vignettes ($n = 44$ of 48 vignettes), the crimes depicted also are violent and personal (murder, attempted murder, rape, kidnapping, armed robbery and child molestation). Sixty-two percent of UM's vignettes ($n = 18$) include violence against persons. For both programs, murder is depicted in 52 percent of the vignettes ($n = 40$).

Ninety-one percent of the vignettes ($n = 70$) depict male criminals. Four percent of the vignettes ($n = 3$) feature female criminals, and these are portrayed as accomplices. Criminals are 30 years or older in 56 percent of the vignettes ($n = 43$), and Caucasians are involved in 64 percent of all vignettes ($n = 44$). African Americans ($n = 9$) and Hispanics ($n = 9$) are featured in 12 percent of the vignettes (see table 2).

Table 1   Number and Percentage of Vignettes that Depicted Offense Types by Program[a]

	Program Vignettes					
Offense	UM ($n = 29$)		AMW ($n = 48$)		Combined UM/AMW ($n = 77$)	
	%	n	%	n	%	n
Murder	41	(12)	58	(28)	52	(40)
Theft/fraud/extortion	21	(6)	8	(4)	13	(10)
Escape	7	(2)	15	(7)	12	(9)
Bank robbery/armed robbery	10	(3)	10	(5)	10	(8)
Illegal arms/terrorism	0		4	(2)	3	(2)
Unexplained death/missing	14	(4)	2	(1)	7	(5)
Rape	3	(1)	6	(3)	5	(4)
Kidnapping	3	(1)	6	(3)	5	(4)
Child molestation	3	(1)	6	(3)	5	(4)
Attempted murder	0		4	(2)	3	(2)
Drug dealing	0		4	(2)	3	(2)
Other[b]	10	(3)	4	(2)	7	(5)

[a] Percentages are based on the total number of vignettes for each program. Note that a vignette may contain depictions of more than one offense type.
[b] The Other category includes bigamy and/or intimidation.

Table 2 **Number and Percentage of Vignettes that Depicted Offender Characteristics by Program**[a]

	Program Vignettes					
	UM		AMW		Combined UM/AMW	
Characteristics	(*n = 29*)		(*n = 48*)		(*n =77*)	
Gender	%	*n*	%	*n*	%	*n*
Male	76	(22)	100	(48)	91	(70)
Female	3	(1)	4	(2)	4	(3)
Unknown/not depicted	21	(6)	0		8	(6)
Age						
20–29	21	(6)	31	(15)	27	(21)
30–39	17	(5)	21	(10)	20	(15)
40–49	21	(6)	31	(15)	27	(21)
50–59	14	(4)	6	(3)	9	(7)
Unknown/not depicted	28	(8)	10	(5)	17	(13)
Ethnicity						
Caucasian	66	(19)	63	(30)	64	(49)
African American	3	(1)	17	(8)	12	(9)
Hispanic	7	(2)	15	(7)	12	(9)
Mixed ethnicity	3	(1)	0		1	(1)
Unknown/not depicted	21	(6)	6	(3)	12	(9)

[a] A vignette may contain depictions of male and female offenders or multiple offenders of the same gender, age, and ethnicity.

Contrary to television drama, criminals are frequently portrayed as professional criminals. Corporate and political criminals are absent from the vignettes. A motivation for crime is offered in over half of the vignettes (*n* = 42). Greed frequently prompts the crime, especially on UM (*n* = 11), while emotional motivations, such as jealousy, are prominent on AMW (*n* = 6). Some crimes are blamed on random violence or mistaken identity (*n* = 9).

AMW and UM provide a social history, re-enacting past key events in the life of the criminal, and describe their current lives. However, these caricatures tend to reinforce existing stereotypes about criminals.

Citizens play a significant role on both programs. The program hosts credit viewers with captures, while the police are depicted as competent and accessible to the viewers. AMW and UM also provide more information about trial and sentencing than usually appears in crime drama.

AMW and UM as Urban Legends

Fear-evoking cues magnified by sophisticated cinematographic techniques enable AMW and UM to construct entertaining programs that fit the standard format of the television crime genre. The vignettes are symbolic morality plays about good and evil.

As in urban legends, the crime portrayed on AMW and UM symbolizes the dangers and complexities of modern life that threaten the social order. Brutal, violent crimes are featured (for example, UM 2-22-89; AMW 2-12-89), and graphic details are shown, including the number and location of a victim's wounds. For example, one victim is stabbed 30 times through the heart (AMW 2-12-89); another victim is shot "5 times and died of massive bleeding" (AMW 2-5-89).

Cinematographic techniques enhance the affective aspects of crime. In some vignettes, the film speed is reduced to slow motion as a criminal draws a gun and shoots the victim, capturing the muzzle flash (AMW 2-5-89, 2-12-89, 4-9-89). One vignette employs fear cues: the host, emerging from the night on a deserted road, references a common fear of driving on a lonely stretch of highway where one's cries for help would go unheeded (UM 4-12-89).

Described are dimensions or harm that go beyond the risk of victimization. Victims are "embarrassed and devastated" (UM 3-15-89), and their families' and friends' lives are tragically disrupted (UM 1-25-89, 3-15-89, AMW 4-2-89). Dramatic irony intensifies the tragedy. Victims are murdered shortly after achieving an important goal (AMW 3-19-89) or on their birthday (UM 3-15-89). Victims do not merely lose property through theft, they lose "a precious family heirloom that was part of their heritage" (AMW 4-2-89). The narrative, the visual, and the soundtrack combine to communicate a sense of tragedy, e.g., the host notes that a slain policeman is buried with full honors. The vignette shows footage of his funeral as "Taps" is played in the background (AMW 2-5-89). Stories are simple and easily dramatized. Twenty AMW vignettes (42 percent) depict random, purposeless crimes often featured in urban legends, while nineteen UM vignettes (66 percent) offer such a depiction.

Criminals. Like the villains of urban legends, criminals are dangerous people who are beyond social control. Thirty-seven AMW vignettes (77 percent) depict criminals in this manner. Nineteen UM vignettes (66 percent) offer such depictions.

Fugitives are characterized as dangerous (for example, AMW 2-5-89; UM 4-12-89), and the bail bond imposed suggests that these criminals should be incarcerated (AMW 2-5-89). The camera often zooms in on a captured fugitive's handcuffs, providing a visual image of the physical restraints that are required to control these individuals (for example, AMW 2-12-89; UM 3-15-89).

Some criminals are traditional urban legend villains, such as drifters (AMW 3-26-89) and hitchhikers (UM 3-1-89). Other criminals are portrayed as satanists (AMW 4-16-89; UM 3-29-89). AMW and UM also feature criminals who are gang members (AMW 2-12-89) and drug dealers (AMW 2-5-89; 4-16-89).

AMW and UM feature frightening criminals who have ambiguous psychological capacity. One criminal is a "crazed killer, a psycho, a maniac" (UM 3-29-89), while others are characterized as "schizophrenic" (AMW 4-2-89) or "emotionally disturbed" (AMW 2-26-89). Both programs feature criminals who "showed no emotion" (for example, AMW 2-5-89, UM 3-29-89), or who demonstrate "a flamboyant disregard of authority" (AMW 4-12-89).

The programs define criminals through their actions, portraying criminality as a master status, noting such deviance is undifferentiated in that the criminal activity is generalized to other aspects of their lives. For example, one criminal "masqueraded as a construction worker but he was really an escaped murderer" (AMW 2-5-89). Another criminal who "appeared to be a model cop was in reality a child molester" (UM 3-1-89).

The program hosts provide physical descriptions of fugitives in derogatory terms, such as "a scraggly beard" (AMW 4-2-89), or "dirty blonde hair" (AMW 2-26-89). Other deviant behaviors unrelated to the crimes are mentioned, such as dabbling in voodoo (AMW 4-2-89). In one vignette, the host invites the audience to view the physical effects of depravity, using a time-lapse technique on a series of photographs in which the criminal's physical appearance deteriorates (AMW 2-26-89).

Victims.   The victims often occupy ambiguous and interstitial roles and statuses and, therefore, are vulnerable to harm. Victims are similar to those of urban legends. Twenty-four AMW (50 percent) and twenty UM vignettes (69 percent) depict such victims. Children are molested and kidnapped (UM 3-1-89, 1-25-89). In this regard, AMW's opening features a visual of an empty playground swing, accompanied by a voice-over of the word "kidnapped."

Women are frequent victims as well. Approximately one-half of the victims whose sex is noted are female, thereby reinforcing the fear of crime and violence that women experience.

AMW and UM offer information about victims designed to achieve viewer empathy. Victims are referred to by their given names, and friends share personal anecdotes. Crimes are re-enacted so as to promote identification with the victim; the camera takes the victim's perspective, reproducing a good/evil dichotomy, with the victim and the audience aligned against the criminal.

The programs focus on the victim's personal and professional worth. In contrast to the criminals, victims are "hard working" individuals (for example, UM 3-15-89; AMW 4-16-89). UM characterizes one victim as a "devoted wife and mother who was active in the community" (UM 3-29-89), and another as "the kind of girl you'd like to have for your daughter" (UM 3-15-89). One vignette featuring wild horses as victims establishes their worth in human terms: "They symbolize the freedom of the American West, and each animal has its own unique personality" (UM 1-25-89).

Modern Danger

Both programs create a sense of modern danger analogous to the fears that urban legends convey. This modern danger is characterized as a world in which no one, no matter how careful, is safe.

Just as urban legends are portrayed as true stories, AMW and UM act as media storytellers of "real life" and the terrible uncertainties of life. The reality program format enhances the sense of modern danger. As entertainment these hybrid programs combine fear cues and cinematographic techniques, and appeal to the conventions of news programming that bolster credibility of reality claims.

An Unsafe World. Good storytellers localize their tales in time and space. AMW and UM program hosts begin their stories with statements like, "27 years ago tonight" (AMW 2-5-89). Exact dates of crimes (UM 1-25-89) and phrases such as "20 days ago" (AMW 3-19-89) provide accessible temporal referents, contributing to reality claims.

Geographic settings are also important. Statements such as "it all started in this house on Chestnut Street" (AMW 2-19-89), or "a quiet blue-collar suburb on the outskirts of Cleveland" (UM 5-31-89) produce an identifiable sense of place. Some locations, such as an unfamiliar area or dark alley, serve as fear cues.

Featured are crimes that occur in safe places, and program hosts draw special attention to such settings. One vignette, set in a conservative Louisiana community, represents, the host notes, an unlikely setting for a crime (UM 3-1-89). In another vignette, "dark forces swirled beneath a small-town facade" (UM 2-22-89). Crimes often violate special places, such as the home. In one dramatization, the camera follows a schizophrenic killer as he observes the sleeping victims (AMW 4-23-89). Another vignette depicts a burglar sneaking through a house while the occupants host a dinner party. Later, a teenage girl showers and her unsuspecting mom works in a bedroom, while the burglar prowls through the house (AMW 4-2-89). When crime occurs in seemingly safe places, a sense of modern danger is enhanced.

Certain predictable people, such as menacing strangers, also serve as fear cues. However, the worst danger portrayed evolves from seemingly trustworthy persons. Likeable and normal people are portrayed as manipulative con artists or crazy (for example, UM 1-25-89; AMW 2-12-89, 4-9-89). In some instances, the unsuspected criminal occupies a special role, such as a policeman who counsels abused children but who also molests these children (UM 3-1-89), or a sociopathic nurse who kidnaps a newborn baby at gunpoint (UM 1-25-89).

The most terrifying criminals hold a special status with respect to the victim. Examples include the husband who murders his wife while she begs him to spare her life (AMW 2-5-89). Other vignettes depict special criminals who hold an interstitial status, such as the "All American" kid who becomes a drug user and murders his parents (AMW 2-26-89). Such vignettes emphasize the thesis that no place is safe; no person is trustworthy.

Random Terror. One message is that the modern world is filled with danger. Random and terrifying danger lurks everywhere, awaiting the victim and, by implication, the viewer. Powerful, emotionally charged vignettes produce images that reinforce a sense of danger that is commonplace in modern society. Some of the vignettes emphasize the criminal. For example, as the host characterizes the criminal as dangerous, the frame freezes, leaving the criminal's intense stare directed at the audience (AMW 4-9-89). Program hosts urge the audience to remember these visually compelling images, and to be on the lookout for the fugitives.

Victims are also emphasized, many of whom are randomly chosen, innocent individuals who are "arbitrarily targeted" (UM 3-29-89) or murdered by mistake (AMW 4-16-89). On occasion a horror movie format is used in which the foolish character opens a door at the top of the stairs as the audience screams "No." People sense the impending danger and warn victims who rarely heed such warnings. Either victims do not appreciate the extent of the danger (AMW 2-12-89, 4-16-89), or they are engaged in common activities that escalate into sudden violence, such as the woman who became involved in a marital dispute and was murdered (UM 1-25-89).

Equally terrifying are the vignettes in which the victims realize their danger. The camera follows an obviously frightened woman leaving her house. Ominous music complements this fear as she nervously scans the street, searching for some threat. She is careful, but she still disappears (UM 1-25-89).

Other careful victims are murdered by maniacal killers (for example UM 3-29-89), or by satanic blood cults (AMW 4-16-89). Emphasizing victim terror, victims often describe their fear (UM 4-12-89). In other instances the host describes the fear, indicating how it feels for a family to be stalked by a prison escapee bent on revenge (UM 4-12-89).

Situational and fear cues heighten the sense of victim terror and audience frustration. Vignettes feature people who are isolated and alone when victimized (for example, UM 4-12-89). In other instances, people are nearby but do not render assistance to the victim. A woman whose baby has been kidnapped screams for help, but no motorist will stop (UM 1-25-89). Careful, normal, and hard-working people are victimized by base, depraved strangers. They are also victimized by their children, spouses, mates, and friends. In this area, AMW and UM programs extend beyond the content of urban legends, suggesting that modern danger is inescapable.

AMW and UM programs portray a world in which crime is so unpredictable and its consequences so devastating that public safety is at issue. Crime is a metaphor for a world gone berserk, for life out of control. The only recourse viewers have is to call the authorities or the program representative with information that will put criminals behind bars. Program updates attribute captures to viewer tips, and footage of captured fugitives supports these claims.

Modern danger legitimizes public surveillance. Forging a partnership between the police, the media, and the audience, these programs encourage wide dispersal of community social control.

Conclusion

Prior research has shown that television dramatizes stereotype depictions of crime and criminals. In the present study the authors conclude that reality programming presents similar images. Crimes are portrayed as violent and personal, and fugitives are portrayed as dangerous people.

However, the present study diverges from the more traditional media crime approach in that the focus is on program meaning. AMW and UM programs present images common to popular urban legends in that crime is used to symbolize the uncertainties of modern life, that criminals are evil, abnormal people, and victims are portrayed as being vulnerable. Such tales nurture the very fears that produce urban legends.

Using a combination of case selection, cinematographic techniques, and claims, these reality programs depict a sense of modern danger. AMW and UM programs present a world in which anyone can be cast into the role of a criminal or victim. Such an image of reality is frightening because the victims are people with whom viewers can identify.

Reality programs nurture audience participation as one solution to the pervasiveness of crime, supporting the notion that viewers can be empowered in the fight against crime. Viewers are encouraged to watch for fugitives and report them either to the police or the program. Both programs claim that such surveillance leads to the capture of fugitives.

Reality program encouragement of surveillance supports the view that control is dispersing more widely into society. Images of dangerous fugitives who participate in a world characterized by violence and uncertainty justify surveillance and reporting to the police. This world view also supports the claim made by Gitlin (1979) and Schattenberg (1981) that crime drama endorses a control orientation.

In sum, AMW and UM's hybrid news and entertainment format continues the trend toward blurred television genres previously noted by media scholars. The influence of television is so great that it has become an important part of the viewer's reality. Participating in reality programs means the audience is a part of that reality, making that reality almost indistinguishable from any other aspects of life.

References

Best, Joel. 1990. *Threatened Children*. Chicago: University of Chicago Press.

Comstock, George. 1978. *Television and Human Behavior*. New York: Columbia University Press.

Davis, James. 1952. "Crime News in Colorado Newspapers," *American Journal of Sociology* 57:325–30.

Douglas, Mary. 1966. *Purity and Danger: An Analysis of Concepts of Pollution and Taboo*. Hammondsworth: Penguin Books.

Ericson, Richard, Patricia Baranek, and Janet Chan. 1991. *Representing Order: Crime, Law and Justice in the News Media*. Toronto: University of Toronto Press.

Fine, Gary. 1980. "The Kentucky Fried Rat: Legends and Modern Society." *Journal of the Folklore Institute* 17:222–43.

Fishman, Mark. 1978. "Crime Waves As Ideology." *Social Problems* 25:531–43.

Garofalo, James. 1981. "Crime and the Mass Media: A Selective Review of Research." *Journal of Research in Crime and Delinquency* 18:319–49.

Gerbner, George, and Larry Gross. 1976. "Living With Television: The Violence Profile." *Journal of Communication* 26:173–99.

Gitlin, Todd. 1979. "Prime Time Ideology: The Hegemonic Process in Television Entertainment." *Social Problems* 26:251–66.

_____. 1985. "Looking Through the Screen." Pp. 3–8 in *Watching Television*, edited by Todd Gitlin. New York: Pantheon Books.

Graber, Doris. 1980. *Crime News and the Public.* New York: Praeger.

_____. 1990. "Seeing is Remembering: How Visuals Contribute to Learning from Television News." *Journal of Communication* 40:134–55.

Hirsch, Paul. 1980. "The 'Scary World' of the Nonviewer and Other Anomalies: A Reanalysis of Gerbner et al.'s Findings on Cultivation Analysis, Part 1." *Communication Research* 7:403–56.

_____. 1981. "The 'Scary World' of the Nonviewer and Other Anomalies: A Reanalysis of Gerbner et al.'s Findings on Cultivation Analysis, Part 2." *Communication Research* 8:3–37.

Humphries, Drew. 1981. "Serious Crime, News Coverage, and Ideology." *Crime and Delinquency* 27:191–205.

Katz, Jack. 1987. "What Makes Crime News?" *Media, Culture and Society* 9:47–75.

Kellner, Douglas. 1990. *Television and the Crisis of Democracy.* Boulder, CO: Westview Press.

Lichter, Linda and Robert Lichter. 1983. *Prime Time Crime.* Washington, DC: The Media Institute.

Merry, Sally. 1981. *Urban Danger: Life in a Neighborhood of Strangers.* Philadelphia: Temple University Press.

Molotch, Harvey, and Marilyn Lester. 1974. "News as Purposive Behavior: On the Strategic Use of Routine Events, Accidents, and Scandals." *American Sociological Review* 39:101–12.

Oring, Elliott. 1990. "Legend, Truth, and News." *Southern Folklore* 47:163–77.

Pandiani, J. 1978. "Crime Time TV: If All We Knew Is What We Saw. . . ." *Contemporary Crises* 2:437–58.

Schattenberg, Gus. 1981. "Social Control Functions of Mass Media Depictions of Crime." *Sociological Inquiry* 51:71–77.

Stanko, Elizabeth. 1990. *Everyday Violence: How Women and Men Experience Sexual and Physical Danger.* London: Pandora.

Tuchman, Gaye. 1978. *Making News: A Study in the Social Construction of Reality.* New York: Free Press.

Wachs, Eleanor. 1988. *Crime-Victim Stories: New York City's Urban Folklore.* Bloomington: Indiana University Press.

Warr, Mark. 1990. "Dangerous Situations: Social Context and Fear of Victimization." *Social Forces* 68:891–907.

Williams, Raymond. 1989. *Raymond Williams on Television: Selected Writings*, edited by A. O'Connor. London: Routledge.

FIVE

STATE MANAGERS, INTELLECTUALS, AND THE MEDIA

A CONTENT ANALYSIS OF IDEOLOGY IN EXPERTS' QUOTES IN FEATURE NEWSPAPER ARTICLES ON CRIME

Michael Welch, Melissa Fenwick, & Meredith Roberts

For several decades, scholarly inquiry into the media has revealed key patterns and tendencies in the production of crime news. In particular, scholars have delineated critical stages in the social construction of crime—all of which contribute to the reification of crime news. First, crime is selected from among many available social issues (e.g., education, employment, poverty) and advanced to the status of a *problem* requiring serious policy consideration. Second, the crime *problem* is sufficiently narrowed to include street crime, thereby neglecting other types of lawlessness and harm (e.g., corporate violence). In the final stage, crime is defined as a criminal justice *problem* (Michalowski 1985), and it is this particular image of crime that typically takes the form of crime news (Kappeler, Blumberg, and Potter 1996; Surette 1992; Tunnell 1992; Schoenfeld, Meier, and Griffin 1979).

Operating within the final stage of the social construction of crime, political leaders and law enforcement officials (also known as *state managers*) enjoy the privilege of offering to the media *primary* as well as ideological definitions of crime (Kasinsky 1994:210; Hall et al. 1978). Thus, critics charge that the media serve propaganda functions within the state's ideological machinery (Herman and Chomsky 1988). In particular, it is through the media that state managers *filter* definitions of crime; as a result of this gatekeeping and various other propaganda techniques (Kappeler et al. 1996:24–26), state managers

Justice Quarterly, Vol. 15, No. 1, March 1998. Permission granted by Taylor & Francis, Ltd. http://www.tandf.co.uk/journals

and the media together determine what is *socially thinkable* (e.g., violence committed solely by individual predators instead of corporate offenders). Benefitting from their elevated position within a hierarchy of credibility (Becker 1973, 1967), state managers also promote and legitimize their "law-and-order" crime control agenda (Ericson, Baranek, and Chan 1991, 1989, 1987; Fishman 1978; Hall et al. 1978; Surette 1992; Humphries 1981).

Although crime news exists as a product manufactured by the media, it is significantly shaped by state managers who contribute to its distinct ideological qualities. Fishman (1978:531) reminds us that "all knowledge is knowledge from some point of view." Crime news, therefore, tends to be *ideological* insofar as it represents a worldview of state managers who distort the reality of crime, specifically by disavowing the causal relationship between crime and social conditions (see Marx 1978; Reiman 1995; Sahin 1980).

State managers (e.g., law enforcement officials) have long refined the art of influencing the course and content of crime news (Fishman 1978). Similarly, intellectuals (e.g., professors) have also realized the importance of participating in the construction of crime news. Marking a significant movement in the field, Barak (1994, 1988) introduced the term *newsmaking criminology* to describe a conscious effort by criminologists to engage in the public discourse on crime (see also Fox and Levin 1993; Greek 1994; Henry 1994). "Newsmaking criminology presupposes that there is no such thing as 'objective' news reporting and interpreting: The presentation of crime and violence in the mass media, for example, cannot be disconnected from the prevailing ideologies of the day" (Barak 1994:261).

In this study—the first of its kind—we administered a content analysis of quoted statements offered by different types of experts on crime; namely, state managers (i.e., politicians and criminal justice practitioners) and intellectuals (i.e., professors and nonacademic researchers). In doing so, we examined the ways in which experts' quoted statements convey two principle dimensions of *ideology* of crime: crime *causation* and crime *control*. This investigation is significant because it specifically identifies the sources, forms, and patterns of ideology in crime news, thereby contributing to an understanding of how the media and the state construct misleading depictions of crime and crime policy.

Techniques of Propaganda and Popular Topics in Crime News

An analysis of the social construction of crime news would not be complete without exploring the importance of propaganda as a mechanism facilitating the misrepresentation of crime. Undoubtedly, the elevation of crime to the status of a social problem depends greatly upon the persuasiveness of propaganda: "a technique for influencing social action based on intentional distortions and manipulation of communications" (Kappeler et al. 1996:24). Moreover, it is through numerous propaganda techniques that the media and the state together inject elements of ideology into distorted images of crime. However, these biased versions of crime are not the result of a conspiracy but rather "the unintended consequence of the process by which information is collected, processed, and prepared for dissemination by mass media, government, and interest groups" (Kappeler et al. 1996:22–23; Tunnell 1992; Marsh 1991; Bohm 1986).

Still, it is crucial to emphasize that not all crime news is the product of conscious attempts at propaganda; nevertheless, many distortions of crime are generated by propaganda tactics deeply institutionalized and widely routinized within the media and the government (Kappeler et al. 1996; Kasinsky 1994; Hall et al. 1978). As we explore various examples of propaganda in this and other sections, we should remain mindful of how ideology shapes misleading images of crime at each stage of social construction.

In this study, our sample reveals 47 separate topics represented among 105 feature articles about crime, thus suggesting a diverse range of crime issues. The most common topic was street crime rates/trends ($n = 15$); the street crime drop in New York City ($n = 8$); youth street crime and juvenile delinquency ($n = 8$); and politicians discussing street crime ($n = 7$). Furthermore, the remaining articles offered an assortment of issues, including the growth in prison population, "three strikes" laws, firearms, carjacking, genetics, gangs, DNA, stalking, urban violence, women offenders, and the war on drugs.

This sample of crime topics illuminates the process of social construction; first, crime is awarded the status of a social problem requiring massive policy attention; second, the crime problem is distinctly narrowed to include street crime while excluding other forms of lawlessness; and finally, street crime is defined in ways that elicit criminal justice intervention. Conforming to this framework, the most striking characteristic of our sample of topics is its disproportionate emphasis on street crime. Despite 47 different topics, only one of these feature articles went beyond street crime to focus on white-collar offenses. Indeed, the media bias toward street crime (especially offenses committed by *individuals*) to the exclusion of white-collar, corporate, governmental, military, and political crime (especially offenses committed by *groups* and organizations) is abundantly evident.

This particular bias toward street crime suggests that the topics selected for these feature newspaper articles are ideologically filtered or screened. Such a distortion is indicative of a propaganda technique by the which the media manage information through the editorial process; consequently, street crime emerges as the preferred construction of crime. In shoring up the information-management technique, biased language is employed to sensationalize and label certain forms of lawlessness (Kappeler et al. 1996:25). In addition to the frequent and vague use of the term "gang," value-loaded language was also found in references to "stalking" (instead of harassment) and "carjacking" (instead of car theft or robbery). Interestingly, even some law enforcement officials were skeptical of the term "carjacking."

We don't even like to say "carjacking" . . . It's robbery and it's been going on for a long time. There's a lot of hype going on right now.

Billy Davis, spokesman for the Chicago Police Department;
New York Times, December 9, 1992:A-18

Thus, the media together with state managers reproduce an image of public disorder that is overwhelmingly based on street crime, especially offenses committed by low-income individuals. Typically, these constructions of crime are also void of meaningful references to the causal relationship between crime and societal conditions. Consequently, the media contribute to one of the most common forms of propaganda—namely, the creation of criminal stereotypes.

The nature of topics in our sample supports the assertion that crime news is not only commodified for public consumption (Tunnell 1992) but also shaped according to the dominant ideology. A principal aspect of the dominant ideology is its insinuation that street offenses are the most costly, dangerous, and threatening form of crime (see Barlow, Barlow, and Chiricos 1995a, 1995b). Financial losses assessed for different types of offenses, however, contradict the dominant ideology's image of crime. It is estimated that the cost of street crime hovers around $4 billion per year whereas the expense of white-collar and corporate crime exceeds that figure fifty times—reaching $200 billion per year (Mokhiber and Wheat 1995:9; Albrecht, Wernz, and Williams 1995). Further, approximately 24,000 homicides were committed in the United States in, for example, 1995. By contrast, during the same period, more than 56,000 workers died as a result of injuries or diseases caused by unsafe working conditions, totaling more than 300 fatalities per day (Mokhiber and Wheat 1995:9; see also Serrin 1991:80; Welch 1996a, 1996b; Reiman 1995).[1]

Therefore, in publishing messages about certain forms of crime news, the media warn the public of some of the threats to their safety (e.g., street offenses), but neglect—due to ideological constraints—other social harms (e.g., white-collar and corporate offenses) (see also Kappeler et al. 1996:141–63). Again, the framework of social constructionism reminds us of the process by which street crime is selected from many available social harms and defined in ways that legitimize the criminal justice machinery. In facilitating these social constructions, techniques of propaganda serve crucial functions by managing information, thus contributing to stereotypes of criminality (i.e., street crime) (Kappeler et al. 1996:24–25; Tunnell 1992; Bohm 1986; Dickson 1968).

In light of this evidence, our study raises questions about how the media define crime, and just as important to our content analysis, how newspapers *index* topics of crime. Since we examined only those articles listed by the selected newspapers as *features* on crime, our sample was dictated by the newspapers' indexing scheme. As noted, these articles were disproportionately devoted to street offenses; thus, our sample is as much a product (and artifact) of newspaper indexing as it is a reflection of the biases in how the media define crime. In a manner of speaking, we decided to accept the "cards we were dealt" by the newspaper indexing procedure. Regrettably, however, we are aware that many other forms of crime were not indexed into our sample including corporate violence, terrorism, and child sexual abuse, just to name a few.

Research Method

Sample of Feature Articles on Crime

The sample of feature articles in this study was drawn from four major newspapers from 1992 to 1995. These newspapers were selected due to their large circulation, their reputation for offering readers a national coverage of news, and because together they contribute to a sense of geographical representation. A total of 105 feature articles about crime were published in these newspapers between 1992 and 1995; specifically, 42 feature articles were published in the *New York Times*, 24 in the *Washington Post*, 23 in the *Los Angeles Times*, and 16 in the *Chicago Tribune*. It should be noted that the greatest number of feature articles about crime appeared in 1994 ($n = 38$) followed by 1993 ($n = 31$), 1992 ($n = 20$), and 1995 ($n = 16$) (refer to table 1).

For the purposes of this study, our sample of newspaper articles about crime includes only those articles indexed as *features* and containing at least one quote from a crime expert. Obviously, there are perhaps hundreds of articles about incidents of crime published by each of these newspapers. However, feature articles on crime were targeted because they typically offer focused discussions of crime in which experts' quotes are particularly relevant. In this vein, the objective of our research was to examine the content of experts' quotes within the context of feature articles on crime.

Table 1   Number of Feature Articles on Crime Per Year by Newspaper

Newspaper	1992	1993	1994	1995	Totals
NY Times	7	12	15	8	42
Washington Post	7	6	6	5	24
LA Times	3	7	12	1	23
Chicago Tribune	3	6	5	2	16
Totals	20	31	38	16	$n = 105$

Procedure

Two major groups of experts were constructed for this study. The first group of experts—state managers—includes politicians and criminal justice officials and practitioners (i.e., police commissioners, police officers, prosecutors, as well as members of "tough on crime" groups who serve as legislation lobbyists). The rationale for combining politicians and practitioners into one group is based on their roles as state managers; indeed, we also found that the contents of their quotes were consistently similar in terms of ideological statements about crime causation and crime control.

The second group of experts—intellectuals—includes university and college professors as well as nonacademic researchers (e.g., analysts at the Rand Corporation). The rationale for combining professors and nonacademic researchers is based on their roles as intellectuals; additionally, we also confirmed that the contents of their quotes were consistently similar in terms of ideological statements about crime and crime control.

The central purpose of this study is to examine systematically the content of quoted statements offered by experts (as the units of analysis) and to sort them according to two principle dimensions of ideology of crime: crime causation and crime control. Borrowing from Barlow et al. (1995a, 1995b), we relied on three perspectives of crime causation. The first perspective of crime causation in our classification scheme was *utilitarianism*, typically surfacing as references to criminal motives in relation to economic gain. From this viewpoint, the following utilitarian notion of deterrence sheds light on the significance of greater opportunity to commit crime coupled with fewer risks of detection.

> Twenty-nine years ago, there was no Medicare, Medicaid and a much smaller pool of (private) health insurance. Doctors were conventionally paid in cash and had greater opportunity to under report income. Today, that's not the case.
>
> David Levine, Chief Economist for New York-based
> Stanford C. Bernstein Co., a securities research firm;
> *Los Angeles Times*, February 13, 1993:A-21

The second perspective of crime causation, *personal pathology*, commonly manifested itself in statements about psychological defects affecting criminals and their inability to control their unlawful behavior. Consider the following item:

> Impulsivity, sensation-seeking, and defiance are all stable traits found among juvenile delinquents that can sometimes be seen as early as preschool.
>
> Denise Gottfredson, associate professor at the
> Institute of Criminal Justice and Criminology,
> University of Maryland at College Park;
> *New York Times*, July 22, 1993:10

Finally, the perspective that *social factors* cause crime served as our third content category; in sum, this grouping of factors included various microsocial circumstances, social influence, social conflict, and macrosocial conditions.

> This is all symbolic. But everybody's avoiding the really tough issues of addressing the fundamental social conditions that are breeding this.
>
> Stuart A. Scheingold, professor at University of Washington;
> *New York Times*, October 24, 1993:4

Also drawing from Barlow et al. (1995a, 1995b), we categorized crime control into two types of strategies. The first content category of crime control was designated for *hard control*, including the expansion of law enforcement, "get-tough-on-crime" campaigns, and preventative measures based on deterrence.

> This is precisely the type of person three-strikes-and-you're-out was aimed at: career criminals. It's a victory for the people of California because this is a thug who has a record of violence in the past—serious felonies—who believes that it's okay to go out and terrorize little kids.
>
> Daniel E. Lungren, California State Attorney General;
> *Washington Post*, March 8, 1995:A-14

The second grouping of crime control intervention was reserved for *soft control*, namely, rehabilitation, decriminalization, gun control, and criminal justice (and social) reform.

> Getting in there with programs is more difficult because of this chasm. The issue is not just that people have moved, but the jobs have moved. And for this and other reasons, inner-city residents don't have the resources to deal with these issues.
>
> Donna E. Shalala, Health and Human Services secretary;
> *Washington Post*, February 12, 1993:A-12

Methodologically, it should be noted that statements critical of hard control were coded as soft control; likewise, statements critical of soft control were sorted into the category of hard control.

In administering a content analysis, we systematically examined each of the experts' quotes to determine whether they conveyed statements about crime causation (as represented by either manifest content or latent content), and, if so, according to which perspective (i.e., utilitarianism, personal pathology, or social factors). Similarly, the quotes also were scrutinized to conclude whether they contained statements about crime control (as indicated by either manifest content or latent content), and, if so, according to which perspective (i.e., hard control or soft control).

Findings

The first task of our content analysis involved identifying and sorting experts' (politicians and practitioners compared to professors and nonacademic researchers) quotes into two principle categories of ideology of crime: crime causation and crime control. Table 2 indicates that our sample includes 162 quoted statements about the cause of crime and 132 quoted statements pertaining to crime control (totaling 294 statements overall). What is noteworthy about these findings is that 61 percent (*n* = 92) of the quotes from politicians and criminal justice practitioners deal with crime control, while 39 percent (*n* = 58) are relevant to crime causation. Conversely, 72 percent (*n* =

Table 2   Number of Quoted Statements About Crime Causation and Crime Control by Politicians & Practitioners Compared to Professors and Nonacademic Researchers*

	Politicians & Practitioners	Professors & Nonacademic Researchers	Totals
Statements about:			
Crime Causation	58	104	162
	(39%)	(72%)	(55%)
Crime Control	92	40	132
	(61%)	(28%)	(45%)
Totals	150	144	$n = 294^{\dagger}$

* Quoted statements drawn from 105 feature newspaper articles on crime in the *New York Times*, the *Washington Post*, the *Los Angeles Times*, and the *Chicago Tribune* from 1992 to 1995.
† Computations for chi-square yield statistical significance at .001 level of probability.

104) of the quotes from professors and nonacademic researchers pertain to causes of crime, whereas 28 percent ($n = 40$) relate to crime control.

Although the number of statements quoted from each grouping of experts is strikingly balanced (150 statements offered by politicians and practitioners and 144 by professors and nonacademic researchers), the differences between the content of statements—as they reflect an ideology of crime—are marked. That is, politicians and practitioners were quoted along lines of crime control, whereas professors and nonacademic researchers were quoted about the causes of crime. Computations for chi-square test yield statistical significance at the .001 level of probability (refer to table 2). Obviously, it is difficult to know whether these differences are the result of fundamental views of ideology of crime (crime causation compared to crime control) or whether these differences stem from how journalists select (or filter and screen) quotes to be used in their feature articles. Given the central importance of this issue in the context of propaganda, we shall return to it later in this section.

Crime Causation

The second task of our content analysis involved identifying and sorting experts' (politicians and practitioners compared to professors and nonacademic researchers) quoted statements into three categories of crime causation: utilitarianism, personal pathology, and social factors. Table 3 shows that we located 26 quoted statements about utilitarianism, 33 quoted statements about personal pathology, and 103 quoted statements about social factors (totaling 162 quoted statements about the causes of crime). What is noteworthy about these findings is that more than 46 percent ($n = 27$) of the quoted statements from politicians and practitioners deal with social factors; 38 percent ($n = 22$) embrace utilitarianism; and 15.5 percent ($n = 9$) address personal pathology. Conversely, 73 percent ($n = 76$) of the quoted statements from professors and nonacademic researchers reflect their view that social factors cause crime; 23 percent ($n = 24$) relate to personal pathology; and 4 percent ($n = 4$) pertain to utilitarianism.

In addition to 14 politicians, this pool of practitioners includes 20 law enforcement officials, 6 prosecutors, 2 corrections officials, 1 judge, 1 defense lawyer, 1 probation official, 1 member of the ACLU, 1 state director of criminal justice, 1 director of criminal justice services, 1 coroner, 1 forensic psychologist, 1 criminal justice advocate, and 1 chief economist at a security firm. Additionally, the pool of experts includes 44 men and 8 women. The pool of intellectuals includes 42 professors and 8 nonacademic researchers. Additionally, the pool of intellectuals was made up of 38 men and 12 women.

The differences between the content of statements—as they relate to crime causation—are compelling. That is, professors and nonacademic researchers tend to endorse the view that crime is caused by social factors. Although politicians and practitioners lend some support to this view, as a group they were also more likely to embrace the perspective of utilitarianism. Computations for chi-square test yield statistical significance at the .001 level of probability (refer to table 3).

The following quoted statements drawn from the sample illuminate the three perspectives on crime causation: utilitarianism, personal pathology, and social factors.

Utilitarianism.   The utilitarian (and deterrence) model of crime was greatly advanced by Cesare Beccaria ([1764] 1981) and Jeremy Bentham ([1789] 1962), who depicted humans as rational, calculative, and motivated by personal (and especially material) gain. Briefly, these classical theorists

Table 3   Number of Quoted Statements About Crime Causation by Politicians & Practitioners Compared to Professors and Nonacademic Researchers*

	Politicians & Practitioners	Professors & Nonacademic Researchers	Totals
Causes of Crime:			
Utilitarianism	22	4	26
	(38%)	(4%)	(16%)
Personal Pathology	9	24	33
	(15.5%)	(23%)	(20%)
Social Factors	27	76	103
	(65.5%)	(73%)	(64%)
Totals	58	104	$n = 162$†

* Quoted statements drawn from 105 feature newspaper articles on crime in the *New York Times,* the *Washington Post,* the *Los Angeles Times,* and the *Chicago Tribune* from 1992 to 1995.
† Computations for chi-square yield statistical significance at .001 level of probability.

proposed that crime could be deterred if penalties for crime outweighed the gain of criminal behavior. In this vein, Bentham further developed the utilitarian perspective by referring to these human tendencies as the pleasure/pain principle and hedonistic calculus. In our sample, numerous sources relied on the utilitarian model to describe their view of crime.

> We've even seen altered lottery tickets made to look as if they were winners. People will try just about anything for money.
>
> Carissa Cragg, document examiner;
> *Chicago Tribune*, February 28, 1993:8

Not only does the next quote refer to the role of police in deterring crime, but it also suggests a much deeper—and darker—view of society.

> People are gonna do what they're gonna do. They commit crimes when you aren't there. I could be on one street, and there might be something happening on the street directly parallel to it.
>
> Jurithia Foust, Washington, D.C. police officer;
> *Washington Post*, September 17, 1993:B-1

In deconstructing a "mean worldview," Surette (1992) and Gerbner et al. (1980, 1979, 1978) point to how the media and state managers depict society as violent and dangerous, consequently compounding attitudes of fear, isolation, and suspicion among citizens. Relying on animal metaphors, the role of police ("sheepdogs") in a "mean world" is to patrol the community and protect the public ("sheep") from the criminal element ("wolves") (Surette 1992:42–44).

In the realm of social constructionism, utilitarian notions of crime in the media rest on the individualistic bias, thus becoming detextualized from the larger social realities of crime causation and social control (Bohm 1986). Indeed, propaganda techniques serve to reinforce the individualistic bias insofar as they contribute to the creation of criminal stereotypes (e.g., offenses committed by low-income individuals) (Kappeler et al. 1996:24).

Personal Pathology. Much like utilitarianism, the perspective of personal pathology as a cause of crime also reinforces the individualistic bias in the social construction of crime (Bohm 1986). Further, the mediated version of personal pathology also promotes criminal stereotypes and, in doing so, contributes to false distinctions between criminals and law-abiding people; for instance, Bohm (1986:200–201) reports that over 90 percent of all Americans have committed some crime for which they could be incarcerated. Personal pathology as a cause of crime stems from early positivism, especially the work of Cesare Lombroso (1876) who proposed that criminals were defective humans. Although the sources of such defects could be genetic, biological, psychological, sociological—or any combination of them—Lombroso's principal assumption was that criminals were pathological, thus different from so-called normal, law-abiding people. With this in mind, several statements from our sample rely on positivism (and even genetic terminology, e.g., "breed") in characterizing some criminals as defective, dangerous, and out of control. One source describes

> . . . a breed of "super-predator" criminal so dangerous that even older inmates working their way through life sentences complain that their youthful counterparts are out of control.

> Professor John J. DiIulio, Princeton University;
> *Los Angeles Times*, May 2, 1995:E-7

While acknowledging the importance of social factors in crime causation, some statements advocate genetic research in locating individual causes of crime. The following source agrees

> . . . that environmental causes are the "overwhelming" reason for high crime rates in blighted neighborhoods, but she believes that genetics might play a role that should be looked into.

> Diana Fishbein, senior researcher at the Department of Justice,
> former criminology professor at University of Baltimore;
> *Washington Post*, September 22, 1995:B-3

In addition to deflecting attention from the social factors in crime causation, the positivistic components of these quotes lend themselves to criminal stereotypes. Further, these remarks are also shaped by another propaganda technique in which opinion is presented as fact (Kappeler et al. 1996:24–25). As a result, such statements promote a degree of fear and terror commonly found in *moral panic*, "a turbulent, excited, or exaggerated response to deviance or a social problem" (Mann 1984:255; Cohen 1972; Hall et al. 1978; Chiricos 1996; Goode and Ben-Yehuda 1995). Although moral panics are projected by the media in a sensationalized, stylized, and stereotypical fashion, as noted, they are also defined as social problems amenable to the criminal justice agenda (Cohen 1972:9; See also Welch et al. 1997).

Social Factors. Social factors causing crime encompass microsociological determinants (e.g., negative family circumstances) and macrosociological and economic conditions (e.g., poverty and unemployment). Consider the following item representative of this perspective of crime causation:

> High-crime areas end up being areas of "disinvestment." These become the areas that need jobs. The cab drivers don't want to go there, the business people don't want to locate there, the tax base erodes. And these are the very areas that require the most services.

> Jerry Abramson, Mayor, Louisville, KY;
> *Washington Post*, July 5, 1994:A-6

Similarly, the socioeconomic aspect of the drug market and its relationships to violence were also addressed in several references to social factors, for example:

> It's also plausible that the drug market has stabilized and been driven indoors, and that the "private commercialization" causes less fighting over territory.

> Jerome Skolnick, visiting criminology professor,
> John Jay College of Criminal Justice;
> *Washington Post*, December 27, 1995:F-2

Several other social factors were the subject of discussion, especially demographics with respect to age:

> Most of the decline that has occurred would have occurred anyway. The baby boom generation, which comprises almost a third of the population is getting older. They are middle-aged, and they are not nearly as aggressive and violent as they were when they were younger.

> Professor James Alan Fox, Northeastern University;
> *New York Times*, July 23, 1995:4

Crime Control

The third task of our content analysis involved identifying and sorting experts' (politicians and practitioners compared to professors and nonacademic researchers) quoted statements into two broad categories of crime control: hard control and soft control. Table 4 shows 132 quoted statements pertaining to crime control. What is worth noting about this particular finding is that 73 percent ($n = 67$) of the quotes from politicians and practitioners support hard control strategies, while 27 percent ($n = 25$) embrace soft control. Conversely, 75 percent ($n = 30$) of the quoted statements offered by professors and nonacademic researchers endorse soft control strategies, whereas 25 percent ($n = 10$) favor hard control.

Table 4   Number of Quoted Statements about Crime Control by Politicians and Practitioners Compared to Professors and Nonacademic Researchers*

	Politicians & Practitioners	Professors & Nonacademic Researchers	Totals
Crime Control Strategies:			
Hard Control	67	10	77
	(73%)	(25%)	(58%)
Soft Control	25	30	55
	(27%)	(75%)	(42%)
Totals	92	40	$n = 132$†

* Quoted statements drawn from 105 feature newspaper articles on crime in the *New York Times*, the *Washington Post*, the *Los Angeles Times*, and the *Chicago Tribune* from 1992 to 1995.
† Computations for chi-square yield statistical significance at .001 level of probability.

The differences between the nature of the statements—as they relate to crime control—are compelling. While politicians and practitioners endorse strategies of hard control in dealing with crime, professors and nonacademic researchers overwhelmingly support measures of soft control. Computations for chi-square test yield statistical significance at the .001 level of probability (refer to table 4).

In addition to 37 politicians, this pool of practitioners includes 15 law enforcement officials, 3 members of the ACLU, 3 criminal justice advocates, 2 prosecutors, 2 corrections officials, 2 judges, 2 defense lawyers, and 1 director of criminal justice services. Additionally, this pool of experts includes 56 men and 12 women.

The pool of intellectuals includes 20 professors and 7 nonacademic researchers. Additionally, the pool of intellectuals includes 25 men and 2 women.

Hard Control.   Hard control measures range from such deterrent strategies as strengthening and expanding the criminal justice system to contemporary retribution imperatives: "get-tough-on-crime" (and on prisoners) and "three strikes, you're out." From this perspective, the following state manager advocates incapacitation for the purpose of reducing violent crime.

> If you can get these violent criminals to serve more time, you will inevitably reduce the violent crime rate. Anyone who is locked up will not commit a crime.

> Representative Bill McCollum, Florida Republican,
> Chairman of the House subcommittee on crime;
> *New York Times*, August 10, 1995:A-14

Returning to classical theory, some experts reiterated the language of Beccaria ([1764] 1981) and Bentham ([1789] 1962) to characterize the nature of punishment as it relates to deterrence. The next passage is firmly rooted in retribution but also contains elements of moral panic underscored with value-loaded language, a common propaganda technique (i.e., the undefined use of the term "gang").

> Punishment has to be swift and certain. When children commit adult crimes, they should be prosecuted as adults. We can't coddle criminals because they are young. We're not just talking about gang members. What we are seeing is total disregard for pain and human life among the young. It's scary, and I predict it will only get worse.

> Jeanine Ferris Pirro, Westchester County [NY] District Attorney;
> *New York Times*, January 30, 1994:15

Interestingly, the following assertion draws on positivist views of criminality; but instead of suggesting rehabilitation in correcting criminal defects, an argument justifying incapacitation is offered. Moreover, the source's presentation of opinion as fact and alarmist use of the terms "new breed" and "predatory street criminal" evidence value-loaded language as a propaganda tactic.

The new breed of predatory street criminal cannot be deterred. They can only be incapacitated.

> Professor John J. DiIulio, Princeton University;
> *Los Angeles Times*, May 2, 1995:E-7

Finally, in the realm of promoting a favorable image of law enforcement and their claim of crime deterrence, the following item claims police effectiveness—a prominent theme in criminal justice propaganda. While presenting opinion as fact, such proclamations justify continued investment in the criminal justice system, especially hard control.

> We [the police] are changing behavior in New York City.

> William J. Bratton, New York City Police Commissioner;
> *New York Times*, November 19, 1995:43

Soft Control. Measures of soft control include efforts to rehabilitate offenders (and drug addicts), decriminalize particular forms of lawlessness (e.g., certain types of drug offenses), impose tighter regulation of gun ownership, and reform the criminal justice system in ways that uphold fairness and reduce discrimination (e.g., addressing racial and socioeconomic biases). Moreover, several statements opposed larger expenditures for hard control strategies (e.g., correctional spending) which flourish at the expense of soft control measures (e.g., social services and education).

> In recent years, the increase in correctional spending for states has been twice that for general fund increases and even larger than in education spending. We have to find new ways to cope with the rate of criminality,

> Jon Felde, studied judiciary issues for the
> National Conference of State Legislatures;
> *Washington Post*, June 2, 1994:3

Finally, the following viewpoint is one of many proposals in our sample that endorsed greater restrictions on gun ownership.

> You have to stop and ask: Would you rather have those 6,000 people able to go into a store and buy a gun? [According to Sarah Brady, the Brady bill is] the cornerstone of a serious gun-control policy in America that will eventually include more restrictions.

> Sarah Brady, Chairwoman of Handgun Control, Inc.;
> *New York Times*, August, 15, 1993:4

Discussion

As noted, it is difficult to conclude whether the differences between state managers and intellectuals are the result of fundamental views of crime (i.e., crime causation and crime control) or whether these discrepancies stem from how journalists select quotes in preparing their feature articles. In light of this uncertainty, a number of unanswered questions remain. For instance, while being interviewed by journalists, do politicians and practitioners devote more discussion to crime control while professors and nonacademic researchers reflect more on the causes of crime? Are journalists asking politicians and practitioners more questions that relate to crime control—conversely, asking professors and nonacademic researchers more questions that pertain to crime causation? Or are journalists deliberately filtering the experts' quotes in ways that lead one to the biased viewpoint that politicians and practitioners shall be quoted for statements about crime control while professors and nonacademic researchers are to be sourced for comments concerning the causes of crime?

If such a bias does exist, it might suggest that the media view professors (and nonacademic researchers) as appropriate sources for remarks about crime causation, whereas politicians and practitioners are perceived as suitable sources for comments about crime control. Consequently, it seems that crime control policy is understood by the media as the domain of state managers, while it appears that professors (as well as some nonacademic researchers) remain in—or are consigned by the media to—the "ivory tower." As a result of this marginalization, academics seem to be restricted to offering so-called "theoretical" and "abstract" notions about crime causation; moreover, such ideas about criminological theory are perhaps taken to mean that they have little relation to the "real" world. In fact, many state managers quoted in our sample vehemently ridiculed criminological research while engaging in crass anti-intellectualism.

> I was not hired to be Arizona's chief social theorist. I was not sent here to sit meditating on Freud or on the latest "root causes" of criminal behavior. The criminal law deals not with theories but with thugs.
>
> Governor Fife Symington, Arizona, Republican;
> *New York Times*, January 24, 1994:B-6

Revealing additional evidence of anti-intellectualism, the law enforcement official attributed to the following statement attacks not only social science in general, but a well-established relationship between aging and declining crime rates in particular.

> When the ball went down in Times Square in 1994, did (the crooks) suddenly age? Or all get locked up? Or kill each other off in that 10 seconds? [he demands, noting that the city's (New York City) youth population was lower in the '80s, when crime was higher.] These excuses are pathetic, worse than sophomoric.
>
> John Maple, NYC Deputy Police Commissioner;
> *Washington Post*, December 27, 1995:F-2

In the event that this bias exists, the media evidently operate on preconceived notions about the appropriate role of intellectuals (i.e., theorists) vis-a-vis state managers (i.e., policy makers) in the manufacturing of crime news. Moreover, this particular bias may very well be reinforced by various techniques of propaganda, including the masking of opinions through sources and selective interviewing (Kappeler et al. 1996:25–26). With this in mind, it is important to question procedures by which the media determine *who* constitutes a source. Kasinsky (1994:210–11) reminds us: "The dominant sources tend to flood the market. Government sources, including local police departments, the Pentagon, and the State Department, can saturate the media with information or disinformation, because information from these sources is considered official and carries with it the assumption of credibility" (see also Ericson et al. 1989; Chermak 1994). In the same manner, this study finds that print journalists rely heavily on government sources—specifically, law enforcement officials—especially in recommending policies for crime control (refer to tables, 2, 3, and 4).[2]

As far as this study of crime news is concerned, our research design is not entirely without limitations. For methodological purposes, we borrowed categories of crime causation and crime control from Barlow et al. (1995a, 1995b). Although dichotomizing statements about the causes of crime according to utilitarianism, personal pathology, and social factors offers methodological advantages, there are also some drawbacks. Specifically, the social factors category might have been too broad; this category encompasses microsociological determinants (e.g., negative family circumstances), macrosociological and economic conditions (e.g., poverty and unemployment), along with demographics (i.e., age) and the socioeconomic aspects of drug market violence. As a result of collapsing micro- and macrolevels of analysis, a particular problem emerges. Grouping microsociological factors with macrosociological conditions diminishes the saliency of truly critical approaches to crime causation (e.g., the role of capitalism in generating crime). Nevertheless, the presence of genuinely radical voices about crime causation (and crime control) in this sample were nonexistent, thus confirming the suspicion that the media's spectrum of worldviews remains decidedly narrow.

Indeed, the exclusion of radical intellectuals from the social construction of crime news might very well be evidence of a common propaganda technique in the media, namely, selective interviewing (Kappeler et al. 1996:26). Even more to the point, preventing radicals from participating in the public discourse on crime reflects another tactic of propaganda in which journalists mask their own opinions through sources who are selected because their views closely resemble—or do not stray too far from—the media's (Kappeler et al. 1996:25). Tables 3 and 4 provide evidence of sourcing patterns by enumerating a heavy reliance on politicians and law enforcement officials.

Additionally, the relative independence of the pool of intellectuals could also be called into question insofar as many professors (and nonacademic researchers) fit the description of *de facto* state managers by virtue of having strong funding connections to the state. Further, the presence of *de facto* state managers in this pool may make the intellectuals seem more conservative than they are.

As another methodological limitation, the lack of separation between microsociological factors and macrosociological forces could explain why state managers appear to be more liberal than expected. According to our classification scheme, statements offered by politicians who view crime causation, for instance, from a "family values" standpoint are grouped into a category of social factors which also includes remarks made by professors targeting unemployment as a cause of crime. Not only does this classification procedure blur fundamental distinctions among views of crime causation, it also affects how the respective strategies of crime control are catalogued. In this respect, the categories for crime control may also have been too inclusive—permitting, for example, "family values" strategies to be sorted into the same group of soft control initiatives as economic strategies. Again, this method of coding could explain why state managers appear to be more liberal with respect to crime control than expected.

At the onset of this study, it was presumed that certain views of crime causation would correspond with particular strategies for crime control. Conforming to this logic, utilitarianism coincides with hard control whereas personal pathology and social factors match the ideals of soft control. However, our classification scheme allows sources to equivocate on their beliefs of crime causation and crime control; in fact, politicians were able to lend support to the view that crime is caused by social factors (e.g., negative family circumstances) while simultaneously endorsing punitive measures of crime control (e.g., advocating incarceration) (refer to tables 3 and 4). This lack of consistency between crime causation and crime control suggests that the media (i.e., journalists) tend to refrain from confronting their sources about apparent incongruities; arguably, this lack of journalistic vigilance facilitates the propaganda process.

Conclusion

Despite its limitations, however, this research sheds light on the roles of the media and the state in the social construction of distorted images of crime which are projected in the form of crime news. To this end, our study shows that the contents of quotes by state managers are significantly more ideological (in both crime causation and crime control) insofar as they neglect the causal connection between social conditions and crime. Additionally, we also find that several state managers repeatedly invoked crime-control mantras which blend elements of political "tough-talk" and "crime-speak" with simplistic views of crime causation. Taken together, these remarks are ideologically self-serving because they reinforce the popular perception that the problem of crime is the sole domain of the criminal justice apparatus, thus excluding other forms of state intervention (e.g., public health services).

> I want to send a message to the violent criminals, that if you commit the crime you do the time.
>
> Governor Bruce King, New Mexico, Democrat;
> *New York Times*, January 24, 1994:B-6

We're sending a message—if you commit a crime, you will do the time.

Governor Ben Nelson, Nebraska, Democrat;
New York Times, January 24, 1994:B-6

If you've done the crime in this state, you will do the time.

Governor Mel Carnahan, Missouri, Democrat;
New York Times, January 24, 1994:B-6

Clearly, these political proclamations about crime share a striking similarity, suggesting that "official" versions of crime are ideologically "prepackaged." Even New Hampshire Governor Stephen Merrill, who conceded that his state was "comparatively free from violence," maneuvered to keep the crime issue in the public mind by insisting, "We will spend more time in 1994 talking about crime, and we should" (*New York Times*, January 24, 1994:B-6).

Overall, the prevailing construction of lawlessness depicted by the media together with state managers is a collage of individual street crimes detextualized from social factors. Surette (1994:148–49) reminds us that "the continuing disparity between the media-constructed reality of crime and justice and the nonmedia reality of crime and justice results in the public receiving an unnecessarily distorted image that supports only one anti-crime policy approach, an expanded and enhanced punitive criminal justice system—an approach lacking evidence of success."

Although macrosociological forces (e.g., politics and economics) significantly shape its content and scope, the social construction of crime news is also subject to meso-level (i.e., organizational) determinants. In this vein, we ought to remain mindful that media (e.g., print and electronic journalism) are formal organizations which administer their tasks in pursuit of institutional goals. Surette (1992:59) insists that "because the market and manipulative models ignore these organizational constraints on the creation of news, they are both inadequate. News is neither a pure picture of society nor a fully controlled propaganda message but instead an organizational product."

In the same manner, the relationship between the media and state managers (serving as primary definers of crime) is structured, in large part, around the organizational needs and routines of journalists. Operating under incessant time restrictions, journalists must rely on institutional resources not only for the purpose of meeting unreasonable deadlines but also to assure the public that information about crime is "officially" confirmed and validated by *credible* sources: law enforcement officials and political leaders (Benedict 1992:10). It should also be emphasized that the relationship between the media and law enforcement agencies is mutually rewarding insofar as police officials help journalists create their product—that is, crime news. According to this *relation of reciprocity*, law enforcement officials not only benefit by serving as primary definers of crime but also gain from publicly promoting their institutional objectives and needs (e.g., financial funding, the hiring of additional employees, and the acquisition of equipment)

(Welch, Fenwick, and Roberts 1997; Chermak 1996, 1994; Kasinsky 1994; Hall et al. 1978).

> In short term, the expenditure of money has to increase. We need more and better cops, more prosecutors.
>
> Eric H. Holder, Jr., U.S. Attorney;
> *Washington Post*, July 5, 1994:A-6

> Each one you catch, evidence shows they have committed a host of other crimes. If you take them out of society, these are cost savings never calculated into what we spend on new prisons.
>
> Bill Jones, Secretary of State, California,
> former assemblyman and author of the "three strikes law";
> *Washington Post*, March 8, 1995:A-14

In sum, the lessons of social constructionism instruct us about the complex process by which crime is not only elevated to the status of a social problem but is distinctly framed in ways that make it amenable to the criminal justice apparatus. Hence, this study contributes to an understanding of this process by illuminating how the state and media collaborate to propagandize distorted images of crime for public consumption.

Finally, social constructionism also teaches us about the significance of a related concept, namely, the *definition of the situation* (also known as the Thomas theorem and the self-fulfilling prophecy). Simply put, what people believe to be real will be real in its consequences (Thomas 1923; Thomas and Znaniecki 1927). Given the power of the media and the state to perceive the world, shape public attitudes and opinions, and manufacture what is socially thinkable (Tunnell 1992; Altheide 1984),[3] we ought not be surprised by the public's willingness to accept ideological views of crime causation (e.g., disavowing the causal relationship between societal conditions and crime) and to lend its support to an expanding criminal justice machinery.

Notes

[1] Reiman (1995), among other scholars, further verifies that white-collar and corporate crime pose greater threats to public safety than street crime: "We have a greater chance of being killed or disabled, for example, by an occupational injury or disease, by unnecessary surgery, by shoddy medical emergency services than by aggravated assault or even homicide (1995:50). In widening the scope of social harm beyond street crime, it should be noted more than 419,000 persons annually die from diseases caused by cigarettes in the United States; similarly, more than two-thirds of homicides and serious assaults involve alcohol (Johnson Foundation, 1993).

[2] Whereas government sources have long been connected to the production of news, professors have recently begun to make inroads into the media. Still, some professors appear in feature articles more frequently than others, thus raising questions about the selection and sourcing of academic experts. It has been suggested that there exists a pool of "usual suspects" consisting of oft-cited academics on whom journalists rely for expert commentary. Although our sample includes a few oft-quoted professors, the dominance of these figures is substantially diminished by the vast number of other professors also quoted in these features. In fact, our sample

contained a relatively large quantity of professors, including academics with national reputations as well as those considered regional and local.

In discussing the matter of sourcing with a prominent (crime news) journalist, he stated that he approaches several different professors for each feature; typically, he tries to match a topic with the expertise of the academician. In the past, many journalists relied on their rolodexes for locating experts; today many reporters turn to Lexis/Nexis and other on-line computer services for tracking professors and their expertise (as indicated by published articles and books on a given topic). Nevertheless, professors most likely to be interviewed are those who remain accessible to journalists—especially those who carry pagers, cellular telephones, and return messages promptly (see Fox and Levin 1993; Barak 1994). (Refer to Welch et al. [1997] for a more elaborate examination of the selection of sources and experts.)

[3] Drawing on the National Crime Survey, Tunnell (1992:295) finds that "96 percent of the respondents reported relying on the news media to learn about crime and criminals, and 49 percent of those surveyed believed that the media gave the right amount of attention to stories about crime." Tunnell also notes: "At that time, more than 50 percent of the news stories were of violent crime, whereas only 6 percent of the actual crimes involved some form of violence. Not surprisingly, 88 percent of those surveyed overestimated the number of crimes they believed involved violence.

References

Abercrombie, N., S. Hill, and B. S. Turner. 1980. *The dominant ideology thesis*. London: Allen and Unwin.

Albrecht, S., G. W. Wernz, and T. L. Williams. 1995. *Fraud: Bringing light to the dark side of business*. Burr Ridge, IL: Irwin Professional Publishers.

Altheide, D. 1984. "TV news and the social construction of justice: Research issues and policy." Pp. 292–304 in *Justice and the Media*, R. Surette, (Ed.). Springfield, IL: Charles C. Thomas.

Barak, G. 1988. "Newsmaking criminology: Reflections on the media, intellectuals, and crime." *Justice Quarterly*, 5:565–87.

Barak, G. 1994. *Media, process, and the social construction of crime*. New York: Garland Publishing.

Barlow, M. H., D. E. Barlow, and T. G. Chiricos. 1995a. "Economic conditions and ideologies of crime in the media: A content analysis of crime news." *Crime & Delinquency*, 41:3–19.

Barlow, M. H., D. E. Barlow, and T. G. Chiricos. 1995b. "Mobilizing support for social control in a declining economy: Exploring ideologies of crime within crime news." *Crime & Delinquency*, 41, 2:191–204.

Beccaria, C. [1764] 1981. *On crimes and punishments*. Translated by Henry Paolucci. Indianapolis: Bobbs-Merrill.

Becker, H. S. 1967. "Who's side are we on?" *Social Problems*, 14:239–47.

Becker, H. S. 1973. *Outsiders: Studies in the sociology of deviance*. New York: The Free Press.

Benedict, H. 1992. *Virgin or vamp: How the Press covers sex crimes*. New York: Oxford University Press.

Bentham, J. [1789] 1962. *An introduction to the principles of morals and legislation*. John Browning, (Ed.). New York: Russell & Russell.

Bohm, R. 1986. "Crime, criminal, and crime control policy myths." *Justice Quarterly*, 3:193–214.

Chermak, S. 1994. "Crime in the news media: A refined understanding of how crimes become news." Pp. 95–130 in *Media, process, and the social construction of crime*, G. Barak, (Ed.). New York: Garland Publishing.

Chermak, S. 1996. "The presentation of drugs in the news media: The news sources involved in social problem construction." An unpublished manuscript. Bloomington: Indiana University.

Chiricos, T. 1996. "Moral panic as ideology: Drugs, violence, race and punishment in America." Pp. 19–48 in *Justice with prejudice: Race and criminal justice in America*, M. Lynch and E. B. Patterson, (Eds.) New York: Harrow and Heston Publishers.

Cohen, S. 1972. *Folk devils and moral panics: The creation of the mods and rockers*. London: MacGibbon & Kee.

Cohen, S. 1985. *Visions of social control: Crime, punishment and classification*. Cambridge: Polity Press.

Cohen, S., and J. Young. 1981. *The manufacture of news*. Newbury Park, CA: Sage Publications.

Dickson, D. 1968. "Bureaucracy and morality: An organizational perspective on a moral crusade." *Social Problems*, 16:143–156.

Ericson, R. V. 1995. *Crime and the media*. Aldershot, VT: Dartmouth.

Ericson, R. V., P. M. Baranek, and J. B. L. Chan. 1987. *Visualizing deviance: A study of news organizations*. Toronto: University of Toronto Press.

Ericson, R. V., P. M. Baranek, and J. B. L. Chan. 1989. *Negotiating control: A study of news sources*. Toronto: University of Toronto Press.

Ericson, R. V., P. M. Baranek, and J. B. L. Chan. 1991. *Representing order: Crime, law, and justice in the news media*. Toronto: University of Toronto Press.

Fishman, M. 1978. "Crime waves as ideology." *Social Problems*, 25:531–43.

Fox, J., and J. Levin. 1993. *How to work with the media*. Newbury Park, CA: Sage.

Gerbner, G., L. Gross, M. Jackson-Beek, S. Jeffries-Fox, and N. Signorielli. 1978. "Cultural indicators: Violence profile no. 9." *Journal of Communication*, 28:176–207.

Gerbner, G., L. Gross, L. Signorielli, M. Morgan, and M. Jackson-Beek. 1979. "The demonstration of power: Violence profile no. 10." *Journal of Communication*, 29:177–96.

Gerbner, G., L. Gross, M. Morgan, and N. Signorielli. 1980. "The mainstreaming of America: Violence profile no. 11." *Journal of Communication*, 30:10–29.

Goode, E., and N. Ben-Yehuda. 1995. *Moral panics: The social construction of deviance*. Oxford: Basil Blackwell.

Gramsci, A. 1971. *Selections from the prison notebooks*. New York: International.

Greek, C. 1994. "Becoming a media criminologist: Is 'newsmaking criminology' possible?" Pp. 265–86 in *Media, process, and the social construction of crime*, G. Barak, (Ed.). New York: Garland Publishing.

Hall, S., C. Critcher, T. Jefferson, J. Clarke, and B. Roberts. 1978. *Policing the crisis: Mugging, the state and law and order*. New York: Holmes and Meiser.

Henry, S. 1994. "Newsmaking criminology as replacement discourse." Pp. 287–318 in *Media, process, and the social construction of crime*, G. Barak, (Ed.). New York: Garland Publishing.

Herman, E. H., and N. Chomsky. 1988. *Manufacturing consent: The political economy of the mass media*. New York: Pantheon.

Hickman, M. 1982. "Crime in the streets—a moral panic: Understanding 'get tough' policies in the criminal justice system." *Southern Journal of Criminal Justice*, 8:7–22.

Humphries, D. 1981. "Serious crime, news coverage, and ideology." *Crime and Delinquency*, 27:191–205.

Israel, M. 1996. "Should ACJS join Cossa?" *ACJS Today*, XIV, 4:1, 12.

Jenkins, P. 1992. *Intimate enemies: Moral panics in contemporary Great Britain*. New York: Aldine De Gruyter.

Johnson Foundation. 1993. *Substance abuse: The nation's no. 1 health problem.* Princeton, NJ: Johnson Foundation.

Kappeler, V. E., M. Blumberg, and G. W. Potter. 1996. *The mythology of crime and criminal justice* (2d ed.). Prospect Heights, IL: Waveland Press.

Kasinsky, R. G. 1994. "Patrolling the facts: Media, cops, and crime." Pp. 203–236 in *Media, process, and the social construction of crime,* G. Barak, (Ed.). New York: Garland Publishing.

Kidd-Hewitt, D., and R. Osborne. 1995. *Crime and the media: The postmodern spectacle.* East Haven, CT: Pluto Press.

Lombroso, C. 1876. *The criminal man.* Milan: Hoepli.

Mann, M. 1984. *The encyclopedia of sociology.* New York: Continuum.

Marsh, H. L. 1989. "Newspaper crime coverage in the US: 1893–1988." *Criminal Justice Abstracts,* September: 506–14.

Marsh, H. L. 1991. "A comparative analysis of crime coverage in newspapers in the United States and other countries from 1960–1989: A review of the literature." *Journal of Criminal Justice,* 19:67–79.

Marx, K. 1978. "The German Ideology." Pp. 146–200 in *The Marx Engels reader* (2d ed.), R. D. Tucker, (Ed.). New York: Norton.

Michalowski, R. J. 1985. *Order, law, and crime: An introduction to criminology.* New York: Random House.

Mokhiber, R., and A. Wheat 1995. "Shameless: 1995's 10 worst corporations." *Multinational Monitor,* December: 9–16.

Reiman, J. 1995. *The rich get richer and the poor get prison: Ideology, class and criminal justice* (4th ed.). Boston: Allyn and Bacon.

Sahin, H. 1980. "The concept of ideology and mass communication." *Journal of Communication Inquiry,* 61:3–12.

Schoenfeld, A., R. Meier, and R. Griffin. 1979. "Constructing a social problem: The press and the environment." *Social Problems,* 27:38–61.

Serrin, W. 1991. "The wages of work." *The Nation,* January 28:80–82.

Surette, R. 1992. *Media, crime & criminal justice: Images and realities.* Pacific Grove, CA: Brooks/Cole Publishing Company.

Thomas, W. I. 1923. *The unadjusted girl.* Boston: Little, Brown.

Thomas, W. I., and F. Znaniecki. 1927. *The Polish peasant in Europe and America.* Chicago: University of Chicago Press.

Tunnell, K. 1992. "Film at eleven: Recent developments in the commodification of crime." *Sociological Spectrum,* 12:293–313.

Welch, M. 1996a. *Corrections: A critical approach.* New York: McGraw-Hill Book Company.

Welch, M. 1996b. "Critical criminology, social justice, and an alternative view of incarceration." *Critical Criminology: An International Journal* 7:43–58.

Welch, M., M. Fenwick, and M. Roberts. 1997. "Primary definitions of crime and moral panic: A content analysis of experts' quotes in feature newspaper articles on crime." *Journal of Research in Crime and Delinquency,* 34: In Press.

PART II

Constructing Crime Problems

SIX

THE GANG INITIATION RITE AS A MOTIF IN CONTEMPORARY CRIME DISCOURSE

Joel Best & Mary M. Hutchinson

Claims regarding social problems inevitably borrow from the broader culture, interweaving both familiar and original elements to construct particular problems. Thus Gamson and his associates speak of *issue cultures*, in which competing viewpoints are organized in packages of cultural elements, including many drawn from the available culture (Gamson and Lasch 1983; Gamson and Modigliani 1987, 1989). Williams (1995) argues that a social movement must mobilize accessible *cultural resources* to make its cause meaningful both to the movement's members and to those they hope to persuade; Benford (1993) suggests that actors in a movement adapt existing vocabularies of motive. Constructionist analyses of *claimsmaking rhetoric* note that persuasive claims incorporate elements from the broader culture (Best 1990; Gusfield 1981; Ibarra and Kitsuse 1993). Although it is generally agreed that discourse on social problems borrows from its cultural context, most analysts focus on the original, problem-specific elements of claims while neglecting the more familiar elements adapted by claimsmakers from the available cultural repertoire. This emphasis on the original aspects of claims overlooks how the familiar elements shape the construction of social problems.

These familiar elements can take various forms, including (but not limited to) metaphors, motives, exemplars, idioms, catchphrases, social types, and motifs. In particular, motifs have received little sociological attention. Folklorists use the term motif to refer to a recurring narrative element; for example, being required to answer a riddle is a common motif in folktales and fairy stories. Although the concept rarely appears in sociological analysis, Ibarra and Kitsuse suggest that it may be useful in analyzing social problems rhetoric:

Justice Quarterly, Vol. 13, No. 3, September 1996, pp. 383–404. Permission granted by Taylor & Francis, Ltd. http://www.tandf.co.uk/journals

> Motifs are recurrent thematic elements and figures of speech that encapsulate or highlight some aspect of a social problem. They are . . . a kind of generic vocabulary conventionally used in claims-making, each term or phrase acquiring distinctive connotations in being situated in one kind of context or another. The study of motifs in social problems discourse ought to focus our attention on how morally imbued metaphors and phrases can be intelligibly applied in claims-making. Some examples of motifs: *epidemic, menace, scourge, crisis, blight, casualties, tip of the iceberg, the war on* (drugs, poverty, crime, gangs, etc.), *abuse, hidden costs, scandal.* (Ibarra and Kitsuse 1993:47; authors' emphasis)

Ibarra and Kitsuse, then, equate motifs with metaphors that can be used to characterize many different social problems. Some motifs, however, such as "welfare queen," are specific to discourse about particular problems. When a problem-specific motif recurs in discussions of a particular social problem, it can shape the definition of that problem and its potential solutions.

Many analyses of social problems construction make at least passing reference to particular motifs (e.g., Gusfield [1981] on "the killer drunk" in claims about drunk driving), but we know of no full-scale analysis of a single social-problems motif. In this article we attempt this task: We examine the "gang initiation rite" as a recurring element—a motif—in three forms of contemporary discourse about crime.

Claims that invoke this motif depict joining a delinquent gang as a formal process marked by a ritual of initiation, in which the prospective member usually must commit some deviant act as a condition of membership. We focus, not on this alleged deviance, but on the motif. That is, our interest is in the claims that certain deviant acts occur as part of gang initiations. Whether such acts actually occur in the course of gang initiation rites is not the analytic issue. Rather, we hope to understand how gang initiation rites figure in discourse about crime.

Methods: Examining Three Forms of Discourse about Crime

Claimsmaking about crime and other social problems occurs in many venues or arenas (Hilgartner and Bosk 1988), and a motif's meaning may vary with the arena.

We compare the imagery of gang initiation rites in contemporary legends (a form of popular discourse), in social scientific research, and in newspaper stories. Gang initiation rites have different meanings in these three forms of discourse; those meanings link contemporary constructions of gangs to their broader cultural context, especially imagery of conspiratorial deviance. After summarizing our methods, we examine how the three forms of discourse use the gang initiation motif; then we discuss the significance of deviant conspiracies in the construction of social problems.

Press Reports

Constructionist researchers often sample the mass media, usually by searching one or more published indexes (e.g., *Reader's Guide to Periodical Literature*, *New York Times Index*, or *Television News Index and Abstracts*). Obviously such analyses depend on the quality of the indexing from which they draw. In attempts to study motifs, however, such indexes are virtually useless; motifs rarely are used as keywords in indexing. Not only is *gang initiation rite* unlikely to be used as an index heading; the motif may not appear in more than a small fraction of the many stories indexed under "gangs," and it may well appear in stories indexed under other headings.[1]

Computerized full-text databases, however, allow researchers to locate even passing references to particular topics. They can search vast collections of material for every use of a particular word or phrase. We used NEXIS, a database that includes press coverage. On September 15, 1995 we searched the MAJPAP and PAPERS files in NEXIS's NEWS library, using the search words *gang initiation* and *rite*. This search identified 114 stories for our analysis.[2]

The use of NEXIS to sample media discourse has limitations. For example, the service is relatively new, so some sources have been part of the database for only a few years; although the service indexes many major newspapers and magazines, coverage is not complete; and slightly different search commands would produce somewhat different samples. Still, it seems reasonable to believe that our search revealed the range of ways in which press reports use the expression *gang initiation rite*.

Popular Discourse

Efforts to learn how the general public talks about social problems present even more daunting obstacles than attempts to sample media coverage. There is no way to identify all popular discourse about crime, no way to systematically sample naturally occurring crime talk. Some social scientists have tried to circumvent these problems by staging discussions about crime problems (Sasson 1995a, 1995b) or by recording individuals' narratives about their personal experiences with crime (Wachs 1988). Such approaches, however, seem ill-suited for analyzing motifs because it would be necessary to examine very large collections of popular discourse to find an adequate sample of even fairly common motifs.

We adopt a different approach: examining contemporary legends that mention gang initiation rites. Contemporary or urban legends are stories, told as true, usually transmitted orally, which often depict dangers in contemporary life (Brunvand 1981; Fine 1992). Folklorists collect and analyze contemporary legends, so we located legends about gang initiation rites by examining recent books and articles by folklorists and by consulting *FOAF-Tale News*, the newsletter of the International Society for Contemporary Legend Research. In addition, our discussion of contemporary legends draws on newspaper articles that we located in our NEXIS search, which debunk specific reports of gang initiation rites as legends or "urban myths." We focus on two recent legends with wide circulation, but we also identify some less familiar stories that incorporate the motif of the gang initiation rite.

Contemporary legends pose their own analytic problems. Usually it is impossible to know which portions of the population tell, hear, or believe these stories. Legends characteristically occur in a wide range of variant forms. Still, contemporary legends—particularly the two core stories—provide evidence of the general public's perception of gang initiation rites.

Social Science Discourse

Research on gangs by sociologists, criminologists, and other social scientists has a long history. Some of these studies make at least passing reference to initiation practices in gangs. We examined several classic and contemporary studies of gangs; here we compare their discussions of gang initiation rites with the discourse of the press and the public.

Gang Initiation Rites in Contemporary Legends

We begin by examining two contemporary legends concerning gang initiation rites that achieved national currency in the early 1990s. Then we turn to other, apparently less widespread legends. Finally, we identify some general themes in folkloric construction of gang initiation rites.

"The Slasher under the Car"

This contemporary legend circulated nationally after 1984 and peaked in late 1992 ("Ankle Slashers" 1993; Brunvand 1993:134–38; "Close Call" 1993; "Urban Yarn" 1991). The story involves a criminal who crawls under a car and lies in wait until someone returns and begins to open the car door. At this point, the criminal grabs the unsuspecting victim's ankles and begins an assault.

This legend is not new; Brunvand (1993:135) suggests that it may have circulated as early as the 1950s. It takes variant forms. The criminal is often, but not always, said to be a gang member; many versions explain the ankle grabbing as a "gang initiation rite" (e.g., the illustrated version in Fleming and Boyd 1994:18). Usually, but not always, the victim is female, and the setting is a parking lot at that hotbed of contemporary legend violence—the shopping mall. Sometimes the criminal is identified as black or southeast Asian. Often the criminal renders the victim helpless by slicing through her Achilles' tendon with a knife or razor; in other cases, the criminal smashes his victim's ankles with a tire iron, or even plants banana peels and waits under the car for the victim to slip and fall into reach. The ankle grabbing leads to various crimes including rape, purse snatching, robbery, and auto theft; in some versions, when the victim reaches toward her ankles, the gang member grabs her hand and cuts off a finger.

"Lights Out"

A second legend, called "Lights Outs" by folklorists ("Blood" 1993; Brunvand 1995; "Lights Out" 1993), circulated widely in 1993–1994 and involves gang members driving at night. When approaching motorists blink their lights to warn the gang members that their lights aren't on or are on high beam, they are followed by the gang members, who attack and (in most versions) kill them. Almost all versions of this story explain these attacks as part of a gang initiation rite. One faxed version declared "This is the time of year for gang initiations" (Brunvand 1995:32); another stated "police departments across the nation are being warned that this is 'blood' initiation weekend. Their intent is to have all new bloods nationwide drive around on Saturday and Sunday nights with their lights off" ("Blood" 1993). This story attracted nationwide attention; police departments received many inquiries. Most authorities denied that this story was anything more than a rumor. Our NEXIS search located stories debunking local versions of this legend in 16 major newspapers.

Other Gang Initiation Legends

Although the ankle-grabbing and "Lights Out" stories apparently reached the largest numbers of people, other contemporary legends also involve gang initiations. One common theme in these stories is gang-initiation violence in shopping malls. In "The Castrated Boy," a legend that achieved wide circulation in the 1960s and 1970s, a small boy enters a public restroom—often in a mall—and is castrated by a group of older children or adults from another ethnic group, "often as part of an alleged ritual or initiation ceremony" (Brunvand 1984:88; Carroll 1987; Dorson 1981:228–30). In 1991, a rumor circulated in Wichita, Kansas:

> . . . gangs of black teens were initiating new members by requiring them to grab white children and throw them over a second-level railing to the level below. Lack of public information was blamed on a conspiracy in which police, newspaper editors, and mall owners hushed up the incidents to keep Christmas shopping high and profitable. ("Mall Mayhem" 1992)

A story in the *Chicago Sun-Times* ("Truth is Floored" 1993) debunked this legend about a South Side mall: "Teen thugs are knocking down young female shoppers and slashing them across the cheeks in a gruesome rite-of-passage demonstration."[3] According to a Pittsburgh story, police had been warned that "two juveniles would be shot as part of a gang initiation rite at an undesignated mall" ("Malls on Alert" 1994). As Halloween approached in 1995, a rumor circulating in Sanger, California, stated that a gang initiation rite would involve drive-by shootings of trick-or-treaters (Gerald T. Horiuchi, personal communication, November 10, 1995).

Another recently circulated tale is a variant of a well-established contemporary legend, "The Killer in the Backseat" (Brunvand 1981:52–53,

1984:214; 1986:58–59). In this story a woman is warned, usually by a service station attendant or another motorist, that a criminal is hiding in the backseat of her car. Recent tellings of this story often include gang initiations: "The police arrive and arrest a teenager who confesses that, as part of his gang initiation, he must sneak into the cars of two women at gas stations in order to rape and kill them" ("Killer" 1993; also see "New Urban Myth" 1993). A Dallas version specified that the initiates must "rape a white woman" ("Don't Take . . ." 1992).

Occasionally the press speculated that other gang initiation stories might be contemporary legends. In St. Louis, police criticized a radio commentator for describing a gang initiation rite in which "wannabes were driving into crowds of pedestrians . . . just for the fun of seeing them scatter"; the story ran under the heading "Urban Legend Dept." (1994). A San Antonio story that "several teen-age girls willingly had unprotected sex with a male gang member who was HIV-positive as part of a gang initiation rite" was labeled "a public health time bomb," or "maybe . . . just the latest urban myth" ("Gang Rites" 1993).

Themes in Contemporary Legends

Certain clear similarities run through the contemporary legends that mention gang initiations. Virtually all of the legendary initiations demand that initiates commit acts of serious, even deadly violence against strangers who are chosen virtually at random. Frequently the victims are women or children, some of society's most vulnerable members. The violence often seems pointless; its only purpose is to fulfill the requirements of the initiation rite. In many cases the gang members are identified as members of ethnic minorities; their victims, implicitly if not explicitly, belong to the white majority. In short, popular discourse, at least in the form of contemporary legends, views gang initiation rites as serious threats to the social order, a cause of unpredictable violence in which deviant gang members attack innocent, respectable citizens. In these stories, the motif of gang initiation provides a motive: "Why kill another driver for blinking headlights?" "Because the initiation rite demands it." The motif makes sense of the senseless.

Although contemporary legends usually are believed to be true by those who tell and hear them, they are considered false as soon as they are labeled "just" rumors or legends.[4] That is, someone (believing the tale to be true) might warn a friend about ankle grabbers at the local mall, but the friend might respond that the story is "just a rumor" (and therefore false). Thus the newspaper stories cited above acknowledged that many people believed these stories about gang initiations, but declared that these particular stories were legends, not true reports. (As we observe below, newspapers have treated other stories about gang initiation rites as true.)

Gang Initiations in the Social Science Literature

The notion of the gang initiation rite is familiar to sociologists and criminologists. Spergel notes:

> According to gang lore, gang initiations have ranged from drinking a large quantity of alcohol to using or selling drugs, fighting other members or running a gauntlet, stealing from a store, and doing a chit" (e.g., shooting a member of an opposing gang). Females may be required to have sex with a male core gang member, or fight a leader or core member of the female gang. (1995:91)

Whereas "gang lore" identifies a wide range of initiation practices, ethnographers' reports on gangs describe a much narrower range of practices, very different from the random violence associated with gang initiations in contemporary legends.

Researchers consistently report that gangs require prospective members to demonstrate toughness and commitment to the gang before they can join. Toughness is a key virtue for gang members; they must be prepared to defend themselves and their territory against rivals (Jankowski 1991; Miller 1958). Most often, gangs initiate new members by making them demonstrate an ability and willingness to fight:

> Although initiation ceremonies are not universal features, many fighting groups of ghetto adolescents have found them attractive over the years. In contemporary Mexican-American barrios, they commonly take the form of brief, casually arranged episodes of submission to group fist pounding. On the East Coast among white ethnics in the fifties and among Puerto Ricans in the sixties, initiation procedures were described as formalized, elaborate, painful, and terrifying. They are rarely mentioned in the ethnographies of black urban gangs of the sixties [but see Keiser, cited below]. When they are performed, initiation rituals most directly work like a metaphysical immigration ceremony, granting membership in an ontologically higher order. (Katz 1988:134)

Similar accounts can be found in a wide array of ethnographic reports of gangs (Jankowski 1991:12, 50; New York City Youth Board 1960:50), including case studies of Hispanic gangs (Horowitz 1983:98–99; J. Moore 1991:49; Padilla 1993:182; Vigil 1993:105), African-American gangs (Hagedorn 1988:90–91; Keiser 1969:21; Shakur 1993:9), suburban gangs (Monti) 1994:68), female gangs (Campbell 1984:25; J. Moore 1991:49), and motorcycle gangs (Wolf 1991:110–14). Such accounts also appear in training materials about gangs, prepared for law enforcement and social welfare professionals:

> There are a variety of ways to become a member of a gang. The most common is through an initiation process of being "jumped in" or "courted in." This means you may have to physically fight two or more members of the gang for approximately 15–60 seconds. If you fight well, show that you are not afraid, and can defend the honor of the gang, you

are accepted as a member. (Operation Safe Streets 1995:37; also see Carondelet Management Institute N.D.:4)

The practice of requiring initiates to fight experienced members may have emerged sometime after World War II. Most of the earlier accounts of gangs do not mention initiation through ritualized fighting; instead an informant in Thrasher's (1927:28) classic study reported: "We took in only two new members . . . but for them we devised a special initiation, copying some of our stunts from the 'Penrod and Sam' stories by Tarkington."[5]

Although some ethnographies discuss initiation rites, the researchers often observe that not all gang members go through these rituals:

> Seven of those we interviewed answered that initiation rites included an act of some sort of "fighting," and two said the new member had to "rip off" something in order to become a member. All others (36) said either that there was no initiation procedure or that it varied with circumstances. (Hagedorn 1988:90. For similarly qualified statements, see Campbell 1984; Jankowski 1991; Keiser 1969; J. Moore 1991; New York City Youth Board 1960; Operation Safe Streets 1995)

In none of the ethnographic accounts do gangs demand that initiates commit crimes of random violence against nongang members. One of Hagedorn's (1988:91) informants specifically denied this possibility: "Nothing like, OK, we wanna see how bad you are—go rob the next corner store you see. Nothing like that." Although some observers charge that gay bashing is a skinhead initiation rite, Hamm's (1993:138) "most unequivocal finding" was that all his interview subjects "denied taking part in an initiation rite of violence." Yablonsky (1970:193) reports, "There is a mythology built up around initiation rites, such as the requirement that a potential member steal something or assault someone, but these entrance demands are seldom fulfilled or really expected to take place."

Themes in the Social Science Literature

Social scientists, then, depict gang initiation rites very differently than contemporary legends. Although random, often lethal violence against nonmembers is a central theme in contemporary legends, virtually all of the violence described by social scientists occurs within the gang as ritualized fighting between initiates and experienced gang members. Serious injuries can occur, but they are uncommon; the point of the ritual is to test—not to harm—the prospective member. In short, the reports of researchers who claim firsthand knowledge of gangs and their initiation rites differ markedly from the accounts in contemporary legends. These legends clearly are not grounded in a reading of ethnographers' accounts.

Gang Initiation Rites in Newspaper Coverage

Most of the 114 newspaper stories that mentioned gang initiation rites fall into one of three distinct categories. First, 29 stories (25 percent) debunk contemporary legends with gang initiation themes. As noted above, these tales tend to feature elaborate but senseless violence: "Lights Out," ankle grabbing, rapists hiding in the backseat, and so on.

Second, the NEXIS search revealed 22 reports (19 percent) of mundane "beat-downs" or "jump-ins"—the violent tests of character described by social scientists in which initiates must fight experienced members. In Seattle, two police officers making a training film on gangs were criticized after they videotaped (with the gang's permission) an initiation rite:

> Between six and eight gang members took turns punching and kicking a youth at a playground . . . as part of a gang initiation rite. . . . Sources say . . . the beating lasted less than one minute, no weapon was used, and the youth suffered only minor bruises and some swelling . . . the officers reportedly heard the youth consent to being beat up. The teenager was struck several times on his arms, legs, and torso. . . . ("County Police" 1992; also see "Ganging Up" 1987)

These fights sometimes had serious consequences. One news story involved a boy killed during an initiation ("Boy was Kicked" 1990). In a notorious Houston case, two young women were raped and murdered when they came upon several gang members who had held an initiation rite earlier in the evening ("Blacks N Whites" 1993). For the most part, however, newspaper accounts of initiation rites pitting initiates against experienced members resembled the descriptions in the social science literature.[6]

In the third and largest category of newspaper articles, 47 stories (41 percent) linked gang initiations to murder, assaults, and other crimes against nongang members.[7] These stories generally lacked the detailed reporting found in stories about initiation by fighting; only six cited gang members' claims that the violence was part of a gang initiation. In contrast, 22 stories in this category speculated that crimes were part of gang initiations:

> Right-wing groups like Skinheads and junior Klan groups . . . might require initiates to attack gay and homeless people. . . . ("Gang Beat-Downs" 1994)

> Police assume Adams [shot in a drive-by] was victim of a gang initiation rite. . . . Adams, the father of two young sons, said he is not considering moving to the suburbs. (Such random violence can happen anywhere in America.) Instead, he and his wife, Carol, are seriously thinking about moving to the southwest coast of Ireland. ("Staunch Advocate" 1994)

The remaining 19 stories in this category attributed crimes to gang initiations. Often they cited a source but did not explain the basis for the attribution:

> A teenage gang in New York City is forcing each of its new recruits to shoot one person in the leg as an initiation rite, the *New York Post* has

reported. . . . The newspaper said members of the gang had denied the
accusations. ("Gang Initiation" 1990)

The FOLKS, the Crips and La Raza in Chamblee have made auto theft
an initiation rite, police said. Those gangs, police say, have targeted suburban malls. ("Where Are You Safe?" 1994)

Many of the stories in this category concerned unsolved crimes or general types
of crime, and accounted for their occurrence by referring to possible gang initiation rites. Often they attributed this explanation to the police.[8] These articles also
mentioned random violence, and cited gang initiation rites as an explanation.

Themes in Newspaper Coverage

Press coverage mentions gang initiation rites in diverse contexts. Some
press reports focus on ritual fights between initiates and experienced members; often these fights become newsworthy only when someone—typically
an initiate or a passerby—suffers a serious injury. Other press reports debunk
contemporary legends; usually these involve extravagant forms of violence
against strangers, as in the "Lights Out" tale. The largest number of stories,
however, attributes shootings, stabbings, arson, and other acts of "senseless,"
"random" violence to gang initiation rites.[9] Although the violence in these
stories tends to be more mundane and less dramatic than the melodramatic
violence in contemporary legends, the two forms of discourse share the view
that gang initiation rites involve unprovoked attacks against strangers. In
other words, the accounts of gang initiation rites promoted by contemporary
legends can be regarded as melodramatic versions of press reports that routinely attribute violence to gang initiations.

Conspiracies of Deviants

In his discussion of ritual in preindustrial social movements, Hobsbawm
notes

> . . . the heightened ceremony which surrounded the initiation of a man
> into a special group of his fellows, one designated to demonstrate its utter
> difference from other groups and to bind him to it by the strongest con-
> ceivable links. It combined awe, the element of testing the candidate and
> that of instructing him in the mysteries of the group, and naturally culmi-
> nated in some form of most solemn declaration—normally an oath—and
> some ceremony symbolizing adoption into the group. (1959:154)

Simmel (1950) observed the centrality of initiation rituals in secret societies;
ethnographers have described rites of passage and other initiation rites in a
wide array of cultures; and theorists have interpreted initiation as a psychological and cultural process (Eliade 1958; La Fontaine 1985). Such analyses
typically focus on the meaning of rituals for the participants, both the initiates
and those who do the initiating.

The interpretation of recent discourse on gang initiation requires a rather different approach. Popular treatments of gang initiation rites in legends and in the press invoke standard themes found in discussions of other initiations: secret ceremonies that admit individuals into a select group; ritual symbolism, sometimes including blood, oaths, renaming, and the like; and trials or tests that demonstrate the individual's commitment to the new identity. The very term *initiation rite* evokes anthropological imagery; it suggests scientific objectivity but has other connotations as well. It hints that gang members might be characterized by various invidious terms for the anthropologist's subjects—*primitives, savages,* and the like. In these ways, claims about gang initiations borrow from generally available understandings of the nature of initiation rituals. As Simmel (1950:360) suggests, "Through the symbolism of the ritual, which excites a whole range of vaguely delimited feelings beyond all particular, rational interests, the secret society synthesizes those interests into a total claim upon the individual." According to legends and press reports about gang initiations, the rituals require prospective gang members to commit terrible crimes; in doing so, the initiates not only demonstrate their capacity for and commitment to the gang's criminality, but also take an irrevocable step into deviance.

Our analysis focuses not on the putative rituals, but rather on these accounts of gang initiation rites—particularly the discourse of the press and the public. We begin by indicating parallels between claims about gang initiation rites and accounts of other conspiracies of deviants; then we offer an interpretation of stories about initiation into deviant conspiracies.

Initiations into Other Deviant Conspiracies

Accounts of conspiracies of deviants often include descriptions of initiation rituals. Frequently these rituals require initiates to commit or join in the commission of serious acts of deviance, as in these examples:

Satanism.   Contemporary claims about a powerful satanic blood cult engaged in tens of thousands of human sacrifices as well as other crimes emphasize cult rituals, including rituals of initiation:

> First a blood relative or trusted friend inducts a child. Secret ceremonies instill a ritualistic fear of evil, accompanied by robed and hooded figures, naked women on altars, hypnotic chants, goblets of animal blood, bottles of human flesh preserved in formaldehyde, and orgies between adults and children and children and animals. The eating of feces, drinking of urine, sacrifices of babies, and taking of pictures for pornographic purposes are other elements. . . . (Larson 1989:122)

These accounts, especially when they depict the initiation of small children, contrast the initiate's innocence with the awful practices required by the rites (Richardson, Best, and Bromley 1991).

La Cosa Nostra.   In his testimony to Senate investigators, Joseph Valachi described his own initiation into a Cosa Nostra organized crime family: a

ritual involving swearing oaths before a gun, a knife, and flame, blood brotherhood, and adoption by a godfather (U.S. Senate 1963:180–84). Although
Valachi denied witnessing other such ceremonies, he insisted that all members went through the same initiation rite (p. 210). His testimony influenced
popular and academic conceptions of organized crime groups as tightly organized, formal criminal organizations with powerful holds on their members
(Smith 1975).

   Other Deviant Conspiracies.   Many other accounts portray initiation
rituals as thresholds to deviant conspiracies. First-century Romans believed
that Christians initiated new members in rituals involving sacrificing and eat-
ing infants (Ellis 1983). Claims of ritualized child sacrifice by Jews (the
"Blood Libel"), witches and other heretics, and other supposed deviant conspiracies have long histories (Dundes 1991; R. Moore 1987). The moral panic
about the criminal "Mohocks" in eighteenth-century London featured claims
about their initiation rituals (Statt 1995). Other accounts describe initiation
rituals among criminals, pirates, and other deviants (Hobsbawm 1959).

Initiation and Conspiracy

   The imagery of conspiratorial deviance emphasizes secrecy, power, purpose, and difference. In contrast to the standard image of deviance as rule
breaking by individuals or small groups of accomplices, claims about conspiracy locate deviance in a larger context:

> Conspiracy implies that members of a confession, party, or ethnicity
> (Jews, Freemasons, communists, pacifists, etc.) are united by an indissol-
> uble secret bond. The object of such an alliance is to foment upheaval in
> society, pervert societal values, aggravate crises, promote defeat, and so
> on. The conspiracy mentality divides people, things, and actions into two
> classes. One is pure, the other impure. These classes are not only distinct,
> but antagonistic. They are polar opposites: everything social, national,
> and so forth, versus what is antisocial or antinational, as the case may be.
> On the one hand, everything normal, lawful, that is, native; on the other
> hand, everything abnormal, unlawful, and hence, alien. The opposing
> groups belong to two distinct universes: a region of daylight and clarity
> versus an opaque and nocturnal milieu. (Moscovici 1987:154)

Most theories of conspiratorial deviants hold that outsiders—especially members of ethnic or religious minorities—band together in the cause of deviance.[10] This conspiratorial alliance is hidden from view, and the secrecy
conceals the web connecting apparently unrelated acts of deviance. Dedicated to advancing the deviant cause, the conspirators are a powerful yet
invisible social force. Such imagery gives rhetorical power to claims about
conspiratorial deviance. It suggests that deviant acts should be understood as
part of a large, powerful, insidious campaign. Thus any deviant act, no matter how mundane it may seem, can be defined as evidence of a major threat
to societal well-being.

Descriptions of deviant conspirators' initiation rites emphasize the gulf between the deviance and respectability. In joining the conspiracy, individuals commit themselves to the deviant cause. The transformation from respectability to deviance is made manifest in the initiation ritual, which usually requires initiates to commit some sort of serious deviant act, thereby demonstrating commitment to deviance and binding the new members to the deviant group.

Ethnographers and historians often dispute conspiratorial interpretations of deviance. Researchers studying organized crime, for instance, criticize Valachi-inspired descriptions of nationally coordinated organized crime for exaggerating the bureaucratization, centralization, and power of organized crime families (Haller 1990; Ianni 1972; Reuter 1983; Smith 1975). Similarly, ethnographies of satanists find no evidence of a powerful, conspiratorial blood cult (Bainbridge 1991; Ellis 1991; Lowney 1995). Proponents of conspiracy claims, however, do not consider such findings compelling: After all, a successful conspiracy would conceal its true workings from naive researchers, or even would enlist researchers as conspirators.

Understanding Claims about Gang Initiation Rites

Contemporary discourse about gang initiation rituals resembles other accounts of conspiratorial deviance. The motif of the gang initiation rite has parallels in claims about initiations into deviant cults and criminal organizations. What accounts for this pattern? How should we interpret contemporary claims linking gang initiation rites to random violence against respectable strangers?

Fear of crime has become a central theme in contemporary American culture. The press, popular culture, and everyday conversation emphasize the threat of crime, especially the risk of random attacks by strangers. This theme runs through claims about serial murder, hate crimes, violence against women, carjacking, sexual predators, freeway shootings, stalking, kids and guns, and other recently constructed crime problems. Claimsmakers promote notions that even very serious crimes are commonplace and virtually patternless—that everyone is at risk of victimization from these threats.

Of course, much social scientific research demonstrates that the risks of victimization are not distributed evenly throughout society. The urban poor, in particular, are far more likely than others to be victimized. Such findings usually lead social scientists to explain crime in terms of inequities in the social structure, but these explanations are relatively unpopular in the society at large. Popular discourse tends to focus not on the victims' poverty but on their respectability and innocence. Thus, typical accounts of criminal violence juxtapose deviant offenders (often portrayed as evil, exploitative, depraved, or irrational) with respectable victims (portrayed as innocent and powerless).

Since the mid-1980s, gangs have played a featured role in discourse about crime because of several interrelated developments, each inspiring claimsmaking campaigns: press coverage of rivalry between large "supergangs," especially confederations of black gangs (e.g., the Crips and the Bloods in Los Angeles; People and Folks in Chicago); the emergence of crack in the ghetto and gangs' involvement in its distribution; the spread of more—and more powerful—firearms among youths; the emergence of what are perceived as new forms of gang-related violence (e.g., drive-by shootings); the rise of popular-culture forms dramatizing inner-city violence (e.g., gangster rap music); and the dramatic rise in adolescent homicide deaths, particularly among African-Americans. Some researchers dispute claims about large, powerful, tightly organized supergangs,[11] but the public, the press, and policy makers attribute much contemporary crime to such conspiratorial groups (Jackson 1993).

In this cultural context, the gang initiation rite makes sense. The motif provides a reason for irrational, random crimes. We don't need to wonder why a respectable citizen is shot or why a car is stolen from a mall; such hard-to-explain crimes, which may seem pointless, can be attributed to gang initiation rites, in which criminal conspiracies require initiates to commit terrible, otherwise senseless crimes. Moreover, the initiation rite is the entryway into gang membership. Presumably gangs that require such crimes of their initiates do so because they are conspiracies dedicated to disorder. Having passed the initiation test, gang members will no doubt be willing and ready to commit other acts of random violence.

Studies of criminal violence commonly reveal that homicide, rape, and robbery have relatively mundane interactional causes; the offenders' motives hardly seem to measure up to the consequences of their acts. Popular discourse rectifies this discrepancy by giving terrible actions terrible motivations. One way to do this is to define the deviant as different in kind; thus varieties of insanity are said to motivate the "serial killer, the "sexual predator," and the "copycat criminal." Another way is to locate the deviant act within a larger conspiracy. Thus a belief in gang initiation rites helps to make acts of random violence explicable.

Motif, Meaning, and Cultural Resources

We began this analysis by contrasting references to gang initiation rites in contemporary legends, in press coverage, and in social science research: Social scientists report that gangs sometimes initiate members by testing their fighting abilities, whereas legends attribute horrific, melodramatic crimes to initiates, and the press uses gang initiations to explain crimes of unknown motivation. We then argued that initiation rites often figure in claims about deviant conspiracies, and noted how contemporary developments have fostered concerns about conspiratorial gangs. This motif constructs society as a locus for disorder, but in doing so, offers an explanation for that disorder.

Our analysis, then, uses a contemporary motif—the gang initiation rite—to link individual events described in legends and press reports to a centuries-old conception of conspiratorial deviance. The initiation of deviant conspirators is a familiar element in the cultural repertoire or "toolkit" (Swidler

1986), an element long used to construct many social problems including (most recently) gang violence. Our analysis reveals how discourse on social problems—even very specific talk about particular events—is embedded in a broader cultural context. Thus a given shooting may be explained by drawing on the familiar, currently popular motif of the gang initiation rite, which in turn evokes traditional imagery of conspiratorial deviance. That imagery gives meaning to the motif, which in turn explains the shooting.

The motif of the gang initiation rite is not new; it has a complex history. Evidence from both folklore and ethnography reveals that it was used in discourse about gangs during the 1960s, if not a decade earlier. It is impossible to know exactly when people first used the expression *gang initiation rite*, to trace its precise evolution, or to know how—or whether—popular discourse, ethnography, and media coverage influenced one another's use of the motif. This motif apparently became prominent in the early 1990s; its visibility seems to be tied to a diverse set of concerns about inequality, racial tensions (particularly middle-class whites' fears about the black underclass), urban unrest, random violence, drugs, assault weapons, and media violence, as well as gangs. Each of these issues became the subject of considerable claimsmaking; each was defined as troubling; each demanded explanation. The image of powerful, conspiratorial gangs helped to explain these problems in a way that focused blame on evildoers, rather than, say, on structural inequities. In this view, gangs were much more than a symptom of ghetto problems; they were a major cause of those problems. The gang initiation rite provided dramatic evidence of the moral gulf between this conspiracy of deviants and respectable society, just as the image of this gulf in turn fostered melodramatic portrayals of gangs in the press and in popular culture. Thus the various contemporary claims about gangs, including references to gang initiation rites, reinforced one another and reaffirmed the gang's threat to respectability.

In no sense is the gang initiation rite motif unique. All talk about social problems borrows from the broader culture, and can be understood only within that cultural and historical context. Moreover, motifs and other claimsmaking elements do not exist in isolation. Although we have chosen to focus on the motif of the gang initiation rite, we recognize that one motif does not a social problem make. Discourse about gang initiation rites commonly incorporates other cultural elements such as ideas about random violence, waves or trends in crime, and rebellious youths. Each of these elements lies embedded in its own cultural context—in understandings about deviance, morality, social order, and so on. These links need not be made explicit; when experienced members of the culture make sense of a particular legend or news report about a gang initiation rite, they draw on their broader understandings of the nature of deviance and social problems. Thus the construction of "new" crimes and other social problems inevitably incorporates familiar cultural elements, while the very familiarity of those elements discourages critical evaluation.

History offers many examples of warnings about conspiracies of deviants; such warnings evoked concerns that later analysts judged to be exaggerated or distorted. In retrospect, witches, Reds, mafiosi, dope peddlers, and white slavers often appear to be less organized, less powerful, and less threatening than claimsmakers imagined, just as the great juvenile gang menace of the 1950s became the stuff of nostalgic musicals. It is easy to debunk nearly forgotten claims, but more difficult to think critically about constructions of contemporary problems. Nonetheless, the familiar, taken-for-granted imagery in today's claims about social problems is consequential, and it demands our attention.

Studies of social problems construction have devoted considerable attention to organizational matters: claimsmakers' interests, mobilizing resources, achieving ownership of problems, and the like. Cultural analyses have focused mostly on rhetoric—overt efforts to persuade. The cultural context of claimsmaking in general, and particularly the role of familiar cultural elements such as motifs, has been largely ignored. Yet the motif of the gang initiation rite suggests that claimsmaking inevitably draws on familiar cultural resources in ways that shape the construction of social problems and, in turn, social policy. Constructionism reminds us that social problems take form through the language of claims. We must ask how this language, including even the most familiar motifs, shapes what we know—or fear.

Notes

[1] In the 1980s, indexing services began using computers to index newspapers and periodicals. These computerized indices relied on the Library of Congress (LC) subject headings that most U.S. libraries use to categorize books. Although LC subject headings can be subdivided, they are generally broad, formal categories, and do not include information at the level of motifs. There is an LC heading for *gangs*, but *gang initiation rites* is not an LC subheading and thus is not used as a heading in most indices.

[2] The search identified 169 stories, but we eliminated 55 of these from our analysis. Among these were four stories from newspapers published outside the U.S. and Canada. We also decided to include only one story about each incident, for example, although 16 stories discussed the 1993 rape-murders of two Houston teenagers, we included only one of these stories in our sample.

[3] This account does not give a detailed description of the cheek slashing, but the tale may be a variant of an English legend involving members of a gang (the "Chelsea Smilers") who cut their victims' "mouths at the sides in a grotesque smile." The report of the English legend does not mention initiation rites, however (Roud 1989).

[4] In general, legend scholars consider the factual truth of legends irrelevant. A legend is a story that is repeated widely by individuals: in the course of transmission, most legends are altered, usually by the claim that the events occurred locally. In some cases a particular incident might have provided the basis for what became a legend, but that initial truth has been lost in the hundreds of variants that evolved.

[5] Booth Tarkington's humorous Penrod stories featured preadolescent middle-class boys: In *Penrod and Sam*, the boys establish a secret society—not a gang—with a "'nishiation'" ritual featuring blindfolds, secret oaths, and paddling (Tarkington 1916).

[6] A few news stories described female initiates choosing or being compelled to have sex with male gang members: "There's a choice you can make as a woman if you want to join a gang. . . . You can either be beaten in, or you can choose to have sex with up to 20 members of the gang" ("Rapes" 1994). The ethnographic accounts do not describe this practice, although Spergel (1995) mentions it as part of "gang lore," and Hopper and Moore (1990:372–73) report that out-

law motorcycle gangs sometimes require male initiates to supply a woman who will have sex with the gang's members.

7 Two additional categories accounted for the 16 remaining stories: five stories (4 percent) attributed violence to gang initiation rites, but it was not clear whether the victim was an initiate (i.e., in a beat-down) or someone outside the gang; the remaining 11 stories (10 percent) did not address gang violence and formed a residual category.

8 Such news reports sometimes resemble contemporary legends. For example, the *Durham (NC) Herald-Sun* ran a front-page story headlined "Police: Gang Rapes Women for Initiation" (1993). This story began: "Durham police believe a gang of teen-agers in Northern Durham has developed a brutal rite of initiation—new members must kidnap and rape a white woman." One week later, a follow-up story explained that some rapes had been committed, but gave no evidence of gang involvement ("Police Chief" 1993). (These stories were not part of our NEXIS sample; we are indebted to Bill Ellis for calling them to our attention.)

9 The following section on initiation rites appears in a popular handbook on gangs published by the National Counseling Resource Center, "a not-for-profit organization started to combat many of the destructive beliefs and behaviors (e.g., gangs, Satanism, etc.) which are plaguing our nation and world.") This list illustrates how these different images can be conflated:

1. Many are *"beat in"* to the group. . . . These beatings are usually very severe.
2. Some are asked to do a *"Drive-by"* killing. . . .
3. Commit a *crime* (e.g., steal, rape, extortion, assault, arson, auto theft, etc.)
4. *Spray paint over enemy graffiti.* . . .
5. Those who grow up with a gang or in gang turf may have *no initiation ceremony.*
6. *Shoot someone in uniform.*
7. *Rob a home with the occupants there.*
8. *Girls* are initiated in a variety [sic] ways:
   a. *"Raped in"* or *"sexed in"* by a predetermined number of guys in the gang, . . . [or] have sex with someone who has AIDS. . . .
   b. They may be *"beat in"* by other girls in the set. . . .
   c. Others are asked to *beat up their mother* [sic] as a way of showing allegiance to the gang. (Larson and Amstutz 1995:42; authors' emphasis).

10 Although claims about conspiratorial gangs fit this model, other popular discourse depicts crime as a product of conspiracies by elites. For example, Turner (1993) and Sasson (1995b) examine how some African-Americans blame conspiracies of government and business elites for street crime, crack, AIDS, and other ghetto problems.

11 The analytic problems identified by researchers include: defining gangs and distinguishing among various types of gangs; assessing the degree to which gangs feature hierarchies of authority, centralized decision making, and other characteristics of formal organizations; determining the nature and strength of ties among gangs; and deciding which deviant acts committed by gang members should be considered "gang-related." In general, ethnographic research (cited above) tends to find gang activities less structured, less rationalized, and less centralized than do descriptions in the press or in popular discourse.

References

"Ankle Slashers at the Mall." 1993. *FOAFTale News* 29:10–11.

Bainbridge, W. S. 1991. "Social Construction from Within: Satan's Process." Pp. 297–310 in *The Satanism Scare*, edited by J. T. Richardson, J. Best, and D. G. Bromley. Hawthorne, NY: Aldine.

Benford, R. D. 1993. "'You Could Be the Hundredth Monkey': Collective Action Frames and Vocabularies of Motive within the Nuclear Disarmament Movement." *Sociological Quarterly* 34:195–216.

Best, J. 1990. *Threatened Children*. Chicago: University of Chicago Press.

"Blacks N Whites Gang Probably Formed Recently, Police Believe." 1993. *Houston Chronicle* July 1, p. A25.

"Blood Initiation Weekend." 1993. *FOAFTale News* 31:6.

"Boy Was Kicked to Death in Gang's Test, Police Say." 1990. *Orlando Sentinel,* November 22, p. A20.

Brunvand, J. H. 1981. *The Vanishing Hitchhiker.* New York: Norton.

_____. 1984. *The Choking Doberman.* New York: Norton.

_____. 1986. *The Mexican Pet.* New York: Norton.

_____. 1993. *The Baby Train.* New York: Norton.

_____. 1995. "'Lights Out': A Faxlore Phenomenon." *Skeptical Inquirer* 19 (March): 32–37.

Campbell, A. 1984. *The Girls in the Gang.* New York: Basil Blackwell.

Carroll, M. P. 1987. "'The Castrated Boy': Another Contribution to the Psychoanalytic Study of Urban Legends." *Folklore* 91:216–25.

Carondelet Management Institute. *N.D. Gangs.* Tucson: Carondelet Health Care.

"Close Call Heightens Fear of Crime." 1993. *Arizona Republic,* October 17, p. F3.

"County Police 'Documentary'." 1992. *Seattle Times,* April 21, p. D1.

"Don't Take Fearful Tale on Faith." 1992. *Dallas Morning News,* December 18, p. 29A.

Dorson, R. M. 1981. *Land of the Millrats.* Cambridge: Harvard University Press.

Dundes, A. ed. 1991. *The Blood Libel Legend.* Madison: University of Wisconsin Press.

Eliade, M. 1958. *Rites and Symbols of Initiation.* New York: Harper & Row.

Ellis, B. 1983. "De Legendis Urbis: Modern Legends in Ancient Rome." *Journal of American Folklore* 96:200–208.

_____. 1991. "Legend-Trips and Satanism: Adolescents' Ostensive Traditions as 'Cult' Activity." Pp. 279–95 in *The Satanism Scare,* edited by J. T. Richardson, J. Best, and D. G. Bromley. Hawthorne, NY: Aldine.

Fine, G.A. 1992. *Manufacturing Tales.* Knoxville: University of Tennessee Press.

Fleming, R. L. and R. F. Boyd Jr. 1994. *The Big Book of Urban Legends.* New York: Paradox Press.

Gamson W. A. and K. E. Lasch. 1983. The Political Culture of Social Welfare Policy. Pp. 397–415 in *Evaluating the Welfare State,* edited by S. E. Spiro and E. Yuchtman-Yaar. New York: Academic Press.

Gamson, W.A. and A. Modigliani. 1987. "The Changing Culture of Affirmative Action." *Research in Political Sociology* 3:137–77.

_____. 1989. "Media Discourse and Public Opinion on Nuclear Power." *American Journal of Sociology* 95:1–37.

"Gang Beat-downs Called Common Initiation Rite." 1994. *Atlanta Journal and Constitution,* March 25, p. F1.

"Gang Initiation Requires Shooting Folks in the Leg." 1990. *Orlando Sentinel,* April 29, p. A18.

"Gang Rites, AIDS and Unprotected Sex." 1993. *Houston Chronicle,* May 2, p. A26.

"Ganging Up." 1987. *Los Angeles Times,* November 30, p. II1.

Gusfield, J. R. 1981. *The Culture of Public Problems: Drinking-Driving and the Symbolic Order.* Chicago: University of Chicago Press.

Hagedorn, J. 1988. *People and Folks: Gangs, Crime and the Underclass in a Rustbelt City.* Chicago: Lake View Press.

Haller, M. H. 1990. "Illegal Enterprise." *Criminology* 28:207–35.

Hamm, M. S. 1993. *American Skinheads: The Criminology and Control of Hate Crime.* Westport, CT: Praeger.

Hilgartner, S. and C. L. Bosk. 1988. "The Rise and Fall of Social Problems." *American Journal of Sociology* 94:53–78.

Hobsbawm, E. J. 1959. *Primitive Rebels: Studies in Archaic Forms of Social Movement in the 19th and 20th Centuries.* New York: Norton.

Hopper, C. B. and J. Moore. 1990. "Women in Outlaw Motorcycle Gangs." *Journal of Contemporary Ethnography* 18:363–87.

Horowitz, R. 1983. *Honor and the American Dream.* New Brunswick, NJ: Rutgers University Press.

Ianni, F. A. J. 1972. *A Family Business.* New York: Russell Sage Foundation.

Ibarra, P. R. and J. I. Kitsuse. 1993. "Vernacular Constituents of Moral Discourse." Pp. 25–58 in *Reconsidering Social Constructionism,* edited by J. A. Holstein and G. Miller. Hawthorne, NY: Aldine.

Jackson, P. 1993. "Moral Panic and the Response to Gangs in California." Pp. 257–75 in *Gangs: The Origins and Impact of Contemporary Youth Gangs in the United States,* edited by S. Cummings and D. J. Monti. Albany: SUNY Press.

Jankowski, M. S. 1991. *Islands in the Street: Gangs and American Urban Society.* Berkeley: University of California Press.

Katz, J. 1988. *Seductions of Crime.* New York: Basic Books.

Keiser, R. L. 1969. *The Vice Lords.* New York: Holt, Rinehart and Winston.

La Fontaine, J. 1985. *Initiation.* New York: Penguin.

Larson, B. and W. Amstutz. 1995. *Youth Violence and Gangs.* Rochester, MN: National Counseling Resource Center.

Larson B. 1989. *Satanism: The Seduction of America's Youth.* Nashville: Thomas Nelson.

"'Lights Out' Gang Initiation." 1993. *FOAFTale News* 31:5–6.

Lowney, K. 1995. "Teenage Satanism as Oppositional Youth Subculture." *Journal of Contemporary Ethnography* 23:453–84.

"Mall Mayhem in Wichita." 1992. *FOAFTale News* 25:11–12.

"Malls on Alert After Rumor of Gang Rite." 1994. *Pittsburgh Post-Gazette,* March 20, p. W1.

Miller, W. B. 1958. "Lower Class Culture as a Generating Milieu of Gang Delinquency." *Journal of Social Issues* 14:5–19.

Monti, D. J. 1994. *Wannabe: Gangs in Suburbs and Schools.* Cambridge, MA: Blackwell.

Moore, J. W. 1991. *Going Down to the Barrio.* Philadelphia: Temple University Press.

Moore, R. I. 1987. *The Formation of a Persecuting Society.* New York: Basil Blackwell.

Moscovici, S. 1987. "The Conspiracy Mentality." Pp. 151–69 in *Changing Conceptions of Conspiracy,* edited by C. F. Graumann and S. Moscovici. New York: Springer-Veriag.

"New 'Urban Myth' Surfaces in Valley." 1993. *Arizona Republic,* October 2, p. A1.

New York City Youth Board. 1960. *Reaching the Fighting Gang.* New York: New York City Youth Board.

Operation Safe Streets. 1995. "L.A. Style: A Street Gang Manual of the Los Angeles County Sheriff's Department." Pp. 34–45 in *The Modern Gang Reader,* edited by M. W. Klein, C. L. Maxson, and J. Miller. Los Angeles: Roxbury.

Padilla, F. 1993. "The Working Gang." Pp. 173–92 in *Gangs: The Origins and Impact of Contemporary Youth Gangs in the United States,* edited by S. Cummings and D. J. Monti. Albany: SUNY Press.

"Police Chief Apologizes for Handling of Rape Warning." 1993. *Durham (NC) Herald-Sun,* January 12, p. A1.

"Police: Gang Rapes Women for Initiation." 1993. *Durham (NC) Herald-Sun,* January 5, p. Al.

"Rapes a Gang Ritual, Police Say." 1994. *Rocky Mountain News,* August 29, p. 5A

Reuter, P. 1983. *Disorganized Crime.* Cambridge, MA: MIT Press.

Richardson, J. T., J. Best, and D. G. Bromley, eds. 1991. *The Satanism Scare.* Hawthorns, NY: Aldine.

Roud, S. 1989 "Chelsea Smilers: Interim Report on a Gang-Violence Rumor." *FOAF-Tale News* 15:1–2.

Sasson, T. 1995a. *Crime Talk: How Citizens Construct a Social Problem.* Hawthorne, NY: Aldine.

_____. 1995b. "African American Conspiracy Theories and the Social Construction of Crime." *Sociological Inquiry* 65:265–85

Shakur, S. 1993. *Monster: The Autobiography of an L.A. Gang Member.* New York: Atlantic Monthly Press.

Simmel, G. 1950. "The Secret Society." Pp. 345–76 in *The Sociology of Georg Simmel,* edited and translated by K. H. Wolff. New York: Free Press

Smith, D.C., Jr. 1975. *The Mafia Mystique.* New York: Basic Books.

Spergel, I.A. 1995. *The Youth Gang Problem: A Community Approach.* New York: Oxford University Press.

Statt, D. 1995. "The Case of the Mohocks: Rake Violence in Augustan London." *Social History* 20:179–99.

"Staunch Advocate of Urban Living Having Second Thoughts after Drive-by Attack." 1994. *Atlanta Journal and Constitution,* March 15, p. D1.

Swidler, A. 1986. "Culture in Action." *American Sociological Review* 51: 273–86

Tarkington, B. 1916. *Penrod and Sam.* New York: Doubleday, Page. Chicago: University of Chicago Press.

The Killer in the Backseat." 1993. *FOOAF Tale News* 33:5–6.

Thrasher, F.M. 1927. *The Gang.* Chicago: University of Chicago Press.

"Truth Is Floored by Urban Rumor." 1993. *Chicago Sun-Times,* January 31, p. 11.

Turner, P. A. 1993. *I Heard It through the Grapevine: Rumor in African-American Culture.* Berkeley: University of California Press.

U.S. Senate. 1963. "Organized Crime and Illicit Traffic in Narcotics." Hearings by the Permanent Subcommittee on Investigations, Committee on Government Operations, Part 1. October 1–2.

"Urban Legend Dept." 1994. *St. Louis Post-Dispatch,* October 30, p. CL1.

"Urban Yarn of 'Mall Slasher' Just Won't Die." 1991. *Chicago Tribune* October 11, p. CL1.

Vigil, D. 1993. "The Established Gang." Pp. 95–112 in *Gangs: The Origins and Impact of Contemporary Youth Gangs in the United States,* edited by S. Cummings and D. J. Monti. Albany: SUNY Press.

Wachs, E. 1988. Crime.Victim Stories. Bloomington: Indiana University Press.

"Where Are You Safe?" 1994. *Atlanta Journal and Constitution,* November 15, p. B6.

Williams, R.H. 1995. "Constructing the Public Good: Social Movements and Cultural Resources." *Social Problems* 42:124–44.

Wolf, D.R. 1991. *The Rebels: A Brotherhood of Outlaw Bikers.* Toronto: University of Toronto Press.

Yablonsky, L. 1970. *The Violent Gang.* Rev. ed. Baltimore: Penguin.

SEVEN

THE PRESENTATION OF DRUGS IN THE NEWS MEDIA

THE NEWS SOURCES INVOLVED IN THE CONSTRUCTION OF SOCIAL PROBLEMS

Steven Chermak

Politicians and criminal justice officials have both a financial and an ideological stake in the way social problems are presented to the public. The issue of drugs, for example, tends to fade in and out of political priority (Peyrot 1984). Most recently, political interest in drugs escalated steadily through the 1980s. Drug enforcement was part of Ronald Reagan's crime control agenda, culminating in his declaration in 1986 that America needed yet another war on drugs (Jensen, Gerber, and Babcock 1991). George Bush retained Reagan's concern for drugs, developing a national drug control strategy, appointing the nation's first drug czar, and using the military to aid interdiction efforts.

The principal response advocated by both presidents, reflecting their political ideology, was to increase criminal justice and military enforcement efforts. Police departments cracked down on sellers, using undercover and "buy-and-bust" operations to increase the number of arrests. Courts cleared their dockets or created special drug courts to process the large influx of drug offenders. Penalties for drug offenses increased, with concomitant growth in prison populations. Moreover, the distinction between the police and the military in fighting the war on drugs eroded (Kraska 1993, 1994). Kraska (1993:161), for example, discusses how the formerly figurative "drug-war metaphor" has become more literal with the significant involvement of the military in foreign and domestic drug-control efforts.

It is significant that the rise and fall of drugs as an important political issue has not coincided with changes in the reported incidence of drug use

Justice Quarterly, Vol. 14, No. 4, December 1997. Permission granted by Taylor & Francis, Ltd. http://www.tandf.co.uk/journals

(Beckett 1994; Jensen et al. 1991; Reinarman and Levine 1995). Beckett (1994:442) discovered that public concern about drugs was affected only by shifts in the level of state-initiated activities. Similarly, Jensen et al. (1991) found that the enactment of federal drug legislation was not related to objective conditions of drug use, but to politicians' efforts to promote drugs as a social problem.

For several reasons, the news media are an effective resource available to claimsmakers when they seek support for policy preferences. First, news images are important because the public's exposure to the political process is limited (Edelman 1964; Kessel 1975). According to McCombs and Shaw (1991:17), "the information in the mass media becomes the only contact many have with politics." Second, media coverage is a cost-efficient way to garner support for a policy position because the public relies heavily on the news media (Graber 1980; Skogan and Maxfield 1981; Tunnell 1992). Third, the news media are an important agent of social control. Claimsmakers need public support to survive, compete, and thrive in the "social problems marketplace" (Best 1990:15), although predicting public preferences is difficult. Because "public perceptions are malleable," influenced by forces such as the mass media (Tittle 1994:32), social control agents are motivated to participate as news sources to transmit their beliefs and values, and also to legitimize themselves with the public.

An event that is presented to the public is shaped by a reporter's perception of it because it is rarely observed directly (Kappeler, Blumberg, and Potter 1996). Reporters rely on authoritative sources, such as political and criminal justice officials, to construct the event (Berkowitz 1987; Berkowitz and Beach 1993; Brown et al. 1987; Chermak 1995; Gans 1979; Sigal 1973). Sigal (1973:123) found that government officials accounted for approximately half of the sources cited in articles published in the New York Times and the Washington Post. Similarly, Chermak (1995:89) found that law enforcement and court officials accounted for more than half of the sources cited in crime stories.

"Although most research agrees with these findings, there are two general explanations for the dominance of official sources in news stories. First, several researchers argue in support of a conflict or structuralist perspective. This explanation emphasizes how the reliance on state officials is determined by macro-level forces. The structuralist perspective assumes that the media are an important symbolic mechanism used in the construction of ideology (Binder 1993; Sacco 1995). It is argued that the ideological power of the media results from their control over consumers' views of the world. Events are framed into standard modes of communication. These frames, according to Binder (1993:754–55), "help receivers make sense of social occurrences because they organize events into recognizable patterns." Consumers rely on this framing of events when deciphering reality; thus alternative viewpoints are eliminated from consideration (Beckett 1994; Binder 1993; Gamson et al. 1992; Gitlin 1980; Sacco 1995).

This macro-level focus deals specifically with questions of power and how power is expressed and distributed in society. It is important to understand the sources involved in the construction of crime because social problems can be framed in many different ways. For our analysis, the key aspect is how the reliance on government claimsmakers allows these sources to make claims and to characterize problems so as to legitimize existing social, cultural, and political relations. Political and economic elites have preferential access to the media because of their hierarchic position in society; they use this access to define the social order, maintain cultural boundaries, and reaffirm the status quo (Hall et al. 1978; Herman and Chomsky 1988).

Second, other researchers explain the reliance on these sources from an organizational perspective. Although news content may support a specific ideology, researchers argue that this is not done intentionally (Berkowitz 1987; Berkowitz and Beach 1993). Instead this reliance results from organizational and economic needs (Benedict 1992; Fishman 1980; Gans 1979; Tuchman 1978). News organizations are structured bureaucratically and rely on decentralized news beats to create news efficiently. Sources able to provide information in an efficient and newsworthy manner receive the opportunity to influence public discourse on crime and social control. Representatives from bureaucratic organizations understand the routine channels of news discourse and make themselves available to reporters. Researchers with this perspective, however, concede that the relied-upon sources do not completely control news images: News personnel accept only images consistent with their own organizational needs and media formats (Ericson, Baranek, and Chan 1987, 1989, and 1991).

Katherine Beckett's (1995) study examining the impact of sources on the presentation of drugs in the media contributes to these theoretical viewpoints and illustrates the importance of examining the presentation of sources in various types of story. In a sample of "hard" and "soft" (editorials, cartoons, opinion columns) drug stories, Beckett linked the sources cited to the "framing" of the issue. She found that the sources' ability to influence the presentation of drugs varied according to the type of story examined. First, she found that state officials affected the issue frames presented in the "hard" news stories and that the frequent presence of these frames resulted in a narrow perspective on the drug issue, supporting conservative "law and order" themes. Second, she found that a wider range of issue frames was presented in the "soft" items, supporting the conclusion that such a range results from state officials' exclusion from stories. These stories are media-generated, and the news personnel producing them are not constrained by the information provided by sources.

Other research examining relations between reporters and sources has rarely considered how these interactions evolve by type of story. Some researchers acknowledge, however, that sources other than routine crime authorities can procure media coverage, thus affecting news content and public attention to social problems (Best 1990; Gitlin 1980; Jenness 1993; Schlesinger and Tumber 1994). Joel Best's (1990) study of crimes against children documents the influence that outsider claimsmakers, such as activists and moral entrepreneurs, can exert on public and political attention to social problems by securing media coverage. Similarly, Valerie Jenness (1993) demonstrated how a group of outsider claimsmakers was able to reshape the "symbolic landscape" of prostitution and challenge the way traditional experts constructed this social problem.

The news process evolves according to the importance of the story. Chermak (1995) found that most stories are routine occurrences produced quickly in order to fill the space or time needs of a news organization. Chermak also found, however, that stories receiving significant amounts of attention are produced differently. Several reporters work on various aspects of these stories, four or five stories are presented to the public when the event is initiated, and the news media follow these stories closely over time (Chermak 1995:28–410.)

Similarly, Mark Fishman (1978:531) discussed how the news media can construct "crime waves," thus contributing to an ideological conception of crime. He found that incidents which could be attached to an ongoing theme of violence against the elderly were more likely to be published and received more attention in the news. Momentum increased as other media organizations tried to capitalize on this theme. Fishman also found that political and criminal justice officials contributed to the construction of this crime wave by taking action that received media coverage, shifting media attention to "how the system [was] working to remedy the situation" (p. 541).

In an analysis of criminal justice case processing, Friedman and Percival (1981:237) identified this "handful of cases at the apex of the system" as "celebrated." Criminal justice officials respond to different cases in different ways, and possess great discretion in deciding the importance of a case (Walker 1989:24–25). Because of the publicity received by these celebrated cases, they can affect public perception of the criminal justice system (Walker 1989:25). In applying this notion to media coverage, Surette (1989) calls the celebrated case a "media trial." Such trials have an impact far beyond their number, Surette argues, "because many viewers believe that the news and its portraits are real and accurate, the image of justice that media trials project has serious implications for public understanding of basic judicial concepts and support for the legitimacy of the entire criminal justice system" (p. 293).

The claimsmakers' involvement in celebrated cases, in contrast to their participation in typical cases, is an important aspect of social constructionism. Although celebrated cases are rare, they provide high-ranking officials with an opportunity to define the "hierarchy of credibility" in society and to reaffirm their position as a "primary definer" of an issue (Fishman 1980; Johnson 1995). Moreover, these cases can be "powerful teachers and preachers of conventional morality" (Friedman and Percival 1981:259). In documenting the sources that participate in celebrated news stories, we clarify how the relationship that results from the production of ordinary stories gives political and criminal justice officials strategic access to media personnel when opportunities arise to institutionalize their authoritative position.

In this article we examine how reporters and sources construct social problems in the news media. Specifically, we examine the sources cited in routine crime stories, in stories linked to a highly visible policy issue, and in stories examining celebrated cases relevant to policy issues. We document the news sources cited in these three types of story to determine whether the relationship between reporters and sources evolves as a story increases in importance. By examining the sources used by news organizations to define what is important about a topic of substantial interest, and then comparing the results with those for other crime stories, we understand more clearly how official sources define social problems in the news.

To illustrate the construction of social problems, we examine the problem of drug abuse, documenting the "primary definers" of the drug problem during a period when it was a high-priority news topic. Schlesinger and Tumber (1994:2) note that "only very recently have questions begun to be asked in a consistent and focused fashion about the tactics and strategies pursued by sources seeking media attention," and researchers on this topic have used only one of two research methodologies. First, most studies employ content analysis, counting and nonofficial sources (Berkowitz 1987; Berkowitz and Beach 1993; Brown et al. 1987; Sigal 1973). Second, other studies examine the relationship between reporters and sources by observing the news production process (Fishman 1978; Gans 1979; Tuchman 1978). Most research fails to link these two research methodologies, although each has limitations when used alone (Ericson et al. 1987). In this study we combine content and observational analysis to precisely document the sources involved in news production and to explain why, and how, political and criminal justice officials are involved in the representation of social problems in the news.

We believe that the theories traditionally used to explain the heavy reliance on official sources for news construction are not in conflict, but operate at different levels of understanding. Considered in this way, these theories are seen to complement one another; this suggests that an integrated theory may be more appropriate for understanding these officials' involvement in news construction. We argue that the relationship between sources and news personnel can evolve, and that it is influenced by the type of story in question. Most stories support the convergence of the bureaucratic goals held by news and source organizations: To make the production of crime news manageable, news media routinize their task by positioning themselves so as to gain easy access to sources that can supply crime news (Berkowitz and Beach 1993; Chibnall 1977; Fishman 1980; Gans 1979; Tuchman 1978). This reliance, in turn, provides these sources with the opportunity to shape the crime images presented in the news, although the information provided must be consistent with the media organization's time, resource, and format concerns (Ericson et al. 1987, 1989, 1991). In keeping with the organizational perspective, we hypothesize that criminal justice officials will dominate coverage of all types of routine crime story.

In addition, in the organizational process used to produce crime stories, news reporting is structured to support existing political, social, and legal systems. Issues that are thematically important or can be linked to celebrated cases provide strong opportunities to reaffirm the status quo. We hypothesize that a different class of social control agents will be used as sources in all drug stories and in celebrated drug cases. Because government claimsmakers have established access to media organizations, they can use specific stories as opportunities to legitimize their position as an important voice of the "deviance-defining elite" and to promote and frame a social problem. We hypothesize that high-ranking officials will be involved more frequently in typical drug cases and in celebrated cases, and will use these types of story to argue in support of a policy position because of the attention received. Drug abuse is a well-established, "recurring" social problem with potential for policy innovation and change (see Best 1990; Scheingold 1984). We examine the involvement of sources in incidents, policies, and celebrated stories about drugs to document whether the organizational constraints of news production place government claimsmakers in a position to use social problems for their strategic advantage.

Research Methodology

To examine the information on drug crimes available to the public, it is important to use various research methodologies. Here we employ content analysis of print and electronic news media to examine how drug crimes, policies, and sources are presented to the public; we also use observational and interview data to understand the origins of these news stories, the motivations of news sources, and the underlying intentions of the parties involved in news production.

We used content analysis to examine the presentation of drug-related crime in newspapers and on television. Content data were collected from six print and three broadcast media organizations, selected by geographic location and city size. We selected news organizations by generating a list of cities that had at least one local newspaper with a circulation greater than 50,000 (*Gale Directory* 1990). We matched the cities according to population size and number of index offenses for 1990, then stratified them into medium, large, and extra-large categories. The media from two cities in each category were selected to represent as many regions of the country and as much variation in crime rate as possible.[1] We examined content from one newspaper in each of the six cities (two medium, two large, two extra-large) and one television station in three of the cities (one medium, one large, one extra-large).

We coded 36 days of newspaper content from six print organizations: the *Albany* (New York) *Times-Union*, the Buffalo *News*, the *Cleveland Plain Dealer*, the *San Francisco Chronicle*, the *Dallas Times Herald*, and the *Detroit News*. Newspaper stories were coded for every fifth day of the first six months of 1990. In addition, we coded the *Cleveland Plain Dealer* for 18 days over a three-month period in 1991. These 18 days were coded for two reasons: First, the additional coding strengthens the reliability of comparisons between newspaper and television samples. Second, it allows for a comparison with the results from the 1990 newspaper sample.

Television content was coded from local evening broadcasts in Albany, Cleveland, and Dallas for an eight-week span from May to July 1991. We recorded and viewed a total of 168 broadcasts in their entirety. Crime stories were transcribed and then content-coded.[2]

We conducted a theme analysis of content, using a combination of coding rules from other research that examined crime content (Ericson et al. 1991; Graber 1980). Source variables, such as who was cited in a news story and that person's position in an organization, were added to the codebook to document precisely how news media present sources. We coded more than 2,500 crime stories.

The second methodology used in this study is ethnography. Ethnographic observation of the crime news production process was conducted in 1991 at one newspaper and one television station in a large metropolitan city; we spent approximately 150 hours in each news agency. These observations help to overcome the limitations of content analysis and demonstrate how decision making in news and source organizations contributes to the way the news is represented to the public.

The newspaper observed, which we will call the *Midwest Tribune,* is a large organization with a daily circulation of about 500,000. Police and court reporters produce most of the crime stories presented in the *Tribune.* Reporters working the police beat, located on the first floor of police headquarters, are responsible for producing stories about any crimes reported to the police. Court reporters are responsible for producing crime stories after an arrest is made and the defendant is arraigned. We made most of our observations on these two beats, but we also spent time with general assignment reporters and editors to broaden our understanding of news production.

Observations were also conducted at a television station in the same city, which we call the Midwest Nightly. All of the Midwest Nightly reporters are general assignment reporters, any of whom could be assigned to cover a given crime story. Reporters are assigned to stories at an afternoon editorial meeting; after these meetings, we asked reporters if we could follow their coverage of a particular story or shadow them as they made their daily routine checks.

We supplemented the ethnographic findings with 40 interviews. In addition to asking specific questions about the production process, we conducted structured, open-ended interviews for a broader perspective on how each media organization produced stories on crime: These included 20 long interviews with crime beat reporters and editors working for the organizations we observed, 15 interviews with news personnel from other organizations, and five interviews with criminal justice and victim sources. These interviews help to increase the generalizability of the observational findings.

Findings

The findings are presented in three sections. First, we establish the heightened attention given to drug crimes during the sample period, and compare the presentation of drugs as incident and policy stories with other types of crime story. Second, we examine the sources cited in typical drug stories, and compare the results with the presentation of sources in all crime stories. Although officials were the most common source cited in all types of story, we found several interesting differences when examining drug stories. Finally, we examine local and national celebrated incidents. These results help to document the importance of such cases in the construction of social problems.

The Importance of Drugs as Incident and Policy Stories

Nearly 75 percent of the crime stories presented were specific incident stories ($n = 1,982$). A law violation is noted, and the reporter discusses who was involved and what occurred. Table 1 lists the 12 types of crime most frequently cited in print and in electronic news media. At least one of these 12 offenses was presented in 70 percent of all the crime incident stories. As in other content studies, these results show that serious violent crimes are presented frequently (Chermak 1995; Ericson et al. 1991; Graber 1980).

Table 1   The 12 Crimes Most Frequently Presented in Print and Electronic Media[a]

	Lead Crime	Crimes Combined	Newspaper Results[b]	Television Results[c]
Murder	28.1%	24.6%	28.3%	27.3%
Drugs	11.1	9.4	11.8	8.2
Rape	4.7	5.0	3.7	8.5
Fraud	3.8	3.7	4.0	2.8
Assault	3.7	3.5	3.7	3.6
Robbery	3.5	4.4	3.8	2.3
Shooting[c]	3.0	2.2	2.5	4.6
Burglary	2.4	2.6	2.6	1.5
Kidnapping	2.2	2.2	1.9	3.4
Extortion	2.2	2.6	2.5	.8
Manslaughter	2.1	1.8	2.3	1.5
Larceny	2.1	2.0	2.4	1.0
	$n = 1,890$	$n = 3,712$	$n = 1,502$	$n = 388$

[a] We coded up to three crimes to document the crimes that news media present as most significant. If more than three crimes were mentioned, we coded the first three crimes presented in a story, using order of presentation as our best indicator of significance. The first column in table 1 presents the results of the first crime mentioned in a specific incident story. The second column in table 1 presents multiple crime results combined into a single category.
[b] According to presentation of the lead crime.
[c] Not specific as to charges filed.

Drug crimes were the subject of the second most frequently cited incident story, accounting for over 11 percent of the stories. Approximately 12 percent of the incident stories in newspapers and over 8 percent of the incident stories in television news focused on drug crimes. These results differ significantly from the findings of research conducted before 1980. Graber (1980:39) found that drug offenses were the tenth most frequently cited crime in the *Chicago Tribune*; they represented less than 1 percent of the total number of offenses when examined as a single-topic category and less than 2 percent when studied as a three-topic category (1980:22). Drugs also were important in policy stories: Changes in the criminal law, usually consisting of proposed sentencing modifications, accounted for nearly 30 percent of the 138 policy stories presented. Drugs were the topic of the second most frequently presented policy story (approximately 16 percent). These results support the conclusion that drugs become more newsworthy in 1990, and presented officials with a social problem of strong public interest (see Jerin and Fields 1995).

The activities of the reporters observed and interviewed here are consistent with these content findings. Early in our observations of the *Midwest Tribune,* for example, we shadowed a reporter recently assigned to the police beat. One of the first steps in his daily news production routine was to peruse the police blotter to select potential stories. He had unrestricted access to these reports, but the pile was more than one inch thick. When we asked him what he was looking for in these reports, he emphasized that violence, crimes with young victims, and drug crimes received priority because they had the potential to win a significant amount of news space. Drugs, he explained, had the potential to evolve into an important news story, especially when large amounts of drugs or cash were confiscated. He ignored most other crimes because they rarely had the potential to be newsworthy.

On the basis of our observations of the *Tribune,* court reporters also considered drug crimes newsworthy and adjusted their newsgathering routines to increase exposure to known drug offenses. As in the news selection techniques used on the police beat, reporters relied on court documents such as motion papers, court calendars, and appellate decisions. Court reporters also established access to returned search warrants to search for drug news. These documents included a detailed inventory of the evidence seized by police officers after the execution of a warrant. Court reporters invested time to peruse these documents because of the potential for payoff in the form of a front-page story.

Reporters learned the news value of specific types of crime by interacting with their superiors. These interactions helped reporters to develop and internalize an understanding of the crimes that should receive attention in their daily work routines. Reporters contacted their superiors early in the day to discuss story selection options. As they developed their stories, they frequently consulted the editors for suggestions on story frames and contacts with sources. These editors then reviewed stories before publication; frequently they changed the structure of a story or altered the presentation. This finding is consistent with that of others who have emphasized that the hierarchical structure of the newsroom has an important effect on news content (Benedict 1992; Ericson et al. 1987).

Similarly, the managing editor of the Midwest Nightly played a particularly important role in determining the stories to be included in the evening's broadcast. His first task every morning was to generate a list of story ideas. Later in the day, the news director, producers, assignment editors, and reporters attended an editorial meeting to decide which of the stories selected by the managing editor would be produced for the evening broadcast. Moreover, he had already made the initial contacts for the potential lead stories, and told reporters when specific sources would be available for an interview.

Sources Cited in Crime and Drug Stories

Table 2 presents the sources cited in specific crime incident stories.[3] Police and court officials account for over 50 percent of the source attributions in all such stories.[4] These results are consistent with other research examining the presentation of crime (Chermak 1995; Sherizen 1978), specific crime topics (Best 1990; Johnson 1995), and other news topics (Sigal 1973).

Our ethnographic results suggest that news organizations rely on police and court officials primarily because this method is most efficient for the organization. Criminal justice organizations provide reporters with access to organizational documents, and supply accommodating sources. The reliance on these sources increased the ability of the *Tribune* and Nightly to fulfill daily crime story quotas.[5] Newspapers utilize decentralized police and court beats to produce crime stories, and allow reporters to interact with official sources. Police beat reporters from the *Tribune* rarely left police headquarters, where they had access to blotter reports, arrest logs, and public relations personnel. Similarly, the court beat was in the courthouse, where reporters had access to various court documents and members of the courtroom workgroup. In general, television stations do not have enough employees to permanently assign reporters to police headquarters or the courthouse, although television reporters speak with these sources by telephone.

Reporters supplemented the information provided in official reports with two or three contacts with police or court personnel; these individuals were presented to the public as authorities on an incident. Police reporters had frequent contact with a departmental spokesperson; court beat reporters relied primarily on attorneys from the prosecutor's office. These representatives were willing to provide information and answer questions, thus contributing to the completion of a story.

A day we spent with a police beat reporter illustrates how reliance on police sources increases efficiency of news production. We shadowed "Carl Sanders" on a day when the other police beat reporter called in sick. Although Sanders was annoyed by his partner's absence, he easily produced three crime stories because of his access to police sources and documents.

Table 2 Sources Used in Specific Incident Stories

Sources	All Crimes	Murder	Drugs	Rape	Fraud	Assault	Robbery	Shooting	Burglary	Kidnapping	Extortion	Manslaughter	Larceny
Police	27.7%	29.1%	26.3%	35.6%	20.7%	54.8%	44.3%	58.9%	50.0%	40.9%	11.7%	13.2%	33.8%
Court	22.9	22.6	31.6	26.0	36.2	14.4	17.9	1.4	12.5	9.1	41.6	28.3	26.5
Defendant[a]	9.5	12.5	8.8	11.0	13.8	4.8	2.1	2.8	5.6	7.6	11.7	13.2	1.5
Victim[b]	8.3	6.5	1.0	11.7	6.0	8.7	11.5	12.3	12.5	13.7	5.2	9.4	16.2
Politician	3.8	1.9	6.4	.0	3.4	1.0	2.1	1.4	2.8	.0	3.9	1.9	2.9
Witness	3.7	4.8	2.7	4.8	2.6	2.9	3.6	5.5	1.4	1.5	2.6	9.4	1.5
Citizen	3.4	3.5	1.3	1.4	3.4	1.9	2.9	2.7	1.4	1.5	2.6	3.8	4.4
Documents	3.4	3.1	5.7	2.7	6.0	1.0	2.1	.0	1.4	1.5	3.9	3.8	2.9
Media	2.0	1.3	1.3	1.4	1.7	.0	1.4	.0	.0	6.1	2.6	7.5	1.5
Experts	2.0	1.7	.7	.0	.9	.0	.7	.0	.0	1.5	.0	.0	.0
Corrections	.8	.9	.0	.7	.0	1.9	1.4		.0	1.5	.0	.0	.0
Other[c]	5.3	4.3	.7	.7	.0	1.0	2.1	4.1	4.2	3.0	.0	3.8	.0
Not Specific[d]	7.0	7.1	10.8	3.4	5.2	5.8	7.9	8.2	4.2	9.1	9.1	5.7	7.4
	n = 5,038	n = 776	n = 297	n = 146	n = 116	n = 140	n = 140	n = 73	n = 72	n = 66	n = 77	n = 53	n = 68

n = Number of sources that commented on the crime incident.
a. Category includes attributions to defendants and acquaintances of defendants.
b. Category includes attributions to victims and acquaintances of victims.
c. Includes attributions to school and church officials.
d. Coded as not specific when attribution was "sources say," "officials say," or "authorities say."

After making his morning calls to sources that might provide breaking news (e.g., police districts, suburban departments, airport security), he examined the blotter reports and asked the departmental spokesperson for reports about four crime incidents: an assault in which the victim's skull was fractured, the robbery of an elderly man, the robbery of a teacher, and the burglary of a county administrative building. We met with the spokesperson, who provided Sanders with the reports for the assault and the burglary, but he also mentioned a shooting that had just occurred. Sanders produced the stories on the assault and the burglary as "local briefs," using verbatim the facts provided in the police reports. In addition, he was able to interview a sergeant and a detective by telephone to ask about the shooting. He tried to contact the victim and the victim's family, but they were unavailable for comment. Sanders produced a third story, about 12 column inches long, from the report and the information provided from the two police sources.

Access to police and court sources and documents increases news efficiency, but this reliance allows sources to protect themselves or to provide information to reporters in a way that benefits themselves. For example, reporters had only limited access to organizational documents. Police reporters did not know whether the blotter reports provided to them included every crime incident, but they did know that only partial information about an incident was included in the reports made available. From the name, age, sex, and type of crime included in these summary reports, reporters determined whether an incident had news potential. They had to request the complete report from an organizational representative, who then decided whether it would be released. Court reporters had unimpeded access to court hearings, but could report only what resulted from informal decision-making processes such as plea negotiations. Some sources refused to cooperate with news personnel. When we interviewed a news director from a television station in a large city he commented, "Sometimes [sources are willing to cooperate], sometimes they're not. It depends what their interests are in a particular story. There are many instances where the police cooperate with us so they get a story out."

Reporters rarely questioned the veracity of the information provided by officials and did not criticize the activities of the source organization. They were more concerned about keeping access to sources and organizational documents than about the reliability of information provided by officials. Loss of access to information affected not only the reporters' decision-making processes but also reporter-editor relationships, decisions about story assignments, and the images presented to the public.

Reporters' concern that sources might obstruct the flow of information was not unfounded. One reporter we interviewed had recently completed an investigative reporting series that criticized a local police department. After the stories were aired, he was denied access to organizational documents and had difficulty finding a police representative who would provide comment on camera. His investigative series also damaged the relationship of this police department with other persons employed by the same news organization.

Table 2 also presents the sources cited in the large number of typical drug stories. The reliance on police and court sources in drug stories is greater than in all other types of crime story, accounting for nearly 58 percent of the information. This heavy use of police and court sources reflects how official sources fulfill organizational needs in the construction of crime news.

Moreover, the fact that drugs are "victimless" crimes narrows the range of sources and perspectives provided in drug stories. When reporters construct crime stories involving victims, they frequently attempt to contact victims or family members for an emotional quotation. This emotion is sometimes directed at officials because of their handling of a case. Reporters rarely have access to victims in drug stories; victims accounted for only 1 percent of the source attributions. Defendants, who could provide alternative perspectives on drug incidents, are difficult to contact; reporters rarely considered them an important source.

Other sources are excluded from drug stories because they cannot meet the immediate needs of story production or provide responses consistent with expected frames. For example, experts such as criminologists and sociologists are rarely cited in crime stories; they accounted for only 2 percent of the source attributions in all crime stories and were cited even less frequently in drug stories (see table 2). Reporters are not likely to have easy access to such sources, and it is unlikely that these sources would state the information in a way that is consistent with the format needs of the news organization.

Politicians are not generally considered standard sources for comment on specific incidents. They accounted for only 3.8 percent of the sources cited when the sources from all crime stories were considered, and were involved even less when almost all of the specific crime categories were examined. These sources are rarely used because their involvement is beyond reporters' daily routines. Politicians, however, accounted for 6.4 percent of the source attributions in drug crimes in early 1990; this, in turn, encouraged politicians to make themselves available for routine coverage of drug incidents.

In several instances, when we observed activities at the *Tribune* and Nightly, politicians used an event such as an arrest or a trial to comment on the effectiveness of current drug policy. Some of these incidents received enormous amounts of attention (see "Sources Used in Celebrated Crime Stories"). Moreover, politicians used isolated incidents as opportunities to publicize policy efforts. When several individuals were arrested for selling drugs, the mayor held a press conference to discuss the incident and link the event to drug crackdown initiatives.

Table 3 displays the results of the sources cited in all types and specific types of policy story. Although politicians are rarely used as authorities in specific incident stories, they are the most frequent source cited in all types of policy story combined and in most individual categories. For example, politicians accounted for 26.6 percent of the source attributions in all policy stories, 45.9 percent in death penalty stories, 37.5 percent in stories about changes in the criminal law, and 20.3 percent in drug policy stories.

Table 3　Sources Used in Policy Stories

Sources	All Policy Stories	Criminal Law Changes	Drugs	Victim	Death Penalty	Police	Guns	Courts	Corrections	Other
Police	11.4%	5.1%	7.8%	16.7%	5.4%	42.1%	36.4%	.0%	.0%	4.8%
Court	24.9	32.3	28.1	23.3	13.5	7.9	.0	52.9	23.5	23.8
Defendant[a]	3.6	1.0	1.6	.0	.0	.0	.0	23.5	.0	4.8
Victim[b]	6.6	4.0	.0	23.3	10.8	5.3	.0	.0	.0	23.8
Politician	26.6	33.3	20.3	16.7	45.9	18.4	54.5	5.9	11.8	23.8
Witness	.0	.0	.0	.0	.0	.0	.0	.0	.0	.0
Citizen	3.3	2.0	.0	.0	5.4	5.3	.0	.0	17.6	9.5
Documents	4.8	4.0	7.8	10.0	.0	.0	.0	11.8	.0	9.5
Media	1.5	1.0	.0	.0	8.1	2.6	.0	.0	.0	.0
Experts	3.3	5.0	7.8	.0	2.7	.0	.0	.0	.0	.0
Corrections	3.0	2.0	1.6	.0	5.4	.0	.0	.0	29.4	.0
Other[c]	3.6	1.0	7.8	3.3	2.7	2.6	9.1	.0	11.8	.0
Not Specific[d]	7.5	9.1	9.4	6.7	.0	15.8	.0	5.9	5.9	.0
	n = 334	n = 99	n =64	n = 30	n = 37	n = 38	n = 11	n = 17	n = 17	n = 21

n = Number of sources

[a]Category includes attributions to defendants and acquaintances of defendants.

[b]Category includes attributions to victims and acquaintances of victims.

[c]Includes attributions to school and church officials.

[d]Coded as not specific when attribution was "sources say," "officials say," or "authorities say."

The media use political, police, or court officials to evaluate the quality of current responses to crime and to recommend specific changes in policy. Nearly 60 percent of the attributions in all types of policy story were sources serving in some official capacity. The explanation for such reliance—consistent with the organizational explanation for the news production of specific incident stories—is that they are available and willing to participate as news sources. Moreover, these sources involve themselves in the production of policy news stories because of the possibility of generating support for their own position. These sources promote specific policy issues by requesting coverage, and then frame what is discussed by participating as news sources.

To further illustrate officials' involvement in news construction, we examined the specific types of police and court sources used in incident and policy stories about crime and drugs. We expected that the upper echelons of the police hierarchy would take an active role in defining what was important about crime, drugs, and crime policy. In addition, we thought that the political members of the courtroom workgroup (prosecutors and judges) would take a more active role in policy news production than would other court sources. The results support both expectations.

When police sources are cited, the dominance of police chiefs, captains, and lieutenants is persuasive. Members of the command staff account for most of the information provided by police organizations; they are cited in at least 20 percent of the police attributions in all types of crime incident story. The upper levels of the police hierarchy accounted for 20.6 percent of the source attributions in drug incident stories. Police chiefs accounted for more than 13 percent of the source attributions in policy stories. We discussed source interactions with a television reporter, who emphasized his reliance on police officials in power:

> I get most of my information by talking with people in charge. Every once in a while, I get a call from somebody who is not of officer rank, with a "tip." I then call the people in charge. They ask, "Where did you get that information?" Primarily the routine daily calls go to those in charge.

The highest ranks of the police involve themselves in the news production process to increase their control of the images of police departments. The bureaucratic structure of police organizations guarantees that only a limited number of sources—individuals with policy-making power—will have the most access to internal organizational information and can choose the information that is funneled to media personnel.

The division of labor in police organizations also "fosters unique accounting strategies" (Cavender, Jurik, and Cohen 1993:153). Information, reports, and statistical data about departments typically are released through spokespersons. These public relations employees, trained by the department in image building, work closely with other officials to represent the department's position favorably; they nurture their relationship with reporters to ensure that this image is presented prominently. *Tribune* police reporters interacted daily with the spokesperson in his office, and Nightly reporters contacted him by telephone when they needed sound bites. The spokesperson was willing to be questioned by reporters to influence the type of coverage presented about the police department.

Prosecutors accounted for at least 25 percent of the court source attributions across all categories of incident crime. When all crime stories were examined, prosecutors accounted for 32.6 percent of the court source attributions, defense attorneys for 24.7 percent, and judges for 12.9 percent. Similarly, prosecutors and judges dominate court source attributions in policy stories. Judges accounted for more than 37 percent of the attributions to court sources in policy stories. This high percentage is impressive because judges are involved in the routine coverage of news only when they allow reporters to record courtroom comments. Judges were cited frequently in all types of policy stories, including more than 40 percent of the court source attributions in drug policy stories. (Most judges are elected officials, who can benefit from positive news coverage.) Prosecutors accounted for 34.1 percent of the remaining court attributions in drug policy stories, but defense attorneys for only 12.1 percent.

Sources Used in Celebrated Crime Stories

The findings on the types of sources presented in crime and drug stories indicate the possibility that officials use specific types of story to define the parameters of social problems. An additional method for examining sources' involvement in construction of social problems is to consider the authorities cited in celebrated drug cases. News space is not a luxury; stories thought to be most attractive to news consumers receive disproportionately large amounts of space. Because celebrated stories are rare events, compared with the traditional, routine "who, what, and where" crime story, the news organization expends valuable resources to cover all angles of these stories and constantly brings news consumers up to date. Because of the space and significance given to celebrated crime stories, they are also important for sources interested in generating public support for policy initiatives. We examine sources' involvement in celebrated cases using two lines of inquiry. First we discuss several local celebrated cases, combining the content and the observational results. Then we examine sources' involvement in two national celebrated cases.

While examining the media content and making observations, we were exposed to several celebrated local cases linked to the heightened interest in drugs. These local events received great amounts of space, were presented on the front page, often with a banner headline, and were revisited constantly as they progressed through the criminal justice system. Moreover, media personnel often were able to link these local scandals to a national drug story, such as a policy proposal or the arrest of a national figure. For example, a story about a federal investigation that resulted in the arrests of five Buffalo police officers was juxtaposed with a story about President Bush's involvement in a Latin American drug summit (Herbeck 1990).

One way to study sources' involvement in the presentation of local celebrated cases is to examine the officials cited in different-sized stories. The size of a story (in column inches or in amount of time) can be used as a proxy for its importance. These data are rather crude, but they indicate that routine sources, such as police and court officials, were presented disproportionately in stories of all sizes. Moreover, these quantitative results show that as the size of a story increased, so did the involvement of high-ranking police officials and politicians.

We suspect that the percentage of source attributions to these officials significantly underrepresents the officials' involvement in construction of social problems. One limitation of examining sources' involvement in quantitative terms is that each attribution to a source is given equal value. This methodology overlooks the possibility that one source may influence the discourse of others or that an official contributes to the framing of social problems by leaking information to officials or other sources. This limitation can be addressed, however, by relying on other methodologies.

Three types of drug story received large amounts of space in the media organizations we examined: the arrest of a large number of individuals involved in a single incident, an innocent victim caught in the crossfire of a drug turf war, and the arrest or trial of a high-profile defendant such as a police officer. Officials linked these celebrated events to an issue, and framed them as supporting their drug policy position or used them to request additional funding. Local celebrated events were explained within a similar framework, regardless of the medium or the media organization considered.

Officials used the first two types of local celebrated incident to advocate a law-and-order response to drugs; they cited them as illustrating the need for additional resources to crack down on drug dealers or as examples of successful efforts. In agreement with the national response to the drug problem, local politicians across the country declared their own localized version of a war on drugs. When a significant arrest occurred or when a bystander was killed, the incident provided an opportunity to seek support for a policy position or to advocate the creation of a task force or special unit.

An example from our observations at the *Tribune* illustrates how politicians used their access to reporters and criminal justice personnel as an opportunity to comment on drug policy. A spokesperson from a suburban police department contacted one of the reporters about a press conference that had been called to announce a major drug bust. A man had been stopped for speeding, but the officer making the stop found a box of cash and a gun in the back seat, and (upon further investigation), a large amount of drugs in the trunk. At the press conference, attended by the mayor and the police chief, the drugs, gun, and cash were displayed for photographers and television news crews. The case was discussed in detail by several police representatives, but the story was always framed within the suburb's efforts to crack down on drugs. The mayor was quoted several times in the story.

In the third and last type of local celebrated event, political and criminal justice officials use their status as standard sources to respond to a scandal (see Cavender et al. 1993). In another incident that occurred during our observations at the *Tribune,* when we arrived at the court beat early one morning, we were told that 30 police officers had been arrested and were being arraigned on drug and gambling charges. At the federal courthouse, we encountered about 25 reporters and 10 videographers in the hallway outside the courtroom, waiting for people to exit. We spent the day with one of several *Tribune* reporters who were assigned to attend the arraignments and two press conferences about this case.

Officials speaking at both press conferences focused on positive attributes of the police department, reassuring the public that the department's position in the community's social control structure was not fundamentally flawed. At the first conference the mayor stated his support for the department and focused on its accomplishments. He also stressed his disdain for the behavior of these officers.

The second news conference was held at the offices of the FBI. Comments were made by the agent in charge of the investigation, the police chief, the director of public safety, and a U.S. attorney. In this second news conference, the police chief's initial comments framed how the newspaper and television organizations presented the incident to the public, and affected how other officials discussed it. In his opening statements, the chief stated that he no longer considered the arrested officers worthy of employment. He also claimed that they were not representative of the department. Most of the questions posed to the panel focused on his statement, allowing him to clarify his position and to discuss the department's efforts to respond to corruption. Moreover, the chief's initial comments provided the lead article in the next morning's newspaper.

The editorial staff coordinated the efforts of the reporters assigned to cover this case. Four stories detailed the investigation and how the combined efforts of the police department and the FBI resulted in the arrests. The primary minority voice presented was a union official; when asked to respond to the chief's statement, he reminded reporters that the officers had not yet been convicted.

Buffalo's police department responded similarly when five of their officers were arrested on drug charges. At the news conference announcing the arrests, a U.S. attorney said that the police commissioner requested the investigation. Moreover, the agent in charge of the sting operation was quoted as saying, "What we found was not a widespread drug problem in the department, but a very, very serious problem involving a fairly small group of officers" (Herbeck 1990).

To conclude this discussion, we present the content results from two national events. Each case is unique, but the results illustrate how relationships between officials and reporters, and access to the "symbolic landscape," provided opportunities to demonize drug use and gain policy support (see

Kraska 1993). One case was used to advocate a crackdown on drug crimes; the other illustrates efforts to respond to scandal on the national level.

In the first case, General Manuel Noriega was indicted for federal drug trafficking charges in February 1988, two months after George Bush began his presidency. On December 19, 1989, when almost two years of political and military pressure had failed to remove Noriega from power, the United States invaded Panama and legitimized the invasion by claiming that it was needed to bring Noriega to trial. Noriega evaded capture for 10 days by seeking refuge in the Vatican embassy, but eventually surrendered and was brought to the United States on January 4, 1990.

The second celebrated case involved Marion Barry. In his third term as mayor of Washington, DC, Barry was arrested and indicted by a federal grand jury on 11 drug and 3 perjury charges. The arrest was made in the Vista Hotel on January 18, 1990 as the result of a drug sting operation set up by federal drug agents. The evidence implicating Barry included videotape of Barry smoking crack from a crack pipe. Barry's case received news attention throughout the sample period, including stories about his arrest, the pretrial motions, and the prosecution witnesses' opening statements and testimony.

Twenty-eight stories about Noriega and 37 stories about Barry fell on the sampled content days, accounting for nearly 30 percent of the drug stories presented. Moreover, the stories about these two cases were generally larger than the other crime and drug stories presented. The stories about Noriega's case averaged over 16 column inches and the stories about Barry averaged over 15 column inches, whereas all stories of specific incidents averaged just over 12 column inches and all other drug stories averaged under 12 column inches.

The incident and defendant sources cited in the stories about these two celebrated cases are presented in table 4. These findings differ dramatically from those on the sources cited in routine crime stories: For example, political sources accounted for 16 percent of the source incident information and 15 percent of the defendant information in the Noriega stories. The presentation of Noriega's case in the news was unique in that it involved high-ranking officials, including President Bush, because of the events leading up to Noriega's arrest. Administration officials, Justice Department spokespersons, State Department officials, White House Press Secretary Marlin Fitzwater, senators, and President Bush were among the politicians quoted in the stories about Noriega that framed the discourse about his case.

These sources used Noriega's arrest to justify current drug policy and to win public approval for a law-and-order response to drug enforcement. In August and September 1989, four months before Noriega's arrest, President Bush had made drugs his primary domestic policy issue and had announced his program to fight them. The President then used the capture of Noriega to generate public support; he reacted immediately to Noriega's surrender and linked his arrest to the need to crack down on drug dealers: "His apprehension and return to the United States should send a clear signal that the United States is serious in its determination that those charged with promoting the

Table 4   Sources Cited in Celebrated Crime Stories

	High-Profile			
	Noriega		Barry	
Sources	Incident	Defendant	Incident	Defendant
Police	1.1	.0	6.5	2.0
Court	56.4	35.0	19.4	10.0
Defendant[a]	3.2	5.0	33.3	48.0
Victim[b]	.0	.0	.0	.0
Politician	16.0	15.0	1.1	6.0
Witness/Jurors	.0	.5	5.4	4.0
Citizen	1.1	20.0	9.7	6.0
Documents	1.1	.0	2.2	4.0
Media	1.1	.0	2.2	6.0
Experts	2.1	5.0	1.1	6.0
Corrections	.0	.0	.0	.0
Other[c]	1.1	5.0	.0	.0
Not Specific[d]	13.8	10.0	19.4	6.0
	$n = 94$	$n = 20$	$n = 93$	$n = 50$

n = Number of sources
[a]Category includes attributions to defendants and acquaintances of defendants.
[b]Category includes attributions to victims and acquaintances of victims.
[c]Includes attributions to school and church officials.
[d]Coded as not specific when attribution was "sources say," "officials say," or "authorities say."

distribution of drugs cannot escape the scrutiny of justice" (Rosenthal 1990:A1). Senator Dole expressed similar sentiments: "Noriega's arrest was good news for our war on drugs" (p. Al). Two months after Noriega's arrest, as approval ratings for President Bush soared, administration officials declared that the U.S. was succeeding in the war on drugs, and cited the arrest as evidence ("U.S. Cites Progress" 1990).

The source results for the Barry stories are very different. Although Barry's case involved a prosecutor with political motivations and high-profile defense attorneys who knew how to benefit from news coverage, Barry himself was the most frequently cited source in stories about his case.[6] One-third of the source incident attributions and nearly one-half of the defendant attributions were direct quotes from Barry or his acquaintances. Barry alone accounted for 25.8 percent of the total source incident attributions about his case.

We believe that Barry was used frequently as a news source for two reasons. First, he had enormous media savvy, which he had developed as a politician in a city where competition for news space is fierce. Barry used his access to the news media, orchestrating news events after his arrest to influence public opinion about his case. He apologized for his actions to the city's children, voluntarily entered drug treatment, announced that he had become a born-again Christian, lashed out at the FBI for endangering his life by allowing him to smoke crack, and reacted to the prosecution's case on the courthouse steps. Second, it could be argued that these two celebrated cases were in direct competition for the daily headlines, and clearly the Noriega case provided a better opportunity for generating support for national drug control policy. The Barry case was less politically appealing and created considerable risk for officials identified with his arrest. Questions of entrapment and racism were important themes in the news about his case.

Our research has identified two complementary processes involved in the representation of social problems in the news media. We will show how these processes can be explained by integrating the bureaucratic perspective of news production with the structuralist perspective. We conclude by elaborating on this integrated theoretical perspective and applying it to the presentation of drugs by the media.

Most crime news is produced through a process that satisfies organizations' bureaucratic goals. Media organizations present several crime stories daily: According to our research, print media present nine crime stories a day, on average, and electronic media four crime stories per day. The heavy demand for crime stories, coupled with the unpredictability of news, generates the need to simplify news production (Tuchman 1978). Efficiency is increased by placing reporters near sources, thus increasing their exposure to documents and to individuals willing to impart their official knowledge of crime. The research results presented here show that police and court sources are cited frequently in all types of crime, drug, and policy stories.

The reliance on these sources affects how crime, and criminal justice organizations, are presented in the news. Sources are willing to expose their organizations to media scrutiny in exchange for the opportunity to influence public opinion by framing issues within a narrow range of discourse. As sources they are given an accepted public forum to define what is important about crime policy. For example, the structured hierarchy of police organizations limits outsiders' access to organizational information and increases the organization's control over the dissemination of information. Police organizations use the upper echelons of the department in the news production process to ensure that the images provided are consistent with the department's goals. Reporters, however, do not blindly accept what the organizations say, but use the information selectively. The resulting images are the product of the interplay between reporters and officials.

The relationship that evolves from source organizations' structured involvement in the routine coverage of news is beneficial to those organizations because it provides strategic access to the media; it allows them to determine and support the traditional frames of events. The organizational features that produce crime stories, including the decentralized beat structure, the developed routines, and the reliance on official sources, all structure news media reporting so as to legitimize the system. This research has illustrated several important characteristics of media constructionism which ensure that the representation of crime supports the status quo.

First, media personnel are not likely to criticize the activities of the source organization because they treat as factual the information provided by official sources (see Fishman 1980). Moreover, the officials' ability to deny access or withhold information from reporters significantly shapes the reporters' decision-making process. Reporters are unlikely to criticize official sources because they fear losing access to information. Helen Benedict's (1992:10) study examining how the media cover sex crimes illustrates how "the habitual hurry and pressure under which reporters work render them particularly susceptible to manipulation." This manipulation is most likely to occur when public and political interest in a problem area is substantial, such as when specific issues or types of crime attract heightened media attention. In such cases, sources have the opportunity to expand the organization's power and to reaffirm their position as agents of social control. Celebrated cases provide officials with opportunities to bring attention to a social problem and to recommend policy initiatives.

Second, the reliance on these officials causes events to be framed in ways that reaffirm standard approaches to crime. Reporters are not likely to question officials' "bureaucratic accounts" because sources provide information consistent with their expectations (Fishman 1980; Gitlin 1980). By interacting with other reporters and with supervisors, reporters learn the established frames that help to legitimize accepted practices. These frames are reinforced by the way stories are reconstructed, where stories are placed, and how much attention is given to a specific crime incident. Moreover, even though officials or a specific individual may not receive attribution in every story about an issue they can still affect its presentation because others are forced to respond to the way officials expect issues to be framed.

Third, news organizations are structured so as to ensure exposure to a limited range of viewpoints. Media routines for the production of crime stories expose reporters primarily to high-ranking political and criminal justice officials. These sources are particularly highly motivated to manage the portrayal of crime news. For example, high-ranking members of the police hierarchy—either the police chief or the public relations spokesperson—dominated the representation of the police in the news. Other sources, such as experts, victims, and defendants, were rarely contacted by reporters because of their inaccessibility and their inability to provide information within expected frames. Also, experts were rarely cited in celebrated cases. Although both the Noriega and the Barry cases presented legal, moral, and political issues of interest to experts, most of the information cited in these stories was provided by politically affiliated sources.

Politicians, police chiefs, prosecutors, and judges participate as news sources when new or recurring social problems arise, because they receive attention and the opportunity to promote themselves or the institution they represent. These powerful sources are expected to comment on important social problems because of their position in an organization and in society: They are "recognized socially to be in a position to know" (Ericson et al.

1989:4). Tittle (1994:50) discussed how [elites] almost always find it necessary to create some sense in others that the elites deserve to be in powerful
positions because they do, or have done, something good for the collectivity."

Moreover, a source's initial involvement in a celebrated case encourages
continued involvement by others. The public, noticing the amount of space
given to celebrated events, assumes that the issue and the person commenting
on the issue are important. News consumers develop psychological relationships with these sources, increasing the sources' credibility and the expectation that they should continue to provide comment about the same and
similar events (Reese, Grant, and Danielian 1994). The media access accorded
to officials and the expectation of continued involvement allow officials to
determine the scope of the debate and ultimately the interpretation and control of the topic (see Hall et al. 1978). Additional and contradictory stories
about a topic might be presented; they will be framed according to what has
been established, however, and the privileged access enjoyed by officials gives
them an opportunity to respond.

Media coverage of drug cases illustrates clearly how the media routines
that result from organizational needs allow politicians and law enforcement
officials to accomplish system-legitimizing goals. Drugs are a well-established social problem; according to Best (1990:13), "most well-established
social problems are owned by well-established claims-makers."

Drug abuse is a social problem that rises and falls in political priority.
When it is popular, sources realize the potential to obtain organizational or
individual benefits by defining themselves as authorities on the issue. Drugs
historically have been used to further law-and-order approaches to crime. In
the 1980s, politicians, including Presidents Reagan and Bush, paid an enormous amount of attention to drugs and defined the drug crisis in a particular
way (Beckett 1994, 1995; Brownstein 1995; Kappeler et al. 1996; Reinarman
and Levine 1995). Drugs have been framed as a criminal justice problem,
with the implication that a law enforcement solution is the most effective.

Police and court officials accounted for a disproportionate amount of the
information provided in incident and policy stories about drugs. The reports'
reliance on these sources for drug stories is consistent with their frequent
involvement in all types of crime story. In addition, politicians were involved
in the social construction of this problem: We found that political officials
increased their involvement in stories about drug crimes in general, in stories
that received a large amount of space, and in stories about the celebrated
arrest of Manuel Noriega.

The reliance on these news sources, coupled with the sources' understanding of standard media operating procedures, provided them with opportunities to determine how the drug issue would be framed for public
consumption. Kappeler et al. (1996:9) discuss how drug wars exemplify the
way crime myths are created, supported, and maintained. Drugs are an easy
political target and offer an opportunity for bureaucratic expansion. Thus the
crisis response that typically accompanies the heightened attention to the

issue can be easily predicted. Politicians pander to popular fear, frame the issue in the "most unyielding terms," and call for more law and more order—the safest political response (Kappeler et al. 1996:167). The message conveyed is the need for another war on drugs, with a crackdown on buyers and sellers regardless of the amount involved. Officials use dramatic examples, such as random acts of drug violence, to typify the problem and to establish consistency in the preferred response. Moreover, when a high-profile event occurs, officials can use it to reaffirm the accepted frames.

Alternative approaches such as drug treatment or drug education programs are much less likely to be presented and supported in the news, in the current political environment. Although a cadre of law enforcement officials, politicians, and economists have argued in support of drug legalization, this has not been presented as a viable alternative in the news media. Legalization was discussed in approximately 30 percent of the drug policy stories presented during the sample period. Legalization, however, was presented only in contrast to the preferred criminal justice response. The great majority of stories, including the celebrated events, were framed in language consistent with a need for law enforcement crackdowns, increased sentences, and zero tolerance.

The particularly important point about the ideological power of the news media is that these frames helped to support and reproduce elite interests. For example, the heightened attention resulted in policy initiatives. Public opinion about the seriousness of the problem peaked in 1990, at about the time when we conducted the content analysis. In 1985 a Gallup Poll survey showed that only 2 percent of respondents mentioned drug abuse as the single most important problem facing the country. In 1990, 38 percent of the respondents cited it as the leading problem (Gallup 1990). Such attention provides the opportunity to implement policy that addresses the problem in response to the way it was framed in the news media.

The sources involved in defining the drug crisis have made substantial financial and political gains. For example, the federal drug budget has quintupled since 1981 (Gardiner and McKinney 1991). According to a national report on drug statistics, the federal drug control budget was nearly 43 dollars per capita in 1991; in 1981 it had been less than 7 dollars. Over half of the available money ($28.24 per capita) was used for law enforcement; the rest was distributed between treatment ($6.91), prevention ($5.85), and research ($1.78) (U.S. Department of Justice 1992:128).

Moreover, treating drugs strictly as a problem of the criminal justice system, and advocating a response involving more arrests and longer sentences, had disproportionate effects on different social and racial groups. Amy Binder (1993:755) describes how the representation of events by the media is ideological—when officials in powerful institutional positions support frames that reinforce unequal social relations. According to research, drug wars have been designed to affect certain groups disproportionately (Currie 1993; Kappeler et al. 1996: Tonry 1995). Reinarman and Levine (1995:147), in examining crack cocaine, illustrate vividly how "drug scares typically link a scapegoated drug to a troubling subordinate group—working-class immigrants, racial, or ethnic minorities, or rebellious youth." They conclude: "Crack was a godsend to the Right. They used it and the drug issue as an ideological fig leaf to place over the unsightly urban ills that had increased markedly under Reagan administration social and economic policies" (p. 170).

Our latest drug war was fought primarily in the inner cities, drug use was associated with the lower classes, and drug policy affected black communities disproportionately (Currie 1993; Tonry 1995). Researchers argue that the policy makers who designed our approach to drugs knew it would affect various groups differently. According to Michael Tonry (1995:123), "the War on Drugs and the set of harsh crime-control policies in which it was enmeshed were launched to achieve political, not policy, objectives, and it is the adoption for political purposes of policies with foreseeable disparate impacts, the use of disadvantaged black Americans as a means to the achievement of politicians' electoral ends, that must in the end be justified, and cannot." Officials attempted to justify the policy response to drugs, and to generate support for their position, by being involved in the social construction of the drug problem.

We conclude that news sources involve themselves in the news production process to further their own social control agendas. In our integrated theory of news production, we assume that the two processes identified are closely linked, and that the negotiations between reporters and sources determine what is presented about social problems in the news. Media organizations rely on official sources to fulfill daily production objectives. These routine stories are irrelevant in terms of their impact on public opinion, and the established news production process ensures that they rarely harm news sources. When public interest is focused on a specific social problem or a celebrated case that can be linked to a policy issue, high-ranking officials use their access to the news production process to frame social problems and to *increase the likelihood* that public opinion will coincide with their own beliefs. Other social problems might present different sources with opportunities to gain support and legitimacy.

Future research should examine how sources use specific types of stories to promote issue frames, how the relationship between reporter and source evolves by type of story, and whether this relationship varies by type of organization. With such knowledge we could comprehend more clearly the involvement of sources in the news production process and the social control functions of the news media.

Notes

[1] Medium-sized cities are those with 100,000 to 400,000 inhabitants and 5,000 to 50,000 index offenses per year; large cities are those with 400,000 to 800,000 inhabitants and 50,000 to 90,000 index offenses; extra-large cities have 800,000 to 1,500,000 inhabitants and register 90,000 to 150,000 index offenses.

[2] Each of the news organizations considered here has an interest in attracting a local audience; therefore this is a study of local media organizations. One would expect that the national offi-

cials' predominance is underestimated because local news presents only wire reports that contain comments from these officials.

[3] Nearly 60% of the stories contained fewer than five cited sources. When a story included a large number of sources, we collected data on as many as nine sources cited: as many as three sources providing comment on the incident, three on the defendant, and three on the victim. In this article we discuss findings on source incidents. Only information that was attributed directly to a source was coded. If more than three sources provided information, we coded the first, third, and fifth sources. We chose the sources at the beginning of stories because we thought these sources represented those whom news organizations deemed the most important voices on a topic; we also wanted to capture as many of the voices cited in crime stories as possible.

[4] These results are consistent across each news organization in the sample. Police and court sources accounted for 57% of the attributions in the *Albany Times Herald*, 56.1% in the *Buffalo News*, 53.6% in the *Cleveland Plain Dealer*, 48.1% in the *San Francisco Chronicle*, 48.7% in the *Dallas Times Herald*, and 48.3% in the *Detroit News*.

[5] No specific amount of space is set aside for crime stories; events either increase or decrease the importance of crime. We argue that crime is an important news topic in general. The content results show that approximately 11% of all news stories were related to crime, the fourth most likely category to be presented. Production of these stories requires a substantial investment of organizational resources.

[6] Although Mayor Barry was a politician at the time of his arrest, we coded his source results in the defendant category because of his role as a defendant.

References

Beckett, K. 1994. "Setting the Public Agenda: 'Street Crime' and Drug Use in American Politics." *Social Problems* 41:425–47.

_____. 1995. "Media Depictions of Drug Abuse: The Impact of Official Sources." *Research in Political Sociology* 7:161–82.

Benedict, H. 1992. *Virgin or Vamp: How the Press Covers Sex Crimes.* New York: Oxford University Press.

Berkowitz, D. 1987. "TV News Sources and News Channels: A Study in Agenda-Building." *Journalism Quarterly* 64:508–13.

Berkowitz, D. and D. W. Beach. 1993. "News Sources and News Context: The Effect of Routine News, Conflict, and Proximity." *Journalism Quarterly* 70:4–12.

Best, J. 1990. *Threatened Children: Rhetoric and Concern about Child-Victims.* Chicago: University of Chicago Press.

Binder, A. 1993. "Constructing Racial Rhetoric: Media Depictions of Harm in Heavy Metal and Rap Music." *American Sociological Review* 58:753–67.

Brown, J. K., C. R. Bybee, S. T. Wearden, and D. M. Straughan. 1987. "Invisible Power: Newspaper News Sources and the Limits of Diversity." *Journalism Quarterly* 64(2):45–54.

Brownstein, H. 1995. "The Media and the Construction of Random Drug Violence." Pp. 45–65 in *Cultural Criminology,* edited by J. Ferrell and C. R. Sanders. Boston: Northeastern University Press.

Cavender, G., N. C. Jurik, and A. K. Cohen. 1993. "The Baffling Case of the Smoking Gun: The Social Ecology of Political Accounts in the Iran-Contra Affair." *Social Problems* 40:152–66.

Chermak, S. M. 1995. *Victims in the News: Crime and the American News Media.* Boulder: Westview.

Chibnall, S. 1977. *Law and Order News.* London: Tavistock.

Currie, E. 1993. *Reckoning: Drugs, the Cities, and the American Future.* New York: Hill and Wang.

Edelman, M. 1964. *The Symbolic Uses of Politics.* Urbana: University of Illinois Press.

Ericson, R. V., P. M. Baranek, and J. B. L. Chan. 1987. *Visualizing Deviance: A Study of News Organization.* Toronto: University of Toronto Press.

_____. 1989. *Negotiating Control: A Study of News Sources.* Toronto: University of Toronto Press.

_____. 1991. *Representing Order: Crime, Law, and Justice in the News Media.* Toronto: University of Toronto Press.

Fishman, M. 1978. "Crime Waves as Ideology." *Social Problems* 25:531–43.

_____. 1980. *Manufacturing the News.* Austin: University of Texas Press.

Friedman, L. M. and R. V. Percival. 1981. *The Roots of Justice: Crime and Punishment in Alameda County, California 1870–1910.* Chapel Hill: University of North Carolina Press.

Gale Directory of Publications and Broadcast Media. 1990. New York: Gale Research.

Gallup, G. G. 1990. *The Gallup Poll Monthly,* No. 298. Princeton, NJ: Gallup.

Gamson, W., D. Croteau, W. Hoynes, and T. Sasson. 1992. "Media Images and the Social Construction of Reality." *Annual Review of Sociology* 18:373–93.

Gans, H. J. 1979. *Deciding What's News: A Study of* CBS Evening News, Newsweek *and* Time. New York: Pantheon.

Gardiner, G. S. and R. N. McKinney. 1991. "The Great American War on Drugs: Another Failure of Tough-Guy Management." *Journal of Drug Issues* 21:605–16.

Gitlin, T. 1980. *The Whole World Is Watching: Mass Media in the Making & Unmaking of the New Left.* Los Angeles: University of California Press.

Graber, D. 1980. *Crime News and the Public.* New York: Praeger.

Hall, S., C. Critcher, T. Jefferson, and B. Roberts. 1978. *Policing the Crisis.* London: Macmillan.

Herbeck, D. 1990. "Drug Probe Nets 5 City Officers: U.S. Undercover Investigation Yields Charges of Cocaine Dealing." *Buffalo News,* February 15, p. Al.

Herman, E. and N. Chomsky. 1988. *Manufacturing Consent: The Political Economy of the Mass Media.* New York: Pantheon.

Jenness, V. 1993. *Making It Work: The Prostitutes' Movement in Perspective.* New York: Aldine.

Jensen, E. L., J. Gerber, and G. M. Babcock. 1991. "The New War on Drugs: Grass Roots Movement or Political Construction?" *Journal of Drug Issues* 21:651–67.

Jerin, R. A. and C. B. Fields. 1995. "Murder and Mayhem in *USA Today:* A Quantitative Analysis of the National Reporting of States' News." Pp. 187–202 in *Media, Process and the Social Construction of Crime: Studies of Newsmaking Criminology,* edited by G. Barak. New York: Garland.

Johnson, J. M. 1995. "Horror Stories and the Construction of Child Abuse." pp. 17–31 in *Images of Issues: Typifying Contemporary Social Problems,* edited by J. Best. New York: Aldine.

Kappeler, V. E., M. Blumberg, and G. W. Potter. 1996. *The Mythology of Crime and Criminal Justice.* 2nd ed. Prospect Heights, IL: Waveland.

Kessel, J. H. 1975. *The Domestic Presidency: Decision-Making in the White House.* North Scituate, MA: Duxbury.

Kraska, P. B. 1993. "Militarizing the Drug War: A Sign of the Times." Pp. 159–206 in *Altered States of Mind: Critical Observations of the Drug War,* edited by P. B. Kraska. New York: Garland.

_____. 1994. "The Police and Military in the Post-Cold War Era: Streamlining the State's Use of Force Entities in the Drug War." *Police Forum* 4(l):1–8.

McCombs, M. E. and D. L. Shaw. 1991. "The Agenda Setting Function of Mass Media." Pp. 17–26 in *Agenda Setting: Readings on Media, Public Opinion, and Policy Making,* edited by D. L. Protess and M. McCombs. Hillsdale, NJ: Erlbaum.

Peyrot, M. 1984. "Cycles of Social Problem Development: The Case of Drug Abuse." *Sociological Quarterly* 25:83–96.

Reese, S. D., Grant, A., and Danielian. L. H. 1994. "The Structure of News Sources on Television. A Network Analysis of CBS News," "Nightline," "Mac-Neil-Lehrer," and "This Week with David Brinkley." *Journal of Communication,* 44(2):84–107.

Reinarman, C. and H. G. Levine. 1995. "The Crack Attack: America's Latest Drug Scare, 1986–1992." Pp. 147–90 in *Images of Issues: Typifying Contemporary Social Problems,* edited by J. Best. New York: Aldine.

Rosenthal, A. 1990. "Noriega Gives Himself Up to U.S. Military: Is Flown to Florida to Face Drug Charges." *New York Times,* January 4, p. Al.

Sacco, V. F. 1995. "Media Constructions of Crime." *The Annals of the American Academy of Political and Social Science,* 539:141–54.

Scheingold, S. A. 1984. *The Politics of Law and Order: Street Crime and Public Policy.* New York: Longman.

Schlesinger, P. and H. Tumber. 1994. *Reporting Crime: The Media Politics of Criminal Justice.* Oxford: Clarendon.

Sherizen, S. 1978. "Social Creation of Crime News: All the News Fitted to Print." Pp. 203–24 in *Deviance and Mass Media,* edited by C. Winick. Beverly Hills: Sage.

Sigal, L. V. 1973. *Reporters and Officials.* Lexington, MA: Heath.

Skogan, W. G. and M. G. Maxfield. 1981. *Coping with Crime: Individual and Neighborhood Reactions.* Beverly Hills: Sage.

Surette, R. 1989. "Media Trials." *Journal of Criminal Justice* 17:293–308.

Television and Cable Factbook. 1991. Washington, DC: Warren.

Tittle, C. R. 1994. "The Theoretical Bases for Inequality in Formal Social Control." Pp. 21–52 in *Inequality, Crime, & Social Control,* edited by G. Bridges and M. Myers. Boulder: Westview.

Tonry, M. 1995. *Malign Neglect: Race, Crime, and Punishment in America.* New York: Oxford University Press.

Tuchman, G. 1978. *Making News: A Study in the Construction of Reality.* New York: Free Press.

Tunnell, K. D. 1992. "Film at Eleven: Recent Developments in the Commodification of Crime." *Sociological Spectrum* 12:293–313.

"U.S. Cites Progress in Latin American Drug War." 19'90. Reuters Wire Service, March 6.

U.S. Department of Justice. 1992. *Drugs, Crime, and the Justice System: A National Report from the Bureau of Justice Statistics.* Washington, DC: U.S. Government Printing Office.

Walker, S. 1989. *Sense and Nonsense about Crime: A Policy Guide.* 2nd ed. Pacific Grove, CA: Brooks/Cole.

EIGHT

THE SOCIAL CONSTRUCTION OF AN ALCOHOL PROBLEM

THE CASE OF MOTHERS AGAINST DRUNK DRIVERS AND SOCIAL CONTROL IN THE 1980S

Craig Reinarman

Social problems have careers that ebb and flow independent of the "objective" incidence of the behaviors thought to constitute them. This is nowhere more amply illustrated than in the history of alcohol issues. I offer here a description of the rise and impact of Mothers Against Drunk Driving—the latest in a long line of social movements that have contended over the definition of alcohol problems—and an interpretation of why this movement managed to make drinking-driving into a major public problem in the conservative ethos of the 1980s.

The anti-drunk driving movement did not spring from any rise in the incidence or prevalence of drinking-driving or in accidents thought to be related to it. In fact, the rate of road accidents in the United States remains lower than in most other Western industrial democracies. It is widely believed that people who drink and drive end up in accidents in which there is tragic and costly loss of life, limb, and property.[1] However, none of the organizations or leaders of the movement against drinking-driving have even suggested that their efforts were prompted by some sudden rash of drinking-driving accidents. On the contrary, all claim that their work arose from the fact that the injustices attributed to drinking-driving have long been a problem and have never been treated seriously by legislatures and courts. Indeed, in the late 1960s and early 1970s, the federal government promoted and funded a variety of drinking-driving countermeasures, and arrests did rise in several states. However, despite a steady stream of accidents and the

Source: *Theory and Society,* 1988, vol. 17, pp. 91–120, © 1988 Kluwer Academic Publishers. Reprinted with kind permission from Springer Science and Business Media.

best efforts of both local civic groups across the country and the National Highway Traffic Safety Administration (NHTSA), it was not until 1981 that a *movement* against drunk driving arose and succeeded in putting the issue in the public policy spotlight.[2]

Thus, the thematic questions addressed in this article: If the carnage along U.S. highways thought to be causally related to drinking-driving has long been part of our culture—and always an unacceptable one—while a national movement against this has never before existed, why all this fuss *now*? How was a problem long held to be merely an unfortunate fact of modern life—or, in Joseph Gusfield's phrase, a "folk crime" (an offense routinely committed by many a "good citizen")—reconstituted into a focal point of public outrage? And why should this occur in the early 1980s?

By making this sort of question central, I am placing my analysis of MADD squarely within the social constructionist tradition in the study of social problems. This tradition has focused on the claims-making activities and structuring practices that, whether or not "objective" human suffering exists or is rising, constitute the *sine qua non* of a social problem.[3] Such an analytic stance draws attention to the role of interest groups and social movements that contend for ownership of a problem and the power to define and give public prominence to it.

The MADD case raises the issue of the *viability* of claims made by social movement organizations about putative conditions being problems.[4] I suggest that the viability of a claim that a problem exists depends upon the *interaction* of at least two factors—the credibility of the claims-makers and the historical context in which such claims become utterable and resonate with the dominant discourse. In the case of MADD, the credibility of those who have lost children to drunk drivers has, quite rightly in my view, never been questioned. But the fact that thousands of such victims and their family members have been heretofore mute is intriguing. After describing the rise and impact of MADD, I shall argue that its foci and tactics succeeded when they did largely (although not merely) because they were in harmony with the morality, policy ideologies, and social-control strategies of the Reagan administration and a renascent right. First, however, it is useful to review briefly the history of earlier constructions of alcohol problems.

The modern understanding of alcohol as a dangerous and problematic substance was first articulated at the end of the eighteenth and the beginning of the nineteenth century in the United States. In the colonial era alcohol consumption was virtually universal and drunkenness common practice. Even the Puritans deemed alcohol "the Good Creature of God." The radical shift in problem definition and public discourse by which the "liquor problem" was constituted began with the writings of Dr. Benjamin Rush. Over the first three decades of the nineteenth century, Rush and a variety of other medical, religious, and business leaders established the anti-alcohol or "temperance" movement and redefined alcohol from the Good Creature to a destructive, demonic, and addictive substance. Temperance authorities scapegoated alcoholic beverages, blaming drink for most of the ills in American society at the dawn of industrialization—poverty, business failure, broken homes, madness, immorality, and crime. The emerging temperance ideology held that alcohol was *inherently* addicting, and that it weakened the moral and mental as well as the physical constitution of drinkers. By the 1830s, such a view spread downward from elites to the middle classes, and later to women in particular, who saw solutions to the alcohol problem as central to a broader moral reformation. As would be the case with MADD a century later, temperance groups frequently held that "mothers and children" were "the innocent victims" of alcohol.[5]

In the twentieth century a new wave of prohibitionist agitation developed in response to new economic and political conditions, although it continued to scapegoat alcoholic beverages for most social ills and to hold out abstention as the only hope. Prohibitionists took on the liquor industry and the saloon in an attempt to use the power of state to eliminate alcohol completely and thus help impose a new order on an increasingly conflict-ridden society. Levine captures this well:

> In the 19th century, the American middle class thought itself hegemonic; temperance was aimed at bringing the lower classes and outsiders into the middle class society and culture. In the 20th century, however, the middle class of small businessmen and entrepreneurs felt increasingly overwhelmed and displaced by the growing corporate, industrial society. Enormous corporations called "trusts" seemed more and more to control America. Further, the undeniable presence of a permanent industrial working class was shattering the dream of America as the land where everyone could achieve middle class success. . . . The old middle class of small businessmen, and the new middle class of professionals and technical experts, as well as representatives of the corporations, all shared the concern with finding new ways of maintaining social, political, and economic order. The growth of middle class support for legislative and Constitutional prohibition should be understood, paradoxically, both as attacks on the symbols of corporate capitalist society, and also as part of a larger . . . "search for order". . . .
>
> To the old 19th century fear of the barroom as the breeding ground of immorality and personal ruin, was added the almost total identification of it as alien and subversive; the saloon was unmiddle class and unAmerican. Saloons were now not only immoral, they were also political evils, where unions were organized, where urban political machines purchased votes, and where anarchists and communists found recruits. The obliteration of the saloon, it was argued, was a precondition for the management of America in the 20th century.[6]

For both material and ideological reasons, the captains of industry had by 1915 thrown their decisive weight behind Prohibition. Business leaders held that in addition to a more productive labor force, prohibition would reduce industrial accidents and workers' compensation costs. Also, because workers would be unable to spend their wages on whiskey, their disposable income would rise such that there would be fewer wage demands, unions, and strikes. Moreover, without alcohol there would be less poverty, disease, madness, and crime, and therefore less need for taxes to support institutions and services. Perhaps as important to a corporate elite then under fire for their avarice was the legitimation to be gained by expressing concern about the nation's social problems—particularly when booze rather than business was construed as culprit. As historian Andrew Sinclair put it, "prohibition became a sort of moral mask for big business."[7] As I will suggest later, this kind of link to business, at least to the alcohol industry, is also critical in understanding MADD.

Little more than a decade would pass before the onset of the Depression, when much of the corporate elite made an about face and began to push for Repeal. As Levine shows, leading figures among the corporate rich wanted taxes on alcohol restored in order to reduce both business and personal tax burdens. Further, many of them began to fear that widespread violations of Prohibition were delegitimating other forms of law as well, including property law. Ironically, many of the same economic arguments used in support of Prohibition were later invoked to justify its repeal. Former Prohibitionist John D. Rockefeller, Jr. was only the most prominent of corporate leaders to argue that a legalized, healthy liquor industry would mean a desperately needed increase in employment and tax revenues that could help pull the nation out of the Depression.[8] In a scant dozen years, spirits were transformed from the source to the solution of economic woes, from panapathogen to panacea.

At the height of the Great Depression, Repeal set the stage for the redefinition of alcohol problems with which we are most familiar, the alcoholism-as-addictive-disease paradigm. This model of alcohol problems was invented (some might say reinvented, as it borrows heavily from temperance ideology) by the founders of Alcoholics Anonymous (AA) in 1935. It had been clear to most Americans since the end of the nineteenth century that the case for alcohol being inherently addicting was weak. Most drinkers, after all, never became drunks, and the notion that chronic drunkenness was at least in part due to individual character was always part of popular understanding. Yet, throughout the conflict over Prohibition the "alcohol problem" had been seen as just that—a problem having to do with the substance itself. AA set in motion a process that soon succeeded in radically transforming the definition of the problem. In the broadest sense, the alcohol problem was, in Gusfield's phrase, reprivatized—the evil shifted from the bottle to the person. AA maintained that people who drank compulsively had a disease, like an allergy to alcohol. This shift did not signify a complete break with temperance thought; the disease still was said to be progressive, its defining symptom a "loss of control" over drinking, its cure abstinence. However, AA and the emerging alcoholism movement established a new discourse about alcohol problems: the individual drinker became the locus of "the alcohol problem," and, equally significant, the range of public problems held to be alcohol-related shrank in proportion to the growing influence of the disease model.[9]

AA and the alcoholism movement rapidly gained important adherents who helped establish the disease concept as the dominant paradigm in both social policy and public discourse. By the close of World War II, Yale had established a Center on Alcohol and a Summer School in Alcohol Studies. The scientists associated with these institutions spread a new, medical rather than moral conception of alcohol problems. With their focus on the plight of the individual alcoholic, they steered an ideological course around all of the public, i.e., social and political, dimensions of alcohol that were so central to and problematic for the earlier temperance and Prohibition movements. Indeed, they held that only by dropping alcohol's political baggage could they overcome the moral obstacles to "scientific" *treatment* for problem drinkers. At the close of World War II, the activist core of the alcoholism movement also established what is now called the National Council on Alcoholism with the express purpose of spreading their new conception of alcoholism.[10] Throughout the post-war period and up to the present, the alcoholism movement has succeeded in maintaining the disease model as the dominant frame through which alcohol problems are viewed in American culture and policy circles alike. As the welfare state grew, this model became ensconced in public agencies at all levels of government, focusing funding, scholarship, and public attention on the disease of alcoholism rather than a range of alcohol problems. In contrast to the morality plays of earlier epochs, on this new "scientific" stage few villains were visible—only victims of a disease in need of treatment.

There are now two generations in the United States who have no personal memory of the "failed" (Herbert Hoover called it "noble in intention") experiment that was Prohibition. They have grown up in a culture in which both drinking and the discourse of disease are taken for granted. If mass-circulation periodicals are any guide, however, there has been more interest in alcohol problems in the past five years than at any time in the past fifty. In its New Year's Eve edition of 1984, *Newsweek*'s cover story, "Alcohol on the Rocks," cited "the new prohibitionists" and "the country's new Temperance movement" as having arisen from the anti-drunk-driving movement. Although a shift toward drinking lighter-alcohol beverages had begun in the late 1970s as the baby boom generation became more health conscious, and despite the fact that the scholarly literature in alcohol studies had begun to focus on a range of drinking problems at about the same time, the anti-drinking-driving movement became the centerpiece of the media's attention to the so-called new temperance.

Following *Newsweek*, *Business Week* (2/25/85) offered a similar cover story called "The Sobering of America," and, not to be outdone, *Fortune* contributed to this emerging news theme by following with "America's New Abstinence" (3/18/85). In April 1985, *Newsweek*'s "On Campus" edition featured "A New Prohibition" as its lead, and told of "a new era of campus prohibition" springing "from the nationwide crusade against drunken driving." The next month, *Time*'s cover, "Cocktails 1985: America's New Drinking

Habits" (5/20/85), referred repeatedly to "the new temperance" in the same terms.[11] These were only the most prominent of hundreds of news articles on alcohol issues, most centering on the movement against drunk driving, particularly the largest, most prominent and powerful organization in that movement, Mothers Against Drunk Driving (MADD).

A Brief History of MADD

In May of 1980, 13-year-old Cari Lightner was walking along a bicycle path in the central valley town of Fair Oaks, California, a suburb of Sacramento. She was struck and killed by a hit-and-run driver who was later found to have been intoxicated. He was, moreover, both on probation for previous Driving Under the Influence (DUI) convictions and out on bail for another hit-and-run DUI offense a few days before hitting Lightner. In discovering these facts and following the defendant through the criminal justice process, Cari's mother, Candy Lightner, a part-time real estate agent, grew increasingly outraged at what she perceived as the extraordinary leniency with which DUI offenses were routinely handled. She began channelling her grief and anger into efforts to get tougher DUI laws passed by the California legislature.[12]

Most of her initial inquiries were met with indifference by policy makers who tended not to define DUI as a politically "hot" issue. Ms. Lightner has often remarked publicly that prior to her daughter's death she had been apolitical—neither registered to vote nor able to distinguish Democrat from Republican. After being shocked by the legal leniency with which her daughter's killer was treated and repeatedly rebuffed by representatives, her eyes were opened to ways political. With the aid of a few sympathetic legislators, she was given a crash course in lobbying. She began holding dramatic press conferences, giving tearful and angry testimony before legislative committees, and organizing what was to become Mothers Against Drunk Driving.

MADD was incorporated as a non-profit organization in August 1980. Lightner worked tirelessly, full-time on building the organization, and invested her daughter's insurance settlement and her own savings to get it off the ground. She enlisted the help of the executive director of the District Attorneys Association, a few legislative aides who were interested in the issue and skilled at political work, and a few friends and dedicated volunteers. The fledgling group pushed then-Governor Jerry Brown to set up a state task force on drunk driving. Like most legislators, he hesitated initially on the grounds that there was not sufficient citizen interest, and assumed that people tended to feel "There but for the grace of God go I." The governor soon sensed, however, that potential support existed (and little if any opposition), so he set up a task force and appointed Lightner to it.

A MADD board of directors was formed from the nucleus of early activists, and they got a small grant from the American Council on Alcohol Problems for a brochure. Next the board wrote a grant proposal and received $65,000 from the National Highway Traffic Safety Administration to organize more MADD chapters. This was quickly followed by an unstipulated $100,000 grant from the Levy Foundation, a principal benefactor of which was an insurance company heir who also had lost a daughter to a drinking driver. By 1982 MADD had begun to employ a direct-mail solicitation firm with experience in mailings to Christian constituencies. With growing media coverage and the power of computerized, direct-mail solicitations, "the money just literally started pouring in," according to an original board member.

From the beginning MADD billed itself as "The Voice of the Victim," a victim's rights organization concerned with advocating for and counseling bereaved relatives, preparing them for a trying adjudication process in which "the rights are with the defendant," and ostentatiously monitoring courtrooms in the hope of insuring more convictions and stiffer sentencing of drinking-drivers.[13] Although the victim remained the focus at local chapters, the strategy of the national organization grew increasingly media oriented. Lightner's preoccupation quickly became the maximization of media attention to what she called the "dirty little secret" of drinking-driving: that 250,000 American lives had been lost in "alcohol-related auto crashes" in the past decade, "70 Americans a day, one every 23 minutes"; that drunk driving was "the leading cause of death for 16–24 year olds," 360 of whom are injured in drunk-driving accidents daily; that a million crippling or serious injuries occur in the United States annually due to drinking drivers; that all this costs more than $5 billion per year; that on an average weekend night one of ten drivers on the road is intoxicated; and, importantly, that of every 2,000 drinking drivers on the road, only one will get arrested, and the chances of even that one getting any "serious" penalty are "mathematically insignificant."[14] Unlike some other groups such as the Center for Science in the Public Interest, whose strategy was to work against the alcohol industry's massive promotion of drinking in general, MADD focused exclusively on the sins of the drinking driver.

In the past, without a visible moral entrepreneur to give a human voice to these figures, drinking-driving tended to be treated matter-of-factly as episodic, unconnected accidents. But with the rise of MADD, the media seemed willing to oblige in recounting such compelling statistics from a dramatic spokesperson such as Lightner. She appeared in front of all manner of legislative committees, on all national and dozens of local television talk shows, and was written about in literally thousands of newspaper and magazine articles. Virtually all this coverage was explicitly supportive, although one media observer offered a more critical interpretation of why, now, the media found this old issue so appealing:

> Television began this groundswell by giving airtime to MADD's painful [Congressional] Hill testimony. . . . It did so not merely because of its perceived importance—important but complex and boring testimony is given all the time without a dream of TV coverage—but because it was emotional, sentimental. No sane news director will pass up a grieving, sobbing mother; it is the basic image of tragedy on which TV thrives. . . .

> It was the beginning of an orgy of attention. In their search for safe issues on which to take a 10-second position, TV editorial directors pounced on drunk driving as if it were an end-zone fumble. They called repeatedly, almost weekly for "stiffer penalties." . . . It was a heaven-sent: instantly graspable and without opposition. . . . At the same time, the National Association of Broadcasters organized a massive public service campaign on the problem. . . . Broadcasters aren't stupid; the motivation behind all this attention was forestalling any efforts to ban [alcohol beverage] ads.[15]

The efforts of Lightner and the national MADD led to explosive growth of the organization. Only a year after it began, the organization had generated income of nearly a half-million dollars and sprouted eleven new chapters in four states. A year later, in 1982, seventy chapters were in operation. By 1985 MADD had over 600,000 members and donors, 360 chapters in all fifty states, and a budget approaching $10 million administered by a full-time professional staff of at least twenty.[16] Throughout 1985, not a week would go by without a MADD story in most major newspapers and magazines.

The media-based organizing strategy of MADD and the media's fascination with Lightner and her organization led to a symbiosis that put floodlights on the issue. Newspaper coverage of drinking and driving grew from a handful of articles in 1978 and 1979 to several hundred articles in both 1983 and 1984. In a 1984 national poll, MADD got 85 percent name recognition—double the percentage of people who could name their congressional representative. A *Washington Post* columnist could claim, without fear of contradiction, that "1984 was the year of the Anti-drunk-driving Campaign," while *Time*'s "Man of the Year" edition cited MADD President Lightner as one of "Seven Who Succeeded" because "MADD is getting just about all the laws it wants." Under the magnifying glass of the media, MADD had effectively made drinking-driving into a "hot" issue.[17]

Perhaps the most substantive impact of the movement was on law and public policy. Under pressure from MADD, Reagan appointed a Presidential Commission on drunk driving (and, like Gov. Brown, appointed Lightner). It recommended legislation to force states to raise the minimum drinking age to 21. A bill to this effect was originally proposed by congressional Democrats in early 1985. But despite a strong endorsement for the anti-drunk driving movement in the 1984 Republican Presidential Platform and his own Commission's recommendation, Reagan opposed the age 21 measure until three weeks before signing it. The *New York Times* noted that "almost everyone involved was stunned by the swift, overwhelming Congressional approval" (81 to 16 in the Senate), and that "the statistics were alarming but had theretofore failed to provoke action." According to this and many other accounts, MADD's dramatic testimony in favor of the bill—echoed by other important groups like the American Medical Association, the Parent Teachers Association, the National Council on Alcoholism, insurance industry lobbies, and the National Safety Council—led Reagan's advisors to argue that drinking-driving had been made into a "sleeping giant" of an "apple pie issue" that he could not afford to oppose. Some conservatives still threatened to block the bill on the grounds that it was yet another mode of "social engineering" and an "unwarranted federal intervention into states' rights," but the President began to sense a natural conservative issue and changed direction. The *Times* gave this account of his reversal: "At first President Reagan criticized the legislation . . . as just another instance of Washington wanting to meddle in the states' affairs. But by last week he sounded like a life-long advocate. . . . Looking on were representatives of such groups as MADD, which had lobbied for the legislation for years." In what can be seen as a well-crafted piece of ideological work, the President turned to smile at Candy Lightner, pen in hand, and announced to the assembled press, "The [drunk driving] problem is bigger than the states . . . [so] we have no misgivings about this judicious use of federal power."[18]

Less noticed but equally striking was the passage of more than 230 new anti-drunk driving laws at the local level. In virtually every state and city, MADD was acknowledged as the leading force behind the new statutes. All fifty states toughened their laws against drinking and driving between 1981 and 1985, and the number of states requiring mandatory jail sentences for first offenders convicted of DUI doubled in the same period. Other states sharply raised fines, began to suspend licenses, curtailed judicial discretion with minimum sentence requirements, or enacted "per se" standards that make driving with certain blood-alcohol content (BAC) levels criminal offenses in and of themselves. More broadly, under the momentum of the MADD movement, an additional one hundred alcohol control statutes were passed between 1981 and 1984, including server liability laws and bans on happy hours.[19]

The Context of Success

Both social movement theory[20] and the social constructionist approach to social problems suggest that the existence of compelling troubles or substantial human suffering may be necessary but not sufficient conditions for the emergency of a successful movement for public action. The history of alcohol problems in general and the long latency of the drinking-driving problem in particular suggest the need for an analysis of the special resonance of MADD in the early 1980s. I will argue in what follows that the remarkable rise of MADD must be understood as a product of the interaction between the strategic focus of claims by this moral-entrepreneurial movement and a historical context marked by a peculiar conjuncture of trends favorable to those claims in both the alcohol arena and the larger political culture.

In the late 1970s health consciousness spread across America. Whether this fitness fetish derives from the greater need to exercise in a service economy that reduces the need for physical exertion while increasing tension, from some deeper narcissism, or from the mere demographic ascendancy of the 1960s generation who popularized health foods, few would deny that hordes of runners are visible everywhere and that the health spa and aerobics industries have enjoyed meteoric growth. Bound up with such developments are changes in what we eat and drink: less red meat and more fish and poultry, fewer spirits and more white wine and "lite" beer. It is also worth noting that this health craze seemed particularly marked among the middle and upper-middle class (it is often referred to as a "yuppie" phenomenon) and that these groups are most likely to vote and otherwise participate in political life. Insofar as this makes them the sort of people about whom legislators (and advertisers) worry, trends in their values and behaviors can be seen as influential.

The alcohol industry has adjusted adroitly to such trends by stepping up its marketing of low-alcohol beverages. Yet, distillers, brewers, and vintners perceived more ominous possibilities in all this that were not so amenable to shifts in product lines and advertising strategies. In addition to declining per capita consumption of alcohol and all the media attention to "the new temperance" and "neo-Prohibitionism," the fiscal crisis and growing budget deficits led many legislators to call for increased taxes on alcohol. This strategy is often advocated by many public health specialists as a means of both reducing alcohol abuse and raising revenues needed to pay for alcohol treatment. Still more threatening to the industry, the Center for Science in the Public Interest (CSPI) launched a national campaign to ban all alcohol advertising in the electronic media (Stop Marketing Alcohol on Radio and Television, or SMART), which had gained endorsements and momentum by 1985. In the context of such developments the alcohol industry began to see the movement against drinking and driving as the lesser of evils.

While other anti-drunk-driving organizations refused industry support, MADD accepted a variety of financial contributions from alcohol interests. Anheuser-Busch and Miller Brewing, for example, both contributed money to the national anti-drunk driving movement. One of MADD's original board members proposed that, as a matter of principle, they refuse to accept money from the alcohol industry. He was out-voted on the basis of Lightner's argument that it is not alcohol itself that causes death and injury but rather irresponsible users and abusers of alcohol. She remained steadfast in her opposition to the idea that widespread promotion of alcohol consumption was in any way related to drinking-driving. Moreover, after Lightner purged the original board of all her adversaries, she appointed to it representatives of the alcohol and broadcasting industries. Unlike many of the lesser known anti-drunk-driving organizations, MADD has not advocated increases in alcohol taxes as a means of reducing consumption or financing prevention and treatment, and it sent a memo to its local chapters stating the official MADD policy against participation in the SMART petition drive. In a position paper, national MADD took the position of taking no position on the debate over regulation of alcohol advertising, save that of urging the industry to "police itself." Further, MADD supported the alcohol and broadcasting industries in their attempt to stave off demands that networks broadcast "counter-messages" to alcohol commercials.[21]

In a context marked by "neo-temperance" sentiments, declining alcohol consumption, and increasing pressure for higher alcohol taxes and tighter controls over alcohol advertising, the advantages of MADD's narrow focus on the drunk driver—on the individual deviant—was not lost on alcohol producers. Indeed, both the alcohol and broadcasting industries "courted" MADD. As the *Wall Street Journal* put it, "In an effort to blunt criticisms of its products and restrict the debate to alcohol *abuse*, the industry has lent its financial support to those combatting drunk-driving." This way, the "new prohibitionism" would not, as one alcohol industry executive put it, "dismember" the beverage alcohol business "one bite at a time."[22] In fairness it must be said that the alcohol industry was never the main source of funding for MADD; nor can it be proven that industry contributions softened MADD's stance. What can be noted, however, is the *affinity* between MADD's strategy of rhetorically locating the source of the problem in individual-level deviant behavior and the alcohol industry's strategies for deflecting attention away from the full range of problems related to consumption of their products in general. One consequence of this affinity was that a potentially powerful form of corporate opposition to MADD was not only neutralized but turned to the organization's financial and ideological advantage.

Other developments on the government side of the alcohol arena also made for fertile soil for the growth of MADD. Although the disease paradigm had been part of state and local government alcohol programs for most of the post-war period, the alcoholism movement first established a national institutional beachhead in the welfare state in the early 1970s—the National Institute of Alcohol Abuse and Alcoholism (NIAAA). By the late 1970s a growing network of state and local alcohol agencies, treatment programs, research centers, and alcohol professionals was funded by NIAAA. They constituted an active, institutionalized constituency, which arguably had created cultural space for and was ready to echo the cry of an anti-drunk-driving movement.[23] More specifically, this network of institutions was by 1980 edging away from the intellectual hegemony of the disease concept toward a "disaggregative" approach to alcohol problems. In this framework a *range* of alcohol-related problems is held to exist, rather than one in which all such problems are conceived as either so many manifestations of an underlying "disease" entity called alcoholism or as the less important, poorer relatives of the disease.

Robin Room's historical analysis of the disease concept notes that "In the last few years, . . . an 'alcohol problems' approach has gained considerable ground in alcohol policy statements [which entails] the abandonment of the assumption of entitivity" underlying the alcoholism-as-disease-entity paradigm. This shift may be seen, for example, in recent policy statements contained in a 1979 report to Congress ("Alcohol problems in the general population do not seem to form a coherent pattern. The problems are too diffuse to be described as part of a single concept of alcohol addiction . . ."). A 1980 World Health Organization Expert Committee Report said much the same thing ("Until recently, there has been a widespread tendency to conceptualize the whole gamut of alcohol problems as manifestations of an underlying entity, alcoholism. . . . Alcohol dependence constitutes only a small part of the total of alcohol-related problems.")[24]

Bound up with these developments is the emergency of a "public health" perspective on alcohol that takes a *preventative* approach to alcohol-related problems.[25] Examples of this include the recent increases in federal funding for prevention education, the sponsorship of national prevention research centers, and the SMART campaign against deceptive alcohol advertising in electronic media. In a related development, the private National Council on Alcoholism experienced an internal rift over what many staff felt was an alcohol industry-induced, excessively narrow focus on the disease and its treatment at the expense of other alcohol problems and solutions. In the end, NCA moved to limit industry involvement on its board and to broaden its perspective toward a general public health view. Such arguable liberal, at least partly progressive developments in the scientific and public policy sides of the alcohol arena seem to have given intellectual elbow room to those calling attention to non-disease alcohol problems such as drinking-driving.

The second set of historical developments that has aided the rise of MADD concerns changes in the broader political arena. Here I shall refer to the political culture of Reaganism and suggest that MADD's claims were ideologically harmonious with the policy rhetoric of the Right. Like the Temperance and Prohibition movements of the nineteenth and early twentieth centuries, neither MADD nor the anti-drunk-driving movement in general are politically monolithic or ideologically homogeneous.[26] It is possible, however, to glimpse MADD's underlying conservatism by contrasting its politics with those of the "Stop Marketing Alcohol on Radio and Television" campaign (SMART). The origins of SMART lie in the consumer movement for *corporate* accountability and responsibility. SMART leaders speak of the "total social costs" of alcohol production and consumption; they explicitly confront corporate power and influence; they propose solutions aimed at the *structural* sources of alcohol-related problems.[27] Their rhetoric evokes notions of *collective* responsibility and social justice, and implies regulatory-state solutions when corporations and industries resist or ignore moral appeals for the public good.

MADD's origins, on the other hand, lie in victims' rights movements, which seek retribution from criminals. MADD's Lightner chose an organization name that ends with "drunk drivers" rather than "driving" and yields an acronym symbolizing moral anger; MADD members repeatedly rail against the "Killer Drunk"; they complain of the neglect of drinking-driving as "America's most frequently committed violent crime," the "only socially acceptable form of homicide."[28] MADD's organizing strategy is explicitly one of personal vilification, and it assiduously avoids attention to corporate interests and structural sources of alcohol problems in favor of a rhetoric of *individual* responsibility, the private moral *choice* of drinkers, and solutions based upon *self*-regulation by both drinkers and the alcohol, advertising, and broadcast industries.[29]

From the MADD perspective, then, the *aperture of attribution* for all the suffering and social costs that they claim are caused by drinking-driving is constricted; only the lone deviant comes into focus. Such constriction, I submit, largely explains industry support for the movement. It tacitly legitimatizes the continued production, promotion, and consumption of alcohol products that are vulnerable to the more structural critique of SMART and other groups. Some forty years ago in the pages of *American Sociological Review*, Alfred McClung Lee offered an analysis of the politics of Prohibition that parallels this point:

> Large contributors to political movements and campaigns found that the Drys offered a more attractive issue than did those who stressed issues more fundamental to the control of our economic and political institutions. The "era of the muckrakers" of about 1901 to 1912 . . . struck many business leaders in particular as having an unsettling tendency. The Prohibitionists merely attacked Booze, the Saloon, the Whisky Trust, and the Brewers, but Lincoln Steffens, Ray Stannard Baker, Upton Sinclair, and others went after the political bosses, the public utilities, patent medicines, advertising, and even capitalism itself. Let the reformers have Booze and the Saloon. Let that keep them busy![30]

MADD's self-image as "the voice of the victim" also lends itself to a narrow and conservative focus. The organization has drawn upon the victims' rights groups that were first given national recognition in the law-and-order campaign of the Nixon administration. Both victims' rights groups and MADD bemoan the injustices victims suffer at the hands of defendants whom they see as overly protected by Miranda rights and other impediments to retribution, which are also anathema to the Reagan/Meese Justice Department. Both MADD and its law-and-order, victims' rights predecessors call for less judicial discretion and an end to plea-bargaining so as to ensure longer sentences. Newspaper accounts of MADD often cite, for example, the "national punishment mentality" in the "very punitive era" of the 1980s as a factor in the organization's rise.[31]

Each of these major facets of MADD's orientation—its individualist focus, its systematic inattention to structural/corporate sources of problems, and its narrow retributive prescriptions—is in ideological harmony with and gains legitimacy from the policies and the rhetoric of Reagan and the New Right. There is also some preliminary evidence on the social base of the movement that supports such an interpretation. Although a substantial number of MADD activists (e.g., chapter officers) are either victims of drinking-driving accidents or members of families with victims, the rate of MADD chapter formation across states and regions of the United States is strongly correlated with standard survey measures of politico-religious conservatism. Moreover, the National Association of Evangelicals pushed for stiffer punishments for drinking-driving and was instrumental in getting a plank to that effect put into the 1984 Republican Presidential Campaign Platform. New Right fundraisers also have targeted people who strongly oppose drinking-driving as people who look to them for leadership.[32]

Of course, neither the shifts in the alcohol arena nor those in political culture can be construed as *causal* in any rigorous, theoretical sense. However, they do suggest that a thorough, textured account of the rise of MADD cannot rest upon the mere existence of drinking-driving accidents and an effective social-movement organization; the former has long existed and it is the effectiveness of the latter that needs to be explained. Rather, this form of anti-drunk-driving movement took off when it did in large part because of its *elective affinity* with a political context dominated by Reaganism and the Right, and also, ironically, with a subtle shift toward what I would construe as more liberal, public health perspectives in the alcohol arena.

Weber's concept of elective affinity seems especially valuable here. His most well-known use of it was to conceptualize the relation between Calvinism and other Puritan sects and the spread of capitalist social organization and accumulation. Weber argued that although the "spirit of capitalism" and the accumulation of "worldly goods" flowed quite naturally from Puritan religious principles designed to ensure the "salvation of the soul," the material results that stemmed from such "purely religious motives" were "unforeseen and even unwished-for." He explicitly rejected both the idea that the Reformation could be deduced "as a necessary historical result" of the rise of capitalism, as well as the converse notion "that the spirit of capitalism [. . .] could only have arisen as the result of certain effects of the Reformation." What he attempted to demonstrate instead were the ways in which the Puritan ethic had *taken part* in the qualitative formation and the quantitative expansion of the spirit of capitalism.[33] Whatever subsequent scholars have made of the specifics of Weber's case, the theoretical and conceptual utility of "elective affinity" has endured. I believe it most closely captures the more or less fortuitous, mutually-informing relation between MADD and elements of the new conservative era in which it grew.

Clearly most people stand firmly against the loss of life, limb, and property at the hands of drivers who have been drinking. But MADD's claims draw much of their support from and resonate strongly among the core constituencies of renascent conservatism. Thus, I would argue that the rather remarkable fortunes of this movement cannot be understood apart from their emergence in an epoch about which it safely could be said, "The notion is gaining that intervention in other people's lives is more legitimate." For the Right, as its leaders proudly profess, is as anxious to intervene in most private moral spheres as it is loath to do so in public economic ones. MADD's approach to drinking-driving fits snugly within this ideological mold.[34]

What MADD Has Wrought, and What It Means

Although changes in the alcohol arena contributed to the emergency of MADD and the anti-drunk-driving movement, it is also true that MADD and the movement have in turn altered the alcohol arena. First and most obvious, both the quantity and quality of anti-drinking-driving weapons have increased. The following measures are all parts of the MADD agenda and most have been enacted in many states: computerized criminal and driving record retrieval systems for police cars; citizen reporting systems; elimination of plea bargaining for DUI offenses; reduction of the blood-alcohol-content standard from .10% to .08% or even .05%, with implied consent from all licensed drivers for BAC testing and "per se" license suspensions on the scene for any who meet that standard; mandatory jail sentences and higher minimum fines; pre-sentence probation investigations of driving records and alcohol-problem assessments, reclassification of alcohol-related injury and death accidents to felonies; "dram shop" (server) liability laws; roadblocks or highway "sobriety checkpoints" to stop vehicles randomly; and a nationwide minimum drinking age of 21.[35] Together such measures open up to surveillance new areas of the private sphere for more and more people, and invite concern about the erosion of civil liberties.

Less obvious are the changes wrought by the movement in the treatment of alcohol problems. In many jurisdictions fee-paying drunk drivers have replaced public inebriates, alcoholics, and other problem drinkers in both public and private treatment programs. With arrests rising and stiffer sentences, fines, and drinking-driver education becoming increasingly mandatory, a brisk business in the treatment of drinking drivers has developed. It is not clear where the old clients of the alcohol treatment system are going instead, if anywhere. This shift in clientele also seems to entail a subtle but important shift in treatment ideology. It had been axiomatic in the alcohol treatment field that alcoholics must "hit bottom," "be ready," and frequently volunteer for treatment if it was to be effective. Now phrases like "constructive coercion," "breaking down denial," and "tough love" have crept into the argot of alcohol treatment professionals, and clients more frequently enter treatment under court sentencing.[36]

The new laws enacted at the behest of the movement have provided treatment programs with a new funding base as well as a new class of clients. Convicted drinking drivers are now assessed fines (often allocated in part to treatment programs) and required to attend treatment programs that charge fees. These developments have fed other treatment trends that began prior to MADD.

The growth of what may fairly be called a treatment industry began in the early 1970s. First, in response to the fiscal crisis many counties began "contracting out" or "privatizing" treatment programs that had previously been public social-service functions. Some states adopted the quasi-partnership role of organizing the efficient distribution of state-referred clients and ensuring "sufficient marketing of provider services . . . [to] demonstrate market demand."[37] Second, during the same period NIAAA and other treatment interests succeeded in getting alcohol and drug problems defined as diseases for purposes of health-insurance coverage. These so-called third-party payments added to the pool of financial resources on which the new treatment industry could draw.[38] Third, in response to rapid growth and high profit margins in the health care industry, many hospitals expanded. This additional bedspace became excess plant capacity, however, when Medicare reforms and other cost-containment measures of the early 1980s reduced many hospital stays. With occupancy rates down and profits squeezed, many corporate hospital chains either started marketing their own alcohol and drug treatment programs or sold franchises for "chemical dependency units" to national companies specializing in this service. All of these supply-side trends created a new growth industry in alcohol and drug treatment.[39] The anti-drunk driver movement has now provided an additional market segment and a new funding base that has furthered the growth of private, for-profit treatment—for a different, more well-heeled clientele with different alcohol problems, for whom treatment is not voluntary and traditional treatment ideology is not designed.

MADD's success also has implications for the criminal justice system. Higher arrest rates, mandatory jail sentences, prohibitions on plea bargaining, and other features of the new laws are putting added stress on courts and jails. A recent National Institute of Justice study, for example, warns that the movement's impact has led to the need for more judges, jail cells, and probation reports, and that such strains should be considered before enacting additional "mandatory confinement" laws.[40] Additional problems are likely to result as more middle-class defendants are caught in the new, wider drunk-driving nets. They are more likely to pay private attorneys and demand jury trials to avoid jail and license revocation. The *Wall Street Journal* reported that under the new laws, defending drinking drivers has become "a booming and lucrative legal speciality," and the "fastest growing area of the law." Such cases are taken more often by senior attorneys (who charge "three to ten times more") because the "stakes are higher." These lawyers are attempting to "put the breathalyzer on trial"; to use physicians who will testify that because alcoholism is a "debilitating disease" the criminal status of drinking-driving is dubious; and to question the constitutionality of arrests on the grounds that people too drunk to drive are incapable of understanding their Miranda rights.[41] While the ultimate success of such strategies and their impact on conviction rates and drinking-driving cannot be known at this writing, it is clear that stiffer penalties have evoked stiffer resistance, that average adjudication times will probably increase, that there will be new legal challenges to drinking-driving statutes and arrest procedures.

Beyond these relatively concrete effects of MADD on the alcohol arena and the criminal justice system, the movement may well have other, more profound implications for problem definition that are less amenable to empirical description and interpretation. First, there is MADD's role in the ongoing construction of alcohol problems. In the post-World War II period the disease concept became the dominant paradigm in alcohol treatment and policy—dominant but not completely hegemonic. Robin Room has argued persuasively that at least in popular culture and public opinion, the notion that problem drinkers of all sorts had a disease about which they had "no choice" (and, implicitly, therefore, reduced responsibility for their actions) has always coexisted with earlier notions about free choice and moral culpability. We have had, that is, something like a dialectic of ambivalence wherein "both choice and compulsion" are juggled, the one or the other invoked as the micro-political exigencies of the situation require. Orcutt suggests that this ideological amalgam of medical and moral frames may be emblematic of a "transitional" stage in the broader historical trend away from moral and toward medical views.[42] This is a useful insight, but just as opiate addiction was effectively demedicalized by pressure from the federal Bureau of Narcotics and Dangerous Drugs, so MADD has further complicated the trend toward medicalization of deviance by again drawing out those ostensibly dormant antagonisms to a pure alcoholism-as-disease paradigm. The movement has successfully claimed that drinking drivers are, first and foremost, "violent criminals" in need of punishment rather than merely victims of a disease in need of treatment. Thus, the march of medicalization may be less inexorable and more circuitous than many have believed. Just as the old moralistic frame was politically supplanted by the scientific alcoholism movement forty years ago, the medicalization of at least some alcohol problems has now become vulnerable to the vicissitudes of politics—this time the retributionism of MADD as it echoes harmoniously with the calls of the New Right for harsher social control.[43]

Such a conceptual-ideological shift carries with it some potentially important implications for public discourse and public policy. To the extent that MADD has captured popular imaginations on drinking-driving issues, and insofar as the alcohol industry continues to counter the myriad threats posed by the so-called New Temperance with support for the anti-drunk-driving movement, then the "evils of drink" will continue to be situated squarely *in the person* rather than *in the bottle*.[44] Thus, another facet of MADD's impact will be to limit discussion of alternative or structural conceptions of alcohol-related problems and the policies that might be brought to bear upon them. In this new delimited discourse, we will hear less and less, for example, about safer automotive design, the lives saved by seat belt laws, the auto industry's success in forestalling air bags, cuts in funding for public transportation, and the dubious advisability of tacitly subsidizing alcoholic drinks by making them tax-deductible "business expenses."[45] Perhaps most important, the rise of MADD has helped to eclipse competing claims about the social costs of unregulated cultural promotion of *drinking-as-intrinsic-to-social-life*. By this I mean the expansion through alcohol advertising the number of spheres and practices in which alcohol is depicted as a natural accoutrement—and this in a society organized around the automobile as the principle mode of transport from one sphere to another.

At the most general level, MADD and the anti-drunk-driving movement it spawned have resurrected a drama that *reaffirms a particular symbolic order.* As Joseph Gusfield renders it,

> The laws against driving under the influence of alcohol constitute a moral drama which states the public definition of moral conduct in American life. In differentiating the drinking driver from the traffic offender these laws create an identity for the moral person and a counteridentity of deviance and guilt. The law in this area symbolizes a public commitment to the centrality of work, safety, and individual responsibility in American society. It supports and enhances a view of a "generalized other," of a "society" committed to the legitimacy of a style of living in which alcohol is a symbol of risk and danger and its control a mark of morality and social responsibility. The modern world has not been the first to discover the joys of inebriety. It is, however, unique in defining these also as woes that call for public actions.[46]

This conflict between the moral safety of self-control and the dangerous immorality of self-indulgence was increasingly camouflaged in the post-World War II years. The combination of the Repeal of Prohibition and the narrowing of alcohol problems to the disease concept normalized drinking in American society. Repeal made drinking acceptable while the success of the alcoholism movement meant that people with alcohol problems had a disease and thus were to be helped and redeemed through science rather than punished and stigmatized.[47] Now that the anti-drunk-driving movement has created a public problem where once there were only tragic "accidents," they have helped define a discourse in which there is, as Gusfield puts it, "the re-emergence of the perception of alcohol problems as those produced by people who make trouble rather than those from troubled people."[48]

Neither the reaffirmation of this symbolic order nor the new discourse that reduces social problems to individual immorality is the handiwork of MADD alone. On the contrary, as suggested above, MADD is but a part of similar and more sweeping shifts in political culture and public policy in the 1980s. While these shifts differ in each sphere of life and realm of public policy, taken together they seem to center on the *re-regulation of pleasure and the constriction of personal liberty*. In the past few years drugs, sex, and rock and roll have all been defined as *dangerous*, and those who indulge in such problematic practices have been subjected to greater surveillance.[49] I am speaking here of more than mass urinalysis testing, the promotion of chastity as public policy, and attempts to censor rock music lyrics. The new minimum drinking age law, for example, central to MADD's legislative agenda, limited the liberties of youth, albeit "for their own good." It is at least arguable that this law is part of a wider network of control measures enacted in the Reagan era, which include greater discipline in school, the renewed use of corporal punishment, adult trials for juvenile offenders, drug searches, dress codes, curfew laws, and "squeal rules" that inhibit the flow of birth control and abortion information to young people. At the risk of oversimplification, I suggest that the 1980s constitute an epoch in which corporation, state, church, and family are all reasserting authority over individual desires, and in the process attempting to reimpose a real or imagined moral *ancien régime* in which social control takes precedence over social welfare as the organizing axis of both ideology and policy.

The kind of relation I have tried to sketch between MADD and its context is neither a simple nor a novel one. Alcohol problems have never been merely problems having to do with alcohol. It is as if battles against alcohol in American history have been the cultural equivalent of the civil conflicts of Third World countries that provide terrain for the proxy wars of distant superpowers. I have tried to show that the movement against drinking-driving, too, is about more than just its stated object, serious though that object is. The problem that remains is how this might be theorized fruitfully. Clearly the moral/symbolic facets of social movements and social problems cannot neatly be reduced to any material/economic core. MADD in some senses did suit the interests of the alcohol, advertising, and broadcasting industries who were facing what they saw as a broader threat, and the movement both aided and was aided by broader conservative currents. Yet, unrelated and arguable progressive shifts in the alcohol arena also abetted MADD. Further, the conflict over drinking-driving has always been largely moral and symbolic in nature, cutting across social classes and having very different implications for different fractions of capital (alcohol, advertising, and autos, versus insurance), different aspects of the state (alcohol treatment versus criminal justice), and different strands of conservative ideology (libertarian versus law and order). Nor does it seem to be the case that MADD designed its focus to fit with the new conservatism or the affected business interests. There is nothing in MADD's organizational history to suggest that its strategies were anything but the instinctual consequence of a bereaved and angry American mother bent on rectifying injustice who then developed a lucrative career as a moral entrepreneur. Yet, although MADD's birth seems quite autonomous, its particular power in adolescence surely owes much to the political and economic circumstances of its development.

Notes

[1] Although they are beyond the scope of this article, it should be noted that there are many questions about both the extent of alcohol-related accidents and the extent of alcohol's role in accidents so categorized; serious doubts exist about the validity of commonly used figures on the number of injuries and fatalities said to be "caused" by drinking-driving. These methodological and measurement problems are well covered, e.g., in J. Gusfield, *The Culture of Public Problems* (Chicago, University of Chicago Press, 1981); D. S. Reed, "Reducing the Costs of Drinking and Driving," in M. Moore and D. Gerstein, editors, *Alcohol and Public Policy: Beyond the Shadow of Prohibition* (Washington, DC: National Academy Press, 1981); H. L. Ross, *Deterring the Drinking Driver: Legal Policy and Social Control* (Lexington, MA: D. C. Heath, 1982); "Social Control Through Deterrence," *Annual Review of Sociology* 10 (1984): 22; and L. Lanza-Kaduce and D. M. Bishop, "Legal Fictions and Criminology: The Jurisprudence of Drunk Driving," *Journal of Criminal Law and Criminology* 77 (1986): 358–78.

[2] Ross, *Deterring the Drinking Driver*, T. Cameron, "The Impact of Drinking-Driving Countermeasures," *Contemporary Drug Problems* 8 (1979): 495–565; "Trends in Alcohol Problems in California, 1950–1979," in N. Giesbrecht et al., editors, *Consequences of Drinking: Trends in Alcohol Problem Statistics in Seven Countries* (Toronto: Addiction Research Foundation, 1983).

[3] From the social constructionist perspective, the thing-to-be-explained, or explananadum, is the crusade against what is known as drunk driving, not the behavior itself. The lineage and theoretical contours of this tradition may be traced in the following: R. Fuller and R. Myers, "The Natural History of a Social Problem," *American Sociological Review* 6 (1941): 320–28; E. Sutherland, "The Diffusion of Sexual Psychopath Laws," *American Journal of Sociology* 56 (1950): 142–48; H. S. Becker, *Outsiders* (New York: Free Press, 1963); *Social Problems: A Modern Approach* (New York: Wiley, 1966); M. Foucault, *Madness and Civilization* (New York: Random House, 1965); T. S. Kuhn, *The Structure of Scientific Revolutions* (Chicago: University of Chicago Press), 1970, 2nd ed.); H. Blumer, "Social Problems as Collective Behavior," *Social Problems* 18 (1971): 298–306; J. Kitsuse and M. Spector, "Toward a Sociology of Social Problems: Social Conditions, Value Judgments, and Social Problems," *Social Problems* 20 (1973): 407–19; M. Spector and J. Kitsuse, "Social Problems: A Reformulation," *Social Problems* 21 (1973): 145–59; *Constructing Social Problems* (Menlo Park, CA: Cummings, 1977); A. L. Mauss, *Social Problems as Social Movements* (Philadelphia: Lippincott, 1975); P. Conrad and J. Schneider, *Deviance and Medicalization* (St. Louis: C. V. Mosby, 1980); J. Schneider, "Social Problems Theory: The Constructionist View," *Annual Review of Sociology* 11 (1985): 209–29. An insightful review of the intellectual cousin of this tradition in psychology is in K. Gergen, "The Social Constructionist Movement in Modern Psychology," *American Psychologist* 40 (1985): 226–75. Works in this tradition specifically on alcohol problems include: J. R. Seeley, "The W.H.O. Definition of Alcoholism," *Quarterly Journal of Studies on Alcohol* 20 (1959): 352–56; J. R. Seeley, "Alcoholism is a Disease: Implications for Social Policy," in D. J. Pittman and C. R. Snyder, editors, *Society, Culture, and Drinking Patterns* (New York: Wiley, 1962); C. MacAndrews and R. Edgerton, *Drunken Comportment* (Chicago: Aldine, 1969); R. L. Chauncey, "New Careers for Moral Entrepreneurs: Teenage Drinking," *Journal of Drug Issues,* 10 (1980): 48–70.

[4] On the viability of claims-making, see Spector and Kitsuse, *Constructing Social Problems.*

[5] This draws heavily upon the key works of Gusfield and Levine. See J. Gusfield, *Symbolic Crusade: Status Politics and the American Temperance Movement* (Urbana: University of Illinois Press, 1963); H. G. Levine, "The Discovery of Addiction: Changing Conceptions of Habitual Drunkenness in American History," *Journal of Studies on Alcohol* 39 (1978): 143–67; "Temperance and Women in 19th Century United States," *Research Advances in Alcohol and Drug Problems* 15 (1980): 26–67; "The Good Creature of God and the Demon Rum: Colonial and 19th Century American Ideas about Alcohol, Accidents, and Crime," in R. Room and G. Collins, editors, *Alcohol and Disinhibition* (Washington, DC: National Institute on Alcohol Abuse and Alcoholism, 1983); "The Alcohol Problem in America: From Temperance to Alcoholism," *British Journal of Addiction* 79 (1984): 109–19. For a useful, class-rooted revisionist interpretation of Gusfield's classic study of temperance as symbolic conflict, see J. J. Rumbarger, *The Social Origins and Function of the Political Temperance Movement in the Reconstruction of American Society, 1825–1917.* Ph.D. dissertation, University of Pennsylvania, 1968 (forthcoming in revised form, State University of New York Press). Note, too, that while women played crucial roles in the temperance movement and were often cast as the victims, the movement was dominated by men.

[6] Levine, "The Alcohol Problem in America," 113. See also Gusfield, *Symbolic Crusade*; and J. H. Timberlake, *Prohibition and the Progressive Movement 1900–1920* (Cambridge: Harvard University Press, 1963).

[7] A. Sinclair, *Era of Excess: A Social History of the Prohibition Movement* (New York: Harper, 1965), 107; see also Timberlake, *Prohibition and the Progressive Movement*; and A. McClung Lee, "Techniques of Social Reform: An Analysis of the New Prohibition Drive," *American Sociological Review* 9 (1944): 65–77.

[8] Levine, "The Alcohol Problem in America."

[9] Ibid.; and Levine, "The Discovery of Addiction."

[10] R. Room, Governing Images of Alcohol and Drug Problems, Ph.D. Dissertation, University of California, Berkeley (1978); "Sociological Aspects of the Disease Concept of Alcoholism," *Research Advances in Alcohol and Drug Problems* 7 (1983): 47–91; C. Wiener, *The Politics of Alcoholism: Building an Arena Around a Social Problem* (New Brunswick, NJ: Transaction, 1971);

Levine, "The Alcohol Problem in America"; J. Schneider, "Deviant Drinking as Disease: Alcoholism as a Social Accomplishment," *Social Problems* 25 (1978): 361–72.

11 See also J. Gusfield, *The Culture of Public Problems: Drinking-Driving and the Symbolic Order* (Chicago: University of Chicago Press, 1981); "Alcohol Problems—An Interactionist View," in J. P. von Wartburg, P. Magnenat, R. Miller, and S. Wyss, editors, *Currents in Alcohol Research and the Prevention of Alcohol Problems* (Berne, Switzerland: Hans Huber, 1985).

12 This historical sketch of MADD is based upon three types of data: First, an archive of journalistic accounts of the organization's founding, growth, and trials and tribulations, which is housed in the library of the Alcohol Research Group at Berkeley, the most important of which are cited directly (Note: there were no journal articles on MADD as of late 1985); second, depth interviews with founding members of the MADD Board of Directors and selected local chapter officers and members from the San Francisco Bay Area; and third, MADD literature, publications, newsletters, and selected board meeting minutes. Although the sketch should not be taken as exhaustive or definitive, it is based upon all information available. Note, too, that since these data were originally compiled and reviewed, MADD founder, president, board chair, and chief executive officer, Candy Lightner, was removed from two of those official posts by the new MADD Board in a power struggle. See R. D. McFadden, "Founder of Anti-Drunken Drive Group Loses 2 Posts," *New York Times* (10/4/85).

13 J. Vejnoska, "Citizen Activist Groups Affecting Policy on Drinking and Driving," *Alcohol Health and Research World* Fall (1987); Mothers Against Drunk Driving, "M.A.D.D." [brochure], n.d.

14 Mothers Against Drunk Driving, "A Summary of Statistics Related to the National Drunk Driving Problem" (Hurst, Texas: MADD, 1984); "Research on Teens: Drinking, Drugs, and Driving" (Hurst, Texas: MADD, 1984). Although MADD collected an impressive array of statistics on which to base their claims, the empirical certainty of their figures is still subject to dispute—although, perhaps surprisingly, no more so than the drinking-driving statistics used by most public health professionals when documenting the horrors of drinking-driving accidents. It is clear that the commonly cited figures on deaths due to drinking-driving are organizationally constructed and rhetorical in character, and that the precise role of alcohol in auto accidents remains unknown; cf. Gusfield, *The Culture of Public Problems*; Ross, *Deterring the Drinking Driver*, and Lanza-Kaduce and Bishop, "Legal Fictions and Criminology."

15 C. P. Freund, "Less Filling, Tastes Great," *City Paper* [Washington, DC], Feb. 1–8, 1985, 1. On the attention given to MADD, see C. Lightner, "MADD at the Court," *Judges' Journal* 23 (1984): 36–39; Insurance Information Institute, *International Symposium on Alcohol and Driving: Conference Report* (Washington, DC: American Insurance Association, 1982): John McCarthy has graphed a 500 percent increase in newspaper coverage of the drinking-driving issue since MADD began; see his "The Causes and Consequences of the Citizens' Movement Against Drunk Driving" [proposal to National Science Foundation] (Washington, DC: Catholic University Center for the Study of Youth Development, 1984). Also note that the Center for Science in the Public Interest was making considerable headway by 1984 in its SMART campaign (Stop Marketing Alcohol on Radio and Television), which was adamantly opposed by the National Association of Broadcasters, the Advertising Council, various liquor lobbyists such as the Distilled Spirits Council, and brewers' associations and vintner groups. See *The Alcoholism Report*, volume XIII, Number 3 (1984): 1 [Minneapolis: The Johnson Institute].

16 Figures on membership, budget, and growth were taken from the following sources: T. Akeman, "Lightner Settles $7,900 Personal Debt to MADD," *Sacramento Bee* (Jan. 1, 1983); "MADD to Add Big D—Moving to Dallas," *Sacramento Bee* (Mar. 29, 1983); Vejnoska, "Citizen Activist Groups"; Lightner, "MADD at the Court"; *Time*, "Man of the Year" (Jan. 7, 1985), 77; Council of Better Business Bureaus, "Philanthropic Advisory Service Report: Mothers Against Drunk Driving," Sept. 24, 1984; and McFadden, "Founder of Anti-Drunken Driver Group Loses 2 Posts."

17 Regarding newspaper coverage, see McCarthy, "The Causes and Consequences of the Citizens' Movement Against Drunk Driving"; S. Cunningham, "Still MADD, but More Strategic," *American Psychological Association Monitor* 15 (1984); M. Jordan, "Drinking and Driving Mar

Merrymaking," *Washington Post* (Dec. 31, 1984); *Time*, "Man of the Year." On the curious courtship between media and movements, see T. Gitlin, *The Whole World is Watching: Mass Media in the Making and Unmaking of the New Left* (Berkeley, University of California Press, 1980).

[18] M. Tolchin, "States Face Carrot or a Stick on the Drinking Age," *New York Times* (July 1, 1984); "Law is Signed to Nudge States on Drinking Age," *New York Times* (July 22, 1985). The law provides that states that do not increase the minimum drinking age to 21 will lose 5 percent of their federal highway funds each year; all but six states had complied as of this writing (April 1987). I have borrowed the notion of "ideological work" from the insightful study by Bennett M. Berger, *The Survival of a Counterculture: Ideological Work and Everyday Life Among Rural Communards* (Berkeley: University of California Press, 1981).

[19] *Time*, "Man of the Year"; *Newsweek*, "Alcohol on the Rocks" (Dec. 31, 1984); *Wall Street Journal*, "Industry Headache—Americans Drink Less, And Makers of Alcohol Feel a Little Woozy: Concerns of Drunk Driving, Health, and Sales to Youths Force Producers to Adapt" (March 14, 1984); *U.S. News and World Report*, "War on Alcohol Abuse Spreads to New Fronts" (Dec. 24, 1984); S. P. Sherman, "America's New Abstinence," *Fortune* (Mar. 18, 1985); M. J. Weiss, "The Crusade Against Drunk Driving," *Ladies Home Journal* (Feb. 1985). MADD was mentioned by name in all these accounts as the leading moral entrepreneur (the term is Howard Becker's [Outsiders]) behind this landslide of legislation. There were other anti-drinking-driving organizations that began a full two years prior to MADD, but none achieved MADD's visibility, size, or stature. By stressing the central role played by MADD here I do not wish to minimize other dynamics—electoral, organizational, or cultural. It is clear, however, that MADD generated the national and local publicity that made it nearly impossible for elected officials and state agencies not to respond. Frances Fox Piven and Richard Cloward have outlined a similar theoretical perspective on political change initiated from the grass roots; see their *Poor People's Movements* (New York: Vintage, 1977), 14–18 et passim.

[20] Both McCarthy and Zald's resource mobilization perspective, which focuses on the capacities for movement organizations to mobilize human and financial resources, and Smelser's notion of "structural conduciveness" suggest the importance of historical context. See J. McCarthy and M. Zald, "Resource Mobilization and Social Movements—A Partial Theory," *American Journal of Sociology* 82 (1976), 1212–1241; N. Smelser, *Theory of Collective Behaviour* (New York: Macmillan, 1963).

[21] MADD, *Newsletter* [national edition], Spring, 1982; "Mothers Against Drunk Driving Position Paper on Alcohol Advertising," Hurst, Texas, 1985; *Advertising Age*, "Lightner Urges Ad Self-Rule" (Apr. 22, 1985); *Wall Street Journal*, "Crusaders Against Drunk Driving Split Over Whether to Fight Alcohol Broadly" (Nov. 6, 1985).

[22] *Wall Street Journal*, "Industry Headache"; *Wall Street Journal*, "Crusaders Against Drunk Driving Split." The National Association of Broadcasters labeled the threat to alcohol-beverage advertising posed by CSPI and their SMART campaign "our number one priority." According to a CSPI representative, the alcohol industry has responded to the threat by casting aspersions on CSPI and public health officials, and by attempting to enhance "alcohol advertisers' public image" by sponsoring public service announcements against drinking-driving. Both quotes from *The Alcoholism Report*, volume XIII, number 3 (1984): 1.

[23] R. L. Chauncey, "New Careers for Moral Entrepreneurs"; P. Morgan, "The State as Mediator: Alcohol Problem Management in the Post-War Period," *Contemporary Drug Problems* 9 (1980): 107–22; C. Wiener, *The Politics of Alcoholism*; R. Room, "Sociological Aspects of the Disease Concept."

[24] Cited in Room, "Sociological Aspects of the Disease Concept," 62. See also R. Room, "Alcohol as Cause: Empirical Links and Social Definitions," in J. P. von Wartburg, P. Magnenat, R. Miller, and S. Wyss, editors, *Currents in Alcohol Research and the Prevention of Alcohol Problems*; Moore and Gerstein, editors, *Alcohol and Public Policy*; and the useful precursors from J. R. Seeley, "The W.H.O. Definition of Alcoholism," and "Alcoholism is a Disease."

[25] See, for example, L. Wallack, "Drinking and Driving: Toward a Broader Understanding of the Role of Mass Media," *Journal of Public Health Policy*, 5 (1984): 471–96; R. Room, "Alcohol Control and Public Health," *Annual Review of Public Health*, 5(1984): 292–317. Cf. H. G.

Levine, "What Is an Alcohol-Related Problem?", *Journal of Drug Issues* 14 (1984): 45–60. It should be noted that this public-health perspective was not necessarily invented de novo in the late 1970s. It may have been in some small way a recrudescence of a strand of temperance rhetoric that held that Prohibition was a preventative public-health measure (James Baumohl, personal communication, 1987), although I know of no evidence that current public-health professionals in the alcohol field knowingly draw upon or consider themselves part of a temperance tradition.

26 On the progressive facets of temperance politics, cf. Gusfield, *Symbolic Crusade*; Timberlake, *Prohibition and the Progressive Movement*; Blocker, *Retreat From Reform*. On the political beliefs and policy preferences of MADD activists, see S. Weed, "Local Chapter Leadership Study for MADD," mimeo (Arlington, University of Texas Center for Social Research, 1985); "Grass-Roots Activism and the Drunk-Driving Issue: A Survey of MADD Chapters," paper presented at the Annual Meeting of the *American Sociological Association*, Washington, DC, 1985.

27 M. Jacobson and R. Collins, "Ads Glamorize Alcohol, Hide Dangers," *New York Times* (Apr. 21, 1985).

28 MADD, "Fact Sheet," n.d.

29 One example of this tendency toward personal vilification was shown in a recent magazine article about MADD. Its lead (a tacit typification that could not have been better suited if created by a novelist) was about a "19 year old sailor" who, drunk *and* drugged, killed two innocents and had to be "hauled to the police station in a drunken rage" while he "cursed" his victims for "having wrecked his car." The article concludes with a quote from a local movement activist: "What he did was no accident. When a person drinks, drives, and kills people, he's a murderer." Weiss, "The Crusade Against Drunk Driving."

30 Lee, "Techniques of Social Reform." It should be noted in passing here that although I found no evidence of direct support of MADD from the auto industry, it is quite clear that the movement's focus on the deviant drinking driver benefits the auto industry insofar as questions about automotive safety design and manufacture are not raised. Moreover, the auto industry was implicated by the National Highway Traffic Safety Administration in their push against drinking-driving in the late 1960s; see Gusfield, *The Culture of Public Problems*, chapters 2–3.

31 For example, D. Cohn, "Reformers of a New Breed Pour It on Against Alcohol," *Los Angeles Times* (Aug. 26, 1984).

32 On membership characteristics, see Weed, "Local Chapter Leadership Study for MADD"; and his "Grass-Roots Activism and the Drunk-Driver Issue"; and S. Ungerleider and S. A. Bloch, "Developing Grass Roots Support for Drinking Driving Countermeasures: A Review of Mothers Against Drunk Driving," *Journal of Traffic Safety Education* (April, 1987): 20–22. On the relation between political and religious conservatism and MADD chapter formation, see F. J. Ritchey and L. L. Daniels, "Regional Variations in Support of the Anti-Drunk Driver Movement," paper presented at the annual meeting of the *Southern Sociological Society*, Atlanta, 1983. With regard to the role of evangelicals and the Republican party platform, see "Battling Drunk Driving," *Christianity Today* 26 (1982): 50–53. Further, the dean of New Right fundraising, Richard Viguerie, wrote in *Conservative Digest* that "people who feel strongly about drunk driving" are a key New Right constituency (cited in Ritchey and Daniels).

33 Max Weber, *The Protestant Ethic and the Spirit of Capitalism* (New York: Scribners, 1958), 90–92, emphasis added. The concept of elective affinity was used explicitly in "Die Wirtschaftsethick der Weltreligionen," *Archiv für Sozialforschung* 41 (1915), translated and edited by H. Gerth and C. W. Mills as "The Social Psychology of the World Religions," in their *From Max Weber* (New York: Oxford University Press, 1946), 284. The utility of the notion is that it does justice to influence without implying strict causality. In this sense it shares some features with the concept of "relative autonomy" as used in neo-Marxian writings.

34 The quotation is from *Business Week*, "The Sobering of America" (Feb. 25, 1985). The implication that state intervention in "private" spheres is a right-wing phenomenon is, of course, overly simple. Clearly the left far more than the right favors intervention against, e.g., "domestic tyrants" who physically abuse their wives or children, just as there are right-wing libertarians who oppose such intervention. Moreover, I am certain that moral outrage against

drinking drivers is shared by people from all ideological camps. My point, however, is that the New Right seems to like to attribute all manner of social problems to individual deviance that is held to be the product of mere moral volition, and that MADD's "theory" of drinking-driving offers just such attributional advantages.

[35] MADD, "National Newsletter," Hurst, Texas (Spring, 1985), 9; *Alcoholism Report*, XI, No. 16, Minneapolis: Johnson Institute (June 16, 1983), 4.

[36] C. Weisner, "The Transformation of Alcohol Treatment: Access to Care and the Response to Drinking-Driving," *Journal of Public Health Policy* 7 (1986): 78–92; C. Weisner and R. Room, "Financing and Ideology in Alcohol Treatment," *Social Problems* 32 (1985): 167–84; R. Speiglman, "Issues in the Rise of Compulsion in California's Drinking Driver Treatment System," in M. R. Valverius, editor, *Punishment and/or Treatment for Driving Under the Influence of Alcohol and Other Drugs* (Stockholm, Sweden: International Committee on Alcohol, Drugs, and Traffic Safety, 1985).

[37] For example, see California Department of Drug and Alcohol Programs, *Alcohol Program Certification and Third-Party Payments*, ADP 82–113 (Sacramento, CA: Health and Welfare Agency, 1982).

[38] C. Holden, "Alcoholism and the Medical Cost Crunch," *Science* 235 (1987): 1132–1133.

[39] See also C. Reinarman, D. Waldorf, and S. Murphy, "Scapegoating and Social Control in the Construction of Public Problems: Cocaine in the Workplace," *Research in Law, Deviance, and Social Control* 9 (1987).

[40] National Institute of Justice, *Jailing Drunk Drivers: Impact on the Criminal Justice System* (Washington, DC: U.S. Government Printing Office, 1985). See also W. L. Hepperle and D. Klein, "An Analysis of the Impact of the 1982 Drunk Driving Legislation on the Alameda County Municipal Courts" (Alameda County, CA: Office of Court Services, 1985).

[41] *Wall Street Journal*, "Lawyers Are Finding Ways to Circumvent Stricter Statutes Against Drunken Driving" (Nov. 2, 1984), 33.

[42] Room, "Sociological Aspects of the Disease Concept." Regarding "choice and compulsion," see R. Roizen, "Barriers to Alcoholism Treatment: Report Submitted to NIAAA," paper #F145, Alcohol Research Group, Berkeley, CA (1977). J. D. Orcutt, "Ideological Variations in the Structure of Deviant Types: A Multivariate Comparison of Alcoholism and Heroin Addiction," *Social Forces* 55 (1976): 419–39. On the ambivalent character of beliefs and the coexistence of multiple belief systems, see M. Edelman, Political Language (New York: Academic Press, 1977); Berger, *The Survival of a Counterculture*; and C. Reinarman, *American States of Mind: Political Beliefs and Behavior Among Private and Public Workers* (New Haven, CT: Yale University Press, 1987).

[43] Professor James Baumohl of McGill University pointed out (personal communication, 1985) that the notion that there has been a transition per se from moral to medical models is in need of complication. While science, particularly medicine, has dominated discourse about alcohol problems since the 1940s, moralism did not so much go away as make an accommodation with the disease model (much as liberal theologians, in accepting science, kept on preaching, and, indeed, argued that science served or even derived from divine purpose). Such an accommodation appears easy enough to forge in the realm of public opinion (see Room, "Sociological Aspects of the Disease Concept") because one gets the "disease," after all, only by repeatedly engaging in what for some people is discrediting behavior. Thus MADD did not have to invent a new ideology in order to claim that drinking-driving stems from free will. For a general discussion of the vicissitudes of medicalization, see Conrad and Schneider, *Deviance and Medicalization*.

[44] This is not meant to imply that MADD has been sole or even senior author of this shift. The convergence of broader trends in alcohol production and consumption and in state policies across several nations led Makela et al. to the following conclusion before MADD was organized: "There is a growing conflict between increased concern about alcohol problems and the economic interests of the alcohol trade that is exacerbated by static or declining markets. In a situation of increased acceptance of drinking in everyday life [in the 1950–1975 period], policies may tend even more toward individual control of deviant drinkers. In an era of con-

tracting public-welfare resources, this tendency may be expressed more in punitive than in treatment-oriented measures." K. Makela et al., *Alcohol, Society, and the State: A Comparative Study of Alcohol Control* (Toronto: Addiction Research Foundation, 1981), 111.

45 Although the deductibility of alcoholic beverages as "business expenses" has been narrowed by the 1987 tax reforms, the tacit subsidy continues on a reduced scale.

46 Gusfield, *The Culture of Public Problems*, 148.

47 Drinking drivers were not generally taken as people having alcohol problems per se, but rather as routine or "folk" criminals; see ibid. They therefore did not often come within the welfare state sphere. Moreover, the U.S. welfare state, in this area as in most others, was and is quite stingy relative to those of other developed capitalist democracies. "Drunks," for example, still cannot get disability benefits despite the disease status of alcoholism. I offer this note only to qualify the more general point about the broader direction of social policy in the post-World War II period, which allowed "drunks" to be conceptualized in other than merely moral terms.

48 Gusfield, "Alcohol Problems—An Interactionist View," 79.

49 See R. Goldstein, "The New Sobriety: What We Risk When We Just Say No." *Village Voice* (Dec. 30, 1986), 23–28; H. Levine and C. Reinarman, "Abusing Drug Abuse: What's Behind 'Jar Wars,'" *The Nation* (Mar. 28, 1987), 388–90. On the expanding panoply of social controls on youth, see T. G. Carpenter, "The New Anti-Youth Movement," *The Nation* (Jan. 19, 1985), 39–41.

COVERAGE OF DOMESTIC VIOLENCE FATALITIES BY NEWSPAPERS IN WASHINGTON STATE

Cathy Ferrand Bullock & Jason Cubert

According to the most recent figures from the Department of Justice's Bureau of Justice Statistics, 1,830 people were murdered by their current or former intimate partners in 1998 (Rennison & Welchans, 2000). Of those, 72% were women (Rennison & Welchans, 2000). Most Americans learn about such violent deaths through the media. News coverage can be framed to give distinctly different views of social problems, influencing how audience members see their world, its problems, and the solutions to those problems (Entman, 1991, 1993; Loseke, 1989; Pan & Kosicki, 1993; Tuchman, 1978). Thus, news coverage can help determine how society views and responds to domestic violence.

This study explores how newspapers portray domestic violence fatalities, how accurately this portrayal reflects the victims' experiences and the broader social problem of domestic violence, and the implications of the patterns of portrayal. Using quantitative content analysis and frame analysis, it examines coverage of domestic violence homicides by newspapers in Washington State during 1998.

Characteristics of Domestic Violence

Studies in intimate partner violence have considered factors such as psychological abuse to be contributors to violent situations in the home. Fagan and Browne (1994) wrote that "psychological abuse, economic deprivation, threats to others in the family, and threats as a method of coercion" (p. 118) exist simultaneously with physical abuse.

From: *Journal of Interpersonal Violence*, vol. 17, pp. 475–499, copyright 2002. Reprinted by permission of Sage Publications, Inc.

Crowell and Burgess (1996) defined *psychological abuse* as verbal abuse (ridicule, harassment, name calling, etc.), isolation, jealousy or possessiveness, and threats or abuse to a victim's children, friends, pets, or possessions. As Martin (1982) wrote, "In many cases, such psychological abuse is a prelude to physical violence. If unchecked violence escalates in frequency and severity sometimes leading to murder" (p. xviii). In roughly 96% of cases studied, death is the culminating event of a long history of interpersonal tension entrenched in violence (Gelles, 1972; Goetting, 1995).

Many researchers focusing on wife battering blame the setup of society and the household (Dobash & Dobash, 1998; Gelles & Straus, 1988; Martin, 1976; Pagelow, 1984). In fact, Gelles and Straus (1988) claimed,

> Our society and our families are organized to not only allow but often encourage violence between intimates. The combination of social attitudes (that sometimes encourage but often just simply allow violence), with the private nature of the modern family, and the socially structured inequality that is part of every household, makes for a tinderbox of emotions and possible violent outbursts. (p. 35)

Little research has been conducted concerning same-sex partnerships and domestic violence; however, current research is focusing on domestic violence other than that by husbands against wives. When women kill their husbands, a high proportion act in self-defense or in reaction to a history of domestic violence by the husband (Klein, Campbell, Soler, & Ghez, 1997; Kurz, 1993; Straus & Hotaling, 1980; Websdale, 1999). This is not to say that women are not abusers or that domestic violence fatalities do not occur at the hands of women; however, some research has taken women's retaliation out of context. Studies have also found that women who were abused as children do not seek out abusive relationships as adults (Cascardi, O'Leary, Lawrence, & Schlee, 1995; Pagelow, 1984). This phenomenon is often seen as the result of self-esteem issues rather than those of conditioning.

Research does affirm that violence is learned at home and that men who beat their partners have most likely seen their fathers beat their mothers (Dobash & Dobash, 1998; Gelles, 1972; Klein et al., 1997; Kurz, 1993; Pagelow, 1984) and have generally experienced a high level of physical brutality throughout childhood (Gelles, 1972).

Characterizations of murderous husbands' having been abused as children often serve as "excuses" or serve to make the men seem deviant, but as research explains, it is the perpetrators' abilities to seem normal that often make recognizing domestic violence such a problem. Herman (1992) wrote,

> The perpetrator's most consistent feature, to both victims and psychologists, is his apparent normality. The perpetrator seeks out situations where his tyrannical behavior will be tolerated, condoned or admired. Few people believe that his crimes can be committed by a man of such conventional appearance. (p. 77)

When police and prosecutors encounter these "normal people" in domestic violence situations, they often view arrest and prosecution as unsuitable. Early writings on police responses to family violence indicated the police's refusal to get involved in family disputes, arrest offenders, or impose criminal sanctions. Many police departments had "hands off policies" stating that arrests were to be avoided whenever possible (Moore, Prothrow-Stith, Guyer, & Spivak, 1994).

When police act, they focus more on offenders than on victims (Martin, 1976; Moore et al., 1994; Pagelow, 1984). Wives are frequently advised to drop charges for fear that they may provoke further violence or lose the family's major economic support (Breci, 1991; Gelles & Straus, 1988). In cases that make it to court, the family is treated as a sacred entity that must be preserved.

News Media and Domestic Violence

American mass media have the power to bring awareness to social issues and, researchers maintain, to provide a picture of events people do not experience directly, teach people about their society, and help structure how people see the world (Hartley, 1982; Manoff & Schudson, 1986; Meyers, 1997; Molotch & Lester, 1974; Sherizen, 1978; Tuchman, 1972). Researchers have developed a long list of factors that may shape the images conveyed through the media. They point to the potential effects of technology, political and economic structures, and news workers' routines, news values, literary forms, and cultural assumptions (for example, see Benedict, 1992; Chermak, 1995; Gans, 1979; Hartley, 1982; Manoff & Schudson, 1986; Meyers, 1997; Molotch & Lester, 1974; Roshco, 1975; Sigal, 1973; Strentz, 1989).

A number of researchers have explored the idea that news is framed in ways that convey certain understandings of reality while excluding others (Cappella & Jamieson, 1997; Entman, 1991, 1993; Pan & Kosicki, 1993; Tuchman, 1978). Entman (1993) offered this definition:

> Framing essentially involves selection and salience. To frame is to select some aspects of a perceived reality and make them more salient in a communicating text, in such a way as to promote a particular problem definition, causal interpretation, moral evaluation, and/or treatment recommendation for the item described. (p. 52)

Journalistic texts can make information more noticeable, meaningful, or memorable through its placement, by repeating it, or by associating it with familiar symbols (Entman, 1991, 1993).

Given the importance of the media in illuminating social issues and their potential to frame news in different ways, it is worth asking how the media have covered domestic violence. "In one sense," said Loseke (1989), "the mass media formally discovered the 'wife abuse' problem in 1974, the first year the *Reader's Guide to Periodical Literature* began listing articles under the special heading of 'wife beating'" (p. 192). Studies indicate that media sometimes create distorted pictures of domestic violence (for example, see Berns, 1999; Consalvo, 1998a, 1998b; Meyers, 1994, 1997).

Meyers (1994, 1997) suggested that news coverage of domestic violence is framed to support the status quo: a system she saw as grounded in patriarchal ideology and designed to sustain male domination over women. Meyers maintained that coverage she examined in several small-scale qualitative studies positioned antiwoman violence in a context of individual and family pathology rather than relating it to social structures and socially approved gender roles. As a result, the coverage blamed women while helping to relieve society of any obligation to act.[1] To her, news coverage of violence against women implies that good girls follow the rules and avoid trouble and bad girls break the rules and get what they deserve. In Meyers's view, attribution of blame grows out of journalists' attempts to explain the "why" of domestic violence; whether the victim or the perpetrator is blamed depends on the underlying ideology.

Researchers also conclude that news coverage of domestic violence is colored by the sources journalists use (Chibnall, 1977; Sherizen, 1978; Sigal, 1973). As Meyers (1997) explained, journalists see the police as legitimate sources whose views are neutral and, thus, do not need to be balanced with information from those representing opposing opinions. However, the police perspective may not be neutral, as suggested earlier by the focus on the offender, and police goals may not serve the needs of the media, the audience, or crime victims and their families (Chibnall, 1977; Meyers, 1997; Sherizen, 1978). The supposedly value-free, outsider's view journalists sometimes say they adopt is often "based on the police perspective and assumes that the cause of the violence resides within the interactive behavior of the woman and man—a position that implicates the woman in her own abuse" (Meyers, 1997, p. 94). Advocates for victims of domestic violence, on the other hand, could bring a different perspective to the coverage (Jones, 1994; Meyers, 1997).

As Entman (1993) suggested, word choice can also help frame the news. Benedict (1992), writing about how the press covers sex crimes, said that the use of sexist vocabulary helps promote traditional images of women. Her research indicates that journalists force set narratives (the woman is a vamp who drove the man to commit the crime or the woman is a virgin sullied by a monster) on sex crimes "through their choice of vocabulary, the slant of their leads, and the material they choose to leave out or put in" (pp. 23–24).

Meyers's (1997) interviews with victims' advocates highlight the importance of labeling in ways that are not misleading. Some advocates objected to phrases such as *domestic disturbance* or *domestic violence*, arguing that these hide that women are generally the victims and men the perpetrators and, thus, separate the crime from societal issues of power and control. Advocates also objected to news coverage that dealt with a domestic violence homicide as just another murder and ignored the context of battering. Meyers wrote, "This denies the pain and abuse that battered women endure, and it makes the cause of death appear inexplicable or the result of a man's suddenly having 'snapped'" (p. 110).

As the research summarized here indicates, news coverage can be framed to convey a particular understanding of reality. This study is built on the idea that journalists can create different pictures of domestic violence and confirm or debunk the myths surrounding it by choosing certain topics, sources, facts, and words over others and by controlling the placement and repetition of information. They can illuminate or obscure domestic violence's role in individual deaths, its importance as a broader social problem, its characteristics and patterns, and its victims' experiences. Our research questions reflect these ideas:

Research Question 1: Did the newspaper coverage acknowledge that this incident involved domestic violence?

Research Question 2: Did the coverage portray the incident as an isolated event or as part of a pattern of abuse between this perpetrator and victim? Also, did it portray the incident as an isolated homicide (or attempted homicide) or as part of a larger social problem of domestic violence?

Research Question 3: Did the coverage give a sense that the case involved physical abuse only or both physical and psychological abuse?

Research Question 4: Did the coverage blame the victim and/or exonerate the perpetrator?

Research Question 5: What sources were used?

The first question grows out of the research that emphasizes the importance of labeling domestic violence in ways that are not misleading. We wondered whether domestic violence would be labeled as such. Questions 2, 3, and 4 were designed to determine whether the coverage passed along some of the common misconceptions about domestic violence, as past studies have suggested, or created a more accurate view. The final question draws on work indicating that the sources journalists use can help determine the frame of an article.

Method

Our analysis focused on coverage of domestic violence fatalities by all community and daily newspapers in Washington State in 1998.[2] With one exception, we included all news and feature articles, companion pieces (such as short articles giving domestic violence fatality statistics), and opinion pieces that dealt primarily with domestic violence-related deaths. The exception was an incomplete clipping for which the full article was not readily available. Approximately 40 of the state's 190 or so newspapers ran domestic violence fatality-related coverage that fit our criteria.[3] Roughly half were dailies; most of the others were weekly newspapers. (See the appendix for a list of the newspapers.)

We examined all coverage through the arraignment, if there was one, in each case. Trial coverage, which presumably would shift toward the legal system and events in court, was omitted because we suspected that it would differ significantly from earlier coverage of the crime. The arraignment formed a natural dividing line often followed by a break in coverage.

To be included in the study, a domestic violence case had to meet two criteria. First, it had to involve people who were or had been romantically involved. Cases in which a woman's former boyfriend killed her current boyfriend were included, as were cases in which one parent killed the children to punish the other parent. Cases in which the perpetrator had not yet been identified were included if a current or former partner was implicated. Second, the case had to involve a death or a clear attempt to kill; we were interested in the coverage of cases that had reached the conclusion of the escalating violence described earlier.[4]

In all, 44 cases met these criteria and were studied. And 3 accounted for a disproportionate amount of the coverage: 55.3% of the units coded. Concerned that these cases might skew the results, we analyzed the 41 smaller cases as a group, the 3 larger cases as a group, and the total data. The 44 cases included 230 articles (119 from the smaller cases and 111 from the larger cases). Almost all were news and feature articles. Of the rest, 4 were letters to the editor, 2 were other types of opinion pieces, and 3 were categorized other.

Articles were broken into units for coding. Headlines, subheads, and leads[5] were coded as separate units. Within the body of an article, each paragraph was coded as a unit. A total of 3,053 units (1,365 in the smaller cases and 1,688 in the larger cases) were coded.

The overall file included a variety of domestic violence cases, as shown by the breakdown of the 42 cases in which the perpetrator had been identified (figures do not total 100% due to rounding error):

> Female victim, male perpetrator: 29 cases (69.0%)
> Male victim, female perpetrator: 9 cases (21.4%)
> Male victim, male perpetrator: 4 cases (9.5%)
> Female victim, female perpetrator: 0 cases (0%)

Of the 9 cases in which women killed men, 5 were described as self-defense, as would be expected based on the literature. The 4 cases in which men killed men all involved women. For example, a woman's estranged husband killed her boyfriend in one case. We found no domestic violence fatalities involving same-sex relationships.

The coverage was analyzed using quantitative content analysis and frame analysis. For the former, we developed a set of quantitative items based on the literature. Measures were pretested several times, and intercoder reliability was 85% or better for all closed-ended items. During the study, coders discussed any questions they had about coding to ensure that reliability remained high.

We used frame analysis to identify the themes or patterns in the coverage. All articles were read at least once by both authors, key ideas were listed, and the ideas were synthesized into the primary frames for the coverage. Because the 3 larger cases included so much coverage, each was analyzed separately.

Results

Quantitative Content Analysis

Key terms signifying that an incident reflects domestic violence were seldom used. Phrases such as *domestic violence, domestic abuse, violent history,* and *battered women* appeared in only 4.3% of the units (3.9% of the units in the 41 smaller cases and 4.7% of the units in the 3 larger cases). These were spread among 22.6% of the articles, or 52 articles. Also, 1 of the 3 large cases accounted for 53.8% of the units that mentioned domestic violence.

Abuse was mentioned even less frequently. For instance, 4 units scattered among 3 articles included the phrase *physical abuse,* and 2 units in 1 article specifically mentioned verbal or emotional abuse. (Psychological abuse was never mentioned.) All 6 units were in 2 of the large cases. However, if the more generic *abuse* is included, the term was mentioned in 33 units, or 1.1% of the total units, distributed among 18 articles (6 from smaller cases and 12 from larger cases). So, the term *abuse* was used in only 7.8% of the articles.

Trauma was specifically mentioned in only 7 units, or 0.23% of the total. These were distributed among 6 articles (2.6%) in 1 smaller case and the 3 larger cases.

To further explore the first research question, we examined whether stories made it clear that they dealt with domestic violence without labeling it as such. Journalistic pieces are generally constructed to make the focus clear by the end of the lead, so we looked at whether the fact that the case involved domestic violence was evident from the headline, subhead (if any), and/or lead. We counted all articles in which (a) domestic violence was specifically mentioned or (b) the victim's current or former romantic partner was implicated in the crime.

By the end of the lead (taking headline package and lead into account), it was evident that 170, or 74.0%, of the stories dealt with domestic violence although it was not labeled as such. The percentage was higher for the large case articles (85.6%) than for the small-case articles (63.0%). As these percentages indicate, a majority of the articles made it clear early on that the story involved domestic violence. This was done by describing the crime and the victim-perpetrator relationship.

We examined seven other items—such as whether there was any evidence of past domestic problems between this perpetrator and victim (other than a protection order), whether the victim had obtained or tried to obtain a protection order against this perpetrator, and whether there was any description of psychological abuse between this perpetrator and victim—to determine whether the idea of domestic violence cropped up indirectly in the coverage. As table 1 indicates, much of the coverage did little to develop the idea that the case involved domestic violence. The most common item, evidence (other than a protection order) of past problems in this relationship, appeared in only 22.6% of the articles. When items were considered together,

30.0% of the articles contained at least one measure that showed domestic violence. More than two thirds of the articles elaborated little on the idea that they involved domestic violence.

In answer to our first research question, the coverage seldom labeled a killing as domestic violence. Instead, it described the crime and the victim-perpetrator relationship early on and largely let readers draw their own conclusions.

Our second research question asked whether the coverage portrayed the incident as an isolated event or as part of a pattern of abuse between this perpetrator and victim. As some of the items in table 1 help illustrate, the coverage tended to omit the idea of a pattern of abuse. In addition, few units and articles indicated that the perpetrator or victim grew up in an abusive home or had been involved in abusive relationships in the past (tables 1 and 2), information that readers might interpret as evidence of a pattern in one or both partners' lives. By not portraying the victim and perpetrator's history, the coverage presented the homicide as an isolated incident.

This research question also asked whether the coverage portrayed the incident as an isolated homicide (or attempted homicide) or as part of a larger issue of domestic violence in society. To address this, we looked at whether the coverage placed the problem in context by mentioning domestic violence not involving this perpetrator and victim (see table 1). Only 2.9% of the units and 10.0% of the articles (14.4% of the large-case articles and 5.9% of the small-case articles) placed domestic violence in a broader context. These cases were generally not presented as part of a larger problem; they appeared to be isolated incidents of violence.

The third research question dealt with whether the coverage showed domestic violence only in terms of physical abuse or whether it also showed psychological abuse. Psychological abuse between perpetrator and victim was described in only 66 units (2.2% of the total) scattered among 39 articles (17.0%). Thus, domestic violence was portrayed overwhelmingly in terms of physical harm, and the psychological component was largely ignored.

Based on the literature, we expected Research Question 4 (Does the coverage blame the victim and/or exonerate the perpetrator?) to be answered affirmatively. Our findings (table 2) contradict this because individual statements showing that the perpetrator had an excuse, that the victim was to blame, or that blame should be shifted to society showed up in few units.

However, analyzing how many articles included any excuse or any form of blame probably provides a more accurate picture. When items were combined, 47.8% of the articles suggested at least one motivation or excuse for the perpetrator (40.3% of the small-case articles and 55.9% of the large-case articles) that could be interpreted as exonerating him or her. A smaller but still noteworthy percentage, 17%, blamed the victim for his or her death (20.2% of the small-case articles and 13.5% of the large-case articles). Overall, only 8.3% shifted the blame to society (2.5% of the small-case articles and 14.4% of the large-case articles).

Table 1   Frequency of Items Indicating That Case Involved Domestic Violence

Item	Unit (Large Case, n = 1,688; Small Case, n = 1,365)		Article (Large Case, n = 111; Small Case, n = 119)	
	Frequency	%	Frequency	%
Past problems in this relationship (any evidence of past domestic problems, other than protection order, between this perpetrator and victim)				
Total	114	3.7	52	22.6
Large/Small	55/59	3.3/4.3	26/26	23.4/21.8
Domestic violence contextualized (cases of domestic violence not involving this perpetrator and victim, domestic violence hot lines, domestic violence agencies and their purposes, etc.)				
Total	89	2.9	23	10.0
Large/Small	71/18	4.2/1.3	16/7	14.4/5.9
Protection order (victim obtained or tried to obtain a protection order against this perpetrator)				
Total	79	2.6	38	16.5
Large/Small	45/34	2.7/2.5	21/17	18.9/14.3
Domestic violence experts used as sources				
Total	74	2.4	11	4.8
Large/Small	67/7	4.0/0.5	10/1	9.0/0.8
Description of psychological abuse (verbal, emotional) between this perpetrator and this victim				
Total	66	2.2	39	17.0
Large/Small	28/38	1.7/2.8	18/21	16.2/17.6
Perpetrator killed victim because victim abused him or her, the children, and so forth				
Total	20	0.7	12	5.2
Large/Small	0/20	0.0/1.5	0/12	0.0/10.1
Perpetrator a domestic abuser of people other than this victim				
Total	11	0.4	6	2.6
Large/Small	5/6	0.3/0.4	2/4	1.8/3.4

Table 2 Frequency of Items That Excuse Perpetrator, Blame Victim, or Blame Society

Item	Unit (Large Case, n = 1,688; Small Case, n = 1,365)		Article (Large Case, n = 111; Small Case, n = 119)	
	Frequency	**%**	**Frequency**	**%**
Perpetrator's motivation and/or excuse				
Perpetrator had mental health problems				
Total	83	2.7	39	17.0
Large/Small	76/7	4.5/0.5	34/5	30.6/4.2
Separation or divorce				
Total	46	1.5	34	14.8
Large/Small	35/11	2.1/0.8	25/9	22.5/7.6
Perpetrator used drugs and/or alcohol				
Total	26	0.9	18	7.8
Large/Small	0/26	0.0/1.9	0/18	0.0/15.1
The death was or may have been accidental				
Total	26	0.9	19	8.3
Large/Small	12/14	0.7/1.0	9/10	8.1/8.4
Money (perpetrator killed for insurance money, to avoid a costly divorce, etc.)				
Total	24	0.8	17	7.4
Large/Small	20/4	1.2/0.3	15/2	13.5/1.7
Perpetrator killed victim because victim abused him or her, the children, and so forth				
Total	20	0.7	12	5.2
Large/Small	0/20	0.0/1.5	0/12	0.0/10.1
Perpetrator was specifically called a victim in this domestic violence case				
Total	8	0.3	7	3.0
Large/Small	2/6	0.1/0.4	2/5	1.8/4.2
Perpetrator had physical health problems				
Total	6	0.2	6	2.6
Large/Small	1/5	0.1/0.4	1/5	0.9/4.2
Perpetrator grew up in an abusive home				
Total	2	0.1	2	.9
Large/Small	0/2	0.0/0.1	0/2	0.0/1.7

(continued)

Table 2   Frequency of Items That Excuse Perpetrator, Blame Victim, or Blame Society *(continued)*

Item	Unit (Large Case, n = 1,688; Small Case, n = 1,365)		Article (Large Case, n = 111; Small Case, n = 119)	
	Frequency	%	Frequency	%
Victim deserved it/brought it on self				
Victim's behavior was unacceptable (victim used drugs or alcohol, was unfaithful, was clingy, etc.)				
Total	72	2.4	35	15.2
Large/Small	28/44	1.7/3.2	14/21	12.6/17.6
Victim was specifically blamed for bringing about his or her death or the attempt on his or her life				
Total	39	1.3	19	8.3
Large/Small	10/29	0.6/2.1	4/15	3.6/12.6
Victim grew up in an abusive home or had been involved in abusive relationships in the past				
Total	4	0.1	2	0.9
Large/Small	2/2	0.1/0.1	1/1	0.9/0.8
Victim had health problems (he or she was unable to care for self)				
Total	2	0.1	1	0.4
Large/Small	2/0	0.1/0.0	1/0	0.9/0.0
Society is to blame				
Society in general is violent				
Total	23	0.8	15	6.5
Large/Small	20/3	1.2/0.2	13/2	11.7/1.7
Perpetrator had easy access to weapons				
Total	6	0.2	5	2.2
Large/Small	5/1	0.3/0.1	4/1	3.6/0.8

The fifth research question dealt with the journalists' sources. As table 3 shows, the coverage relied heavily on factual information not attributed to a source and on information from official sources such as the police, court documents, and legal personnel. Articles drew much less on sources who could put a human face on domestic violence, such as victims' and perpetrators' family members, friends, and employers. This is consistent with the literature, as is the fact that domestic violence experts were rarely used as sources. Such experts appeared in only 11 articles: 10 large-case articles and 1 small-case article (table 1).

Table 3   Frequency of Use of Various Sources

Source	Unit[a] (Large Case, $n = 1,688$; Small Case, $n = 1,365$)		Article[b] (Large Case, $n = 111$; Small Case, $n = 119$)	
	Frequency	%	Frequency	%
Factual, unattributed information and official sources				
Factual statement not attributed to a source, unattributed opinion of writer				
Total	1569	51.4	229	99.6
Large/Small	866/703	51.3/51.5	110/119	99.1/100.0
Police or police records, sheriff, Federal Bureau of Investigation, and so forth				
Total	510	16.7	134	58.3
Large/Small	232/278	13.7/20.4	60/74	54.1/62.2
Court documents or official documents other than police records				
Total	164	5.4	59	25.7
Large/Small	131/33	7.8/2.4	40/19	36.0/16.0
Prosecutor or other member of prosecution team				
Total	134	4.4	66	28.7
Large/Small	71/63	4.2/4.6	40/26	36.0/21.8
Defense lawyer or other member of defense team (other than defendant)				
Total	39	1.3	21	9.1
Large/Small	30/9	1.8/0.7	16/5	14.4/4.2
Firefighters, emergency medical technicians, coroner, and so forth				
Total	34	1.1	22	9.6
Large/Small	11/23	0.7/1.7	7/15	6.3/12.6
Generic authorities ("authorities," "officials," "court officials")				
Total	28	0.9	24	10.4
Large/Small	15/13	0.9/1.0	12/12	10.8/10.1

(continued)

Table 3   Frequency of Use of Various Sources *(continued)*

Source	Unit[a] (Large Case, *n* = 1,688; Small Case, *n* = 1,365)		Article[b] (Large Case, *n* = 111; Small Case, *n* = 119)	
	Frequency	**%**	**Frequency**	**%**
Multiple official sources[c]				
Total	14	0.5	13	5.7
Large/Small	8/6	0.5/0.4	8/5	7.2/4.2
Judge, magistrate				
Total	3	0.1	2	0.9
Large/Small	2/1	0.1/0.1	1/1	0.9/0.8
Personal sources				
Neighbor, acquaintance, friend				
Total	143	4.7	46	20.0
Large/Small	77/66	4.6/4.8	29/17	26.1/14.3
Relative of victim but not perpetrator				
Total	57	1.9	14	6.1
Large/Small	16/41	0.9/3.0	2/12	1.8/10.1
Relative of perpetrator and victim				
Total	36	1.2	4	1.7
Large/Small	4/32	0.2/2.3	1/3	0.9/2.5
Victim's employer, coworker, business associate, adviser, etc.				
Total	27	0.9	10	4.3
Large/Small	16/11	0.9/0.8	7/3	6.3/2.5
Perpetrator's employer, coworker, business associate, adviser, etc.				
Total	19	0.6	8	3.5
Large/Small	17/2	1.0/0.1	6/2	5.4/1.7
Perpetrator				
Total	19	0.6	10	4.3
Large/Small	1/18	0.1/1.3	1/9	0.9/7.6
Relative of perpetrator but not victim				
Total	5	0.2	3	1.3
Large/Small	2/3	0.1/0.2	2/1	1.8/0.8
Domestic violence experts[d]				
Victim's advocate[e]				
Total	67	2.2	7	3.0
Large/Small	60/7	3.6/0.5	6/1	5.4/0.8
Medical professional (psychiatrist, psychologist, therapist, doctor, trauma specialist, etc.)				
Total	4	0.1	2	0.9
Large/Small	4/0	0.2/0.0	2/0	1.8/0.0

Table 3   Frequency of Use of Various Sources *(continued)*

Source	Unit[a] (Large Case, n = 1,688; Small Case, n = 1,365)		Article[b] (Large Case, n = 111; Small Case, n = 119)	
	Frequency	%	Frequency	%
Domestic violence survivor				
Total	4	0.1	1	0.4
Large/Small	4/0	0.2/0.0	1/0	0.9/0.0
Women's group/policy				
Total	3	0.1	2	0.9
Large/Small	3/0	0.2/0.0	2/0	1.8/0.0
Generic domestic violence experts ("many in the domestic violence field," "some domestic violence experts")				
Total	2	0.1	2	0.9
Large/Small	2/0	0.1/0.0	2/0	1.8/0.0
Miscellaneous				
News accounts				
Total	17	0.6	10	4.3
Large/Small	7/10	0.4/0.7	6/4	5.4/3.4
Anonymous source				
Total	6	0.2	4	1.7
Large/Small	2/4	0.1/0.3	1/3	0.9/2.5
Other				
Total	129	4.2	40	17.4
Large/Small	101/28	6.0/2.1	28/12	25.2/10.1
More than one source used[f]				
Total	20	0.7	14	6.1
Large/Small	6/14	0.4/1.0	4/10	3.6/8.4

NOTE: Figures do not total 100% due to rounding error.
[a] If a unit contained factual, unattributed information plus information attributed to a source, it was coded for the source. Units that included two or more sources were placed in the more-than-one-source-used category unless (a) one or more of the sources were domestic violence experts or (b) all of the sources were official sources. In the first case, the unit was coded for the appropriate domestic violence category. In the second, it was coded multiple official sources.
[b] Article percentages total more than 100% because each article and case can contain multiple sources.
[c] Multiple official sources includes units in which more than one source was used and all were official sources.
[d] No units used batterers' treatment personnel as sources, so this category was omitted from the table.
[e] Victim's advocates includes units in which more than one source was used and at least one source was a victim's advocate.
[f] More than one source used does not include units in which at least one of the sources was a domestic violence expert and units in which all sources were official sources.

Frame Analysis

Certain frames appeared to misrepresent the broader social problem of domestic violence, providing common-sense solutions to complex problems. These were the police frame, a frame indicating that the people involved were somehow different, a frame that blamed the victim and/or excused the perpetrator, and a frame that perpetrators/abusers were not "normal" and should be easily identifiable.

The police frame adhered to the "just the facts" approach. It described how the homicide played out (who, what, where, when, and how) with no speculation about the nature of the relationship between the perpetrator and the victim and no indication that the killing or its attempt was part of a larger problem between those involved or in society in general (why). The police frame did not indicate domestic violence as a family situation that needed intervention but rather as a legal situation that was already under control. As a result, the domestic violence fatality was not presented as the culmination of events but as an isolated incident to which the police responded. Two- and three-paragraph stories that only used police and doctors as sources reinforced ideas of the competence and authority of police and emergency services while failing to suggest any of the complexity or history of domestic violence.

Journalists also portrayed those involved as different. This frame indicated that domestic violence only happens to certain types of people. Both the perpetrators and victims were usually represented as being from different cultures, either ethnically or provincially, and from a low social class. Their criminal pasts and/or involvement with drugs and alcohol were highlighted, implying that those involved in domestic violence situations were already "troublemakers." For example, 1 article indicated that of the perpetrator and victim, "Neither was a stranger to crime. Celsa was convicted of manslaughter in 1978 for the death of their 2-year-old daughter, and Manuel was convicted for his involvement. Manuel was also a heroin dealer" (Johnson, 1998).

In addition, quiet, nonsocial couples and individuals were set apart from those more neighborly or social. This helped characterize such people as likely to be involved in domestic abuse. One article used quotes from neighbors who saw one couple as "weird" because "these people never talked to each other" (Broberg, 1998).

An interesting related frame implied that perpetrators should be easily identifiable. Many articles expressed surprise that a perpetrator seemed normal, despite literature that supports this phenomenon. In 1 story, a neighbor indicated surprise that the perpetrator of a murder-suicide could also be such a "well-rounded, upbeat person" (Westfall, 1998), and in another, people were shocked because the perpetrator was a "clean-cut, very nice guy" (Castro, 1998b, p. B2).

Instead, articles sought to characterize the perpetrator as deviant and thus presented the notion that domestic violence radiates from a certain type of person. For example, one headline read, "Murderer accused of being deceitful, nasty" (Harvey, 1998). In another case, the daughter of one victim and perpetrator reacting to media attention stated that the perpetrator is "not this monster like everyone portrays him" (Coffidis, 1998).

Another frame blamed the victim or excused the perpetrator for what had happened. Some articles framed in this manner seemed to indicate that women maintained and almost sought out relationships with abusers. For example, in one article, a victim's ex-sister-in-law noted that "Ronnie had a habit of getting with men that abused her" (Castro, 1998a, p. C7).

This frame provided perpetrators with excuses as well. This was most evident in cases of self-defense. In these articles, the perpetrator was represented as defending himself or herself against what was already an abusive situation perpetuated by the victim. Also by highlighting mental or physical illness in their characterizations of the perpetrators, journalists gave reasons for the murders of intimate partners. One case discussed the perpetrator's Gulf War illness, which shifted focus from what he did to an excuse for why he did it (Castro, 1998b; Costigan, 1998; Ellig, 1998). Cases in which the victim or perpetrator was abusing drugs or alcohol implicated the substance abuse as a possible motivation or excuse in addition to characterizing the drug or alcohol abuser as different.

In the three larger cases, some of the same frames reemerged; however, much of the reporting was handled differently. As coverage continued over time, the journalists moved away from the initial incident reports and developed the story more fully in news, news-feature, and feature articles. This is consistent with Chermak's (1995) discussion of what he called *primary stories*, those placed in the best sections of the newspaper and given more leeway in terms of space. As he explained, it takes time for a crime to work its way through the criminal justice system. Thus, crime stories are ongoing, and a story, especially a primary one, may be recycled as the case progresses. In addition, he said, a primary story may spawn related articles.

One of the large cases retold the story of a woman murdered while trying to get out of a domestic violence relationship (e.g., Barker, 1998; Ho, 1998; Tibbets, 1998). In this case, the system, not the victim, was blamed. By explaining the steps the victim took to get out of the abusive situation and by examining the system in place to protect her, the articles showed domestic violence as a larger societal problem. Still, in their characterizations of the victim and the perpetrator, journalists set up a classic story of good versus evil. The articles seemed to remove human characteristics from both parties and construct their story as a morality tale rather than as a slice of life. For example, the victim was characterized as a "vibrant young woman who did everything right" (e.g., Ho, 1998; Tibbets, 1998). A neighbor even stated, "I met her walking the dog and she was just lovely" (Ho, 1998). The perpetrator, on the other hand, was a man with a "criminal history and a violent past," a "tyrant" who "lived and breathed her fear" (Santana & Barker, 1998).

Another large case blamed both the perpetrator and the victim for the failure of the marriage, which ultimately ended in homicide. In the process, the articles uncovered aspects of their lives that might distance them from a normal reader. One article noted, "According to King County Superior Court documents, she [the victim] is alleged to have met men through a chat room. And prosecutors allege that Durall [the perpetrator] met women in a similar manner" (Bartley, 1998, p. A8). That they were both involved in Internet affairs made them seem sneaky, perverted, and removed from more accepted social outlets. The perpetrator even went so far as to use the Internet to research how to murder his wife. Beyond this, no aspects of their relationship were explained except that they were getting a divorce; the reasons why were never explored. Domestic violence and its patterns were not acknowledged although controlling and jealous behavior by the perpetrator was often mentioned in passing.

The largest case introduced the idea that domestic violence only happens in certain places. In this coverage, the community was painted as serene and rural, a place where neighbors knew each other and where these things almost never happen. One resident remarked, "This would be normal for California, but not here" (Church, 1998).

Another frame indicated that the crime only happens to certain people. These articles took the stance that these people were normal; it *should not* have happened to them. The perpetrator was a successful doctor, the victim was a philanthropist and devoted mother, and together they were popular in their community. However, because of the perpetrator's position at the local hospital (a factor that helped make the story newsworthy; see Chermak, 1995), the articles developed a frame that he mattered most to that community. Articles included quotes such as the following: "'I am personally shocked by these events,' Stegbauer said. 'My understanding is he is well regarded by his peers. This is definitely a tragedy'" (Kelly, 1998).

Rather than deal with the perpetrator and the victim as a couple, the journalists focused more on the perpetrator. Articles detailed his mental condition before and after the crime, mentioned his status as a doctor frequently, and even used his title to identify the victim. For example, the headline of the article quoted above simply read "Doctor's Wife Slain" (Kelly, 1998). Because of these portrayals and because the crime was framed as an isolated incident with no details about the relationship prior to the murder, that the perpetrator snapped was viewed as the ultimate tragedy.

Discussion

In general, the coverage leaves audience members to make the connection between the case and domestic violence, abuse, or trauma. In addition, the coverage fails to provide readers with the vocabulary with which to discuss domestic violence.

For a variety of reasons (including the reliance on unattributed factual information and official sources, use of the police frame, omission of information on the victim and perpetrator's history together, and lack of information on psychological abuse), much of the coverage gives no sense of the victim's experience. This presents a grossly distorted picture of domestic violence, potentially portraying the case as one that can be equated with homicide in general.

Some of the coverage framed the victim and/or perpetrator as different, blamed the victim, or excused the perpetrator. This, too, raises questions about the adequacy of the portrayal of domestic violence fatalities.

With the exception of one large case, the coverage tended to portray the incidents as lone murders rather than as part of a larger social problem. This calls to mind the contention of some feminists that positioning domestic violence in terms of individual and family pathology rather than in terms of social structures and socially sanctioned gender roles blames women and helps relieve society of the obligation to act.

Consistent with the literature, we found that the newspapers relied heavily on official sources of information and often used a police frame. This tends to dehumanize the crime by omitting information from people who knew the victim and perpetrator and by emphasizing things such as the what, where, when, and how of the crime. Also, it places the case within the context of law enforcement rather than the context of domestic violence as a social problem, potentially portraying the situation as one that the police will take care of or that is under control.

Our results lend support to Meyers's (1997) idea that news coverage maintains gender myths and stereotypes. For example, coverage that blames the victim sometimes seems to imply that good girls avoid problems and bad girls get what they deserve. Also, as the feminist literature suggests, by presenting a domestic violence fatality as just another homicide and ignoring the victim and perpetrator's history and the social context, the coverage sidesteps the issues of male control, manipulation, and abuse of women.

The results raise questions about how readers respond to coverage of domestic violence fatalities. It appears that the coverage has the potential to insulate readers from the idea of domestic violence, allowing them to conclude that it could not happen to them and that there is no need to discuss it or take action. Whether readers respond in this way remains for future study.

Few articles in the group of 230 portray domestic violence as a social problem that can affect every reader. However, a handful help prove that domestic violence fatalities can be more accurately portrayed within the boundaries of current journalistic norms and practices. For example, some articles illustrate domestic violence as a social problem by tying in other domestic violence cases, quoting domestic violence experts, discussing the work of domestic violence-related agencies, or including domestic violence hot line numbers. Some carefully describe the victim and perpetrator's history of physical and psychological abuse. Some put a human face on the crime through family members, friends, and others who knew the victim and perpetrator.

Clearly, newspapers have the potential to more accurately reflect the reality of domestic violence, and our results point to some ways that might be accomplished. However, we built the study on the assumption that all or most domestic violence deaths included the patterns of physical and psychological abuse described in the literature. It is possible that these patterns do not apply in some cases, that the perpetrator really just snapped with no warning. In such cases, the current coverage may more accurately portray the crime.

Our study is also limited by its dealing with cases and coverage from only 1 year in one state. In addition, it includes only coverage up through the arraignment, leaving future research to analyze postarraignment coverage.

As Sherizen (1978) suggested, media serve as sense makers to the world. This casts a sobering light on our findings that at least some newspaper coverage yields an incomplete, potentially misleading picture of domestic violence fatalities. However, it appears that a more accurate reflection of the reality of domestic violence as a social problem is possible within current journalistic norms and practices. Within those norms, journalists could include information and choose sources and words that place a domestic violence incident within the broader social context and more accurately portray the victim's experience.

Appendix

List of Washington State Newspapers That Included Domestic Violence Fatality Coverage

Battleground Reflector
Bellingham Herald
The Chronicle (Centralia)
Columbia Basin Herald (Moses Lake)
The Columbian (Vancouver, Washington)
Daily Record (Ellensburg)
Daily World (Aberdeen)
Eastside Journal (Bellevue)
The Evergreen (Pullman)
Grant County Journal (Ephrata)
The Herald (Everett)
The Island's Sounder (Eastsound)
The Issaquah Press
The Journal of the San Juan Islands (Friday Harbor)
Millcreek View
The News Tribune (Tacoma)
News-Standard (Coulee City)
Nisqually Valley News (Yelm)
Northwest Asian Weekly (Seattle)
The Olympian (Olympia)
Peninsula Daily News (Port Angeles)
Peninsula Gateway (Gig Harbor)
Pierce County Herald (Puyallup)

Port Townsend Leader
Renton Reporter
Seattle Post-Intelligencer
Seattle Post-Intelligencer / Times combined Sunday edition
The Seattle Times
Seattle Weekly
The Sequim Gazette
Shelton-Mason County Journal
South County Journal (Kent)
South Pierce County Dispatch (Eatonville)
The Spokesman-Review (Spokane)
Stanwood / Camano News
The Sun (Bremerton)
The Tribune (Deer Park)
Tri-City Herald (Kennewick)
Walla Walla Union-Bulletin
The Wenatchee World

Notes

[1] Work by Maxwell, Huxford, Borum, and Hornik (2000) found that articles focused primarily on domestic violence tended to cover specific incidents, often placed blame and solutions with individual victims and perpetrators, and tended not to offer broader solutions. However, when the researchers included articles in which domestic violence was secondary, they found that a higher percentage of the articles were socially focused rather than incident focused.

[2] The Washington State Coalition Against Domestic Violence hued a clipping service to save all domestic violence fatality-related articles from all Washington State newspapers. The coalition made this file of almost 2 years of coverage available for analysis. To keep the study manageable, we used coverage from 1 calendar year.

[3] The clipping service did not include the newspaper's name on 1 article, so the newspaper was coded unknown. This category was not counted among the 40 newspapers.

[4] A suicide that is a victim's response to and means of escape from an abusive relationship fits this criterion. However, we found no such cases.

[5] A lead was defined as the opening of the article through the paragraph in which the journalist stated the point of the piece. With news articles, the lead was often the first paragraph; with feature articles, the lead sometimes ran several paragraphs. Brief pieces that reported domestic violence statistics sometimes included no formal lead and were coded accordingly.

References

Barker, K. (1998, December 23). Killer "lived and breathed" his estranged wife's terror. *The Seattle Times*, pp. B1–B2.

Bartley, N. (1998, September 5). Internet cited in new charges. *The Seattle Times*, p. A8.

Benedict, H. (1992). *Virgin or vamp: How the press covers sex crimes.* New York: Oxford University Press.

Berns, N. (1999). "My problem and how I solved it": Domestic violence in women's magazines. *The Sociological Quarterly*, 40, 85–108.

Breci, M. G. (1991). The changing police response to domestic violence. In J. E. Hendricks (Ed.), *Crisis intervention in criminal justice / social service* (pp. 19–39). Springfield, IL: Charles C Thomas.

Broberg, B. (1998, July 22). Quiet Redondo couple found shot dead in condo. *South County Journal.*

Cappella, J. N., & Jamieson, K. H. (1997). *Spiral of cynicism: The press and the public good.* New York: Oxford University Press.

Cascardi, M., O'Leary, K. D., Lawrence, E. E., & Schlee, K. A. (1995). Characteristics of women physically abused by their spouses and who seek treatment regarding marital conflict. *Journal of Consulting and Clinical Psychiatry, 63,* 616–623.

Castro, H. (1998a, December 6). Abuse ruled her life—And maybe her death. *The News Tribune,* pp. C1, C7.

Castro, H. (1998b, September 16). Fife grad, children slain. *The News Tribune,* pp. B1–B2.

Chermak, S. (1995). *Victims in the news.* Boulder, CO: Westview.

Chibnall, S. (1977). *Law-and-order news: An analysis of crime reporting in the British press.* London: Tavistock.

Church, J. (1998, March 3). Slaying stuns neighbors. *Peninsula Daily News.*

Coffidis, J. (1998, April 11). Erin Revay renews bond with father. *The Olympian.*

Consalvo, M. (1998a). Hegemony, domestic violence, and *Cops*: A critique of concordance. *Journal of Popular Film and Television, 26,* 62–70.

Consalvo, M. (1998b). "3 shot dead in courthouse": Examining news coverage of domestic violence and mail-order brides. *Women's Studies in Communication, 21,* 188–211.

Costigan, T. (1998, September 16). Quadruple murder stumps residents. *The Tribune.*

Crowell, N. A., & Burgess, A. W. (Eds.). (1996). *Understanding violence against women.* Washington, DC: National Academy.

Dobash, R. E., & Dobash, R. P. (Eds.). (1998). *Rethinking violence against women.* Thousand Oaks, CA: Sage.

Ellig, T. (1998, September 14). Murdered mom, kids from area. *The Spokesman-Review.*

Entman, R. M. (1991). Framing U.S. coverage of international news: Contrasts in narratives of the KAL and Iran Air incidents. *Journal of Communication, 41*(4), 6–27.

Entman, R. M. (1993). Framing: Toward clarification of a fractured paradigm. *Journal of Communication, 43*(4), 51–58.

Fagan, J., & Browne, A. (1994). Violence between spouses and intimates: Physical aggression between women and men in intimate relationships. In A. J. Reiss Jr. & J. A. Roth (Eds.), *Understanding and preventing violence: Vol. 3. Social influences* (pp. 115–292). Washington, DC: National Academy.

Gans, H. J. (1979). *Deciding what's news: A study of CBS Evening News, NBC Nightly News,* Newsweek, *and* Time. New York: Pantheon.

Gelles, R. J. (1972). *The violent home: A study of physical aggression between husbands and wives.* Beverly Hills, CA: Sage.

Gelles, R. J., & Straus, M. A. (1988). *Intimate violence.* New York: Simon & Schuster.

Goetting, A. (1995). *Homicide in families and other special populations.* New York: Springer.

Hartley, J. (1982). *Understanding news.* London: Methuen.

Harvey, P. A. (1998, March 4). Murderer accused of being deceitful, nasty. *The Journal of the San Juan Islands,* p. A5.

Herman, J. L. (1992). *Trauma and recovery: The aftermath of violence from domestic abuse to political terror.* New York: Basic Books.

Ho, V. (1998, December 11). Abuse victim did everything right. *Seattle Post-Intelligencer,* pp. A1, A17.

Johnson, T. (1998, April 10). Bellevue police may have solution to 1981 slaying. *Eastside Journal,* pp. A1, A10.

Jones, A. (1994). *Next time she'll be dead: Battering and how to stop it.* Boston: Beacon.

Kelly, C. (1998, March 3). Doctor's wife slain. *Pierce County Herald,* pp. A1–A2.

Klein, E., Campbell, J., Soler, E., & Ghez, M. (1997). *Ending domestic violence: Changing public perceptions halting the epidemic.* Thousand Oaks, CA: Sage.

Kurz, D. (1993). Physical assaults by husbands a major social problem. In R. J. Gelles & D. R. Loseke (Eds.), *Current controversies on family violence* (pp. 88–103). Newbury Park, CA: Sage.

Loseke, D. R. (1989). "Violence" is "violence" . . . or is it? The social construction of "wife abuse" and public policy. In J. Best (Ed.), *Images of issues: Typifying contemporary social problems* (pp. 191–206). New York: Aldine de Gruyter.

Manoff, R. K., & Schudson, M. (Eds.). (1986). *Reading the news.* New York: Pantheon.

Martin, D. (1976). *Battered wives.* New York: Pocket.

Martin, D. (1982). Introduction. In G. Nicarthy (Ed.), *Getting free: A handbook for women in abusive relationships.* Seattle, WA: Seal.

Maxwell, K. A., Huxford, J., Borum, C., & Hornik, R. (2000). Covering domestic violence: How the O. J. Simpson case shaped reporting of domestic violence in the news media. *Journalism & Mass Communication Quarterly, 77,* 258–272.

Meyers, M. (1994). News of battering. *Journal of Communication, 44*(2), 47–63.

Meyers, M. (1997). *News coverage of violence against women: Engendering blame.* Thousand Oaks, CA: Sage.

Molotch, H., & Lester, M. (1974). News as purposive behavior: On the strategic use of routine events, accidents, and scandals. *American Sociological Review, 39,* 101–112.

Moore, M. H., Prothrow-Stith, D., Guyer, B., & Spivak, H. (1994). Violence and intentional injuries: Criminal justice and public health perspectives on an urgent national problem. In A. J. Reiss Jr. & J. A. Roth (Eds.), *Understanding and preventing violence: Vol. 4. Consequences and control* (pp. 167–216). Washington, DC: National Academy.

Pagelow, M. D. (1984). *Family violence.* New York: Praeger.

Pan, Z., & Kosicki, G. M. (1993). Framing analysis: An approach to news discourse. *Political Communication, 10,* 55–75.

Rennison, C. M., & Welchans, S. (2000). *Intimate partner violence* (Bureau of Justice Statistics Special Report NCJ 178247). Washington, DC: U.S. Department of Justice.

Roshco, B. (1975). *Newsmaking.* Chicago: University of Chicago Press.

Santana, A., & Barker, K. (1998, December 13). Slaying suspect had gun permit. *Seattle Post Intelligencer,* pp. B1–B2.

Sherizen, S. (1978). Social creation of crime news: All the news fitted to print. In C. Winick (Ed.), *Deviance and mass media* (pp. 203–224). Beverly Hills, CA: Sage.

Sigal, L. V. (1973). *Reporters and officials: The organization and politics of newsmaking.* Lexington, MA: D. C. Heath.

Straus, M. A., & Hotaling, G. T. (1980). *The social causes of husband-wife violence.* Minneapolis: University of Minnesota Press.

Strentz, H. (1989). *News reporting and news sources: Accomplices in shaping and misshaping the news.* Ames: Iowa State University Press.

Tibbets, G. (1998, December 20). Fearful of husband, victim still tried to follow the rules. *The News Tribune,* pp. C7–C8.

Tuchman, G. (1978). *Making news: A study in the construction of reality.* New York: Free Press.

Websdale, N. (1999). *Understanding domestic homicide.* Boston: Northeastern University Press.

Westfall, B. (1998, February 10). Man apparently kills woman, then himself. *The Columbian.*

TEN

THE MEDIA CONSTRUCTION OF STALKING STEREOTYPES

Brian H. Spitzberg & Michelle Cadiz

Introduction

The term "crime victim" tends to evoke a set of archetypal images: Innocence, violence, powerlessness, weaponry, and tragedy. The iconicity of these archetypes is in no small part a product of media typifications rather than the factual data of victimization. Various media are used to penetrate people's everyday lives with images that not only aid in defining what society deems relevant and true, but also in the sculpting of society itself. With techniques ranging from graphic pictures to vivid language, the media are able to reach vast audiences with any particular message or perspective. Television, newspapers, and magazines are just a few examples of media that have been investigated in order to understand their social impacts. One of the most investigated areas of media imagery is crime. From streetwalkers to stalkers, most people have prototypical images of certain types of socially "deviant" persons and criminal forms of activity, and these cognitive prototypes in turn bear varying degrees of correspondence to reality. This analysis excavates some of the correspondences between the media archetypes of stalking and the actual phenomenon of stalking.

Any effects the media have on people's views of the world are likely to be greater to the extent people rely on the media for their information on that topic. Crime is one of the arenas in which the public has traditionally relied on the media for its information. From Jack the Ripper to Al Capone to the stalking of Madonna and the murder trial of O. J. Simpson, people often rely on the media to give them an image of the criminal, the crime, and the risk and nature of victimization. The analysis presented here examines the image of the victim constructed by the media, especially in reference to the phenom-

Source: *Journal of Criminal Justice and Popular Culture*, Vol. 9, No. 3, 2002, pp. 128–149, © 2002 by the University of Albany School of Criminal Justice. Reprinted with permission.

enon of stalking. The images of stalking in the media appear prismatic. View-ing stalking through the lenses of the media produces many different biased reflections of the phenomenon. These reflections are often reinforcing, but sometimes inconsistent. Understanding how biases and stereotypes are formed and influenced should aid in the understanding of the actual risks of victimization. It will also allow for an understanding of how a crime such as stalking is portrayed by the media and how this portrayal of the crime may affect the public conception of the crime.

The assumption that the news media somehow serve as a value-neutral or objective representation of the world in general, and crime victimization in particular, has long been discredited (Meyers, 1997). News workers inevita-bly operate with some form of ideology. This ideology in turn "structures the meaning of an event by providing the background assumptions used to understand what is to be treated as an event, what constitutes fact, and inter-pretation of that fact" (Voumvakis & Ericson, 1984, p. 42). For example, Meyers (1994, p. 48) concluded that "news coverage of battering is socially distorted, rooted in assumptions, myths, and stereotypes that link it to indi-vidual and family pathology rather than to social structures and gendered patterns of control" (p. 48). Female victimization, therefore, appears to be a productive arena within which to examine the role of societal and journalistic ideology on the formulation of a stereotype such as stalking.

Gate-Keeping Constructions

Crime depictions in the media result from a multifaceted process involv-ing many people and organizations. The fragmented origin of crime report-ing has no single anchor in the "factual" world (Chermak, 1995). Although justice systems and news representatives may have a clear understanding of what crime is, the news production process can distort the image of crime, creating confusion and resulting in messages different than originally intended. News organizations and reporters monitor society for disruptions that occur within people's lives (Aust & Zillmann, 1996). Crimes, especially violent crimes, represent prototypical disruptions. "Crimes without death, blood, or battering are generally not found in the news" (Chermak, 1995, p. 70). Given the entrepreneurial and competitive nature of news organizations, it is little surprise, therefore, that the media philosophy has come to be sum-marized pithily as: "If it bleeds, it leads." Under the aegis of contributing to public safety, media organizations give extensive coverage of violent crime, even if the actual personal risk of violent crime is relatively minor. Violent crimes possess a high degree of sensationalistic and dramatic content (Mey-ers, 1997, p. 90).

Public fascination and potential identification of personal risk with such stories provide indirect guidance to media organizations in their story selec-tion process. Newscasts take the role of messenger, providing the general pub-lic with the sensational information of the day. Newsrooms and news programs serve as gate-keepers, monitoring what is seen and heard about any given event. The media also influence public perceptions because of the required selectivity involved in media story selection. Out of the thousands of potential stories that occur every day, the gate-keeping function of media organizations extracts only some as sufficiently newsworthy to present in the appropriate and limited venues of media production (Shoemaker, 1996). The criteria by which some stories are included for broadcast or print, and others excluded, inevitably reflect the priorities of the news organizations, which in turn reflect perceived priorities of the consuming media marketplace.

Rhetorical Constructions

Crimes are, among other things, narratives. As such, crime typifications in the media may follow a variety of rhetorical stylistic conventions. Crimes are also a genre of reporting, and therefore reveal certain institutional and strategic conventions:

> Typically, media coverage of new crimes follows a standard pattern: (1) it typifies the crime by offering detailed accounts of particular, usually dramatic, incidents, . . . ; (2) it describes the crime in compelling terms . . . ; (3) it explains some of the crime's causes; (4) it offers interpretations of the crime's meaning and significance; and (5) coverage continues as long as the crime can be approached from fresh angles . . . or until some other story demands attention. (Best, 1999, p. 63)

In general, novelty and titillation potential are important factors affecting whether or not crimes are reported (Meyers, 1997). A more cynical interpretation is that the media "focus on 'hot topics' of entertainment value" until a "media frenzy develops that results in expanded coverage of isolated and unique events. . . . Isolated incidents thus become social issues and, through politicization, eventually crime problems" (Kappeler & Potter, 2005, pp. 6–7). Prototypical representations of crime tend to trade in "(1) the identification and targeting of a distinct deviant population; (2) the presence of an 'innocent' or 'helpless' victim population; (3) the emergence of brave and virtuous heroes; and (4) the existence of a substantial threat to established norms, values, or traditional lifestyles" (Kappeler & Potter, 2005, p. 23). When males are suspects and women are victims, the story takes on greater newsworthiness (Pritchard & Hughes, 1997), perhaps because it resonates with larger cultural narratives. Such news not only conforms to cultural myths, but assists in enforcing them as well (Altheide, 1997). Cultural narratives of crime serve the function of providing warnings and suggestions for personal risk management and sense making (Wachs, 1988).

Other narrative rhetorical conventions can subtly affect impressions of a crime. For example, whether reports are primarily derived from police rather than directly from the victims can affect the personalization of the crime. Word choice can affect attribution of responsibility. Reporting in rape cases that a victim was "taking a shortcut through a ravine late at night, hitchiking [sic], accepting a ride home from a stranger, dressing provocatively, leaving her door unlocked, drinking alone in a bar, sunbathing in a secluded area by herself, and taking a man home from a bar" may seem descriptively incidental, but by implication suggest the victims' role in their own victimization (Voumvakis & Ericson, 1984, p. 23). In a story about a murder-suicide, Meyers (1994) points out that the husband was portrayed as "obsessive" and had a difficult time dealing with the separation from his wife. Such language removes partial blame from the husband's shoulders. In contrast, being obsessive and having a difficulty with separation lend themselves to the explanation that he could not control himself and was driven to shoot both himself and his estranged wife. A content analysis of newspaper reports of domestic violence found that 47.8 percent "suggested at least one motivation or excuse for the perpetrator" (Bullock & Cubert, 2002, p. 484).

Voumvakis and Ericson's (1984) study of newspaper accounts of attacks on women indicated predominant attributions were:

> 1) to the victim, especially in terms of how victim precautions can serve as a major device for crime prevention; 2) to the criminal justice system, especially how more and improved laws, policing, and punishment is another major crime prevention device; and 3) to offender pathology, especially how there is a need to identify and control "dangerous" individuals in society. (p. 43)

The tendency to identify the pathological villain and the helpless victim in such crime stories serves several rhetorical functions. "The archetypes are social predators not bound or restrained in any way by normal social rules and values. In contrast, the media portray victims of crime as passive and helpless" (Surette, 1998, p. 40). As such, (1) anyone may be a victim, especially if that person plays an unwitting role in eliciting victimization, (2) increased law enforcement and personal attention to protection are needed, and (3) attention to ongoing media coverage is vital to stay apprised of the risks of such a crime.

Audience Constructions

Another arena in which media typifications are constructed, and indirectly reinforced, is in the public's perceptions of the media reports. Crimes such as rape, murder, and robbery evoke strong images in the media-consuming public that reflect various cultural, ethnic, and gender-based stereotypes. Such public stereotypes serve to filter what is processed when the media report crime stories, and indirectly feed back to the media organizations' values regarding what the public "wants."

Furthermore, in an increasingly complex communication environment, the public cannot process all available information and news. To manage the deluge of information in the environment, people develop cognitively efficient schemata for processing sensory stimuli. "Perceptions and judgments are subject to distortion because of shortcuts . . . [that is,] fast and expedient paradigms used to cognitively cope with massive amounts or fast-paced information" (Aust & Zillmann, 1996). When crime narratives are distributed to the mass public, the value orientations of these narratives are filtered through millions of personal schemata, and subsequently through millions of informal interpersonal conversations in which new versions are negotiated, reinforced, and passed on to others.

In such information rich environments, media consumers may increasingly rely on the media to structure and simplify reality into more manageable forms. For example, heavy consumption of sexual images appears to decrease sensitivity toward sexual aggression victims (MacKay & Covell, 1997), and repeated exposure to filmed violence against women similarly produces desensitization effects (Dexter, Penrod, Linz, & Saunders, 1997). Gender role stereotypes portrayed in the media coexist with gender stereotypes in society (Signorielli, 1989), and these stereotypes in turn interact with stereotypes of crime and victimization. Rape tends to be portrayed as perpetrated by sadistic, psychopathic, or disturbed persons preying on the relatively helpless (Bufkin & Eschholz, 2000).

The similarity media consumers perceive with reported crime victims plays a role in how people attribute blame to a victim. "A person who sees herself as personally similar to the victim and thus a potential victim will attribute catastrophe to chance or some other factor, and not the victim" (Dexter et al., 1997, p. 2151). The more similar a victim is to a person, the less likely the person is to attribute responsibility of the crime to the victim. Contrariwise, the less the victim is similar to the person, the more likely the person will attribute blame to the victim. Importantly, desensitization, which can be strongly influenced by media typifications and exposure, appears to mediate women's empathy with victims of violence (Dexter et al., 1997). Similarly, males exposed to sexually objectifying films appear less sympathetic to rape victims than males not exposed to such films (Millburn, Mather, & Conrad, 2000).

The finding that similarity between a victim and a perceiver affects the perceiver's attribution of blame has at least three implications. First, although most crime stories mention neither the race nor the socio-economic status of the victim, among those stories that do, most victims are reported as white and middle to upper class (Kappeler & Potter, 2005; Meyers, 1994). Therefore, media consumers who do not identify with these victims are less likely to be sensitized to the victim, and thereby, to the crime itself. Second, the media can bring unfavorable aspects about a victim to light. This can have the effect of diffusing attributed responsibility for the crime, allowing people to be less empathetic to victims of crimes, and implicitly creating a climate of tolerance toward the violence itself. For example, to the extent that stalking victims are portrayed as celebrities, the media consumers may not internalize either empathy or sense of personal risk. Third, and related, relevant parties can distance themselves both from the crime and the societal agenda that would seek to regulate the crime. For example, "the very common view that men who rape, murder, or otherwise commit acts of violence against women are 'sick' or in some way pathological ignores the social roots of this violence. . . . The representation of the assailant as a monster or psychopath also allows men to distance themselves from the perpetrators of these crimes" (Meyers, 1997, p. 10). Thus, for example, to the extent stalkers are portrayed as obsessed, delusional, or mentally ill, the public may distance their own courtship activities from such crazed and deviant actions, thereby licensing their own intrusive behaviors, and not seeking protection or redress against such actions from others.

In regard to crime, the more unusual the crime, the more media exposure it tends to receive (Meyers, 1997). This leads to a media paradox. The media tend to report highly unusual, unlikely, but vivid events that nevertheless provide a "disproportionate influence on . . . subsequent judgments through their increased memorial availability" (Ruscio, 2000, p. 22). Media consumers not only find such reports interesting, but their enhanced memorial availability and sensational nature make such stories more likely to be reproduced in everyday conversation with others. Such interpersonal effects thereby serve to reinforce the selective biases of the media. Thus, the media are selective in what they portray of reality, what they portray reflects both organizational ideologies and cultural stereotypes, and these biases are in many ways reinforced through public interpersonal processes of conversational topical reproduction.

In one of the clearest evidences of the mediated construction of reality, research has repeatedly shown that media consumption is significantly correlated with biased perceptions of personal risk of crime victimization. That is, because crime is more likely than other events to end up being portrayed in the media, heavy media consumers tend to perceive personal risks of crime victimization that are many times greater than their actual statistical risk (Chiricos, Eschholz, & Gertz, 1997; O'Keefe & Reid-Nash, 1987). This enculturation effect suggests that the proportion of media exposure to crime enabled by content selection processes shapes the domain of relevance in people's minds, thereby restricting alternative interpretations of reality.

Media Effects on Reality

News media use statistics in order to get across the importance of a crime or newsworthy event. Yet researchers have found that the media often misrepresent the numbers, or otherwise bias how the numbers are presented and, therefore, interpreted by the consumer. For example, perhaps due to an understanding of recency effects, percentages and rates of crime are usually cited toward the end of a story (Berger, 1998). Furthermore, especially in reference to crime, the most dramatic estimates tend to be selected rather than the most conservative numbers. One study, for example, concluded that the media foster the perception that crime rates are constantly increasing, and even downplaying the amount of nonviolent crime (Kappeler & Potter, 2005). The media in particular appear to be eager and complicit partners with police and political bodies in the construction of "crime waves" (e.g., Brownstein, 1996). Such exaggerations help make a story more newsworthy and interesting. Exaggeration raises viewers' concern and allows the media to spend more time or space on the events (Glassner, 1999).

The media both systematically and unsystematically distort the images they relay to society, for example, in portraying an epidemic of violent crime (Kappeler & Potter, 2005). Yet, the media use such fear evoking images because they invoke a preexisting framework of expectations in which people identify with potential victims and are able to attribute such problems to manageable causes (Altheide & Michalowski, 1999). Apparently, "the success of a scare depends not only on how well it is expressed, but also . . . on how well it expresses deeper cultural anxieties" (Glassner, 1999, p. 208). In parallel to the maxim, "if it bleeds, it leads," it seems to follow that "if it terrorizes, it mesmerizes."

The Media Portrayals of Stalking

By any historical measure, stalking is a paradigm example of social and media construction of a crime. Despite the occurrence of stalking since antiquity (Kamir, 2001), it was not recognized as a crime until California passed an anti-stalking law in 1990. Indeed, the media appear responsible for the labeling of the crime itself (Keenahan & Barlow, 1997; Lawson-Cruttenden, 1996). Despite a lack of any scientific evidence of widespread prevalence or risk in society at the time, and in the murky legal context of prohibiting behaviors that may be constitutionally protected (Hueter, 1997), in less than a decade all 50 states in the U.S. passed some form of anti-stalking legislation. The media played no small part in this avalanche of political activity in a context best known for a more glacial pace of social reform. "The new language of stalking was born in the sensationalism of the media who first appropriated the term stalker to name the persistent pursuers of celebrities. . . . Now stalking forms part of legal and scientific discourses as well as having acquired a privileged status among the descriptors of our society's categories of fear" (Mullen, Pathé, & Purcell, 2000, p. 1). Stalking has generated at least three interrelated domains of discourse: Popular (media), legal, and scientific (Lowney & Best, 1995; Mullen et al., 2000). These discourses will be analyzed as they inform, or fail to inform, each other. First, a couple of specific instances of claims about stalking located at the nexus of these domains are examined for their lack of substance. Second, the research literature on stalking is briefly summarized so as to provide a point of contrast to the media portrayals of stalking. Third, some general critiques regarding media typifications of stalking are presented.

Case Studies in Constructing the Stalking Problem[1]

One of the most oft-cited claims about stalking is that 90 percent of women who are killed by former intimates were stalked prior to the murder (see table 1). This statistic has been reconstituted in hearings before Congress, in the popular press, and extensively in law review articles on stalking legislation. If the credibility of a statistic is in any way based upon its repetition, this "finding" must be true. In an attempt to trace the origins of this statistic, several steps were pursued. First, available databases and search engines were employed to locate any additional information that could provide leads to this statistic's original source. The additional articles found through these search engines proved to be of no use for this purpose. Second, an attempt was made to locate the original person quoted for this statistic. Its derivations always seemed to lead back to William S. Cohen, Ruth Micklem, or Melinda Beck (who first quoted Micklem). The trail turned out to be more circuitous than any precise and oft-quoted statistic ought to be. Examining references to this statistic, the earliest sources appeared to be from one of two primary candidates: (1) studies reported to Congress, or (2) an interview in a popular news magazine.

The "Detroit and Kansas City" Link

Senator Cohen (1993) claimed in testimony during the Judiciary Committee on Anti-stalking Legislation in 1992 that "There are studies in Detroit and Kansas City that reveal that some 90 percent of all those who are murdered by their intimate partners called the police at least once, and more than

---

Table 1   Exemplars of a Mythic Statistic

Beck et al. (1992, July 12, p. 61): "Nearly one third of all women killed in America are murdered by their husbands or boyfriends, and, says Ruth Micklem, codirector of Virginians Against Domestic Violence, as many as 90 percent of them have been stalked."

Holmstrom (1992, Dec. 22, p. 1): "Of all those women murdered by their ex-husbands or boyfriends, studies indicate that 90 percent had called the police at least once for protection, and more than half had called five times or more."

Geberth (1992, p. 139): "According to Ruth Micklem, co-director of Virginians Against Domestic Violence, 'Nearly one third of all women killed in America are murdered by their husbands or boyfriends, and as many as 90 percent of them have been stalked.'" (*Newsweek*, July 13, 1992).

Cohen (1993, p. 8): "There are studies in Detroit and Kansas City that reveal that some 90 percent of all those who are murdered by their intimate partners called the police at least once, and more than half have called five times or more."

Cordes (1993, p. 13): "A study by the Federal Bureau of Investigation reported that 90 percent of women killed by their husbands or boyfriends in 1991 were stalked before the attack."

Morin (1993, p. 125): "Statistical information from Kansas City and Detroit reveals that 90 percent of these women [who were killed by their husbands or boyfriends] made police contact at least once for assistance. Over 50 percent called a minimum of five times" (citing Cohen's [1993] congressional testimony).

Strikis (1993, p. 2772): Note 19: "It is possible that as many as ninety percent of women killed by former lovers or husbands have been stalked by the murderer prior to the attack (citing Melinda Beck et al., "Murderous obsession," *Newsweek*, July 13, 1992, at pp. 60, 61).

Tucker (1993, p. 614): Note 37: "It is estimated that up to 90 percent of women killed in the United States by intimate or former intimate partners have been stalked by them" (apparently citing Joanne Furio, "Can new state laws stop the stalker," *Ms.*, Jan.–Feb., 1993, p. 90; and Geberth, 1992, p. 139).

Gross (1994, 1998, 2000, p. 5): "In fact, 90 percent of the 1,500 women killed by their current or former mates each year in this country were stalked before being murdered" (citing Kenneth L. Woodward, "Murderous obsession," *Newsweek*, July 13, p. 61).

Kappeler & Potter (2005, p. 104): "There were estimates that . . . 90 percent of the women killed by their spouses or former boyfriends were stalked prior to their murder" (Beck, 1992).

Coleman (1997, p. 420): "Ruth Micklem, director of Virginians Against Domestic Violence, estimates that as many as 90 percent of women murdered by boyfriends or husbands may have been stalked prior to their deaths" (Beck et al., 1992).

Davis & Chipman (1997, p. 168): "A total of 90 percent of women murdered by boyfriends or husbands were stalked by their killers" (citing Wells, 1996; and National Institute of Criminal Justice Project . . . , 1993).

Hueter (1997, p. 216): "As many as ninety percent of women killed by their former partners have been stalked prior to their murder" (citing Beck, 1992).

Snow (1998, p. 12): "National statistics show that 90 percent of the women killed every year by current or former spouses were stalked by these men before being murdered" (citing Gross, 1994, p. 9).

Best (1999, pp. 53–54): "In spite of the intense interest in stalking, as late as 1993 there were only two published scholarly studies of stalkers: an examination of LAPD TMU files (Zona et al., 1993); and a typology of 'criminal stalkers' (Holmes, 1993). Neither offered much original data, so antistalking crusaders routinely borrowed data from research on domestic violence to characterize stalking: . . . 'Studies in Detroit and Kansas City reveal that 90 percent of those murdered by their intimate partners called police at least once' (Senator William Cohen in Congressional Record 1992: 59527); 'Nearly one third of all women killed in America are murdered by their husbands or boyfriends, and, says Ruth Micklem, co-director of Virginians Against Domestic Violence, as many as 90 percent of them have been stalked' (Beck 1992: 61). The juxtaposition of the latter two quotes reveals how evidence used to define new crimes evolves: Senator Cohen cited a finding that 90 percent of women killed by husbands or lovers had previously called the police; when later advocates repeated that statistic, they equated having called the police with being stalked, ignoring the likelihood that many women called to complain about abuse by partners living in the same residence (and therefore not stalkers)."

Schell & Lanteigne (2000, p. 19): "Ruth Micklem, director of Virginians Against Domestic Violence, estimates that as many as 90 percent of women murdered by abusive husbands and boyfriends may have been stalked prior to their deaths" (Beck et al., 1992).

half have called five times or more" (p. 8). Best (1999) later surmised that this claim was casually reinterpreted to imply that if calls were made, the victims were being stalked. He correctly noted the fallacy of the inference, given that calls can be made in reference to a current cohabitant, which strains the definition of stalking.

As it turns out, Senator Cohen took liberties with his representation of the studies from Kansas City and Detroit. A focused search of *Criminal Justice Abstracts* eventually yielded the source of Cohen's mysterious statistic. A study published by the Police Foundation (Wilt et al., 1977) investigated police involvement in domestic violence situations in Kansas City and Detroit. The Kansas City study revealed, based on 1970 and 1971 data, that 95 percent (in 1970) and 84 percent (1971) of homicides had previous disturbance calls to the same address, with 52 percent (1970) and 46 percent (1971) having been called to the address five or more times. For aggravated assaults, 87 percent (1970) and 81 percent (1971) had previous disturbance calls, with 50 percent (1970 & 1971) involving five or more calls to the same address. However, in the post-episode interviews, "close to half of the homicide and assault sample reported that they had never called the police for a disturbance" (p. 32). The Detroit data were even more mixed. Of 144 assault victims interviewed, 56 percent indicated they had been victims of previous conflict-based assaults and had reported these assaults to the police. Based on interviews of the perpetrators, only four percent of the homicide cases reported previous calls to the police.

Contrary to Cohen's testimony, therefore, (1) the data are not entirely consistent across both "Detroit and Kansas City," (2) the actual statistic is closer to 85 percent rather than 90 percent in Kansas City, and closer to 56 percent in Detroit, (3) the data refer to both domestic assault and homicide, thereby confounding the far more serious crime of murder with all domestic assaults, (4) the data were two decades old when Cohen reported them, (5) the data could only be linked to an address, and therefore could not be specified according to a "victim" or "perpetrator" in terms of who initiated the call, and (6) the data quite enigmatically suggest that the assaults and homicides were potentially relational, in that there was no difference in calls due to "victim" or "offender" status. Indeed, interviews in the Detroit data led to the conclusion that "in 145 (45.5 percent) of the homicides resulting from arguments, the victims initiated the conflicts, while offenders did so in 123 (38.6 percent) instances. In another 26 (8.3 percent) cases, victims and offenders together started the trouble, while in 25 (7.8 percent) cases someone other than offenders or victims did so" (p. 36). The relational instigation and reciprocity implicit in these latter findings seem ill suited to the attribution of stalking. Thus, although the "Detroit and Kansas City" studies are intriguing in their potential relevance to stalking, they require an excessive amount of extrapolation to be directly evidentiary. Furthermore, as is indicated below, these studies ultimately were clearly revealed not to be the source of the actual statistic in question.

The "Virginians against Domestic Violence" Link

The original source for the 90 percent quote turned out to be Ruth Micklem in an article in *Newsweek*, written by reporters Beck et al. (1992). After this article's debut, Micklem's statistic was subsequently cited in many other articles (see table 1). In the article by Beck et al., Micklem was quoted as co-director of Virginians Against Domestic Violence (VADV). An Internet search eventually yielded contact information for the VADV, including Micklem's office phone number, fax number, and e-mail. Ruth Micklem was contacted, whereupon the following conversation ensued, as reconstructed from the interviewer's[1] notes of the conversation:

"Hello, this is Ruth, what can I do for you?"

"Hi my name is Marian and I am assisting my professor who is a behavioral scientist currently involved in studying the area of stalking . . ."

"Oh, yes?"

"Are you the Ruth Micklem who gave the statistic of 90 percent . . ."

Micklem immediately recognized where the inquiry was going. She claimed having received hundreds of calls on the *Newsweek* statistic ever since it had been published. She apologetically explained that the statistic is basically an inaccurate extrapolation. "There is no study whatsoever that the figure was derived from because there was no study anywhere in the country at that time [concerning stalking]." The 90 percent figure was merely the response to the reporter's question: "How many of the women that you work with are stalked?"

In short, this statistic, which has been cited repeatedly, is at best based on an offhand judgment regarding women who are not necessarily murdered and associated with a particular organization and with a highly self-selected population. Indeed, the only hard empirical data available through standard search engines appear in three recent studies. Moracco, Runyan, and Butts (1998) found that 23.4 percent of femicide cases had experienced "stalking" prior to the incident. McFarlane et al. (1999) found that 76 percent of femicide and 85 percent of attempted femicide cases involved "at least one episode of stalking within 12 months of the violent incident" (p. 308). Morton, Runyan, Moracco, and Butts (1998) conducted a study of partner murder-suicides. In the prototypical episode, 45 percent experienced partner separation or attempted separation as a precursor, and one third of victims had sought protection from the legal system in the form of a restraining order or arrest warrant. "In nearly 70 percent of cases in which the victim and perpetrator were separated, the perpetrator had harassed, followed, or otherwise monitored the activities of the victim in the weeks or days preceding the homicide-suicide event" (p. 96). The evidence of pre-murder stalking appears to be 70 percent of 45 percent, or 32 percent in this admittedly rather specialized sample. Thus, repetition and emphasis of startling quotes such as "90 percent of women murdered by their partner were stalked" illustrate the complicit discourses of the media, legal, and expert domains in the construction of crime myths (Kappeler & Potter, 2005). Stalking would hardly seem to need embellishment, but receives it nonetheless.

The Science of Stalking

Statistics originally produced as an "educated guess" by the profiler and clinical psychologist Park Deitz during congressional hearings made it into the popular press (Mullen et al., 2000). Specifically, he estimated that there were as many as 200,000 stalkers in the U.S., and that as many as 1 in 20 women would be stalked in their lifetime. These estimates began taking on a life of their own in all three discourses—popular, scientific, and legal (Best, 1999, p. 52; Lowney & Best, 1995, p. 42; Mullen et al., 2000, p. 29). That the media would latch on to such precise guesses is not surprising, because a decade ago there was virtually no scientific research on stalking.

As of this writing, there are over 100 studies available across several countries. Reviews of this research, as well as descriptive meta-analytic data on stalking studies, reveal the following picture of the stalking phenomenon (Spitzberg, in press; Spitzberg & Cupach, 2001, 2002, in press). Across studies, approximately 21 percent of people have been stalked or obsessively pursued to some degree. The more that fear or threat are required as definitional elements of pursuit to consider it stalking, the lower this percentage gets. Women (approximately 24 percent) appear victimized more than men (approximately 11 percent), but this difference tends to disappear in younger, college-based samples (e.g., Spitzberg, Nicastro, & Cousins, 1998; Spitzberg & Rhea, 1999). Proportionately about 75 percent of all stalking victims are female, and about 25 percent of all victims are male, although again there are exceptions based upon sampling method and type of sample. A representative adult sample found high proportions of men stalking men, although little is yet understood about what this finding means (Tjaden & Thoennes, 1998). Finally, approximately 75 percent of victims are acquainted with their pursuer, and about 25 percent of pursuers are former romantic partners. Only about a fifth to a quarter of pursuers are complete strangers or unknown to the victim. If the early estimates of societal risk were significantly biased, the accuracy of other media representations of stalking deserve examination.

Media Typifications of Stalking

To date, surprisingly there have been no general surveys of the public's beliefs or stereotypes of stalking, and there has been only one systematic content analysis designed to examine trends in media reporting of stalking (Lowney & Best, 1995). There are several stereotypes that nevertheless appear to litter the media landscape. The most prominent stereotypes, often closely interrelated, seem to be that (1) stalking is a particular problem of celebrity, (2) stalkers tend to be strangers, (3) stalking is a gendered crime, (4) stalkers tend to be mentally disturbed and dangerous, and (5) stalking is mutually exclusive of normal courtship.

Stalking as Celebriphilic

Prior to 1989–1990, stalking legally did not exist, and was rhetorically constructed under the aegis of harassment, obsession, and psychological rape (Lowney & Best, 1995, p. 37). However, with the sensationalistic media coverage of the stalking murder of actress Rebecca Schaeffer, along with the association of this crime in the public and media with Theresa Saldana, Jodie Foster, and several, non-celebrity stalking murders in Southern California, watershed "anti-stalking" legislation was passed in California.

In their study of media typifications of stalking, Lowney and Best (1995) note: "During 1989 and 1990, national magazine articles and television broadcasts presented 16 typifying examples of stalking; 11 (69 percent) involved celebrity victims" (p. 39). An article in *Entertainment Weekly* illustrates the continued lack of connection between media reports of stalking and the actual phenomenon. In the wake of the murder of Robert Blake's wife Bonny Bakley, the article examined "inappropriate pursuit in the entertainment industry." In a surprising twist, it claimed that these people "are not stalkers" because "unlike stalkers and groupies, people like Bakley generally don't develop crushes on the stars they pursue—it's fame itself that flames their desires" (Svetkey, 2001, pp. 44, 47). This claim is odd in several respects. First, it suggests that stalking tends to be motivated by romantic "crushes." Studies show, however, that as a population stalkers have many motives, including revenge, attention, romance, and fantasy (see Spitzberg & Cupach, 2001, 2002, in press). Second, the report seems to imply that stalking is defined motivationally rather than behaviorally. The motive behind unwanted pursuit, presuming the pursuit is intentional, is largely irrelevant to its criminality. Regardless, media reports eventually moved away from a dominant image of stalkers as exclusively experiencing "celebriphilia" (Svetkey, 2001). It is a good bet that any episode of stalking of any prominent celebrity, whether in politics, entertainment, or sports, would receive media attention, whereas stalking among non-celebrities likely would not be covered, short of a serious attendant crime (e.g., kidnapping, murder, etc.). Despite the allure of celebrity for both stalkers and the media, Lowney and Best (1995) found that reports in the media between 1992–1994 occurred far more frequently than in previous years, and stalking was finally depicted as something that affects the public at large.

Stalking as the Return of the Stranger

A corollary of the celebriphilic stereotype is the mythic image of violent crime in general: The lurking stranger lying in wait to inflict harm on the unsuspecting victim. Indeed, people appear to believe there is greater risk of danger from strangers than from intimates (Harris & Miller, 2000). The media equip the public with a stereotypical stalker profile. In the early period of popular media reporting of stalking (1989–1991), victims were most likely to be portrayed as celebrities (Lowney & Best, 1995). The image of stalking seems to persist of "a cunning stranger who has targeted an innocent victim for prey" (Kappeler & Potter, 2005, p. 101). This image seems to represent a corrupted vision of courtship, in which love is disjunctive and exploitative in nature. "The public is captivated by the idea of a total stranger becoming obsessed with a victim" (Hall, 1998, p. 114). If love with a stranger is often romanticized in popular culture (e.g., romance novels), love from a danger-ous stranger may evoke deeper fantasies of taboo and risk in an otherwise cul-turally preferred courtship process.

Stalking as Gendered

One of the notable shifts in media portrayals of stalking is that victims are typically depicted as female while stalkers are typically depicted as male (Lowney & Best, 1995). This shift invokes common societal stereotypes about the nature of criminality and victimization. Combined with the early portrayals of stalking, "the most popular image is that of a celebrity who is stalked by a crazed fan or a battered woman who has left a physically abusive relationship and is now being stalked by the ex-lover" (Hall, 1998, p. 114). The research, indeed, clearly shows that stalking is a fairly gendered activity. Approximately 75–80 percent of stalking victims are female and approxi-mately 75–80 percent of stalkers are male (Spitzberg, in press). Research in some populations, however, shows relatively no or small sex differences in either the victimization by, or perpetration of, unwanted pursuit (e.g., Adams, Pitre, & Smith, 2001; Brownstein, 2001; Langhinrichsen-Rohling, Palarea, Cohen, & Rohling, 2000; Logan, Leukefeld, & Walker, 2000; Sin-clair & Frieze, 2000; Spitzberg & Cupach, 2001, 2002; Spitzberg, Nicastro, & Cousins, 1998; Spitzberg & Rhea, 1999). It seems that Hollywood pursues some movies that depict stalking episodes in ways that violate these gender stereotypes, such as showing a female stalking a male (e.g., *Fatal Attraction*), a female stalking a female (e.g., *Single White Female*), or a male stalking a male (e.g., *The Fan*). Such depictions may be viewed as sensational precisely because they violate traditional gender stereotypes for such a crime.

The media also portray stalking as relatively premeditated and, therefore, the victims as relatively helpless (Kappeler & Potter, 2005). The image of the helpless victim is consistent with both common stereotypes of women as reactive rather than proactive in courtship, and as less capable of taking care of themselves and in need of protection. In a potential double bind, another common stereotype is that women victims of violent crimes, especially sexual crimes, "ask for it" by the way they dress, or how much alcohol they may consume enables many to distance themselves from victims of violent crimes (Cuklanz, 1996). These stereotypes are not very consistent with the actual research on stalking that shows approximately 75 percent deriving from the context of existing relationships, the majority of which were previously inti-mate (Meloy, 1996; Spitzberg, in press). That is, stalking emerges from con-texts in which the participants often pursued voluntarily and comfortably a mutually preferred relationship, which only later became exploitative, poten-tially due to mutually reinforced problems in the relationship.

Stalking as Psychopathic and Violent

Lowney and Best (1995) found in their content analysis of early reports of stalking (circa 1989–1990) that "claimsmakers depicted star-stalkers as mentally disturbed, inappropriately obsessed with their celebrity victims" (p. 39). Later (mid-1990s), stalking was most likely to be depicted as leading to homicide, suggesting that the "if it bleeds, it leads" priority took over once the crime was no longer as novel and unusual in the public consciousness. The movie industry capitalizes on the fears and curiosities evoked by the images of mental disturbance and violence (e.g., *Pacific Heights, The Body Guard, The Thin Line Between Love and Hate, Stalked*). Such sensationalistic dramas reflect, and may reinforce, news reporting biases of reporting more on the glamorous, thrilling aspects of stalking than on the common, more normative, aspects of the crime. Research shows that stalkers brought to the attention of law enforcement do commonly have psychological disorders (see Meloy, 1996, 1999; Meloy & Gothard, 1995; Meyers, 1997). However, to date there is substantial evidence that processes of unwanted pursuit, even often threatening pursuit, occur in relatively "normal" populations (Cupach & Spitzberg, 1998; Cupach & Spitzberg, 2000; Spitzberg, in press). Intersect-ing with the previous stereotypes, these data indicate that victims of stalking have less to fear from strangers than from intimates.

Stalking as Clearly Distinguishable from Courtship

At the same time the media horrify stalking, the media ironically tend to glorify stalking-like actions. Romance narratives commonly entail romantic idealizations and adventurous endeavors overcoming great odds and involv-ing great personal sacrifice, as the one obsessed with another invests in a campaign of pursuit despite the rejections by the object of affection (de Becker, 1997). Reflecting a common cultural romantic theme that persistence in courtship eventually pays off (Lowney & Best, 1995, p. 50), stalkers' Quix-otic quests are given vivid narrative life. Indeed, that the average duration of stalking tends to be approximately two years (Spitzberg, in press) indicates persistence is a hallmark of stalking and unwanted pursuit. Consequently, actions romanticized as persistence may in many cases exceed the boundaries of propriety. Research demonstrates that even relatively mild to moderate forms of unwanted pursuit and intrusion are often perceived as threatening (Cupach & Spitzberg, 2000). Thus, glorifying such events in the media makes identifying them for the public at large a more difficult task.

Discussion

Several interrelated media-fostered stereotypes of violent crime in general, and stalking in particular, have been suggested by this analysis. By way of summary, it appears that the media create, or at least reinforce, the following portrayals: Stalking is celebriphilic; Stalkers are strangers; Stalking is gendered; Stalkers are disturbed; Stalking is violent; and Stalking is culturally deviant. Specifically, stalking is portrayed as threatening and violent, despite data that suggest violence occurs in a minority of stalking relationships. Stalking is portrayed as a product of sick, psychopathic individuals, despite data indicating that most stalking results from preexisting relationships, suggesting the relative normality of the perpetrators. Stalking is often portrayed as a social and cultural aberration, something bizarre and deviant. Yet, stalking itself is little more than an extreme version of existing norms and rituals of courtship. Stalking is portrayed as a highly gendered crime, in which women are at higher risk and threat than males, and males are portrayed as the primary perpetrator. While data support the statistical norms for this stereotype, and despite some notable Hollywood exceptions (e.g., *The Fan*, *Fatal Attraction*, the stalking of Steven Spielberg, David Letterman, etc.), in general women are portrayed as the more prototypical victim, and at much greater risk, and men are portrayed as the prototypical perpetrator. Such stereotypes may ultimately undermine the possibility, let alone the credibility, of male victims and female perpetrators. Finally, stalking continues to be associated with stars and status. In part, simply because those with high status are more likely to be considered newsworthy, stalking stories will disproportionately imply this link. In the process, however, the vastly more common stalking of the far more common person becomes a relatively hidden crime.

An important caveat to any attempt at depicting media typifications and trends is that there is the risk of overgeneralizing the overgeneralizations. The media are far from univocal in their activities and tendencies. Furthermore, while "it is too simplistic to seek a mono-dimensional stereotype of a victim, so too is it too simplistic to seek a mono-dimensional stereotype of a stalker" (Keenahan & Barlow, 1997, p. 294). Thus, an effort has been made to reflect some of the complexity of the process of media portrayals. To characterize any tendency in the media as a whole is a process fraught with ironic potential.

Examining stalking under the light of previous research literature that examines crime depictions in the media allows for an understanding of how stalking is often misunderstood by society. For example, in Great Britain Sheridan and Davies (2001) compared legislative definitions of stalking with public perceptions of stalking, and found significant differences between the two. In another study, subjects clearly distinguished stalking from non-stalking behaviors, and the clusters identified were viewed as "constituents of stalking as recently portrayed by the media" (Sheridan, Gillett, & Davies, 2000, p. 276). However, these authors also found that verbal forms of pursuit and intrusion were largely lacking from people's perceptions of stalking, and concluded that only 20 of the 40 behaviors examined achieved greater than 70 percent shared agreement as stalking behaviors. Hills and Taplin (1997) found in an experimental scenario study that females tend to perceive stalking behaviors as less threatening than males, a finding suggested by Tjaden, Thoennes, and Allison's (2000) report that men who meet the legal definition of being victims of stalking are less likely to view themselves as stalking victims. Perhaps most telling is that police, who should be far more informed than the average person, face many difficulties responding to stalking cases (Spitzberg, 2002). One study presented a stalking scenario to police officers and only slightly over half of them considered treating it as a stalking incident (Farrell, Weisburd & Wyckoff, 2000). A study of actual case files found that out of 285 domestic violence police reports containing narrative elements of stalking, only one resulted in a formal charge of stalking (Tjaden & Thoennes, 2000).

Some have suggested that there are powerful institutional forces at work to "manufacture" victims and victimization (e.g., Dineen, 1996). Indeed, it has been argued that it was the intense media attention to stalking that created sufficient public consciousness to find "political expression in a series of anti-stalking laws" (Mullen et al., 2000, p. 11). "New crimes offer government officials opportunities for media coverage; . . ." and experts, activists, and the media thereby obtain visibility and resources (Best, 1999, p. 67). The argument of self-interested manufacture of public policy, however, appears largely based on two important assumptions. First, it is assumed that economic motives (e.g., law enforcement budgets, political agendas to pander to public interest in the rhetoric of safe streets, psychologists' profit motive in maintaining a steady stream of clients, etc.) equate to actual political collusion in creating victims *ex nihilo*. Second, such an institutional collusion hypothesis assumes that estimates and diagnoses of victimization are exaggerated relative to the facts. The first assumption seems paranoid *a priori*, and is not evidenced by actual exemplars of collusive discourse or paper trails. The second assumption, even if true, hardly denies the existence of a large number of victims, whether counted in the thousands, tens of thousands, or millions. In short, as Spitzberg (1999) suggested in his meta-analysis of studies of rape and sexual coercion prevalence, even if the estimates are lower than some studies and authors have claimed, the best estimates summarized across almost 100 studies still make it obvious that the problems are real and significant *enough* to stop debating *whether* there is a problem (Spitzberg, in press).

One of the obvious biases in the media typifications of stalking is that reporters' crime beats are dominated by police as information sources about crime (Chermak, 1995). Yet, research reveals that women consistently experience gender-specific difficulties in their experiences with police as a source of assistance with their victimization (e.g., Chaudhuri & Daly, 1992; Fischer & Rose, 1995; Gondolf, McWilliams, Hart, & Stuehling, 1994; Kaci, 1994; Keilitz, Davis, Efkeman, Flango, & Hannaford, 1998; Klein, 1996; Spitzberg, in press; Wallace & Kelty, 1995; Zoellner et al., 2000). Victims often are sufficiently traumatized by their experience that they neither seek nor want greater exposure under the media spotlight. Lowney and Best (1995) found that medical, mental health, and legal, criminal justice experts were far more likely to be cited as authorities in stalking reports than were women's victims movement experts. Furthermore, Chermak's (1995) research on crime reports showed that "psychological effects were mentioned in approximately one percent of the sampled stories" (p. 70). In short, stalking reporting is likely to be framed from a law enforcement perspective rather than a victims' perspective. Such a bias may emphasize issues of motive, method, and narrative rather than elaborate victims' sense-making and coping in the face of such unwanted pursuit.

Thus, the official version of crimes often come only from the police, or from clinical psychologists, who have a motive and a worldview to construct crimes as non-routine and products of sick, pathological, and unpredictable individuals. Once again, this would seem to distort the "normality" of stalking in society, and the extent to which it may at once be both a crime perpetrated by men and women, and yet a crime that allows men to terrorize women through routine stalking activities so long as they do not cross the intangible lines that would elicit police response. Police can only report on crimes that come to their attention, and only the most egregious stalking crimes are likely to come to their attention, which are also likely to be those stalking crimes that involve women as victims and psychologically disturbed, male perpetrators. Furthermore, men may be embarrassed to report stalking victimization, especially if it is at the hands of a woman. Such victimization may be considered emasculating by men. This permits men in society to (1) distance themselves and their own mundane relational intrusions from the crime of stalking, and (2) be deterred from ever seeking police intervention in their own stalking victimizations for fear that such incidents would not be regarded as real crimes. At the same time, (3) women would still be likely to experience a background of everyday terrorism by the realization that the next man they say hello to may be a psychopath as depicted in the media (Brockway & Heath, 1998; Ferraro, 1996; Kelly & DeKeseredy, 1994; Stanko, 1985, 1990).

As a potentially paradoxical contrast, once a crime of stalking has come to the attention of the police and media, subsequent instances of arrest, sentencing, and imprisonment are all disproportionately likely to suggest a veil of regulated order and protection. By contrast, in fictional crime shows "estimates put the solution rate on television at greater than 90 percent" (Surette, 1998, p. 21). Only a relatively small fraction of all stalking is likely to be reported to police, subsequently prosecuted, and subsequently resulting in actual punishment of the perpetrator (e.g., Tjaden & Thoennes, 1998). Indeed, it is difficult to locate cases of romantic stalking reported in the media in which the perpetrator was not already apprehended at the time of the report.

One area for future research will be investigation of media effects due to format of presentation. For example, Chermak (1995) reports that television and newspapers differed in their coverage of crimes in a variety of ways. Crime was the second most covered topic on television news, but fifth in newspapers. But certain stages of crimes are more visual, and thus more likely to be covered by television (e.g., police investigation) relative to what is covered by newspapers (e.g., court proceedings). Given the extended time period and intentionally stealthy nature of stalking, it may be a relatively "non-visual" crime unless it ends in a particularly violent manner. Sensational stalking events may be covered more by television, and less violent, routine stalking events may be more covered by newspapers. To the extent that television continues to dominate newspapers as a primary source of news, such a difference between media in their coverage of stalking may perpetuate the sensationalistic stereotypes regarding stalking processes.

A second important arena for research is to conduct random and representative samples of media reports of stalking. These data could then be systematically coded for narrative content and structures, as well as visual content. Such analyses, especially if sensitive to time, could reveal whether stalking reportage has, indeed, evolved (e.g., Lowney & Best, 1995). Furthermore, if these analyses could then be yoked to public opinion surveys regarding fear of stalking as a crime, then a much more comprehensive picture could emerge regarding the role that media and their consumers play in the co-construction of crime stereotypes.

Research is only now coming to grips with the need for scientifically reliable information on stalking, only slightly beyond a decade after the crime splashed onto the headlines and television screens of American culture (e.g., Meloy, 1999; Mullen et al., 2000; Spitzberg, in press; Spitzberg & Cupach, 2001, 2002, in press). It is never easy to strip away fact from myth in the domain of media portrayals, as all such efforts come from an ideological position that interacts imperceptibly with the ideological positions being critiqued. Such efforts, however, provide vital insight both into the process of media influence of public perception, and into the phenomena portrayed, such as stalking.

Note

[1] The authors would like to extend appreciation to Marian Cabuto, a communication student at San Diego State University, who was instrumental in tracking down the original sources for the claims examined under this heading.

References

Adams, S. J., Pitre, N. L., & Smith, A. (2001). Criminal harassment by patients with mental disorders. *Canadian Journal of Psychiatry, 46,* 173–176.

Altheide, D. L. (1997). The news media, the problem frame, and the production of fear. *Sociological Quarterly, 38,* 647–668.

Altheide, D. L., & Michalowski, R. S. (1999). Fear in the news: A discourse of control. The *Sociological Quarterly, 40,* 475–503.

Aust, C. F., & Zillmann, D. (1996). Effects of victim exemplification in television news on viewer perception of social issues. *Journalism and Media Communication Quarterly, 73,* 787–803.

Beck, M., Rosenberg, D., Chideya, F., Miller, S., Foote, D., Manly, H., & Katel, P. (1992, July 13). Murderous obsession. *Newsweek,* 60–62.

Berger, C. (1998). Processing the quantitative data about risk and threat in news reports. *Journal of Communication, 48,* 87–106.

Best, J. (1999). *Random violence: How we talk about new crimes and new victims.* Berkeley, CA: University of California Press.

Brockway, J. H., & Heath, L. (1998). Risk at night: Contextual effects of perceived control on fear of rape. *Representative Research in Social Psychology, 22,* 52–60.

Brownstein, H. H. (1996). *The rise and fall of a violent crime wave: Crack cocaine and the social construction of a crime problem.* Guilderland, NY: Harrow and Heston.

Brownstein, A. (2001, December 8). In the campus shadows, women are stalkers as well as the stalked: New studies on college victim rates prompt debate. *Chronicle of Higher Education,* A40–A42.

Bufkin, J., & Eschholz, S. (2000). Images of sex and rape: A content analysis of popular film. *Violence Against Women, 6,* 1317–1344.

Bullock, C. F., & Cubert, J. (2002). Coverage of domestic violence fatalities by newspapers in Washington State. *Journal of Interpersonal Violence, 17,* 475–499.

Chaudhuri, M., & Daly, K. (1992). Do restraining orders help? Battered women's experience with male violence and legal process. In E. S. Buzawa & C. G. Buzawa (Eds.), *Domestic violence: The changing criminal justice response* (pp. 227–252). Westport, CT: Greenwood.

Chermak, S. M. (1995). *Victims in the news: Crime and the American media.* Boulder, CO: Westview Press.

Chiricos, T., Eschholz, S., & Gertz, M. (1997). Crime, news and fear of crime: Toward an identification of audience effects. *Social Problems, 44,* 342–357.

Cohen, W. S. (1993). Antistalking proposals. *Hearing before the Committee on the Judiciary,* United States Senate (J–103–5). Washington, D.C.: U.S. Government Printing Office.

Coleman, F. L. (1997). Stalking behavior and the cycle of domestic violence. *Journal of Interpersonal Violence, 12,* 420–433.

Cordes, R. (1993). Watching over the watched: Greater protection sought for stalking victims. *Trial, 29,* 12–13.

Cuklanz, L. M. (1996). *Rape on trial: How the mass media construct legal reform and social change.* Philadelphia: University of Pennsylvania Press.

Cupach, W. R., & Spitzberg, B. H. (1998). Obsessive relational intrusion and stalking. In B. H. Spitzberg & W. R. Cupach (Eds.), *The dark side of close relationships* (pp. 233–263). Hillsdale, NJ: Erlbaum.

Cupach, W. R., & Spitzberg, B. H. (2000). Obsessive relational intrusion: Incidence, perceived severity, and coping. *Violence and Victims, 15,* 357–372.

Davis, J. A., & Chipman, M. A. (1997). Stalkers and other obsessional types: A review and forensic psychological typology of those who stalk. *Journal of Clinical Forensic Medicine, 4,* 166–172.

de Becker, G. (1997). *The gift of fear: Survival signals that protect us from violence.* Boston: Little, Brown and Co.

Dexter, H. R., Penrod, S., Linz, D., & Saunders, D. (1997). Attributing responsibility to female victims after exposure to sexually violent films. *Journal of Applied Social Psychology, 27,* 2149–2171.

Dineen, T. (1996). *Manufacturing victims: What the psychology industry is doing to people.* Montreal: Robert Davies Multimedia Publishing.

Farrell, G., Weisburd, D., & Wyckoff, L. (2000). Survey results suggest need for stalking training. *The Police Chief, 67*(10), 162–167.

Ferraro, K. J. (1996). Women's fear of victimization: Shadow of sexual assault? *Social Forces, 75,* 667–690.

Fischer, K., & Rose, M. (1995). When "enough is enough": Battered women's decision making around court orders of protection. *Crime and Delinquency, 41,* 414–429.

Geberth, V. J. (1992). Stalkers. *Law and Order, 40,* 138–143.

Glassner, B. (1999). *The culture of fear.* New York: Basic Books.

Gondolf, E. W., McWilliams, J., Hart, B., & Stuehling, J. (1994). Court response to petitions for civil protection orders. *Journal of Interpersonal Violence, 9,* 503–517.

Gross, L. (1994). *To have or to harm: From infatuation to fatal attraction.* New York: Warner Books.

Gross, L. (2000). *Surviving a stalker: Everything you need to know to keep yourself safe* (rpt., previous title: *To have or to harm*). New York: Marlowe & Company.

Hall, D. M. (1998). The victims of stalking. In J. R. Meloy (Ed.), *The psychology of stalking* (pp. 113–137). San Diego, CA: Academic Press.

Harris, M. B., & Miller, K. C. (2000). Gender and perceptions of danger. *Sex Roles, 43,* 843–863.

Hills, A. M., & Taplin, J. L. (1998). Anticipated responses to stalking: Effect of threat and target-stalker relationship. *Psychiatry, Psychology and Law, 5,* 139–146.

Holmstrom, D. (1992, Dec. 22). Efforts to protect women from "stalkers" gain momentum at state, federal levels. *Christian Science Monitor,* p. 1.

Hueter, J. A. (1997). Lifesaving legislation: But will the Washington stalking law survive constitutional scrutiny? *Washington Law Review, 72,* 213–240.

Kaci, J. H. (1994). Aftermath of seeking domestic violence protective orders: The victim's perspective. *Journal of Contemporary Criminal Justice, 10,* 204–219.

Kamir, O. (2001). *Every breath you take: Stalking narratives and the law.* Ann Arbor, MI: University of Michigan Press.

Kappeler, V. E., & Potter, G. W. (2005). *The mythology of crime and criminal justice* (4th ed.). Long Grove, IL: Waveland.

Keenahan, D., & Barlow, A. (1997). Stalking: A paradoxical crime of the nineties. *International Journal of Risk, Security, and Crime Prevention, 2,* 291–300.

Keilitz, S. L., Davis, C., Efkeman, H. S., Flango, C., & Hannaford, P. L. (1998, January). *Civil protection orders: Victims' views on effectiveness* (National Institute of Justice Research Preview). Washington, D.C.: U.S. Department of Justice.

Kelly, K. D., & DeKeseredy, W. S. (1994). Women's fear of crime and abuse in college and university dating relationships. *Violence and Victims, 9,* 17–30.

Klein, A. R. (1996). Re-abuse in a population of court-restrained male batterers: Why restraining orders don't work. In E. S. Buzawa & C. G. Buzawa (Eds.), *Do arrests and restraining orders work?* (pp. 192–213). Thousand Oaks, CA: Sage.

Langhinrichsen-Rohling, J., Palarea, R. E., Cohen, J., & Rohling, M. L. (2000). Breaking up is hard to do: Unwanted pursuit behaviors following the dissolution of a romantic relationship. *Violence and Victims, 15,* 73–90.

Lawson-Cruttenden, T. (1996). Is there a law against stalking? *New Law Journal, 6736,* 418–420.

Logan, TK, Leukefeld, C., & Walker, B. (2000). Stalking as a variant of intimate violence: Implications from a young adult sample. *Violence and Victims, 15,* 91–111.

Lowney, K. S., & Best, J. (1995). Stalking strangers and lovers: Changing media typifications of a new crime problem. In J. Best (Ed.), *Images of issues: Typifying contemporary social problems* (2nd ed., pp. 33–57). New York: Aldine de Gruyter.

MacKay, N. J., & Covell, K. (1997). The impact of women in advertisements on attitudes toward women. *Sex Roles, 36,* 573–583.

McFarlane, J., Campbell, J. C., Wilt, S., Sachs, C. J., Ulrich, Y., & Xu, X. (1999). Stalking and intimate partner femicide. *Homicide Studies, 3,* 300–316.

Meloy, J. R. (1996). Stalking (obsessional following): A review of some preliminary studies. *Aggression and Violent Behavior, 1,* 147–162.

Meloy, J. R. (1999). Stalking: An old behavior, a new crime. *Forensic Psychiatry, 22,* 85–99.

Meloy, J. R., & Gothard, S. (1995). Demographic and clinical comparison of obsessional followers and offenders with mental disorders. *American Journal of Psychiatry, 152,* 258–263.

Meyers, M. (1994). News of battering. *Journal of Communication, 44,* 47–63.

Meyers, M. (1997). *News coverage of violence against women: Engendering blame.* Thousand Oaks, CA: Sage.

Millburn, M. A., Mather, R., & Conrad, S. D. (2000). The effects of viewing R-rated movie scenes that objectify women on perceptions of date rape. *Sex Roles, 43,* 645–664.

Moracco, K. E., Runyan, C. W., & Butts, J. D. (1998). Femicide in North Carolina, 1991–1993. *Homicide Studies, 2,* 422–446.

Morin, K. S. (1993). The phenomenon of stalking: Do existing state statutes provide adequate protection? *San Diego Justice Journal, 1,* 123–162.

Morton, K., Runyan, C. W., Moracco, K. E., & Butts, J. (1998). Partner homicide-suicide involving female homicide victims: A population-based study in North Carolina, 1988–1992. *Violence and Victims, 13,* 91–106.

Mullen, P. E., Pathé, M., & Purcell, R. (2000). *Stalkers and their victims.* Cambridge: Cambridge University Press.

O'Keefe, G. J., & Reid-Nash, K. (1987). Crime news and real-world blues: The effects of media on social reality. *Communication Research, 14,* 147–163.

Pritchard, D., & Hughes, K. D. (1997). Patterns of deviance in crime news. *Journal of Communication, 47,* 49–67.

Ruscio, J. (2000). Risky business: Vividness, availability, and the media paradox. *Skeptical Inquirer, 24,* 22–26.

Schell, B. H., & Lanteigne, N. M. (2000). *Stalking, harassment, and murder in the workplace: Guidelines for protection and prevention.* Westport, CT: Quorum Books.

Sheridan, L., & Davies, G. M. (2001). What is stalking?: The match between legislation and public perception. *Legal and Criminological Psychology, 6,* 3–17.

Sheridan, L., Gillett, R., & Davies, G. M. (2000). "Stalking"—Seeking the victim's perspective. *Psychology, Crime & Law, 6,* 267–280.

Shoemaker, P. J. (1996). Media gatekeeping. In M. B. Salwen & D. W. Stacks (Eds.), *An integrated approach to communication theory* (pp. 79–92). Mahwah, NJ: Erlbaum.

Signorielli, N. (1989). Television and conceptions about sex roles: Maintaining conventionality and the status quo. *Sex Roles, 21,* 341–360.

Sinclair, H. C., & Frieze, I. H. (2000). Initial courtship behavior and stalking: How should we draw the line? *Violence and Victims, 15,* 23–40.

Snow, R. L. (1998). *Stopping a stalker: A cop's guide to making the system work for you.* New York: Plenum Trade.

Spitzberg, B. H. (1999). An analysis of empirical estimates of rape and sexual coercion. *Violence and Victims, 14,* 241–260.

Spitzberg, B. H. (2002). In the shadow of the stalker: The problem of policing unwanted pursuit? In H. Giles (Ed.), *Law enforcement, communication, and the community* (pp. 173–200). Amsterdam: John Benjamins.

Spitzberg, B. H. (in press). The tactical topography of stalking victimization and management. *Trauma, Violence, and Abuse: A Review Journal.*

Spitzberg, B. H., & Cupach, W. R. (2001). Paradoxes of pursuit: Toward a relational model of stalking-related phenomena. In J. Davis (Ed.), *Stalking, stalkers and their victims: Prevention, intervention, and threat assessment* (pp. 97–136). Boca Raton, FL: CRC Press.

Spitzberg, B. H., & Cupach, W. R. (2002). The inappropriateness of relational intrusion. In R. Goodwin & D. Cramer (Eds.), *Inappropriate relationships* (pp. 191–219). Mahwah, NJ: Erlbaum.

Spitzberg, B. H., & Cupach, W. R. (in press). What mad pursuit: Conceptualization and assessment of obsessive relational intrusion and stalking-related phenomena. *Aggression and Violent Behavior: A Review Journal.*

Spitzberg, B. H., Nicastro, A. M., & Cousins, A. V. (1998). Exploring the interactional phenomenon of stalking and obsessive relational intrusion. *Communication Reports, 11,* 33–48.

Spitzberg, B. H., & Rhea, J. (1999). Obsessive relational intrusion and sexual coercion victimization. *Journal of Interpersonal Violence, 14,* 3–20.

Stanko, E. (1985). *Intimate intrusions: Women's experience of male violence.* London: Routledge & Kegan Paul.

Stanko, E. (1990). *Everyday violence: How women and men experience sexual and physical danger.* San Francisco: Pandora/HarperCollins.

Strikis, S. A. (1993). Stopping stalking. *Georgetown Law Journal, 81,* 2771–2813.

Surette, R. (1998). *Media, crime, and criminal justice: Images and realities.* Belmont, CA: Wadsworth Publishing.

Svetkey, B. (with Wiener, A. H.). (2001, June 22). Dangerous game. *Entertainment Weekly,* 42–48.

Tjaden, P., & Thoennes, N. (1998). *Stalking in America: Findings from the National Violence Against Women Survey.* Washington, D.C.: National Institute of Justice and Centers for Disease Control and Prevention (NCJ 169592).

Tjaden, P., & Thoennes, N. (2000). The role of stalking in domestic violence crime reports generated by the Colorado Springs Police Department. *Violence and Victims, 15,* 427–441.

Tjaden, P., Thoennes, N., & Allison, C. J. (2000). Comparing stalking victimization from legal and victim perspectives. *Violence and Victims, 15,* 7–22.

Tucker, J. T. (1993). Stalking the problems with stalking laws. *Florida Law Review, 45,* 609–707.

Turell, S. C. (2000). A descriptive analysis of same-sex relationship violence for a diverse sample. *Journal of Family Violence, 15,* 281–293.

Voumvakis, S. E., & Ericson, R. V. (1984). *News accounts of attacks on women: A comparison of three Toronto newspapers.* Toronto, Canada: University of Toronto.

Wachs, E. (1988). *Crime-victim stories: New York City's urban folklore.* Bloomington: Indiana University Press.

Wallace, H., & Kelty, K. (1995). Stalking and restraining orders: A legal and psychological perspective. *Journal of Crime and Justice, 18,* 99–111.

Wilt, G. M., Bannon, J. D., Breedlove, R. K., Kennish, J. W., Sandker, D. M., & Sawtell, R. K. (1977). *Domestic violence and the police: Studies in Detroit and Kansas City.* Washington, D.C.: Police Foundation.

Zoellner, L. A., Feeny, N. C., Alvarez, J., Watlington, C., O'Neill, M. L., Zager, R., & Foa, E. B. (2000). Factors associated with completion of the restraining order process in female victims of partner violence. *Journal of Interpersonal Violence, 15,* 1081–1099.

ELEVEN

THE ROLE OF TELEVISION NEWS IN THE CONSTRUCTION OF SCHOOL VIOLENCE AS A "MORAL PANIC"

Donna Killingbeck

Abstract

This work examines the representation of school shootings in the television news media and how these representations have contributed to the construction of school violence as a "moral panic." A review of the literature as it pertains to the media and the social construction of moral panics is provided as well as an overview of the news making process. The discussion is situated within Stanley Cohen's stages of a "moral panic." The article concludes that the presentation of specific events (i.e., school shootings) and elements of popular culture have contributed to increasing levels of fear, misguided political policy, and the development of an industry focused on school violence. In addition, an integrative, broader definition of school violence is suggested.

Introduction

During the 1997–1998 school year, the American public was riveted by magnified coverage of highly unusual crime stories of school shootings that turned into what some news outlets described as an "all too familiar story." Rather than providing context, the media's labeling of these shootings as "a trend" has tended to exacerbate people's fears about the safety of their children and youth in schools. The result is that misdirected public policy is being generated to safeguard the schools, even though the real threat may lie elsewhere. To remedy the purported "crisis" of classroom violence, politicians have proposed solutions ranging from posting additional police officers

Source: *Journal of Criminal Justice and Popular Culture*, Vol. 8, No. 3, 2001, pp. 186–202, © 2001 by the University of Albany School of Criminal Justice. Reprinted with permission.

in our schools, to eliminating any minimum age at which children may be tried as adults, to expanding the death penalty to juveniles.

According to Barak (1994:6): "The consideration or examination of the interrelationships between media, society and criminology is essentially a dynamic and complex enterprise. It involves the interaction of journalists, sources and audiences that co-exist within a diverse and eclectic cultural and social system." To add value, the study also requires attention to the developing political economy and the sociohistorical experience of news production that exist within the larger organization of mass media. In an attempt to provide equal attention to these interactions, this paper begins with a review of the research concerning the media's role in the construction of moral panics. Next, the discussion turns toward the historical representation of criminals and crime in the film and television genre and how these representations have changed over time and is then followed by an outline of the news making process. Finally, the article considers the social impact and importance of the news media's role in policy making and the construction of societal fears, focusing particularly on political and corporate decisions in response to the increasing fears of school violence and how each of these are situated in the framework of a moral panic.

The Construction of Moral Panics

In 1971 Stanley Cohen investigated a series of "moral panics." Cohen (1980) used the term "moral panic" to characterize the reactions of the media, the public, and agents of social control to youth disturbances. This work, involving the Mods and Rockers, demonstrated how agents of social control amplified deviance. According to Cohen (1980), these groups were labeled as being outside the central core values of consensual society and as posing a threat to both the values of society and society itself, hence the term "folk devils." In addition to Cohen's work, Jock Young's (1971a) book, *The Drugtakers*, also demonstrated the role of the media in the amplification of deviance and thus drew attention to the ideological role of the media in actively constructing meanings, rather than simply reflecting a shared meaning. When discussing the public concern about statistics showing an apparent alarming increase in drug abuse, Young (1971b) observed that the "moral panic over drug taking results in setting up of police drug squads, which in turn produces an increase in drug related arrests." This observation highlights the effect produced by the interaction of the media, public opinion, interest groups, and the authorities, which gives rise to a moral panic.

According to Cohen (1980:9), the key elements or stages in a moral panic are:

1. Someone or something is defined as a threat to values or interests;

2. This threat is depicted in an easily recognizable form by the media;

3. There is a rapid build up of public concern;

4. There is a response from authorities or opinion makers;

5. The panic recedes or results in social changes.

It was through Stuart Hall's (1978) approach to ideology that the media's use of moral panics to both define and distort social problems was fleshed out into a general critique of the media's construction of social reality. For instance, mugging was presented in the media as a new and growing phenomenon, when in fact the crime was not new, only the label was. Official statistics did not support the view that mugging was rapidly growing; however, with a name for the crime now in existence old offenses were categorized as such, creating the impression of growth. According to Hall et al. (1978), the media whipped up a moral panic around the issue which served to legitimate an increase in punitive measures; they conclude that the media played a key role in developing and maintaining the pressure for law and order measures.

According to Hall et al. (1978), the media obtain their information from the primary definers of social reality, those in powerful and authoritative positions. The media (secondary definers) amplify the perceived threat to the existing social order, and the police and courts then act to eliminate the threat. The media ensure that the dominant ideas or ideologies are constantly reproduced by relying on the information of the definers of the dominant ideology. Thus, Hall and his colleagues demonstrate the media's ability to enlarge the state's influence into everyday life, the moral panic becoming the vehicle for transmission of the dominant ideology. In other words, "the media tend to reproduce the definitions of the powerful" (Hall et al. 1978: 57). They faithfully reproduce, symbolically, the existing structure of power in today's institutional order. However, Hall et al. (1978) argue that this is not conspiratorial; the media do not set out to divert attention from root problems, such as economic problems. But these economic problems create strain and the media responds by amplifying the symptoms of the strain.

The term "moral" implies that the perceived threat is not something mundane, but is a threat to the social order itself or an idealized conception of it. The threat and its perpetrators are regarded as evil "folk devils" and excite feelings of righteousness. The response is likely to be a demand for greater social regulation or control and a demand for a return to traditional values. Although there is some disagreement on what constitutes a "panic," there is some agreement on the characteristics of concern and hostility. Concern is over the behavior of a certain group or category of people and hostility, or an increase in fear, is directed toward the group or category regarded as a threat. In addition to hostility and concern, other characteristics such as volatility and disproportionality may be emphasized. Volatility means that the moral panics are likely to appear suddenly and that the level of feverish concern is not likely to last, even if the problem is long-standing. Finally, disproportionality refers to an assumption that the threat or danger is more substantial than is warranted by a realistic appraisal (Goode and Ben-Yehuda 1994). During a moral panic, public anxiety is amplified by publicity in the press which portrays these events as signifying a widespread and deeper moral malaise and as a sign of social disintegration. However, public concern about an issue, in complex societies, seldom results from the indignation of the citizenry alone, but as a result of the roles of many contributors, including the role of the moral entrepreneurs.

Howard Becker (1963) emphasizes the role of "moral entrepreneurs" in defining behavior and individuals as deviant and criminal. Becker (1963) asserts that the public is often stirred up through the mass media by efforts of moral entrepreneurs or moral crusaders, who attempt to rouse public opinion through the media by leading social movements and organizations to bring pressure on the authorities to exercise social control and moral regulation. Becker (1963) describes the moral crusader as fervent and righteous and holding to an absolute ethic; what he or she sees is truly evil with no qualification.

Joseph Gusfield (1963), in his study of prohibition, explains the success of moral crusades in terms of Max Weber's status defense. Gusfield (1963) argues that these crusades stand in for the social discontents of particular social classes or groups. By controlling status issues, the group feeling threatened reasserts its power and values through legislation. Although this single factor explanation is far too simplistic to explain the persistence and rise of moral panics, it does, however, add to the understanding of contextual factors that contribute to moral panics.

Philip Jenkins (1992) contributes the role of "symbolic politics" and "politics of substitution" to the understanding of moral panics. Jenkins (1992) argues that claims makers draw attention to a specific problem, in part because it symbolizes another issue. For example, school shootings raise issues concerning gender relations, without ever actually stating it. Whether an accused shooter is from a dual working parent family or a single parent family, simply reporting the shooter's family arrangement says something about the breakdown of the traditional family structure; thus, the idea is conveyed that someone (usually the mother) has done (or hasn't done) something that either led to this situation or allowed it.

Historical Trends in Media Representation of Crime and Criminals

Film was introduced in 1895 and by 1923 was the most influential entertainment medium in America. The images were universally available, widely consumed, and came to shape and reflect American culture. Film affected the public's values, political views, social behavior, consumption patterns, and worldviews. Film was the first mass medium with the ability to create a mass public—a homogenous group made up of people with different social, economic, and ethnic backgrounds. From 1920 to 1950 criminals, whether heroic or villainous, were portrayed as decisive, intelligent, and attractive individuals (Surette 1992).

Enter Television

The growth and public acceptance of television since the 1950s has been enormous and with that acceptance the impact on society's norms, values, consumption, social behavior, public policy, and expectations has been shaped and reflected. In 1987 approximately one quarter of all prime time shows were crime related, whether factual or fictional. According to Ray Surette (1992:32): "The popular mass entertainment media, first in the form of film and today led by television, have thus become a significant social factor, conveying thematic messages and lessons about whom to emulate and fear in society, what the basic causes of crime are and how crime should be fought." Concerns about the images and messages portrayed have steadily risen. The entertainment media do not claim to be an accurate portrayal of reality, nor do they accurately portray crime and its causation. However, society's ability to discern between fact and fiction is often blurred, resulting in inaccurate perceptions of whom to fear, the basic causes of crime, and the appropriate responses. Media repeatedly convey misleading messages and lessons, consistently pointing to individual predatory traits as the cause of crime. Media criminals have consistently become more violent, animalistic, irrational, and predatory and their crimes are increasingly senseless, more violent, and random. Criminality is viewed as an individual choice and other social and economic explanations are irrelevant and ignored (Surette 1992).

Understanding the Newsmaking Process

In order to investigate cases of apparent moral panic, it is necessary to understand how news is developed. The distortions of reality conveyed by the entertainment media are not surprising; they are fiction. However, the similarities between entertainment media and news media, which are expected to depict an accurate and objective view of reality, are unsettling considering the enormous impact of the latter on the social construction of reality.

The images and messages put forth by the news media are remarkably similar to those of the entertainment media. There are two models used to describe the process and criteria by which news media content is created. Realistically, news agencies do not fit neatly into either model but operate somewhere in the middle. At one end is the market model, where the newsworthiness of an event is determined by what is of interest to the public; the facts are objectively reported and realistic information about the world is reproduced. The other extreme is the manipulative model, where newsworthiness is determined not by what is of interest to the public, but by what is of interest to the news agency owners. The ability of the news media, operating under a strict manipulative model, to shape and distort the image of reality is frighteningly apparent (Cohen and Young 1981).

However, it is far too simplistic to assume that these models are the norm in the arena of news reporting. An organizational model of news processing contains components of both the manipulative and market models (Surette 1992). Similar to the manipulative model, under the organizational model news is selected based on the needs of the agency. The periodicity, or timing, of the events and how they match the scheduling needs of the agency is a consideration when determining what is reported. Consonance, or how the story ties into prior news themes and explanations, is also a consideration. It is at this point that routinization allows for a threat to be depicted in an easily recognizable form by the media, one of Cohen's (1980) elements of a moral panic. The organizational model differs from the manipulative and market models in that it is not totally reactive (market) or totally proactive (manipulative). The agency reacts to non-routine events yet takes part in the creation process for the rest of the news.

In the process of routinization, news agencies rely on respected social institutions or officials who are credible and provide reliable information. This easy influx of news allows the news agencies to utilize their financial resources elsewhere. However it also, as Hall et al. (1978) suggest, leads to the reproduction of the definitions of the powerful. This results in news that is dominated by information and interpretations that tend to support the status quo. It also reinforces the respectability of the institutions and organizations providing the information (Chibnall 1981). Hall et al. (1978) also suggest that it is this process that symbolically reproduces the existing power structure.

Crime news makes up a large part of the entire news. Being prepackaged (manipulative) and popular (market), it helps the news organization in its routinization process. Thus, a cycle of newsworthiness is created in which one type of crime is defined as news and will continue to be news. "If this focus on a particular type of event becomes industry wide, a media crime wave results. The crimes chosen as news during this span in effect become the typical 'atypical' event for that period" (Surette 1992:63). Since the traditional definition of news is "that which is uncommon or new," violent crime is seen as more newsworthy because it occurs less frequently. This focus on a particular type of event leads to disproportionality, or the belief that the threat is more substantial than it is truly, a characteristic of a moral panic.

The social importance of these media constructed crime waves is, according to Fishman (1978:533): "(1) They enable the media to influence policy by raising public outrage affecting everything from sentencing and preventative measures to society's level of fear. (2) By operating around these themes, other, more often serious significant events or issues do not become news." Therefore, they are less likely to receive public attention, raise concern or fear, or receive resources. Hall et al. (1978) argue that the media do not consciously set out to divert the attention, yet the end result is the same. The root problems are often neglected and do not receive attention.

Local Television News

Homicide rates have continued to decrease since 1993, yet one out of every seven news stories covered the topic. Coverage of murder has increased

700 percent while overall crime coverage has tripled since 1993. According to a recent survey by Louis Harris for the Center for Media and Public Affairs, local television newscasts are the public's number one source of news. Not only do they get the biggest ratings, but people also rank them as higher in quality and credibility than network news, local newspapers, and any other news source (Grossman 1997). A study conducted by the Rocky Mountain Media Watch found that crime occupied 30 percent of what little time was actually devoted to news (40 percent) in 100 local television newscasts in 56 cities. Incidentally, 36 percent of the airtime was spent on commercials and promos; sports and weather filled 22 percent and another two percent was anchor chatter (Grossman 1997). However, what is most significant and follows from Fishman's (1978) assertion that "more serious and significant events do not become news" is the absence of social and economic investigations, such that the national and local political scene was entirely absent from these newscasts.

Crime has become the focus of local television news for several reasons, and each is consistent with the characteristics of the manipulative, market, and organizational models outlined by Surette (1992). Local television newscasts are relatively cheap to produce and a major profit maker for stations. The "eyewitness news" formula has become the standard thematic scheme and there is a lack of pressure on broadcasters to serve their community's needs and interests (Grossman 1997). Marty Haag, Senior News Vice President for the A. H. Belo stations, reports that: "Covering crime is the easiest, fastest, cheapest and most efficient kind of news coverage for T.V. stations. News directors and station owners love crime because it has a one to one ratio between making the assignment and getting a story on the air" (Grossman 1997). The crime scene doesn't move; no matter when the reporter arrives, there is always a picture to shoot. There is no need to spend time and money researching; when the cameras arrive, so do supposed witnesses.

National News

On the national network news, the story is much the same. In the school year 1997–1998 there were 6,146 deaths by firearms for the age group 15–24 (Hoyert, Kochanek, and Murphy 1999:68). Thirty-five of these deaths were a result of school shootings. School shootings represent .5 percent of the gun related deaths for this age group (National School Safety Center 2001). Network evening news crime coverage for 1998 reported 1392 stories about crime on NBC, CBS, and ABC. Stories on two school shootings—Jonesboro, Arkansas, on March 24, 1998, and Springfield, Oregon, on May 21, 1998—represented nine percent of ALL network evening news crime coverage in 1998 (Center for Media and Public Affairs 1999). This is a significant amount of news coverage for a topic that represents only .4 percent of homicides. There were a total of 126 network evening news stories on these two events. In comparison, there were 113 stories on all environmental issues

(Center for Media and Public Affairs 1999). The leading cause of death for the age group 15–19 was accidents with a total of 13,367, more than double the amount of homicides; however, accidents only made up five percent of news reports (Hoyert, Kochanek, and Murphy 1999). Thirty-five deaths in a single school year is horrifying and tragic, yet small when compared to the approximately 6,000 youth homicides that didn't become national news (these numbers do not include the number of talk show, infotainment shows, and news magazine shows who ran specials on the school shootings).

Increasing Fear

The effects of the "media crime wave," which the Center for Media and Public Affairs (1997) has deemed number 10 on the "Top Ten List of Media Distortions of the 20th Century," are apparent throughout the nation. One element of a moral panic, a rapid build up of public concern, is evidenced in public opinion polls. Eighty-five percent of Oklahomans in both rural and urban areas report being "very concerned about school violence," while actual incidents of school violence are rare. The number one reason that police come to school isn't violence in the school building, but to take reports of violence in the home. School officials in Tulsa, Oklahoma, confirmed that major incidents of school violence elsewhere are exaggerating perceptions of armed and violent students (Associated Press 1998).

Cohen (1980) asserts that a key stage in the development of a moral panic is that there is a response from authorities and/or opinion makers. President Clinton added to the fear of school shootings in this 1997 speech: "We've got about six years to turn this juvenile crime thing around or our country is going to be living with chaos." This said, he then acknowledged that the youth violent crime rate had fallen 9.2 percent the previous year (Center on Juvenile and Criminal Justice 1999). While youth violence continued to decline, CNN reported: "Teenage time bomb's becoming increasingly more commonplace in America." NBC's *Today Show* news anchor Ann Curry introduced a child psychologist to the audience by asking him to address parents on this "new trend in our schools, shooting each other." When he stated that children are safer in school than anywhere else, she reminded him that this was the fourth incident. Vincent Schiraldi, the director of the Justice Policy Institute, reminded viewers that three times as many people were struck by lightning as were killed in school shootings, while *Today Show* host, Katie Couric, declared that "today's youth are more likely to pull a gun than make a fist" (Glassner 1999:xiv). Lead-ins and sound bites such as these are a complete contradiction of the truth. According to the Bureau of Justice Statistics and the National Center for Education Statistics (1999), an average of 50 percent of all schools report fights without a weapon; only 12.5 percent of all schools report fights with a weapon and those weapons are not necessarily guns. These newscasters are opinion makers and the interviews are with authority figures, filling two of Cohen's (1980) elements of a moral panic. . . . [Newscasters defining] . . . guns and kids as a threat to the values and interests of society is also a stage in the development of a moral panic.

Policy Implications

Schools are safer than all other locations where kids congregate, including cars and homes. However, municipalities continue to raise taxes to buy state of the art surveillance cameras, metal detectors, and police mini-stations for schools in response to concerns raised by media reports that proclaimed: "The coming of Super-Predators—teenage boys who have no respect for human life and kill and maim on impulse, without any tangible motive" (Associated Press 1995:3A). Responses by authorities and claims makers, a stage in the development of a moral panic, are evidenced by the reactions of several school districts and officials. School districts across the country are taking steps to improve the security of students, faculty, and staff. A boom has erupted in the school security business such that security technology has become a major budget topic for school administrators as well as politicians. Proposed changes in policy are occurring across the country. For instance, [former] California Governor Gray Davis proposed spending $100 million of a budget surplus to strengthen school safety programs in his state. The money would allow districts to purchase more metal detectors, video surveillance, and other security devices. [Former] Washington Governor Gary Locke wanted legislators to allocate $9 million for a grant program to improve school safety. In Wisconsin, it has been proposed that spending on safety measures be exempt from fiscal limits placed on schools. In San Francisco, [former] Mayor Willie Brown asked for an additional $1.5 million in his budget to put 26 more police officers in public schools; 56 officers were already deployed in San Francisco schools (Kennedy 1999).

President Clinton, at the White House Conference on School Safety, proposed $12 million for project SERV, the School Emergency Response to Violence, which responds to school violence in a similar way that FEMA responds to emergencies. The president also issued a $65 million initiative to hire 2,000 community police and school resource officers to work in schools and a minimum of $25 million in grants to develop and implement community-wide school safety plans (Clinton 2000). Just as Jock Young's (1971b) work demonstrated how the media's amplification of an issue can result in a moral panic leading to the legitimization of punitive policy measures, the amplification of school shootings has led to both legal and economic changes. These changes are what Cohen (1980) listed as the final stage in a moral panic.

School Safety is Big Business

With the large amounts of dollars available, a business that once served private investigators, retail companies, and corporate security details has found an entirely new customer base: schools and government funds. Capitalizing on the fears of citizens, and the policy changes that attempt to alleviate these fears, is big business. Companies not only compound the fears through advertising, but also shape the types of solutions that are offered.

The types of equipment available range in cost and effectiveness, and numerous companies offer consulting and safety plan designs. Emergency communication devices, according to Mike Fickes (1999) of Roland Borg Corporation, are needed because "conventional telephones are inadequate in an emergency. Intercom systems with emergency calling capabilities are vandal proof and one does not need to dial emergency numbers." The company recommends a station in every room, in hallways, and in offices. The cost is $300 per station. Experts also recommend photo badging systems using bar codes. Not only do these systems act as an alarm system (students, faculty, and staff will notice any unbadged person and report them to security), they are also used to control access. Cards cost approximately $2.50 each, midrange card printers cost $3800, and the camera badging station and its software cost $1800. However, these access control systems require an initial investment of $10,000 and approximately $4000 per year in maintenance (Fickes 1999:22). In the 1997–1998 school year, there were approximately 54 million students; if each student were issued a photo badge (this does not include teachers and staff or the initial investment, maintenance fees, and the expense of printers), the cost would be $135 million. Sensormatic Electronics Corporation recommends closed-circuit television (CCTV) monitors at the cost of $10,000 per four cameras, monitor, and videocassette recorder. While CCTVs are mainly used for reactive proposes such as illegal entry and vandalism, schools across the country are purchasing them in hopes of preventing violence. As for metal detection and x-ray screening, experts disagree on which is the best method; however, they agree that one or both are necessary. Handheld units for random searches begin at $150.00 and walk-through units at $2500. Prices for x-ray screening equipment range from $15,000 to $30,000 (Fickes 1999:31). In the 1997–1998 school year there were 136,012 public and private elementary and secondary schools across the nation. If each school bought only one handheld metal detector, the cost would be approximately $20 million. If each school in the country bought four cameras (CCTV), the cost would be a whopping $1.36 billion. With these large sums of potential revenues available, it is no wonder that companies such as Siemens Building Technologies have begun to address society's unwarranted fears with advertisements such as "maintaining a safe and secure environment for our schools and our children requires solutions that work." Best Access Systems advertises expertise in "securing a world where kids are free to learn." Finally, Mosler offers the assertion that "schools today need all the answers technology can give them, and then some" (Fickes 1999:30).

All of this comes despite a special report issued by the Office of Juvenile Justice and Delinquency Prevention (Bilchik 1999) in which the reader is told that in the school year 1997–98: "Juvenile violence peaked in the after school hours on school days and in the evening hours on non school days." The violent victimization of juveniles is greatest between 3 and 9 p.m. The highest percent of violent incidents involving a firearm for those under 18 years old, nine percent, occur between 8 and 9 pm followed by seven percent occurring between 3 and 4 pm (Bilchik 1999).

School Shootings in Context

In the academic school year 1997–1998, there were 44,351 public and private secondary schools and 91,661 public and private elementary schools for a total of 136,012 schools (Moody 1998). There are on average 180 days of school per year when schools are in session for a total of 24.5 million school sessions. The nine school shootings in this year represent .00003 percent of the approximately 24.5 million times school was in session for the day somewhere in America. As horrific and tragic as each of these events was, given the number of days individual schools in America are in session, on most days and in most places it is safe for a child to go to school.

Despite the small numbers and percentages of school shootings, stories of youth violence are used by the news media to present a distorted image of the true state of affairs in our schools. In fact, in 1998 the Bureau of Justice Statistics reported that 29 percent of all teenagers believed drug use/abuse was the biggest problem facing kids their age, followed by social pressures, good grades, and sexual issues; only five percent listed crime and violence in school as the biggest problem (Maguire and Pastore 1999). In 1997, parents listed lack of funding and discipline (15 percent each) as the biggest problems facing schools; violence came in fourth behind drug use/abuse. However, in 1998, at a time when teens believed drugs were the biggest problem, parents' fear of school violence rose to 20 percent (Maguire and Pastore 1999). According to Ray Surette (1992:88): "the media emphasis on crime has frequently been credited with raising the public's fear of being victimized to disproportionate levels, hence giving crime an inappropriately high ranking on the public agenda." Surette (1992) concludes that the importance of the relationship between mass media news and the criminal justice system may be greater today than ever before.

Columbine

In 1999 crime news jumped into second place on the list of broadcasts for ABC, NBC, and CBS. Crime news followed the "War in Kosovo" by only two broadcasts. The Columbine High School shooting topped the list of crime stories covered on those evening broadcasts with 319 stories, more than five times the total of any other incident (Center for Media and Public Affairs 2000). After the smoke cleared, 16 students and one teacher were dead, including the shooters. Students and faculty at Columbine High School, as well as reporters, referred to the shooters as members of the "Trench Coat Mafia." For weeks following the shootings, reports about these modern-day "folk devils" saturated the news. These students were labeled "outsiders," "different," and even "strange." Just as Cohen's (1980) Mod and Rockers were easily identifiable, so were the members of the "Trench Coat Mafia." They wore black clothes and makeup, listened to rocker Marilyn Manson, played violent video games, and designed elaborate web pages. Claims makers, including [former] first lady Hillary Rodham Clinton, used this event to draw attention to the breakdown of traditional values, to attack the entertainment industry, and to rail against those who opposed gun control legislation. "We can no longer shut our eyes to the impact that the media is [sic] having on all of our children," said Mrs. Clinton (Fleeman 1999). Criminologist Jeff Ferrell (1998:148) asserts that "as the production and consumption of popular culture lay the foundations for contemporary social life, they also become the basis for a variety of contemporary controversies." It is interesting that not only has popular culture become the basis of controversies, but these controversies are also used by claims makers to argue their beliefs on other issues. These controversies include attempts by politicians, legal authorities, religious leaders, and others to criminalize popular culture.

The late 1980s and 1990s saw the rise of a booming economy, low interest rates, a dot.com generation, latchkey children, a war fought in a faraway land but portrayed via the media using video game like re-creations of bombings, and the potential to become extremely rich through technology and start-up Internet companies. In addition to computerized everything, there was an aging generation of authority figures, claims makers, and moral entrepreneurs who found themselves out of the loop due to the widespread use of a communications system (the computer and the Internet) that was not what they were used to. In the 1950s rock and roll was blamed for the breakdown of teenage morality and their outrageous behaviors; today Marilyn Manson and rockers like him, video games, and the computer are the elements of popular culture that moral entrepreneurs attempt to criminalize or at least censor.

School shootings, and more generally school violence, have become what Jenkins (1992) calls "symbolic politics" or the "politics of substitution." Politicians and claims makers draw attention to these specific events because they represent other issues such as gun control, censorship, and morality. One week after the Columbine shootings, President Clinton introduced legislation requiring background checks on sales of explosives and holding parents liable when their children commit crimes with guns. White House Press Secretary Joe Lockhart said: "Clinton is counting on outrage over the shootings to help push the legislation through, unfortunately oftentimes it takes tragic events to catalyze work here in Washington" (Sobieraj 1999). Cohen (1980) suggests that one response to a moral panic is a call to return to traditional values. This is echoed in both Joe Lockhart's comment as well as Senator George Voinovich's (R-Ohio) statement: "There is something wrong with our society. I think a lot of it has to do with a return to traditional morals and values. Youngsters are not getting the kinds of moral and religious training they once got at home" (Lowy 1999).

Conclusion

The public has not received the kind of analysis or examination from the media that is needed to give worried parents or concerned policy makers the context with which to judge safety in schools. In reality, kids are more likely to be shot by adults. Adults kill 90 percent of homicide victims under the age of 12 and 75 percent of homicide victims age 12–17 are killed by adults (Donohue, Schiraldi, and Zeidenberg 1998). This is not to say that children face no threats to their safety in school; however, America cannot set rational public policy in the important area of child killings without better information from the media. No one expects the press to ignore tragic killings of kids, whether they occur on school grounds or in other places. But the data contained in this report show that the public and policy makers are done a great disservice if they are led to believe that schoolhouses are a primary locus for juvenile homicides in America (Donohue, Schiraldi, and Zeidenberg 1998).

As other school shootings occur and/or the juveniles involved in the previous shootings are brought to trial, the public discourse could tremendously benefit from the presentation of a broader perspective on juvenile killings. To provide greater context to such cases, the media should at least explain: (1) that school killings are not on the increase; (2) that such killings make up a small minority of all killings of and by juveniles; (3) that children are three times more likely to be killed by adults than by other juveniles; and (4) that there is no trend toward younger and younger juvenile killings. These data are readily available and would tremendously benefit the public's understanding of youth crime.

Nine incidents of school shootings in the 1997–1998 school year provided the opportunity for news agencies to develop a thematic routinization of incidents of school violence. What was an atypical event, hence newsworthy, became the typical event; therefore, under the organizational process model, it became routinized and increased in newsworthiness. The results of this media constructed crime wave shaped public opinion, increasing fear of school shootings, contributing to fears of violent teens, fueling public policy such as government funded school safety, and prompting public consumption patterns and an increase in security technology purchases that fulfilled Fishman's (1978) assertion: "Media constructed crime waves can influence public policy by raising public outrage, effecting preventative measures and levels of fear."

According to Cohen's (1980) stages of a moral panic, school shootings can be included in the long list of moral panics that arise in all modern societies. The results and effects of this panic can be seen in misdirected policies and changes in the behaviors and actions of school officials, parents, and students. According to Barak (1994:35): "Nothing can be more important than the mass content of crime and justice news. The omission of certain types of criminality is equally, if not more important than the types of criminality included." One omission that stands out is a broad definition of school violence. The images associated with school violence, via news broadcasts, are bloody and emotional and involve physical attacks. The perpetrators are associated with death, darkness, and some form of "differentness," whether it is appearance or moral. News production is caught up in the need for dramatic structuring and according to Barak (1994:33): "Crime news is over simplified and reduced to subtle and not so subtle forms of stereotyping that socially construct criminals and victims alike." In the process it erases considerations of structure and political economy that may deconstruct reality and thereby destabilize our sense of order (Barak 1994). These omissions and lack of considerations contribute to a moral panic.

A Broader Integrative Definition of School Violence

In light of the dramatic and often detrimental effects a moral panic has on policy decisions and levels of societal fear, it is imperative that the images and definitions of school violence be expanded and integrated. For example, the current definition is one-dimensional and involves physical force or intimidation. Missing in the news media's coverage of school violence are several elements of harm. According to Stuart Henry (2000): "the omission of these broader dimensions causes us to miss much of the content and many of the causes of violence in schools." Henry (2000) asserts that these missing elements of harm include: (1) the emotional and psychological pain that results from the domination of some over others, (2) the focus on interpersonal relationships that ignore the violence of social processes which produce systemic social injury, such as that perpetuated through institutionalized racism, sexism, and classism, and (3) the symbolic violence of domination, or the subtle form of violence that brings coercion through power exercised in hierarchical relationships. It is not until the media apply this multilevel definition to the problem of school violence that a multilevel causal analysis and a comprehensive policy response that takes account of the full range of constitutive elements will follow. In addition to the inclusion of these dimensions, it is important to realize that, as Barak (1994:ix) argues: "Crime and justice news are subject to and inseparable from political, economic and social struggle." These dimensions must be included in representations of school violence if a broader understanding and effective policy decisions are to develop and the news media are to become forums that promote understanding and social movement rather than moral panic.

References

Associated Press. 1995. "U.S. Children: Armed and Dangerous." *The Baltimore Sun*, September 8, p. 3A.

Associated Press. 1998. "School Violence Worries Oklahomans." *Amarillo Globe-News*. Retrieved August 19, 2001 (http://www.amarillonet.com/stories).

Barak, Gregg (Ed.). 1994. *Media, Process and the Social Construction of Crime: Studies in Newsmaking Criminology*. New York and London: Garland Publishing.

Becker, Howard. 1963. *Outsiders*. New York: Free Press.

Bilchik, Shay. 1999. "Violence after School." Washington, DC: Department of Justice, Office of Juvenile Justice and Delinquency Prevention. Retrieved August 19, 2001 (http://www.ncjrs.org/html/ojjdp/9911_1/contents.html).

Bureau of Justice Statistics and National Center for Education Statistics. 1999. "Indicators of School Crime and Safety, 1998." Bureau of Justice Statistics. Retrieved August 19, 2001 (http://www.ed.gov/pubs/AnnSchoolRept98/index.html).

Center for Media and Public Affairs. 1997. "Network News in the Nineties: The Top Topics and Trends of the Decade." *Media Monitor,* 11(3). Retrieved August 19, 2001 (http://www.cmpa.com/Mediamon/mm070897.htm).

———. 1999. "1998 Year in Review: TV's Leading News Topics, Reporters, and Political Jokes." *Media Monitor,* 13(1). Retrieved August 19, 2001 (http://www.cmpa.com/Mediamon/mm010299.htm).

———. 2000. "1999 Year in Review: TV's Leading News Topics, Reporters and Political Jokes." *Media Monitor,* 14(1). Retrieved August 19, 2001 (http://www.cmpa.com/Mediamon/mm010200.htm).

Center on Juvenile and Criminal Justice. 1999. "School House Hype: Links to Hyperbolic Coverage of Kids." *Justice Policy Institute.* Retrieved August 19, 2001 (www.cjcj.org/jpi/thehype.html).

Chibnall, S. 1981. "The Production of Knowledge by Crime Reporters." In *The Manufacture of News: Deviance, Social Problem, and the Mass Media,* edited by S. Cohen and J. Young. Newbury Park, CA: Sage.

Clinton, William J. 2000. "New Initiatives Announced at the White House Conference on School Safety." Safe and Drug Free Schools Program. Retrieved August 19, 2001 (http://www.ed.gov/offices/OESE/SDFS/initiati.html).

Cohen, Stanley. 1980. *Folk Devils and Moral Panics: The Creation of the Mods and Rockers* (New Edition). Oxford, UK: Martin Robertson.

Cohen, Stanley and Jock Young (Eds.). 1981. *The Manufacture of News: Deviance, Social Problem, and the Mass Media.* Newbury Park, CA: Sage.

Donohue, Elizabeth, Vincent Schiraldi, and Jason Zeidenberg. 1998. "School House Hype: School Shootings and the Real Risks Kids Face in America." Washington DC: Justice Policy Institute. Retrieved August 19, 2001 (http://www.cjcj.org/jpi/schoolhouse.html).

Ferrell, Jeff. 1998. "Criminalizing Popular Culture." In *Popular Culture, Crime, and Justice,* edited by F. Y. Bailey and D. C. Hale. Belmont, CA: Wadsworth.

Fickes, Mike. 1999. "The ABC's of Security Technology." *Under Siege: Schools as the New Battleground.*

Fishman, Mark S. 1978. "Crime Waves as Ideology." *Social Problems,* 25: 531–543.

Fleeman, Michael. 1999. "Colorado Shootings Spur Debate on Entertainment's Role in Youth Violence." *Times Record News,* April 24.

Glassner, Barry. 1999. *The Culture of Fear: Why Americans are Afraid of the Wrong Things.* New York: Basic Books.

Goode, Erich and Nachman Ben-Yehuda. 1994. *Moral Panics: The Social Construction of Deviance.* Oxford & Cambridge, MA: Blackwell.

Grossman, Lawrence K. 1997. "Why Local TV News Is So Awful." *Columbia Journalism Review.* Retrieved August 19, 2001 (http://www.cjcj.org/year/97/6/grossman.asp).

Gusfield, Joseph. 1963. *Symbolic Crusade: Status Politics and the American Temperance Movement.* Urbana, IL: University of Illinois Press.

Hall, Stuart, C. Critcher, T. Jefferson, J. Clark, and B. Roberts. 1978. *Policing the Crisis: Mugging, the State, and Law and Order.* London: Macmillan.

Henry, Stuart. 2000. "What Is School Violence? An Integrated Definition." *The Annals of the American Academy of Political and Social Science*, 567: 16–29.

Hoyert, Donna, Kenneth D. Kochanek, and Sherry L. Murphy. 1999. "Deaths: Final Data for 1997." *National Vital Statistics Report*, 47(19). Retrieved August 19, 2001 (http://www.cdc.gov/nchs/products/pubs/pubd/nvsr/47-pre/47-pre.htm).

Jenkins, Philip. 1992. *Intimate Enemies: Moral Panics in Contemporary Great Britain.* New York: Aldine de Gruyter.

Kennedy, Mike. 1999. "The Changing Face of School Violence." *Under Siege: Schools as the New Battleground.*

Lowy, Joan. 1999. "A New Push for Gun Control after School Shooting." *Scripps Howard News Service*, April 21.

Maguire, Kathleen and Ann Pastore (Eds.). 1999. *Sourcebook of Criminal Justice Statistics.* Washington, DC: U.S. Department of Justice, Bureau of Justice Statistics

Moody, W. (Ed.). 1998. *Patterson's American Education.* Mount Prospect, IL: Educational Directories.

National School Safety Center. 2001. "Report on School Associated Violent Deaths." Retrieved August 19, 2001 (http://nsscl.org/).

Sobieraj, Sandra. 1999. "Clinton to Propose Explosives Restrictions." Associated Press, April 27.

Surette, Ray. 1992. *Media, Crime, and Criminal Justice: Images and Realities.* Pacific Grove, CA: Brooks/Cole Publishing.

Young, Jock. 1971a. *The Drugtakers: The Social Meaning of Drug Use.* London: MacGibbon and Kee.

———. 1971b. "The Role of the Police as Amplifiers of Deviance: Negotiators of Drug Control as Seen in Notting Hill." In *Images of Deviance*, edited by S. Cohen. Harmondsworth, UK: Penguin.

TWELVE

CONSTRUCTING "CRIME"

MEDIA COVERAGE OF INDIVIDUAL AND ORGANIZATIONAL WRONGDOING

William S. Lofquist

Media coverage of crime is a matter of growing academic interest, and criticism of this coverage is widespread. In covering traditional or street crimes, media are accused of focusing on sensational cases (Barlow, Barlow, and Chiricos 1995b; Benedict 1992; Chermak 1994; Kappeler, Blumberg, and Potter 1996), overrepresentation of minorities as offenders (Sheley and Ashkins 1981; Smith 1984), emphasizing socially favored victims (Benedict 1992; Fishman 1978; Graber 1980), decontextualizing crime (Barlow et al. 1995a, 1995b; Garofalo 1981; Humphries 1981; Sherizen 1978), misrepresenting the extent and types of crime (Barlow et al. 1995b; Garofalo 1981; Reiman 1995; Sherizen 1978), misportraying the operations of the criminal justice system (Gorelick 1989), and exaggerating the incidence of stranger-based crimes (Chermak 1994; Kappeler et al. 1996; Tunnell 1992). All of these themes come together most clearly in media coverage of several recent prominent cases: the Charles Stuart murder case in Boston, the Susan Smith murder case in South Carolina, and the O.J. Simpson murder case in California.

Coverage of corporate crime has received much less academic attention. In this type of coverage, media are accused of minimizing corporate liability (Morash and Hale 1987; Wright, Cullen and Blankenship 1995), minimizing attention to causes of outcomes in favor of attention to consequences (Wright et al. 1995), ignoring or underestimating the costs of corporate crime (Hills 1987; Kappeler et al. 1996; Reiman 1995), reluctance to use the term *crime* to describe this misbehavior (Bohm 1993; Lynch, Nalla, and Miller 1989; Wright et al. 1995), attaching blame to secondary or spurious causes (Wright et al. 1995), and inadequately understanding the complexity of corporate crime (Levi 1994;

Justice Quarterly, Vol. 14, No. 2, June 1997, pp. 243–263. Permission granted by Taylor & Francis, Ltd. http://www.tandf.co.uk/journals

Randall 1987; Randall, Lee-Sammons, and Hagner 1988). These charges are illustrated clearly by several prominent cases of corporate wrongdoing including the General Motors pickup truck cases, the Ford Pinto case, the Kentucky school bus case (see Kunen 1994), and the Imperial Food Products case.

Though these inadequacies and biases are numerous and wide ranging, it can be argued that media coverage of these very different types of crime is unified by reliance on a hegemonic narrative (Ewick and Silbey 1995; also see Gamson et al. 1992).[1] Whatever the type of crime and whatever the fact scenario, media coverage tends to follow and reproduce a narrative composed of traditional, system-legitimizing assumptions and assertions (Bohm 1986; Tunnell 1992). When crime is restricted to interpersonal relationships and is portrayed as largely the result of pathological individual actions (Kappeler et al. 1996) unrelated to the conditions or actions of dominant institutions such as the family, business, or politics, or race, class, or gender relations, these institutions and the criminogenic inequalities within them are reproduced. Alternatively, a subversive narrative about crime challenges these institutions and relations, implicating them as important, even central in understanding the occurrence of crime.

In this article I present the results of content analyses of newspaper coverage of two widely reported "crimes" that occurred in the Rochester, New York area in 1994.[2] The analyses relied on local newspaper coverage, though each case also generated some regional and national coverage. The first case is the disappearance of Kali Ann Poulton, a four-year-old girl, from the street in front of her home in May 1994. Throughout the period of this study, Kali Ann had not been found and her disappearance had not been explained. The second case is the collapse and gradual flooding, in March 1994, of a large salt mine owned by Akzo Nobel Salt, a multinational conglomerate based in Holland.

These cases differ in that one deals with an individual as the central figure while the other focuses on a business. In many other respects, however, these cases are remarkably similar and thus provide a fortuitous research opportunity. Both occurred in the same year and in the same area. Both were subject to numerous possible explanations ranging from accident to crime. Both were investigated carefully. Both were unresolved at the time of the research in that the cause had not been determined. Holding these factors constant provides an opportunity to examine media coverage of two very different types of behaviors, each of which is potentially definable as crime. The unresolved nature of these cases allows us to examine whether hegemonic assumptions are used to "fill in the blanks" left by the incomplete fact scenarios.

Missing Children: A Hegemonic Project

Katherine Beckett (1994) makes the argument that the intensity and patterning of the War on Drugs are so far out of proportion to the extent and patterning of drug use that its continuation represents a hegemonic project (also see Chambliss 1994; Currie 1993; D. Gordon 1994; Reinarman 1996; Tonry 1994).

In avoiding evidence for the ineffectiveness of a supply-side, deterrence-based strategy and for the macro-level causes of drug use and the associated crime, policy makers are engaged in an ideologically based effort to undermine the welfare state, and liberalism more generally, by fostering an image of the drug user as undeserving (Gans 1995; Katz 1989; Kleniewski 1995).

A similar argument can be made about missing children. We have strong evidence that missing children are largely runaways or (less often) are abducted by family members or acquaintances. Thus the enormous attention focused on abductions by strangers raises questions about the entire project of publicizing missing children. A substantial social scientific literature has developed, which analyzes this moral panic (see Best 1987, 1990; Forst and Blomquist 1991; Kappeler et al. 1996). Its primary point is that abductions of children by strangers are exceedingly rare, accounting for far less than 1 percent of all missing children. Public, political, and media portrayals of this issue, however, focus disproportionately on these rare cases, implying that most missing children were abducted by strangers.[3] This conclusion has been strengthened by irresponsible claims by politicians, such as Rep. (later Senator) Paul Simon's (D-IL) assertion that at least 50,000 children are abducted each year by strangers (U.S. House 1981; also see Thornton 1983).

Public and media perceptions of missing children have also been shaped by the public forum provided for claims of stranger abduction through frequent congressional hearings and interest group initiatives, particularly in the 1980s. The extensive attention given to these rare but tragic cases has brought widespread visibility and influence to the Adam Walsh Foundation, the National Center for Missing and Exploited Children, Marc Klass (the father of stranger-abducted and murdered Polly Klass), and other activists, and has fostered the perception that the problem of missing children is largely synonymous with the problem of stranger abductions. Another component of this construction is the view of the offender as irrational, disturbed, or pathological (Best 1987)—a pedophile or a childless woman. Such a construction is hegemonic in that it calls forth more social control, as in the increasingly punitive lawmaking associated with crimes against children. A family-based or culture-based construction of missing children would focus on the overwhelming class- and race-based pattern of runaways and abductions by acquaintances, as well as on the physical and sexual abuse that is often a precipitating factor (Currie 1985; Forst and Blomquist 1991). Such a construction is more likely to suggest redistributive (and therefore subversive) social welfare policies.

Corporate Crime: A Project Suggesting Hegemony by Neglect

In a 1993 cover story, *U.S. News & World Report* detailed the enormous costs of crime to Americans. Criminal justice system expenditures, medical costs, lost productivity, and other costs were all included in a price tag of $674 billion. In this putatively comprehensive analysis, however, the harms and costs of corporate crimes were not considered. A more recent, academic consideration of the costs of crime placed the price at $450 billion (Butterfield 1996); again, though media reports of this research did not specify the omission, the researchers excluded corporate crime from consideration. This inattention to corporate crime suggests hegemony by neglect.

Research on corporate crime further supports this view. Direct financial costs of corporate crime are frequently estimated at $200 billion[4] (Clinard and Yeager 1980; Kappeler et al. 1996; Reiman 1995; Simon and Eitzen 1993); human costs in terms of injuries and deaths, though not subject to precise measurement, are widely held to be greater than those associated with street crime (Beirne and Messerschmidt 1991; Clinard and Yeager 1980; Frank and Lynch 1992; Kappeler et al. 1996; Michalowski 1985; Reiman 1995). Thus corporate crime inarguably represents a serious social harm and legal problem.

At the same time, however, corporate crime has a low political, media, criminal justice, and public profile. Congressional hearings on the subject are few. The seemingly endless parade of crime bills gives no attention to corporate crime. Corporate misdeeds are rarely defined publicly or legally as crime. Further, as suggested by recent research on the savings and loan crisis (Calavita and Pontell 1994), it is those corporate crimes that threaten business and business confidence in the economy, not those that threaten consumers, employees, the environment, or other stakeholders, that receive media and enforcement attention.

Methodology

Sample

The articles used in this research were taken from the Rochester *Democrat and Chronicle,* the major daily newspaper for the Rochester and western Finger Lakes region. The only other daily paper in the region is the *Times Union,* the afternoon sister paper to the *Democrat and Chronicle;* both are Gannett publications. The same stories are often carried in both papers. I chose to examine the *Democrat and Chronicle* because it is the only print media outlet that gave sustained, detailed daily coverage to each of these stories.

I conducted content analyses on every relevant story published in the three-month period following each event. I developed story lists by contacting the newspaper, which provided a computer printout of all relevant headlines. I decided on a three-month period because it seemed to provide ample time for developments in each story and for consideration of their causes. Also, three months represents a natural point after which coverage diminished; after that period, relevant stories appeared only sporadically. This is particularly true in the Kali Ann Poulton case: the absence of new information led to a substantial decrease in coverage after one month, and to a further decrease after three months.

Content Categories

Borrowing substantially from the content analysis by Wright et al. (1995) of media coverage of the Imperial Food Products fire, I used three major content categories (cause, harm, and responsibility) as the basis of this analysis. Then I examined each story for some reference to each category and for the nature of that reference. Within each content category, I developed several subcategories to account for the various narratives available to tell each story. Because of this methodology, some content categories might not appear in a particular article or multiple subcategories might be mentioned in a particular article. Expanding on the methodology of Wright et al. (1995), I included two additional content categories (focus and sources) to provide additional insights into the construction of each case.

Cause.   The cause of each of these events can be understood in several ways. The first is as an accident—an event beyond the control of, or unforeseeable by, any individual or group of individuals. Kali Ann Poulton, for example, could have wandered off and become involved in an accident that reduced her ability to return or be found. The Akzo mine collapse could have been the result of an earthquake, as initially reported, or of some other unforeseeable and uncontrollable situation such as the anomalous geological formations, the explanation preferred by Akzo (Bellaby 1995a, 1995c). Each outcome also can be understood as negligence: the result of inadequate parental or community supervision in the Poulton case, or of inadequate managerial or labor supervision of mining conditions or practices in the Akzo case. Finally, each outcome may be portrayed as a crime. Kali Ann Poulton's disappearance could be explained as a kidnapping. The mine collapse could be explained as the result of criminal negligence or wrongdoing on the part of Akzo management, the miners, or some outside party.

Harm.   Each of these events caused an array of harms to a variety of parties. By identifying the harms that are featured in media coverage, one gains insight into the larger narrative into which each story was fitted. For example, as noted by Swigert and Farrell (1980–81), discussion of the harms to consumers in cases of corporate wrongdoing accompanies portrayals of those wrongdoings as criminal. The underlying logic is that a narrative or vocabulary of crime is more likely to be adopted, insofar as corporate wrongdoings resemble traditional violent crimes. In this study I analyzed each article for references to three different types of harm. *Direct harm* refers to harm experienced by the immediate parties to the events. In the Poulton case, direct harm refers to those harms experienced by Kali Ann. In the Akzo case, harms experienced by the corporation, its management, and its employees were identified as direct. *Residual harm* refers to harms experienced by these parties' families. *Community harm* refers, in the Poulton case, to insecurity, anxiety, or strain experienced by members of the Rochester community. In the Akzo case, community harms are those experienced by local property owners, business persons, other community members, and the natural environment.

Responsibility.   In the three causal scenarios identified above, responsibility may be located in different places. As a result, attention to responsibility clarifies the details of narrative construction. I identified three levels of responsibility to facilitate this analysis. *Primary responsibility* is located in those parties closest to the event; Kali Ann Poulton's family and close friends and Akzo management were primary actors. *Secondary responsibility* focuses on nonsupervisory parties; in the Poulton case, any stranger is a secondary party, while laborers are secondary in the Akzo case. *Tertiary responsibility* refers to official regulatory agents, as in articles that identify regulatory inadequacy—whether insufficient police presence or lax or "captured" mine regulatory officials—as responsible to some extent for either outcome.

Focus.   I use an additional content category, developed for this analysis, to examine the narrative focus of each article. Preliminary analysis revealed that much of the coverage of the Kali Ann Poulton case in particular did not focus on the events of the case or provide news about the progress of the investigation but concentrated on tangential issues, such as the picnic held to help relieve the searchers' stress. Therefore I developed a content category distinguishing between articles with a primary and a secondary focus. *Primary focus* refers to articles in which the case is in the foreground: the discussion advances the reader's understanding of the case and related developments. In articles with a *secondary focus,* the case is merely the backdrop for events generated by the extent and character of news coverage and public interest regarding the story. The number of secondary stories suggests the value of the case as a media phenomenon beyond its value as a news story.

Sources.   The sources used in constructing a narrative are important in shaping and revealing that narrative. Because of the magnitude of the events discussed here, the media had access to a broad range of sources in researching and writing their accounts. Therefore it is important to examine the types of sources used in the articles and the extent of reliance on these sources. I identified seven types of sources. *Party* refers to those directly involved in the case, including members of the Poulton family and Akzo management and miners. *Community* includes any person identified as living in the affected area and not identified as belonging to any organization of stakeholders. *Regulatory* sources are official state sources such as police officers, mine safety or environmental officials, or local lawmakers.[5] *Activists* are persons identified as belonging to a nonstate organization active in promoting a particular set of interests affected by the case, such as members of the Adam Walsh Foundation in the Poulton case, or members of local environmental organizations in the Akzo case. *Experts* are individuals with credentials suggesting technical competence in the issues relevant in the case, who are not identified as affiliated with regulatory or activist organizations. These individuals usually occupy academic positions. *Business* sources refer to members of the community identified as business persons and speaking in that capacity. Finally, *media* sources are media professionals.

In addition to these substantive categories, the form of presentation of the stories was subject to quantitative analysis. I collected data regarding the frequency of coverage, as measured by the number of distinct stories with a substantial focus on the event in question.[6] I also analyzed the location of each story in the paper. Whether the story began on the front page, the editorial page, the front page of a section, or an interior page signifies the emphasis placed on the story by the newspaper. Front-page and editorial-page stories signify greatest importance, followed respectively by sectional front-page and interior-page coverage. Also, I measured the length of each story by counting the number of lines of coverage. Finally, to examine trends in coverage over time, I divided each story into three one-month periods for further analyses.

Findings

Form of Coverage

As shown in table 1, the Kali Ann Poulton case received somewhat more coverage than the Akzo case. As measured by story placement, the Poulton case was also given a higher priority: 43.5 percent of the articles were placed on the front page or the editorial page, compared with 36.6 percent in the Akzo case. The trends in coverage, however (see table 2) reveal a somewhat different picture. Table 2 makes clear that coverage of the Poulton case was skewed dramatically toward the first month after the event. During this period, 73 articles were published, sometimes three or four in a single day. Coverage declined dramatically after the one-month anniversary of the case. In contrast, the Akzo case received more consistent coverage over time; coverage declined steadily from Period 1 to Period 3. Also interesting in the Akzo case is the change of placement in the paper: during Period 1, front-page articles predominated; in Period 2, most articles appeared on the front page of the Region section; by Period 3, the story had moved to the inside of the paper.

Table 1   Form Analyses of Kali Ann Poulton and Akzo Stories

	Kali Ann Poulton		Akzo	
	N	%	*N*	%
Placement				
Front page	32	37.6	25	35.2
Regional front page	12	14.1	22	31
Editorial page	5	5.9	1	1.4
Other inside page	36	42.4	23	32.4
Total	85	100	71	100
Length				
Number of lines	9,577		6,238	
Mean	111.5		87.9	
Median	95		80	

These trends in coverage reflect differences in the development of each case more strongly than the interest of the media in covering the cases. The Poulton case was characterized by a frustrating lack of new information; apart from a serious hoax and a number of unsubstantiated sightings, the media reported no important clues or progress at any point. As a result, the media could not sustain the story despite considerable efforts through reliance on secondary articles. In contrast, the Akzo case continued to present new developments over the course of this analysis. The mine collapse caused an aquifer to drain into the mine, slowly flooding it. This event generated considerable news: Akzo endeavored to stop the flooding, local wells dried up as a result of aquifer drainage, and the movement of water through the mine eroded salt pillars, causing sinkholes and property damage.

Although these stories developed differently over time, the Poulton case received more attention per article than the Akzo case throughout the period of this research. Overall, mean and median story lengths were 15 or more lines greater than in the Akzo case. Further, table 2 shows that although few Poulton stories were printed after the first month, mean and median story lengths remained longer for the Poulton case than for Akzo, particularly during the second month of each story.

Table 2   Form Analysis of Kali Ann Poulton and Akzo Stories, by Period

	Period 1		Period 2		Period 3	
	N	%	N	%	N	%
Kali Ann Poulton						
Story Placement						
Front page	30	41.1	2	33.3	0	0
Regional front page	7	9.6	0	0	5	83.3
Editorial page	5	6.8	0	0	0	0
Other inside page	31	42.5	4	66.7	1	16.7
Total	73	100	6	100	6	100
Length						
Number of lines	8,309		755		413	
Mean	113.8		125.8		68.8	
Median	102		139		61	
Akzo Story Placement						
Front page	20	57.1	4	17.4	1	7.7
Regional front page	5	14.3	13	56.5	4	30.8
Editorial page	1	2.9	0	0	0	0
Other inside page	9	25.7	6	26.1	8	61.5
Total	35	100	23	100	13	100
Length						
Number of lines	3,812		1.674		752	
Mean	108.9		72.8		57.8	
Median	114		69		68	

Content of Coverage

Cause.   In the content of media coverage, as summarized in table 3, several notable points emerge. In regard to cause, the two narratives contrast sharply. The Kali Ann Poulton story was constructed quickly and strongly as a crime. Within hours, the media were portraying Kali Ann's disappearance not only as a crime but as a crime committed by a stranger. Quoting "an unnamed source close to the investigation," the *Democrat and Chronicle* reported on May 25, 1994, "I think we might have the worst-case scenario, an abduction by a stranger" (Finnerty et al. 1994:1A). Alternative causes received no print coverage at this early point, and were mentioned only briefly in later months.

The Akzo story, on the other hand, was constructed immediately and almost unvaryingly as an accident; this construction appeared in every story on the case, though it was accompanied by suggestion of negligence in 11.3 percent of all stories. It was never suggested that a crime may have occurred when the mine collapsed. The "accident" narrative remained resistant to change in the following months, even as the fact scenario changed. This version of events was aided initially by reports that an earthquake caused the collapse. This explanation, however, was dismissed within five days in favor of the universally accepted view that the collapse caused the appearance of an earthquake. Yet even as this latter view emerged, media coverage still was dominated by the view that the collapse was itself the product of an accident. In a particularly interesting feat of obfuscation, the story line that emerged was that the collapse caused the problems in the mine; little independent consideration was given to the cause of the collapse.

Table 3   Content Analyses of Kali Ann Poulton and Akzo Stories

	Kali Ann Poulton			Akzo		
	Story %	Category %	N	Story %	Category %	N
Cause						
Accident	1.2	1.5	1	100	89.9	71
Negligence	1.2	1.5	1	11.3	10.1	8
Crime	76.5	97	65	0	0	0
Harm						
Direct	100	79.4	85	26.8	21.3	19
Residual	12.9	10.3	11	1.4	1.1	1
Community	12.9	10.3	11	97.2	77.5	69
Responsibility						
Primary	7	12.5	6	11.3	80	8
Secondary	49.4	87.5	42	0	0	0
Tertiary	0	0	0	2.8	20	2
Focus						
Primary	37.6		32	94.4		67
Secondary	62.4		53	5.6		4

Harm. Examination of the harm category reveals another interesting pattern. In the Poulton case, the dominant harm was to Kali Ann herself. Harms experienced by her family and by the surrounding community were each mentioned in 12.9 percent of all stories, seemingly little attention for such an intensively examined event.

In the Akzo case, on the other hand, emphasis was placed on the harm experienced by the mine and, in a related vein, by the natural environment. Harms experienced by Akzo management and miners were mentioned in 26.8 percent of stories; harms experienced by their families were mentioned in only 1.4 percent of the articles. Harms experienced by members of the community, though included in the community subcategory, received much less attention than harms to the environment. This pattern of coverage is instructive in light of Swigert and Farrell's research (1980–81) on the identification of corporate wrongdoing as crime. They argued that corporate wrongdoing comes to be publicly and legally defined as crime insofar as the harms associated with it resemble the harms associated with street crime. By giving little attention to the property damage, declining property values, and community stress and incivility associated with the mine collapse (harms also associated with street crime), the media weakened the relationship between this event and crime.

Responsibility. Media coverage of responsibility for these two events provides the key component of the larger narrative construction of these cases. In the Poulton case, in the 49.4 percent (42) of all the stories in which responsibility for Kali Ann's disappearance was discussed, that responsibility was placed on a stranger. In six of these 42 stories it was suggested that a member of her family might be responsible, though this was never the dominant implication of an article. Viewed in conjunction with the cause category, the Poulton case clearly was very quickly constructed to fit the "stranger abduction" narrative. This occurred even in the absence of any publicly disclosed evidence privileging this explanation or precluding alternative explanations.

Because the Akzo case was framed primarily as an accident, responsibility received little attention: it was mentioned in only 11.3 percent (8) of all the stories. In these eight stories, responsibility was focused on Akzo management; regulatory failure was also suggested in two of these stories. Rather than focusing on responsibility, media attention was focused on the consequences of the collapse, a hegemonic approach in that it reinforced the accident scenario and drew attention away from corporate responsibility.

Focus. Confirming the impression gained in my preliminary analysis, most of the coverage of the Poulton case (62.4% of the articles) focused on secondary events and issues. The limited progress made in the investigation provided little news, but the very high public consciousness of this case, aided strongly by the intense media coverage in the first few weeks after the disappearance, created a large volume of secondary stories. Thus the story was kept in the news even when the case itself provided nothing new to report. In this way the extent of secondary coverage becomes a means by which the newsworthiness of a story, in terms of its amenability to hegemonic interests, can be maintained and measured. The Akzo case generated only four second-ary stories (5.6 percent of all articles); though this story is also hegemonic, the construction of the case as an accident gives it little news value beyond the occurrence of new developments. The Poulton case, on the other hand, fits into one of the most powerful and most pervasive hegemonic narratives of recent years: innocent, law-abiding individuals, particularly children, as the prey of pathological strangers.

Sources. The Poulton and the Akzo case are remarkably similar in the extent of their reliance on sources: An average of 3.53 different sources was cited in each Poulton article and an average of 3.51 in each Akzo article (see table 4). This general similarity masks the substantial and revealing differ-ences in the types of sources used in constructing each narrative. Most nota-bly, the Poulton narrative relies much more strongly on activists—in this case hegemonic activists, particularly those associated with the Adam Walsh Cen-ter. These sources strongly supported the "stranger abduction" narrative and quickly coupled this case with well-known actual and alleged stranger abduc-tions such as the cases of Polly Klass, Adam Walsh, and Sara Anne Wood.[7] I also found a much greater reliance on community members, who shared the sense of threat and loss communicated in the hegemonic narrative, and much less reliance on parties than in the Akzo case.

In the Akzo narrative, the dominant sources of information (68.8 percent of the total) are "official" sources from Akzo or from relevant regulatory agencies. These sources overwhelmingly support hegemonic interests in their orientation toward the events; the absence of a regulatory agency concerned with mining techniques limited the likelihood that Akzo would encounter regulatory opposi-tion and allowed Akzo to be characterized favorably by regulatory officials.[8] Activists in the Akzo case received much less attention than in the Poulton case[9] and were primarily subversive environmental groups and community members; many of the latter included adversely affected property owners. These patterns suggest that in each case, the media preferred predictable, hegemonic voices.

Table 4 Sources Used by Media

Source	Kali Ann Poulton Case		Akzo Case	
	N	%	N	%
Party	17	5.6	74	29.8
Community	96	32	34	13.7
Regulatory	110	36.8	97	39
Activist	42	14	7	2.8
Expert	17	5.6	31	12.3
Business	12	4	5	2
Media	6	2	1	.4
Total	300	100	249	100
Avg. Sources/Story	3.53		3.51	

Discussion and Conclusions

In a series of essays on Darwin's theory of evolution, Stephen Jay Gould (1980) points out that the substantial gaps in the fossil record of human evolution were "filled in" by Darwin and others with a linear trajectory suggesting steady evolutionary progress. More recent research suggests that these gaps cannot properly be connected by a straight line; rather, evolutionary progress is uneven, disrupted, even revolutionary. Darwin, Gould argues, filled the gaps in the fossil record in a hegemonic fashion; in the absence of evidence he favored order and predictability over disorder and revolution. The results of the present research suggest a similar conclusion: media create and reproduce hegemonic understandings of events. In the case of substantial uncertainty about the causes of two dramatic events in the Rochester area, the media framed these events in a manner consistent with established interests.

The most interesting aspect of these cases is that in each the hegemonic narrative runs contrary to the most likely fact scenario; that is, maintaining that narrative requires considerable effort. In the Poulton case, the statistical evidence is quite clear that Kali Ann was most likely abducted by a family member or acquaintance. Nothing in the evidence released to the community counters this scenario. In fact, maintaining the hegemonic narrative also required minimizing or ignoring the efforts of police and others to suggest the subversive narrative. Somewhat contrary to earlier research which suggests that crime reporters rely heavily on police sources and reproduce the police views of crime (Benedict 1992; Best 1990; Chermak 1994; Sheley and Ashkins 1981; Sherizen 1978), the present research suggests that the media will maintain the hegemonic narrative even when police do not support it.[10]

Four early articles are relevant in this regard. In an article offering expert advice to parents in helping their children deal with the Poulton case (McNamara 1994), pediatricians and child psychologists advised parents that children must be taught to have a "reasonable wariness" of strangers. They implied that Kali's disappearance was the result of an abduction by a stranger, even while they also mentioned that children are "overwhelmingly more likely" to be endangered by someone they know. The message of the story is that stranger abductions are a serious concern, and that the Poulton case, though rare, is an example. In an editorial appearing on the same day (*Democrat and Chronicle* 1994b), statistics on missing children showed that stranger abductions are a small percentage of all cases; nonetheless, the editorial concluded that "knowing the statistics doesn't help us deal with cases like that of . . . Kali Poulton." Again it is clearly implied that the rare event occurred in this case. Two days later, in a story that had little impact on the overall tone of coverage of the story, an expert was quoted as stating that "the information sheriff's investigators have released so far points to an abduction by someone who knew Kali" (Sopko and Smith 1994). On the same day, another article offered parents further expert advice on helping their children to be cautious around strangers (*Democrat and Chronicle* 1994c).

The Akzo case contains abundant evidence for inappropriate mining practices including the unprecedented size of the collapse, the miners' well-known objections to working in the area before the collapse, the closing of the area just before the collapse, subsequent expert findings relating to the mining methods used in the area, and Akzo's previous knowledge of the dangers of these methods (Bellaby 1995c; Petersen 1993).[11] Instead of developing this subversive counternarrative, the media presented the collapse as the cause of the mine disaster without considering the causes of the collapse itself. After the initial observation that "what caused the collapse is unknown" and that this knowledge was essential to stopping mine flooding *(Democrat and Chronicle* 1994a), coverage focused heavily on efforts to stop the flooding. In the face of continuing uncertainty about the cause of the collapse, the story line that emerged and was sustained throughout the 90-day period of this research was that the collapse was the precipitating event. In a manner typical of the coverage of this event, one reporter (Orman 1994) stated that "the leak was triggered by the March 12 mine collapse." This account is hegemonic in communicating that the collapse was an unforeseen and unforeseeable natural occurrence; Akzo fostered and favored precisely this version of events, which allowed attention to focus on the consequences of the collapse.

The media, rather than focusing on the background of the collapse, emphasized the consequences; this explains the frequency of articles that mention neither cause nor responsibility. Within two days of the collapse, the dominant story line was the flooding of the mine and the efforts to stop the flooding. This focus portrayed Akzo management as a victim of events beyond its control, much like the American media portrayal of Union Carbide in the aftermath of the Bhopal disaster (Lynch et al. 1989). This approach also casts Akzo as part of an aggressive but ultimately futile effort to save the mine. This version of events can be found in an article that depicts Akzo as fighting a battle to "survive a March 12 collapse" through a "step-by-step" process requiring the corporation to "win" approval from regulators (Rosenberg 1994).

Stories do not tell themselves. Rather, the aftermath of unanticipated events includes a period in which the definition of the situation is fluid. During this period, efforts at social construction are most active, entailing aggressive attempts to apply a stable and favorable understanding to the event in question. James Kunen (1994) illustrates this process in considerable detail in examining the efforts of different interests to construct the Kentucky school bus crash as the result of drunk driving or an unsafe bus. After initial media attention to the unsafe features of the bus, corporate, governmental regulatory and investigatory, media, religious, and community groups worked aggressively to fit the crash into the drunk-driving narrative that prevailed at the time (see Gusfield 1981; Ross 1984). In the present research I argue that this process also occurred in the Akzo and Poulton cases; media treatment of these events located them within dominant narratives about children and business, making it possible to tell these stories and to reproduce elite interests through their telling.

The swift emergence of stabilized, ratified, hegemonic understandings of the Kali Ann Poulton and Akzo cases testifies to the power and influence of their larger narratives. The 1980s and 1990s have been characterized by substantial national concern about children's well-being, evidenced most prominently by the attention to missing children. Children represent vulnerability and the future (Best 1990); our concern that they may be threatened expresses our concern about the society we have created. Representing the pathological individual as the specific threat—in this society but not of it—provides for a recognition and admission of threat, and allows media and other interests to be responsive to public concerns. At the same time, however, policy initiatives pursuant to this construction are limited to system-legitimizing efforts such as incarceration, "stranger danger" education, and public awareness programs. Broader, well-documented threats to children, such as poverty, illiteracy, infant mortality, educational inequality, and inaccessibility of health care, receive far less public and media attention. These threats, a product of social rather than interpersonal relations, are thus not amenable to a vocabulary of crime (Bohm 1993). They are ignored because of their subversive potential or are recast hegemonically as products of irresponsible parents and larger subcultural values.

The last two decades also have seen tremendous growth in the power, status, and profitability of corporations, accompanied by increasing security and declining wages for workers (D. M. Gordon 1996; Schor 1992). As more intense public and public policy scrutiny has been directed toward individuals, attention has been turned away from corporations. Explanations for declining wages, increasing debt, and lost leisure time focus on consumers' choices and on the putatively inevitable process of globalization rather than on the anti-union and low-wage strategies of corporations. Record corporate profits and executive salaries are hardly scrutinized; the media pass over their relationship to layoffs and declining wages in favor of concern about an "overheated economy," associated fears of inflation, and unrelenting attention to fluctuations in the stock market. A more clearly hegemonic framing of economic news is difficult to imagine. In a related area, deregulation of corporate conduct has been substantial. Because of increasingly conservative political administrations and growing economic concerns, the state today is more openly solicitous and supportive of corporations than in the recent past. In this context, organizational wrongdoing is obscured; the weakness of regulation and of media scrutiny limits the likelihood of "naming and blaming," and allows a vocabulary of accident to prevail.

Epilogue

On August 9, 1996 Mark David Christie apparently confessed to police that he had kidnapped and killed Kali Ann Poulton. Her body was found on

August 10, in a large liquid storage tank where Christie formerly was employed.[12] He lived next door to the Poultons at the time of the kidnapping. According to police, Christie disclosed that he killed her within minutes of kidnapping her and managed to remove her body from the scene in the hours immediately following her disappearance. He confessed to the police after first confessing to his wife and his employer, who turned him in.

By the time Kali Ann Poulton was found, media coverage had lessened substantially; stories appeared only to mark the anniversary of the case. The one-year anniversary was marked by the publication of a long article describing the futility of the investigation and the suffering experienced by the family. Accompanying the text was a picture of the most recent poster detailing the case, headlined "Stranger Abducted Child." This and other posters identifying Kali Ann as missing and stranger-abducted were common throughout the area until she was found. It was hardly noted that this case, in its ultimate tragic conclusion, did not fit the narrative into which it was so assiduously placed.

The Akzo mine collapse is also understood more fully, though organizational cases generally lack the neat resolutions provided by the arrest of an offender. In the summer of 1995, the federal Mine Safety and Health Administration released the findings of its investigation of the causes. A banner headline at the top of the front page stated "Akzo declared blameless" (Bellaby 1995a). The article made clear that Akzo was blameless in the sense that it "followed proper steps to ensure that no miners were injured"; workers' safety is the concern of this regulatory agency. However, because "we don't have a standard that says you can't lose your own mine" (p. A1), no federal or state regulatory agency explored the propriety of the mining methods used by Akzo. Subsurface mining techniques are unregulated; only workers' health and safety are subject to regulation.

Several weeks later, a report prepared for the New York Department of Environmental Conservation by a private consultant was released to the public. According to another front-page article, under the headline "Study faults Akzo method," the small-pillar mining technique used by Akzo contributed to the collapse (Bellaby 1995b). Akzo disputed this conclusion, arguing that anomalous geologic conditions were responsible. (Interpretations still differ.) The mine was fully flooded and closed by early September 1995.

In 1996, after making considerable progress in gaining permission to open a new mine several miles away, and after receiving more than $50 million in local and state subsidies to do so, Akzo announced that it was ceasing all mining operations in the area.

Notes

[1] An alternative and perhaps complementary critique of media reporting practices emphasizes how the production of news is influenced by features of media organizations, including race and gender compositions of newsrooms, financial constraints, and deadline pressures (see Benedict 1992; Gans 1979; Tuchman 1978). This meso-level approach specifies the organizational means by which macro-level elite interests are reproduced.

[2] In view of evidence that newspaper coverage of crime correlates more strongly with public perceptions of crime than does coverage by other media (Sheley and Ashkins 1981), the coverage examined here probably approximates closely the public perceptions of these events.

[3] See Forst and Blomquist (1991) and Best (1990) for extended discussions about estimates of the size of the missing children problem and the politics accompanying these estimates.

[4] This figure represents direct costs to consumers. It does not include the secondary costs, such as law enforcement and other protective measures, cited by *U.S. News & World Report* in its estimate of the costs of crime. Also excluded are the substantial but not easily quantified environmental costs and the costs associated with loss of public and consumers' confidence.

[5] New York State lacks any regulation of subsurface mining techniques, precisely the issue in the Akzo case. Instead the state's mining regulation focuses on workers' safety and health, which were not major issues in the Akzo case.

[6] This step required some judgment calls, particularly in the Kali Ann Poulton case. Because of the prominence of this case, it quickly became a focal point of community concern and therefore a reference point in community discussions of crime, threats to children, and related issues. The several stories that made only passing reference to the case were excluded from this analysis.

[7] The Sara Anne Wood case is well known in the New York area and the Northeast. Sara Anne Wood, a 12-year-old girl, was last seen riding her bike near her rural upstate New York home in August 1993. She is believed to have been abducted and killed by a stranger.

[8] On August 10, 1995, as its lead story at the top of the front page, the *Democrat and Chronicle* ran as its headline "Akzo declared blameless: U.S. says owner of collapsed mine upheld safety rules." As pointed out in the story, however, workers' safety was never the major issue in the collapse. Highlighting the regulatory lacuna, Mine Safety and Health Administration official David Park is quoted as saying: "We don't have a standard that says you can't lose your own mine. . . . You just can't hurt any miners when you do it" (Bellaby 1995a).

[9] Two local environmental groups were promoting subversive understandings of the mine collapse and other Akzo-related issues and were readily available for comment. In addition, members of the local college faculty were available to comment on the mine collapse from their various disciplinary perspectives. The absence of these generally subversive voices from media coverage suggests that organizational explanations relating to time and resource constraints on media are inadequate in explaining the construction of the Akzo story.

[10] The subversive narrative of a family abduction of Kali Ann Poulton was not prominent in police accounts of this event, though when this narrative was mentioned, it was usually the police who mentioned it. Activists, readily available to the media through the Adam Walsh Center, provided regular and consistent support for the stranger abduction narrative.

[11] Reports available to Akzo before the collapse (Petersen 1993) and reports released well after the event (Bellaby 1995b, 1995c) make it clear that the danger of a collapse had been well known to Akzo before it occurred.

[12] All of the research and most of the writing for this article were completed before Kali Ann Poulton's body was discovered.

References

Barlow, M H., D. E. Barlow, and T. G. Chiricos. 1995a. "Economic Conditions and Ideologies of Crime in the Media: A Content Analysis of Crime News." *Crime and Delinquency* 41:3–19.

_____. 1995b. "Mobilizing Support for Social Control in a Declining Economy: Exploring Ideologies of Crime within Crime News." *Crime and Delinquency* 41:191–204.

Beckett, K. 1994. "Setting the Public Agenda: 'Street Crime' and Drug Use in American Politics." *Social Problems* 41:425–47.

Beirne, P. and J. Messerschmidt. 1991. *Criminology.* New York: Harcourt Brace Jovanovich.

Bellaby, M. D. 1995a. "Akzo Declared Blameless." *Democrat and Chronicle,* August 10, p. A1.
_____. 1995b. "Study Faults Akzo Method." *Democrat and Chronicle,* August 26, pp. 1A, 5A.
_____.1995c. "Akzo Collapse Scrutinized." *Democrat and Chronicle,* October 16, p. B1.
Benedict, H. 1992. *Virgin or Vamp: How the Press Covers Sex Crimes.* New York: Oxford University Press.
Best, J. 1987. "Rhetoric in Claims-Making: Constructing the Missing Children Problem." *Social Problems* 34:101–21.
_____. 1990. *Threatened Children: Rhetoric and Concern about Child Victims.* Chicago: University of Chicago Press.
Bohm, R. 1986. "Crime, Criminal and Crime Control Policy Myths." *Justice Quarterly,* 3:193–214.
_____. 1993. "Social Relationships That Arguably Should Be Criminal Although They Are Not: On the Political Economy of Crime." Pp. 3–29 in *Political Crime in Contemporary America,* edited by K. D. Tunnell. New York: Garland.
Butterfield, F. 1996. "Survey Finds That Crime Costs $450 Billion a Year." *New York Times,* April 22, p. A1.
Calavita, K and H. N. Pontell. 1994. "The State and White-Collar Crime: Saving the Savings and Loans." *Law and Society Review* 28:297–324.
Chambliss, W. J. 1994. "Policing the Ghetto Underclass: The Politics of Law and Law Enforcement." *Social Problems* 41:177–94.
Chermak, S. M. 1994. "Body Count News: How Crime Is Presented in the News Media." *Justice Quarterly* 11:561–82.
Clinard, M. B. and P. C. Yeager. 1980. *Corporate Crime.* New York: Free Press.
Currie, E. 1985. *Confronting Crime: An American Challenge.* New York: Pantheon.
_____. 1993. *Reckoning: Drugs, the Cities, and the American Future.* New York: Hill and Wang.
Democrat and *Chronicle.* 1994a. "Just Hope Experts Can Contain Damage at Akzo." March 23, p. 10A.
_____. 1994b. "A Little Girl Is Missing and a Community Rallies." May 26, p. 12A.
_____. 1994c. "Experts Help Parents Deal with Anxieties." May 28, p. 11A.
Ewick, P. and S. S. Silbey. 1995. "Subversive Stories and Hegemonic Tales: Toward a Sociology of Narrative." *Law and Society Review* 29:197–226.
Finnerty, B., G. Livadas, S. McNamara, and A. Morrell. 1994. "Authorities Voice Fear Girl Was Abducted." *Democrat and Chronicle,* May 25, pp. 1A, 5A.
Fishman, M. 1978. "Crime Waves as Ideology." *Social Problems* 25:531–43.
Forst, M. L. and M. E. Blomquist. 1991. *Missing Children: Rhetoric and Reality.* New York: Lexington.
Frank, N. K. and M. J. Lynch. 1992. *Corporate Crime, Corporate Violence.* New York: Harrow and Heston.
Gamson, W. A., D. Croteau, W. Hoynes, and T. Sasson. 1992. "Media Images and the Social Construction of Reality." *Annual Review of Sociology* 18:373–93.
Gans, H. J. 1979. *Deciding What's News: A Study of CBS Evening News, Newsweek and Time.* New York: Pantheon.
_____. 1995. *The War against the Poor: The Underclass and Antipoverty Policy.* New York: Basic Books.
Garofalo, J. 1981. "Crime and the News Media: A Selective Review of Research." *Journal of Research in Crime and Delinquency* 18:319–50.

Gordon, D. 1994. *The Dangerous Classes.* New York: Norton.

Gordon, D. M. 1996. *Fat and Mean.* New York: Free Press.

Gorelick, S. 1989. "'Join Our War': The Construction of Ideology in a Newspaper Crimefighting Campaign." *Crime and Delinquency* 35:421–36.

Gould, S. J. 1980. *The Panda's Thumb: More Reflections on Natural History.* New York: Norton.

Graber, D. A. 1980. *Crime News and the Public.* New York: Praeger.

Gusfield, J. R. 1981. *The Culture of Public Problems: Drinking-Driving and the Symbolic Order.* Chicago: University of Chicago Press.

Hills, S., ed. 1987. *Corporate Violence.* Totowa, NJ: Rowman and Littlefield.

Humphries, D. 1981. "Serious Crime, News Coverage, and Ideology: A Content Analysis of Crime Coverage in a Metropolitan Newspaper." *Crime and Delinquency* 27:191–205.

Kappeler, V., M. Blumberg, and G. W. Potter. 1996. *The Mythology of Crime and Criminal Justice.* 2nd ed. Prospect Heights, IL: Waveland.

Katz, M. 1989. *The Underserving Poor.* New York: Pantheon.

Kleniewski, N. 1995. "The War against Welfare Moves to the States." *Research in Politics and Society* 5:193–215.

Kunen, J. S. 1994. *Reckless Disregard: Corporate Greed, Government Indifference, and the Kentucky School Bus Crash.* New York: Simon and Schuster.

Levi, M. 1994. "The Media and White-Collar Crime." Presented at the annual meetings of the American Society of Criminology, Miami.

Lynch, M. J., M. K. Nalla, and K. W. Miller. 1989. "Cross-Cultural Perceptions of Deviance: The Case of Bhopal." *Journal of Research in Crime and Delinquency* 26:7–35.

McNamara, S. 1994. "What Do You Tell Kids?" *Democrat and Chronicle,* May 26, p. 10A.

Michalowski, R. J. 1985. *Order, Law, and Crime.* New York: Random House.

Morash, M. and D. Hale. 1987. "Unusual Crime or Crime as Unusual? Images of Corruption at the Interstate Commerce Commission." Pp. 129–49 in *Organized Crime in America: Concepts and Controversies,* edited by T. S. Bynum. Monsey, NY: Criminal Justice Press.

Orman, D. 1994. "Akzo Can Continue Drilling at Mine." *Democrat and Chronicle,* March 27, p. 1A.

Petersen, G. 1993. Letter to Kurt Kiser, Superintendent, AKZO, from Rock Mechanics Assist, Nov. 22.

Randall, D. M. 1987. "The Portrayal of Business Malfeasance in the Elite and General Public Media." *Social Science Quarterly* 68:281–93.

Randall, D. M., L. Lee-Sammons, and P. R. Hagner. 1988. "Common versus Elite Crime Coverage in Network News." *Social Science Quarterly* 69:910–29.

Reiman, J. 1995. *The Rich Get Richer and the Poor Get Prison: Ideology, Crime, and Criminal Justice.* Boston: Allyn and Bacon.

Reinarman, C. 1996. "The Social Construction of Drug Scares." Pp. 224–34 in *Social Deviance,* edited by E. Goode. Boston: Allyn and Bacon.

Rosenberg, E. 1994. "Akzo Salt Gets OK to Build a Pump Station." *Democrat and Chronicle,* April 3, p. 3B.

Ross, H. L. 1984. *Deterring the Drunk Driver.* Lexington, MA: Lexington Books.

Schor, J. B. 1992. *The Overworked American.* New York: Basic Books.

Sheley, J. F. and C. D. Ashkins. 1981. "Crime, Crime News, and Crime Views." *Public Opinion Quarterly* 45:492–506.

Sherizen, S. 1978. "Social Creation of Crime News: All the News Fitted to Print." Pp. 203–24 in *Deviance and Mass Media,* edited by C. Winick. Beverly Hills: Sage.

Simon, D. R. and D. S. Eitzen. 1993. *Elite Deviance.* 4th ed. Boston: Allyn and Bacon.

Smith, S. J. 1984. "Crime in the News." *British Journal of Criminology* 24:289–95.

Sopko, J. L. and V. Smith. 1994. "Police Usually Mum about High-Profile Cases." *Democrat and Chronicle,* May 28, p. 10A.

Swigert, V. L. and R. A. Farrell. 1980–81. "Corporate Homicide: Definitional Processes in the Creation of Deviance." *Law and Society Review* 15:161–82.

Thornton, J. 1983. "The Tragedy of America's Missing Children." *U.S. News & World Report,* October 24, pp. 63–64.

Tonry, M. 1994. *Malign Neglect.* New York: Oxford University Press.

Tuchman, G. 1978. *Making News: A Study in the Construction of Reality.* New York. Free Press.

Tunnell, K. 1992. "Film at Eleven: Recent Developments in the Commodification of Crime." *Sociological Spectrum* 12:293–313.

U.S. House of Representatives. 1981. "Missing Children's Act." Hearings before the Subcommittee on Civil and Constitutional Rights, Committee on the Judiciary, November 18, 30.

Wright, J. P., F. T. Cullen, and M. B. Blankenship. 1995. "The Social Construction of Corporate Violence: Media Coverage of the Imperial Food Products Fire." *Crime and Delinquency* 41:20–36.

THIRTEEN

"ROAD WARRIORS" ON "HAIR-TRIGGER HIGHWAYS"

CULTURAL RESOURCES AND THE MEDIA'S CONSTRUCTION OF THE 1987 FREEWAY SHOOTINGS PROBLEM

Joel Best

Theories of social problems construction argue that the concerns policy-makers and the public have about particular social problems are not simply a reflection of objective facts about social conditions (Blumer 1971; Spector and Kitsuse 1977; Schneider 1985; Hilgartner and Bosk 1988). Rather, social problems emerge—become a focus for concern—through a process of claims-making. This process determines not only which phenomena come to be designated social problems but the characteristics ascribed to those problems. Problems can always be depicted in more than one way: rape as a sex crime or a crime of violence; marijuana as a cause of psychosis, a precursor to hard drugs, or a threat to economic productivity; and so on. Explaining how and why particular images of problems emerge has become a central task for constructionist analysts (Best 1989).

Typically, constructionist explanations examine the organization of the claimsmaking process, assuming that claims originate with activists, professionals, or others with vested interests in bringing attention to an issue and/or promoting a particular image of the problem. The news media then transform the primary claims of these individuals and relay the resulting secondary claims to the public (Fishman 1978; Fritz and Altheide 1987; Stallings 1990). According to this two-stage model, the resulting images of problems depend, in part, on the primary claimsmakers' interests and ideol-

Source: *Sociological Inquiry*, Vol. 61, No. 3, August 1991, pp. 327–345. © 1991 by the University of Texas Press. Reprinted with permission.

ogy, the constraints imposed by the media's routines, and the rhetoric adopted in making both primary and secondary claims (Best 1990).

Although others' primary claims usually shape news coverage of social issues, the media's role need not be reactive; the press can act as primary claimsmaker, discovering and constructing social problems on its own. In such cases, there might seem to be few constraints on how the media characterize the problem. Yet in practice, the press usually presents these problems within familiar frameworks and describes them in familiar terms. Shootings on Los Angeles freeways offer an example: during the summer of 1987, the press discovered, promoted, and then dropped this problem. Examination of this coverage reveals conventional elements, common to discussions of many other social problems. The conventional nature of this coverage is this article's topic. Unconstrained by independent primary claimsmakers, the press might have characterized freeway violence in many different ways. In fact, the media's treatment of freeway violence resembles most other social problems coverage. What accounts for this standardized, taken-for-granted treatment?

Sociological studies of the news media suggest that the answer lies in the nature of news work: reporters and editors work within constraints (e.g., television news broadcast time limits) for which they develop routines (e.g., television news favors stories which can be illustrated with videotape) (cf. Gans 1979; Gitlin 1980; Tuchman 1978). No doubt such routines helped shape the media's treatment of freeway violence, but they alone cannot account for the particular way the problem was described.

The press's coverage also drew upon a fund of cultural resources. In constructing freeway violence as a social problem, the media adopted a familiar template of elements routinely used in social problems coverage, borrowed familiar cultural images, and otherwise located the problem within a taken-for-granted cultural framework. Examining the use of cultural resources in claimsmaking about freeway shootings reveals the role of cultural concerns in the larger process of social problems construction.

Methods

This article analyzes the imagery used to construct the 1987 freeway violence problem in three major news media: newspapers (including all relevant stories, editorials, columns, and cartoons from the *Los Angeles Times, Los Angeles Herald Examiner, San Francisco Chronicle,* and *New York Times* as well as selected items from other papers and interviews with two reporters who wrote key stories); magazines (including all stories indexed in the *Reader's Guide to Periodical Literature*); and national television broadcasts (videotapes of all eleven network news stories indexed in *Television News Index and Abstracts,* as well as a printed transcript for ABC's *Nightline* [July 30]). While not a systematic sample of press coverage, the sources examined include many of the most significant treatments—both local and national—of the freeway violence problem.

This analysis does not try to contrast the media's construction with the "reality" of freeway shootings, if only because it is impossible to convincingly draw such a contrast. Media coverage is virtually the only source of information about freeway violence; the short-lived problem produced no official records, victimization surveys, or public opinion polls, and only a single social scientific study of the phenomenon.[1] In 1987, for instance, no agency kept official statistics on the incidence of freeway shootings, nor was there any way to determine whether the rate of incidents had changed from the preceding years. Reporters covering the story compiled their own lists of violent incidents and argued that these incidents reflected a new social trend. The issue is not whether this was a "real" trend—a largely unanswerable question—but how journalists used "trend" and other language to characterize freeway shootings.

Evaluation of the freeway violence problem begins by examining the template—the standard elements of description, explanation, and interpretation—used in new stories about social problems. Then the author considers three sorts of imagery—popular culture, humor, and random violence—used as cultural resources in constructing freeway violence as a social problem and suggests some circumstances which affect claimsmakers' choices of images. Finally, an explanation is offered for the emergence and disappearance of freeway shootings as a social problem.

Freeway Shootings and the Template for Social Problems Stories

The 1987 freeway shootings problem seems to have been discovered in a June 26 *Los Angeles Times* column, "No Shelter From Freeway Violence," which suggested "there is a malevolence loose on those roads . . ." (Sauter 1987a). A month later, freeway violence received nationwide notice: all three television networks broadcast stories on their evening news programs; all three major newsweeklies ran stories; and feature articles, columns, and editorial cartoons appeared in newspapers throughout the country (see Appendix). After about three weeks, the national media turned to new topics, although freeway shootings occasionally resurfaced, e.g., a November, 1987 *Glamour* self-help article ("How to Handle On-the-Road Hostility"), and a 1988 exploitation movie (*Freeway*).

While short-lived, the media's treatment of freeway violence resembled coverage of other, better-established social problems. The press described freeway shootings as a social phenomenon, offered explanations for the violence, and located the problem within familiar interpretive schemes. These elements—description, explanation, and interpretation—form a template for social problems coverage. Although most contemporary news stories about social problems fit this template, the emphasis on description, explanation, and interpretation is socially constructed. Different news templates occur in other times and places, such as framing news stories in moralistic or ideological terms (Hallin and Mancini 1984).

Describing the Problem

On June 24, the *Los Angeles Times* ran a brief story, "2nd Freeway Shooting Incident Is Investigated," noting that there had been two apparently unrelated shootings during the previous weekend (Stewart 1987). This story seems to have performed a central task in social problems construction: it established a new category (freeway shooting), thereby redefining the two *incidents* as *instances* of a new problem. In Fishman's (1978, p. 534) language, freeway violence became a "news theme," which "presents a specific news event, or a number of such events, in terms of some broader concept." The new category inspired the June 26 column which claimed there had been "four unrelated freeway shootings over the past 10 months" (Sauter 1987a). Sauter later explained that this column reflected "a desire to seize on a trendoid—the journalistic category reflecting something new, potentially interesting and possibly—just possibly—indicative of a trend" (1987b). *Times* reporters recall that they were now "watching for a trend." An editor assigned reporter Lonn Johnston to write a feature article on the topic. Completed after a few days, the story "was held [i.e., not published] for a couple weeks" (Bill Billiter and Lonn Johnston, telephone interviews, 1989).

Journalists have a rule of thumb: once a third thing happens, you have a trend. The July 20 *Times* news story—"Traffic Dispute Results in Third Freeway Shooting"—revived the concept (Billiter 1987). The next day, Johnston's feature article (amended with a "new top" referring to the newest incident) appeared, shifting the focus from news reports about particular incidents to a general analysis of the freeway violence problem ("a new kind of urban warfare") (Johnston 1987). The same day, the *Los Angeles Herald Examiner*'s (1987) editorial cartoon showed a motorist shopping for "the ultimate freeway defense vehicle"—a tank.

The category was now familiar. A July 26 story began: "While police searched for suspects in the latest highway shooting . . ." (Kendall 1987); it was the first of four front-page *Times* pieces over five days. (The *Herald Examiner* ran front-page freeway violence stories on twelve of the fourteen days from July 21 to August 3.) As the story received more attention, the freeway shootings category began showing elasticity: not all reported incidents occurred on freeways, and not all involved shooting. Some reporters began using broader terms to refer to the problem; e.g., "traffic-related shootings" or "roadway violence," and a variety of incidents were presented as instances of the category, including rocks thrown at windshields (ABC *Nightline*, July 30) and:

> . . . one copycat has moved from the freeways to the busy Southern California skyways. The pilot of a Cessna says he was threatened by the pilot of another plane, who flew close—alongside—and pointed a handgun. (CBS, August 5)

Press reports described freeway shootings as a series of incidents—"sudden evolution," "trend," "wave," "spate," "spree," "upsurge," "fad," "rash"—an "epidemic," "plaguing Southern California," "reaching alarming proportions." However, some reporters acknowledged that it was impossible to document increasing freeway violence. The category had no official standing; no law enforcement agency kept records of freeway shootings as such, and the press had no way to measure shifts in incidence. Instead, reporters quoted officials to the effect that violence seemed more common and referred to a running total of incidents, usually beginning with shots fired at a motorcyclist on June 18 (a case not mentioned in any of the early *Times* stories). By August, the list included over forty incidents.

Descriptions of the shootings emphasized that they began with mundane traffic disputes, that they seemed random, without clear motive, irrational. CBS anchorperson Dan Rather noted, "authorities are dealing with, literally, murderous rage" (CBS, July 24), but other stories spoke of copycats and "triggermen out for a cruel joke" (NBC, July 29). The result, reporters suggested, was freeways becoming "shooting galleries," "scenes of combat," "war zones," or a "terror zone."

If freeway shootings were random and senseless, then their context was irrelevant. For instance, the first network news story about freeway violence featured a typifying example:

> REPORTER JERRY BOWEN: Nineteen-year-old Jiang Nan was shot by another motorist last month during a race for a freeway exit. [video: shots of Nan in hospital bed] (CBS, July 24)

Three nights later, Nan reappeared in a story on another network:

> REPORTER KEN KASHUIHARA: Jiang Nan was shot in the arm because, he says, he honked his horn at another driver. [video: Nan walking, bandaged]
>
> NAN: You can't go around people, shooting people because people just honk your horn. You know. That's not right. [video: close-up of Nan speaking, sitting in car's driver's seat, labeled "Jiang Nan—Victim"] (ABC, July 27)

CBS and ABC used Jiang Nan's experience to exemplify the randomness of freeway violence. In contrast, the *Los Angeles Times* story about the same incident offered more information about its context:

> Alhambra Police Detective Jim Varga said Sunday's shooting occurred after two cars approached the New Avenue freeway on-ramp in Alhambra at about the same time, and the drivers "began jockeying for position to see who would get on first."
>
> Once on the freeway, occupants of both cars threw paper cups and other items at each other, and the other driver tried to prevent Nan from changing lanes, Varga said. When Nan headed for the Atlantic Boulevard exit, the gunman opened fire, striking Nan in the arm. (Stewart 1987)

This description makes the shooting seem less random, less an irrational response ("shooting people because people just honk your horn"), and more like the escalating "character contests" which often precede interpersonal violence (Luckenbill 1984). While the press did not offer detailed accounts of every incident, other reports showed violence emerging from a context of conflict. For instance, the aerial gun-waving incident mentioned above involved rival planes engaged in fish-spotting (Trippett 1987). Some reporters seemed to restrict the concept of freeway shootings to random incidents: "investigators believe that as many as four of the recent shootings involved gang activity or narcotics and may not have been examples of random roadway violence" (Kendall and Jones 1987, p. 20). In other words, not all shootings on freeways were "freeway shootings." (In 1987, the media attributed five deaths to freeway violence, but the CDC researchers, after eliminating cases involving prior disputes, found only two [one on a freeway] [Onwuachi-Saunders, Chukwudi, Lambert, Marchbanks, O'Carroll and Mercy 1989].)

If freeway shootings were random and on the rise, then all motorists were potential victims. The media reported that fear was widespread, that some motorists were buying bulletproof windshields or arming themselves to fight back, and that there had been a "courtesy surge by drivers fearful of reprisals" (Dean 1987, Gest 1987).

In short, the media described freeway shootings as a growing problem, characterized by random violence and widespread fear. Without official statistics or public opinion polls bearing on the topic, reporters relied on interviews with their sources to support these claims. Thus, the eleven network news stories used thirty-eight clips from interviews: eleven with law enforcement officials promising to take action or advising caution; thirteen victims describing their experiences; ten person-in-the-street interviews revealing public concern; and four experts offering explanations.

Explaining the Problem

Having discovered and described freeway violence, the press sought to explain this new social problem. These explanations came from interviews with experts, mostly psychiatrists and social scientists who offered some version of frustration-aggression theory (cf. Dollard, Miller, Doob, Mowrer, and Sears 1939):

> Maybe you have a short fuse. Maybe you have a gun in a car. You're wrapped in steel armor, plenty of power under your foot, but constantly boxed in by traffic. A feeling of impotence and anger, and then someone cuts you off. That, authorities say, is how the shootings began. Then perhaps some people began firing for fun. (NBC, August 3)

In this view, driving in congested "creep-hour traffic" produced stress and frustration which, in turn, led to anger and escalated into shootings and other violent acts (Lobue 1987).[2] Almost all press reports offered some version of this explanation; some added secondary accounts. Several stories suggested that a car's anonymity made aggression less risky ("It's the private bubble that brings out Mr. Hyde" [Johnston 1987, p. 3]); others implied that media coverage encouraged copycat crimes. Still others alluded to the effects of summer heat, "increased levels of violent crime in general, the prevalence of violence on television, drug and alcohol abuse, and even the breakdown of the family" (Armstrong, 1987, p. 4).

Interpreting the Problem

If freeway violence was a social problem, what sort of problem was it? There were several answers to this question, examples of what Gamson and Modigliani (1989) call interpretive packages:

> A package has an internal structure. At its core is a central organizing idea, or *frame*, for making sense of relevant events, suggesting what is at issue. . . . Finally, a package offers a number of different condensing symbols that suggest the core frame and positions in short-hand, making it possible to display the package as a whole with a deft metaphor, catch-phrase, or other symbolic device. (Gamson and Modigliani 1989, p. 3—emphasis in original)

These interpretations offered different orientations to understanding freeway violence and had different implications for social policy.

Perhaps the most straightforward interpretation treated freeway shootings as a *crime problem*. Government and law enforcement officials emphasized this theme. One Highway Patrol officer declared: "These are difficult crimes to try to stop for law enforcement. These are ty—, these are crimes of passion which are akin to the types of crime that occur, uh, between family members" (NBC, August 3). If freeway violence was a crime problem, then its solution lay in increased patrols, better investigations, and more effective prosecution. All three freeway-violence bills which became law fit this model: A.B. 2416 added officers to the Highway Patrol; A.B. 2142 forbade probation for convicted offenders; and S.B. 117 created an additional five-year penalty for persons convicted in freeway shootings (Gillam 1987).

Other analysts portrayed freeway violence as a *traffic problem*, a product of congested highways. While Los Angeles Police Chief Daryl Gates (1987) warned of a "breakdown in self-discipline," his op-ed piece concentrated on ways to improve traffic flow, e.g., closing rush-hour freeways to single-occupant cars. Interpreting freeway violence as a traffic problem implied a need for new freeways, mass transportation, or other means of reducing congestion, although such long-term solutions rarely received detailed discussion.

Still others treated freeway violence as a *gun problem*, one more consequence of the ready availability of firearms. Newspaper editorial pages favored this interpretation; the *Times* (1987a; 1987c) and *San Francisco Chronicle* (1987b) editorials on freeway shootings advocated gun control, and the *Washington Post* (1987) ran a Herblock cartoon, showing a roadside gun stand with signs reading "Last Chance to Reload Before Freeway" and "NRA Freeway Special."

Several commentators spoke of a *courtesy problem*; they viewed the violence as a product of aggressive, hurried, self-centered driving habits. One "recovering Type A" urged people to change their habits: "It takes self-confidence to be a freeway wimp" (Brenner 1987). The CDC researchers offered a *medical* interpretation: "the full public health impact of roadway violence has never been investigated. Roadway assaults could have an enormous emotional impact on drivers in Los Angeles County as well as throughout the United States" (Onwuachi-Saunders et al. 1989, p. 2264). Finally, there were suggestions that freeway shootings were really a *media problem*, "a combination of coincidence and media hype" (Royko 1987a). But even these critics seemed to agree that more than hype was at work; after describing the "media circus," *Newsweek* went on to discuss traffic congestion—"the real cause of L.A.'s sudden evolution from 'Have a Nice Day' to 'Make My Day'" (Kaus 1987).

The Template for Social Problems Coverage

In covering freeway violence, the press concentrated on description, explanation, and interpretation. These are, of course, standard elements for stories about social problems; they form a template for social problems coverage. Because the press places a premium on the novel and the exotic, description is central to the construction of new social problems. Explanation and interpretation offer accounts for these problems. Some analysts argue that, while the American press is overtly nonideological, its underlying message is hegemonic (Gitlin 1980). In this view, freeway violence would be an attractive candidate for press coverage, because it could be explained as a problem caused by the flawed characters of deviant individuals rather than by flawed social institutions.

The only unusual feature of the press coverage was the diversity of interpretive schemes presented. Stallings (1990, p. 90) argues that the media prefer noncausal explanations; while early press coverage may offer competing interpretations, "later accounts tend to converge on a single factor." This failed to happen in the case of freeway violence, probably because the media continued to play the role of primary claimsmaker. Most social problems coverage follows the lead of the independent primary claimsmakers who promote a particular interpretation. Because the press discovered freeway violence, there was no single authoritative interpretation, commentators adapted several familiar interpretive packages, albeit from within a limited ideological range. Thus, interpretations of the problem came from both conservatives (crime problem) and liberals (gun problem), but there was no radical critique, challenging important institutional arrangements. Moreover, there were no parties who chose to make the issue their own, who made determined efforts to promote their interpretation over rival viewpoints.

Culture and Claims

Constructionist analysts suggest that it is easier to promote claims which "fit closely with broad cultural concerns" (Hilgartner and Bosk 1988, p. 64), which "resonate with larger cultural themes" (Gamson and Modigliani 1989, p. 5). The media's treatment of freeway shootings was noteworthy for the ease with which it incorporated imagery from other sources. Often, claimsmakers who presented different interpretations of freeway violence drew upon similar images.

Popular Culture

Discussions of freeway violence frequently borrowed images from violent films. Reporters invoked references to crime thrillers ("Make My Day"), action pictures set in post-Vietnam ("Freeway Rambos") or post-apocalyptic society ("Road Warriors," "A Mad Max mentality"), and Westerns ("hair-trigger impulses reminiscent of the frontier West" [Cummings 1987]). These images fit nicely with interpretations of freeway shootings as a crime or gun problem.

The importance of the film industry to Los Angeles no doubt encouraged these allusions to contemporary movies, and the frequent use of violent automotive chase scenes in action pictures must have helped forge the link between freeway shootings and movie imagery. But references to popular culture are not uncommon in constructions of social problems; most obviously, "Star Wars" has become a standard referent in defense policy debates.

Popular culture is a readily available cultural resource, offering a vast array of familiar images which are easily adapted to claimsmaking. There are advantages to using these images: they suggest that the claimsmaker is clever or up-to-date and they make claims more accessible or more interesting to a wider audience. But these advantages come at a cost. When popular cultural images typify a problem, they shape perceptions of it.

Thus, suggestions that freeway shootings somehow resembled the extraordinary violence in formula films implied an ambivalence toward violence, since popular culture simultaneously celebrates and deplores violence. And, since U.S. popular culture tends to locate good and evil within individual heros and villains, the movie imagery may have helped define freeway shootings in terms of deviant individuals. Finally, likening brief incidents of freeway violence to the prolonged, dramatic violence found in films implied a level of violence far greater than that found in press reports of particular freeway shootings. Although the references to Mad Max and Rambo were playful, they exaggerated the problem's seriousness.

Humor

Reports of freeway violence also inspired cartoonists and humor columnists. Most often, their work used exaggeration to make the problem seem ridiculous. Instead of depicting freeways as scenes of criminal violence, cartoonists militarized the problem (e.g., depicting a middle-class couple in a car, with the middle-aged female passenger wearing a Rambo-style headband and aiming a rocket launcher [*Los Angeles Times* 1987b], or showing a traffic reporter's helicopter under fire [*San Francisco Chronicle* 1987a]). Playing on reporters' references to war zones and Rambo, these cartoons extended the problem to a ridiculous extreme, showing ordinary people taking extraordinary violence for granted. Other cartoons contrasted freeway violence with earthquakes and drunk driving (*Los Angeles Times* 1987d, 1987e), suggesting that shootings were just one added problem faced by long-suffering urbanites. The humor lay in the implication that freeway shootings were mundane, not at all extraordinary, that random danger is simply another hazard of urban life. (Compare the analogous cartoons about nineteenth-century English crime waves in Pearson [1983]).

Other humor depended on freeway shootings having emerged in Los Angeles, notorious for its heavy, fast-moving freeway traffic. Thus, a CBS (July 24) story began: "It's always been crazy on the Southern California freeways—a real zoo—but these days the animals are armed and dangerous," while columnist Lewis Grizzard (1987) noted, ". . . there are more crazy people in Los Angeles than anywhere else in the country." Here, stereotypes of Southern California provided a cultural resource for the humorists. Other humorists warned that the roots of freeway violence were mundane, that aggressive driving was widespread, and that it was only a small step from everyday hostility to extraordinary violence (cf. Royko 1987b). Thus, all parties—and the larger culture—were to blame when incidents escalated to violence. As these examples suggest, claimsmakers incorporated humor into almost all of the competing interpretations of freeway violence.

Random Violence

The humorists' treatments of freeway shootings, like the reporters' references to Rambo, suggest a failure to take the problem completely seriously. However, most of the humor was not pointed; it made fun of the phenomenon, rather than the people involved. At the same time, press reports emphasized the random, senseless qualities of freeway violence, warning that ordinary drivers, going about their everyday business, were potential victims. This drew upon a more general, contemporary concern with irrational, capricious villains. The 1980s saw the construction of other villains said to strike at random, including serial murderers, strangers abducting children, and product-tampering copycats. (The movie *Freeway* illustrates the ease with which these typifications can be blended: its villain is an ex-priest, ex-mental-patient serial killer who shoots other motorists while talking to a radio psychiatrist on a car phone. The film was previewed under the title *Drive-By* [an allusion to the "wave" of "drive-by shootings" linked to Los Angeles gangs—another problem defined in terms of random violence]).

In the 1960s and 1970s, asserting randomness became a standard tactic for claimsmakers seeking to raise social concern; defining all children as potential child-abuse victims or all women as potential rape victims gave the widest possible audience an interest in confronting these problems. But it is easy to move from saying "X happens to all sorts of people," to "X can happen to anyone," to "X occurs randomly." And defining events as random encourages people to ignore or deny patterns in social life. Thus, claims that freeway shootings were random linked this problem to those involving other menacing deviants, while discouraging critical analysis of the problem's nature.

Incorporating Cultural Images

Because there were no independent primary claimsmakers guiding the interpretation of freeway shootings, the media had a relatively free hand in constructing the problem. However, rather than treating freeway violence as a unique phenomenon, the press located the problem within a set of existing—and not necessarily consistent—cultural concerns. Freeway shootings were said to resemble violent elements in popular culture, to have humorous features, and to reflect the random impulses of violent criminals. Confronted with a "new" problem, the media borrowed established cultural images to discuss it, with advocates of very different interpretations adopting similar imagery.

The problem's Southern California setting explains the frequent references to the film industry, the Los Angeles freeways, and the character of Californians. Not surprisingly, a different imagery characterized media coverage of an earlier "outbreak" of freeway violence in Houston, Texas in 1982 (King 1982; Ivey 1983). In particular, there were references to the frontier West ("gunfighter," "posse"), while the most prominent explanation held that Houston's economic boom had attracted "Texas newcomers," producing a "clash of cultures on the highway." A 1987 *Houston Post* article ("Freeway free-for-all: Why on Los Angeles' highways and not Houston's?") argued that, while Houston led the nation in traffic congestion, the city's recent economic slowdown had reduced the influx of newcomers and slowed the "frantic pace of life," causing a decline in freeway shootings (Flood 1987).

The contrasting treatments of freeway violence in Los Angeles and Houston suggest that primary claimsmaking by the media will usually draw from a pool of available imagery. This resembles Swidler's (1986, p. 273) model of culture "as a 'tool kit' of symbols, stories, rituals, and worldviews, which people may use in varying configurations to solve different kinds of problems." In this view, "individuals select the meanings they need . . . from the limited but nonetheless varied cultural menu a given society provides" (Schudson 1989, p. 155). Thus, reporters covering the 1987 freeway shootings incorporated familiar images—references to recent films, expertise from psychiatrists and social scientists, humorous stereotypes about Californians and their freeways, and warnings about random violence. If nothing else, the time constraints of news work make this sort of borrowing likely.

The problem with this tool-kit model is that it does not help us predict which images will be used to construct which problems (Schudson 1989). But claims do not emerge in a vacuum; they have an organizational context which affects the choice of imagery in at least three stages of the claimsmaking process. First, primary claimsmakers have ideologies, professional training, perceived interests, and other concerns which shape their construction of social problems. Claimsmakers' identities affect their characterization of problems; where moralists see sin, medical authorities detect disease.

Second, primary claimsmakers find themselves competing with one another for media attention. Not all claims receive coverage, and the press favors those which are dramatic, sponsored by powerful groups, and "relate to deep mythic themes" (Hilgartner and Bosk 1988, p. 64). Thus, bigots, political radicals, religious fundamentalists, and others outside the political and cultural mainstream have trouble getting the press to listen to their claims and often complain that the coverage they do receive distorts what they have to say. The media's role as a filter is less obvious when (as in the case of freeway violence) they act as primary claimsmakers. Here, reporters have insiders' knowledge of what makes a good story; they understand the template for social problems stories and shape their reports to fit.

In turn, media coverage shapes the reactions of policymakers and the public. Gamson and Modigliani (1989) discuss this third stage, arguing that the impact of claims depends upon the rhetoric and activities of primary and secondary claimsmakers and upon whether the claims have "cultural resonance." Claims presented in terms which are unfamiliar or ill-matched to the larger culture's concerns have little impact.

In short, while primary claimsmakers may seem to have a great deal of freedom in composing claims, they are in practice constrained by their own perceptions of the problem, the expectations of the press, and the concerns of policymakers and the public. Even so, the language and imagery used by independent primary claimsmakers is likely to be more diverse than the rhetoric adopted when the press serves as primary claimsmaker. When not prompted by outside claimsmakers, reporters and editors construct social problems within the familiar limits of news-work conventions. These constraints help explain why, in the case of freeway violence, the media adapted familiar explanations, interpretations, and images in their presentation of the problem. Still, the impact of those claims depended on a set of contingencies which shaped the rise—and fall—of the freeway shootings problem.

The Natural History of a Short-Lived Social Problem

Three contingencies accounted for the emergence of freeway violence as a social problem. First, the "freeway violence" category had to be discovered; someone had to define separate incidents as part of a larger pattern. The resulting category had its own appeal: it offered both drama (as a violent crime) and immediacy (i.e., most people were part of freeway traffic and therefore at risk). Yet freeway violence was not controversial; the media's construction of the problem did not threaten any powerful interest. And television had little difficulty illustrating the problems with videotape of dense traffic, bullet holes in cars, and interviews with victims. Once discovered, freeway violence fit several of the media's requirements for a good social problems story.

Still, these features alone cannot explain freeway violence becoming a focus for national attention. Most crime waves attract only local news coverage (Fishman 1978). Other outbreaks of freeway shootings—in California in 1977 (*Los Angeles Times* 1987a), Detroit in 1989 (*New York Times* 1989), and Houston in 1982—failed to attract as much national attention as the 1987 Los Angeles incidents.

This suggests the importance of a second contingency: the *Los Angeles Times* discovered freeway shootings. As the most authoritative newspaper in its state and region, it sets the agenda for Southern California print and electronic news coverage; a story treated seriously by the *Times* is likely to be picked up by radio and television stations, as well as other newspapers (Best 1986). (The fact that Van Gordon Sauter, the author of the first *Times* column on freeway shootings, was a former president of CBS News may have given the story additional authority.) Moreover, as a major metropolitan region and the center for the entertainment industry, Los Angeles has more than its share of reporters. Major newsmagazines and newspapers station correspondents there. All three television networks own and operate affiliates in Los Angeles, and the network news programs favor reports from owned and operated stations (Epstein 1973). Moreover, the widespread perception that Southern California often sets styles for the rest of the country makes it more likely that a Los Angeles "trend" will receive coverage in the national press.

Third, timing may have been important. There seem to have been relatively few stories competing for media attention. Journalistic folklore speaks of summer "dog days" and the "silly season" when news is slow, reporters must look harder for stories, and marginal stories are more likely to receive coverage. It may well be easier to gain coverage for social-problems claimsmaking during the summer. Consider the "crack epidemic" of 1986, freeway shootings in 1987, and the interest in polluted beaches in 1988. Claimsmakers must compete for media attention but, to the degree that this competition is seasonal, there may be periods when relatively weak claims can rise to visibility.

Taken together, these contingencies—the discovery of the category, by the *Los Angeles Times*, during a slow news season—help account for the rise of freeway violence to national prominence. Because the freeway shootings emanated from Southern California—often a source for new trends—the media anticipated that violence would spread. On CBS (August 5), Dan Rather asked: "Is it a local phenomenon, or does it indicate something in the country as a whole, something in society at large?" Broadcasting from Chicago, ABC's (August 6) Peter Jennings noted, "There haven't been any incidents here in the Midwest. . . ." But the *Wall Street Journal* argued that the violence was nationwide: "the nation's freeways now resemble something out of the Wild West" (Gonzales 1987). In its August 17 issue, *Time* noted: "Highway officials in Arizona, Washington, Utah, and Northern California reported armed confrontations last week" (Trippett 1987); three months later, a short item reported freeway violence "appears to have faded on the West Coast but is all the rage in southern Illinois and is spreading to eastern Missouri" (*Time* 1987). However, these isolated reports were apparently insufficient to maintain media interest in freeway violence as a spreading problem.

The failure to document a dramatic spread in freeway shootings helps account for their disappearance as a social problem. Freeway violence both emerged and disappeared quickly. Why? The news media constructed the problem, but the story did not develop in any of the ways which might have let it remain visible. The light-hearted tone of some coverage may have discouraged people from taking the problem seriously. The press did not find sufficient cases to portray freeway violence as spreading throughout the country, nor did reporters find a growing number of incidents in Los Angeles; there was no dramatic new news to keep the story alive. Moreover, there were no independent primary claimsmakers interested in pursuing and promoting the story. The media brought freeway violence to public attention without prompting from outside claimsmakers. Once the problem achieved visibility, it might have been adopted by claimsmakers outside the press, but this did not happen, probably because the principal interpretations of the problem called for solutions which seemed unworkable. Whatever the arguments for expanded freeways, mass transportation, or other long-term solutions to Los Angeles traffic problems, few advocates expected progress, let alone solutions, in the near future. And defining freeway shootings as a gun problem offered little advantage; the tiny number of freeway homicides could not affect the entrenched debate over gun control. In other words, no constituency emerged to adopt the newly-constructed freeway shooting problem, to nurture it and help it develop into a well-established social problem.

Conclusion

Freeway violence offers an example of a short-lived social problem in which the media acted as primary claimsmakers. This problem was discovered and constructed by enterprising reporters and press commentators. In 1987, theirs were the only voices to be heard on the subject. Because they had a free hand in constructing this problem, we can view the result as a prototype of social-problems construction as practiced by the media. Most striking are the similarities between the construction of freeway shootings and the media's treatment of other social problems. The press framed its coverage within a standard structure, using a template of elements—description, explanation, and interpretation—usually found in contemporary social-problems stories. Moreover, the media adapted a variety of cultural resources, such as references to popular culture and random violence, to depict freeway shootings. The particular construction which emerged—a frightening yet funny spectacle of Los Angelinos, pushed beyond endurance by the frustrations of freeway driving, turning to random shootings and somehow incorporating this violence into their everyday lives—was engaging enough (and the immediate competition for media attention weak enough) to catapult freeway violence into national visibility. However, there was little to sustain the media's interest, and the attention soon faded.

By mid-August, 1987, freeway violence had disappeared from national news coverage. Still, the problem retains some familiarity and remains the subject of occasional asides (e.g., an article describes how Japanese drivers respond to a traffic jam, then notes: "this passivity is better than gunning other motorists down, as in Los Angeles" [Fallows 1989, p. 52]). Freeway shootings, then, have become a cultural resource in their own right, available for use in the construction of other social problems.

Appendix

Chronology of Principal 1987 Coverage of Freeway Violence
(June 24–August 11)

Wed., June 24   —*L.A. Times* story about "2nd Freeway Shooting"

Fri., June 26   —*L.A. Times* column about "freeway violence"

Mon., July 20   —*L.A. Times* story about "Third Freeway Shooting"

Tue., July 21   —*L.A. Times* feature article on "War Out There"

Fri., July 24   —CBS story (2:10)

Sat., July 25   —ABC story (2:00)

Sun., July 26   —NBC story (:20); *S.F. Examiner* front-page feature article on "Road Warriors"; *L.A. Herald Examiner* front-page feature article on "Hair-Trigger Highways"

Mon., July 27   —ABC story (2:40); *N.Y. Times* article

Wed., July 29   —NBC story (2:20)

Thu., July 30   —ABC *Nightline* episode

Fri., July 31   —*L.A. Times* front-page feature article on "Coping with Violence"; *L.A. Herald Examiner* front-page feature article "Shedding Light on Dark Side of L.A. Drivers"

Sun., August 2   —ABC story (1:40); NBC story (:30); *S.F. Examiner* feature article on "Freeway 'Rambos'"

Mon., August 3—NBC story (1:50); *Christian Science Monitor* and *Wall Street Journal* articles

Tue., August 4   —*Newsweek* article—"Gunplay on the Freeway"; *U.S. News* article—"Rambo's Brothers Cruise Clogged Expressways"

Wed., August 5—CBS story (2:40)

Thu., August 6   —ABC story (2:00); NBC story (:20)

Tue., August 11—*Time* article—"Highway to Homicide"

Notes

[1] Researchers from the Centers for Disease Control (CDC) compared summertime "roadway firearm assaults" in Los Angeles, 1985–87. They searched law enforcement records for reported incidents involving "the shooting or brandishing of a firearm at occupants of a moving vehicle on any freeway, highway, or surface street," then eliminated cases deemed gang-related or "the result of preexisting domestic quarrels" (Onwuachi-Saunders et al. 1989, p. 2262). They found 137 incidents in 1987 (49 on freeways)—an increase over 1985 (32 incidents, 4 on freeways) and 1986 (91 incidents, 15 on freeways).

[2] Novaco (1987) noted an important flaw in this explanation: "The road assaults are not being done by commuters. . . ." Many incidents occurred, not during heavily-congested rush hours, but at night or on weekends—a pattern common to other violent crimes. For instance, four of the five fatalities attributed to freeway violence occurred on weekend nights, two in a single incident at an intersection with a stop sign (i.e., not on a freeway). The CDC researchers note that "more than two-thirds (69%) of the 1987 assaults occurred outside of the hours of peak traffic flow," although they "found a positive association between freeway congestion and freeway firearm assaults" (Onwuachi-Saunders et al. 1989, p. 2264).

References

Armstrong, Scott. 1987. "Southern California Freeway Shootings Test Drivers, Police." *Christian Science Monitor* (August 3):3.

Best, Joel. 1986. "Famous for Fifteen Minutes." *Qualitative Sociology* 9:372–82.

_____. 1989. *Images of Issues*, edited by Joel Best. New York: Aldine de Gruyter.

_____. 1990. *Threatened Children*. Chicago: University of Chicago Press.

Billiter, Bill. 1987. "Traffic Dispute Results in Third Freeway Shooting." *Los Angeles Times* (July 20):13.

Blumer, Herbert. 1971. "Social Problems as Collective Behavior." *Social Problems* 18:298–306.

Brenner, Martin. 1987. "Power to the Freeway Wimps." *Los Angeles Times* (August 5): 117.

Cummings, Judith. 1987. "On Congested Highways, California Motorists Turn to Violence." *New York Times* (July 28): I10.

Dean, Paul. 1987. "Defensive Driving." *Los Angeles Times* (August 5): V1.

Dollard, J., N. E. Miller, L. W. Doob, O. H. Mowrer, and R. R. Sears. 1939. *Frustration and Aggression*. New Haven: Yale University Press.

Epstein, Edward Jay. 1973. *News from Nowhere*. New York: Random House.

Fallows, James. 1989. "Containing Japan." *Atlantic Monthly* 263 (May): 40–54.

Fishman, Mark. 1978. "Crime Waves as Ideology." *Social Problems* 25:531–43.

Flood, Mary. 1987. "Freeway Free-for-All." *Houston Post* (August 9): 1A, 20A.

Fritz, Noah J., and David L. Altheide. 1987. "The Mass Media and the Social Construction of the Missing Children Problem." *Sociological Quarterly* 28:473 92.

Gamson, William, and Andre Modigliani. 1989. "Media Discourse and Public Opinion on Nuclear Power." *American Journal of Sociology* 95:1–37.

Gans, Herbert J. 1979. *Deciding What's News*. New York: Pantheon.

Gates, Daryl F. 1987. "Highway Hostility Must Be Stopped." *Los Angeles Times* (August 23): V5.

Gest, Ted. 1987. "Rambo's Brothers Cruise Clogged Expressways." *U.S. News and World Report* 103 (August 10): 6.

Gillam, Jerry. 1987. "Bills Signed to Combat Violence on the Freeways." *Los Angeles Times* (September 27): I21.

Gitlin, Todd. 1980. *The Whole World Is Watching*. Berkeley: University of California Press.

Gonzales, Monica. 1987. "Motorist Mayhem." *Wall Street Journal* (August 3): 1, 14.

Grizzard, Lewis. 1987. "How to Avoid Getting Shot." *Atlanta Constitution* (August 2): B1.

Hallin, Daniel C., and Palolo Mancini. 1984. "Speaking of the President." *Theory and Society* 13:829–50.

Hilgartner, Stephen, and Charles L. Bosk. 1988. "The Rise and Fall of Social Problems." *American Journal of Sociology* 94:53–78.

Ivey, Mark. 1983. "Where the Commuter Is A Gunfighter." *Business Week* (May 1): 20A, B.

Johnston, Lonn. 1987. "Stress on Freeways Sparks 'War Out There'." *Los Angeles Times* (July 21): I3.

Kaus, Mickey. 1987. "Gunplay on the Freeway." *Newsweek* 110 (August 10): 18.

Kendall, John. 1987. "Death Raises Level of Fear on Highways." *Los Angeles Times* (July 26): I1.

Kendall, John, and Jack Jones. 1987. "4 Men, Woman Held in Highway Shooting Death." *Los Angeles Times* (July 29): I1, 20.

King, Wayne. 1982. "'Unfriendly Driving' Explodes into Violence on Texas Freeways." *New York Times* (December 17): A16.

Lobue, Ange. 1987. "Mayhem on the Freeways." *U.S. News and World Report* 103 (September 28): 9.

Los Angeles Herald Examiner. 1987. Editorial cartoon (July 21): A14.

Los Angeles Times. 1987a. "Guns and Tire Irons" (editorial). (August 6): I10.

_____. 1987b. Editorial cartoon. (August 8): I12.

Los Angeles Times. 1987c. "Guns in Cars" (editorial). (August 23): I14.

_____. 1987d. Editorial cartoon. (August 23): V5.

_____. 1987e. Editorial cartoon. (October 10): II9.

Luckenbill, David F. 1984. "Character Coercion, Instrumental Coercion, and Gun Control." *Journal of Applied Behavioral Science* 20:181–92.

New York Times. 1989. "Outbreak of Road Shootings Plagues Detroit." (February 12): 27.

Novaco, Raymond W. 1987. "Highway Violence Has Numerous Triggers." *Los Angeles Times* (August 2): V5.

Onwuachi-Saunders, E. Chukwudi, Deborah A. Lambert, Polly A. Marchbanks, Patrick W. O'Carroll, and James A. Mercy. 1989. "Firearm-Related Assaults on Los Angeles Roadways." *Journal of the American Medical Association* 262:2262–2264.

Pearson, Geoffrey. 1983. *Hooligan.* New York: Schocken.

Royko, Mike. 1987a. "California 'Trend' Strictly a Misfire." *Chicago Tribune* (August 4): 3.

_____. 1987b. "Were They Cruising for a Shooting?" *Chicago Tribune* (August 10): 3.

San Francisco Chronicle. 1987a. Editorial cartoon. (August 10): 54.

_____. 1987b. "Limiting Guns in Motor Vehicles" (editorial). (August 21): 72.

Sauter, Van Gordon. 1987a. "No Shelter from Freeway Violence." *Los Angeles Times* (June 26): V1.

_____. 1987b. "Too Much Ado about Freeway Shootings." *Los Angeles Times* (August 3): I15.

Schneider, Joseph W. 1985. "Social Problems Theory." *Annual Review of Sociology* 11:209–29.

Schudson, Michael. 1989. "How Culture Works." *Theory and Society* 18:153–80.

Spector, Malcolm, and John I. Kitsuse. 1977. *Constructing Social Problems.* Menlo Park, CA: Cummings.

Stallings, Robert A. 1990. "Media Discourse and the Social Construction of Risk." *Social Problems* 37:80–95.

Stewart, Jill. 1987. "2nd Freeway Shooting Incident Is Investigated." *Los Angeles Times* (June 24): II1.

Swidler, Ann. 1986. "Culture in Action." *American Sociological Review* 51:273–86.

Time. 1987. "Homicide on the Highway." 130 (November 23): 31.

Trippett, Frank. 1987. "Highway to Homicide." *Time* 130 (August 17): 18.

Tuchman, Gaye. 1978. *Making News.* New York: Free Press.

Washington Post. 1987. Editorial cartoon. (August 3): A14.

PART III

Effects of Constructing Crime

FOURTEEN

CRIME, NEWS AND FEAR OF CRIME

TOWARD AN IDENTIFICATION
OF AUDIENCE EFFECTS

Ted Chiricos, Sarah Eschholz, & Marc Gertz

In July, 1993 two teenaged girls in Houston took a shortcut home through a wooded area, crossed paths with six gang members to whom "life means nothing," and were raped and brutally murdered (*Newsweek*, 1993a). Two weeks later, the national newsmagazines ran cover stories on violent crime, and a media feeding frenzy was underway. Typical stories included: "Teen Violence: Wild in the Streets" (*Newsweek*, 1993b); "Danger in the Safety Zone" (*Time*, 1993a); "In a State of Terror" (*Newsweek*, 1993c); "Taming the Killers" (*Time*, 1993b), and "Florida: State of Rage" (*U.S. News*, 1993a).

The explosion of attention to this issue extended to other news outlets as well. Television and newspaper stories about violent crime and juvenile violence increased more than 400 percent between June and November of 1993 (figure 1). In the wake of this extraordinary burst of media coverage, public concern about crime rose dramatically. Americans ranking crime or violence as the nation's foremost problem jumped from 9 percent to 49 percent between January 1993 and January 1994 (Gallup 1994:6). Politicians at every level rose to the "challenge" of keeping up with public opinion. Proposals to stem the seeming "epidemic" of violence included everything from castration to caning, from fingerprinting school children to incorporating military technology in the latest "war on crime." That levels of violent crime actually were declining was apparently irrelevant.

In this article, we examine relationships between fear of crime (FEAR) and the news consumption reported by 2,092 persons living in a state capital who were randomly sampled at the peak of the media frenzy about violent crime. We consider four sources of news: television, radio, newspapers, and

Social Problems, Vol. 44, No. 3, August 1997, pp. 342–357. Permission granted by University of California Press Journals.

weekly newsmagazines. We examine the relationship between news consumption and FEAR, controlling for age, gender, race, victim experience, and other crime perceptions, including the perception of risk. That perception is often misinterpreted as fear itself (Ferraro 1995).

Most importantly, we explore the possibility that relationships between fear of crime and news consumption vary in ways that reflect socially patterned differences among respondents. In the manner of "reception research" (Dahlgren 1988) we assume that meaning does not reside entirely in media messages; rather, it is variably received and interpreted by audiences in distinctive social situations. Young African-American women likely bring a different set of experiences and interests to the construction of media meaning about crime than, for example, older white men. We assume that diverse cat-

Figure 1   Violent Crime and Media Coverage of Violent Crime

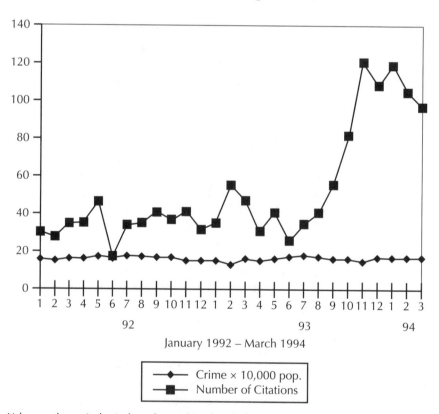

January 1992 – March 1994

Crime × 10,000 pop.
Number of Citations

Values on the vertical axis show the combined total of newspaper and television stories involving violent crime or juvenile violence and the rate of UCR violent crime per *10,000* population.

Sources: U.S. Department of Justice (1993,1994,1995) for Violent Crime. Dialog Information Service (1994) for coverage of 26 major newspapers. Burelle's Transcripts (1994) for coverage of CBS, NBC, and FOX networks.

egories of social existence frame orientations to media messages, and as Fiske (1986:405) noted, "contradictions in society reproduce themselves in subjectivities" (1986:405).

When patterned "subjectivities" coalesce around issues like crime and fear, they may form what some have termed "interpretive communities" (Jensen 1990; Lindlof 1988). The latter affirms "the complexity and variability of audience responses to media messages" and situates the "individual reader or viewer within broader social and cultural contexts" (Carragee 1990:86). In contrast with more structural interpretations of media effects (Gitlin 1979), this approach posits an active audience and, if not polysemic media messages (Fiske 1986), then at least polyvalent (Condit 1989) interpretations of them.

It has yet to be established that shared experiences of gender, race, age, income, and fear are sufficient to constitute "interpretive communities." Even so, if the relationship between fear and news consumption is patterned by gender, race, age, etc., we may begin to understand how news consumers "actively produce meaning from . . . within the context of their everyday lives" (Dahlgren 1988:289–90). In this article we examine whether "fear" is differentially produced by consumers of news who are distinguished by gender, race, age, income, and victim experience.

Prior Research: Media, Audiences and Fear of Crime

A recent review of "mass media and fear of crime" research by Heath and Gilbert concludes that the relationship is contingent on "characteristics of the message, of the audience, and of the dependent measure" (1996:384). Relevant message characteristics include the proportion of a newspaper devoted to crime (Gordon and Heath 1981), whether the crime is local versus distant (Heath 1984), whether the crime is random or is the subject of sensational crime reports (Heath 1984; Liska and Baccaglini 1990; Williams and Dickinson 1993) and whether there is "just" closure of a crime on television drama (Wakshlag 1983). Concerning dependent measures, Heath and Gilbert (1996: 380–384) report stronger links between media and fear when the issue is "societal concern" as opposed to personal fear (Tyler and Cook 1984) for apprehension about "the world out there" versus the immediate neighborhood (Heath and Petraitis 1987) and for urban as opposed to rural settings (Zillmann and Wakshlag 1985).

Audience characteristics are the focus of this study. On this issue, Heath and Gilbert conclude that: ". . . belief in the reality of television drama (Potter 1986) and viewer apprehension about crime victimization (Tamborini et al. 1984; Wakshlag 1983; Zillmann and Wakshlag 1985) affect the relationship with fear of crime" (1996:384). These are the only audience traits discussed by Heath and Gilbert. The remainder of this review examines other audience attributes that appear relevant in prior assessments of media relationships to FEAR. It should be noted that several of the best studies of crime news and fear (Heath 1984; O'Keefe 1984; O'Keefe and Reid-Nash 1987;

Williams and Dickinson 1993) are not concerned with audience characteristics *per se*, while several studies of TV drama do raise issues of variable audience reception that warrant attention.

One potentially salient factor in the reception of media crime messages is whether audience members have direct victim experience or share characteristics making them more likely crime victims. Gunter argues that indirect sources of information, such as media accounts, will be more consequential "when direct experience is lacking" (1987:61). Though limited to 108 university students, Weaver and Wakshlag's (1985) study of crime-related television watching and "crime-related anxiety" demonstrated precisely that point.

Similarly, Liska and Baccaglini hypothesized that newspaper crime stories will have their strongest fear effects for those "least likely to experience victimization" such as "whites, the elderly and females" (1990:363). Their content analysis of newspapers and 1974–75 NCVS fear measures (perceived safety) for twenty-six cities, showed FEAR related only to local homicide stories in the first part of the paper. While this finding held for diverse demographic groups, the media influence was "weakest for those statuses [non-whites, young, males] most likely to experience victimization" (Liska and Baccaglini 1990:372).

Doob and MacDonald's (1979) frequently cited research comes to a different conclusion about the relationship between victim likelihood and media influence. Their interviews with 300 Toronto residents established the number and type of television programs watched in the previous week, as well as perceived chances of victimization (called fear). Overall, when age, sex, and neighborhood type were controlled, there was no relationship between television watching and "fear." However, in urban "high crime" neighborhoods, "fear" was significantly higher for those who watched the most television and significantly lower for those who read newspapers. No such relationships were found in "low crime" neighborhoods; people outside high crime urban neighborhoods "do not feel that the violence on television has any relevance for them . . ." (1979:177).

This is what Gerbner et al. (1980) termed "resonance" in their studies of television's ability to "cultivate" a violent and threatening view of the world. Much of their early work (e.g. Gerbner et al. 1978) argued for "across the board" consequences—with "heavy" television viewers more likely to describe a violent and fearsome world. Later, apparently in response to Doob and MacDonald (1979), Gerbner et al. hypothesized that when a particular television audience receives messages "congruent with everyday reality (or even perceived reality), the combination may result in a . . . powerful 'double dose' of the television message . . ." (1980:15). In short, media effects should be stronger when they "resonate" real life experience.

Gerbner et al. (1980) used their findings from a national survey (N = 3903) to illustrate the "resonance" hypothesis. They noted that "city dwellers . . . show the strongest association" between amount of television viewing and FEAR. However, their data also showed that watching television makes a bigger difference for women and whites (who have low victim risk) than it does for men and non-whites. In fact, for non-whites and those with the lowest incomes (and higher victim risk) the relationship between FEAR and total television watching was actually *negative,* though not significant (Gerbner et al. 1980:21).

Another possibility raised by Gerbner and his associates could be described as audience "affinity." This approach posits that "we may be especially receptive to seeing how characters like ourselves . . . fare in the world of television" (1978:186). Since Gerbner's (1978) analyses of programs in the 1970s showed women, older women, and blacks (men and women) to be most victimized in television drama, Hirsch (1980) hypothesized that heavy television viewing should cultivate the greatest fear among these groups. Yet, his analysis of 1502 respondents to a national survey in 1977 revealed that "none of the expected . . . effects obtains in any of these groups" (12).

Skogan and Maxfield suggested that "vulnerability" to attack—as opposed to victim risk *per se*—could make some audiences "more sensitive to messages" that others discount. They hypothesized that "women and the elderly . . . would be more responsive to personal or media messages about crime." Their 1977 telephone survey (N = 1389) of San Francisco, Chicago, and Philadelphia residents "failed to find any support for this notion" since the relationship between fear and ability to recall a recent crime story (television or newspaper) "was constant among more vulnerable and less vulnerable groups" (1981:179).

Finally, Heath and Petraitis (1987) conducted telephone interviews with 372 respondents in twenty-six medium sized U.S. cities. They found that total TV viewing increased respondents' fear of distant, urban settings—but only among *males.* Viewing crime drama increased the perceived likelihood of victimization in New York City and in one's own neighborhood—again, only for *males* (105–109). They suggested that the absence of a media relationship for women could be due to their consistently high fear levels and a kind of "ceiling effect" that mitigates additional influences. They also raise the prospect that "affinity" is a plausible interpretation for their findings (121).

From the foregoing, five audience circumstances can be identified with potential to influence the media/FEAR relationship. They are listed here with examples of the kinds of people who were (or could be) expected to experience those circumstances.

> *Substitution:* Lacks victim experience or has reduced victim likelihood: (Women, elderly, whites, non-victims)
>
> *Resonance:* Has victim experience or higher victim likelihood: (Urban, high-crime neighborhood residents, males, young, blacks)
>
> *Vulnerability:* Less able to defend against attack: (Women, elderly)
>
> *Affinity:* Shares characteristics of more likely media victims: (Women, older women, black women, victims)
>
> *Ceiling Effect:* Has such high fear that media can have little influence: (Women, blacks)

Depending on the rationale employed, one could *expect* stronger media/FOC relationships for women, men, young, old, victims, non-victims, blacks, or whites. As we have seen, the *evidence,* though limited, is only slightly less equivocal than theoretical expectations.

More surprising than the inconsistency of theory and evidence on this issue, is the paucity of research dealing directly with audience traits, *news* consumption, and fear of crime. Only Doob and MacDonald (1979) and Liska and Baccaglini (1990) are relevant in this regard. Both use data from the 1970s. But, only Doob and MacDonald connect the specific news consumption of individuals to *their* fear. Liska and Baccaglini linked NCVS rates of "fear" (perceived safety) in twenty-six cities to newspaper content in those communities. While useful, such data cannot tell us whether those most fearful even read newspapers. In short, only one study relating *news* consumption by *individuals* to *their* fear uses audience characteristics to specify that relationship. That study was done in Canada almost twenty years ago (Doob and MacDonald, 1979). The audience trait at issue was living in an "urban high crime neighborhood" (N = 83) or not.

Methods

Between January and March, 1994, we surveyed 2,092 adults in Tallahassee, the state capital of Florida—a state featured prominently in the frenzy of news accounts of violent crime noted above. Respondents were randomly chosen from adults (18 years or older) having the most recent birthday in households accessed by random digit dialing.[1] The sampling frame—the county where the city is located (1994 population: 212,107)—was stratified by telephone trunk numbers to insure proportional representation from all community areas. The demographics of the sample and sampling frame (in parentheses) are: female 55 percent (52%); African-American 18 percent (24%); median age: 37 (29) years; median household income $30,000 ($30,512) per year. The slight overrepresentation of women, white, and older respondents is not unusual in telephone surveys (Lavrakas 1987).

Dependent Variable: Fear of Crime

As recommended by Ferraro (1995), Ferraro and LaGrange (1987), Warr (1990) and others, we operationalize FEAR in a manner that is direct and crime specific. Respondents were asked:

> On a scale of one to ten, with ten representing the most fear and one representing the least fear, how much do you fear being robbed by someone who has a gun or knife . . . (someone breaking into your house to steal things; someone stealing your car; someone attacking you physically?)

Responses for auto theft did not correlate well with the other offenses and so the remaining crimes (robbery, assault, and burglary) were combined into a FEAR index with an alpha of .81 which is employed as our measure of crime fear.

Independent Variables

There are six measures of news consumption employed here. The first three use "a typical week" as a frame of reference: PAPER indicates the number of days a respondent reads a newspaper in a typical week. TVNEWS is the number of days that news is watched on television; and RADIO is the number of days the respondent listened to radio news. A fourth news variable, MAGAZINE, asks how often in a "typical month" a respondent reads a "national newsmagazine like *Time, Newsweek* or *U.S. News and World Report?*" Responses of "weekly," "a couple times a month," "less frequently" and "never" were coded from three to zero.

A fifth news measure, DETAIL, addresses how much information could be recalled about three highly publicized, seemingly random, *inter*racial crimes. The questions asked were: Have you read, seen or heard anything about . . .(1) "the attack on the truck driver in Los Angeles?" (2) ". . . the murder of tourists in Florida?" (3) ". . . people being shot on a train?" The first referenced the assault on Reginald Denny during the riot following the acquittal of policemen accused of beating Rodney King.[2] The second could have referred to the murder of a German tourist in Fort Lauderdale or the murder of a British tourist at a rest stop on I-10 in northern Florida. The third referenced the so-called "Massacre on the Long Island Railroad" (*Newsweek* 1993d) in which a gunman killed five people and wounded eighteen. For each incident, if respondents indicated awareness, they were asked what details they remembered. Up to six details were recorded for each incident and scores on this variable ranged from zero to 18.

The final news variable, LOCALTV, is dichotomous and reflects persons who say they *only* watch local television news (score = 1) and those who *only* watch national television news (score = 0). There are only 397 of these "exclusive" TV news watchers, since most (N = 1573) say they watch both and are treated as missing cases. While the (N) limits the use of this variable in specifying audience subsamples, its relevance is well established and warrants attention (Heath 1994; Liska and Baccaglini 1990).

Other independent variables initially used to model FEAR in this study include FEMALE (male = 0), AGE, BLACK (white = 0), INCOME, and whether a member of the respondent's household has been a crime VICTIM in the past six months (yes = 1). FEMALE is the individual trait most consistently related to fear of crime in existing research (Bankston and Thompson 1989; Ferraro and LaGrange 1992). Regarding AGE, older persons *had* been reported most fearful (Clemente and Kleiman 1976; Jaycox 1978) but recent assessments question that understanding (Bankston and Thompson 1989; Ferraro 1995).

It is often found that FEAR is greater for blacks than for whites (Skogan and Maxfield 1981; Parker and Ray 1990). This is attributed either to victimization risk (actual or perceived) or the presence of "incivilities" in predominantly black or poor neighborhoods (Covington and Taylor 1991; LaGrange et al. 1992). For similar reasons, we include INCOME (self-reported for household) in our models.

On the premise that *cognitive* judgments relating to risk (Ferraro 1995; Ferraro and LaGrange 1987) could influence the *affective* state of fear, we include several judgments in our models. The first, SAFE, is operationalized with two questions: "How safe would you say you feel being out alone in your neighborhood at night? . . . (home alone at night?)" Responses from these two questions ranging from 'very safe' to "not at all safe" were combined in an index (alpha = .70). Values on SAFE ranged from 2 (most safe) to 6 (least safe). Ferraro (1995) among others, argues that assessments of safety or risk are distinct from the *affect* of fear, but play an important role in predicting fear. Other judgments include estimates of whether crime in the neighborhood (CRIMEN) and in the county (CRIMEC) has increased (yes = 1) in the past year.

Research Findings

Ordinary least squares regression is used to estimate the net relationship between news consumption and fear of crime. Residual plots indicate no violations of the assumption of homoskedasticity. Bi-variate correlations among independent variables show none in the full model higher than .27 and, with tolerance levels in excess of .86, there is no apparent problem of multicollinearity. Except for media variables, only those predictors with significant coefficients are included in these equations. It is particularly notable that INCOME and VICTIM dropped out of almost all estimates of FEAR. In tables 1–3, unstandardized (b) and standardized (Beta) coefficients are shown, with corresponding levels of significance.

Table 1 reports seven estimates of FEAR.[3] The first six introduce individual news measures separately, and for each equation the distinctive media variable is listed at the top of the relevant column. The seventh estimate combines RADIO and TVNEWS and that model (FINAL) is used in subsequent efforts to identity "media effects" for diversely constituted audiences.

Looking first at non-media control variables, AGE has a significant *negative* relationship with FEAR in every equation. The fact that older respondents report lower fear is consistent with recent findings questioning the presumption that older people fear crime most (Bankston and Thompson 1989; Ferraro 1995). Women and African Americans are significantly more fearful than men and whites respectively and FEAR is consistently elevated for those who feel less SAFE or perceive crime to be increasing in their neighborhood (CRIMEN) or in the county (CRIMEC).

More importantly, table 1 shows that when AGE, FEMALE, BLACK, and several cognitive perceptions of crime are controlled, both RADIO and TVNEWS have a significant independent effect on crime fear. That is, people who more often listen to radio news or watch television news express significantly higher levels of FEAR. The same effect appears for LOCALTV. The fact that people who *only* watch local television news have higher fear lends support to patterns established in the work of Heath (1984) and Liska and Baccaglini (1990).

In contrast, the frequency of *reading* newspapers or newsmagazines has no apparent relationship to FEAR. This is consistent with Doob and Mac-Donald's (1979) finding that reading newspapers lowered crime fear for residents of high crime areas but was not significant when age and gender were controlled. Finally, table 1 shows that attention to DETAIL in relation to several highly publicized, non-local, "random" violent crimes has no bearing on crime fear.

Table 1   Regression of Crime Fear on News Media Variables and Other Controls

Variable	(1) Paper ß (Beta)	(2) Radio ß (Beta)	(3) TV News ß (Beta)	(4) Magazine ß (Beta)	(5) Detail ß (Beta)	(6) Local TV ß (Beta)	(7) Final ß (Beta)
Age	−.064** (−.147)	−.064** (−.146)	−.066** (−.150)	−.061** (−.139)	−.060** (.138)	−.106** (−.202)	−.069** (−.158)
Female	2.12** (.145)	2.10** (.144)	2.14** (.146)	2.07** (.141)	2.08** (.142)		2.17** (.149)
Black	1.19** (.064)	1.48** (.079)	1.16** (.063)	1.26** (.068)	1.27** (.068)		1.37** (.074)
Crimen	1.54** (.086)	1.60** (.089)	1.57** (.087)	1.58** (.088)	1.59** (.089)		1.58** (.088)
Crimec	1.81** (.106)	1.89** (.111)	1.76** (.103)	1.83** (.107)	1.84** (.107)	1.56** (.100)	1.82** (.106)
Safe	2.35** (.375)	2.31** (.368)	2.32* (.371)	2.34** (.373)	2.34** (.373)	2.29** (.375)	2.29** (.366)
Paper	.077 (.028)						
Radio		.115* (.045)					.102* (.040)
TV News			.138* (.042)				.135+ (.041)
Magazine				.089 (.014)			
Detail					.008 (.003)		
Local TV						1.47* (.103)	
R²	.265	.267	.266	.262	.263	.233	.270
(N)	1914	1897	1919	1932	1935	382	1881

Note: * p < .05   ** p < .01   + p = .052

Disaggregating Audiences

In the following sections, we examine a variety of contexts to assess whether there are discernible social patterns to the news/FEAR relationship. These analyses seek to determine whether audiences of disparate social composition find meaning in news media reports about crime. Equation (7) had the highest R^2 value in table 1 and it is used in estimates for the disaggregated subsamples in the remaining tables. In table 2, estimates are done separately for women and men, blacks and whites, and respondents from three age groups. Despite its theoretical relevance and significance in table 1, LOCALTV had too many missing values to be useful in these analyses. To provide comparability across audience subsamples, variables are included in estimates for a particular category (e.g. gender) only if they are significant for one of its subsamples (e.g. male or female).

The frequency of watching television news is significantly related to *higher* FEAR levels for women, whites, and respondents between the ages of 30–54. Though not significant, television news is associated with *lower* FEAR levels among men, blacks, and those under 30 and over 55. Tests of significance for the difference between subsample slopes[4] show that TVNEWS effects[5] are significantly different (p<.01) for men and women and for mid-

**Table 2   Regression of Crime Fear on Radio and TV News
for Audience Subgroups**

Variable	Male ß (Beta)	Female ß (Beta)	Black ß (Beta)	White ß (Beta)	Under 30 ß (Beta)	30 to 54 ß (Beta)	55+ ß (Beta)
Age	−.053** (−.129)	−.081** (−.187)	−.054* (−.111)	−.071** (−.165)			
Female			2.15** (.140)	2.11** (.147)	2.23** (.162)	1.98** (.135)	2.21** (.139)
Black	1.17* (.066)	1.51** (.083)			.847 (.055)	1.36* (.067)	2.49* (.107)
Crimen	1.78** (.105)	1.51** (.086)	.110 (.006)	1.92** (.110)	.862 (.053)	1.84** (.098)	2.29* (.121)
Crimec	1.03* (.070)	2.45** (.135)	1.21 (.069)	1.89** (.113)	.661 (.043)	2.60** (.153)	1.58 (.069)
Safe	2.40** (.385)	2.21** (.349)	2.71** (.420)	2.22** (.357)	2.29** (.373)	2.52** (.395)	1.97** (.320)
Radio	.043 (.018)	.159* (.063)					
TV News	−.099 (−.032)	.305** (.093)	−.139 (−.036)	−.185* (.058)	−.057 (−.018)	.246** (.076)	−.063 (−.013)
P Level Slope Difference	.002	.057	.017	.111			
R^2	.224	.227	.218	.264	.223	.300	.204
(N)	819	1062	360	1559	684	879	356

Note: * p < .05   ** p < .01

dle-aged (as opposed to younger) respondents. The difference between black and white respondents fails to achieve statistical significance—even though the TVNEWS and FEAR relationship is positive and significant for whites and negative and non-significant for blacks. The only significant relationship between FEAR and listening to RADIO news is reported for women.

Table 3 examines the relationship of television and radio news to fear of crime for audiences with disparate household incomes, crime victim experience, and neighborhood racial composition. Incomes are divided into less than $30,000; $30–50,000; and above $50,000. Victim experience refers to anyone in the respondent's household being victimized in the past six months. Neighborhood racial composition—which has been variably linked to FEAR (Covington and Taylor 1991; Liska et al. 1982)—is a *perceptual* measure that asks respondents to estimate the percentage of blacks among those living within a mile of their home.[6] Because blacks comprise 24 percent of the population in the community studied, audience members are divided into those living in neighborhoods perceived to be above or below this criterion.

In table 3, TVNEWS is significantly related to FEAR for those *with* recent victim experience, a *low* household income, or living in neighborhoods perceived to be disproportionately *black*. Subsample slope differences in

Table 3   Regression of Crime Fear on Radio and TV News for Audience Subgroups

Variable	Victim ß (Beta)	Non Victim ß (Beta)	Black Low Pct ß (Beta)	Black High Pct ß (Beta)	Under $30,000 ß (Beta)	$30,000 to $50,000 ß (Beta)	Over $50,000 ß (Beta)
Age	−.045	−.065**	−.065**	−.077**	−.071**	−.053**	−.081
	(−.092)	(−.149)	(−.154)	(−.162)	(−.173)	(−.113)	(−.147)
Female	1.93*	2.15**	2.21**	2.16**	1.85**	2.48**	2.22**
	(.132)	(.147)	(.156)	(.147)	(.126)	(.176)	(.156)
Black	−1.49	1.58**	1.99*	1.01*	1.39**	1.84*	−.205
	(−.074)	(.086)	(.071)	(.063)	(.088)	(.083)	(−.007)
Crimen	1.32	1.54**	1.90**	1.48**	1.60**	2.41**	1.02
	(.088)	(.082)	(.107)	(.084)	(.093)	(.135)	(.055)
Crimec	2.24*	1.68**	1.66**	1.92**	1.50**	2.11**	2.35**
	(.134)	(.098)	(.097)	(.113)	(.090)	(.125)	(.135)
Safe	2.83**	2.26**	2.26**	2.19**	2.23**	2.56**	2.70**
	(.443)	(.360)	(.363)	(.346)	(.357)	(.340)	(.416)
Radio			.053	.169*	.067	.292*	.008
			(.021)	(.068)	(.027)	(.111)	(.003)
TV News	.454*	.077	−.002	.271**	.201*	.039	.148
	(.146)	(.023)	(−.000)	(.081)	(.061)	(.012)	(.045)
P Level Slope Difference	.023	.018	.171	.375			
R²	.337	.258	.272	.250	.237	.285	.309
(N)	246	1653	899	932	902	449	463

Note: * p < .05   ** p < .01

TVNEWS effects are significant for the victim, nonvictim comparison (p<.05) and for the racial composition of neighborhood comparison (p<.02). Apparent differences for income subsamples are not significant. RADIO is also a predictor of FEAR in neighborhoods perceived to be disproportionately black and for audiences above the median income.[7]

To this point, significant TVNEWS effects are found for female, white, and middle age audiences and for those with recent victim experience, low income, and living in disproportionately black neighborhoods. But these audience traits are not mutually exclusive and audiences are not one-dimensional. To pursue a more complete identification of those for whom news/FEAR relationships may be significant, we next consider audience composition in multi-dimensional terms.

Table 4 displays the results of estimating the FEAR and TVNEWS relationship for gender/race specific groups, with a series of other characteristics taken one at a time. To illustrate: for black females, FEAR equations were estimated with subsamples further specified sequentially by categories of age, victim experience, perceived safety, income, and neighborhood racial composition. This was also done for white females, black males, and white males.

Table 4 lists forty-eight audience subsamples and for each, indicates whether TVNEWS has a significant relationship with FEAR after controlling for other variables (using equation 7 from table 1). Because so many estimates are involved, we show only whether the FEAR coefficient is significant at p<.05 (YES) for each subsample. Full equations are available on request.

The first thing apparent in table 4 is that *all* television "news effects" are limited to *women*. There are no audience traits associated with males—black or

Table 4   Significant Relationships: Fear and TV News for Specified Audience Subgroups*

Variable	Black Females		White Females		Black Males		White Males	
Under 30	YES	(99)	no	(263)	no	(78)	no	(227)
30 to 54	no	(81)	YES	(412)	no	(50)	no	(324)
55 and over	no	(31)	no	(176)	no	(13)	no	(127)
Victim	no	(20)	YES	(127)	no	(15)	no	(79)
Non–Victim	no	(189)	YES	(715)	no	(123)	no	(593)
Low Safety Perception	no	(57)	YES	(348)	no	(77)	no	(451)
High Safety Perception	no	(154)	YES	(503)	no	(64)	no	(227)
Less than $30,000	no	(158)	YES	(366)	no	(106)	no	(272)
$30,000 to $50,000	no	(29)	no	(213)	no	(22)	no	(185)
More than $50,000	no	(15)	YES	(237)	no	(10)	no	(201)
Low Percentage Black	no	(39)	no	(474)	no	(21)	no	(365)
High Percentage Black	no	(164)	YES	(359)	no	(114)	no	(295)

Note:
* YES indicates positive and significant (p < .05) TVNEWS effect.
( ) N size.

white—for which TVNEWS has a significant relationship to FEAR. Moreover, almost all TVNEWS effects are limited to *white women*. (The only contrary instance—with a relatively small N (99)—involves *young* (<30) black women). In fact, among white women a significant link between FEAR and TVNEWS is sustained whether or not they have recent victim experience, whether or not they perceive their neighborhoods to be safe or have high or low incomes. The news/ FEAR relationship is concentrated, among *middle-aged* white women (30–54) and those living in disproportionately black neighborhoods.

Table 2 indicates that a positive relationship between TVNEWS and FEAR exists for whites, women, and middle-aged audiences. Table 4 shows that it exists specifically and *only* for white middle-aged women—and for no one else among whites and almost no one else among women. While table 3 indicates that the news/FEAR relationship is significant for those with victim experience, low income, and those living in disproportionately black neighborhoods; table 4 shows that it is *only* white women in those groups who manifest a "news effect."

These data clearly indicate that the relationship between television news and fear of crime is exclusive to women and almost entirely exclusive to white women. The question we address in the remainder of this article is: what explains this concentration of media effects?[8]

Discussion

Several ways that audience traits could inform construction of the media/FEAR relationship were discussed above. These included: (1) the "*resonance*" of personal experience with media messages which increases their salience (Doob and MacDonald 1979; Gerbner et al. 1980); (2) the lack of experience with crime or its immediate threat, which allows media messages to "*substitute*" as a prime information source (Gunter 1987; Liska and Baccaglini 1990; Weaver and Wakshlag 1986); (3) the "*affinity*" that may exist between audience members and the characteristics of victims portrayed by media (Gerbner 1978; Hirsch 1980); (4) the differential "*vulnerability*" to crime of some audience members which makes them "more sensitive" to media crime messages (Skogan and Maxfield 1981), and (5) a "*ceiling effect*" which leaves little room for media influence among audience types with already high levels of fear (Heath and Petraitis 1987).

At first glance, the pattern of current findings appears to rule out the relevance of "ceiling effects" (Heath and Petraitis 1987). Women in our sample have levels of FEAR (17.6) that are 25 percent higher than men (13.9) and still, all "news effects" involve women. Looking closer, it happens that white, middle-aged women—who manifest virtually all of the TVNEWS effects in this sample—have FEAR levels (16.5) lower than black women (19.6) and substantially lower than middle-aged black women (20.3). If "ceiling effects" are real, they may apply here to black women and may help to explain the lack of a news/FEAR relationship for that group.

The issue of "vulnerability" has had a prominent place in discussions of FEAR (Baumer 1985; Garofalo 1981). A presumption that women and the elderly can less well defend against attack is sometimes used to explain the "seeming paradox" of higher fear levels despite lower risk and experience of crime. It has also prompted the hypothesis that the most "vulnerable" will be most responsive to media messages (Skogan and Maxfield 1981). Even if the elderly and women are less able to ward off attacks—not altogether certain with increased gun ownership and "advances" in self-defense technology—this issue seems not to explain the pattern of TVNEWS effects reported here. White middle-aged women should be no *more* "vulnerable" than black middle-aged women or *older* women of either race. In fact, in terms of the ability to resist victimization, it is not certain that a thirty-five-year-old white woman would be more vulnerable than, for example, a seventy-year-old man of either race. In our sample, there are no TVNEWS effects for older females who presumably would feel the most vulnerable.

A concentration of TVNEWS effects among white middle-aged women is not entirely consistent with a "resonance" interpretation (Doob and MacDonald 1979; Gerbner et al. 1980). In general, white, middle-aged women have consistently low victim risk (U.S. Department of Justice 1996) and for most, media messages would not resonate their experience. Of course, there are some white middle-aged women with experience as victims. In this sample, TVNEWS is significantly related to FEAR among white women *with* recent victim experience, and for those with *low* income or living in disproportionately black neighborhoods—a pattern consistent with "resonance." This interpretation would have greater relevance if males and blacks with those same characteristics also had significant TVNEWS effects. They do not.

Since white women *without* recent victim experience and living in *high* income circumstances also show significant TVNEWS effects, it seems likely that for them, something other than resonance is at work. A possibility to explain news/FEAR relationships among these white women (high-income or no victim experience) is that media messages "substitute" for lived experience in the genesis of fear (Gunter 1987; Liska and Baccaglini 1990).

It may be plausible that "substitution" explains the news/FEAR relationship for some white women (high-income, no victim experience) and "resonance" explains it for other white women (low-income, victim experience). However, neither of these explanations account for the more basic fact that, except for white women, virtually no TVNEWS effects are found.

A final interpretation of these findings could be that an *affinity* exists between the audience for whom TVNEWS effects are found (white women) and the content of televised news messages. The rationale, as Gerbner et al. (1978:186) note in their discussion of the "cultivation" of fear, is that "we may be especially receptive to seeing how characters *like ourselves* . . . fare in the world of television" (original emphasis). Hirsch hypothesized that television "viewers from subgroups whose members are most often victimized or killed should appear more afraid" than others (1980:10).

We have additional data that may be relevant to this hypothesis. Eighteen months *after* the FEAR survey discussed here, we did a content analysis of televised evening news programs in Tallahassee. For nine weeks, three teams of three judges (graduate students) recorded various features of crime incidents reported on local and network news. A detailed study of those incidents in relation to a FEAR survey taken at the same time is underway. Assuming the demographics of TV news victims changed little in eighteen months, what we learned about their race and gender may help to explain the present findings. When both race and gender could be identified, the profile of TV news victims was: 32 percent—white female; 26 percent—white male; 12 percent—Hispanic female; 11 percent—black male; 6 percent—black female; 3 percent—Hispanic male; 10 percent—other.

The distribution of TVNEWS victims is consistent with an *affinity* interpretation of the relationship found in this study between TVNEWS and FEAR. The audience most likely to see itself victimized in the news—white women—is the only audience for which significant TVNEWS effects are found. This suggests that regardless of actual victim experience (table 4), seeing people like themselves victimized frequently in televised news may have substantially contributed to the fear of crime among white women.

The purpose of the present analysis has been to underscore the importance of attending to specific "audience effects." Without doing so, we may ask the wrong questions. The issue is not whether media accounts of crime increase fear, but which audiences, with which experiences and interests, construct which meanings from the messages received. We have found that the construction of fear from the messages of television news is limited to middle-aged white women. Since white women are most often shown as victims on the news in this television market, an "affinity" explanation for the relationship of media consumption to fear is supported. In their early studies of television and the "cultivation" of fear, Gerbner and his associates noted that "it is important who scares whom and who is 'trained' to be the victim" (1980:715). They further observed that televised violence in particular, demonstrates "the realities of social power . . . generates fear, insecurity and dependence and thus serves as an instrument of social control" (1980:715). In the present study, white women see victims "like themselves" on TVNEWS and are more fearful. It is for them that "the realities of social power"—implicit in crime—have the most salience. It is in them that "fear, insecurity and dependence" are cultivated, and it may be for them that TVNEWS serves as an instrument of social control (Gerbner et al. 1980:715).

Notes

1 The survey was conducted by The Research Network, Inc., in Tallahassee, using a two-stage Mitofsky-Waksberg sampling design. Business, fax and disconnected numbers were eliminated and a response rate of 80 percent for those beginning the survey was realized.

2 The attack took place in 1992, but the trial of alleged assailants was underway in the summer of 1993. Helicopter video of the attack was replayed almost nightly for several weeks.

[3] An eighth estimate combined five of the news variables (excluding LOCALTV). In this presumably misspecified model, none of the news variables achieved significance at p<.05.

[4] The conventional formula for assessing differences in regression coefficients across sub-groups takes into account the sample sizes of each of the sub-groups (Kleinbaum et al. 1988:266). With large samples this formula is shown to asymptotically converge to: $(b1-b2) / (se (b1)^2 + se (b2)^2)1/2$ (Kleinbaum & Kupper, 1978: 101). Given the magnitude of our sample sizes, it is appropriate to use this latter formula, and we have done so.

[5] It is possible that what we are calling TVNEWS effects are the *consequence* of FEAR, rather than its antecedent (Gunter, 1987; Sparks, 1992). That is, people who are more fearful (e.g. women) may watch more television. In the absence of panel data (O'Keefe and Reid-Nash 1987) this possibility cannot be tested.

[6] The rationale for including percent black is given by the extent to which popular rhetoric has typified the crime problem in racial terms (Anderson 1995). In 1992, for example, Senator Bill Bradley observed that "fear of black crime covers the streets like a sheet of ice" (Skogan, 1995: 60).

[7] The remaining discussion is limited to TVNEWS because its meaning is less ambiguous than RADIO. The latter may be a very different input, for example, to someone listening to NPR and someone listening to music with news briefings at the top of every hour.

[8] One explanation could be that men admit fear less often, which would truncate the distribution of their responses relative to women, thereby reducing the likelihood of significant relationships. Because differences in standard deviations on FEAR, however, range from 6.4 (white males) to 7.2 (white females), this is not a likely explanation for the observed pattern.

References

Anderson, David C. 1995. *Crime and the Politics of Hysteria*. New York City: Random House.

Bankston, William B., and Carol Y. Thompson. 1989. "Carrying firearms for protection: A causal model." *Sociological Inquiry* 59:75–87.

Baumer, Terry L. 1985. "Testing a general model of fear of crime: Data from a national sample." *Journal of Research in Crime and Delinquency* 22:239–55.

Burrelle's Transcripts. 1994. *Burrelle's Index of Broadcast Transcripts*, Annual Edition. Livingston, NJ: Burrelle's Information Services.

Carragee, Kevin M. 1990. "Interpretive media study and interpretive social science." *Critical Studies in Mass Communication* 7:81–95.

Chiricos, Ted. 1995. "Moral panic as ideology: Drugs, violence, race and punishment in America." In *Justice with Prejudice: Race and Criminal Justice in America*, Michael J. Lynch and E. Britt Patterson, (eds.), 19–48. New York: Harrow & Heston.

Clemente, Frank, and Michael Kleiman. 1976. "Fear of crime among the aged." *Gerontologist* 16:207–10.

Comstock, George, Steven Chaffee, Nathan Katzman, Maxwell McCombs, and Donald Roberts. 1978. *Television and Human Behavior*. New York: Columbia University Press.

Condit, Celeste M. 1989. "The rhetorical limits of polysemy." *Critical Studies in Mass Communication* 6:103–122.

Covington, Jeanette, and Ralph B. Taylor. 1991. "Fear of crime in urban residential neighborhoods: Implications of between- and within--neighborhood sources for current models." *The Sociological Quarterly* 32: 231–49.

Dahlgren, Peter. 1988. "What's the meaning of this?: Viewers plural sense-making of TV news." *Media, Culture & Society.* 10:285–301.

Dialog Information Service. 1994. Newspaper and Periodical Abstracts. [Online], January 1992–June 1994. Ann Arbor, MI: UMI. Available: DIALOG File: Newspaper and Periodical Abstracts (484).

Doob, Anthony N., and Glenn E. MacDonald. 1979. "Television viewing and fear of victimization: Is the relationship causal?" *Journal of Personality & Social Psychology* 37:170–79.

Ferraro, Kenneth A. 1995. "Fear of Crime: Interpreting Victimization Risk." Albany, NY: SUNY Press.

Ferraro, Kenneth A., and Randy LaGrange. 1987. "The measurement of fear of crime." *Sociological Inquiry* 57:70–101.

_____. 1992. "Are older people afraid of crime?: Reconsidering age differences in fear of victimization." *Journal of Gerontology: Social Sciences* 47:233–44.

Fiske, John. 1986. "Television, polysemy and popularity." *Critical Studies in Mass Communication* 3:391–408.

Gallup, George Jr. 1994. *The Gallup Poll*, No. 341 (February). Wilmington, DE: Scholarly Resources.

Garofalo, James. 1979. "Victimization and the fear of crime." *Journal of Research in Crime and Delinquency* 16:80–97.

_____. 1981. "The fear of crime: Causes & consequences." *Journal of Criminal Law and Criminology* 72:839–57.

Gerbner, George, Larry Gross, Marilyn Jackson-Beeck, Suzanne Jeffries-Fox, and Nancy Signorielli. 1978. "Cultural indicators: Violence profile No. 9." *Journal of Communication* 28:176–207.

Gerbner, George, Larry Gross, Michael Morgan, and Nancy Signorielli. 1980. "The 'mainstreaming' of America Violence profile No. 11." *Journal of Communication* 30:10–29.

Gitlin, Todd. 1979. "Prime time ideology: The hegemonic process in television entertainment." *Social Problems* 26:251–66.

Gordon, Margaret, and Linda Heath. 1981. "The news business, crime and fear." In *Reactions to Crime*, Dan Lewis, ed., 227–50. Beverly Hills: Sage.

Gunter, Barrie. 1987. *Television and the Fear of Crime*. London: John Libbey.

Gunter, Barrie, and J. Wakshlag. 1986. "Television viewing and perceptions of crime among London residents." Paper presented at the international Television Studies Conference, Institute of Education, London, July.

Hall, Stuart. 1981. "Notes on deconstructing the popular." In *People's History and Socialist Theory*, R. Samuel, (ed.), 227–39. London: Routledge and Kegan Paul.

Hall, Stuart, Chas Critcher, Tony Jefferson, John Clarke, and Brian Roberts. 1978. *Policing the Crisis: Mugging, the State and Law and Order*. London: MacMillan.

Heath, Linda. 1984. "Impact of newspaper crime reports on fear of crime: Multi methodological investigation." *Journal of Personality and Social Psychology* 47:263–76.

Heath, Linda, and John Petraitis. 1987. "Television viewing and fear of crime: Where is the mean world?" *Basic and Applied Social Psychology* 8:97–123.

Heath, Linda, and Kevin Gilbert. 1996. "Mass media and fear of crime." *American Behavioral Scientist* 39:379–86.

Hirsch, Paul M. 1980. "The 'scary world' of the nonviewer and other anomalies: A reanalysis of Gerbner et al.'s findings on cultivation analysis, part 1." *Communication Research* 7:403–56.

Hughes, Michael. 1980. "The fruits of cultivation analysis: A reexamination of some effects of television watching." *Public Opinion Quarterly* 44: 287–302.

Jaycox, Victoria. 1978. "The elderly's fear of crime: Rational or irrational?" *Victimology* 3:329–34.

Jensen, Klaus B. 1990. "Television futures: A social action methodology for studying interpretive communities." *Critical Studies in Mass Communication* 7:129–46.

Kleinbaum, David G., and Lawrence L. Kupper. 1978. *Applied Regression Analysis and Other Multivariate Methods*. North Scituate, MA: Duxbury Press.

Kleinbaum, David G., Lawrence L. Kupper, and Keith E. Muller. 1988. *Applied Regression Analysis and Other Multivariate Methods*, second edition. Boston: PWS-KENT Publishing Company.

LaGrange, Randy, Kenneth F. Ferraro, and Michael Supanic. 1992. "Perceived risk and fear of crime: Role of social and physical incivilities." *Journal of Research in Crime and Delinquency* 29:311–34.

Lavrakas, Paul J. 1987. *Telephone Survey Methods*. Newbury Park, CA: Sage.

Lindlof, Thomas R. 1988. "Media audiences as interpretive communities." In *Communication Yearbook*, Jay Anderson, (ed.), 2:81–107. Newbury Park, CA: Sage.

Liska, Allen E., Joseph J. Lawrence, and Andrew Sanchirico. 1982. "Fear of crime as a social fact." *Social Forces* 60:761–70.

Liska, Allen E., and William Baccaglini. 1990. "Feeling safe by comparison: Crime in the newspapers." *Social Problems* 37:360–74.

O'Keefe, Garrett J. 1984. "Public views on crime: Television exposure and media credibility." In *Communication Yearbook*, R. Bostrom, (ed.), 8:514–35. Beverly Hills: Sage.

O'Keefe, Garrett J., and Kathaleen Reid-Nash. 1987. "Crime news and real-world blues: The effects of the media on social reality." *Communication Research* 14:147–63.

Newsweek. 1993a. "Life means nothing." (July 19):16–17.

_____. 1993b. "Wild in the streets." (August 2):40–47.

_____. 1993c. "In a state of terror." (September 27):40–41.

_____. 1993d. "Death ride: Massacre on the LIRR." (December 20):26–31.

Parker, Kenneth D., and Melvin C. Ray. 1990. "Fear of crime: An assessment of related factors." *Sociological Spectrum* 10:29–40.

Potter, W. James. 1986. "Perceived reality and the cultivation hypothesis." *Journal of Broadcasting and Electronic Media* 30:159–74.

Skogan, Wesley. 1995. "Crime and the racial fears of white Americans." *The Annals of the American Academy of Political and Social Science* 539:59–71.

Skogan, Wesley G., and Michael G. Maxfield. 1981. *Coping With Crime*. Beverly Hills, CA: Sage.

Sparks. 1992. *Television and the Drama of Crime*. Philadelphia, PA: Open University Press.

Tamborini, Ron, Dolf Zillmann, and Jennings Bryant. 1984. "Fear and victimization: Exposure to television and perceptions of crime and fear." In *Communications Yearbook*, R. Bostrom. (ed.), 8:492–513. Beverly Hills: Sage.

Time. 1993a. "Danger in the safety zone." (August 23):29–32.

_____. 1993b. "Taming the killers." (October 11):58-59.

Tyler, Tom R., and Fay L. Cook. 1984. "The mass media and judgments of risk: Distinguishing impact on personal and societal level judgements." *Journal of Personality and Social Psychology* 47:693–708.

U.S. Department of Justice. 1993. *Crime in the United States—1992*. Washington, DC: U.S. Government Printing Office.

_____. 1994. *Crime in the United States—1993*. Washington, DC: U.S. Government Printing Office.

_____. 1995. *Crime in the United States—1994*. Washington, DC: U.S. Government Printing Office.

_____. 1996. *Criminal Victimization in the United States, 1993.* Washington, DC: Bureau of Justice Statistics.

U.S. News and World Report. 1993. "Florida: The state of rage." (October 11):40–44.

Wakshlag, Jacob. 1983. "Viewer apprehension about victimization and crime drama programs." *Communications Research,* 10:195–217.

Warr, Mark. 1990. "Dangerous situations: Social context and fear of victimization." *Social Forces* 68:891–907.

Weaver, James, and Jacob Wakshlag. 1986. "Perceived vulnerability to crime, criminal experience and television viewing." *Journal of Broadcasting and Electronic Media* 30:141–58.

Williams, Paul, and Julie Dickinson. 1993. "Fear of crime: Read all about it?" *British Journal of Criminology* 33:33–56.

Zillmann, Dolf, and Jacob Wakshlag. 1985. "Fear of victimization and the appeal of crime drama." In *Selective Exposure to Communication,* Dolf Zillmann and Jennings Bryant (eds.), 141–56. Hillsdale, NJ: Lawrence Erlbaum.

Perceived Fears

The Reporting Patterns of Juvenile Homicide in Chicago Newspapers

John G. Boulahanis & Martha J. Heltsley

It is a seeming paradox: Homicides involving juvenile offenders have been declining, and yet there remains a high fear of crime by youth (Heide, 1999). Although the late 1980s and early 1990s saw an increase in violent offenses involving juveniles, the increase peaked in 1994 and has declined steadily ever since. The years of increased juvenile crime led to a change in the perception of juveniles. Mahini (2000) suggests that a juvenile was no longer perceived as a petty criminal but as a serious and motivated offender. Heide (1996) suggests that news media have played a substantive role in this perception in that they have portrayed today's juvenile as "more dangerous to society than [his or her] predecessors" (p. 27). Utilizing a constructionist approach, this study examines the accuracy in reporting patterns of juvenile homicide in Chicago newspapers. Juvenile homicide cases that have received coverage in the *Chicago Sun-Times* and *Chicago Tribune* from 1992 to 2000 are compared to those that were not covered in the papers. The results indicate any discrepancies between actual homicides reported to the Chicago Police Department (CPD) and the homicides selected for coverage by the newspapers. A constructionist approach posits that overreporting of certain types of homicide may affect perceptions of fear; as well, focusing on atypical elements of the crime may further perpetuate false perceptions about offenders and victims.

Media and Social Construction

The power of the media to shape public perceptions of crime depends on the type and depth of coverage given a particular offense. Gusfield (1981)

From: *Criminal Justice Policy Review*, vol. 15, no. 2, pp. 132–160, copyright 2004. Reprinted by permission of Sage Publications, Inc.

suggests the media are an "image-making industry" (p. 439), and Barak (1994) argues that the media are "the principal vehicle by which the average person comes to know crime and justice in America" (pp. 3–4). The result of overreporting particular crimes increases the chances of what Cohen (1972) calls moral panics. Moral panics are conditions shaped by experts about the increasing dangerousness and growth of a particular episode that generates intense fear in society (Cohen, 1972; Goode & Ben-Yehuda, 1994). Often these claims have been unfounded or grossly exaggerated, such as missing children (Best, 1990), serial murder (Jenkins, 1994), and drug use (Reinarman, 2000). The recent anthrax scare is a more recent example of an exaggerated problem causing fear in society.

The media does have internal and external constraints on their coverage. Internal constraints, such as format, limit the space given to a particular article, and the time spent covering a particular case is governed by publishers rather than reporters (Altheide, 1985; Chermak, 1994; Ericson, Baranek, & Chan, 1991; Gans, 1979). External constraints include the practice of media hegemony or the preference for certain images, symbols, and subjects that reflect the views of sponsors or the audience (Altheide, 1985). News items are also constrained by the type and amount of information reporters receive. Often a mutual dependency is established between the police and the media. The media rely on the police to inform them of crimes and, conversely, the police are dependent on the media for supporting their needs (Barak, 1988; Chermak, 1994; Ericson et al., 1991; Fishman, 1978). The newsmaking process is not random, and many variables influence the type of information the public receives. News reports are "neither a pure picture of society nor a fully controlled propaganda message, but is instead an organizational product" controlled by a few key individuals (Surette, 1998, p. 62).

The Reporting of Crime: A Focus on the "Atypical"

Speaking on news reporting, Elikann (1999) suggests that "if it bleeds, it leads" (p. 55). Numerous studies have suggested the media tends to overreport murder and other serious crimes (Davis, 1952; Ericson et al., 1991; Graber, 1980; Hubbard, DeFleur, & DeFleur, 1975; Jerin & Fields, 1994), but few have attempted to differentiate between adult and juvenile crime. According to Sprott (1996), juveniles have not been studied as intensely as adult crime. Sprott's (1996, p. 280) content analysis on juvenile cases in Canada found violent crimes were overreported and focused primarily on "the impact of crime on others." A survey accompanying Sprott's study found that almost three-fourths of respondents tended to overestimate the amount of crime, believed homicides involving juvenile offenders had increased (while they had actually decreased), and most viewed the juvenile court as "too lenient" (p. 280). However, most studies concerning the overreporting of crime have been conducted on adults rather than juveniles since violent crimes committed by youth are statistically rare events. It is also common knowledge that property crimes occur far more frequently than homicides; yet they receive very little newspaper coverage. Other atypical features of the crime influence newsworthiness and these include demographic variables such as race, gender, and age.

Race

Race is problematic as a variable when analyzing newspaper accounts because it is no longer a journalistic practice to indicate the race of the offender or victim in articles. Race is less of a problem when the medium is television. Some studies examining television news reporting have indicated the overreporting of African Americans as offenders (Dixon & Linz, 2000; Grabe, 1999). However, in a New Orleans study, Sheley and Ashkins (1981) found very little disparity between cases reported to the police and cases reported on television and in newspapers. Race of the victim may also play a role in whether a case receives media attention. Johnstone, Hawkins, and Michener (1994) examined the victim characteristics of homicides reported in Chicago newspapers to those reported to the CPD and found that African American and Hispanic victims were underreported in the newspapers. Boulahanis, Esmail, and Heltsley (2000) interviewed reporters from the *Chicago Tribune* and *Chicago Sun-Times* and found that race often determined the value given the homicide cases. They quote one reporter as stating the following:

> I'm sorry to say that race influences whether or not to run the story. This is not to say that we are racist, but because we know that the vast majority of homicides are committed by African-Americans so they become run-of-the-mill.

The explanation offered by another reporter suggested that certain individuals within the CPD take it upon themselves to determine what is newsworthy, and race is often a criterion:

> Many desk sergeants in Area headquarters referred to cases that involved African-American offenders and victims as "blue cases" and these cases were usually not reported. Many times I would call the desk sergeant to see if anything interesting had happened to report and they would respond by saying something to the effect that we just had a couple of blue cases, and that would be the end of it.

Both statements suggest that crimes committed by African Americans are less appealing in terms of newsworthiness because they occur more frequently. Thus, homicides perpetrated by offenders that are atypical in regard to racial composition are the cases that receive more attention. Given this, it is likely that race may well play a role in newspaper accounts; however, due to the current formatting of newspaper articles, it is sometimes impossible to accurately determine the race of the offender or victim.

Gender and Age

Unlike race, gender can easily be established when reading newspaper accounts. Research examining gender and crime has consistently indicated that most crimes involve male offenders and victims. Cases involving females are rare; thus, when they occur, they are perceived to be more newsworthy and are more likely to receive media coverage (Chermak, 1995; Katz, 1987; Madriz, 1997; Naylor, 1995). In a particular study examining the reporting patterns of female offenders, Naylor (1995, p. 80) concluded that although female offenders constitute about 10% of the crimes reported to the police, they made up about one third of the violent cases reported in newspapers, warning that the depiction of females may lead others, and particularly females, to be more fearful of women as potential offenders. As one of her research subjects stated, "All you have to do is read the newspapers or watch the news on TV and see how women have become worse than men" (p. 26). Likewise, the gender of the victim plays an important role in the newsworthiness of the case for much of the same reason. Chermak (1995) argues, "Society thinks females, like children, are more vulnerable and feels crimes committed against them are more newsworthy" (p. 130). If the atypical is given more coverage, female victims should be disproportionately represented in the media.

The age of the offender and victim also influence media coverage. According to Chermak (1995), the majority of crimes are committed by individuals between the ages of 17 and 24, but these cases are reported disproportionately less often then cases involving younger and older offenders. Because of their rarity and perceived vulnerability, cases involving victims who are children or elderly get an exorbitant amount of attention. To test whether the age of the victim is a determinant in deciding newsworthiness, we divided the victim's ages into the following aggregates: younger than 14, 14 to 19, 20 to 29, 30 to 49, 50 to 64, and 65 and older. Thus, we should expect to find the greatest coverage given to victims younger than 14 and older than 65.

The literature thus suggests that the media are guilty of overreporting cases containing atypical features. This prompts us to examine the impact these patterns have on public perception and fear of crime. Fear of crime due to media consumption is by no means a neglected topic in the social science literature. A brief review of some previous findings is provided in the following section.

Media and Fear of Crime

Various studies of media influences on fear of crime have been conducted, yielding mixed results. In one study, Jaehnig, Weaver, and Fico (1981) compared levels of fear of violent crime to exposure to newspaper depictions of crime in three cities (Evanston, Illinois; Indianapolis, Indiana; and Lebanon, New Hampshire). Based on interviews conducted with randomly selected panels in each city, the researchers concluded that levels of reported fear were more consistent with the images portrayed in the newspapers rather than the actual amount of crime committed in each community. Findings suggest that the reported levels of fear were highest in the community that had the highest rate of violent victimization and the highest percentage of crime-related news in the newspaper, and lowest in the community that had the least amount of violent crime reported in the newspaper.

In a study conducted in Britain, Williams and Dickinson (1993) observed a positive relationship between reading the newspapers and fear of crime. The researchers analyzed 10 papers in a 1–month period (May to June 1989) to examine the types of criminal cases reported in each newspaper. Their findings indicated that, on average, 12.7% of the news reported on a daily basis was crime-related. Furthermore, of these articles, 64.5% were devoted to violent crime (Williams & Dickinson, 1993, p. 40). Williams and Dickinson also sent out 1,000 questionnaires to addresses around the newspapers' circulation area to estimate the level of fear of crime among individuals who subscribed to the newspapers. The majority of respondents who reported being fearful of the possibility of an attack attributed that fear to previous stories they had heard about in the media.

Heath (1984), in an attempt to measure reporting patterns of the media and levels of fear, conducted a content analysis of 36 newspapers throughout selected cities in the United States for a week. Furthermore, she measured the effects of the newspapers' claims by conducting telephone interviews of randomly selected individuals residing in the selected cities. Perceived fear was assessed by asking respondents general questions such as "How safe do you feel out in the streets of your neighborhood at night?" (p. 266). The findings revealed marked differences between females and males who read the paper. Overall, females reported higher levels of fear of crime when compared to males. In examining the location of the crime, Heath (1984) concluded that females were more fearful of local crimes than of nonlocal cases. Building on Heath's study, Liska and Baccaglini (1990) examined the impact of the media on reported levels of fear of crime by analyzing the content of newspapers in 26 cities throughout the United States during 1974 and 1975 and using fear of crime data collected for the National Crime Survey. To measure whether the location of the story (i.e., the page number the story appeared on) influenced public perception, the researchers separated stories by whether they appeared on the first 15 pages or the last 15 pages of the newspaper. The researchers concluded that homicide cases were overreported in the media; although homicides comprised .02% of all index crimes, they constituted 29.9% of all crime stories reported in the newspapers (pp. 366–367). Additional findings from the study indicated that local homicide stories tended to produce high levels of fear among all respondents (African American, Caucasian, young, middle-aged, and elderly), whereas nonlocal stories tended to reduce levels of fear among all respondents. Consistent with Heath, Liska and Baccaglini attributed reduced levels of fear among nonlocal cases of homicide to the possibility that readers felt safer in their community by comparing it to other areas. However, Liska and Baccaglini noted that nonlocal stories might reduce reported levels of fear because an increase in reporting of nonlocal homicide means a decrease in reporting of local homicide cases because there is limited space in the paper.

Various studies have focused on perceptions and reported level of fear of crime among individuals who reside in high-crime areas and are exposed to these accounts by the news media. In one such study, O'Keefe and Reid-Nash (1987) compared fear of crime generated by reading newspaper depictions versus televised news in high-crime areas. In doing so, the researchers were able to test the "cultivation hypothesis" (p. 148). The cultivation hypothesis postulates that individuals exposed to the type of images of violence portrayed by the media cultivate a similar image of crime in the real world (Gerbner & Gross, 1976, cited in O'Keefe & Reid-Nash, 1987). The findings supported the cultivation hypothesis, revealing that individuals who watched televised news reported higher levels of fear than those who relied solely on newspaper accounts.

Chiricos, Eschholz, and Gertz (1997) tested whether the characteristics of the audience influenced fear of crime. They suggested that individuals perceive things differently based on various characteristics, such as race, gender, age, and previous victimization history. The researchers measured fear of crime by posing "direct" and "crime specific" questions such as: "On a scale of one to ten . . . how much do you fear being robbed by someone who has a gun or a knife?" (p. 347). Respondents were further asked to report the frequency with which they read the newspaper, watched the news on television, and listened to the news on the radio per week. Regression results, derived from a random sample of Tallahassee, Florida, residents, indicated a positive relationship between televised news exposure and reported fear of crime among White, middle-aged females. In examining the type of cases depicted in the media, the researchers observed that most cases involved White, middle-aged victims, thus causing them to conclude that "white women see victims 'like themselves' on TV news and are more fearful" (p. 354). However, 3 years later, in a similar study conducted on a statewide basis, Chiricos, Padgett, and Gertz (2000) reported somewhat conflicting results. Although the earlier study (Chiricos et al., 1997) showed a significant positive relationship between viewing televised news and increased levels of fear solely among White, middle-aged females, the statewide examination revealed a significant relationship between reported levels of fear and exposure to televised news among both African American and Caucasian females. Chiricos et al. (2000) attributed the discrepancy in the findings to a possible bias effect in the initial study due to a rash of reported cases in Tallahassee, Florida, involving White, middle-aged female victims reported in the news media at that time.

The Current Study

In summary, fear-of-crime research has suggested that increased exposure to the media can be positively correlated to increased levels of fear. However, very few studies have differentiated between crimes committed by adults and juveniles. Additionally, no study, to our knowledge, has used mapping techniques to examine the spatial distribution of the reporting patterns of the media and measured perceptions and fear of areas that are overreported and underreported by the newspapers. This is what we attempt to do in this study.

Methodology

To determine the characteristics of juvenile homicides (i.e., homicides involving an offender younger than 17) reported to the CPD, police department data was utilized.[1] The selection of these data was facilitated by three factors. First, because Chicago is one of the four leading cities with respect to the number of reported annual homicides, it was preconceived that enough cases would be readily available for statistical analysis. Second, the data set is one of the most complete data sets in existence. Finally, due to the serious nature of homicide, and because these data were reported directly by the CPD, they are fairly accurate.

The purpose of analyzing these data was to provide some descriptive characteristics of juvenile offenders and their victims in Chicago, as reported in the *Chicago Sun-Times* and *Chicago Tribune*, and to compare this profile with the juvenile homicide cases that did not receive coverage in the newspapers. In doing so, variations on the type of weapon, age, gender, and race of offenders/victims are examined and compared.

Full-text articles were accessed using keyword searches (such as "juvenile murder," "juvenile homicide," "youth murder," and "youth homicide") on *WestLaw.* We used 1992 to 2000 as our time frame, and examined every story reported during this period. However, not every story pertained to an actual murder by a juvenile in Chicago. Several of the articles were excluded because they either dealt with juveniles who were murdered by adults, or discussed juvenile homicide in general terms without focusing on a specific case. Others were omitted because they occurred outside Chicago city limits. Additionally, it is quite possible that some cases were excluded simply because *WestLaw* did not pick up these cases. We minimized this threat by using multiple keyword searches when retrieving the cases.

Of all the articles sampled, 117 stories from the *Chicago Sun-Times* and *Chicago Tribune* together met the criteria for this research—actual homicides committed by juvenile perpetrators within the CPD's jurisdiction.[2] These stories were matched to the CPD data using date, age of the victim, and age of the offender as grouping variables. Weapons were separated into the categories of guns, knives, and other.

To examine the spatial distribution of homicides reported in the newspapers, homicide data was converted into ArcView, and maps depicting the spatial distribution of homicide cases both reported and unreported were created. This procedure took the geographical district of each reported homicide (which was a variable already provided by the CPD in the reported data and coded in the newspaper data) and matched it using the X and Y coordinates of the centroid of each district, thus plotting it on a map of Chicago. Once plotted, we were able to determine the spatial distribution of the reporting patterns citywide in each of the 25 police districts in the city of Chicago.

Fear of crime was measured using a mail-survey questionnaire modeled after the National Crime Prevention Survey. Individuals were randomly selected from the 2001 Chicago telephone directory and were asked various questions geared toward measuring their perception and fear of juvenile homicide and the amount of exposure they have to the news media.

Findings

From 1992 to 2000, 535 juvenile homicides were reported to the CPD. Figure 1 displays the number of juvenile homicide cases reported to the CPD from 1992 to 2000. As this figure indicates, homicides increased from 1992 to 1994, peaked in 1994, and steadily declined thereafter. Whereas 535 individual cases were reported to the police, only 117 (around 22%) of these received newspaper coverage.[3] Figure 2 displays the trend in this reporting, showing that newspaper coverage rose steadily from 1992 to 1994, declined from 1994 to 1995, increased sharply from 1996 to 1998, declined in 1999, and increased slightly in 2000. Taken together, these two figures indicate that although the total number of homicides involving juvenile offenders has declined in relatively linear fashion since 1994, the number of cases receiving newspaper coverage mostly increased over the same time period.

**Figure 1   Number of Juvenile Homicide Cases Reported to the
              Chicago Police Department (CPD), 1992 to 2000**

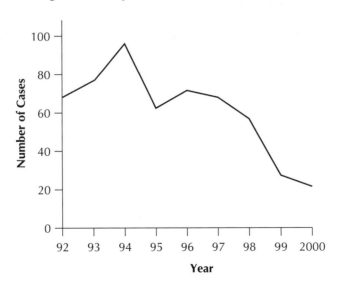

Figure 2   Number of Juvenile Homicide Cases Reported in the Newspapers, 1992 to 2000

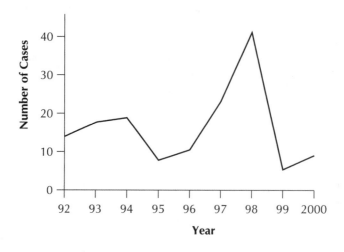

To compare the cases that were reported in the newspapers to those cases that did not receive coverage, we computed a chi-square statistic (see table 1) and a logistic regression model (see table 2). These findings are discussed in greater detail below.

Age of the Offender

The most significant predictor in whether the homicide received newspaper coverage was the age of the offender and victim. Because our sample consists of juveniles, we are dealing with young offenders to begin with; however, the findings revealed that the newspapers favored homicides committed by young children, rather than those that involved adolescent offenders. Consistent with previous research, cases that involved extremely young offenders were more likely to receive coverage (14.23 vs. 15.21, $t = 7.839$, $p < .05$). The age difference was even more evident when cases were categorically defined to include offenders younger than 14 and those between the ages of 14 and 16. The majority of homicides in Chicago, both reported (82.9%) and unreported (94.3%), involved offenders older than 13. However, although offenders younger than 14 make up 5.7% of the unreported cases and 8.2% of the total number of homicides reported to the CPD from 1992 to 2000, they constituted 17.1% of the cases that received news media attention. More important, more than 45% of the cases involving offenders younger than 14 were reported by the newspapers, whereas less than 20% of the cases involving older perpetrators (aged 14 to 16) received news coverage.

Table 1 A Comparison of Age, Race, Gender, and Type of Weapon among Reported and Unreported Cases

| | Reported Status in Newspapers (%) | | |
	Unreported	Reported	Chi-Square
Age of the victim			
Younger than 14	39.1	60.9	
14 to 19	78.9	21.1	
20 to 29	85.7	14.3	
30 to 49	85.4	14.6	
50 to 64	80.0	20.0	
65 and older	58.3	41.7	52.432***
Race of the offender			
Caucasian	40.9	59.1	
African American	79.5	20.5	
Latino	83.0	17.0	
Asian/Other	50.0	50.0	20.858***
Race of the victim			
Caucasian	67.6	32.4	
African American	79.8	20.0	
Latino	77.3	22.7	
Asian/Other	50.0	50.0	4.771
Gender of the offender			
Male	79.6	20.4	
Female	64.4	35.6	5.386*
Gender of the victim			
Male	80.8	19.2	
Female	62.0	38.0	12.510***
Type of weapon used			
Gun	79.0	21.0	
Knife	84.6	15.4	
Other	69.9	30.4	3.224
Total	419	117	

$*p < .05.$ $***p < .001.$

As table 2 suggests, the age of the offender entered negatively into the model. The findings suggest that for every 1-year increase in age, we decrease the odds-ratio of reporting by 0.725. In other words, every 1-year increase in offender age corresponded to a 27.49% reduction in the odds of receiving newspaper coverage.

Age of the Victim

Not unlike age of the offender, newspapers overreported cases that involved youthful victims as well. On average, cases reported in the newspapers involved victims with a mean age of about 21, whereas unreported cases

Table 2   Predicting the Reporting Patterns of the Newspapers

Variable	Attribute	B	SE	Exp (ß)
Offender's age		−0.3214**	0.1020	0.7251
Victim's age	Younger than 14	1.7576***	0.4201	5.7986
(0 = 20 to 29)	14 to 19	0.3783	0.2917	1.4598
	30 to 49	−0.0958	0.3954	0.9087
	50 to 64	−0.8412	1.2033	0.4312
	65 and older	0.8246	0.7313	2.2816
Offender's race	African American	−1.4929*	0.5867	0.2247
(0 = Caucasian)	Latino	−1.8639***	0.5685	0.1551
	Asian/Other	−0.2650	1.6889	0.7672
Victim's race	African American	−0.6361	0.5517	0.5293
(0 = Caucasian)	Latino	−0.2533	0.5625	0.7763
	Asian/Other	0.1131	1.2027	1.1198
Offender's gender	Female	0.7709*	0.3948	2.1616
Victim's gender	Female	0.7300*	0.3164	2.0751
Type of weapon	Knife	−0.5174	0.6214	0.5960
(0 = gun)	Other	−0.2906	0.4240	0.7478
White in district (%)		−0.0272	0.201	0.9731
Black in district (%)		−0.0319	0.0203	0.9686
Latino in district (%)		−0.0212	0.0139	0.9790

Note: Nagelkerke r^2 = .2188, model χ^2 = 81.305***, df = 19, n = 534.
*$p < .05$. **$p < .01$. ***$p < .001$.

involved slightly older victims with a mean age of about 24, a mean difference of about 3 years (t = 1.975, df = 533, $p < .05$). Prompted by previous research that has indicated that the news media overreport homicides committed against children and the elderly (Chermak, 1995), we collapsed victim age into categories that included those younger than 14, 14 to 19, 20 to 29, 30 to 49, 50 to 64, and 65 and older. In doing so, it was discovered that victims younger than 14 disproportionately represented almost one fourth of the cases reported by the news media, whereas they constituted only 4.3% of the unreported cases and 8.6% of the total cases reported to the CPD. Furthermore, of the 46 cases that involved victims younger than 14, almost 61% were reported by the newspapers, compared to just 21.1% of those aged 14 to 19, 14.3% aged 20 to 29, 15.7% aged 30 to 49, and 20% aged 50 to 64. As indicated in table 2, homicides that involved victims younger than 14 were around 480% more likely to receive coverage than cases that involved victims aged 20 to 29. No significant differences were observed among homicides committed against the elderly.

Race of the Offender and Victim

The vast majority of juvenile homicides in Chicago involved African American offenders (75.5%). This held true for both cases that received news media attention (72.1%), as well as those that received no attention at all (76.6%). Significant differences were noted between the racial characteristics of the offender and the reporting status of the case where Caucasian offenders received disproportionately higher coverage than did African Americans and Latinos. More than 59% of the cases involving Caucasian offenders received newspaper coverage, compared to roughly 21% and 17% of the cases involving African American and Latino offenders, respectively. The race of the offender also entered significantly into the logistic regression model. Homicides involving Latino and African American offenders were about 85% and 78% less likely to be reported in the newspapers when compared to cases that involved Caucasian offenders.

Although significant differences were noted between the race of the offender and the reporting status of the case, none were noted between the race of the victim and whether the case received coverage. Quite similar to the characteristics of the offender, the majority of homicides involved African American victims (72.3%); Latinos (20.5%), Caucasians (6.4%), and Asian/Other (0.8%) victims followed, respectively.

Gender of the Offender

As found in previous research, male perpetrators committed the vast majority of cases. Past research on the reporting patterns of crime by the media have suggested that cases involving female participants (either victim or offender) have generated more coverage because their statistical rarity has made them more newsworthy (Chermak, 1995; Katz, 1987; Madriz, 1997; Naylor, 1995). From 1992 to 2000, 535 juvenile homicide cases were reported to the CPD, of which 490 (around 91%) involved male offenders. In comparing gender differences between reported and unreported cases in Chicago, variation was noted. Slightly more than 20% of the cases involving male perpetrators received news media attention, whereas almost 36% of the cases involving female offenders received coverage. As indicated in table 2, this difference proved to be significant in our model, suggesting that homicides committed by female perpetrators were more likely to receive newspaper coverage than cases committed by males.

Gender of the Victim

When gender differences between cases that were reported in the newspapers were compared to nonreported cases, significant differences were observed. Female victims, although involved in only slightly more than 13% of the homicides reported to the CPD, make up almost one fourth of the cases reported in the newspapers. On average, homicides committed against females were 2.08 times more likely to receive media coverage than cases that involved male victims, a finding consistent with previous research.

Geographical Coverage of Cases

Although various studies have examined the reporting patterns of newspapers by focusing on variables such as age, gender, and race, very few have explored the location in which the homicide occurred. We believe location is an important variable to consider, especially in Chicago because it acts as a proxy for race and income. While Chicago is a racially diverse city, it is still segregated in that each district is relatively homogeneous. As figure 3 indicates, the majority of residents in the southernmost districts of the city are African American, whereas those in the northern districts are predominately Caucasian. Latinos makeup the majority in the central portion of the city in Districts 10, 12, 13, and 14.

Besides racial differences between the north and south side of the city, economic differences are present as well. The south side is marked with greater poverty and violence than the north. If rarity is an element in the newsmaking process, we would expect to see disproportional reporting in the northern districts of the city.

Figure 4 provides a depiction of the distribution of juvenile homicides reported in the papers to the total number of cases reported to the CPD. Because population varies from district to district, the raw number of homicides

Figure 3   Racial Demographics by District in Chicago

Figure 4   Rates of Juvenile Homicide and Percentage of Cases Reported in Each District, 1992 to 2000

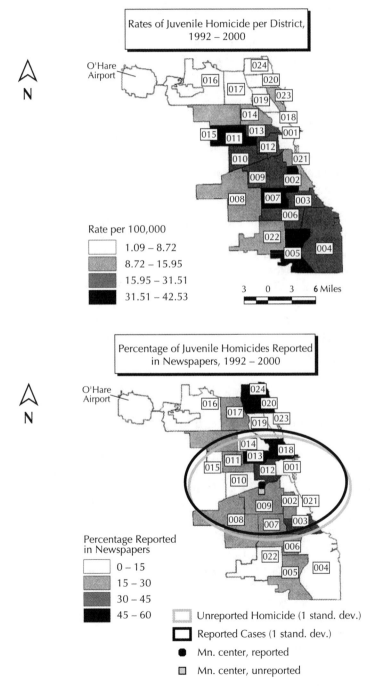

reported was converted into a rate per 100,000. As this figure illustrates, homicides reported to the CPD ranged from a low of 1.09 (District 16) to a high of 42.53 per 100,000 (District 2), with a mean homicide rate of 20.45 per 100,000 citywide. The percentage of juvenile homicide cases reported in the newspapers in each district ranged from a low of 0 (Districts 1 and 16) to a high of 60 (District 20). With few exceptions, our findings suggest that the reporting patterns of the newspapers correspond with the reported homicide rates in each district. From 1992 to 2000, very few homicides in the northern districts were reported to the CPD. Similarly, these areas received less attention by the media.

There was some noticeable variation in the spatial distribution of reported juvenile homicides. For example, northern Districts 17, 18, 20, and 24 were better represented by the newspapers when compared to Districts 4 and 5, the southernmost districts. Better representation in the north was further evident when standard deviational ellipses were mapped out. Map 2 in figure 4 depicts the geographical location of reported and unreported cases. Each ellipse represents one standard deviational unit—meaning that roughly 68% of the cases fall within the geographical boundaries of each ellipse. As figure 4 illustrates, there is much agreement in the geographical location of reported and unreported homicides. Both ellipses center on District 9 and encompass much of the same geographical location; however, there is one noticeable difference. The ellipse representing the homicides reported in the papers shifts slightly to the north, whereas the lower boundary of the ellipse representing unreported cases shifts to the south. In other words, the papers tended to slightly overreport from the northern districts. This fording is not that surprising, given that fewer cases occur in the north; thus, when they occur, they are more likely to be seen as newsworthy.

Type of Weapon

No significant differences were noted between the type of weapon used in the homicide and whether the case received media attention (see table 1). Most juvenile homicides involved the use of some type of firearm or gun (84.7%). Similarly, the majority of homicides reported in the newspapers were gun-related as well (81.9%). It should be noted, however, that cases that received increased newspaper coverage in the form of multiple stories tended to involve atypical, "other" weapons.

In summary, significant differences were noted between the juvenile homicide cases that received newspaper coverage versus those that did not. Newspapers favored cases that involved Caucasian, young, female victims and offenders. In examining the location of the homicide, the newspapers favored homicides reported in the northern districts. This raises the following questions: What impact, if any, do the reporting patterns of homicide have on public perception and fear? Do individuals subscribe to the news media's claims to begin with? And if so, does this resonate fear in their everyday life? This is addressed in the concluding sections below.

Fear of Crime

To measure public perception and fear of crime, a mail survey was conducted. As noted earlier, 500 respondents were randomly selected and a questionnaire (both English and Spanish) was mailed to their home. Of the 500 questionnaires sent, 126 were returned, a response rate of slightly more than 25%. This is a dangerously low response rate and, as such, the findings presented here should be viewed only as suggestive.

The majority of respondents were female (53.2%). Additionally, 70.2% of the sample reported their race as Caucasian; African Americans (21.8%), Latinos, and Asian/Other followed, respectively. Most participants reported to be between the ages of 30 to 49 (31.7%); 25 to 29 (23%), 50 to 64 (23%), 65 and older (15.9%), and 18 to 24 (6.3%) followed, respectively. None of the respondents was younger than 18.

Respondents were asked to respond to various questions geared toward measuring their perceptions of juvenile homicide, their exposure to the newspapers, and their fear of crime. More than 81% of the sample reported reading either the *Chicago Tribune* or the *Chicago Sun-Times* on at least a weekly basis, whereas 42% reported the newspaper as their primary source of crime-related information. When asked if the newspapers did an adequate job in reporting juvenile homicides, roughly 62% of the respondents said "yes." When asked whether they believed homicides involving juvenile offenders had increased, decreased, or stayed the same, more than 56% believed that it had increased, whereas only 13% reported that it had declined (see figure 5).

Figure 5 Within the Past 5 Years, Have Juvenile Homicides Increased, Decreased, or Remained Unchanged?

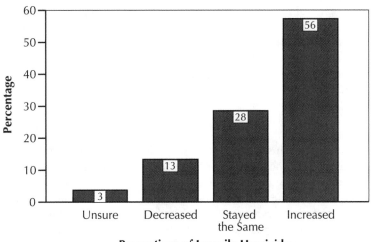

Perceptions of Juvenile Homicide

Fear of crime was measured using 14 Likert-type scale questions. These questions (see table 3 for a list of questions used in scale) were scaled, and a composite "fear of juvenile crime" score was calculated.[4] Fear scores ranged from a low of 14 to a high of 64, with a mean score of 26.27. Scores were dichotomized into a *low fear* and *high fear* category, using 33 as a natural break. In other words, individuals who reported scores ranging from 14 to 33 were labeled as *low fear*, and those who scored 34 to 64 were labeled as *high fear*. Of those who reported higher levels of fear, 59% resided in the southern districts of Chicago (see figure 6 for fear distribution).

Using variables such as respondent age, gender, race, number of years lived in Chicago, type of neighborhood (low, medium, or high crime), and exposure to the media, a logistic regression model was computed (see table 4). The model accurately predicted 83.62% of the cases and was significant ($\chi^2 = 32.403$, $df = 12$, $p < .01$), whereas the Hosmer and Lemeshow goodness-of-fit test revealed that the model's estimates fit the data at an acceptable level ($\chi^2 = 12.6268$, $df = 7$, $p = .0817$). The race of the respondent proved to be the best predictor of fear, with African American respondents reporting a higher level of fear than Caucasian participants. Statistically, being African American increased the odds-ratio of reported levels of fear 9.43 times.

Whether individuals received most of their crime-related news from the newspapers was also a significant variable in the model. Reporting that the primary source of crime information was newspapers increased the odds-ratio of reported fear 7.28 times, when compared to those who received their information from either other mediums or friends/family members.

As noted earlier, we included a geographical variable to control for the juvenile homicide rate. Districts were categorically defined into *low, moderate,* and *high rate* groups based on their respective rate of juvenile homicide per 10,000 residents. Although this variable did not prove to be significant at the .05 level, it approached significance ($p = .08$, Wald = 2.93) and in all probability would have reached it had the sample size been larger. The findings indicated that residing in areas that had moderately high juvenile homicide rates increased the odds-ratio of reported fear 3.23 times. Paradoxically, living in an area with a high rate of juvenile homicide was not a significant predictor of fear. One possible explanation is that individuals who reside in high-crime areas see violence on a daily basis, become somewhat desensitized to it, and are therefore less fearful.

Discussion

The purpose of this research was twofold. The first purpose was to examine the accuracy of the reporting of juvenile homicide cases in two Chicago newspapers. In particular, we questioned whether the public was getting a clear perception of the characteristics associated with juvenile offenders and their victims. If the newspapers are guilty of overreporting atypical cases, this led us, as a second purpose, to ponder the impact this has on public perceptions and fear of juvenile homicide.

Table 3 Frequency Distribution of Responses to Fear of Crime and Safety Questions (in percentages)

Question	Very Safe	Fairly Safe	Neither Safe Nor Unsafe	Unsafe	Very Unsafe
1. How safe do you feel walking alone in the area of your home at night (1 mile)?	22.2	33.3	20.6	6.3	17.5
2. How safe do you feel walking alone in the area of your home at night 0.5 mile)?	27.0	36.5	18.3	6.3	11.9
3. How safe do you feel walking alone in the area of your home during the day (1 mile)?	51.6	35.7	7.9	3.2	1.6
4. How safe do you feel walking alone in the area of your home during the day (0.5 mile)?	59.5	29.4	5.6	2.4	2.4
5. How safe do you feel when you walk by a group of youth you do not know?	13.6	37.6	30.4	9.6	8.8
6. How safe do you feel in your home?	64.0	28.8	4.0	2.4	0.8

Question	Not Afraid	Slightly Afraid	Moderately Afraid	Mostly Afraid	Very Afraid
7. How afraid are you of being victimized in the area of your home at night (1 mile)?	31.7	38.1	19.0	5.6	5.6
8. How afraid are you of being victimized in the area of your home at night (0.5 mile)?	35.7	39.7	15.1	4.0	5.6
9. How afraid are you of being victimized in the area of your home during the day (1 mile)?	61.1	28.6	7.1	2.4	0.8
10. How afraid are you of being victimized in the area of your home during the day (0.5 mile)?	68.3	25.4	3.2	2.4	0.8
11. How afraid are you of being attacked by a juvenile offender near your home?	41.3	31.0	16.7	6.3	4.8
12. How afraid are you of being murdered by a juvenile offender near your home?	55.6	21.4	9.5	9.5	4.0
13. How afraid are you of being attacked by a juvenile offender in your home?	69.0	16.7	6.3	3.2	4.8
14. How afraid are you of being murdered by a juvenile offender in your home?	73.8	13.5	4.8	1.6	6.3

Figure 6   Spatial Distribution of Fear

Overall, cases receiving press coverage from the *Chicago Sun-Times* and *Chicago Tribune* were significantly different than cases not receiving coverage in terms of the offender and victim's age, race, and gender. The most significant variable predicting newspaper coverage was the age of the offender. Because the focus of this study is on juveniles, we are already dealing with young offenders to begin with. However, homicides committed by 16- and 17-year-olds were not as newsworthy as cases committed by young offenders and, as such, were less likely to receive coverage. A similar pattern was noted with respect to the age of the victim. If the homicide involved a victim younger than 14, it increased the odds of receiving newspaper coverage by 480% when compared to cases involving victims between the ages of 20 and 29. Our findings with respect to age are consistent with previous studies. Chermak (1995), for example, suggested that cases involving young children receive disproportionate amounts of coverage by the press because they are perceived to be more vulnerable and incapable of protecting themselves; thus, when a case involving a child victim occurs, it elevates the importance of the case.

Table 4 Predicting Fear: A Logistic Model

Variable	Attribute	B	SE	Exp(β)
Age (0 = 18 to 24)	25 to 34	−0.9025	1.2980	0.4055
	35 to 49	1.5402	1.3505	0.2143
	50 to 64	−1.2933	1.4024	0.2744
	65 and older	−1.8608	1.5289	0.1556
Race (0 = Caucasian)	African American	2.2439***	0.8725	9.4300
	Other	−0.5419	1.2531	0.3428
Gender	Female	−0.2051	0.5788	0.8145
Newspaper		1.9850*	0.7744	7.7290
Television		0.9356	0.7145	2.5487
Live in Chicago (0 = less than 20 years)	20 or more years	0.8011	0.7622	2.2279
Homicide rate in neighborhood (0 = less than 0.72)	0.72 to 2.11	1.1734	0.6849	3.2329
Black in district (%)		0.1621	0.9522	1.1760

Note: Nagelkerke r^2 = .368, model χ^2 = 32.408*, df = 12, n = 120. *p < .05. **p < .01. ***p < .001.

The race of the offender was also a significant predictor of newspaper coverage. Homicides committed by Latino and African American offenders were less likely to be reported than cases committed by Caucasian offenders. This finding is consistent with previous research conducted by Johnstone et al. (1994) and Boulahanis et al. (2000). However, we should note that although significant differences were noted, the newspapers' portrayal of race was not that different from the cases reported to the CPD. Overall, 75.7% of all homicides reported to the CPD involved an African American offender and 72.2% of all cases reported in the papers involved an African American as well. Cases involving Latino offenders constituted nearly 20% of the cases reported to the police and 15.7% of the cases printed in the newspapers. Caucasians, on the other hand, comprised slightly more than 4% of all cases reported to the CPD, yet they made up 11.3% of the stories in the newspapers. Taken together, these findings suggest that although the percentage of homicides committed by Caucasians were disproportionately covered, the majority of actual stories depicted in the newspapers involved African American and Latino offenders.

With regard to gender, the findings suggest that the media disproportionately covered cases involving female victims and offenders. One of the most consistent findings in homicide research is that homicide is by far a male-dominated act. We found this to be the case as well. More than 91% of the cases reported to the CPD involved a male offender and almost 87% involved a male victim. Of the cases reported in the newspapers, 86% and nearly 77% involved male offenders and victims, respectively. As was the case with race, the newspapers' audience is getting elements of the typical cases involving male offenders and victims, as well as the overreporting of the atypical female offender and victim cases.

In examining the spatial distribution of the reporting patterns of the news media, we noted much agreement between the geographical location of homicides reported in the newspapers and those not reported. The majority of cases in Chicago occurred in the southern districts, and the majority of cases reported in the papers reflect this as well. There was, however, a slight northern shift in reported cases, indicating that the newspapers tended to favor homicides in the northern portion of the city. There are clear racial differences between the north and south side of the city. Individuals residing in the north are predominately Caucasian, whereas the south is predominately African American. The increased exposure given to the north by the newspapers may have influenced public perceptions by the population residing there.

In an attempt to measure public perceptions of fear, we sent out a mail survey to residents in Chicago. Our findings revealed that 81% of the sample reported reading either the *Chicago Sun-Times* or *Chicago Tribune* on a weekly basis. The findings also revealed that 84% believed that homicides involving juvenile offenders had either increased or stayed the same during the past 5 years. In examining fear, the findings indicated that African Americans tended to be more fearful than Caucasians and those who reported receiving most of their crime-related news from the newspapers were more fearful than those who received this information from other mediums or friends and family.

Overall, our findings suggest that the newspapers overreported certain atypical cases. Additional findings revealed that increased exposure to the newspapers is associated with increased fear. It is obviously primitive to suggest that the reporting patterns of the media caused this fear, as there are many variables that influence perceptions and fear. Because this study only investigated present-day perceptions of fear, it is impossible for us to examine any longitudinal effects in reaction to atypical characteristics. The majority of cases that received coverage were ordinary, suggesting that newspaper reporting is fairly accurate. However, by overreporting the atypical, the readers receive a steady diet of both typical and atypical, thus making it difficult to uncover patterns of victimization. In the absence of discernable patterns, the image of the type of juvenile likely to be an offender or victim becomes convoluted and fear is more broadly dispersed. For example, Riedel (1998) concludes that fear of serial killers rests on the inability of law enforcement to either identify the offenders and the media's portrayal of these homicides. The uncertainty produces a fear that anyone can be a victim and anyone can be a perpetrator. We suggest that this may also be occurring in the case of juvenile homicide. Although police data have suggested that homicides involving juvenile offenders have declined in recent years, the atypical cases remain to be sensationalized and distort perceptions in a number of ways. First, juvenile homicides are a statistical rarity and are therefore newsworthy. The more bizarre, the greater the chances of receiving media attention. Second, juvenile homicides represent a problem with America's youth, a problem that is perceived to be growing. Children can and do kill, and for many this is an indication of throw-away youth, poor parenting, spoiled children, or lax juvenile laws. The generation gap between children and adults is further increased when it comes to the commission of senseless crime resulting in death. Third, the sensationalized representation of atypical cases suggests the offenders and victims could be anyone. This also may be the result of the various locations in which these homicides occur, which was not examined in this research: the school classroom, the playground, the street, or in the home. There are patterns, but unless these patterns are identified in the press, the levels of fear may intensify. This is not to suggest that atypical cases should not receive attention, but rather, responsible reporters should identify them as rarities.

In turn, public perceptions often influence lawmakers, and a better-informed public audience would be less likely to overexaggerate the problems with today's youth.

Limitations of the Study

There are a few limitations to this study that should be addressed. First, characteristics of the cases in the article were examined independently. That is, we analyzed the data on race, gender, age, and weapon as distinct properties that we compared to the cases unreported in the media. There are clear patterns noted in juvenile homicide cases in Chicago. Offenders are generally males using guns, and are disproportionately African American. Victims, more often than not, are males older than 14 and African American. The majority of cases examined in this study confirms those statements but indicate that there are some significant differences found when analyzed separately. Focusing on the atypical features of the news story without viewing the article as a composite of many separate elements may exaggerate the importance of these features. In examining the cases receiving press as a composite, we suggest that future researchers may find that most cases have some atypical features. For example, we found one story in which a male African American offender used a gun to kill an African American male victim. It sounds rather typical at first glance, but this case involved a "pedal-by" shooting by a juvenile too young to drive a car. Another case involved several African American teenage males that killed an African American man by setting him on fire; only method of murder is unusual. In still another story, gang violence broke out and a young female was caught in the crossfire—the innocent victim is the unusual element in this story. Thus, cases like these have more typical features than atypical. Only one element is necessary to make a case appear atypical in regard to statistical analysis, and we suggest future researchers should take a more qualitative approach to analyzing this data.

A second limitation is a methodological one. We compare reported to unreported homicides without examining cases that received multiple stories. Our findings indicated that only about 20% of the juvenile homicide cases reported to the CPD received newspaper coverage. Obviously, if all stories were reported, individuals would be exposed to five times as many cases and fear could be intensified. However, by not examining the type of case that received increased attention in the form of multiple and follow-up stories, we may be de-emphasizing the effects the atypical stories may have had on perceived fear. Future studies should consider including multiple and follow-up stories, as well as determining the type of case that generates this level of interest.

It is our hope that this research will fill a void in the constructionist and media studies literature. Although much research has been conducted on the reporting patterns of homicide by the media, very few studies have examined the reporting patterns of cases involving juvenile offenders. Understanding the reporting patterns of juvenile homicide is a necessary first step in examining current perceptions and public policy dealing with juveniles. The timing for research could not be more perfect for additional research on this subject. Data sets are readily available to examine the increase and decline in juvenile crime, and media accounts are at a more manageable level since the decline in homicide rates. Furthermore, no study, to our knowledge, attempts to use Geographic Information System technology to map out the reporting patterns of homicide by the media, as we have attempted to do. Future studies should consider this technique as a valuable tool to map reporting patterns of the media.

Notes

[1] See Block, Block, and the Illinois Criminal Justice Information Authority (1998). Data from 1992 to 1995 came directly from the Chicago Homicide data set. Data from 1996 to 2000 was made available by the Chicago Police Department. We are indebted to Superintendent Terry G. Hillard, Lieutenant Lemmer, and Rachel M. Johnston of the Chicago Police Department.

[2] Because the majority of cases involved lone victims and offenders, only the first offender and victim in each case was selected. In other words, multiple offenders and multiple victims were excluded from these analyses.

[3] Some cases received multiple follow-up coverage. No multiple stories are used in these analyses.

[4] A Cronbach's alpha level of 0.9364 indicated that the questions measured a strong univariate construct, thus allowing us to effectively create a scaled score.

References

Altheide, D. L. (1985). *Media power.* Beverly Hills, CA: Sage.

Barak, G. (1988). Newsmaking criminology: Reflections on the media, intellectuals, and crime. In G. Barak (Ed.), *Media, process, and the social construction of crime: Studies in newsmaking criminology.* New York: Garland.

Barak, G. (1994). Media, society, and criminology. In G. Barak (Ed.), *Media, process, and the social construction of crime: Studies in newsmaking criminology.* New York: Garland.

Best, J. (1990). *Threatened children: Rhetoric and concern about child-victims.* Chicago: University of Chicago.

Block, C. R., Block, R. L., & the Illinois Criminal Justice Information Authority. (1998). *Homicides in Chicago, 1965–1995* (4th ICPSR version) [Computer file]. Ann Arbor, MI: Inter-University Consortium for Political and Social Research.

Boulahanis, J. G., Esmail, A., & Heltsley, M. (2000, November). *An examination of juvenile homicides and perceptions of violence in Chicago: A true phenomenon or constructed reality caused by the media.* Paper presented at the American Society of Criminology, San Francisco.

Chermak, S. (1994). Crime in the news media: A refined understanding of how crimes become news. In G. Barak (Ed.), *Media, process, and the social construction of crime: Studies in newsmaking criminology.* New York: Garland.

Chermak, S. (1995). *Victims in the news: Crime and the American news media.* Boulder, CO: Westview Press.

Chiricos, T., Eschholz, S., & Gertz, M. (1997). Crime, news, and fear of crime: Toward an identification of audience effect. *Social Problems, 44,* 342–357.

Chiricos, T., Padgett, K., & Gertz, M. (2000). Fear, TV news, and the reality of crime. *Criminology, 38,* 755–786.

Cohen, S. (1972). *Folk devils and moral panics: Creation of mods and rockers.* London: MacGibbon and Kee.

Davis, E. J. (1952). Crime news in Colorado newspapers. *American Journal of Sociology, 57,* 325–330.

Dixon, T. L., & Linz, D. (2000). Overrepresentation and underrepresentation of African Americans and Latinos as lawbreakers on television news. *Journal of Communication, 50,* 131–154.

Elikann, P. (1999). *Superpredators: Demoralization of our children by the law.* New York: Plenum.

Ericson, R. V., Baranek, P. M., & Chan, J. B. L. (1991). *Representing order: Crime, law, and justice in the news media.* Toronto, Canada: University of Toronto Press.

Fishman, M. (1978). Crime waves as ideology. In S. Cohen & J. Young (Eds.), *The manufacture of news: Social problems, deviance, and the mass media.* Beverly Hills, CA: Sage.

Gans, H. J. (1979). *Deciding what's news: A study of CBS Evening News, NBC Nightly News,* Newsweek, *and* Time. New York: Pantheon Books.

Goode, E., & Ben-Yehuda, N. (1994). *Moral panics: Social construction of deviance.* Cambridge, UK: Blackwell.

Grabe, M. E. (1999). Television news magazine crime stories: A functionalist perspective. *Critical Studies in Mass Communication, 16,* 155–171.

Graber, D. A. (1980). *Crime news and the public.* New York: Praeger.

Gusfield, J. R. (1981). *The culture of public problems: Drinking-driving and the symbolic order.* Chicago: University of Chicago Press.

Heath, L. (1984). Impact of newspaper crime reports of fear: Multimethodological investigation. *Journal of Personality and Social Psychology, 47,* 263–276.

Heide, K. (1996). Juvenile homicide in the United States: Trends and contributing factors. In M. Riedel & J. G. Boulahanis (Eds.), *Lethal violence: Proceedings of the 1995 Research Working Group.* Ottawa, Canada: U.S. Department of Justice.

Heide, K. M. (1999). Youth homicide: An integration of psychological, sociological, and biological approaches. In M. D. Smith & M. A. Zahn (Eds.), *Homicide: A sourcebook of social research* (pp. 221–238). Thousand Oaks, CA: Sage.

Hubbard, J. C., DeFleur, L. B., & DeFleur, M. L. (1975). Mass media influences on public conceptions of social problems. *Social Problems, 23,* 22–34.

Jaehnig, W. B., Weaver, D. H., & Fico, F. (1981). Reporting crime and fearing crime in three communities. *Journal of Communication, 31,* 88–96.

Jenkins, P. (1994). *Using murder: Social construction of serial homicide.* New York: Aldine De Gruyter.

Jerin, R. A., & Fields, C. B. (1994). Murder and mayhem in *USA Today:* A quantitative analysis of the national reporting of states' news. In G. Barak (Ed.), *Media, process, and the social construction of crime: Studies in newsmaking criminology.* New York: Garland.

Johnstone, J. W. C., Hawkins, D. E., & Michener, A. (1994). Homicide reporting in Chicago dailies. *Journalism Quarterly, 71,* 860–872.

Katz, J. (1987). What makes crime "news"? *Media Culture and Society, 9,* 47–75.

Liska, A. E., & Baccaglini, W. (1990). Feeling safe by comparison: Crime in women's lives. *Social Problems, 37,* 360–374.

Madriz, E. (1997). *Nothing bad happens to good girls: Fear of crime in women's lives.* Berkeley: University of California Press.

Mahini, R. B. (2000). There's no place like home: The availability of judicial review over certification decisions invoking federal jurisdiction under the Juvenile Justice and Delinquency Prevention Act. *Vanderbilt Law Review, 53*(4), 1131–1354.

Naylor, B. (1995). Women's crime and media coverage: Making explanations. In R. E. Dobash, R. P. Dobash, & L. Noaks (Eds.), *Gender and crime.* Cardiff, UK: The University of Wales Press.

O'Keefe, G. J., & Reid-Nash, K. (1987). Crime news and real-world blues: Effects of the media on social reality. *Communication Research, 14,* 147–163.

Reinarman, C. (2000). The social construction of drug scares. In P. A. Adler & P. Adler (Eds.), *Constructions of deviance: Social power, context, and interaction* (3rd ed.). Belmont, CA: Wadsworth.

Riedel, M. (1998). Serial murder, communities, and evil: A review essay. *Criminal Justice Review, 23,* 220–232.

Sheley, J. F., & Ashkins, C. D. (1981). Crime, crime news, and crime views. *Public Opinion Quarterly, 45,* 492–506.

Sprott, J. B. (1996). Understanding public views of youth crime and the youth justice system. *Canadian Journal of Criminology, 38*(3), 271–290.

Surette, R. (1998). *Media, crime, and criminal justice: Images and realities.* Belmont, CA: West/Wadsworth.

Williams, P., & Dickinson, J. (1993). Fear of crime read all about it? The relationship between newspaper crime reporting and fear of crime. *British Journal of Criminology, 33,* 33–56.

"ALL THE NEWS THAT'S FIT TO PRINT"

A CONTENT ANALYSIS OF THE CORRECTIONAL DEBATE IN THE *NEW YORK TIMES*

Michael Welch, Lisa Weber, & Walter Edwards

Since the 1970s, scholars have generated significant research document-ing various ways in which the media projects official images of crime and criminal justice (Barak, 1988, 1994; Chermak, 1994, 1997; Ericson, Baranek, & Chan, 1987, 1989, 1991; Fishman, 1978; Hall, Critcher, Jefferson, Clarke, & Roberts, 1978; Humphries, 1981; Kidd-Hewitt & Osborne, 1995; Surette, 1992). In particular, those investigations show that mediated information about crime is commonly traced to government sources; namely, political leaders, law enforcement officials, and other state managers. By occupying elevated positions within the hierarchy of credibility, politicians and govern-ment officials enjoy the privilege of offering to the media primary—and self-serving—definitions of crime (Becker, 1967, 1973). As a result of this social arrangement, the media afford political and government leaders valu-able opportunities for advancing a criminal justice agenda that serves the state's political, ideological, and economic interests by generating public sup-port, legitimizing power, and garnering funds for resources and manpower (Fishman, 1978; Hall et al., 1978; Kasinsky, 1994). The reciprocal relations between the state and the media contribute to the projection of governmental (or official) versions of crime to the public, producing what is *socially thinkable* about the nature of crime and strategies to control it.

Given the pivotal role of politicians in manufacturing the news, critics accuse the media of carrying out propaganda functions for the government's ideological machinery (Herman & Chomsky, 1988; Kappeler & Potter, 2005;

From: *The Prison Journal*, vol. 80, no. 3, pp. 245–264, copyright 2000. Reprinted by permission of Sage Publications, Inc.

Tunnell, 1992). Similarly, our previous research uncovered important elements of ideology (i.e., beliefs on crime causation and crime control) contained in crime news (Welch, Fenwick, & Roberts, 1997, 1998). Those studies, the first of their kind, were based on a content analysis of experts' quotes appearing in feature articles about crime in four major newspapers (i.e., the *New York Times*, the *Washington Post*, the *Los Angeles Times*, and the *Chicago Tribune*). In sum, we discovered further evidence of journalism's reliance on politicians and law enforcement officials as news sources who in effect serve as primary definers of crime. Compared to intellectuals (i.e., professors and non-academic researchers) also sourced in those articles, politicians spoke more ideologically about crime causation and crime control insofar as they routinely disavowed the relationship between social conditions and crime.

Applying a similar method of content analysis, this investigation examines newspaper articles devoted to corrections—a widely neglected area in media studies (Marsh, 1989, 1991). While remaining attentive to which issues comprise the corrections agenda, the study tracks chief patterns of news sourcing, particularly among sources supporting the government's correctional strategies vis-à-vis sources opposing such policies. In doing so, we set out to weigh the relative balance of press coverage in the debate over corrections, thus shedding a critical light on agenda setting in criminal justice.

Sample

While being able to generate mass attention to social issues, the media possesses a unique power to shape the nature of debate by defining parameters and selecting key items for public discourse. The debate over corrections presented in the press adheres to that pattern of news production, especially considering the selection process by which certain correctional issues are deemed more newsworthy than others. To further our understanding of how the correctional debate is framed by journalists, we turned our attention to the most circulated and arguably most influential newspaper in the nation.

Ranking first among metropolitan newspapers, the *New York Times* reports a daily circulation figure of 1,074,741, which surpasses its chief competitors, the *Los Angeles Times* (1,050,176), the *Washington Post* (775,894), and the *New York Daily News* (721,256) (Detroit Free Press, 1998). Largely due to its vast circulation, the *New York Times* is considered a highly influential newspaper that commands the attention of political, government, and business leaders, as well as the public. Given such influence, the *New York Times* has the capacity to present social issues in ways that dictate the nature of debate on matters of social policy. With this idea in mind, we set out to examine the manner in which corrections is covered by the *New York Times*.

To learn the extent to which correctional issues appeared in the *New York Times*, we administered a computerized literature search using the terms *corrections* and *prisons* as key words in locating appropriate articles. The search was limited to medium (6 to 18 column inches) and long (exceeding 18 column inches) stories to ensure depth of coverage. Between 1992 and 1995, the *New York Times* published 206 articles on corrections, spanning a wide array of 19 issues.[1] Institutional violence ($n = 40$) and correctional programs ($n = 34$) were the most frequently covered topics, constituting 19% and 17% of all articles, respectively. Other notable correctional issues included health care ($n = 17$, 8%), "get tough" policies ($n = 16$, 8%), and privatization/corrections as industry ($n = 16$, 8%). By comparison, less attention was directed at overcrowding ($n = 10$, 5%), drugs (including the war on drugs) ($n = 9$, 4%), famous (and celebrity) inmates ($n = 9$, 4%), community concerns (including fear) ($n = 8$, 4%), correctional budgets ($n = 8$, 4%), and institutional issues ($n = 8$, 4%). Furthermore, even less coverage was aimed at juveniles ($n = 6$, 3%), officers ($n = 6$, 3%), the death penalty ($n = 4$, 2%), detention in Immigration and Naturalization Service (INS) centers ($n = 4$, 2%), contraband ($n = 3$, 1%), early release ($n = 3$, 1%), women prisoners ($n = 3$, 1%), and prison history ($n = 2$, 1%) (see table 1).

Method

A principle objective of the study was to examine in-depth the manner in which the *New York Times* covers corrections; in particular, we set out to eval-

Table 1 Correctional Issues in the *New York Times*, 1992 to 1995: Number of Articles and Percentages ($N = 206$)

Issue (abbreviation)	Number of Articles[a]	Percentage
Violence (VI)	40	19
Programs/rehabilitation (PR)	34	17
Health care (HC)	17	8
Get tough (GT)	16	8
Privatization/industry (PI)	16	8
Overcrowding (OC)	10	5
Drugs (DR)	9	4
Famous inmates (FI)	9	4
Budgets (BU)	8	4
Community concerns (CC)	8	4
Institutional issues (II)	8	4
Juveniles (JV)	6	3
Officers (OF)	6	3
Death penalty (DP)	4	2
Immigration and Naturalization Service (IN)	4	2
Contraband (CB)	3	1
Early release (ER)	3	1
Women (WM)	3	1
History (HI)	2	1

Note: Figures do not total 100% due to rounding.

[a]Totals exceed the number of articles due to cross-listing of overlapping topics.

uate the relative balance of coverage by attending to news sourcing. To achieve this undertaking, we administered a content analysis on the sample of 206 articles by identifying and coding all sources along with their direct quotes and attributed statements. While acknowledging the identity of every source (e.g., politicians, corrections officials, reform advocates), we analyzed the content of their quotes to determine whether they supported or opposed the government's correctional strategies. It should be noted that the research design relied on mutually exclusive categories dichotomizing support and opposition to the government's correctional strategies.

Interestingly, there were no quotes that could be construed as neutral; perhaps the lack of neutrality stems from the nature of interview questions presented by journalists who force news sources to take firm positions on issues in the correctional debate. Each correctional issue (e.g., institutional violence, correctional programs) was scrutinized according to the classification scheme, thereby permitting us to ascertain whether the debate over corrections in the *New York Times* appeared balanced or biased. Upon delineating the pattern of sourcing, we delved further into the qualitative content of the articles to extract nuances of news coverage aimed at corrections.

Findings

Comparing various news sources in the correctional debate presented in the *New York Times*, we found that 62% ($n = 593$) of the sources supported the government's correctional strategies whereas 38% ($n = 363$) opposed them. A similar pattern also was evident among the sample of quoted statements: 62% ($n = 1486$) endorsed the government's prison policies whereas 38% ($n = 893$) expressed criticism of them (see table 2). By examining the relative proportion of sources and quotes within each category of issues, table 2 demonstrates that the number of sources (and their quotes) supporting the government's correctional strategies consistently exceeded the sources (and quotes) voicing opposition; this pattern emerged in 15 of the 19 topics studied. On only four correctional issues (i.e., overcrowding, famous inmates, INS, and history) did the sources (and quotes) expressing opposition outnumber those supporting the government's stance on corrections. And on only one issue (i.e., budgets) did the number of sources (and statements) representing both sides of the debate reach parity.

The largest margin of imbalance emerged in articles on programs and rehabilitation (34 articles), a bias favoring the government's position with 83% ($n = 174$) of the sources and 84% ($n = 392$) of the quotes. The second widest gap was found in the articles on privatization/corrections as industry (16 articles); on that issue, 72% ($n = 49$) of the sources and 74% ($n = 121$) of the quotes supported the government's position. In due course, we shall explain precisely what the government's position is on each of the issues examined, thus allowing us also to interpret more fully the scope of the correctional debate in the *New York Times*. Nevertheless, in the next section we delineate the emergent pattern of sourcing that illuminates the perspectives from which the correctional debate is framed.

Sources and Quotes Supporting the Government's Correctional Strategies

Overall, 23 types of news sources ($N = 593$) supporting the government's correctional strategies were identified, altogether generating 1,486 total quotes. The leading sources in this category are officials in political and government positions (elected and appointed officials, e.g., legislators, attorneys general), accounting for 24% ($n = 144$) of the sources and 22% ($n = 325$) of

Table 2 Support for Government Compared to Opposition, Number of Sources and Quotes per Issue: *NY Times* 1992 to 1995 ($N = 206$)

Issue (abbreviation)	n	Sources				Quotes			
		Support	(%)	Oppose	(%)	Support	(%)	Oppose	(%)
Violence (VI)	40	95	(59)	66	(41)	266	(63)	153	(37)
Programs/ rehabilitation (PR)	34	174	(83)	35	(17)	392	(84)	74	(16)
Health care (HC)	17	36	(56)	28	(44)	100	(59)	69	(41)
Get tough (GT)	16	36	(53)	32	(47)	128	(61)	82	(39)
Privatization/ industry (PI)	16	49	(72)	19	(28)	121	(70)	53	(30)
Overcrowding (OV)	10	22	(44)	28	(56)	49	(44)	63	(56)
Drugs (DR)	9	38	(53)	34	(47)	79	(51)	78	(49)
Famous inmates (FI)	9	11	(32)	23	(68)	34	(29)	82	(71)
Budgets (BU)	8	17	(50)	17	(50)	19	(37)	33	(63)
Community concerns (CC)	8	21	(55)	17	(45)	41	(55)	33	(45)
Institutional issues (II)	8	22	(64)	13	(36)	50	(63)	30	(37)
Juveniles (JV)	6	20	(66)	10	(34)	86	(86)	14	(14)
Officers (OF)	6	13	(59)	9	(41)	30	(47)	34	(53)
Death penalty (DP)	4	9	(60)	6	(40)	21	(50)	21	(50)
Immigration and Naturalization Service (IN)	4	6	(43)	8	(57)	15	(36)	27	(64)
Contraband (CB)	3	10	(59)	7	(41)	16	(57)	12	(43)
Early release (ER)	3	6	(55)	5	(45)	14	(50)	14	(50)
Women (WM)	3	7	(64)	4	(36)	20	(71)	8	(29)
History (HI)	2	1	(33)	2	(67)	5	(27)	13	(73)
Totals	206	593	(62)	363	(38)	1486	(62)	893	(38)

the quotes. The second and third leading sources supporting are corrections officials (e.g., correctional commissioners, deputy commissioners) (20%, $n =$ 116) and correctional managers (e.g., wardens, deputy wardens) (13%, $n =$ 76), accounting for 24% ($n = 352$) and 15% ($n = 220$) of the total quotes, respectively. It should be noted that this emerging constellation of sourcing conforms to the government's hierarchy of state managers; indeed, the highest ranking officials were the most often quoted, followed by those officials occupying the lower strata of government power. The dominance of these groups is especially significant because they comprise 57% of the sources and 60% of the quotes endorsing the government's position on corrections. Interestingly, the fourth largest group of sources supporting the state version of corrections consists of inmates, representing 13% ($n = 76$) of all sources and 12% ($n = 174$) of all quotes. The remaining 19 types of news sources clearly remained underrepresented; still, together they contribute substantially to the overall support of the government's position on corrections (comprising 43% of all sources and 40% of all quotes). Other sources include the following: health care professionals ($n = 33$), correctional staff (e.g., officers and various staff members, $n = 26$), prosecutors ($n = 16$), volunteers ($n = 14$), religious personnel (e.g., chaplains and various religious leaders, $n = 12$), judges ($n = 12$), program directors ($n = 10$), reform advocates (e.g., correctional watchdogs, civil liberties activists, $n = 9$), researchers ($n = 7$), professors ($n = 7$), residents ($n = 6$), attorneys representing inmates ($n = 6$), corrections union officials ($n = 6$), relatives of crime victims ($n = 5$), teachers of inmates ($n = 5$), "tough on crime" advocates ($n = 4$), a labor arbitrator ($n = 1$), an attorney representing corrections officers ($n = 1$), and a relative of an inmate ($n = 1$).

Sources and Quotes Opposing the Government's Correctional Strategies

Overall, 24 types of news sources ($N = 363$) opposing the government's correctional strategies were identified, altogether contributing to 893 total quotes. Perhaps expectedly, the leading critics were reform advocates (e.g., correctional watchdogs, civil liberties activists) who represented 18% ($n = 67$) of all critics, offering 20% ($n = 175$) of all quotes. The second largest group of critics consisted of officials in political and government positions (elected and appointed officials, e.g., legislators, attorneys general), accounting for 15% ($n = 55$) of all sources and 12% ($n = 105$) of all quotes. Inmates ($n = 52$, 14%) emerged as the third most prevalent source of criticism, attributed to 20% ($n = 180$) of all statements, and attorneys representing inmates were the fourth most cited critics ($n = 44$, 12%, offering 95 quotes or 10%).

The government's correctional policies and practices also were called into question by numerous other critics, including 27 professors (7%), 21 corrections union officials (5%), 16 correctional staff members (e.g., officers) (4%), 14 corrections officials (e.g., correctional commissioners, deputy commissioners) (4%), 12 judges (3%), 12 residents (3%), 11 health care professionals (3%), 9 correctional managers (e.g., wardens, deputy wardens) (2%), 5 religious personnel (e.g., chaplains and various religious leaders) (1%), 3 program directors (0.8%), 2 researchers, attorneys representing correctional officers, "tough on crime" advocates, teachers of inmates, and prosecutors (0.5% each), as well as a collector, an auctioneer, a juror, a newspaper editor, and a volunteer (0.2% each).

Interpreting the Nature of the Debate Over Corrections

Reaching beyond a basic quantification of sources and quotes, this study also set out to explore in-depth the content of articles on corrections, drawing more fully on the qualitative aspects of the data. This approach enables us to offer additional interpretations about how the correctional debate is formulated by the *New York Times*, while remaining attentive to the pattern of sourcing. In this section, we concentrate primarily on the five most prevalent correctional issues: institutional violence ($n = 40$ articles), programs and rehabilitation ($n = 34$), health care in corrections ($n = 17$), get-tough campaigns ($n = 16$), and privatization/corrections as industry ($n = 16$).

Institutional violence and riots. As the most common correctional topic, institutional violence (and riots) ($n = 40$) comprises 19% of the articles in the sample. Upon closer scrutiny, however, it should be noted that there are distinct subtopics in this category. For instance, 10 articles were devoted to institutional violence occurring at Rikers Island jail complex (New York City); 8 articles focused on the 1993 prison riot at Lucasville, Ohio; 3 articles covered the questionable deaths in Mississippi jails; 3 articles followed the controversy surrounding prison disturbances that observers claimed were precipitated by the disparity in sentencing for crack (versus powdered) cocaine; finally, 3 articles chronicled the beatings and mistreatment of detainees held by the INS.

Not surprisingly, incidents of institutional violence were covered primarily as *events* (e.g., a particular riot, disturbance, or incident); by comparison, most other articles in our sample were presented as discussions or debates over certain correctional issues. Also prevalent in most of the articles in this category were exposés and other forms of investigative journalism, a type of media coverage rarely found among the other topics, except for a few articles on drugs, contraband, and the INS.

As table 2 illustrates, there is considerable reliance on sources supporting the government's correctional policies in this category (accounting for 59% of the sources and 63% of the quotes). Interestingly, the nature of opposition in several of those articles unveils an otherwise uncommon coalition in the correctional debate. Correctional watchdogs, attorneys representing inmates, prisoners, and correctional officers unions linked institutional violence (or the threat of violence) at Rikers Island to a lack of adequate funding and allocation of resources. Together, those groups opposed New York City's correctional policy that reduced spending for municipal jails. In the words of William H. Booth, chairman of the Board of Correction (a watchdog group),

"I'm not one to predict riot, but I know very well when you make cuts like this and take away people's services and rights, they're going to react and you never know how" (Clines, 1994, p. B1). In response, New York City Mayor Giuliani adamantly defended the government's budgetary cuts for the city's jails, accusing the union of issuing "unfounded warnings" for the purpose of "budget manipulation" (Clines, 1994, p. B8). Stan Israel, president of the Correction Officers Benevolent Association injected further the alarming claim that "gang organization is on the rise" at Rikers Island (Clines, 1994, p. B8). As if in riposte, the Commissioner of Correction, Anthony Schembri, announced after a visit to Rikers Island that "a correctional officer, not an inmate had been arrested in possession of contraband—four razor blades and a sharpened knife blade presumably intended for sale to inmates" (Clines, 1994, p. B8). In projecting the government's interpretation of crime expressed through the media, Surette (1992, pp. 42–44) reminds us that animal metaphors abound in criminal justice rhetoric insofar as the role of police and corrections officers ("sheep dogs") is to protect the public ("sheep") from the criminal element ("wolves") (also see Welch, 1996, 1999; Welch et al., 1997, 1998). The wolf pack metaphor is especially popular in reference to gang violence. Conforming to this pattern of hyperbole, union president Israel referred to Hispanic and Black gangs at Rikers Island as "out-of-control wolf packs roaming the prison at will and attacking any rival before correction officers can intervene" (Sullivan, 1994, p. B3).

As the debate on this issue suggests, even in articles about institutional violence, a theme of correctional economics is unmistakable. Moreover, political rhetoric and hyperbole is not only issued by the government to justify increased spending on corrections, but also by corrections officers unions who deploy similar tactics to protest budget cuts that affect adversely their membership. Equivocally, corrections officers unions either support or oppose the government's correctional policies depending on how it best serves their interests. It should be noted that the voices of correctional unions were heard early and often in the *New York Times*; union representatives were sourced in 7 of 10 articles about violence at Rikers Island.

Programs and rehabilitation. Although adequate funding for correctional programs has been denied greatly for the past three decades, contrary to the claims of some correctional pundits, the issue of rehabilitation is far from dead (see Clear, 1994; Flanagan, 1996; Welch, 1995, 1996, 1999). As a rough indicator of the degree to which correctional rehabilitation resonates in the mind of the press, our sample features 34 articles (17%) on programs, the second most common topic. Even more to the point, this grouping of articles generated more sources ($n = 209$) and quotes ($n = 466$) than other correctional topics in our sample; undoubtedly, the correctional debate over programs and rehabilitation is very much alive (see table 2).

Consistent with the economic motif already acknowledged, the most common types of programs specified in these articles ($n = 6$) were those related to the promotion of meaningful work and gainful employment as a means of rehabilitation. Similarly, the subtopic of employment also alluded to the correctional value of instilling a work ethic. Perhaps underscoring the unspoken spiritual importance of a work ethic, an equally common subtopic in this section was religion as a source for reform ($n = 6$ articles). The next largest subsets of articles were devoted to the debate over the treatment of sex offenders ($n = 5$ articles) and for substance abusers ($n = 4$ articles). Although the virtues of the vocational, moral, and medical models were fairly well represented in this subsample, the education model, however, remained conspicuously neglected ($n = 3$ articles).

News sources (83%) and their quotes (84%) favoring the government's policies and practices overwhelmingly outnumbered voices of opposition; still, the government's stance on rehabilitation requires clarification. Remarkably, in all 34 articles, the government supported rehabilitation and programs, including those designed for sex offenders. The nature of criticism, however, centered typically on the complaint that correctional programs should be more available and better funded; likewise, many government officials concurred. Interestingly, opposition in the form of advocating harsher punishment rather than rehabilitation was minimal. More significantly, in 24 articles there was not a single news source (or quote) rejecting the government's claim that rehabilitation is an important aspect of its correctional strategy.

Upon reflection, the near absence of opposition on this issue could very well mean that the debate over rehabilitation constitutes a *false polarity*, insofar as it is more universally supported by citizens than politicians realize. Indeed, public opinion polls demonstrate that citizens generally favor correctional rehabilitation, especially in the form of substance abuse treatment (Maguire & Pastore, 1995, pp. 165, 176, 198; also see Cullen, Cullen, & Wozniak, 1988; Flanagan, 1996; Welch 1997a, 1997b; Welsh, Leone, Kinkade, & Pontell, 1991). True, citizens may also demand punishment (Maguire & Pastore, 1995), but contrary to the mind-set of politicians who exploit the crime issue for campaign purposes, rehabilitation and punishment really do not exist as mutually exclusive categories (see Clear, 1994).

Similarly, Wilkins (1991) refers to false polarities in criminal justice by pointing to "just deserts": the idea that offenders ought to receive the punishment that they justly deserve. Elaborating on what he means by a false polarity, Wilkins insists that it is precisely the popularity of "just deserts" that diminishes its value as a principle of jurisprudence, "since no one can really oppose the idea of 'just deserts' due to the absurdity of calling for unjust undeserved punishment" (1991, p. 2). In light of overwhelming public approval for correctional programs—along with the government's endorsement—the debate over rehabilitation often seems superficial, constituting a false polarity. Rather than depicting rehabilitation as a hotly contested issue, the *New York Times* appears to reflect a wide consensus supporting correctional programs.

Health care in prisons. Given the amount of concern and anxiety about health care in the general population, it is of little surprise that medical issues in corrections ranked third among the topics in our sample ($n = 17$, 8%). The most common subtopic in this category was the issue of AIDS/HIV ($n = 8$), followed by tuberculosis (TB) ($n = 4$) and smoking in correctional facilities ($n = 3$).[2] As table 2 illustrates, news sources (56%) and quotes (59%) supporting the government's strategy for prison health care outnumbered the voices of opposition.

Consistent with the coverage on many of the topics, the theme of correctional economics is clearly evident in articles on health care. Indeed, the government's policies on prison health care were predicated largely by economic initiatives that, in turn, polarized the correctional debate. The government's plan to privatize prison medical services was staunchly opposed by correctional staff unions. Similarly, the government's policy requiring inmates to pay for health care was criticized by reform advocates and attorneys for inmates as well as inmates themselves. Government sources commonly pointed to the rising costs of medical care, including staffing and medication (especially for AIDS/HIV and TB) as reasons to reduce health care expenses.

Issues of correctional debate also included controversial prison management practices, particularly in the realm of AIDS/HIV, TB, and smoking. In 1992, the Erie County, N.Y. jail was sued by Louise K. Nolley, an inmate (charged with passing a check with insufficient funds and forgery) who was subjected to humiliating and improper treatment by correctional staff. The county government approved an institutional policy confining inmates with AIDS to an isolation unit, requiring them to wear plastic gloves while using the typewriter in the prison library and having their belongings labeled with red stickers identifying them as being infected with AIDS. Defending the county's correctional policy on AIDS, jail superintendent John Dray argued that the red stickers were introduced in 1986 when "AIDS became the epidemic that was terrorizing everybody in the business" and they are still necessary "to protect the 13,000 inmates we have in our system every year" (Sullivan, 1992, p. B4). Prisoners and reform advocates challenged the county's correctional policy and practice on AIDS. Eventually the courts intervened on behalf of the prisoners. Judge John T. Curtin of the Federal District Court in Buffalo, N.Y., awarded Nolley $155,000, commenting that, "there is no question that the red-sticker policy was developed, not in response to contagious diseases in general, but specifically in response to the hysteria over HIV and AIDS" (Sullivan, 1992, p. B4).

In its coverage of smoking in prisons, the *New York Times* clearly pointed out that the government's correctional policies and practices included defending itself against inmates suing prisons for illnesses caused by secondhand smoke. In *Helling v. McKinney* (1992), a Nevada prisoner sued the state department of corrections for being housed (in a six-by-eight foot cell) with a cell mate who smoked five packs of cigarettes a day. The U.S. Supreme Court ruled in the case that prisoners who can show that exposure to smoking is a threat to their health may have a constitutional right not to be confined with a chain-smoking cell mate.

On the issue of smoking in prisons, the government's stance is particularly revealing. During the initial stages of litigation involving *Helling v. McKinney*, the Bush administration as well as 34 states petitioned the Court to rule against the prisoner, insisting that "smoking is wide-spread in society" and that "smoking is a habit that is deeply rooted in our history and experience" (Greenhouse, 1993, p. A8). The Bush administration further argued that "there was no basis for ruling that exposure to secondhand smoke could even theoretically violate the Eighth Amendment" (Greenhouse, 1993, p. A8). Whereas the *text* (or manifest content) of the debate appears to focus on the issue of health in correctional facilities, the *subtext* (or latent content) seems to be geared toward the Bush administration's (along with 34 state governments') support for the tobacco industry.

Get-tough campaigns. The fourth largest grouping of articles (*n* = 16, 8%) was devoted to get-tough campaigns, a punitive social movement that significantly impacts the form and function of corrections. A principle theme of those articles centered on the retributionist claim that correctional facilities are not tough enough to fulfill their mission of imposing punishment, instilling discipline, and deterring lawbreakers from committing future offenses. Advocates of get-tough campaigns insinuate that corrections coddles inmates and, confounding the issue, imply that high rates of recidivism are the result of institutional conditions that are inadequately punitive. While being driven by a staunch sense of retribution, those campaigns also are inspired by nostalgic sentiments involving criminal justice (Garland, 1990; Jameson, 1991; Simon, 1995; Stauth & Turner, 1988). Get-tough proposals include "three strikes" legislation, the return to hard labor (e.g., breaking rocks), chain gangs, correctional boot camps, the reduction or elimination of institutional amenities (e.g., programs, televisions, weight lifting), and the construction of super-maximum security penitentiaries.

The nostalgic worldview in corrections has emerged as a reaction to the modern and so-called liberal American prison where convicts are afforded certain constitutional protections, allowed to participate in institutional programs, and permitted to keep personal belongings while incarcerated (e.g., civilian clothes, televisions, coffee, cigarettes, snack food). Critics argue that depictions of prisons as country-clubs (or "three hots and a cot") are wildly exaggerated, inaccurate, and politically manipulative (Welch, 1997b, 1999). Nostalgia marks a return to harsh images of prison life, similar to those projected in such classic movies as *Cool Hand Luke*. In describing support for the get-tough campaigns in Arizona, Governor Fife Symington waxed his personal nostalgia with movie imagery which includes a sheriff's 400 member "executive posse" patrolling Phoenix in search of lawbreakers: "I remember, going way back, watching Tom Mix and Gene Autry and Roy Rogers . . . and I always remember the sheriff swearing in business people on a horse as posse men and saying, 'Go after the horse thieves'" (Mydans, 1995, p. A6; see Koppes & Black, 1987). Sounding the alarm of perceived lawlessness, social disorder, and moral panic, the nostalgic view of corrections expresses a need to regain control of convicts and penal institutions, as well as a return to a simpler society. In doing so, notions of retribution and deterrence are politicized to the extent that the locus of power is personified in criminal justice officials. Sheriff Joseph M. Arpaio, who was elected in 1992 to administer the Maricopa county jail, Arizona, announced to the press, "I want everybody in this country to know that if you commit a crime, you are going into a very bad jail. . . . I want people to say: 'I hate that sheriff. I hate his jails'" (Mydans, 1995, p. A6). Correspondingly, Sheriff Arpaio proudly boasted his beliefs about the virtues of expanding the criminal justice system, saying, "My whole philosophy is, put more people in jail. We've got a vicious crime problem out there, and the answer is to take them off the streets and educate them through punishment" (Mydans, 1995, p. A6).

Illuminating the tendency for elected leaders to resort to political hyperbole in justifying the government's financial commitment to increasing the criminal justice apparatus, Georgia Congressman Newt Gingrich proclaimed, "We should build as many stockades as necessary, and as quickly as though this were wartime and people were dying, because they are" (Berk, 1994, p. A9). Likewise, California Governor Pete Wilson blended populism and correctional economics into his personal vernacular of political crime-speak: "There's really no dispute that these reforms will require considerable additional expense for building prisons and operating them. That is an expense, I submit, that the public is willing to pay. We cannot afford not to pay" ("California Governor," 1994, p. A16). Joining the prevailing political mantra to expand the correctional machinery, New York Governor George F. Pataki pleaded to his constituents, "We cannot fail to build new [correctional] facilities if public safety requires it" (Levy, 1995, p. B4).

Whereas the divide between news sources supporting the government's correctional strategy of getting tough (53%) and its opposition (47%) was narrower than others, the total number of statements favored the government (61%; see table 2). Nevertheless, many dissenters offered insightful and reasonable criticisms of get-tough campaigns. In particular, a critic of Alabama's revived chain gangs and rock-breaking ritual pointed to the futility of those practices. Dalmus Davidson, a highway director in Alabama, reported that the Department of Corrections' rock-breaking program would "provide no financial benefit to the state, which already has contracts with quarries to crush rock in various sizes that can be used along highway shoulders and for some road construction" ("Alabama to Make Prisoners," 1995, p. A5). In essence, get-tough campaigns often resort to a form of prison labor that ironically is void of utility and profit, suggesting that such penal exercises take on a purely punitive significance (Foucault, 1979; Welch, 1999).

Privatization and corrections as industry. Correctional economics evident in the growing correctional-industrial complex remained a principle theme in articles on privatization ($n = 9$) and corrections as industry ($n = 6$) (1 additional article focused on the privatization of health care; together these articles comprise 8% of our sample). Overall, 72% of news sources ($n = 49$) and 70% of quotes ($n = 121$) supported the government's correctional strategy advocating both privatization and the use of corrections as local industry. While downsizing the armed services and closing military bases, a move that erodes the economic base of those communities, the government has endeavored to offset local financial loss by installing penal institutions that promise to boost the local economy.

A case in point: In 1992, the federal government announced the closing of Fort Dix, N.J., army base, sending shock waves through a community that had deep financial ties to the military. (In fact, nearly 4,000 civilians worked at Fort Dix, one of the nation's largest employers.) An agreement between the Pentagon and the Federal Bureau of Prisons, however, softened the blow by converting Fort Dix into the federal system's biggest prison (housing 3,200 inmates). An estimated 700 new jobs were created, albeit little compensation for the massive civilian layoffs caused by the closing of the army base. According to Daniel R. Dunne, a spokesman for the Federal Bureau of Prisons,

> It's a win-win-win situation for everyone involved. . . . It's an excellent opportunity for the taxpayers. We'd move into a facility that's already established. Both organizations see the importance and economic significance this has and are looking to make it work. (Hanley, 1992, p. 33)

Similarly, in other articles describing the support for corrections as local industry, a Weed, California, city councilwoman retorted, "prisons don't go out of business" ("Residents of Dying," 1994, p. 28) whereas a resident in Appleton, Minnesota, quipped, "It's not a smoke-stack industry. . . . It's a renewable resource" (Terry, 1993, pp. 1, 14).

On the other side of the debate, relatively few sources were quoted opposing the government's correctional strategy of privatization and use of prisons to generate revenue ($n = 19$ articles, 28%; $n = 53$ quotes, 30%). Six of the 16 articles did not cite a single source (or statement) of criticism, and in 4 articles, only one critic was quoted. Still, some critics of the government's correctional policies did shed light on the ironic nature of correctional economics contributing to the proliferation of the correctional enterprise.

> Ideally, prisons should be trying to put themselves out of business by doing everything in their power to reduce the recidivism rate. . . . But the very function of a for-profit prison company is to keep people locked up, as long as possible because the companies are paid a certain amount per prisoner, per day. (Jenni Gainsborough, spokeswoman for the National Prison Project of the American Civil Liberties Union [ACLU], quoted in Van Natta, 1995, p. A24)

In a similar vein, Alvin Bronstein, executive director of the National Prison Project of the ACLU, cited criminal justice as one of the few growth industries in the United States, adding, "Corrections today is a gigantic cash machine" (Holmes, 1994, p. 3).

Conclusion

Proponents of dominant ideology theory argue that the media's manu-facturing of news relies heavily on government sources who, in turn, exploit public access to reinforce state power (Abercrombie, Hill, & Turner, 1980; Hall et al., 1978; Herman & Chomsky, 1988). From a Marxian view of the media, the power of the ruling class extends beyond the ownership and con-trol of the means of material production by exerting influence over the means of mental production. Public pronouncements ratifying the government's criminal justice apparatus, for instance, are mental products transmitted in line with the imperatives of the dominant ideology (see Gramsci, 1971; Lar-rain, 1983; Marx, 1978; Sahin, 1980).

This research discovered considerable evidence of the politicization of punishment and criminal justice agenda setting. Emulating the hierarchy of state managers, political and government leaders were quoted considerably more often on correctional issues than any other news source, even correc-tions officials and prison managers. Our findings suggest that media dis-course on corrections provides additional opportunities for high-ranking government figures to institutionalize their authoritative position (Becker, 1967, 1973; Chermak, 1997; Hall et al., 1978). In our sample, government sources pronounced repeatedly their agenda to expand the correctional sys-tem and to harshen the nature of incarceration, both of which are prominent features of coercive social control. Whereas political posturing on corrections serves to cultivate public support for criminal justice policy, it also functions to legitimize state power through the distribution of punishment (Foucault, 1979; Welch, 1999). By serving as primary news sources, politicians and gov-ernment officials benefit ideologically, insofar as they determine what is *socially thinkable* about crime and criminal justice; likewise, they also gain materially by promoting their institutional goals and needs (e.g., increased spending on prison construction, maintenance, resources, and personnel) (see Chermak, 1994, 1997; Fishman, 1978; Hall et al., 1978; Humphries, 1981; Kappeler & Potter, 2005; Kasinsky, 1994; Surette, 1992; Tunnell, 1992).

The politicization of punishment and criminal justice agenda setting in the media have significant implications to correctional policy and practice. The correctional debate presented in the *New York Times*, whose motto is "All the news that's fit to print," concentrates heavily on issues of institutional vio-lence and correctional programs. To a lesser degree, the *New York Times* addresses prison health care, get-tough policies, and privatization/corrections as industry, while neglecting other important correctional issues (e.g., capital punishment, juveniles, and female prisoners). More to the point of agenda setting, which influences correctional policies, those selected issues are intro-duced more often from the viewpoint of politicians and government officials whose perspectives determine the fate of policy and the flow of funding.

The phenomenon of agenda setting in corrections is highly relevant to criminal justice research, especially considering that popular notions about crime and criminal justice are constructed by the media, often according to the political views of government leaders. Criminal justice scholars entering the public debate over corrections should assess critically what is being reported in the media, remaining attentive to which issues are subject to discussion and which issues are ignored. Equally important, scholars should ascertain which groups serve as the dominant news sources and decipher their recommendations for correctional policy and practice. In doing so, it is crucial that scholars be mindful of the biases among news sources and confront the numerous myths and misconceptions shaping the government's correctional strategies.

In sum, our analysis of newspaper articles on corrections yields findings consistent with previous research documenting the media's dependence on government sources in manufacturing images of crime and criminal justice (Barak, 1994; Chermak, 1994, 1997; Ericson et al., 1987, 1989, 1991; Fishman, 1978; Hall et al., 1978; Humphries, 1981; Kasinsky, 1994; Surette, 1992; Welch, Fenwick, & Roberts, 1997, 1998). However, we also revealed that the press tends to include voices challenging the government's correctional strategies, suggesting perhaps a sense of pluralism. In fact, 38% of the sources (and their quotes) in our sample opposed the government's correctional policies and practices. Still, the degree of diversity evident in this study must be interpreted cautiously. Our examination of news sourcing was confined to the *New York Times*; as a result, the extent of pluralism in our findings may be unique to that newspaper. Additional research is needed to determine whether these findings are representative of other newspapers and media outlets. Despite these limitations, our investigation contributes further to a critical understanding of the social construction of crime news by offering an analysis of corrections: a vital component of criminal justice, though widely neglected by media researchers.

Notes

[1] In keeping to our task of evaluating the relative balance of press coverage on corrections in the United States, we eliminated articles on international corrections ($n = 23$), leaving 206 articles in the sample.

[2] Newspaper articles on drug and alcohol treatment were assigned to the previous section on programs.

References

Abercrombie, N., Hill, S., & Turner, B. S. (1980). *The dominant ideology thesis.* London: Allen and Unwin.

Alabama to make prisoners break rocks. (1995, July 29). The *New York Times*, p. A5.

Barak, G. (1988). Newsmaking criminology: Reflections on the media, intellectuals, and crime. *Justice Quarterly, 5*(4), 565–587.

Barak, G. (1994). *Media, process, and the social construction of crime.* New York: Garland.

Becker, H. S. (1967). Whose side are we on? *Social Problems, 14,* 239–247.

Becker, H. S. (1973). *Outsiders: Studies in the sociology of deviance.* New York: Free Press.

Berk, R. (1994, January). G.O.P. sees crime as a major issue. The *New York Times*, p. A9.

California governor expected to back life terms for repeated felons. (1994, March). *The New York Times*, p. A16.

Chermak, S. (1994). Crime in the news media: A refined understanding of how crimes become news. In G. Barak (Ed.), *Media, process, and the social construction of crime* (pp. 95–130). New York: Garland.

Chermak, S. (1997). The presentation of drugs in the news media: The news sources involved in the construction of social problems. *Justice Quarterly, 14*(4), 687–718.

Clear, T. R. (1994). *Harm in American penology: Offenders, victims, and their communities.* Albany: State University of New York Press.

Clines, F. X. (1994, November 17). Rikers is tense as cuts loom, and official warns of crisis. *The New York Times*, pp. B1, B8.

Cullen, F. T., Cullen, J. B., & Wozniak, J. F. (1988). Is rehabilitation dead? The myth of the punitive public. *Journal of Criminal Justice, 16*, 303–317.

Detroit Free Press. (1998). 100 largest U.S. newspapers [Online]. Available: http://www.fieep. com/jobspage/links/top100.htm

Ericson, R. V., Baranek, P. M., & Chan, J. B. L. (1987). *Visualizing deviance: A study of news organizations.* Toronto, Canada: University of Toronto Press.

Ericson, R. V., Baranek, P. M., & Chan, J. B. L. (1989). *Negotiating control: A study of news sources.* Toronto, Canada: University of Toronto Press.

Ericson, R. V., Baranek, P. M., & Chan, J. B. L. (1991). *Representing order: Crime, law, and justice in the news media.* Toronto, Canada: University of Toronto Press.

Fishman, M. (1978). Crime waves as ideology. *Social Problems, 25*, 531–543.

Flanagan, T. J. (1996). Reform or punish: Americans' views of the correctional system. In T. J. Flanagan & D. R. Longmire (Eds.), *Americans view crime and justice: A national public opinion survey* (pp. 75–92). Thousand Oaks, CA: Sage.

Foucault, M. (1979). *Discipline and punish: The birth of the prison.* New York: Vintage.

Garland, D. (1990). *Punishment and modern society: A study in social theory.* Chicago: University of Chicago Press.

Gramsci, A. (1971). *Selections from the prison notebooks.* New York: International.

Greenhouse, L. (1993, June 19). Court offers inmates a way to escape prison smokers. *The New York Times*, p. A8.

Hall, S., Critcher, C., Jefferson, T., Clarke, J., & Roberts, B. (1978). *Policing the crisis: Mugging, the state and law and order.* New York: Holmes and Meiser.

Hanley, R. (1992, August 30). Fort Dix may become federal prison. *The New York Times*, p. 33.

Helling v. McKinney, 61 U.S. LW 3445 (1992).

Herman, E. H., & Chomsky, N. (1988). *Manufacturing consent: The political economy of the mass media.* New York: Pantheon.

Holmes, S. A. (1994, November 6). The boom in jails is locking up lots of loot. *The New York Times*, p. 3.

Humphries, D. (1981). Serious crime, news coverage, and ideology. *Crime and Delinquency, 27*, 191–205.

Jameson, F. (1991). *Postmodernism or the cultural logic of late capitalism.* Durham, NC: Duke University Press.

Kappeler, V. E., & Potter, G. W. (2005). *The mythology of crime and criminal justice* (4th ed.). Long Grove, IL: Waveland Press.

Kasinsky, R. G. (1994). Patrolling the facts: Media, cops, and crime. In G. Barak (Ed.), *Media, process, and the social construction of crime* (pp. 203–236). New York: Garland.

Kidd-Hewitt, D., & Osborne, R. (1995). *Crime and the media: The postmodern spectacle.* East Haven, CT: Pluto.

Koppes, C., & Black, G. (1987). *Hollywood goes to war: How politics, profits, and propaganda shaped the World War II movies.* New York: Free Press.

Larrain, J. (1983). *Marxism and ideology.* London: The Macmillan Press.

Levy, C. (1995, December 12). Pataki proposes a ban on parole in violent crimes. The *New York Times,* pp. A1, B6.

Maguire, K., & Pastore, A. L. (1995). *Sourcebook of criminal justice statistics 1994.* Washington, DC: U.S. Department of Justice, Bureau of Justice Statistics, U.S. Government Printing Office.

Maguire, K., & Pastore, A. L. (1996). *Sourcebook of criminal justice statistics 1995.* Washington, DC: U.S. Department of Justice, Bureau of Justice Statistics. U.S. Government Printing Office.

Marsh, H. L. (1989, September). Newspaper crime coverage in the U.S.: 1893–1988. *Criminal Justice Abstracts,* pp. 506–514.

Marsh, H. L. (1991). A comparative analysis of crime coverage in newspapers in the United States and other countries from 1960–1989: A review of the literature. *Journal of Criminal Justice, 19,* 67–79.

Marx, K. (1978). The German ideology. In R. D. Tucker (Ed.), *The Marx Engels reader* (2nd ed., pp. 146–200). New York: Norton.

Mydans, S. (1995, March 4). Taking no prisoners, in a manner of speaking. The *New York Times,* p. A6.

Residents of dying California town see future in a prison. (1994, May 8). The *New York Times,* p. 28.

Sahin, H. (1980). The concept of ideology and mass communication. *Journal of Communication Inquiry, 61,* 3–12.

Simon, J. (1995). They died with their boots on: The boot camp and the limits of modern penality. *Social Justice, 22*(2), 25–48.

Stauth, G., & Turner, B. S. (1988). Nostalgia, postmodernism, and the critique of mass culture. *Theory, Culture, and Society, 52–53,* 509–526.

Sullivan, R. (1992, August 26). Ex-inmate wins award in bias case: Woman with AIDS granted $155,000. The *New York Times,* p. B4.

Sullivan, R. (1994, December 20). 7 stabbings and 5 others hurt in Rikers clash. *New York Times,* p. B3.

Surette, R. (1992). *Media, crime & criminal justice: Images and realities.* Pacific Grove, CA: Brooks/Cole.

Terry, D. (1993, January 3). Town builds a prison and stores its hope there. The *New York Times,* p. 1.

Tunnell, K. (1992). Film at eleven: Recent developments in the commodification of crime. *Sociological Spectrum, 12,* 293–313.

Van Natta, D. (1995, August 12). Despite setbacks, a boom in private prison business. The *New York Times,* p. A24.

Welch, M. (1995). Rehabilitation: Holding its ground in corrections. *Federal Probation: A Journal of Correctional Philosophy and Practice, 59*(4), 3–8.

Welch, M. (1996). *Corrections: A critical approach.* New York: McGraw-Hill.

Welch, M. (1997a). A critical interpretation of correctional boot camps as normalizing institutions: Discipline, punishment, and the military model. *Journal of Contemporary Criminal Justice, 13*(2), 184–205.

Welch, M. (1997b). The war on drugs and its impact on corrections: Exploring alternative strategies to America's drug crisis. *Journal of Offender and Rehabilitation, 25*(1–2), 43–60.

Welch, M. (1999). *Punishment in America: Social control and the ironies of imprisonment.* Thousand Oaks, CA: Sage.

Welch, M., Fenwick, M., & Roberts, M. (1997). Primary definitions of crime and moral panic: A content analysis of experts' quotes in feature newspaper articles on crime. *Journal of Research in Crime and Delinquency, 34*(4), 474–494.

Welch, M., Fenwick, M., & Roberts, M. (1998). State managers, intellectuals, and the media: A content analysis of ideology in experts' quotes in featured newspaper articles on crime. *Justice Quarterly, 15*(2), 219–241.

Welsh, W., Leone, M. C., Kinkade, P., & Pontell, H. (1991). The politics of jail overcrowding: Public attitudes and official policies. In J. Thompson & G. L. Mays (Eds.), *American jails: Public policy issues* (pp. 131–147). Chicago: Nelson-Hall.

Wilkins, L. T. (1991). *Punishment, crime and market forces.* Brookfield, VT: Dartmouth.

SEVENTEEN

DOMINANT IDEOLOGY AND DRUGS IN THE MEDIA

Craig Reinarman & Ceres Duskin

"Jimmy is 8 years old and a third-generation heroin addict, a precious little boy with sandy hair, velvety brown eyes and needle marks freckling the baby smooth skin of his thin brown arms."

So began a front page feature in the *Washington Post* on Sunday, Sept. 28, 1980. The reporter, Janet Cooke, claimed that Jimmy had "been an addict since the age of five." She told of how Jimmy "doesn't usually go to school, preferring to instead to hang with older boys." When he did go, Cooke wrote, it was "to learn more about his favorite subject—math," which he planned to use in his drug dealing career. She noted the "cherubic expression" on Jimmy's face when he spoke about "hard drugs, fast money and the good life he believes both can bring." He sported "fancy running shoes" and an "Izod shirt." "Bad, ain't it, I got me six of these," the child reportedly told Cooke.

She described Jimmy's house in detail. There were addicts "casually" buying heroin everyday from Ron, Jimmy's mother's "live-in-lover," cooking it and then "firing up" in the bedrooms. "People of all shapes and sizes," a "human collage" including teenagers, "drift into the dwelling . . . some jittery, uptight and anxious for a fix, others calm and serene after they finally 'get off.'" These things were, Cooke wrote, "normal occurrences in Jimmy's world."

"And every day, Ron or someone else fires up Jimmy, plunging a needle into his bony arm, sending the fourth grader into a hypnotic nod." Cooke then quoted Ron on how he first "turned Jimmy on": "He'd been buggin' me all the time about what the shots were and what people was doin' and one day he said, 'When can I get off?'" She described Ron as "leaning against the wall in a narcotic haze, his eyes half-closed, yet piercing," and quoted him as answering Jimmy, "'Well, s—, you can have some now.' I let him snort a little and, damn, the little dude really did get off."

Reprinted from *International Journal of Drug Policy*, vol. 3, no. 1, Craig Reinarman and Ceres Duskin, Dominant Ideology and Drugs in the Media, pp. 6–15, 1992 with permission from Elsevier.

"Six months later," Cooke wrote, the 5-year-old "was hooked." She quoted the boy as saying, "I felt like I was part of what was goin' down. . . . It (heroin) be real different from herb (marijuana). That's baby s——."

Cooke also quoted Jimmy's mother: "I don't really like to see him fire up. But, you know, I think he would have got into it one day, anyway. Everybody does. When you live in the ghetto, it's all a matter of survival. . . . Drugs and black folk been together for a very long time."

The mother had been routinely raped, Cooke wrote, by her mother's boyfriend, one such instance leading to Jimmy's birth and then to heroin use to blot out her growing pain. When her drug sources dried up after a bust, she turned to prostitution to support further heroin use. Cooke quoted the mother as saying that she wasn't alarmed by her son's dealing ambitions "because drugs are as much a part of her world as they are of her son's."

Cooke made the more general point that heroin use had "become part of life" among people in poor neighborhoods people who "feel cut off from the world around them"—often "filtering down to untold numbers of children like Jimmy who are bored with school and battered by life." Many kids "no older than 10," Cooke claimed, could "relate with uncanny accuracy" dealer names and drug nomenclature.

Cooke's story then offered a familiar litany of quotes to bolster and contextualize her story. Drug Enforcement Agency officials noted the influx of "Golden Crescent heroin." Local medical experts spoke of the "epidemic" of heroin deaths in Washington. Social workers observed how the lack of "male authority figures" and peer pressure combine to make such childhood tragedies common.

"At the end of an evening of strange questions about his life," Cooke concluded, "the calm and self-assured little man recedes" to reveal a "jittery and ill-behaved boy" who was "going into withdrawal." Ron then left the room, according to Cooke, and returned with "syringe in hand, and calls the little boy over to his chair." He grabbed Jimmy's "left arm just above the elbow, his massive hand tightly encircling the child's small limb. The needle slides into the boy's soft skin like a straw pushed into the center of a freshly baked cake. Liquid ebbs out of the syringe, replaced by bright red blood. The blood is then re-injected into the child." The final scene in Cooke's drama depicted little Jimmy "looking quickly around the room" and climbing into a rocking chair, "his head dipping and snapping upright again in what addicts call 'the nod.'"

The Story Becomes the Story

The Washington Post is not prepared to identify
young Jimmy; Mayor Barry orders a city-wide search.

Two days after Cooke's story appeared, the *Washington Post* ran a fascinating follow-up article entitled, "D.C. Authorities Seek Identity of Heroin Addict, 8." Such a tragic tale of young life lost to drugs, so compellingly conveyed by Cooke and so prominently published by the *Post*, led to hundreds of outraged calls and letters to the paper and to local officials.

The then Mayor Marion Barry was "incensed" by the story and assigned a task force of hundreds of police and social workers to find Jimmy. It was later learned that the police intensively combed the city for nearly three weeks. Teachers throughout Washington checked the arms of thousands of young students for needle marks. Citizens from housing projects called in offering to help. A $10,000 reward was offered. The police, supported by the mayor and the U.S. Attorney, threatened to subpoena Cooke in an effort to find and "save" the boy. The *Post* refused to identify Jimmy, citing First Amendment rights to protect confidential sources (*New York Times,* 4/16/81, p. Al).

The *Post* assigned an 11-member reporting team to cover all this, six of whom were told to search for another Jimmy, "on the theory that if there is one, there must be others" (Green, 1981:A13). Cooke and one of her editors searched for Jimmy's house for seven hours. For some unexplained reason, they never found it. Neither the police nor anyone else found Jimmy either. And, neither the other *Post* reporters nor anyone else ever found any other child addict.

Meanwhile, *Post* publisher Donald Graham congratulated Cooke. Bob Woodward, a senior editor who eight years earlier had broken the Watergate scandal, promoted her. The *Post* went on with its normal coverage of drug issues.

Six months later, on April 13, 1981, "Jimmy's World" resurfaced in a ceremony at Columbia University in New York, where it was announced that Janet Cooke had won the Pulitzer Prize in Feature Writing for her story. The next day, the *Post* published a piece proudly announcing Cooke's prize and reprinted "Jimmy's World" in honor of the occasion. The story noted that "Jimmy's World" had first met with shock and disbelief. But despite the fact that none of the massive follow-up efforts had ever turned up Jimmy, or anyone like him, the *Post* asserted that experts had confirmed the fact that heroin addicts of Jimmy's age were common.

For any American reporter, winning a Pulitzer—the journalist's equivalent of a Nobel Prize—is as good as it gets. Such prizes make careers, catapult people out of the grind of routine reportage into prestigious positions, often to fame and fortune. Journalism students fantasize about such feats. Competitive cub reporters across the country covet chances for front-page stories that might get noticed and nominated. Janet Cooke should have been ecstatic. As the world would soon learn, she wasn't.

Two days later, on April 16, the *Washington Post* published another front-page piece on "Jimmy's World":

> The Pulitzer Prize Committee withdrew its feature-writing prize from *Washington Post* reporter Janet Cooke yesterday after she admitted that her award-winning story was a fabrication. . . . It was said to be based on interviews with the boy, his mother and his mother's boyfriend. Cooke now acknowledges that she never met or interviewed any of those people and that she made up the story of Jimmy. . . .

The *Post* lead editorial that day, "The End of the 'Jimmy' Story," began with a phrase unusual for papers of the *Post*'s stature: "We apologize." It went on to say that "This newspaper, which printed Janet Cooke's false account of a meeting with an 8-year-old heroin addict and his family, was itself the victim of a hoax—which we then passed along in a prominent page-one story taking in the readers as we ourselves had been taken in. How could this have happened?"

To find out, Executive Editor Ben Bradley invited the *Post*'s ombudsman, Bill Green, to conduct an independent "full disclosure" investigation. Green learned that the *Post* had been running many more routine stories about drug problems in Washington, and that Cooke had been researching the local heroin problem for some time. She took extensive notes to City Editor Milton Coleman. In describing her material she mentioned in passing an 8-year-old addict. Recognizing the print media equivalent of "dramatic footage," Coleman stopped her right there and said, "That's the story. Go after it. It's a front-page story."

Green discovered that when Cooke followed Coleman's instructions she was unable to come up with the young addict. Coleman sent her back out to find him. Again she could not. A week later Cooke told him that she had found another 8-year-old addict, "Jimmy," by going to elementary school playgrounds and passing out her cards. She told her editor that one of her cards found its way to a mother, who called and angrily asked, "Why are you looking for my boy?"

Cooke then extracted promises of confidentiality for "Jimmy's" mother and told her editors that she had visited the child's home, according to Green's report. She soon turned in a 13-page draft of the story. She rendered the furnishings and other aspects of the home and "Jimmy's" life in such delicious detail, Green found, that no editor had ever asked for "Jimmy's" or his mother's identity. Editor Coleman later told Green that he went over the story carefully: "I wanted it to read like John Coltrane's music. Strong. It was a great story, and it never occurred to me that she could make it up. There was too much distance between Janet and the streets."[1]

Green came to feel that the *Post* had been blinded by its ambition for a dramatic feature and by the fine prose of a reporter who was black and thus assumed trustworthy on such matters. Editors dismissed doubts and decided to run "Jimmy's World." It was not until Cooke was awarded the Pulitzer that the story started to unravel. Even then, questions centered on her background, not her story.

The first clue emerged when Cooke's earlier employer, the *Toledo Blade*, wanted to run the prizewinning story. In setting up a sidebar on Cooke's Toledo roots, *Blade* editors discovered that the biographical information they had received over the Associated Press wire "did not jibe" with what they knew of Cooke's background. Her "official" resume—sent in by the *Post*, released by the Pulitzer Committee, and carried with the AP story—had Cooke graduating from Vassar magna cum laude, studying at the Sorbonne, earning a masters degree from the University of Toledo, speaking four languages, and winning half a dozen Ohio newspaper awards.[2] When the editors at the *Blade* called AP to check on the discrepancies, AP editors began to ask questions of their own. They discovered other discrepancies. No Sorbonne. No masters degree. They called Cooke. She asserted that her official resume was correct. AP knew at this point, according to ombudsman Green's report, that "something was wrong."

Prompted by the AP inquiry, Green discovered, the *Post*'s editors compared her personnel file and the Pulitzer biography form she filled out. After discovering that the two did not match in several respects, Bradley told Coleman to "take her to the woodshed." Coleman took Cooke for a walk and grilled her. Cooke eventually admitted she had not graduated from Vassar but continued to insist that everything else, especially the Jimmy story, was true.

Coleman phoned his superior with these answers, according to Green's report. Bradley told him to bring Cooke back to the *Post* via a side entrance "to avoid being conspicuous" and to sequester her in a vacant office three stories above the newsroom. Bradley came up and grilled her. He asked about the foreign language skills she had listed on her resume: "Say two words to me in Portuguese," Green quoted Bradley as saying. She couldn't. Her French wasn't much better. He asked about the journalism prizes. Her answers were inconclusive. Bradley said, "You're like Richard Nixon, you're trying to cover up."

In another office, Assistant Managing Editor Bob Woodward joined deputy Metro Editor David Maraniss, and another editor to go over the 145 pages of Cooke's notes and two hours of tape-recorded interviews. According to Green's report, they found "echoes" of the "Jimmy" story, but no evidence that she had actually spoken with a child addict.

Meanwhile, under pressure of intense questioning, Cooke gave Coleman what she claimed were the real names of Jimmy, his mother, and her boyfriend, as well as their address. Coleman and Cooke went there, but, as had been the case six months before, she somehow could not find the house. (Forgotten at this point in the investigation was the fact that in the immediate aftermath of her story, Cooke had been unable to find the house, returning the next day claiming to have found it but that the family had moved.)

It was nearly midnight when they got back to the *Post*. By this time, according to Green, each of the editors who had bought the story all along had become convinced that she was lying. Woodward then confronted Cooke: "It's all over. You've gotta come clean. The notes show us the story is wrong. We know it. We can show you point by point how you concocted it." Cooke continued to deny it. The more Woodward yelled, the more stubbornly she stuck to her story.

Exhausted from failed interrogations, they left Cooke in the room with only her closest colleague, Maraniss. Cooke knew that he knew, according to Green. They talked quietly for an hour about how tough it was to succeed at a national newspaper (Bradley called it "major-league journalism" or "hardball") and how far they had come. After she had tiptoed all around a confession, Maraniss gently pushed Cooke by asking her what he should tell the others.

She broke down. "Jimmy's World" was, she finally admitted, "a fabrication." "There was no Jimmy and no family. . . . I want to give the prize back," Green quoted her as saying. Maraniss told the others. Bradley asked him to get a written admission and a resignation. Cooke complied.

The Lessons Learned

Where does the blame lie: breakdown in editorial procedure,
pathological ambition or systematic prejudice?

The ombudsman's report (Green, 1981) was the second longest article ever published in the *Post*. Its conclusions were that warning signals were ignored, that senior editors were uninformed, that competition for prizes had pushed an ambitious young reporter too hard, and that the result was "a temporary lapse." The majority of the *Post* editors and reporters interviewed agreed, interpreting this lapse in terms of ambition and competition.

The *Post* editorial accompanying the first admission of the fraud framed the whole affair in terms of the breakdown of normal journalistic editing procedures—"quality control," Green later dubbed it. The writers thus implied that this was the ultimate cause of the fraud and expressed the hope that it would be seen as the aberration it was, thereby leaving intact the *Post*'s "prized credibility" (*Washington Post*, 4/16/81).

Other newspapers, of course, closely covered the scandal and offered similar interpretations. The *San Francisco Chronicle* (4/19/81) blamed the *Post* editors for trusting their reporters too much. The *Los Angeles Times* (4/19/81) blamed the fraud on the growing use of unnamed sources, a practice it claimed arose during the Vietnam and Watergate debacles. A few days later an *L.A. Times* columnist went further to opine that the lesson of the Cooke fraud was that the Watergate-era spirit of "gung-ho press investigators" needed to be reversed (4/23/81).

According to the *New York Times* (4/23/81, p. 16), the 600 editors who attended the annual convention of the American Society of Newspaper Editors a week after the scandal broke talked of little else. They expressed a variety of concerns about the "loss of credibility for all newspapers." But almost all supported the ombudsman's principal conclusions that the scandal stemmed from "internal pressures" to "produce sensational articles and to win prizes" and from the failure to use the editing and checking "system that should have detected the fraud." Some editors added that the scandal had "forced them to re-examine" the procedures for checking the background of new reporters and the use of unidentified sources.

The *Post* itself (4/18/81, p. A3) published a summary of what other papers said about the Cooke affair. The core themes were the same: failure to check confidential sources and the risks of putting sensationalism above editorial judgment. The *Post* story also quoted a *Wall Street Journal* piece which asked whether in all of these investigations "the hard questions" would be raised, but did not say what those questions were. The *Post*'s summary closed with a *Chicago Tribune* editor's rotten apple theory—like many others, he blamed the whole affair on "one highly unethical person."

Strangely, none of these accounts mentioned anything about the media's general assumptions and beliefs about drugs and drug users, which ultimately allowed Cooke's concoction to slip into print. For us, this is the hardest question, and it was neither asked nor answered in any of the press post mortems.

What of the Pulitzer Prize jury? Surely if the *Post*'s editors could suffer a "temporary lapse," at least one of the esteemed editors and journalists selected to serve on the prestigious Pulitzer jury should have detected some flaw in Cooke's story. As it turns out, a few of the jurors were concerned. One questioned Cooke's guarantee of confidentiality when a child's life seemed at stake. A second was troubled by the lack of attribution, but accepted Cooke's piece "on faith" because "it had gone through the editing process on a reputable newspaper." A third overcame her doubts because she felt the article "spoke to a very compelling problem of our time. We did not suspect that it was not what it seemed to be. *We had no reason to*" (*Washington Post*, 4/17/81, p.9; emphasis added).

Still other jurors expressed doubts after the fact, but these centered largely on the unusual procedure by which Cooke's article had won. The *Post* had submitted it in the "general local reporting" category. The local reporting jury picked "Jimmy's World" second. The Pulitzer Board agreed with the jury, awarding that prize to another reporter. However, several Board members felt that the Cooke piece belonged in the feature category. After discussion, board member Joseph Pulitzer suggested that it be re-considered later in that category (Green, 1981).

Meanwhile, the jury for the feature-writing prize had selected three finalists and submitted them to the Board. None had ever seen the Cooke article. When the Board discussed overruling the jury in favor of "Jimmy's World," some members raised the familiar questions about the article. Their opposition "evaporated," however, when one member, distinguished African-American journalist Roger Wilkins, "eloquently" argued "that he could easily find child addicts within 10 blocks" of where the Board was meeting at Columbia University (*Washington Post,* 4/17/81, p. 9). Just as no one at the *Post* had challenged an articulate African-American reporter six months earlier, no juror challenged Wilkins' assertions about addiction in the inner city. Whatever questions they may have had about "Jimmy's World" were dropped. The Board overruled the jury and unanimously awarded Janet Cooke the Pulitzer Prize in feature writing.[3]

The Lessons Not Learned

What happens to the editorial 'crap detector' when
newspaper editors are confronted with a drug story?

In all of this, no one ever turned up any concrete evidence that a child addict such as "Jimmy" existed. It is, of course, statistically possible that America's inner cities may somewhere contain a few 8-year-old addicts whose mothers' boyfriends shoot them full of heroin every day. But it is a virtual certainty that if such child addicts exist at all they are exceedingly rare. So for us, the most curious part of the Cooke scandal is that in the ensuing decade and throughout the dozens of press accounts we analyzed, no one has yet critically examined the underlying ideology that allowed her bizarre claim that such child addicts are common to pass unnoticed into publication and on to a Pulitzer.

No one doubts that Janet Cooke was a talented writer. No one disputes that the "Jimmy" story was compelling. And certainly no one questions that tragic drug problems persist across the USA, particularly in inner cities. Was it not reasonable, then, for the *Post*'s editors to have been "taken in," and for even the prestigious Pulitzer jury to have become "victims of a hoax"? Who could have seen through a fraud perpetrated by an otherwise fine reporter whose pathological ambition led her to such thorough deceit?

We wish to suggest that the "Jimmy" story was, in fact, rather unreasonable on its face, and that the media would not have been "taken in" by it had they not been blinded by bias. We think that the *Post* editors and Pulitzer jurors—and virtually all the others in the news business who interpreted the scandal—*missed the point.*

The "hoax" to which the American media became "victim" was one they played a central role in making. Drug scares have been a recurring feature of American history. From the early nineteenth century until Prohibition passed in 1919, many in the press were willing handmaidens to the zealous moral entrepreneurs in the Temperance crusade. Newspapers and magazines often uncritically repeated wild claims that alcohol was the direct cause of most of the crime, insanity, poverty, divorce, "illegitimacy," business failure, and virtually all other social problems afflicting America at the time of its industrialization (Levine, 1984).

Throughout the twentieth century the media helped foment a series of drug scares, each magnifying drug menaces well beyond their objective dimensions. From the turn of the century into the 1920s, the yellow journalism of the Hearst newspapers, for example, offered a steady stream of ruin and redemption melodramas. These depicted one or another chemical villain, typically in the hands of a "dangerous class" or racial minority, as responsible for the end of Western civilization (see Musto, 1973; Mark, 1975; Morgan, 1978). In the 1930s, newspapers repeated unsubstantiated claims that marijuana, "the killer weed," led users, Mexicans in particular, to violence (Becker, 1963). In the 1950s, the media spread a story of two teenagers in Colorado who had gotten high accidentally by inhaling model airplane glue. This led to nationwide hysteria, which in turn spread the practice of glue-sniffing (Brecher, 1972).

In the 1960s, the press somehow re-made "killer weed" into "the drop-out drug" (Himmelstein, 1983), and spread other misleading reports that LSD broke chromosomes and yielded two-headed babies (Becker, 1967; Well, 1972). The media that might have served as a source of credible warnings about the risks of drug abuse were dismissed with derision by the very users they needed to reach. In the 1970s, the press again falsely reported that "angel dust" or PCP gave users such superhuman strength that the police needed new stun guns to subdue them (Feldman et al., 1979). In 1986, the press and politicians once again joined forces on crack use among the black underclass. The drug was unknown outside of a few neighborhoods in a few cities until newspapers, magazines, and TV networks blanketed the nation with horror stories that described the crack high (Reinarman and Levine, 1989).

In each of these drug scares the media has consistently erred on the side of the sensational and dutifully repeated the self-serving scare stories of politicians in search of safe issues on which to take strong stands. And in each scare, including the current "war on drugs," reporters and editors have engaged in the *routinization of caricature*—rhetorically recrafting worst cases into typical cases, and profoundly distorting the nature of drug problems in the interest of dramatic stories.

A century from now historians may ponder this construction of drug demons just as they now ponder the burning of witches and heretics.[4] But what is already clear is that a century's worth of scapegoating chemical bogeymen left even the very best journalists quite prepared to believe the very worst about drug users, especially inner-city addicts. Given such a deep structure of bias prevailing within media institutions, it is little wonder that Janet Cooke's story elicited so little of the press's vaunted skepticism.

Thus, her immediate editor Milton Coleman told the *Post*'s investigating ombudsman that he "had no doubts" about "Jimmy's World" and that "it never occurred to me that she could make it up." Assistant managing editor and former Pulitzer winner Bob Woodward admitted similarly that "my skepticism left me," that his "alarm bells simply did not go off," and that "we never really debated whether or not it was true." The few doubts of the distinguished Pulitzer jury were washed away when one black voice asserted that "Jimmys" were everywhere in the ghetto. Even after the scandal broke wide open, ombudsman Green's thoroughly detailed report never really asked *why,* as he put it, "None of the *Post*'s senior editors subjected Cooke's story to close questioning."

These things were possible, we contend, precisely because America's guardians of truth had no touchstone of truth on drug problems apart from their own scare stories. In this the *Washington Post* was no worse than most media institutions in the USA. When seen as part of the historical pattern of news "coverage" of drug issues, the Pulitzer Prize-winning fraud was less a "lapse" than part of a long tradition. On almost any other subject, editors' "crap detectors" would have signaled that something was amiss.

The evidence for this contention oozed from every pore of Cooke's tale and was bolstered at every turn in the follow-up investigations. First, there were the shaky assumptions about addiction. Cooke alleged that "Jimmy" was "addicted" to heroin at age 5 and that he smoked marijuana before that. Children are curious creatures, so it is theoretically possible that a 4- to 5-year-old might push himself to learn to inhale foul-tasting smoke and hold it deep in his lungs repeatedly. It is even possible, although even less likely, that a 5-year-old could learn to enjoy snorting heroin powder into his nostrils day after day. What is hardly possible and highly unlikely is that a 5-year-old would ask to have a needle stuck into his "thin brown arms" more than once a day for the weeks it would take him to become addicted. One needn't be a drug expert for such claims to set off "alarm bells," one need only have seen a doctor try to vaccinate a child.

All this aside, if any journalists had checked, they would have found that most heroin users experience serious nausea the first few times they use. In addition to the difficulties posed by needles and nausea, a mildly skeptical editor easily could have discovered that drug effects are rarely unambiguously pleasurable early on. Drug "highs" are in many important respects acquired tastes that are teamed over time through processes that 5- or 8-year-olds are exceedingly unlikely to endure (Becker, 1953; Zinberg, 1984). Yet, after all of journalism had put this story-scandal under its microscopes, no one had even asked about such things.

Cooke's fiction contained a second set of what Green called "red flags," which had to do with assumptions about addicts. How moronic could addicts have to be (even crass "junkie" stereotypes depict them as shrewd) to allow a reporter from a top newspaper to witness them "firing up"? Even if criminalization had not made paranoia an occupational hazard of addicts, there is no evidence that they are proud of their habits. And in a home Cooke herself described as a dealing den and shooting gallery full of other addicts, no known drug is capable of inducing the magnitude of stupidity necessary for an adult addict to show a reporter how they inject heroin into their small child.

Let us leave this aside, too, and examine a third set of red flags. Neither *Post* editors nor Pulitzer jurors nor any of the other editors who both reprinted Cooke's article and later dissected the scandal ever seemed to question Cooke's claims that "Ron" routinely injected "Jimmy" and that his "mother" tacitly approved of this. Not even the tallest tales of Temperance crusaders gave us such villainous villains. What sort of people would knowingly and repeatedly inject heroin into a child that they clothed, fed and bathed?

There is nothing in the scientific literature to suggest that addicts recommend addiction to anyone, much less their own kids. The media apparently knew so little about heroin they could simply assume it induced depravity and transformed users into the sort of vile subhumans who think nothing of doing such things. Thus the media smuggled into their stories a simplistic sort of pharmacological determinism. Clearly heroin can be powerfully addicting, but even if it were capable of morally lobotomizing all addicts, why would such addicts give away the very expensive stuff for which they reputedly lie, cheat, and steal?[5]

Almost any street junkie could have served as an expert informant (a "Deep Throat," if you will) and saved the *Post* from scandal. If the editors had picked ten addicts at random and asked them if a junkie would give away precious junk to a child, nine would have thought it absurd, moral qualms aside. Asked to read the Cooke story, most addicts could have told the *Post* immediately that is was concocted. Even if one accepted all of the other demonstrably dubious assumptions upon which the story rested, it made no sense even according to the perverse logic attributed to addicts.

A final set of red flags shot up immediately after "Jimmy's World" was published. According to the *Post*'s own follow-up stories, hundreds of police officers and social workers scoured the city looking for "Jimmy." Elementary school teachers inspected thousands of small student arms. Aroused citizens from housing projects in neighborhoods like "Jimmy's" all over Washington hunted for him. As Green's (1981) report put it, "The intense police search continued for 17 days. The city had been finely combed. Nothing." Half a dozen *Post* reporters also searched in vain for any other child addict. Our point here is not merely that none of these myriad searches turned up so much as a clue as to "Jimmy's" specific whereabouts. More significant is that with everyone so certain that "untold numbers of children like Jimmy" existed, no one found any child addict—not an 8-year-old, not a 10-year-old, not a 12-year-old.

For some reason these journalistic findings were not considered newsworthy. Presented with the choice of publishing the recalcitrant facts uncovered by their reporters or what they wanted to believe, *Post* editors and their print brethren chose to print the more ideologically compliant assertion that 8-year-old heroin addicts are common in America's inner cities. The Cooke affair thus suggests that the *Post* had more in common with President Reagan than it liked to believe. Reagan was fond, for example, of attacking "welfare chiselers" for buying vodka with their food stamps. No matter how many times his own experts told him this was untrue due to food-stamp redemption rules, he continued to tell the tale because it suited his ideological purposes. Lies uttered as political demagogy are one thing, but we expect more from the great newspapers on which we rely to expose such lies. In continuing to insist that "Jimmys" were everywhere in the face of their own evidence to the contrary, the *Post* seemed to be saying, â la Reagan, that if "Jimmy's World" doesn't exist in reality, then it can be made to exist in ideology.

Unfortunately, the nonfictional lives of African Americans in our inner cities and of growing numbers of other poor Americans are sufficiently harsh that some of them seek solace, comfort and meaning in drugs. But editors seem to believe that readers don't like to be reminded that there is something fundamentally wrong with the social system from which most of them benefit. Editors and readers alike, it seems, feel more comfortable believing that the worsening horrors of our inner cities are caused by evil individuals from a different gene pool—"addicts." Thus, a story about how crushing poverty and racism give rise to despair that sometimes leads to drug use, abuse or addiction is not considered "newsworthy." Stories that simply depict addicts as complicated, troubled human beings would be neither comforting enough for readers nor dramatic enough for prizes. To us, this sin of omission is more the real pity of this story than Janet Cooke's sin of commission.

About a week after the story first appeared and months before the scandal broke, *Post* publisher Donald Graham sent Cooke a congratulatory note on her "very fine story" (Green, 1981). It said, in part, that "The *Post* has no more important and tougher job than explaining life in the black community in Washington." Here he was as close to the ideal of journalism as Cooke's tale was distant from it.

Graham went on to praise the struggle of "black reporters who try to see life through their own eyes instead of seeing it the way they're told they should." In calling attention to the importance of independent reporting, Graham again articulated an important ideal. Ironically, Cooke had so internalized the way reporters in general "are told they should" see drug users that she gave a whole new meaning to the idea of seeing things through her "own eyes."

Finally, Graham wrote of how Cooke's article displayed the "gift" of "explaining" how the world works. "If there's any long-term justification for what we do," he wrote, it is that "people will act a bit differently and think a bit differently if we help them understand the world even slightly better. Much of what we write fails that first test because we don't understand what we're writing about ourselves." Here Graham displayed unintended prescience. For what he took to be a grand exception turned out to be a glaring example of his rule.

Cooke's concoction led readers to misunderstand the lives of addicts "in the black community." But hers was only an egregious case of the press's cultivated incapacity for understanding drug problems. If the *Post* scandal has value, it inheres in the accidental glimpse it affords into the nominally hidden process by which media institutions force the untidy facts of social life through the sieve of dominant ideology (Molotch and Lester, 1974). We submit that it is this process that allowed Cooke's tale to sail undetected past *Post* editors, Pulitzer jurors, and the hundreds of other journalists who analyzed the fraud. And we suggest that this process continues to camouflage the ways our world produces drug problems in the first place, and thereby helps to forge a public prepared to swallow the next junkie stereotype and to enlist in the next drug war.

Notes

[1] By all accounts in Ombudsman Green's investigation, Janet Cooke was not street-wise. She was middle-class and upwardly mobile. Her immediate supervisor told Green that Cooke "was not really street-savvy—she was Gucci and Cardin and Yves St. Laurent—she didn't know the kinds of people she was dealing with, but she was tenacious and talented" (Green, 1981:A12).

2 The Vassar degree had caught Editor-in-Chief Ben Bradley's eye, causing him to sift Cooke's resume from the hundreds he receives each week and to set in motion the hiring process which brought her to the *Post* (Green, 1981:A12).

3 The Pulitzer Board drew its own lesson from the Cooke scandal. Seven months later it adopted new procedures to guard against such problems. Pulitzer juries would henceforth deliberate for two days instead of one *(New York Times,* 11/22/91).

4 The authors are indebted to Dr. Peter Cohen for the analogy to witches and heretics. Personal communication, 1991.

5 To be fair, we did find one article *(New York Times,* 4/16/81) that at least mentioned the idea that addicts might not want to give away their heroin, but this lead was not pursued. Also, Mayor Marion Barry told the *Post* after the city-wide search that he doubted "the mother or the pusher would allow a reporter to see them shoot up" (Green, 1981:A13).

References

Becker, Howard S. 1953. Becoming a marijuana user. *American Journal of Sociology,* 59:235–43.

Becker, Howard S. 1963. *Outsiders: Studies in the Sociology of Deviance.* New York: Free Press.

Becker, Howard S. 1967. History, culture, and subjective experience: An exploration of the social bases of drug-induced experiences. *Journal of Health and Social Behavior,* 8:162–76.

Brecher, Edward M. 1972. *Licit and Illicit Drugs.* Boston, MA: Little, Brown.

Cooke, Janet. 1980. Jimmy's World—8-year-old heroin addict lives for a fix. *Washington Post,* Sept. 28, A1.

Feldman, Harvey, Michael Agar, and George Beschener. 1979. *Angel Dust.* Lexington, MA: D.C. Heath.

Green, Bill. 1981. Janet's world—The story of a child who never existed—How and why it came to be published. *Washington Post,* April 19, Al.

Himmelstein, Jerome. 1983. *The Strange Career of Marihuana.* Westport, CT: Greenwood Press.

Levine, Harry Gene. 1984. The alcohol problem in America: From temperance to Prohibition. *British Journal of Addiction,* 79:109–19.

Los Angeles Times. 1981. Story that was fabricated found a friend on Pulitzer board. April 17, I, 9.

Los Angeles Times. 1981. A matter of confidence. April 19, IV, 5.

Los Angeles Times. 1981. Finally, the Watergate spirit is dead in America. April 23, II, 11.

Los Angeles Times. 1981. Pulitzer fiasco's ripples spread too far. April 24, II, 1.

Mark, Gregory. 1975. Racial, economic, and political factors in the development of America's first drug laws. *Issues in Criminology,* 10:56–75.

Molotch, Harvey and Marilyn Lester. 1974. News as purposive behavior: On the strategic uses of routine events, accidents, and scandals. *American Sociological Review,* 39:101–12.

Morgan, Patricia. 1978. The legislation of drug law. *Journal of Drug Issues,* 8:53–62.

Musto, David. 1973. *The American Disease: Origins of Narcotic Control.* New Haven, CT: Yale University Press.

New York Times. 1981. *Washington Post* gives up Pulitzer, calling article on addict, 8, fiction. April 16 A1.

New York Times. 1981. Paper's false article is a major topic at convention of newspaper editors. April 23, A16.

New York Times. 1981. Pulitzer prize board adopts new procedures. November 22, A38.

Reinarman, Craig and Harry Gene Levine. 1989. Crack in context: Politics and media in the making of a drug scare. *Contemporary Drug Problems,* 16:535–77.

San Francisco Chronicle. 1981. *Washington Post* blames its editors for Pulitzer fiasco. April 19, A6.

Washington Post. 1980. D.C. Authorities seek identity of heroin addict, 8. September 30, A11.

Washington Post. 1981. *Post* writer wins Pulitzer for story on child addict. April 14, A1.

Washington Post. 1981. The end of the "Jimmy" story. April 16, A18.

Washington Post. 1981. *Post* reporter's Pulitzer Prize is withdrawn. April 16, A1.

Washington Post. 1981. The district line: The problem is all too real. April 17, C13.

Washington Post. 1981. "Jimmy" episode evokes outrage, sadness. April 17, C13.

Washington Post. 1981. Nation's editors plumb "Jimmy's World." April 18, A3.

Washington Post. 1981. Putting the creator of "Jimmy's World" in context. April 19, D1.

Well, Andrew. 1972. *The Natural Mind: An Investigation of Drugs and the Higher Consciousness.* Boston, MA: Houghton Mifflin.

Zinberg, Norman. 1984. *Drug, Set and Setting: The Basis for Controlled Intoxicant Use.* New Haven: Yale University Press.

EIGHTEEN

BREAKING NEWS

HOW LOCAL TV NEWS AND REAL-WORLD CONDITIONS AFFECT FEAR OF CRIME

Ronald Weitzer & Charis E. Kubrin

Fear of crime is a major problem in the United States. In 2000, for instance, 40% of Whites and 47% of Blacks reported that they were afraid to walk alone near their homes at night (Bureau of Justice Statistics, 2001, p. 120). At the same time, there has been growing public concern about the role of the mass media—especially television—in promoting violence in American society. While public beliefs about crime and fear of victimization come from various sources, the media appear to play a substantial role in shaping these beliefs and fears. As one review concluded, the "evidence on public perceptions of crime and media distortion of crime news is strikingly corroborative" (Warr, 2000, p. 468). Most Americans identify the media as their primary source of information about crime—95% in one study (Graber, 1980, p. 50)—and the media may also be a major predictor of fear of personal victimization. This study examines the effect of several types of news consumption on citizens' fear of crime. The findings address four theoretical perspectives on the relationship between media and audience perceptions.

Theoretical Background

People's fear of crime may be influenced by several factors, including their personal victimization, city or neighborhood levels of crime, and mass media coverage of crime. Competing theoretical perspectives highlight different sources of fear. We begin by briefly describing two general approaches to fear of crime, and then turn to two more complex perspectives.

Justice Quarterly, Vol. 21, No. 3, September 2004, pp. 497–520. Permission granted by Taylor & Francis, Ltd. http://www.tandf.co.uk/journals

One major approach—the real-world thesis—portrays fear of crime as largely or entirely shaped by objective conditions, such as criminal victimization, neighborhood characteristics, or city-level crime rates. According to this perspective, the media play little or no role because media reports are typically far removed from the audience's everyday lives and often cover atypical, serious, or spectacular crimes, whereas personal victimization and crime conditions are more immediate and salient (Rubin, Perse, & Taylor, 1988; Tyler, 1984). Regarding victimization, some studies find that prior victimization is positively associated with fear (Skogan & Maxfield, 1981; Stafford & Galle, 1984; Tyler, 1984). Paradoxically, however, most find that persons who have the lowest victimization rates (such as women and the elderly) express the greatest fear of crime, whereas those with higher rates (e.g., young Black males) express less fear (Warr & Stafford, 1983). Regarding type of neighborhood, it appears that racial composition of a neighborhood influences residents' fear, with residents of minority communities more likely to fear crime (Eschholz, Chiricos, & Gertz, 2003). Another neighborhood factor thought to influence fear is the amount of crime or disorder in the community (Covington & Taylor, 1991; LaGrange, Ferraro, & Supancic, 1992; Lewis & Maxfield, 1980). Disorder includes both signs of physical disorder (e.g., graffiti, abandoned cars) and low-level street deviance (rowdy youth, panhandlers, public drinking)—conditions that may cause residents to fear for their safety. One review concluded that "nearly all studies report a significant relationship between incivility [disorder] and fear of crime" (LaGrange et al., 1992, p. 313).

The role of the media is not considered in some of these studies, making it impossible to determine if the apparent real-world effects on fear of crime persist once media exposure is factored into the equation. In other studies that examine both real-world and media variables, some have found real-world effects, indicating that researchers should continue to test the real-world thesis.

The role of the media is the focus of the second major perspective—the cultivation thesis. This approach portrays the media world as very different from the real world, with the implication that heavy consumption of media messages distorts audience beliefs about the world and influences cognitive and emotional states (Gerbner, Gross, Morgan, & Signorielli, 1980; Morgan & Signorielli, 1990). In this view, the greater one's exposure to the media, the more likely it is that one's perceptions of the real world will match what is most frequently depicted in the media. With regard to crime, the media disproportionately report on violent crime (especially murder), largely neglect crime patterns, give little attention to the causes of crime, and leave the impression that crime is often random and inexplicable (Surette, 1998). This media world, especially television, differs greatly from the real world of crime and may cultivate a perception that the world is a scary place. Repeated exposure to media coverage of crime may thus generate fear and insecurity among viewers (Gerbner & Gross, 1976).

While some empirical support exists for cultivation (Gerbner et al., 1980), critics—now including Gerbner himself—regard it as somewhat limited because it assumes that media messages have a uniform effect on audiences. Audience characteristics (race, gender, age, etc.) and experiences (e.g., victimization) may play an important role in how media content is received. The field of communication studies has increasingly regarded the reception of media messages as a dynamic process in which viewers actively interpret and perhaps reconstruct those messages in light of their personal backgrounds and experiences (Dahlgren, 1988; Gunter, 1987). While relatively few studies of media and fear of crime examine audience characteristics, those that do have found that media messages are variably interpreted by persons with distinctive social characteristics (Eschholz, 1997; Heath & Gilbert, 1996).

Audience differences are central in two other approaches, which specify the conditions under which media messages may contribute to fear of crime. One approach—the substitution thesis—is a variant of the cultivation perspective that is sensitive to audience and contextual differences. The substitution thesis predicts that heavy exposure to media portrayals of crime has particularly strong effects on those with no direct experience of crime; for these individuals, media images of crime become a surrogate for real-world experience (Gunter, 1987). This view is consistent with the larger "proposition that media effects are most powerful for issues that are outside a subject's personal experience" (Surette, 1998, p. 205). Persons who are well insulated from crime (e.g., the affluent, the elderly, women, residents of low-crime communities) should therefore be more susceptible to crime messages in the media. Few empirical studies have tested the substitution thesis. One found that crime victims were not influenced by crime-related television viewing (television dramas and documentary programs), whereas nonvictims were, and developed greater fear of crime (Weaver & Wakshlag, 1986). In accordance with the substitution thesis, "greater exposure to exaggerated depictions of crime on television, in the absence of other more direct sources of information, may lead to the assimilation of elevated crime-related perceptions" (Weaver & Wakshlag, 1986, pp. 153–154).

A fourth perspective—the resonance thesis—predicts the opposite of the substitution thesis (Gerbner et al., 1980). The resonance thesis holds that when media images are consistent with lived experience (e.g., criminal victimization, residing in a high-crime community), media and experience mutually reinforce citizens' fear. As Eschholz (1997) writes, "individuals who live in high-crime areas may be particularly sensitive to crime on television because of their direct knowledge of a crime problem in their neighborhoods" (p. 47). Because many high-crime communities are predominantly African American and because African Americans are disproportionately victimized by crime, the resonance thesis would predict a stronger media-fear relationship among Blacks than among Whites (Chiricos, Padgett, & Gertz, 2000). That is, exposure to crime news in the media, coupled with greater personal vulnerability or experience of neighborhood crime, should produce a heightened fear of crime among Blacks.

The resonance perspective is supported in a few studies. One found that fear increased with greater television watching, but only in high-crime neighborhoods. Television exposure had no effect on fear in low-crime neighborhoods, leading to the conclusion that television only becomes salient when it interacts with neighborhood crime conditions (Doob & MacDonald, 1979). A similar finding is reported by Heath and Petraitis (1987), who studied the effect of exposure to television crime dramas. Viewing such programs increased fear for residents of high-crime but not low-crime neighborhoods in Chicago. Similarly, a study that examined the effect of city-level crime rates in 242 Florida cities found that local television news consumption had the strongest effect on fear in cities with high crime rates, lending further support to the resonance hypothesis (Chiricos et al., 2000). "These people receive a 'double dose' of messages that the world is violent," as Gerbner et al. (1980, p. 20) state, "and consequently show the strongest associations between viewing and fear."

If the media do influence fear of crime, there are reasons to expect that media effects will be strongest for those who are exposed to local television news, compared to other news sources. The following section indicates why this might be the case.

Disaggregating the Media

One problem with much of the literature on media and fear of crime is that most studies examine the effects of only one medium. The few studies that examine two or more media indicate that "the media" need to be disaggregated and examined separately and comparatively (Eschholz, 1997; Heath & Gilbert, 1996). In these studies, some media appear to influence consumers' perceptions, values, and concerns, while other media do not.

Why should this be the case? First, the style and content of reporting differs across the various media. Stylistically, television is a highly visual format, and seeing something on television may have a much stronger emotive impact than hearing about it on the radio or reading about it in the newspaper. Second, the resources available to different media vary considerably, which has implications for depth of investigation and for how news stories are packaged. Pressure for ratings and advertising revenue is greater for television news than for newspapers, which leads to a greater stress on marketable, shocking news in television (Chermak, 1995, p. 111). Third, some media sectors experience greater internal competition than others (e.g., several local television stations vs. one major newspaper in a city), which can lead to more crime coverage and more sensationalized coverage on television news (Chermak, 1995; Sheley & Atkins, 1981). Fourth, the audience is able to take a more active role in relation to some media than others. Newspaper and Internet readers exercise considerable selectivity in what they read, whereas television and radio news audiences are more passive and less selective in their reception of newscasts (Heath & Gilbert, 1996).

The research literature suggests that the different media vary in their capacity to influence audience feelings and beliefs. Only a couple of studies find that exposure to television crime dramas affects fear (Eschholz, 1997).

Regarding newspapers, some research finds that newspaper consumption increases readers' fear, but others find no such effect (Eschholz, 1997; Heath & Gilbert, 1996). Newspapers, however, vary significantly in the amount and quality of their coverage of crime. Readers of tabloids (which tend to be sensational) are much more likely than readers of broadsheet newspapers to perceive violent crime as being common and to feel unsafe walking alone at night (Williams & Dickinson, 1993). Similarly, fear is more strongly associated with reporting on crime in one's own city rather than elsewhere in the nation; in fact, "coverage of crime in other cities makes people feel safe by comparison" (Heath, 1984; Liska & Baccaglini, 1990, p. 372). In other words, "news of distant, sensationalistic, random crime allows people to reduce their anxiety about local crime by allowing them to compare themselves with others who are seen as worse off" (Surette, 1998, p. 208).

Most researchers study a single medium in isolation from others; very few compare two or more media. Single-medium studies are limited by their inability to determine whether some types of media are more consequential than others. The few existing comparative studies point to substantial variation in audience effects by media type, with some sources having greater effects on audience perceptions than others. A comparison of newspaper and television news consumption found that fear of crime increased only with exposure to television news (O'Keefe & Reid-Nash, 1987). Another study found that fear of crime increased with frequent exposure to television and radio news, but not to newspapers or television news magazines (e.g., *60 Minutes*) (Chiricos, Eschholz, & Gertz, 1997). A third study found a positive association between fear of crime and frequent exposure to local television news, crime dramas, tabloid shows (e.g., *Hardcopy*), and reality crime programs (e.g., *COPS*), but not to national television news or news magazines (Eschholz et al., 2003). One problem with these studies is that they only assess the frequency of exposure to each medium and neglect salience—that is, which medium is most important for the respondent. This is problematic when individuals, for example, watch both local and national television news and read newspapers, but form their impressions about crime based largely on one medium. Regardless of this shortcoming, it is noteworthy that the few studies comparing local and national television news find that fear increases with exposure to local but not to national television news (Barzagan, 1994; Chiricos et al., 2000; Eschholz et al., 2003; an exception is Gross and Aday's [2003] finding that neither medium affects fear).

In addition to the results of the latter studies, there are sound substantive reasons to expect local television news to have a stronger effect on perceptions than other types of news media. Local television news coverage is literally "close to home" for viewers,[1] whereas national television news stories tend to be far removed from viewers' everyday lives. Local television news also operates by the maxim, "If it bleeds, it leads." A 1997 study of 100 local television stations found that 72 began their evening newscasts with a crime story (Klite, Bardwell, & Saltzman, 1997). Approximately one-fourth of all local television news stories deal with crime (Project for Excellence in Journalism, 1999, 2001), and, compared to newspapers and radio, local television news broadcasts are often televised live from crime scenes and presented in a graphic, sensational, or disturbing manner. The public sees this local television news reporting as believable. When asked in a 1996 Harris poll (N = 3,004) what percentage of local television evening news they "believed," the mean for a sample of Americans was 74%; the mean for national network television evening news was 69% (cited in Center for Media and Public Affairs, 1997). It is understandable, therefore, why local television news has been thought to have the most pronounced and ongoing effects on audience perceptions of crime, victimization, and criminal justice (Lipschultz & Hilt, 2002). Compared to other types of news media, local television news is both proximate to the audience and realistic. Other sources may satisfy either the proximity or realism test, but not both—i.e., national news (distant), crime dramas (fictional)—while others such as newspapers and radio programs lack the visual dimension of local television news.

In sum, the literature offers mixed support for the hypothesis that exposure to the media increases fear of crime. Findings vary by type of medium, by audience characteristics, and by the control variables examined (Eschholz, 1997; Heath & Gilbert, 1996). Yet, there are also a number of deficiencies and unanswered questions in the media-fear literature. Many studies fail to examine both real-world and media variables. In studying media and fear, it might seem obvious to control for crime (e.g., prior victimization, neighborhood crime conditions), but only a handful of researchers have done so. Analyses of two or more media are rare, but without comparative studies it is difficult to determine which media type has the strongest effect on audience perceptions. And, finally, few studies examine the effect of audience characteristics on the reception of news media reports, though some find that race, gender, and age influence the reception of media messages (Chiricos et al., 2000; Eschholz et al., 2003).

The present study builds on, and fills some gaps in, the literature by (1) examining several types of media genres (local television, national television, newspapers, radio, the Internet), (2) assessing whether demographic factors (e.g., race, gender) and real-world conditions (e.g., neighborhood crime, personal victimization) interact with media exposure to influence fear of crime, and (3) using two measures of media exposure—both frequency of consumption and salience (i.e., the "most important source of news" to respondents).[2]

The study will address the theoretical perspectives discussed above. Support for the real-world perspective would be found if objective crime conditions (i.e., personal victimization, neighborhood crime), but not media exposure, increase fear of crime.[3] Support for cultivation would be found if media exposure (i.e., frequency or salience), but not real-world crime conditions, increases fear. Support for the substitution thesis would be found if fear of crime is heightened among individuals with high media exposure and low personal or neighborhood experience with crime. Support for resonance would be found if fear of crime is increased among those with both high media exposure and personal and/or neighborhood experience of crime. The data analyzed in the present study do not permit an exhaustive test of these four perspectives, but the findings may be interpreted as evidence in support of one or another thesis.

Methods

Data for the study come from a telephone survey of 480 residents of Washington, DC.[4] The survey was conducted in March–April 2001 by the Center for Survey Research at George Washington University. Random digit dialing was used to contact households. When a call was answered, an interviewer asked to speak to the "youngest male, 18 years or older, who is now at home." If no eligible male was present, the interviewer asked to speak with the "oldest female, 18 years or older, who is now at home." This selection technique has been used in Pew polling, and prior research has established that it produces more demographically representative samples than alternative techniques and also increases the proportion of attempted interviews that are completed (Keeter & Fisher, 1997; Srinivasan, Christiansen, & Tortora, 1996). The demographic characteristics of the sample, with comparable Washington, DC population data from the 2000 census in parentheses, are as follows: 57.7% Black (60%); 62.5% female (53%); median age 43 (35). The slight oversampling of female and older respondents is not uncommon in telephone surveys (Lavrakas, 1993).

Our dependent variable—fear of crime—has been operationalized in several ways in previous studies, including respondent's concern about crime or proxies for crime (e.g., safety concerns), perceived risk of victimization, and anxiety about being outside during the day or at night (Ferraro, 1995; Warr, 2000). Although some measures do not explicitly mention crime, crime is often implicit in the wording of the question, as it is in the present study. Our respondents were asked, "How comfortable are you walking alone at night within two or three blocks of your home? Are you very comfortable, somewhat comfortable, somewhat uncomfortable, or very uncomfortable?"[5] Being "very uncomfortable" or "somewhat uncomfortable" are rough measures, in the present study, of concern about crime. People who feel uncomfortable are likely to be concerned with becoming a victim of crime. We recognize that such anxiety is not equivalent to fear of crime, but it arguably taps into emotional concerns about personal safety when "walking alone at night," and safety concern has often been used as a proxy for fear in other research (Ferraro & LaGrange, 1987). For instance, one of the most frequently asked fear-of-crime questions is the NCVS question, "How safe do you feel or would you feel being out alone in your neighborhood at night?"

In our sample, 36.5% (N = 175) stated they were very comfortable while walking alone at night near their homes, 30% (N = 144) were somewhat comfortable, 16% (N = 77) were somewhat uncomfortable, and 14.8% (N = 71) were very uncomfortable.

There are several problems or gaps in the literature that our research design addresses. One serious problem, mentioned earlier, is that prior studies on the relationship between media exposure and fear of crime have typically examined only one medium at a time. The present study incorporates several media (national and local television, newspapers, radio, and the Internet). Another design deficiency is the common practice of measuring respondents' overall exposure to a medium (e.g., newspapers) without considering the content of what people take in. Broad measures, such as overall exposure to a medium, may thus include people who read only the business section of the newspaper or television viewers who watch the local news simply for sports or weather—thereby limiting their exposure to crime news. Our design specifically captures exposure to the news content of the media. A final problem is that researchers have measured media exposure solely in terms of frequency (e.g., hours of television watching, days of newspaper reading), and have not considered news source salience. To our knowledge, ours is the only study to use both frequency and salience measures (Potter & Chang, 1990).

Respondents were first asked how frequently, if ever, they: (1) "watch national evening news programs such as *World News Tonight* with Peter Jennings or cable news programs like CNN;" (2) "watch local television news for information other than weather and sports;" (3) "read the news or editorial sections of a daily newspaper;" (4) "listen to radio shows that invite listeners to call in to discuss current events, public issues, and politics;" and (5) "go online to get information on current events, public issues, and politics."[6] Respondents were then asked: "What would you say is the most important source of news for you? Would you say it is national television news, local television news, daily newspapers, radio, or the Internet?" Not surprisingly, there was substantial variation in which medium was the most important news source for respondents with 19.2% of the sample answering national television, 30.2% local television, 26.7% daily newspapers, 7.1% radio, 12.3% Internet, and 3.1% "other medium." This distribution underscores the importance of disaggregating the media into subtypes when studying whether media exposure influences fear of crime; more than 20% of respondents indicated that the radio, Internet, or other medium—sources almost never examined in the literature—was most important. The question regarding respondents' most important source of news is the independent variable of primary interest in this study.[7]

Because some studies find that certain demographic attributes (such as gender and race) influence fear of crime, we include the following independent variables in our models: respondents' age (measured continuously), age^2 (because the slope for age is nonlinear), gender, race (Black, White, other race, with White as the omitted category), education (college graduate or not), family income (seven categories),[8] and victimization by violent crime (ever) or property crime (in the past year). Respondents were asked: "Have you ever personally been a victim of a violent crime? By violent crime we mean, for example, assault, mugging, rape, or battery." Respondents were also asked: "During the past year, have you personally been a victim of a property crime such as having your house or car broken into?"

Another variable of interest is perceived risk of criminal victimization. It has been argued that risk of crime and fear of crime are different constructs that may vary independently or be causally related. Risk of victimization is a cognitive perception whereas fear of crime is an affective state (Ferraro, 1995). This conceptual distinction is supported in research that treats risk of crime as an independent or control variable: a review of 20 studies found that perceived risk of crime was a predictor of fear of crime (Ferraro, 1995, p. 31; cf. Chiricos et al., 2000; Rountree & Land, 1996). The present study, accordingly, treats perceived risk of victimization as a possible predictor of fear, using three risk measures.[9] Respondents were asked: "Now I am going to read you a list of items relating to safety risks to you and your family. Would you say that you and your family are at almost no risk, slight risk, moderate risk, or high risk from [violent crime/property crime/street drugs]?"[10] Respondents may associate "risk from street drugs" with the violence surrounding street-level drug markets, concerns about children getting involved in the drug trade, or other by-products of street drug markets, such as disorderly behavior or intimidation of residents. Street-level drug use is among the "incivilities" that have been found to increase perceived risk and/or fear of crime among neighborhood residents (LaGrange et al., 1992; Lewis & Maxfield, 1980).

Finally, we control for the respondent's local crime conditions: violent crime rate (murder, rape, robbery, and assault) and property crime rate (burglary, larceny, auto theft, and arson). These rates are measured at the police district level, unlike some prior studies that measure crime at the city level (Chiricos et al., 2000). The respondent's zip code was matched to one of the seven police districts in Washington, DC whose crime rates vary significantly. The Metropolitan Police Department provided police district crime data for 2000, which we used to compute local violent and property crime rates.

Results

Table 1 provides descriptive statistics for each independent variable and its bivariate correlation with fear of crime. Of importance are the significant positive relationships between frequency of exposure to local television news and fear ($R = .15$) and between local television as respondents' most important news source (i.e., salience) and fear ($R = .15$). No other news source is significantly positively correlated with fear, and some sources (daily newspapers, radio, Internet, and other medium) are negatively associated with fear. Other significant positive correlates include age and age^2 ($R = .14, .17$), female ($R = .21$), Black ($R = .24$), perceived risk of violent and property crime and street drugs ($R = .16, .17,$ and $.18$), property crime victimization ($R = .18$), and the local violent crime rate ($R = .21$). Other significant negative correlates are college graduate and family income logged (both $R = -.14$). Surprisingly, being a victim of violent crime is not significantly associated with fear of crime.

To further test the relationship between exposure to news media and fear of crime, the data are analyzed using OLS regression.[11] The first analyses assess whether local television news influences fear of crime, controlling for other factors, and compares local television news to the other types of news media. The second analyses examine the effects of local television news for Blacks and Whites separately, given the finding of race differences in previous research (Chiricos et al., 1997; Chiricos et al., 2000). The final analyses determine whether real-world factors (local crime rates, personal victimization) interact with local television news to affect fear of crime.[12]

Table 2 displays the results of the first regression analyses. Model 1 excludes all media types except local television to determine whether this media source, relative to all others combined, is significantly related to fear of crime. Results show that salience, but not frequency, of exposure to local television news is a significant predictor of fear. Those who list local television as their most important news source are significantly more fearful of crime ($\beta = .097$; $p < .05$). The relationship between salience of local television news and fear holds after controlling for the respondents' characteristics (age, race, gender, education, income), perceived risk of violent and property crime and street drugs, prior violent and property victimization, and local violent and property crime rates.

Turning to the other predictors, Model 1 shows that females ($\beta = .192$; $p < .001$) and Blacks ($\beta = .150$; $p < .05$) are more fearful. The negative coefficient for age and the positive coefficient for age^2 suggest that fear of crime initially decreases with age and then increases for older respondents, as one would predict. Those who believe that they are at a higher risk for property crime ($\beta = .128$; $p < .05$) as well as those who have been victims of property crime in the past year ($\beta = .154$; $p < .01$) are also more fearful. Finally, the local violent crime rate is significantly associated with increased fear ($\beta = .124$; $p < .05$) but violent victimization is not. The adjusted R^2 for the model is .20.[13]

Model 2 provides a more nuanced examination of the role of local television news relative to each of the other media types; in this model, local television is the omitted category. As such, one can assess whether those who

Table 1   Descriptive Statistics for Regression Model Variables

Variable	Mean	S.D.	Min.	Max.	r Fear	Description
Local TV	.30	.46	0	1	.15*	Local TV most important news source for R
National TV	.19	.39	0	1	.01	National TV most important news source for R

Daily Newspaper	.27	.44	0	1	−.06	Newspaper most important news source for R
Radio	.07	.26	0	1	−.05	Radio most important news source for R
Internet	.12	.33	0	1	−.05	Internet most important news source for R
Other Medium	.03	.17	0	1	−.12*	Other medium most important news source for R
Frequency Local TV	4.04	1.34	1	5	.15*	Frequency of watching local TV for R
Age	45.15	16.95	17	86	.14*	R's age
Age^2	2325.02	1668.59	289	7396	.17*	R's age squared
Female	.63	.49	0	1	.21*	R is female
Black	.58	.50	0	1	.24*	R is Black
Other Race	.11	.31	0	1	−.04	R is race other than Black or White
College Graduate	.41	.49	0	1	−.14*	R is college graduate
Family Income	10.55	.73	9	12	−.14*	R's family income logged
Risk Violent Crime	2.31	1.02	1	4	.16*	R's perceived risk for violent crime
Risk Property Crime	2.50	1.02	1	4	.17*	R's perceived risk for property crime
Risk Street Drugs	2.07	1.16	1	4	.18*	R's perceived risk for street drugs
Victim Violent Crime	.28	.45	0	1	−.01	R ever violent crime victim
Victim Property Crime	.22	.42	0	1	.18*	R property crime victim in past year
Local Violent Crime Rate	16.53	6.28	3.37	23.30	.21*	R's police district violent crime rate per 1,000
Local Property Crime Rate	61.93	33.01	36.77	136.20	−.04	R's police district property crime rate per 1,000

*p < .05

list, say, daily newspapers as their most important news source are less likely to be fearful, compared to those who list local television as their most important source.

Findings from Model 2 further support the effects of local television news on fear, but they also suggest that local television news significantly increases fear only when compared to certain other media sources. Those who identify

Table 2 Regression of Fear of Crime on News Media

Variable	Model 1			Model 2		
	Beta	b	(SE)	Beta	b	(SE)
Local TV most important news source	.097*	.222	(.107)	—		
National TV most important news source	—			−.096^	−.264	(.139)
Daily newspapers most important news source	—			−.116*	−.277	(.127)
Radio most important news source	—			−.041	−.174	(.208)
Internet most important news source	—			−.026	−.081	(.167)
Other most important news source	—			−.107*	−.667	(.281)
Frequency local TV	.010	.008	(.040)	.010	.008	(.040)
Age	−.939***	−.060	(.017)	−.889**	−.057	(.017)
Age^2	1.070***	.0007	(.000)	1.041***	.0007	(.000)
Female	.192***	.419	(.098)	.190***	.414	(.098)
Black	.150*	.323	(.139)	.149*	.320	(.139)
Other Race	.040	.139	(.171)	.035	.120	(.172)
College Graduate	.045	.096	(.119)	.051	.109	(.119)
Family Income	−.036	−.052	(.071)	−.040	−.058	(.073)
Risk Violent Crime	.028	.029	(.057)	.018	.019	(.057)
Risk Property Crime	.128*	.133	(.052)	.130**	.136	(.052)
Risk Street Drugs	.085	.078	(.048)	.087	.080	(.048)
Victim Violent Crime	.035	.084	(.107)	.038	.090	(.107)
Victim Property Crime	.154**	.393	(.118)	.158**	.402	(.118)
Local Violent Crime Rate	.124*	.021	(.010)	.133*	.023	(.010)
Local Property Crime Rate	−.025	−.0008	(.002)	−.038	−.001	(.002)
Constant	2.161**	—	(.795)	2.370**	—	(.813)
Adjusted R^2	.200			.203		
N	433			433		

^p < .06 *p < .05 **p < .01 ***p < .001

national television as their most important news source are less likely to be fearful than those who select local television news ($\beta = -.096$; $p < .06$). The same is true for those who list daily newspapers as their most important news source ($\beta = -.116$; $p < .05$) as well as those who select the "other" category ($\beta = -.107$; $p < .05$). Those who list the radio or the Internet as their most important news source also tend to be less fearful than those who select local television, though the findings are not statistically significant.

To test the relative effects of each media source, we ran additional analyses (now shown here) where each source served as the omitted category. The findings show that, in comparison to the other types, no media source is significantly associated with fear of crime (that is, aside from local television news). The only significant finding is that, relative to those who mention the Internet as their most important news source, those whose most important news source is "other medium" are less likely to be fearful ($\beta = -.103$; $p < .05$).

Race and Local Television News

Consistent with previous research, we uncovered significant race effects, with Blacks being more fearful than Whites, even after controlling for other personal characteristics and prior victimization. Of interest is whether there are race differences in selection of the most important news source, and whether these differences help explain, in part, why Blacks are more fearful. An examination of the data reveals that 40.8% of Blacks in the sample report that local television is their most important news source, compared to only 11.2% of Whites (a plurality of Whites—37.1%—selected daily newspaper as their most important news source).

The resonance thesis would predict a significant interaction between consumption of local television news and membership in a group that has high vulnerability to crime (e.g., Blacks). The substitution thesis would predict an interaction for those who are not vulnerable to crime (e.g., Whites).

Results from regression analyses disaggregated by race are displayed in table 3. With the exception of the measure of salience of local television, predictors that were nonsignificant in all models are not shown in the table. The results confirm that local television news matters most for Blacks. Local television news is significantly related to fear of crime for Blacks ($\beta = .139$; $p < .05$) but not for Whites. This fording is underscored when considering that prior violent victimization and local violent and property crime rates matter less for Blacks than does local television news. Other predictors of fear for Blacks include age, being female, property crime victimization, and perceived risk for street drugs. For Whites, the single most important predictor of fear is the perception of being at risk for violent crime (but not actually having been a victim of violent crime). The effect of this variable is quite large ($\beta = .317$; $p < .01$). Although fewer of the predictors explain Whites' compared to Blacks' fear, the adjusted R^2 is much greater in the model for Whites (.239) than Blacks (.111).

Table 3   Regression of Fear of Crime on News Media for Subsamples

Variable	Blacks			Whites			Violent Crime								
							Low			Medium			High		
	Beta	b	(SE)	Beta	b	(SE)	Beta	b	(SE)	Beta	b	(SE)	Beta	b	(SE)
Local TV most important news source	.139*	.313	(.142)	-.021	-.054	(.220)	.003	.008	(.305)	.130^	.300	(.170)	.150*	.331	(.166)
Age	-.847*	-.057	(.024)	-1.237*	-.069	(.029)	-2.454**	-.141	(.049)	-.753^	-.045	(.024)	-.906*	-.062	(.030)
Age^2	1.008**	.0007	(.000)	1.212*	.0007	(.000)	2.367**	.001	(.000)	.972*	.0006	(.000)	.949*	.0007	(.000)
Female	.155*	.359	(.144)	.254**	.440	(.146)	.346**	.610	(.226)	.235**	.517	(.150)	.128^	.280	(.164)
Black		—			—		.101	.348	(.500)	.202*	.445	(.216)	.121	.288	(.251)
College Graduate	.063	.166	(.184)	-.058	-.122	(.187)	-.128	-.264	(.259)	.175*	.380	(.187)	-.064	-.149	(.205)
Risk Violent Crime	-.058	-.061	(.078)	.317**	.332	(.099)	.196	.197	(.136)	-.044	-.047	(.093)	.059	.062	(.089)
Risk Property Crime	.103	.110	(.074)	.124	.111	(.092)	.068	.060	(.126)	.119	.125	(.086)	.194*	.201	(.082)
Risk Street Drugs	.133^	.120	(.063)	-.084	-.079	(.086)	-.079	-.084	(.138)	.156^	.146	(.078)	.097	.085	(.072)
Victim Property Crime	.183**	.507	(.177)	.126	.256	(.179)	-.036	-.079	(.297)	.119	.305	(.193)	.248**	.615	(.186)
Constant	2.557*		(1.239)	1.346		(1.124)	2.471		(1.589)	2.640		(1.397)	1.773		(1.308)
Adjusted R^2	.111			.239			.196			.193			.139		
N	253			129			65			181			187		

^p < .10 *p < .05 **p < .01 ***p < .001

Do demographic characteristics besides race interact with local television news to increase fear of crime? The substitution thesis predicts that the effects of media on fear will be greater for groups least vulnerable to victimization—women, the elderly, and the affluent. To test this thesis, we ran additional interaction analyses disaggregating the sample by gender, age, and income.[14] The results reveal no interaction effects, and thus provide no support for the substitution thesis.

Crime and Local Television News

The final analyses examine the interactions between two possibly salient real-world characteristics and local television news exposure. The resonance thesis predicts that people who (1) live in neighborhoods with high violent crime rates or (2) have been personally victimized, and for whom local television is their most important news source, will be especially fearful of crime. Living in such neighborhoods or having been a crime victim is likely to affect residents' experiences, observations, or perceptions of crime, which may amplify the effect of local television news on fear.

First, we grouped respondents into low, medium, or high violent crime communities based on the violent crime rate of the police district in which they lived. Given the city's average violent crime rate of just over 15 violent crimes per 1,000 population, police districts whose rates were less than 14 were classified as low, those whose crime rates were between 14 and 19 were classified as medium, and those whose rates were greater than 19 were classified as high. The results from the interaction analyses are shown in the third, fourth, and fifth columns of table 3. In communities with high violent crime rates, the significant positive relationship between local television news and fear (β = .150; p < .05) indicates that—controlling for personal and other factors—people who live in such communities and who rely on local television as their most important news source are especially fearful of crime. Results from regression analyses for residents of communities with low levels of violent crime show that local television news does not affect fear of crime in such communities. Residents of communities with medium levels of violent crime are more likely to be fearful but the interaction is significant only at the p < .10 level.[15] Other important correlates of fear in areas with high violent crime include age and age^2 (β = −.906, p < .05 and β = .949, p < .05), property crime victimization (β = .248, p < .01), and perceived risk for property crime (β = .194; p < .05). In neighborhoods with low violent crime rates, age and gender are the only significant predictors of fear.

Second, interaction analyses (not reported here) reveal that criminal victimization does not interact with local television news exposure to influence fear. This finding, like the earlier finding that property crime victimization, but not violent crime victimization, influences fear (see table 2) is inconsistent with the resonance perspective. But, as noted above, the literature is inconclusive regarding the association between victimization and fear of crime; some studies find that victimization increases fear while other studies find no such relationship. In addition, the different effects of property vs. violent crime victimization in the present study may be explained, in part, by the time period for the question. Respondents were asked if they had ever been a victim of a violent crime. If earlier violent victimization, which may have occurred many years ago in other cities or states, is less salient for respondents than more recent victimization, then this would explain the nonsignificant relationship between violent victimization and fear. Still, we find some support for the resonance thesis in our findings on neighborhood crime effects.

Discussion

Our findings suggest that the media play a substantial role in shaping beliefs and fear of crime. We found that those who identify local television as their most important news source are more fearful compared to those who selected national television, daily newspapers, and "other medium." This is consistent with a body of literature described earlier in the paper, which predicts that local television news should have a particularly strong impact, compared to other media, on audience perceptions and fears. The results speak to the importance of disaggregating the media when studying its effect on audience perceptions. Similarly, the findings confirm the need to disaggregate audiences; media messages are not received in the same way by different people. Our analysis shows that media and real-world conditions have different effects on White and Black respondents and on respondents from communities with different levels of violent crime.

These findings bear on the four perspectives discussed earlier. The real-world, cultivation, substitution, and resonance theses predict different kinds of outcomes from exposure to the media. The real-world thesis holds that objective conditions trump media messages and that the latter have no appreciable impact on the values, beliefs, or fears of the audience. By contrast, the cultivation approach predicts that media messages overwhelm all other possible influences. The assumption is that heavy exposure to the media is such a powerful influence that it overshadows other factors, including audience characteristics or contextual variables. Both substitution and resonance assert that the impact of media messages is conditional, depending on whether those messages are consistent with audience members' experiences and living conditions, such as past victimization or neighborhood crime conditions. Substitution predicts that media messages will have the greatest effect on those who lack personal or neighborhood experience with crime, while resonance predicts the opposite.

For the total sample, the results show strong support for neither the cultivation nor the real-world thesis, because both media and real-world conditions influence fear (table 2). Furthermore, the interaction analyses suggest a more complex and conditional relationship among the media, real-world factors, and fear of crime (table 3). When the sample is broken down by race, the findings lend support to both the resonance and the real-world theses, depending on the racial group. Whites' fear of crime is influenced not by the media but instead by their perceived risk of violent criminal victimization. Insofar as perceived risk can be considered a "real-world" indicator (see Footnote 3), the real-world thesis is partially supported for Whites, though other real-world factors such as personal victimization and risk of other types of crime are not significant.

Blacks are influenced both by local television news and by real-world conditions—namely, property crime victimization and perceived risk of street drugs to themselves and family members. That Blacks are concerned about street drugs is understandable in a city like Washington, DC, where street-level drug markets are concentrated in poor Black neighborhoods. For Blacks, the combined effect of local television news and the above crime factors provides support for the resonance thesis.

When the sample is disaggregated by neighborhood violent crime level, residents of communities with high violent crime rates are especially likely to be affected, in their fear of crime, by local television newscasts. By contrast, local television news exposure does not increase fear for residents of low violent-crime communities. The finding that local news effects are stronger for residents of high violent crime areas is consistent with findings from some previous studies (Chiricos et al., 2000; Doob & MacDonald, 1979; Heath & Petraitis, 1987), and lends further support to the resonance thesis.

No support is found for the substitution thesis, which predicts that groups that have a low victimization risk—women, the elderly, and the affluent—will be especially susceptible to media influences. In the interaction analyses disaggregated by each of these characteristics, local television news was not a significant predictor of fear.

There are three possible limitations of the study. The first has to do with the interpretation of the findings for the interaction analyses. It should be kept in mind that the interaction analyses did not yield statistically significant interracial and neighborhood differences, as reported in Footnote 15. That is, while the effect of local television news on fear of crime was significant for Blacks and not for Whites, the coefficients across the Black-White models were not statistically significantly different from each other. Similarly, while local television news was associated with increased fear in high violent crime areas but not in low violent crime areas, differences across the models were not statistically significant. These results, therefore, should be interpreted with caution.

Second, our measure of fear of crime differs from that employed in other studies, including those that operationalize fear as perceived "safety" or as being "afraid." We believe that our measure—level of comfort while walking alone at night near one's home—taps into the same emotional state as measures that ask about one's safety concerns and fear, but we also recognize that these variables are not equivalent. This means that similarities between our findings and those reported in some other studies must be qualified, even as they point to a similar relationship between media and other factors in their influence on audience perceptions.

The third limitation has to do with generalizability. Although our results are limited to one city and therefore cannot be generalized to other contexts, we have no reason to expect that the nature of the city or its media would produce unique patterns in the findings. While the city's dominant newspaper, the *Washington Post*, gives somewhat more coverage to national political events than might be true for other cities, it also has plenty of local crime coverage. Also, despite being the nation's capital, local television newscasts in Washington focus almost exclusively on the city, and much of that reporting is crime related.

An unanswered question has to do with how the media, and local television news in particular, increase fear of crime. There is considerable speculation in the literature about this, but little research on the mechanisms involved—e.g., whether fear is triggered by the visual images portrayed, by a particular kind of (dramatic) story line, by the types of crimes most frequently covered, or by the episodic nature of the coverage, leaving the impression that crime is a random, unpredictable event. We know relatively little about how crime stories are interpreted, a question that could be explored with more qualitative and experimental research on audience reactions to media messages.

The finding that local television news is the medium with the greatest effect on fear, coupled with what we know about the selective and distorted presentation of crime on local television newscasts, raises some policy implications. Critics frequently argue for less sensationalized and more contextualized reporting, as well as for less coverage of atypical and predatory crimes and more coverage of corporate crime. An important policy question has to do with the role of media crime reporting on the public's preferences regarding crime control. The limited existing literature indicates that people who are "heavy viewers of television crime shows . . . are disposed to support the law enforcement system . . . and favor crime control over due process policies" (Surette, 1998, p. 213). The same may also be the case for heavy viewers of local television newscasts, but research is needed to determine whether exposure to television news has this same effect on crime policy preferences.

Notes

[1] One study reported that 84% of local news coverage of crime dealt with local crime and the remainder dealt with crime elsewhere in the country (Project for Excellence in Journalism, 2001).

[2] A study using the same database tested only the frequency measure, neglecting the important issue of media salience (Gross & Aday, 2003).

[3] One question is whether perceived risk of crime qualifies as indicative of real-world conditions or is purely a subjective assessment. Risk of crime may be viewed as a quasi-objective phenomenon, which is apt to be strongly associated with real neighborhood crime conditions or personal victimization, but is clearly more subjective than either of these.

[4] These data are part of a larger survey of the greater Washington, DC metropolitan area (N = 921). For the entire sample, 8,199 phone numbers were called, 59% (N = 4,878) of which were reached. Of those, 42% were viable while the remaining numbers were either disconnected or were linked to businesses or fax machines. For numbers that were not initially reached, up to

five callbacks were made. The final response rate, defined as completed interviews / (completed interviews + refusals), was 45%. We use only the DC portion of the sample (N = 480) because neighborhood crime data were not available for the surrounding suburbs. Although we cannot calculate the response rate for just the DC sample (because the phone numbers were pooled), the Center for Survey Research has informed us that the response rate is likely to be very similar.

5 This variable is coded as 1 = "very comfortable," 2 = "somewhat comfortable," 3 = "somewhat uncomfortable," and 4 = "very uncomfortable."

6 Coding of this variable ranges from 1 to 5, with 1 = "never," 2 = "several times a month," 3 = "once or twice a week," 4 = "most days," and 5 = "every day."

7 Distinguishing between local and national news is not always simple. Most crime news stories carried on national news are "local" stories somewhere and more importantly, local newscasts sometimes report crime stories from elsewhere in the state or nation (16% of the time, see Footnote 1) that have no direct connection to the local news market (Chiricos et al., 2000, p. 764). While it is difficult to control for such overlap, the measures used in the present study clearly distinguish local from national television broadcasts. In reading the question on national television news, the interviewer stated: "We are interested in national news programs; this is different from the local news shows about the area where you live."

8 The log of this variable is used to correct for skewness.

9 A recent study using the same database unfortunately combined the three risk items with the fear measure to produce a fear of crime scale (Gross & Aday, 2003). In accordance with the literature, we treat risk of victimization and fear of crime as qualitatively distinct variables that should not be conflated because the former is a possible predictor of the latter.

10 This variable is coded as 1 = "almost no risk," 2 = "slight risk," 3 = "moderate risk," and 4 = "high risk."

11 Given the nature of the dependent variable, we also ran ordinal regression in SPSS, which allows one to model the dependence of a polytomous ordinal response on a set of predictors (see McCullagh, 1980). The results from these analyses were nearly identical to the results from the OLS analyses. For ease of interpretation, we report the OLS regression results. Results from the ordinal regression analyses are available from the authors upon request.

12 We considered using HLM to model contextual effects, but one important limitation of this approach is the rigid requirement concerning the size of the nested files. In order for HLM to operate successfully, the number of individual-level cases per aggregate unit must be sufficiently large; small numbers of cases make it difficult to obtain reliable measures, and aggregate units with too few cases are dropped in the analyses. Because of our relatively small sample size, there were too few cases per aggregate unit to successfully run HLM models.

13 Collinearity diagnostics suggest that there are no problems of multicollinearity in the regression analyses. None of the VIF scores were above the conventional threshold of 4.

14 Income was broken down into three categories based on the distribution of the variable. Low-income respondents were classified as having incomes of $25,000 or less (N = 140), medium-income respondents $25,001 to $87,499 (N = 256), and high-income respondents $87,500 or greater (N = 84). With regard to age, the sample was broken into three categories—young (ages 18–30, N = 116), middle-aged (ages 31–59, N = 253), and elderly (ages 60 and over, N = 100).

15 We used the equation $t = b_1 - b_2 / \sqrt{(SEb_1^2 + SEb_2^2)}$ (Paternoster, Brame, Mazerolle, & Piquero, 1998) to test whether the local television news coefficients were significantly different from one another across the models (i.e., Blacks vs. Whites and low violent crime neighborhoods vs. high violent crime neighborhoods). The results indicate that they are not significantly different at the p < .05 level.

References

Barzagan, M. (1994). The effects of health, environmental, and socio-psychological variables on fear of crime and its consequences among urban black elderly individuals. *International Journal of Aging and Human Development, 38,* 99–115.

Bureau of Justice Statistics. (2001). *Sourcebook of criminal justice statistics, 2000.* Washington, DC: U.S. Government Printing Office.

Center for Media and Public Affairs. (1997). *What the people want from the press.* Washington, DC: Author.

Chermak, S. (1995). *Victims in the news: Crime and the American news media.* Boulder, CO: Westview.

Chiricos, T., Eschholz, S., & Gertz, M. (1997). Crime, news, and fear of crime. *Social Problems, 44,* 342–357.

Chiricos, T., Padgett, K., & Gertz, M. (2000). Fear, television news, and the reality of crime. *Criminology, 38,* 755–785.

Covington, J., & Taylor, R. (1991). Fear of crime in urban residential neighborhoods. *Sociological Quarterly, 32,* 231–249.

Dahlgren, P. (1988). What's the meaning of this? Viewers' plural sense-making of television news. *Media, Culture, and Society, 10,* 285–310.

Doob, A., & MacDonald, G. (1979). Television viewing and fear of victimization. *Journal of Personality and Social Psychology, 37,* 170–179.

Eschholz, S. (1997). The media and fear of crime: A survey of the research. *University of Florida Journal of Law and Public Policy, 9,* 37–59.

Eschholz, S., Chiricos, T., & Gertz, M. (2003). Television and fear of crime: Program types, audience traits, and the mediating effect of perceived neighborhood racial composition. *Social Problems, 50,* 395–415.

Ferraro, K. (1995). *Fear of crime.* Albany: State University of New York Press.

Ferraro, K., & LaGrange, R. (1987). The measurement of fear of crime. *Sociological Inquiry, 57,* 70–101.

Gerbner, G., & Gross, L. (1976). Living with television: The violence profile. *Journal of Communication, 26,* 173–199.

Gerbner, G., Gross, L., Morgan, M., & Signorielli, N. (1980). The mainstreaming of America: Violence profile No. 11. *Journal of Communication, 30,* 10–29.

Graber, D. (1980). *Crime news and the public.* New York: Praeger.

Gross, K., & Aday, S. (2003). The scary world in your living room and your neighborhood. *Journal of Communication, 53,* 411–426.

Gunter, B. (1987). *Television and the fear of crime.* London: John Libbey.

Heath, L. (1984). Impact of newspaper crime reports on fear of crime. *Journal of Personality and Social Psychology, 47,* 263–276.

Heath, L., & Gilbert, K. (1996). Mass media and fear of crime. *American Behavioral Scientist, 39,* 379–386.

Heath, L., & Petraitis, J. (1987). Television viewing and fear of crime. *Basic and Applied Social Psychology, 8,* 97–123.

Keeter, S., & Fisher, K. (1997). A comparison of "last birthday" and youngest male/oldest female respondent selection procedures. Paper presented at the annual meeting of the American Association for Public Opinion Research, Norfolk, VA.

Klite, P., Bardwell, R., & Saltzman, J. (1997). Local television news: Getting away with murder. *Press /Politics, 2,* 113–119.

LaGrange, R., Ferraro, K., & Supancic, M. (1992). Perceived risk and fear of crime: The role of social and physical incivilities. *Journal of Research in Crime and Delinquency, 29,* 311–334.

Lavrakas, P. (1993). *Telephone survey methods.* Newbury Park, CA: Sage Publications.

Lewis, D., & Maxfield, M. (1980). Fear in the neighborhoods: An investigation of the impact of crime. *Journal of Research in Crime and Delinquency, 17,* 160–189.

Lipschultz, J., & Hilt, M. (2002). *Crime and local television news.* Mahwah, NJ: Lawrence Erlbaum.

Liska, A., & Baccaglini, W. (1990). Feeling safe by comparison: Crime in the newspapers. *Social Problems, 37*, 360–374.

McCullagh, P. (1980). Regression models for ordinal data. *Journal of the Royal Statistical Society, Series B, Methodological, 42*, 109–142.

Morgan, M., & Signorielli, N. (1990). Cultivation analysis. In N. Signorielli & M. Morgan (Eds.), *Cultivation analysis* (pp. 13–34). Newbury Park, CA: Sage Publications.

O'Keefe, G., & Reid-Nash, K. (1987). Crime news and real-world blues: The effects of the media on social reality. *Communication Research, 14*, 147–163.

Paternoster, R., Brame, R., Mazerolle, P., & Piquero, A. (1998). Using the correct statistical test for the equality of regression coefficients. *Criminology, 36*, 859–866.

Potter, J., & Chang, I. (1990). Television exposure measures and the cultivation hypothesis. *Journal of Broadcasting and Electronic Media, 34*, 313–333.

Project for Excellence in Journalism. (1999). *Local television news.* Washington, DC: Author.

Project for Excellence in Journalism. (2001). *The look of local news.* Washington, DC: Author.

Rountree, P., & Land, K. (1996). Perceived risk versus fear of crime: Empirical evidence of conceptually distinct reactions in survey data. *Social Forces, 74*, 1353–1376.

Rubin, A., Perse, E., & Taylor, D. (1988). A methodological examination of cultivation. *Communication Research, 15*, 107–134.

Sheley, J., & Ashkins, C. (1981). Crime, crime news, and crime views. *Public Opinion Quarterly, 45*, 492–506.

Skogan, W., & Maxfield, M. (1981). *Coping with crime.* Beverly Hills, CA: Sage Publications.

Srinivasan, R., Christiansen, E., & Tortora, R. (1996). Comparative study of three respondent selection techniques for telephone survey research. Paper presented at the annual meeting of the American Association for Public Opinion Research, Salt Lake City, UT.

Stafford, M., & Galle, O. (1984). Victimization rates, exposure to risk, and fear of crime. *Criminology, 22*, 173–185.

Surette, R. (1998). *Media, crime, and criminal justice.* Belmont, CA: Wadsworth.

Tyler, T. (1984). Assessing the risk of crime victimization: The integration of personal victimization experience and socially transmitted information. *Journal of Social Issues, 40*, 27–38.

Warr, M. (2000). Fear of crime in the United States: Avenues for research and policy. In D. Duffee (Ed.), *Criminal justice 2000: Vol. 4. Measurement and analysis of crime and justice* (pp. 451–489). Washington, DC: National Institute of Justice.

Warr, M., & Stafford, M. (1983). Fear of victimization: A look at the proximate causes. *Social Forces, 61*, 1033–1043.

Weaver, J., & Wakshlag, J. (1986). Perceived vulnerability to crime, criminal victimization experience, and television viewing. *Journal of Broadcasting and Electronic Media, 30*, 141–158.

Williams, P., & Dickinson, J. (1993). Fear of crime: Read all about it. *British Journal of Criminology, 33*, 33–56.

EPILOGUE

A potential pitfall of studying crime, particularly when its reality is forged through the media, is that some may get the impression that the complex processes leading to the construction of crime can be captured in formulaic fashion. It might seem that with enough careful scientific study, a matrix or model of media-crime construction will emerge. Working through the research can leave one with a sense that a significant scientific project is underway. Certainly scholarship on the media and crime has generated a detailed inventory of the practices, actors, and effects of crime construction. Because of the imagination and effort of many researchers, we can now list and describe media practices that contributed to the social construction of crime—the creation and spread of news "themes" and "crime waves" (Fishman, 1978); the use of "motifs" and "typifications" (Best, 1990; Ibarra & Kitsuse, 1993) to culturally situate crime; and the media's overreliance on sources and practices closely tied to the crime control industry to generate a reality of crime (Kappeler & Potter, 2005; Welch, Fenwick, & Roberts, 1998).

We can enumerate some of the many actors in the social production of crime—the press, politicians, law enforcement officials, action groups, activists, and individuals and mythic incidents that are transformed into "folk devils" and "urban legends" (Cohen, 1980; Fine, 1980, 1992). Likewise, we can recount and analyze the often complex effects of media-crime presentations—public fear, collective insecurity, changes in lifestyle, and support for a growing web of social control (Carlson, 1995; Gerbner, 1994; Liska & Baccaglini, 1990). Yet, this rich and detailed inventory cannot lead to a precise formula, comprehensive matrix, or conclusive scientific explanation for the social reality of crime (Kappeler & Potter, 2005). We can use broader brushes to paint the media's reality of crime as "panics," "morality plays," or "crime dramas" (Cavender & Bond-Maupin, 1993; Cohen, 1972). Even so, these portraits capture only a limited view of the entire landscape of crime reality.

Unlike researchers, the media are not bounded by the logic of science. Media workers care little about the assumptions of linearity or temporal sequence, and they certainly are not concerned with selective observation or overgeneralization. In fact, these are some of the practices used to construct crime waves, moral panics, and epidemics. Mark Fishman (1978, p. 34) observes that "the crime wave dynamic is necessary for a theme to grow into a wave: There must be a continuous supply of crime incidents that can be

367

seen as instances of a theme." Of course, justice officials provide the media with highly selective crime reports, and journalists arrange the spatial and temporal sequences of these incidents to match their themes.

For social researchers, however, even isolating a unit of study is a particularly vexing problem. Should researchers analyze national stories, regional news, or local broadcasts? If one of these levels is selected, how does one take into account interactive media constructions of crime that cross all of the levels? Not only do local newspapers and television stations repeat the stories selected by the Associated Press or the major networks, but they also resituate national problems in local contexts. That is, the local media introduce viewers and readers to a localized version of a crime problem or the local personification of some folk devil. As Gray Cavender and Lisa Bond-Maupin (1993) remark, "Good storytellers localize their tales in time and place" (p. 52).

When focusing on media constructions of crime, should researchers isolate television from newspapers or advertisements from the news? Can we even draw a line between what is "news" and what is entertainment? Can the interests of business, media, politics, and the construction of crime be disentangled? The media are "embedded in a configuration of institutions" (Fishman, 1978, p. 25). Five corporations—Time Warner, Disney, News Corporation, Bertelsmann, and Viacom—control the vast majority of the media industry in the United States. Let's consider two of these corporations to get a sense of their size and scope of influence.

Time Warner, the world's largest media company, owns well-known brands like HBO, CNN, Warner Brothers Entertainment, Time, Inc., America Online, Turner Broadcasting System, and Time Warner Cable. The corporation owns cable television stations, film and TV production/distribution companies, and over 150 magazines ranging from parenting to leisure and investment publications. It controls at least 20 online services including Netscape, Moviefone, and MapQuest. Viacom, another media giant, owns more than 100 networks around the world. They are one of the world's largest creators of programming across all media platforms, including Internet companies, book publishers, and film production and distribution companies. Some of their well-known holdings include Paramount Pictures, MTV, VH1, and DreamWorks. These media giants control what we see, hear, and read. Their influence and power, however, is not limited to the media arena. They are also intermingled with government and an array of industries.

Of the 10 largest media conglomerates, 118 people sit on nearly 288 different and overlapping corporate boards (Thornton, Walters, & Rouse, 2005). These board members are among some of the most powerful people in the world. They move freely from industry to industry and back and forth between government and private sector positions. These boards fuse the interests of media, business, and government. For example, former political leaders like Sam Nunn (who voted against using racial statistics in death penalty appeals) served on the boards of General Electric, Chevron-Texaco, and Coca-Cola. General Electric has a history of anti-union activity, was a forerunner in exporting jobs, and has a major stake in weapons manufacturing. It has overlapping board director positions with Disney, which owns ABC, which shares board members with Halliburton, Boeing, and Pfizer. William Cohen (who as a senator assisted in spreading the hysteria over stalking and who served as secretary of defense) served on the board of directors for the NASDAQ and Viacom. Viacom is linked to Verizon Communications, which has overlapping membership with Procter and Gamble, which shares a board member with Lockheed Martin. The media are linked through institutionalized relationships to the way business and governing is done in the United States. Media constructions of crime come at us from many directions and origins and are related to an array of interests. Our most public images of crime are influenced reciprocally by media business practices and organization of information and by how our society organizes activities. Is it possible to disentangle the modern web of media, crime conceptions, and society?

Understanding the social construction of crime problems is perhaps even more problematic when researchers attempt to use tools designed for measuring the physical world. These tools are not always conducive to measuring changing social constructions. We know, for example, that the processes and techniques used by the media are not static and the consequences of these processes are less than predictable. Sometimes moral panics center around marginalized or unpopular groups, other times the media-amplified victimization of a celebrity causes a national panic. While physical objects wait for careful researchers to calibrate their measurements, media practices and the configuration of business relationships change as fast as sound bites are produced.

Even media-generated moral panics defy uniformity. Some crime problems emerge, develop, hold public interest, have long lives, and result in social policy; others never fully mature. Occasionally, immature panics resurface in media loops. Road rage is an example of an immature crime problem that only occasionally resurfaces in the media (Roberts & Indermaur, 2005). Likewise, as we prepare to make our measurements, the media can capriciously abandon a current panic to concentrate on another story—perhaps a celebrity trial, the death of a prominent person, or some natural disaster. We know very little about the processes that displace or diffuse emerging crime panics. Attempting to map the terrain of the cause-and-effect relationships between media constructs and behavior or even making useful generalizations in a territory where the boundaries are constantly changing is problematic at best. The matter is further complicated because media constructions occur within the equally volatile environment of constantly changing corporate configurations, governmental leaders, and power relationships. Perhaps we can account for some of these contradictions by broadening the focus a bit beyond the media-crime landscape.

Ideology, Media, and Crime

As mentioned in the introduction, the primary functions of ideology are to explain and to create meaning and understanding. Ideology situates us within the social world by providing ready-made understandings of our roles and relationships. It gives "understandable meanings to all kinds of social events, activities, and trends that otherwise appear unintelligible. It places them within a frame of reference that constitutes a defined context which assigns meanings to them" (Olsen, Lodwick, & Dunlap, 1992, p. 19). From ideology, we learn what is expected of us in a given situation, how others will respond to our words and behaviors, and even how to think about our experiences.

Ideology is a pattern of ideas about the social order expressed in the creation, arrangement, and presentation of seemingly natural symbols developed in the epoch in which a people live. The purpose of ideology is to explain social relations, practices, and institutions as well as the desired methods and techniques for understanding social change from the position and perspective of the group that creates it. Ideology is used to create the conceptual space in which people think and act. It serves as the marching orders for members of society (Gramsci, 1971). Ideology has an internal logic that allows contradictions to be masked, refuted, or reconciled, thus creating a system of thought for its adherents. The collective system provides the values, attitudes, and convictions to sustain itself and the means of characterizing and refuting any challenges.

The social order of any society is maintained through a balance of twin forces—consent and coercion. Consent is manufactured by the development and dissemination of ideology through social institutions like the family, schools, churches, and the media. These institutions collectively generate and maintain an ideology that defines and maintains social relations. In the modern age, the media is one of the most powerful producers of consent. We learn about crime from ideology, and we learn ideology from the media. When ideology falters and when consent is not freely given, coercion maintains the social order. The military, police, courts, and corrections are all institutions that bring force to bear when the manufacturing of consent cannot maintain existing social relations. In the furthering of domestic order, the criminal justice system is the most powerful of coercive institutions. So the media and the criminal justice system share a relationship in maintaining the social order. Crime and its depiction in the media play an especially important role in developing consent and representing both social relations and the use of the criminal justice system.

Ideology can bridge differences between social groups and define social relations in configurations that establish a dominant order. When ideology is shared across large groups as a natural view of the social world, when it assigns meaning for social relations within and across groups, when it provides personal identity within a specific configuration of social relations, and when it becomes a binding together of groups with a shared vision of the social order, it becomes a hegemonic ideology (Gramsci, 1971). In this case, the rich and the poor, the laborer and the professor, and the criminal and crime-fighter are bound together in a shared conception of the social world.

The media furthers this conceptualization of the world, and crime plays a central role in its construction.

The media play an important role in producing hegemony in society. Hegemony is the predominance of one group's views over interests of other groups or classes. The media projection of this dominant worldview causes most of us to accept the ideology as "common sense." Common sense has been defined as "the way a subordinate class lives its subordination" (Alvarado & Boyd-Barrett, 1992, p. 51). This kind of common sense is not etched in stone. It has to be redefined and transformed almost daily, and this is the role of the mass media (Hall, 1980).

Ideology aligns the world of representation and ideas with experience. With our understanding of experience guided by ideology, human choice is limited to a range of behaviors that fall within prescribed bounds. Media depictions play a central role in defining the range of these bounds. Because ideology defines acceptable beliefs and practices and brackets out alternative interpretations of experience, it directs behavior by limiting choice to that which is formulated and advanced by social elites to justify their interests. So while ideologies are "widely used by established elites to explain and legitimate their exercise of power and control and their privileged status" (Kinloch, 1981 cited in Olsen, Lodwick, & Dunlap, 1992, p. 18), they also explain the role and place of subordinated groups.

Ideologies are structured to maintain power while reducing conflict and the need for force to sustain the social order. Ideology not only explains the relationships within a given social order but also reduces resistance to it. Ideology is control of the mind, which reduces the need to use force to control behavior and relationships because we self-regulate through the way we think. Ideology is the symbolic use of violence that, through the proliferation of the ideals of the powerful, manufactures a shared consensual control (Althusser, 1971; Gramsci, 1971; Herman & Chomsky, 2002). The target of this control is not just the criminal or the deviant, although they are convincing narrative subjects for naturalizing and objectifying ideology. The criminal law is one of the most obvious forms of consensual ideological control. As Robert T. Ford (2005) remarks,

> the most important function of criminal law is not how it affects the criminal (punishment or therapy) or even the potential criminal (deterrence), but how it affects, by defining, the law-abiding citizen: criminal law defines the boundaries of acceptable conduct in a society, and in so doing it attempts to give a society an identity. The law is in this sense both a regulative and an epistemological technology: it generates the rationale for the monitoring of citizens (the prevention of crime) while its rules and decisions produce norms of behavior, the texts in which society writes, reads—and therefore knows—itself. Thus while proponents of draconian sentencing provisions inevitably claim that the new laws will "send a message to criminals," the real recipient of the message is society itself. (pp. 150–151)

An adequate ideology uses signs, values, and language to legitimate a given social order and to direct our thoughts about the world in a way that lends acceptance to existing configurations of power and privilege. For those who consent, it produces the notions of self and place in the relationship of ideas that cage them; it forces those who refuse consent into the role of criminals, deviants, and dangerous persons.

When ideology fails to regulate our behaviors, when we punch a hole in the ideological veil, or when we begin to resist the dominant order, overt violence is used to control behavior. Resistance often comes in the form of crime, and control surfaces in the form of criminal justice. Ideology contains within it all the necessary rationalizations for using force and invoking the criminal justice system when it can no longer reduce resistance to meaningless exercises devoid of the potential for altering existing power configurations. Crime as depicted by the media confines our behaviors to a narrow range that matches the interests of the powerful and justifies a coercive response to failure to conform. The justifications for the use of force and the rationalizations used for organized violence when the interests of the powerful are threatened are all contained in the media construction of crime. The elite response to resistance comes in the form of law, police, power, coercion, and prisons. Ideology of "dominant elites, leaders of a social movement, a powerful social class, . . . purposely use it as a means of supporting and furthering their power, privileges, actions and goals. In short, an ideology is always a symbolic political weapon" (Olsen, Lodwick, & Dunlap, 1992, p. 17). When this symbolic weapon fails, we invoke the violence of criminal justice.

The Transformational Media and Commodified Society

The media are beset by transformational obsolescence. As soon as movie theaters became the dominant form of entertainment in the 1930s, radio brought entertainment into the home. The social construction process now had two players capable of reaching mass audiences. The visual images of the movies were somewhat displaced by the more readily available audio messages. Then in the 1950s television pervaded daily life. Even the hardware that disseminates media images and messages overlaps to make distinctions difficult. One can listen to radio broadcasts through television speakers and watch the news on a computer monitor. Viewers can now interact with the media through computers, becoming part of the reality produced through the mix of "live" participation with mediated images. The proliferation of technology combines all the modern communication sources into a multimedia "spectacle" where image, sound, and interactions are possible (Debord, 1970, 1990). The media itself becomes part of the story. This participation can range from media personalities interviewing each other about the bias of the "liberal media," to a network advertising itself as "FOX, fair and balanced," to communication companies providing government officials with private information to assist in crafting new communications laws to control the

Internet to protect children from "cyber stalkers" and pornography. (Remember the political players who were involved in the initial stalking panic and the interlocking ownership and interests of many Internet services and companies reviewed earlier.)

Mass communication makes it increasingly difficult to distinguish the viewer from the viewed. We watch ourselves entering department stores on large-screen security cameras. At sporting events, student sections cheer wildly as soon as the red light indicates the television camera is panning the audience. Television and the media industry are more accurately described as a "mirrored looking glass" than a "window on the world." We actually see only our own distorted image reflected back. The media portray viewers as well as the world around them by selectively capturing and framing images. The media capture human desires for predictability, safety, order, security, and power; they also transform, frame, and make the foundation of those desires obsolete. The media estrange us from reality and treat us like commodities—producing and satisfying desires that no longer correspond with any underlying reality. The media, in this sense, create a phantom "public" where individuals and their desires are amassed into a uniformity of thought destroying "all personality" (Kierkegaard, 1978, 1982) in favor of a "marketable personality" (Fromm, 1947). The media not only construct crime but also the audience, their desires, and their responses—all with an eye toward an amalgamation of political and economic interests.

The mass-market place of production and consumption generates "abstractions" from reality (Kierkegaard, 1978) and tends to erase difference and magnitude in favor of global appeal, intensity, and fantasy. Striving for universal appeal, the media erase distinctions between forms of reality and between social class, social groups, and political ideology in favor of composite abstractions. We can all go with Kathy Lee Gifford on a Caribbean cruise; we are all, along with our credit cards, "accepted wherever we go"; and we can all "rock the vote" with our participation. The media also introduce us to the universalized dangers of living. This seems particularly evident in the media construction of drug panics. "Drug scares typically link a scapegoat drug to a troubling subordinate group—working-class immigrants, racial, or ethnic minorities, or rebellious youth" (Reinarman & Levine, 1995, p. 147). Media reality extends the threat beyond these urban groups to suburban, white, middle-class teenagers and women, as with stories about heroin use shifting from inner-city shooting galleries to affluent small-town teenagers. To match the constructed market, the language describing the "new" forms of drug use adds the term "designer"; parties where drugs are consumed become "raves." Methamphetamine has reportedly become so dangerously addictive that stories about "hidden labs" and peopling cooking meth in the presence of children in the rural South and Southwest have been overshadowed by stories about the laws that now require over-the-counter allergy and cold medications to be placed behind pharmacy counters and subjected to careful monitoring and written records of purchases in Chicago.

In essence, just as advertisers use technology to blend race and ethnicity to construct human faces that have universal marketing appeal, the media now mix and blend behaviors, places, and populations into a composite danger. The media no longer need to instruct us about "urban danger," or specific "different ones." They create for us a symbolic "dangerous world" (Cavender & Bond-Maupin, 1993; Kappeler & Potter, 2005) where the symbol is detached from its reality. The camera lens pulls back to create global danger; differences and particularities are dissolved in abstraction. Because the desire for safety is universal, the new reality consumes us despite the absence of any anchors to individual reality. So child abductors hiding in the dark, waiting to whisk away our children, are transformed into terrorist sleeper cells waiting to attack—we have come to know all about hidden evils and predatory criminals. Our borders become passages for terrorists and danger to the sovereign rather than the recruiting paths for cheap labor. In these transformational processes, reality is erased as the desire for safety and predictability is assumed and magnified.

Of course the media instruct us where safety and predictability can be sought. FOX, for example, announces, "It's 10 o'clock. Do you know where your children are?" After a short pause the announcer states, "FOX—safe at home!" There is contradiction in the messages sent by the media. Previously that evening viewers might have watched a crime info-commercial that reenacted some criminal slaughter committed in someone's home, a case of a mother who drowned her children, or a child exposed to the toxic fumes of a parent cooking meth in their home. The media first project obscure and sensational incidents as universal dangers to attract attention and then calm the sensations aroused to retain their market—you're safe at home in front of the television. Both messages are, of course, absurd. The construction creeps into everyday life and common sense. The television industry has an economic interest in keeping people in their homes and in front of their television sets. The needs of the marketplace are transformed into the necessity of safeguarding one's family. The ritualistic enactment of prudent behaviors and the simulation of taking action (by not leaving home) are intertwined. We are projected into the very spectacle we consume.

Technological changes, media constructions, and the processes of mass communication are primary participants in the process by which the reality of crime and everyday life is manufactured. The media comprise a cultural industry that blends production, information, and technology into complex forms of domination that remove us from reality. A few crime incidents are transformed into waves. The adage that "once you have three things you have a trend" plays into the spectacle of modern media (Best & Hutchinson, 1996, p. 192). The media can construct crime and social problems based on their own fabrications and abstractions. The urban legend or folk devil need not be featured; it is already embedded in the abstraction. We have consumed so many images of criminals and constructions of the appropriate responses that we no longer need the missing abstraction—we unconsciously supply it.

Today, the media are both a part of the reality collected and the reality projected. The media become a source of "cultural stock" from which the industry draws to create the next abstraction.

Reproducing Crime in Everyday Life

The allure of the sensationalism that drives the media captures everyone, including those who study the media and crime. While the media's construction of gangs, drunk drivers, road warriors, and drug epidemics are important issues deserving both attention and debunking, we seem less attracted to how crime is folded into everyday life. This is understandable given the richness and the sensational properties of media-based crime presentations—as well as our obsession with them. Yet, crime and the social order are reproduced in far more mundane occurrences. A less sensational example illustrates the pervasive effects. The following newspaper column appeared on the front page of a small-town newspaper.

> Christmas season is a time for joy, but it is also a time for car thefts and personal burglaries, police officials said. During the holiday season while Madison County residents are shopping, they need to take extra caution of where they put their packages, Richmond Police Officer David Pence said.
>
> While at malls and shopping centers, Pence said he recommends hiding Christmas packages either in the trunk or under blankets and locking vehicle doors. "It is too tempting [for the burglars]," Pence said. "We're not living in Mayberry society. You want to take care of your belongings. You don't want to make it so easy for people to take your stuff.
>
> "Think about personal safety. You want to make sure you don't give people the opportunity to rip you off."
>
> When approaching a vehicle that should be parked in a lighted area, Pence said the owner of the vehicle should scan under the vehicle and in the back seat to make sure no one is near their car.
>
> During this time of year, Pence said police also talk to businesses about anti-theft safety and do extra patrols of 24–hour convenience stores.
>
> Because the holiday times are also a time for depression and pressure for many people, Pence said robberies and burglaries tend to rise. Pence said he recommends businesses to not obscure their windows with decorations so police officers can see clearly if the clerk is safe. (Gay, 1997, p. 1)

In these dozen sentences of general instructions, latent urban legends are invoked, legal misconstructions of criminality promote fears of serious danger, media constructions of safe and dangerous places are regenerated, and contemporary patterns of production and consumption are embedded. The journalist uses the holiday as a backdrop for official commentary on crime—the perfect "idiom for expressing urban fear and a corresponding sense of danger" (Cavender & Bond-Maupin, 1993, p. 46). The police officer uses the opportunity to transmit official beliefs and values and to legitimize himself as a source of knowledge about crime, prevention, and control. All the elements and linkages are present in their symbolic forms. "These links need not be made explicit; when experienced members of the culture make sense of a particular legend or news report . . . , they draw on their broader understandings of the nature of deviance and social problems" (Best & Hutchinson, 1996, p. 98).

The journalist conveys and transforms the law enforcement construction of a common event (located at the center of the modern spectacle of consumption, the shopping mall) into media reality that elicits fear with the predictable use of dark, isolated areas and menacing strangers. The petty thief merges with the armed robber. The latent legends of the "slasher" and the "killer in the backseat" reemerge without the need to mention any specifics. This all, of course, takes place "in a parking lot, the hotbed of contemporary legend violence—the shopping mall" (see, Best & Hutchinson, 1996, pp. 86–87). In the abstraction, the officer does not refer to a real small town as a basis of comparison; rather, he chooses a television reality—this is no "Mayberry."

This media abstraction needed no sensational incident, no repeated instances of behavior to create a crime wave, and no real town to reproduce a reality of crime in an everyday aspect of social life. The abstraction based on a generic dangerous world was sufficient. It is doubtful that the officer being interviewed ever encountered a real case of the urban legends he promotes—either "slasher" or "killer in the backseat." Even if shoppers faithfully adhere to the instructions to park in well-lighted areas, what are the probabilities that a police cruiser will pass by at just the precise moment to thwart an attack? It is likewise doubtful that the dutiful shopkeepers who keep their windows unobstructed will be fortunate enough to thwart a burglary or robbery because the "extra patrol" passes by just in time. The officer is merely providing common-sense reality; the advice reproduces the abstraction forged from an ideology of crime long since divorced from the social circumstances that created it.

Abstract danger legitimizes public surveillance and regimented personal action by forging the spectacle between the media, the audience, and comprehensive social control. The real power to control crime pales in comparison to the illusion of control and the universalized desire to control the "evil" that is inscribed in even the most insipid media accounts of crime. These techno-cultural rituals reaffirm faith in control and the "administration" of justice. The perpetrator walk—marching the accused person in handcuffs before a crew of reporters and cameras—feeds the desire for justice. The criminal is reduced to the glare of publicity, caught by the system of control that protects all of us. It is a compelling drama for the media to project to an audience eager to believe that the system of control works. The spectacle of reality produced by mass-media images reduces life, justice, and the real crimes that exist to something less than the abstraction.

Certainly we need to study the construction of crime waves and urban legends—and to unmask the organizational forces within the media industry that forge our common-sense notions of crime, but we must also begin to expand the landscape of crime construction beyond the manufacturing of sensational images projected on our television screens and the journalistic practices that create the words that appear in newspapers and magazines. We must begin to understand how crime plays a central role in the spectacle of social life as it reproduces patterns of behavior, production, and consumption in a society increasingly attracted to the abstraction of reality.

References

Althusser, L. (1971). Ideology and ideological state apparatuses. In L. Althusser (Ed.), *Lenin and philosophy and other essays*. London: New Left Books.

Alvarado, M., & Boyd-Barrett, O. (Eds.). (1992). *Media education: An introduction*. London: BFI/Open University.

Best, J. (1990). *Threatened children*. Chicago: University of Chicago Press.

Best, J., & Hutchinson, M. M. (1996). The gang initiation rite as a motif in contemporary crime discourse. In this volume, pp. 95–114.

Carlson, J. (1995). *Prime time enforcement*. New York: Praeger.

Cavender, G., & Bond-Maupin, L. (1993). Fear and loathing on reality television: An analysis of *America's Most Wanted* and *Unsolved Mysteries*. In this volume, pp. 59–69.

Cohen, S. (1972). *Folk devils and moral panics*. London: MacGibbon and Kee.

Cohen, S. (1980). *Folk devils and moral panics: The creation of the Mods and Rockers*. New York: St. Martin's Press.

Debord, G. (1970). *The society of the spectacle*. Detroit, MI: Black and Red.

Debord, G. (1990). *Comments on the society of the spectacle*. New York: Verso.

Fine, G. A. (1980). The Kentucky fried rat: Legends and modern society. *Journal of Folklore Institute*, 17, 222–243.

Fine, G. A. (1992). *Manufacturing tales*. Knoxville: University of Tennessee Press.

Fishman, M. (1978). Crime waves as ideology. In this volume, pp. 42–58.

Ford, R.T. (2005). *Notes from the outfield—Regarding "three strikes" criminal sentencing proposals*. Appendx, 3: 148–161.

Fromm, E. (1947). *Man for himself*. New York: Holt, Rinehart and Winston.

Gay, T. (1997). Police urge safety techniques during holidays. *The Richmond Register*, 106(328), p. 1.

Gerbner, G. (1994). Television violence: The art of asking the wrong question. *Currents in Media Thought* (July), 385–397.

Goode, E., & Ben-Yehuda, N. (1994). *Moral panics*. Cambridge, MA: Blackwell.

Gramsci, A. (1971). *Selections from the prison notebooks* (Q. Hoare & G. N. Smith, Eds. and Trans.). New York: International Publishers.

Hall, S. (1980). Encoding/decoding. In Centre for Contemporary Cultural Studies (Ed.), *Culture, media, language: Working papers in cultural studies, 1972–79* (pp. 128–138). London: Hutchinson.

Herman, E. S., & Chomsky, N. (2002). *Manufacturing consent: The political economy of the mass media*. New York: Pantheon.

Ibarra, P. R., & Kitsuse, J. I. (1993). Vernacular constituents of moral discourse. In J. A. Holstein & G. Miller (Eds.), *Reconsidering social constructionism* (pp. 25–58). New York: Aldine.

Kappeler, V. E., & Potter, G. W. (2005). *The mythology of crime and criminal justice* (4th ed.). Long Grove, IL: Waveland Press.

Kierkegaard, S. (1978). *Two ages: The age of revolution and the present age.* Princeton: Princeton University Press.

Kierkegaard, S. (1982). *The corsair affair.* Princeton: Princeton University Press.

Liska, A., & Baccaglini, W. (1990). Feeling safe by comparison: Crime in the newspapers. *Social Problems, 37,* 360–374.

Olsen, M. E., Lodwick, D. G., & Dunlap, R. E. (1992). *Viewing the world ecologically.* Boulder, CO: Westview Press.

Reinarman, C., & Levine, H. G. (1995). The crack attack: America's latest drug scare, 1986–1992. In J. Best (Ed.), *Images of issues: Typifying contemporary social problems* (pp. 147–190). New York: Aldine.

Roberts, L. D., & Indermaur, D. (2005). Social issues as media constructions: The case of "road rage." *Crime Media Culture, 1*(3), 301–321.

Sacco, V. F. (1995). Media constructions of crime. In this volume, pp. 29–41.

Thornton, B., Walters, B., & Rouse, R. (2005). Corporate media's corporate America. In P. Phillips (Ed.), *Censored 2006: The top 25 censored stories.* New York: Seven Stories Press.

Welch, M., Fenwick, M., & Roberts, M. (1998). State managers, intellectuals, and the media: A content analysis of ideology in experts' quotes in feature newspaper articles on crime. In this volume, pp. 70–92.

INDEX